IBec → Danny McCoy
ISme → Mark fielding
Cif → Tom Parlon

SfA - Patricia
Callan

Sections

8 → Defines employee
trade dispute
T.U, worker
strike

9 Individual Actions
w'draw Immunities

11 clarifies & restrict
the provision of 1"
Picketing

12 - Conspiracy
Immunities

13 T.U. Immunities

14 Balloting
Provision

19 Injunctions
Ex parte
Interim
Interlocutory

INDUSTRIAL RELATIONS
IN IRELAND
Third Edition

7

Joseph Wallace, Patrick Gunnigle
and Gerard McMahon

D1381910

Gill & Macmillan

To Verona Stellet, Aileen and Michael (Wallace), Theresa, Eoin, Sean and Tadhg (Gunnigle); and Monica, Laura, Alison and Kevin (McMahon) with thanks for your patience and good humour

Gill & Macmillan
Hume Avenue
Park West
Dublin 12
with associated companies throughout the world
www.gillmacmillan.ie

© Joseph Wallace, Patrick Gunnigle and Gerard McMahon 2004
0 7171 3574 8

Index compiled by Cover to Cover
Print origination in Ireland by TypeIT, Dublin

The paper used in this book is made from the wood pulp of managed forests. For every tree felled, at least one is planted, thereby renewing natural resources.

A catalogue record is available for this book from the British Library.

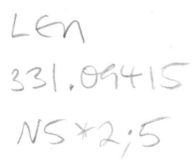

CONTENTS

CHAPTER 4: THE INSTITUTIONAL FRAMEWORK OF INDUSTRIAL RELATIONS

CHAPTER 5: TRADE UNIONS

CHAPTER 6: EMPLOYER ASSOCIATIONS

CHAPTER 7: THE NATURE OF INDUSTRIAL ACTION

CHAPTER 10: NEGOTIATIONS

CHAPTER 12: PARTNERSHIP AND OTHER DEVELOPMENTS IN COLLECTIVE WORKPLACE INDUSTRIAL RELATIONS

CHAPTER 13: THE PROCESS OF COLLECTIVE BARGAINING IN IRELAND

CHAPTER 14: STRATEGY, HUMAN RESOURCE MANAGEMENT AND INDUSTRIAL RELATIONS

ACKNOWLEDGMENTS

For helping us complete this text we would like to acknowledge the help and contribution of a number of individuals and organisations.

Various external organisations and individuals provided data and assistance. In particular we would like to thank the following:

- Andrew Powell, and the staff of the Central Statistics Office
- John Fitz Gerald, Economic and Social Research Institute
- Brian Sheehan, Editor, *Industrial Relations News*
- Anne Fedigan, Research Department, Services Industrial Professional and Technical Union (SIPTU)
- John McCartney, Education and Training Department, SIPTU College
- Professor Bill Roche and Teresa Brannick, Smurfit Graduate School of Business, University College Dublin
- Tony Dundon, National University of Ireland, Galway
- Michael McDonnell and Wendy Sullivan, Chartered Institute of Personnel and Development in Ireland
- Kevin Foley, Declan Morrin and Larry O'Grady, Labour Relations Commission
- Joe O'Shea, Labour Court
- The library staff at the Dublin Institute of Technology, Aungier St, and at the Central Statistics Office
- Damian Thomas and Larry O'Connell, National Centre for Partnership and Performance
- Brendan McPartlin, National College of Ireland
- Brendan Lyons, Collette Devlin and Dan Millar of the Partnership Learning Network
- Paul Joyce, Labour Law Practitioner, Free Legal Advice Centre
- Tom Hayes of European Employee Relations Consultants

Colleagues at the University of Limerick were most helpful. Teresa Murray provided extensive research assistance for a large number of chapters. She also made a substantial contribution to the final work through her extensive comments and assistance with preliminary proofreading of the full text and validation of material. David Collings and Michelle O'Sullivan (Government of Ireland Doctoral Scholars, at the University of Limerick) commented on drafts of chapters and provided research assistance. David Collings assisted with research on the legal chapters and the institutional arrangements. Michelle O'Sullivan worked especially on the material on trade union membership and recognition, employer associations, strikes and the institutional arrangements. David

Collings and Lorraine White provided extensive assistance in the preparation of the PowerPoint slides for the website. We would like to thank Gerard Fitzgerald for his work on the previous edition of the book. Mike Morley and Tom Turner provided much information and advice for which we are extremely grateful. Work undertaken by Linda Edgeworth in her role as Teaching Assistant contributed to the preparation of several diagrams and tables. Daryl D'Art, Christine Cross, Patrick Flood, Tom Garavan, Noreen Heraty, Sarah Moore and Sarah MacCurtain all helped in various ways, not least through their own research and publications. Special thanks goes to Geraldine Floyd and Maria O'Connell, departmental co-ordinators in the Department of Personnel and Employment Relations.

The library staff in the University of Limerick assisted with numerous requests. Our appreciation goes out especially to Aoife Geraghty, Kemmy Business School Librarian for her 'archaeological' skills. We are indebted to Vincent Cunnane, Vice President Research, University of Limerick for research funding assistance.

We would also like to mention the contributions of the staff of Gill & Macmillan, especially Marion O'Brien, Deirdre Nolan and Hubert Mahony, for their help and practical advice in bringing this work to fruition. Kristin Jensen provided a professional proofreading service and Yann Kelly indexed the work. We are indebted to both.

Finally, our greatest debt is to our families.

JW, PG and GMcM, July 2004

LIST OF FIGURES AND TABLES

CHAPTER 1

Industrial Relations:
A Contextual and Theoretical Overview

INTRODUCTION: WHAT DO WE MEAN BY INDUSTRIAL RELATIONS?

The subject area of industrial relations is one of the most-discussed specialist areas of organisational and national economic management. The public prominence of the topic is primarily attributable to its ability to make headlines when in the throes of industrial action, mass redundancy and wage bargaining activities. These events materialise at plant, industry and national level, commanding extensive media coverage and widespread public interest and concern, e.g. the teachers' diputes of 2000–2002, the nurses' dispute of 1997, the Garda Síochána 'blue flu' strike in 1998, the Ryanair trade union recognition strike in 1998 and the Bus Éireann and Aer Rianta disputes in 2004. However, the subject is largely shrouded in confusion and anxiety at the expense of insightful analysis – a factor contributing to the common public pronouncements urging dramatic (and often ill-conceived) policy changes, e.g. to outlaw strikes. Frequently, states of 'moral panic' consume the nation, when other more pervasive and injurious work-related phenomena, like health and safety issues, absenteeism levels or a new European Directive might be judged more consequential. Of course, issues of conflict and disharmony, allied with workers' exposure to aspects of industrial relations during their working lives, give the subject considerable public appeal.

Industrial relations does not easily lend itself to definition. However, the primary focus of the subject is on the employment relationship of over 1.5 million employees in the Republic of Ireland, working across all employment sectors and entity types. These include national or local government, private companies extending from multinational subsidiaries to local corner shops, semi-state companies, single domestic employers and co-operatives, spanning both union and non-union enterprises. Even the term 'industrial relations' itself has connotations of the traditional unionised blue-collar working environment in the manufacturing sector, while the term 'employee relations' conjures up images of the non- or less unionised white-collar services sector. In this text, for ease of classification the terms are assumed by the authors to be synonymous.

As with most subjects, a narrow conception does not facilitate genuine understanding. Therefore, the subject of industrial relations can best be understood and interpreted in the wider context of the historic, political, social and economic processes which have shaped the regulation of working lives. The broad base of the subject draws upon a range of disciplines to facilitate the development of an understanding of both individual and collective relationships in white- and blue-collar work environments and at plant sector, national and international levels. The complexity of the area has necessitated the adaptation of a vast array of other specialist subject areas, such as labour law and labour economics, to accommodate a comprehensive analysis of all the issues that affect people at work. Other disciplines, such as political scientists, sociologists, historians and psychologists, have all addressed the topic using their own particular perspectives. In this text we will draw on all of these subject areas.

Traditionally, the subject matter has been preoccupied with considerations about trade unions. This emphasis, while understandable, fails to appreciate the importance of contextual matters and contrasting (non-union) perspectives on the same phenomena. Both the context of and perspectives on industrial relations are addressed in this opening chapter. In addition to developing an appreciation of the main contextual influences and theoretical perspectives, familiarity with the following range of institutions and issues is necessary to develop an informed view of the nature and scope for change in our industrial relations system.

- **Institutions**: Trade unions; trade union section and branch committees; union confederations/national affiliations; the Irish Congress of Trade Unions (ICTU); employers' organisations; the Irish Business and Employers' Confederation (IBEC); trades councils; the Labour Relations Commission (LRC); the Labour Court; Rights Commissioners; the Employer Labour Conference (ELC); the Employment Appeals Tribunal (EAT); the law courts; the European Commission (EC); European Parliament and European Union (EU); Joint Labour Committees (JLCs); Joint Industrial Councils (JICs); government departments; the Equality Authority; the National Centre for Partnership and Performance; Health and Safety Authority (HSA); specially appointed commissions, e.g. on industrial relations, health and safety; relevant educational and research institutes; etc.

- **Role players:** Shop stewards and shop steward organisation; full-time trade union and employer organisation officials; personnel or human resource specialists; arbitrators; conciliators; adjudicators; Equality Officers; human resource consultants; other third-party actors; government ministers; etc.

- **Processes/procedures**: Third-party referrals; strikes and other forms of industrial action; union recognition; establishing and maintaining closed shops and non-union entities; disciplinary, grievance and dispute-handling procedures; consultation; involvement; participation and negotiation processes and skills; etc.

- **Issues**: The roles of the state, the European Commission, Parliament and Union; the role of collective and individual labour law; the future roles of trade unions and employer organisations; political decision making and national-level economic and social bargaining; economic (including industrial and employment) policy; strikes, lockouts and picketing; pay levels and payment systems; terms and conditions of employment; union recognition and avoidance phenomena; health and safety; new technology; employee flexibility; total quality management and world-class manufacturing; employee involvement/participation; management styles or approaches to employee relations; etc.

Insofar as is possible, this text outlines and analyses the various dimensions of the subject listed above, attempting to adopt a factual and unbiased approach to the study of industrial relations. The very nature of the subject matter inevitably means that many aspects of the topic are contentious. Accordingly, an effort is made to steer a middle line while outlining the central strands of the differing viewpoints that have been expressed on the various aspects of the subject. Of course, a most attractive aspect of the topic is that it allows students to develop their own opinions and to make up their own minds as to the merits of the contrasting perspectives outlined. Opinions need to be informed and this text adopts a *research-based* approach to the topic of industrial relations. The text gives a general overview of the more significant contextual, theoretical, institutional, substantive and procedural aspects while reviewing what are generally judged in the literature to be the more salient trends in this labour relations arena. We also engage with the more contentious, or debatable, dimensions of the subject, including the range of political arguments and the plethora of factual data, which on occasion lend themselves to a number of possible interpretations. The intention is to encourage students to engage in debate and to form their own views on the matters in question.

It is important that the development of particular viewpoints and perspectives be embedded in an appreciation of the many central features and facts in and around which the system of industrial relations operates. Accordingly, we endeavour to provide a balanced and comprehensive treatment of the topic without undue emphasis on any specific area. It is designed to address both practical and theoretical aspects of the subjects, with practical exercises combined with theoretical discussion. Thus the text is suitable for both introductory and advanced courses. Chapters 1, 2, 3, 4, 5, 6 and 12 will be particularly useful for introductory courses. Chapter 10 is a specialist chapter suitable for skills development in negotiation and discipline and grievance handling in either specialist or generalist courses. As such this chapter has more of a prescriptive element to it than other chapters; nonetheless the material is based on research and as such is not totally value driven. The remaining chapters delve deeper into the subject matter of industrial relations, discussing and evaluating the rich vein of contemporary research material that has become available through the activities of fellow researchers in recent years. Where students wish to further explore particular topics for projects and theses, extensive references and a full bibliography are available to facilitate this. Students are encouraged to visit this original research material, which will allow a more nuanced understanding of particular approaches to the study of industrial relations.

Figure 1.1 presents a working model or overview of the Irish system of industrial relations. Each component of this model is outlined and critically evaluated at an appropriate point in the text. In this opening chapter the main contrasting theoretical perspectives and contextual factors which have determined the current – and which will influence the future – shape of the industrial relations system are reviewed. The system itself can be viewed from many different angles or perspectives. However, no single view can yield a perfect understanding, but each can add to our insights. The location of five theoretical perspectives on the outer perimeter of Figure 1.1 is designed to convey the potential of each and all of these theories to provide their own insights on the whole system, or aspects of same. That is, these theoretical perspectives or frames of reference

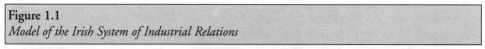

Figure 1.1
Model of the Irish System of Industrial Relations

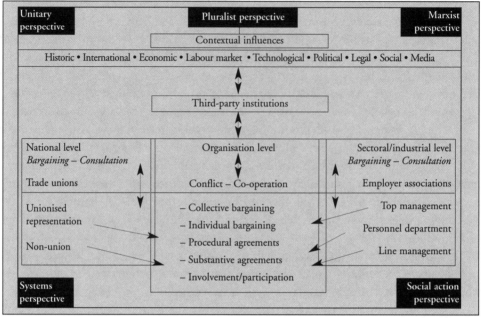

offer contrasting explanations of the same phenomena or various parts of the industrial relations system. Despite the academic orientation of these theories, their relevance should not be underestimated. The decision to support one or other of the theories may well be reflected in:

- the nature of legislation introduced by a government;
- the approach to union recognition adopted by the general manager or his/her board of directors; or
- the intransigence and readiness to recommend industrial action by the worker representative and his/her union.

The prevalence of dual-direction arrows attempts to depict the relationship between the various components of the system. This may be reflected in a vast array of exchanges, such as:

- trade union opposition to legal intervention on grounds of history or tradition;
- the reform of third-party dispute-settling agencies owing to the nature and volume of conflict cases coming before them;
- the impact of the terms of a collective agreement reached at national, industrial or organisational level by employees and employer(s) (or their representative organisations) on the state of the economy; or even
- the content of a plant-level procedural agreement on disciplinary action resulting from national and international political influences, culminating in legislative decisions as to what constitutes an unfair dismissal.

THE CONTEXTUAL SETTING OF INDUSTRIAL RELATIONS

Any initiative designed to analyse and prescribe the area of Irish industrial relations requires some familiarity with the prominent influences which have helped or forced the system to adopt its present shape and character. Hence we have Salamon's (1998) definition of 'industrial relations' as 'a set of phenomena, operating both within and outside the workplace, concerned with determining and regulating the employment relationship'.

The structure and nature of trade unions, employer organisations, specialist government-funded institutions in the area, workplace practices and managerial styles, legislative initiatives and the plethora of voluntary arrangements in place can be more gainfully assessed from a knowledge base spanning three centuries which have thrown up a vast range of economic, political and social changes. While there has been an astonishing range of such interrelated influences, this section attempts to accommodate the more salient of such influences under the inter-related headings of history, economics, the labour market and politics. Of course, such coverage does not purport to be either comprehensive or detailed, but rather to provide some limited insight into the more salient influences shaping the nature and development of the contemporary Irish system of industrial relations.

History and Industrial Relations

Historical factors are of particular relevance in developing an understanding of industrial relations, particularly trade unionism, in Ireland today. As the Industrial Revolution swept Britain in the nineteenth century, the advent of factory cum machine types of production and the further concentration of population in the large industrial cities and towns allowed trade unions to emerge and grow. This was an attempt to redress the perceived imbalance wrought by private enterprise capitalism and the prevalent laissez-faire economic orthodoxy. At the time this orthodoxy or economic system was underpinned by the belief that the market was the only means by which all prices, including wages, profits and economic priorities, should be determined.

Therefore, trade unions were identified as a real threat to the prevalent economic, social and political order. In fact, the unions of Britain and Ireland are among the oldest economic institutions of the modern world. Defining a trade union as a 'continuous association of wage earners for the purpose of maintaining and improving the conditions of their working lives', Sidney and Beatrice Webb have identified the earliest such union as an association of London hatters in the reign of Charles II. In the Webbs' opinion – two of the very first writers on the subject of industrial relations – the Journeymen Hatters' Trade Union of Great Britain and Ireland could trace its origins back to that early association of London hatters (Boyd 1984). The first Irish trade union to be identified by name was the Regular Carpenters of Dublin, which it is estimated was founded in 1764.

There is also evidence that there were several unions or 'combinations' active in the Cork area in the middle of the eighteenth century. Their activities included organising strikes, picketing, destroying tools, materials and machinery and ostracising employers who would not give in to their demands. Eventually Parliament declared that anyone in Cork city found guilty of being a member of an unlawful trade union should be 'imprisoned not above six months, whipped in public and released only on giving recognisance of good behaviour for seven years' (Boyd 1972). From 1770 there is an account of two weavers who were found guilty of 'combination' and were whipped through the streets of Dublin from Newgate Prison to College Green. In 1780 the Irish Parliament passed further legislation for the suppression of all trade unions, an initiative which predated similar legislation in Britain by twenty years. The debate in Parliament was marked by a demonstration of 20,000 trade unionists in Dublin city. Even members of the Irish clergy had condemned unions as 'iniquitous extortions' (Boyd 1972).

Yet despite the legal and social pressures, unions maintained their influence, as individual employers disregarded the legal scenario and negotiated with them. The state's role at this time was deemed to be one of facilitating the unfettered operations of the free market and to confront and control any challenge that was considered to be in 'restraint of trade', e.g. trade unions. Consequently, by the beginning of the nineteenth century a series of statutory and judicial decisions (dating back to 1729) had served to make unions illegal under a variety of headings.

The official hostility toward trade unions may be primarily attributed to the laissez-faire economic 'religion' of the time, which debarred any interference with the laws of supply and demand in the marketplace. However, the minority ruling class also feared the onset of civil disturbance. This had already been witnessed in the Irish rural context with such secret societies as the Whiteboys and the Ribbonmen, and had been central to the outbreak of the French Revolution of 1789 and the ideas of democracy and republicanism which subsequently spread throughout Europe.

Nevertheless, Irish craft workers' trade unions continued to surface, to a large extent as a branch of their unions in the United Kingdom, of which Ireland was a part at that time. According to O'Grada (1994), in the earlier part of the nineteenth century most crafts in Irish towns and cities appear to have been highly unionised. In fact, a wide-ranging survey conducted by the Fiscal Inquiry Committee indicates that in 1914 Ireland's skilled workers were paid almost as much as their British peers, whereas the wage gap for unskilled work was substantial (O'Grada 1994). In a society plagued by unemployment, destitution and illness the skilled tradesmen enjoyed a relatively privileged place in society by virtue of their comparatively high wages and permanent employment. For the purpose of maintaining that position they sought to increase the value of their trade by restricting access to it via an apprenticeship system. Such apprenticeships were generally confined to relatives. In addition, the craft unions endeavoured to increase their members' security by providing mutual unemployment and sick benefits.

Inter-union co-operation in Ireland formally emerged for the first time in the shape of trades councils, i.e. organisations representing trade unionists in individual towns and cities. Such trades councils were founded in Belfast in 1881 and in Dublin in 1884, and though primarily concerned with the interests of craft workers, their unification was a significant step in the overall development of the Irish trade union movement.

With Irish representatives' growing disenchantment at the lack of priority accorded their business by the British Trade Union Congress, in 1894 the Irish Trade Union Congress (ITUC) was established. By 1900 a total of 60,000 workers were members of the ITUC. By contrast Boyle (1988: 105) notes that unionisation among unskilled workers was extremely limited, estimating that 'the total membership of Irish labourer's unions did not exceed four thousand at any one time during the years from 1889 to 1906'.

From 1871 to 1906 the British Parliament passed a series of key enactments that granted legality to trade unions, protected union funds from court action, recognised collective bargaining and legalised peaceful picketing. Around this time the first real efforts to organise unskilled workers began. At the end of the nineteenth century Ireland was in the throes of the Land League disturbances – a mass movement designed to elevate tenants to land owners. Together with the lessons learned from the experiences of their British general worker counterparts and from their rural counterparts via the Land League, mass organisation, solidarity and organised struggle arrived on the trade union agenda at the behest of unskilled general workers. Unlike the craft unions, the general workers' unions were open to all, charged low subscription rates, provided no mutual benefits, had no control over access to work, were more inclined toward frequent and aggressive industrial action and retained quite explicit and radical political links.

However, the struggle to extend union membership and recognition beyond the relatively privileged craft workers was a bitter and often bloody affair, occasionally involving the police and army in a series of repressive measures taken on behalf of employers. For example, major confrontations occurred in Belfast in 1907, Dublin in 1908, Cork in 1909 and Wexford in 1911 (McNamara *et al.* 1994). Directly related to these events was the establishment of the Irish Transport and General Workers' Union (ITGWU) in 1909 by James Larkin. Probably the most renowned confrontation that this union became involved in was the 1913 Dublin lockout (Yeates 2000; Nevin 1994). On 21 August 1913, 200 tramway workers who had refused to leave the union were sacked (locked out). This was the first significant event in a bitter five-month conflict between the ITGWU, led by Larkin, and the Dublin Employers' Federation, established by the prominent businessman William Martin Murphy. Within a month of the lockout starting, over 400 employers and 25,000 workers were in the midst of a violent confrontation. In the face of police assaults the workers established a self-defence group, called the Irish Citizens' Army. A key tactic of the employers' group was to starve the strikers and their families into submission – a tactic that was eventually to prove successful.

However, it was arguably a Pyrrhic victory. In the strike's immediate aftermath the union reorganised and eventually grew to become the largest trade union in the country (Larkin 1965). The strike failed primarily because there were too many workers chasing too few casual jobs and they weren't in a position to bring any large or crucial industry to a permanent standstill. However, the strike marked a sea change in workers' attitudes and the union was to grow rapidly afterwards. The employers' federation involved in this dispute had actually been established in 1911, two years after its Cork counterpart, on which it was modelled. It subsequently played a major role in the 1942 founding of the Federated Union of Employers (FUE), subsequently renamed the Federation of Irish Employers (FIE), which later merged with the Confederation of Irish Industry (CII) to become the foremost Irish employers' representative organisation, the Irish Business and Employers' Confederation (IBEC).

The emergence of general unions was a slow process, as the lack of extensive secondary industry in rural Ireland discouraged the formation of large groups of organised workers in the towns, and those which existed seldom extended beyond a single town. Yet by 1920 the ITGWU could boast a membership of 120,000 members (Roche and Larragy 1986), of whom nearly 50,000 were newly recruited farm labourers. Furthermore, affiliation levels to the Irish TUC jumped from 110,000 in 1914 to 300,000 by 1921.

By this time the central objectives of trade unionism had been clearly established: to secure recognition, to procure collective agreements covering the terms and conditions of employment of their members and to influence the state's legislative and policy-making process in such areas as employment conditions, housing, health care, social welfare and education. The labour movement was effectively accepting the emerging industrial society, though exerting its effort to mould it to its advantage. Such developments were inevitably accompanied by a significant change in the state's attitude toward trade unionism – from one of hostility, intransigence and legal suppression to one of recognition and accommodation – subject to its acceptance of the main economic, political and social structures of society.

The Trade Union Act of 1941 sought to reorganise the union movement and rationalise bargaining structures. It had the tacit support of the ITGWU, which stood to benefit from it. However, James Larkin's newer Workers' Union of Ireland (WUI) and a large number of British-based unions opposed it. The long-standing acrimony between the charismatic firebrand Larkin and the more conservative William O'Brien, treasurer of the ITGWU, which was part ideological and part personal, came to a head in 1944–1945. The union movement and the Irish Labour Party split in two. Just as the 'national question' and related tensions have played, and continue to play, a central role in Irish political matters, so too was it inevitable that such considerations would affect the operation and current shape of the industrial relations system right up to the present time. Nevertheless, by 1959 the ITUC split was resolved and the Irish Congress of Trade Unions (ICTU) was established to represent the vast majority of trade unions operating in this country. Furthermore, union membership almost doubled between 1945 and 1959, with union density peaking in 1980 at just under sixty-two per cent of the civilian labour force.

Economics and Industrial Relations

The policies and practices adopted by Irish trade unions over the years have been characterised by constant adaptations to the reality of political, economic and industrial life in the country. Changes in these spheres have primarily prompted a reactive and pragmatic response, as the trade union movement adjusts its priorities, postures and principles in what is perceived to be in the best interests of its membership and potential membership, i.e. the unemployed, at the time. However, this adaptability also reflects an inability on its part to hugely influence or determine the nature and consequent shape of the Irish economy. It tends to resign itself to a practical role of persuasion within the accepted political and economic framework. While such pressure-group persuasion may adopt various guises, the more significant stakes are primarily pursued through ICTU's influence on government policies, e.g. on job creation, pay determination and labour law. Though individual trade unions may participate in this process, either through ICTU or in an independent capacity, their primary preoccupation inside the prevalent economic parameters is to protect and improve the pay and conditions of their membership at plant, industry and national levels via collective bargaining, and similarly to secure the best deal for their clientele in the face of an entity's economic efficiency drive. It is no surprise then that some authorities to the right of the political spectrum had little hesitation in ascribing the rampant inflation of the 1960s and 1970s, together with subsequent unemployment levels, to the unreasonable pay demands and labour market rigidities respectively sought, secured and imposed by trade unions.

The relatively slow growth of Irish trade unionism in the nineteenth and earlier part of the twentieth centuries may be attributed to the somewhat belated onset of the Industrial Revolution. The absence of high-grade coal and iron ore, at least in comparison with Great Britain, was a contributory factor in this tardy development. However, one cannot disregard the historical issues, such as England's colonisation of Ireland, which proceeded from the middle of the sixteenth century onwards and undoubtedly prevented the growth of industry well before the Industrial Revolution. Such restrictions, which included a period of tariff impositions and export restrictions, prevailed up to 1922, as Ireland was perceived as not just a political but also an economic threat to Britain. By the time British policy had embraced free trade in the earlier part of the nineteenth century, years of colonial exploitation had so severely weakened Irish industry that it was generally incapable of competing internationally. Consequently, throughout the nineteenth and early twentieth centuries Ireland remained primarily an agricultural economy. In fact, the Cumann na nGaedheal government of 1922 had no industrial policy, believing agriculture to be the mainstay of the economy. Half the workforce was in agriculture, food and drink made up most exports and there was a huge market 'next door' in Britain. The belated transition to a modern industrial economy was a hesitant and slow process.

Over the 1914–1920 period trade union membership increased from 110,000 to 250,000 (Roche and Larragy 1989a: 21), but declined again with the depression in agriculture and trade during the 1920s. This was inevitably accompanied by declining wages and rising unemployment. Enjoying the legal tolerance secured by their British counterparts (which had been incorporated into the new state's legislature), trade unions surfaced hesitantly, addressing themselves to issues of growth, consolidation and adaptation to the prevalent and primarily hostile economic order. Indeed, such was the stagnant nature of society and the related lack of vision amongst the nation's leadership that considerable trade union energy was devoted to the establishment and maintenance of differentials, rather than the attainment of any wider economic and social goals. That is, a status rather than a class consciousness prevailed.

Throughout the 1930s significant moves toward economic development were taken inside protectionist economic policies. These were designed to promote greater national economic self-sufficiency and proved effective in securing the development of new industries and the expansion of older ones. However, the onset of World War II and the consequent material supplies shortage contributed to a decline of over a quarter of industrial output during this period. In fact, as late as 1946 agriculture accounted for forty-seven per cent of total employment, services for thirty-six per cent and industry for just seventeen per cent. Even that seventeen per cent was predominantly characterised by small establishments so that by 1958 only forty concerns outside the public service employed more than 500 workers (Lee 1980).

Over the 1945–1950 period a short post-war recovery was experienced, which was accompanied by an increase of about seventy per cent in both strike frequency and union membership levels. However, the recovery of the late 1940s concealed the limitations of the protectionist strategy adopted in 1932. Unlike the remainder of Europe, the 1950s proved to be a miserable decade for the Irish economy. Economic performance was disappointing – marked by emigration, balance of payments difficulties and virtual stagnation – with an actual decline in national output in the last half of the decade. In O'Hagan's (1987) assessment:

> at Government level and at civil service level, there were serious deficiencies in the quality of economic policy making, and a lack of purpose, of energy and of leadership, which was all too readily reflected at other levels of society … There was in fact a policy vacuum, which was all too readily filled by short-term and short-sighted measures to preserve or bolster up uneconomic employment.

While the level of trade union membership increased by over seven per cent during the 1950s, undoubtedly benefiting from state intervention in the economy, strike frequency dropped significantly from its post-war heights, as trade unions resigned themselves to the economy's stagnation or lack of growth. The fact that by 1960 there were 123 operating trade unions – of which eighty-four had an enrolled membership of less than 1,000 – yields some insight into the priority still being accorded status and relativity factors in the mind of the Irish worker in preference to class consciousness or solidarity considerations (Lee 1980).

In the late 1950s Ireland entered a period of sustained economic growth. A sharp reversal of policies and the adoption of a new development strategy saw economic isolationism and the self-sufficiency goal abandoned in favour of free trade, as 'Ireland opened a wider window on the world' (MacSharry and White 2000). The 1960s and 1970s were periods of sustained and unprecedented improvements in living standards and of considerable growth in the Irish economy. By 1964 advertisements placed by the Industrial Development Authority (IDA) in *Fortune* magazine in America featured a small Irish boy scrawling 'Yanks please come over' on a brick wall. Significant emphasis was placed on attracting direct foreign investment and foreign-owned companies were given generous incentives to locate new facilities in Ireland. Commenting upon the changing social climate of the 1960s McCarthy (1973) famously suggested that it was

> a decade of upheaval. We are probably as yet too close to it to recognise its uniqueness. It was a period of national adolescence. The old structures of society were breaking down, the Second Vatican Council had shattered the timeless authoritarian image of the Roman Catholic Church. New attitudes were being painfully developed and new structures and institutions to reflect them. Television mirrored and magnified all that we did.

Indeed, this period witnessed the demise of 'the deferential worker', as previously accepted values, attitudes and institutions were challenged. The expansion of educational opportunities and media influences increased awareness of the outside world and facilitated a greater readiness to question previously sacrosanct practices. Allied to this awakening was an opening up of educational and social possibilities that were previously denied or non-existent.

The 1970s were a time of unprecedented rapid wage increases and an approximation to nearly full employment for craftsmen. Trade union membership levels rose by nearly fifty per cent between the mid-1960s and the late 1970s, while strike frequency levels escalated significantly between 1960 and the mid-1970s. The barriers of pay relativity which had been established were now being reinforced, as both white- and blue-collar workers engaged in some of the most notorious industrial actions in Irish industrial relations history as they clamoured to preserve their differentials and position on the social ladder (McCarthy 1973; McCarthy *et al.* 1975). Two of the main influences on this dramatic turnaround were the increased level of government expenditure and a revised industrial development policy that encouraged overseas companies to establish bases in Ireland. By 1983 almost 1,000 such foreign operations, with a labour force of 87,600, had set up in Ireland.

During the 1960s and 1970s, following in the path of its main trading partners, the Irish government opted to relegate the laissez-faire approach to economic affairs and adopt a Keynesian approach to economic growth management and planning. This involved the government in the stimulation of demand through budgetary deficits and increased expenditure, yielding higher levels of economic activity (via the multiplier effect) and reduced levels of unemployment. Successive governments during this period pursued this strategy of manipulating aggregate demand, public spending and budget deficits for the attainment of full employment levels.

However, this route to the idyllic economy brought with it a new set of ills. Chief amongst these was the spiralling level of inflation, which the social partners attempted to halt via a series of national-level pay agreements for the nation's workforce that came into effect from the beginning of 1971. In addition, the surge in economic confidence brought with it a drift of power to the workplace, with shop stewards dominating the collective bargaining scene at plant level. An upsurge in unofficial strike action materialised as workers seized upon the boom climate created by economic expansion, demand buoyancy and high employment levels.

By the 1980s two significant problems had materialised. First, the accumulated foreign debt had grown from £126 million in 1972 to £7,900 million by 1985, bringing with it an increase of over £730 million in annual debt interest payments. Second, unemployment levels had escalated from about six per cent to seventeen per cent during the years from 1971–1986 – with worse to follow. In brief, the Irish economy was under severe pressure from an explosive national debt, oppressive taxation, high emigration and rising unemployment. Hence the concern amongst Ireland's political and banking community at this time that the International Monetary Fund would step in to impose the economic stringency which the politicians had failed to apply (MacSharry and White 2000). Once again, following international trends, the government opted for 'fiscal rectitude' through monetarist policies, primarily designed to tackle the balance of payments deficit and the attainment of international competitiveness. The policies of particular relevance in the industrial relations context included moderate pay rises and reduced government spending – with consequences for welfare benefit levels, government subsidies and public sector employment. In effect this constituted a neo-laissez-faire economic route, involving reduced state intervention in an economy left largely to the devices of the marketplace.

The advent of this 'new realism' in the 1980s and early 1990s was accompanied by reduced trade union bargaining power, expressed in falling membership levels, spiralling unemployment and an upsurge in managerial confidence, together with instances of 'macho management' practices. As the international recession heightened coming into the 1990s, a persistent balance of payments problem, further increased unemployment and rising interest rates combined to create real constraints and tensions. A consequence of this downturn in economic prosperity was the intensification of divisions within society, as unemployment spiralled and public expenditure on welfare benefits and services declined at the time when the need for them was greatest. Nevertheless, the various indices used to measure industrial action or strike levels reveal a general downward trend, accompanied by sharp declines in trade union density.

For example, the proportion of the workforce in trade union membership fell from a high of fifty-five per cent in 1980 to about forty-three per cent by 1997. The decline in trade union density in the 1980–1987 period is generally attributed to economic factors, particularly recession, increased unemployment and structural changes in the distribution of employment (decline/stagnation of employment in typically highly unionised sectors such as 'traditional' manufacturing and the public sector) and growth in the service and foreign industry sectors, some of which have historically posed difficulties for union penetration (see Chapters 14 and 15). On the industrial action front, an atmosphere of harmony was evident, reflected in the 1996 quarterly returns that reveal the lowest-ever figure for days lost due to strike action up to that time. Reflecting on the social and political impact of the crisis which liberal capitalism found itself in, Bew *et al.* (1989) observed

the relative lack of class conflict. The profound changes in social and economic life ... were not reflected in the emergence of radical politics, industrial militancy or in any fundamental change in the nature of Irish society. Ireland remained a conservative society imbued with the values of Catholicism, nationalism and ruralism, although less stridently so than in earlier periods.

However, by the late 1990s the 'Celtic Tiger' had arrived, with a new economic confidence and aura. This was reflected in such factors as the fastest growth rates in the EU (equivalent to twice the OECD rate), the healthiest Exchequer returns ever, a large balance of payments and current budget surplus, low mortgage interest rates, declining unemployment, booming profits and incomes and the lowest crime rate for nearly twenty years. No economic model had predicted such a reversal of fortune. For example, in 1993 the Bank of Ireland's chief economist pessimistically observed that 'perhaps Ireland's misfortune is to be a small and peripheral part of a structure that is, historically speaking, pretty useless at creating jobs for its people' (O'Grada 1994). The timing of such pronouncements couldn't have been worse, with aggregate employment rising by seven per cent between 1989 and 1995, and the Central Statistics Office predictions of a rise of between 7.2 and 12.9 per cent in employment levels between 1996 and 2006. Indeed, the evidence presented in Tables 1.1 and 1.2 indicates an overall rise of about twenty-five per cent in employment levels over the 1985 recession era to the 1997 boom era. According to O'Donnell and O'Reardon (1996), 'the social partnership approach produced the much-needed recovery from the disastrous early and mid-1980s and has underpinned a sustained period of growth since then'. While the 'social partnership' role in this recovery is often lauded, it is also the case that it coincided with a booming American economy, providing firms there with the profits to invest abroad; a ten per cent tax on manufacturing profits to attract them to Ireland; the lure of a large pool of well-educated and skilled workers; the creation of a single European market easily accessed from English-speaking Ireland together with a credible and conservative macroeconomic policy (O'Hagan 2000).

Allied to this, of course, was the wage restraint (and industrial peace) produced by the social partnership model, which unions traded in return for an input to the wider economic and social agenda. Unlike many of their international counterparts, as Sweeney (1998) points out, the trade unions now had an input to tax matters and a host of other consequential aspects of the economy and society, including fiscal policy. The Economic and Social Research Institute's (ESRI) Medium Term Review for the Irish economy for the 1997–2003 period warned that the biggest domestic danger to economic growth was an excessive rise in expectations. These would feed into wage inflation or insupportable demands on the Exchequer. It was agreed that if the notion of 'pay-back time' were to become the dominant spirit of pressure groups, then the economy and society would have to pay for it in the future by way of higher unemployment and lower real incomes. Sweeney (1998) also identified this type of break-up of the 'national partnership approach' to pay determination as a serious threat to the Celtic Tiger's health. Whatever the future may hold, the economic success of the Irish economy in recent years has been outstanding. This is particularly evident when compared with the recessionary 1980s, with our own fraught economic history or, indeed, with the performance of most other nations. Even the boom of the 1960s pales in comparison with this 'Tiger' period. Indeed, despite the downturn in economic fortunes on both national and international fronts in the early years of the new millennium, the much-feared 'boom and bust' cycle has not transpired to convert the Celtic Tiger into the Celtic Titanic, while the social partnership process has prevailed with the new agreement, i.e. Sustaining Progress, being signed off by the social partners in early 2003.

Whether such a development could herald another 'boom and bust' cycle in the EMU environment, with declining structural funds, remains to be seen. By mid-2002 the National Economic and Social Council warned that negotiations on a successor to the then operative Programme for Prosperity and Fairness would be fraught with concerns about slower economic growth, an unstable international financial environment and Ireland's own infrastructural limitations. By early 2004, however, there was a noticeable turnabout with economic commentators predicting growth rates of the order of 3.5 to 4.5 per cent. Inflation was also under control, but the price was an appreciating euro, which threatened the competitiveness of exports.

The Labour Market and Industrial Relations

Though a central component of the economic framework, such is the impact of the labour market on the evolution and operation of the Irish industrial relations system that it warrants separate consideration. In 2004, out of a population of about four million, over 1.9 million were in the labour force, of whom about ninety-six per cent were employed. Reflecting the change in Ireland's economic fortunes between 1971 to 2004, there was an increase of approximately two-thirds in the size of the labour force (see Table 1.3). This is attributable to a combination of the underlying growth in the population aged fifteen years and over, immigration and increasing female participation in the workforce. Up to 1993, despite the proliferation of government-sponsored training and education schemes, the out-of-work figure rose steadily. For example, in 1971 unemployment stood at 5.5 per cent, but by 1986 it had risen to over seventeen per cent. In fact, between 1979 and 1993 unemployment jumped by more than 150 per cent. The main causal factors giving rise to this 1980s decline were the impact of the long-running international recession and the increasing size of the labour force. Recent years have witnessed significant improvements on this front. While many of the jobs created are less secure, more low paid, part-time, fixed-term or based on fixed-term contracts, the overall trend reveals a 'significant upgrading of the occupational structure' (O'Connell 1998) as many of the newer jobs required qualifications, skills and levels of flexibility quite different to that of traditional industry.

The three key influences on the size of the labour force are the numbers in the population in each age group, the percentages in each age (and sex) group that are active in the labour market and levels of emigration or immigration. The size of the labour force has constantly increased over the past twenty-five years and, despite the significant decline in the birth rate since 1980, this trend is set to continue. For decades the Irish unemployment problem has been masked by high emigration rates. However, when this option narrowed in the 1980s, unemployment rates rose, even when total employment levels were rising. On the matter of activity rates at this time, there is evidence that the youth, i.e. fifteen- to twenty-four-year-olds, were increasingly opting to remain inside the educational system; males over fifty-five years were opting for early retirement; and there was a significant increase in the participation rate of (primarily married) females in the twenty-five to forty-four years of age bracket. Leddin and Walsh (1990) attempted to explain these phenomena, which 'can be understood as responses to economic factors. High unemployment undoubtedly encouraged young people to postpone entry into the labour force, while many older people were offered early retirement by firms that were anxious to reduce their labour force'. The relatively low participation rates for both sexes in the fifteen- to nineteen-year age group (at less than twenty-five per cent) was explained by high participation in education, while the steep rise between this age group and those aged twenty to twenty-four years (at about seventy-five per cent) marks the transition from education to the labour force.

Table 1.1		
Labour Force Classification by Males, Females and Married Females, 1977–2003 (in thousands, percentages in parentheses)		
Year	Males (as % of Total Employed)	Females (as a % of Total Employed)
1977	755 (72)	288 (28)
1981	816 (71)	335 (29)
1985	743 (69)	331 (31)
1989	738 (68)	352 (32)
1992	740 (65)	399 (35)
1997	826 (62)	513 (38)
2002	1,015 (58)	730 (42)
2003	1,040 (58)	757 (42)
Source: Central Statistics Office (www.cso.ie)		

The increasing number of married women in the paid labour force (see Table 1.1) reflects more complex factors, including the fall in the birth rate and higher levels of educational attainment among women. It also seems that more job opportunities have been available in the occupations where women are traditionally employed. There have also been changes in legislation, making it harder to exclude women from employment. The relative decline in male employment levels, together with the associated expansion in female employment, as a proportion of all employees is also evident from Table 1.1. The level of female participation in the labour force has escalated from twenty-eight per cent in 1971 to approximately forty-two per cent in 2002. This trend is mainly evident in retail distribution, insurance, financial/business, professional and personal services.

Related to this trend is the substantial shift in employment levels from the agricultural to the services sector (see Table 1.2). The period since 1926 has witnessed major changes in the relative employment shares of the three broad sectors of economic activity: agriculture, industry and services. The diminishing importance of agriculture is clearly evident, as is the growth of the services sector since 1971.

According to Gunnigle and Morley (1993), 'the most notable changes in the Irish labour market over the past twenty years have been the dramatic fall in numbers employed in agriculture and the consistent growth in employment in the services sector, which now accounts for almost sixty per cent of all employees'. In fact, in contrast with trends elsewhere, the Irish industrial sector has grown in recent years. After large job losses in the 1980s, numbers grew again during the 1990s and early years of the new millennium (see Table 1.2). However, the composition of industrial employment has altered significantly, with contractions in many of the older, labour-intensive, indigenous sub-sectors, such as textiles, clothing and footwear, and expansions in more technology-related, export-oriented and foreign-owned employments, such as chemical and engineering.

Table 1.2
Employment Changes by Sector, 1961–2002 (in thousands, percentage in parentheses)

Year	Agriculture	Industry	Services
1961	380 (36)	257 (25)	414 (39)
1975	238 (22)	337 (31)	498 (47)
1979	221 (19)	365 (32)	559 (49)
1985	171 (16)	306 (28)	602 (56)
1989	163 (15)	306 (28)	621 (57)
1992	153 (13)	318 (28)	668 (59)
1997	134 (10)	386 (29)	818 (61)
2002	122 (7)	494 (28)	1,130 (65)

Source: Central Statistics Office (www.cso.ie)

Consequently, the occupational structure of those at work has also altered, with the demise of traditional industry and its associated skills and their replacement through the emergence and growth of newer ones. Most striking in this context is the overall decline of male manual jobs in the manufacturing sector – job types that have traditionally provided rich pickings for trade union organisers. This relative decline in the potential market of the trade union movement is also reflected in the fact that between 1988 and 1995 the number of full-time jobs increased by eight per cent, while at the same time the number of part-time jobs increased by eighty per cent and the number of occasional jobs by nearly seventy-six per cent. The number of jobs held by women increased by over thirty-one per cent, whereas the number held by men only rose by six per cent. Taking a wider perspective, over the 1971–2002 period, participation by males in the labour force declined steadily from eighty-two per cent to seventy-one per cent. Historically, male labour force participation rates have greatly exceeded those of females, peaking at 87.4 per cent in 1946, but declining thereafter to stand at seventy-one per cent by 2002 (see Table 1.3).

Related to this trend is the effect of technology on such matters as the size, spread, location and duration of employment. The quickening pace of technological change is having a dramatic impact on the structure and nature of the labour market and all job types therein. A key dimension of this trend is the aforementioned move away from manual work. However, the creation of replacement job opportunities – up to the mid-1990s resulting from the 'electronics' revolution of microchips, lasers, computers and new technical systems – was too low, volatile and of the wrong type to compensate for the attrition rate in the other industries.

Table 1.3 *Main Labour Market Indicators, 1971–2003*				
Year	Persons in the Labour Force (000s)	Labour Force Participation Rate (%)		Unemployment Rate (%)
		Male	Female	
1971	1,125	82	28.2	6.7
1981	1,271	76.4	29.7	10.5
1986	1,330	74.0	32.2	17.9
1991	1,383	71.7	35.9	16.9
1996	1,534	70.7	40.7	14.8
2002	1,825	70.5	48.7	4.4
2003	1,885	70.9	49.6	4.7
Source: Central Statistics Office (www.cso.ie)				

In summary, the most significant implications to emerge from this overview of labour market trends are rising employment levels and an associated decline in unemployment, together with increases in the size and changing composition of the active labour force. The prime beneficiaries of these changes are (mainly married) female part-time workers in the services sector of the economy. The decline in male manual full-time employment in recent years is also notable. From an industrial relations perspective these changes have had their fall-out in terms of 'atypical' work patterns, trade union recognition disputes, changes in such matters as working methods, job content, wage differentials and skill protection practices. The impact on industrial relations is also evident in the growth in part-time work, which is primarily a female phenomenon. Women now outnumber men by a ratio of over 3:1 in this category. This has implications for the rising incidence and extent of low pay, minimal job security and decreasing union membership cum collective bargaining strength, as trade unions continue to find it difficult to penetrate this market segment.

In recognition of these trends and the reality of the marketplace, ICTU (1996) sought comparable treatment for full-time and part-time workers, a national minimum wage for atypical workers, the elimination of 'zero-hour' contracts, the extension of existing protective legislative provisions to this 'atypical' category and an accessible and amenable legal route to the procurement of recognition cum negotiation rights at plant level. Indeed, it is also argued that a 'new realism' wrought by the 1980s recession and political developments has been recognised by a trade union movement. This is shown in its readiness to repeatedly commit itself to relatively modest pay increases, agreed at national level since 1987, in anticipation of a beneficial return in the form of greater employment generation efforts and lower levels of taxation on income. Since the mid-1980s pay settlements (and arguably as a consequence inflation levels) have been at appreciably lower levels than during the 1960s or 1970s. During the 1960s and 1970s unemployment figures were significantly lower and trade union density and negotiating strength were greater. Recent economic and labour market developments, however, raise new issues for trade unions, like the increased prominence of non-union policies. These are particularly evident amongst the newer industrial high-tech and service sector employments. It is suggested that sophisticated human resource management (HRM) practices pre-empt the need for a trade union among employees. In this context it is interesting to note that although union membership levels rose between 1987 and 2001, the density level (as a proportion of the employment workforce) declined from over fifty-seven per cent to forty-one per cent (Wallace 2003). This represents the lowest figure for union density since 1950. While the public sector remains a rich source of recruitment for unions, their limited penetration of the private sector (Wallace 2003; Gunnigle *et al.* 2002b) poses a real challenge for unions in the future. Furthermore, the reality of these changes has also forced unions to expand their range of services and to focus more upon the needs of part-time and female workers in negotiations with management and government for the purpose of maintaining their authority, influence and membership levels.

By the middle of the 1990s, the Irish economy began to experience skill shortages in the labour market, the likes of which had not been witnessed for nearly twenty years. For example, regarding immigration (or the use of non-nationals) it has now been officially acknowledged that immigration can make a significant contribution to meeting the nation's labour force needs. This is evidenced by the fact that the number of work permits issued by the government almost trebled to 18,000 during 2000, while a further 1,387 streamlined work visas/authorisations were issued to computer, nursing and construction professionals (McCall 2001). This economic buoyancy also brought to bear pressures on the labour market, in instances obliging employers to pay rapidly escalating 'market rates' for some staff categories, e.g. computer programmers – see Higgins (1997). Indeed, this phenomenon was so wide-scale that under the 2000–2003 Programme for Prosperity and Fairness the government and ICTU established a 'benchmarking' body, charged with levelling public and private sector remuneration levels to compensate for a perceived upward drift in private sector rates over pubic sector rates during the economic buoyancy phase.

Accordingly, recent years have also seen a growth in the number of non-Irish people attracted to this country. These include not just the much-publicised asylum seekers, but a large number of skilled European Union (EU) and non-EU nationals sought by companies eager to fill staff shortages, particularly in information technology and language areas. Whether this pressure on the labour market can be eased in the future remains to be seen. The availability of young people to the jobs market is set to be squeezed over the coming years by both increasing education and a general fall in the number of young people in the population. We have seen that the number of women workers in the labour market accelerated in the 1990s to almost four times the speed of increase in the two previous decades. Women now account for almost forty-two per cent of those in work – a rise very much in tandem with employment growth in the services sector.

Ultimately, however, the principle of neo-classical economics suggests that the impact of a tightening labour market serves to increase the relative power of the employee in the employment relationship. This has an inevitable impact on the industrial relations system. Current labour market developments pose major challenges to the system. For example, integrating non-nationals, protecting 'atypical' workers, tapping the intellectual potential of the workforce via participation or involvement measures, the matter of union recognition and the management of change (and labour costs via social partnership or otherwise) are all matters on the immediate agenda. However, reflecting on a possible decline in collective solidarity among workers due to changes in the occupational structure (with more highly educated and professional workers), the growth of the service sector (again with more highly educated and professional workers) and the growth of the service sector with more female and part-time workers in smaller-scale employments, D'Art and Turner (2002a) counsel caution regarding the demise of trade unions, concluding that in Ireland 'the evidence (of this) is sparse and inconclusive'.

Politics in Industrial Relations

The role of the state in the industrial relations arena has been quite significant over the twentieth century which has seen it adjust from the casting of trade unions as illegal entities to an accommodation in a social partnership or neo-corporatist model, with union involvement in the national-level decision-making processes covering the entire gamut of economic and social affairs. Though the state aspires to the role of independent referee and regulator of labour relations matters, as it addresses the worst excesses of liberal capitalism it would be inappropriate to evaluate its role as that of an impartial facilitator. In any democratic society the state reflects the differences in power between capital and labour and endeavours to side with whomever yields the greatest political influence. In effect, then, through their various powers and agencies, successive Irish governments have upheld the established norms, values and culture of liberal capitalism.

Nevertheless, over time the state has been cautious to refine the extremes of laissez-faire ideology and concede the more modest demands of trade unions, so long as they are peacefully presented and pursued, constitutional and maintain due deference to property rights and industrial capitalism, e.g. freedom of association (as provided for under the Constitution of 1937), rights to collective bargaining and to take industrial action. However, the first Free State government did display some disdain for entitlements granted by their British predecessors, as it proceeded to alienate most working-class voters and reject the application of Whitley procedures to Ireland, i.e. the provision of arbitration machinery for the civil service. In 1922 Michael Collins, as Minister for Finance, received (and denied the requests of) a delegation of staff representatives urging the retention of arbitration in the Free State. In fact, it was not until 1950 that advances of any significance were made in this regard. It is also argued that the policies of this Cumann na nGaedheal government in the 1920s increased the gap between rich and poor (O'Grada 1997). When Fianna Fáil eventually succeeded it in 1932, the new government's policy was adjudged to be far more indulgent and populist in its attitude to welfare matters.

In line with the eventual adherence to an 'auxiliary' or accommodative strategy, the state largely supported the voluntarist principle in labour relations by mainly confining legal interference to the provision of mediation services. Such a strategy, while successfully isolating trade union militancy and dampening popular support for the route to revolutionary socialism, has forced the trade union movement to (generally) separate and seek its ideologically driven aspirations through a political wing, i.e. the Labour Party or via tripartite or corporatist structures.

The Irish Labour Party was established in 1912 at the initiative of James Connolly and James Larkin at the Trade Union Congress. However, between a preoccupation with the burning 'national' question, which has consumed the overwhelming majority of political thought and action over many centuries, and a negligible industrial base (at least until the 1960s), the scope for the development of strong working-class communities and culture was severely restricted. Of some further relevance to the relatively modest influence of the Labour Party is the fact that the party, together with the Irish Trade Union Congress (ITUC), decided not to contest the 1918 general election. This decision has been attributed to the party's lack of funds, interested candidates, political organisation and political direction. There was also a definite reluctance among trade union and labour leaders to oppose the Sinn Féin candidates – who secured seventy-three of the 105 parliamentary seats in the eventual election. However, it is now argued that 'this policy of abstention removed Labour from centre stage in Irish politics for many years, as it sidestepped the great issue of the time which was the struggle for independence' (Kavanagh 1987). In fact, as Fitzpatrick (1977) suggests, attempts to examine Labour's efforts to remain distinct from the mainstream Republican politics becomes a review of 'the process whereby Labour and the Republican movement were sucked together', so prominent has the national question been.

In any case, a working class consumed by sacrosanct relativities and occupational status was unlikely to fill the ranks of a vibrant left-wing opposition along Western European lines. A striking consequence of this void is that there has been little substantial difference in policy stances between successive governments on economic and social issues. Given the ideological similarities across the main political parties and governments, there has been relatively mild opposition to the directions, policies and actions of the governmental process.

The absorption of working-class demands into the existing industrial and political structures has also facilitated the maintenance of widespread support for those parties representing the values and beliefs of liberal capitalism. Indeed, for the larger part of the twentieth century the state adopted such an 'auxiliary' role as it avoided direct coercive interference in the industrial relations process, leaving the parties to resolve their own differences via free collective bargaining. Furthermore, following on the British example, the government addressed itself to the social problems arising from the deficiencies of industrial capitalism, opting for greater intervention to protect and improve the quality of people's lives. In this regard it is interesting to recall O'Grada's (1994) comparison of the Cumann na nGaedheal government's 'flintier' attitude to welfare payments, leading him to conclude that 'Fianna Fáil became the party of the working class'.

The progressive creation of a welfare state in the decades succeeding World War II reflected a belief within society that the state should accept responsibility for the provision of education, health and related social services – effectively the 'haves' supporting the weak or 'have nots', with equality rather than ability of access dominating public policy. This perspective also dominated the economic arena, as the government maintained and persisted with the nationalisation of essential industries and manipulated the economic levers at its disposal to create unprecedented high levels of employment. Of course, the gradual creation of a welfare state facilitated the maintenance of political consensus, stability and legitimacy. The emergence of a corporatist or interventionist ideology was accompanied by an integration of political, economic and social decision making. From the 1960s onwards the state's policy of corporate control came into evidence as trade union representatives were invited to sit on consultative bodies with a role in economic planning, e.g. the National Industrial and Economic Council and the Committee on Industrial Organisation. The advent of tripartite consultations was judged important, given the need for economic adaptation, restructuring and the establishment of appropriate and realistic planning targets. The government therefore had to fall back on those interests involved on the ground in order to acquire the necessary information and understanding, as well as to secure their co-operation in the implementation of policy. The relegation of plant/entity-wide free collective bargaining and the emergence of national-level tripartite bargaining involving government, employers and trade unions marked a new phase in the state/trade union movement relationship.

The decision to enter the European Economic Community (EEC) with effect from 1973 was another important development in the political environment of industrial relations. An immediate impact was felt in areas of industrial development and individual labour law. The influx of multinational enterprises is commonly accredited with a greater level of professionalism in the area of personnel or human resource management, together with an increase in both trade union membership cum pre-production employment agreements and non-union establishments (McMahon 1990). Significant revisions were also prompted in such areas as dismissal, employment equality, mass redundancy and worker participation legislation. This development has certainly facilitated the emergence of prominent players on the industrial relations pitch in the form of the EU and the European Parliament. Furthermore, few doubt that the Community will play a key role in shaping the political agenda of the future. The passage of the Single European Act and the Amsterdam Treaty has focused the minds of most pressure groups in society on the implications of greater economic and political union across the member states. Amongst the scope of influences on the industrial relations environment, considerable attention is being devoted to the social dimension, or Social Charter, which spans a range of social and employment rights, including health and safety, equitable remuneration, equality, information and consultation entitlements and freedom of movement.

The advent of contemporary national-level partnership arrangements – covering a host of economic (including pay) and social issues – can be traced back to the maintenance men's dispute of 1969–1970. According to the Dublin Chamber of

Commerce, this was 'the greatest crisis in industrial relations ever experienced in the history of the state', producing a twenty per cent wage rise over eighteen months (O'Grada 1997). The expectations sparked by this settlement promptly raised industrial relations on the government's agenda. Such a large settlement threatened the government's economic management aspirations in the desire to control incomes and inflationary pressures, thus eventually giving rise to the national tripartite arrangements. Prior to the suspension of such arrangements, over the 1982–1987 period they had expanded in scope to accommodate a plethora of economic and social affairs under the title of 'national understandings'. The temporary demise of the consensus approach at national level during the 1980s can be primarily attributed to a hardened negotiating stance on the part of both employers and the state. Related to this was a change in government, with the more populist or pragmatic Fianna Fáil party being replaced by a Fine Gael/Labour coalition. A subsequent change of government facilitated the resurgence of the social partnership approach from 1987 onwards. National-level agreements emerged again to embrace a range of economic and social issues. It is interesting to contrast the fact that while their British counterparts were left out in the cold during the 1980s and most of the 1990s, the Irish trade union movement played a central role in decisions on not just pay increases, but national economic and social strategy and planning as well. Effectively, the economic recession of the 1980s served to direct Ireland further down the road to corporatism, establishing a pattern that has endured to date. In the opinion of von Prondzynski (1988), however, the progress down this road – the price of participation (in the 1987 Programme) – ought to be costed against

> every evidence that the Programme was designed as a back-up to the Government's programme of expenditure cut-backs and income restraint; the intention was primarily to tie the hands of the trade unions in particular and make difficult any serious militancy in opposition to these policies … this approach is working rather well.

However, in this regard it is also pertinent that the prevailing monetarism or neo-laissez-faire economic policies espoused particularly by Thatcher's Conservative British and Regan's Republican American governments prevailed. Looking to our influential British neighbours, the lesson from the failure of Scargill's miners' union (Crick 1985) – a union assumed to have the ability to topple the government – was not lost. The choice for the Irish unions, in an era of declining membership and rising unemployment, spanned likely futile industrial action or participation in the nation's key decision-making fora. The participative model, therefore, initiated by Seán Lemass in the late 1950s, now appears to be accepted in principle by at least the upper echelons of the trade union and employer organisations. This is reflected by their involvement in a variety of industry- and national-level tripartite fora. However, this commitment to a participative approach, reflected for example in the establishment of the National Centre for Partnership and Performance, is less evident at firm level (Geary 1999; McMahon 2000a, 2000b). The focus of attention on both sides of the industrial relations process at this level tends to be the size of the wage settlement – an element well capable of exposing the fragility of interest group solidarity.

By the early 1990s, the sad state of many important national economic indicators, pressures exerted by a persistent international recession and constraints on remedial initiatives imposed by membership of, and adherence to, the EU and single European market, respectively, combined to apparently signal a new era in the management of industrial relations. Political developments in many industrialised economies – including the resurgence of laissez-faire individualism with its emphasis on monetarism, free enterprise, open markets, deregulation and privatisation – and the demise of socialist economies in Eastern Europe forced the recall and revision of many left-wing and trade union ideological aspirations. This helped reinforce the merits of operating inside the neo-corporatist model for the trade union movement and the furtherance of its more immediate demands under the auspices of the prevalent liberal capitalist political system. Indeed, it may be argued that the status of the trade union movement in a centralised, corporatist state has cushioned it from the trends visible elsewhere in recent times.

The *quid pro quo* exchange was particularly evident in the Celtic Tiger phase. Given the contention that 'trade unions are usually more militant in times of prosperity' (Sweeney 1998), relative industrial peace continued to prevail. According to MacSharry and White (2000), 'social partnership could well be regarded as the crowning achievement of the Celtic Tiger economy'. Against this, however, the absence of greater equity in areas like wealth distribution, health, housing and education poses a formidable challenge to future relationships amongst the social partners (see Chapter 13).

By the late 1990s, however, it was apparent that industrial relations had reached another crossroads. While the resurgent national economic and labour market environment depicted above had contributed to this, the British and French general elections in 1997, the re-election of the Democrats' nominee in the US presidential election and the increasing 'Europeanisation' of industrial relations made it an ever-changing melting pot for subjects and observers alike at the turn of the century. However, by 2002 the political stability associated with the re-election of the Irish government and the prevalence of 'single-ideology states' across the developed world (Pilger 2002) contrasts with the fluidity of the international political landscape. This was apparent in a more 'hawkish' Republican American president, the rise of political parties with xenophobic tendencies across Europe and the imminent expansion of the EU itself – with particular relevance to a more open labour market.

While drawing attention to the Europeanisation of industrial relations, it is important to stress that this does not constitute a European model of industrial relations, nor is there a prospect of one being forthcoming (Biagi *et al.* 2002). Indeed, there are trends in the opposite direction. For instance, Rojot (2001: 79) predicts that with the enlargement of the EU institutional differences across European countries 'will certainly increase'. There is no evidence of transnational European wage bargaining and the competition for mobile capital investment sees differing countries pursue differing strategies in relation to areas such as taxation policy, union recognition and worker democracy. Ireland has opposed common taxation policy because of the perceived advantage of our low corporate taxation rates in attracting multinational investment. While a European industrial relations system does not exist, Biagi *et al.* (2002) argue that 'it is possible to identify an increasing convergence on European issues'. This they see arising as 'a result of growing Europe-wide cooperation in the economic, monetary and employment spheres … In this respect we can say that European industrial relations are changing and they change in a perspective of increasing "Europeanisation"'. Others, however, see this Europeanisation as weak and under threat from the alternative model of capitalism in the US, which is driven not by balancing the interests of various stakeholders – shareholders, workers and managers – but by the often short-term dictates of the stock market.

THE ROLE OF THEORY IN INDUSTRIAL RELATIONS

The role of theory in industrial relations is intended to facilitate the analysis and appraisal of the subject's processes, structures and institutions in as objective a manner as is possible with any of the social sciences. Therefore, this section of the text outlines and evaluates the main academic theories that have been developed in an effort to provide a logical and consistent means of understanding and interpreting industrial relations realities. Over the past twenty years in particular there has been a series of prescriptions for change designed to improve the conduct of industrial relations in this country, e.g. changes in strike laws, worker participation/involvement schemes and trade union rationalisation. Such proposals can often be highly contentious and the theoretical principles and value judgments upon which they are founded are rarely made explicit. Accordingly, this section introduces and assesses the main theoretical perspectives and related value judgments on the nature of the world of work.

Familiarity with the underlying values of the various theoretical perspectives shall help in our analysis of aspects of the changing nature of the employment relationship. As each theory originates from a different base or set of assumptions, it would be inappropriate to insist upon a single 'best' theory of industrial relations or to force the student down a 'pick-and-choose' road in the construction of an analytical framework to fit with their own particular values, perspective or insight. While insisting upon this discretionary prerogative it would be remiss not to acknowledge the traditional primacy of the pluralist analysis in Irish industrial relations practices and debates. This is reflected in the high levels of union density together with the central role of, and preoccupation with, collective bargaining – and its institutions – at establishment, industrial and national levels.

Pluralist Analysis

The pluralist and related analyses of industrial relations systems in Western societies have been in pole position for over thirty years now. This framework or model is based upon the existence of a post-capitalist society, where industrial and political conflict have become institutionally separated, ownership is distinguished from management and authority and power in society are more widely distributed. In effect, such an analysis acknowledges that society is comprised of a range of individuals, interest and social groups, each in pursuit of their own objectives. As in society, the employing entity is comprised of an accommodation or alliance of different values and competing sectional interests, so it is only through accommodation that work organisations can attempt to operate with any degree of continuity and success. Just as the political system is institutionalised and regulated through a party political and parliamentary process, so also is the industrial system institutionalised and regulated through representative organisations and appropriately structured processes. The existence of these competing organisational values and interests then facilitate 'a complex of tensions and competing claims which have to be "managed" in the interests of maintaining a viable collaborative structure' (Fox 1973).

Hence the emergence of a succession of temporary compromises (or collective agreements) as the opposing aspirations for higher profits and productivity or efficiency are aligned with improved pay and working condition demands. As Dubin (1954) summarises, 'collective bargaining is the great social invention that has institutionalised industrial conflict. In much the same way that the electoral process and majority rule have institutionalised political conflict in a democracy, collective bargaining has created a stable means for resolving industrial conflict'. That is, conflict necessitates the establishment of 'accepted procedures and institutions which achieve collaboration through comprehensive, codified systems of negotiated regulation' (Salamon 2000). Such arrangements are a recognition of the fact that the pluralist organisation is in 'a constant state of dynamic tension arising from conflicts of interest and loyalty which require to be managed through a variety of procedures' (Rose 2001).

Such a perspective acknowledges the legitimacy of trade union organisation, interests and the right to contest the managerial prerogative. In any case, 'greater stability and adaptability is given to industrial relations by collective bargaining than by shackling and outlawing trade unions' (Clegg 1975). The structures, formats and processes of labour relations are perceived as the manifestation of the power relations and conflict between employers, managers and trade unions. Accordingly, conflict is viewed as a logical and inevitable feature of the world of work and consequently requires management by a variety of role players or representatives, procedures, processes and specialist institutions.

A central feature of this post-capitalist perspective is that the class conflict by-product of the Industrial Revolution has now abated. The Marxist analysis of the powerful capitalists and weak wage earners – of the socially elite and the socially weak – is no longer an appropriate model, at least in the developed Western world. It is argued that contemporary society is more open and mobile, with the franchise extended for the further democratisation of politics, greater accessibility of educational opportunity opening hitherto closed occupational routes and the advent of the welfare state serving to alleviate the worst extremes of deprivation and inequality. Such societal developments have combined to effectively undermine and point to the need for a replacement of the Marxist prognosis. Furthermore, the spread and diffusion of property ownership, status and authority in the post-capitalist society have irretrievably removed the sharp divisions between those who were once industrially and politically powerful and their counterparts, who were weak and powerless in both these crucial spheres.

Accordingly, with the separation of industrial and political conflict, collective bargaining has become the focus of attention at the workplace for the regulation of relations. With the emergence, structuring and regulation of representative organisations, on both sides of industry appropriate fora have now been established to address the tensions and conflicts arising at all levels between these sectional interest groups. Trade unions compete with employers and government for an input to national-level economic and social decision making via social partnership in return for wage restraint, co-operation with change and industrial peace. In the event of failure to resolve differences at plant level, a range of third-party institutions provides a generally acceptable route for the resolution of contrasting objectives and conflict. In conjunction with this system it is argued that the development of employee involvement, or participative practices, serves to emphasise the distribution or diffusion of power and authority in industry. According to Dahrendorf (1959), these developments are well reflected in:

(1) the organisation of conflicting interest groups itself; (2) the establishment of 'parliamentary' negotiating bodies in which these groups meet; (3) the institutions of mediation and arbitration; (4) formal representations within the individual enterprise; and (5) tendencies towards and institutionalisation of workers' participation in industrial management.

Pluralists then acknowledge the inevitability of conflict, but point to the relative stability of a society that institutionalises, manages and contains any differences via collaboration, negotiated compromises and mediation.

Unitary Analysis

The basic premise of the unitary perspective on the employee relations system is that all employment units are, or should be, cohesive and harmonious establishments with a total commitment to the attainment of a common goal. Being unitary in structure and purpose, with shared goals, values and interests and one source of (managerial) authority, the staff relations are set upon a plinth of mutuality and harmony. That is, there is no conflict between those contributing the capital, i.e. the owners, and the contributors of labour, i.e. the employees. Consequently, all staff members agree unreservedly with the organisation's aspirations and the methods and means deployed to achieve these targets. Through this team or complementary partnership approach, it is assumed that both sides of the equation can satisfy their common goals of high profitability and pay levels, job security and efficiency. Notwithstanding same, it is implicitly acknowledged that, as with any team approach, competent and strong leadership or management are a prerequisite to the pursuit of organisational effectiveness. In practice this may give rise to elements of paternalism and/or authoritarianism on the part of management in their approach to employee relations matters.

Paternalism may be reflected in a managerial concern for staff needs together with a rejection of union recognition and collective bargaining practices. Authoritarianism may also materialise in a dominant managerial value system, characterised by minimal concern for employee welfare and outright opposition to union recognition and collective bargaining initiatives. For example, during the nineteenth century many employers adopted an aggressive unitary stance, actively excluding unions while employing women and children on low pay for long hours in unsanitary working conditions. In either scenario, trade unionism is opposed as a threat to the organisation's unity of purpose and the (legitimate and rational) managerial prerogative because it competes for employee loyalty and commitment. The consequent rejection of collective bargaining is based upon management's perceived legitimate prerogative to proceed without the incumbency of negotiation to attain consent to their decision-making initiatives and responsibility. In such a setting it is assumed that management will insert an appropriate communications structure to alert staff to organisational priorities and to manage the expectations of staff in respect of same. In response, staff effectuate these instructions as they display their loyalty to the entity for the realisation of their common goals, e.g. job security.

In essence the unitary theory rejects the concept of enduring conflict or organisational factionalism since such collision, competition or opposition distracts from what are assumed to be non-competing co-operative initiatives. The existence of conflict is not perceived to be a structural feature of organisational life, but

> is either (a) merely frictional, e.g. due to incompatible personalities or 'things going wrong', or (b) caused by faulty 'communications', e.g. 'misunderstandings' about aims or methods, or (c) the result of stupidity in the form of failure to grasp the communality of interest, or (d) the work of agitators inciting the supine majority who would otherwise be content (Fox 1966).

The unitary philosophy is therefore predominantly managerial in that it legitimises their authority under the heading of commonality, largely attributes the source of conflict to subordinates and serves as a means of justifying their decisions to any interested parties while explaining opposition to same as either ill-informed or perverse. The undoubted increase in levels of opposition to trade union recognition and the associated rise in the number of non-union establishments has significantly strengthened the prevalence and validity of this particular analytical model on the national scene in recent years. Accordingly, this unitarist model provides the subconscious foundation for managers in their choice of issues upon which they are prepared to negotiate and those upon which they are only prepared to consult. Furthermore, it provides a *raison d'être* for many of the now-prevalent human resource management practices in Irish employments.

Classical Marxist Analysis

Though Marxist analyses of industrial relations are more of a by-product of a theory of capitalist society and social change than of labour relations, they do have considerable implications and provide a useful framework for the interpretation of the relationship between capital and labour. That is, Marxism is more concerned with the structure and nature of society than with the actual workplaces society accommodates. Of course when the original Marxist analysis of the nature and structure of society was conceived, the phenomena of trade unionism and collective bargaining were barely established. Consequently, the application of the original Marxist analysis to contemporary labour relations institutions and phenomena is problematic. Classical Marxism saw capitalism as an advanced stage in societal development. However, because of class conflicts over the distribution of the surplus value of workers' efforts, there was an irreconcilable antagonism between capital and labour. Classical Marxism predicted the impoverishment of an ever-growing working class, which would lead to revolutionary change after capitalism had reached a mature stage.

This body of theory is essentially an analysis of the evolution of society, of which the capitalist (or bourgeois state) is only one phase. In other words, Marxism depicts a series of developments, or phases of social change, from the initial state of primitive communism through an era of feudalism to capitalism, which it is predicted would give rise to a class war (between the bourgeoisie and the proletariat), culminating in a dictatorship of the proletariat before progressing to socialism and eventually a utopian classless society.

In the terminology of modern game theory, Marxism saw society and the workplace as a zero sum gain. In the event revolution, when it came, occurred not in the developed West, but rather in the less developed East and under conditions of the uncertainties which arose from capitalist wars. A number of the predictions of classical Marxism have failed to materialise, yet the growth of large-scale business, or monopoly capital, is one of the areas of Marxist analysis which resonates even in our time. Furthermore, capitalism has been enormously successful in developing wealth in certain parts of the globe, but it has not worked so well in other areas. Even with increased wealth the distribution of that wealth remains an issue with which many neo-Marxists and radical writers have been concerned.

Neo-Marxism and Radicalism

These sources attribute the industrial relations system with a limited role via the resolution of pay and condition issues and the delineation of the boundaries of managerial prerogative. Conflict in the industrial relations arena is seen as a reflection of the opposing economic interests engendered by capitalism.

In essence, the Marxist perspective is based upon the premise that class, i.e. capital and labour, conflict is at the root of societal change. This conflict is not a simple consequence of contrasting demands and tensions at the workplace, but rather is the product of an inequitable distribution of power and wealth in wider society. Such inequity is also reflected in society's social and political institutions that serve to maintain the position of the dominant establishment group, i.e. the owners of the means of production. Therefore, social and political conflict – and social change – is the result of these central economic inequities and divisions within society between the owner of capitalist and labouring classes. Accordingly, conflict reflects the difference between these social classes with their diametrically opposed economic and political interests. Class and political conflict are therefore inextricably linked with industrial conflict, which the Marxist perspective judges to be a permanent feature of capitalism. This persistent and unavoidable conflict is the result of these competing interests seeking to consolidate and advance their relative positions in the economic power structure as they contest the distribution of the entity or society's power, wealth and 'surplus value'.

In effect, then, the industrial relations system is a marginal forum for the conduct of a class war. While some Marxists continue to suggest this will ultimately spill out and over into a more fundamental political revolution, others do not. Radical writers, such as Fox (1977), do not see any such development in prospect and suggest that conflict is contained by the social and political system and the trade-offs made to ensure its stability. In other words, the institutions of industrial relations serve to institutionalise conflict. Trade unions are viewed in this context as a collective response to the exploitation of the capitalist system and may perform a central role in the wider political process for the attainment of significant alterations to the economic and social system on behalf of the proletariat (workers). The operation of national, industrial and enterprise-based bodies of joint regulation, however, with their agreed procedures and processes, are judged by Marxists to accommodate, consolidate, legitimise and effectively enhance the managerial prerogative and power position, while projecting an image or veneer of power sharing. That is, the collective bargaining process is perceived to at least temporarily accept, facilitate and ultimately support the inherent contradictions of capitalism. Furthermore, the state's legislative framework is perceived by Marxists to be a related piece of armoury designed to support management's interests (Hyman 1975).

In summary, when evaluating prescriptions arising from other perspectives, Marxists would argue that economic and political issues cannot be separated. Marxists place great emphasis on the antagonistic interests of capital and labour and, in sharp contrast with alternative analytical frameworks, focus on the importance of assessing the power held by opposing interests. For an insightful appreciation of the industrial relations system, focus on the relative 'power' positions of competing (or conflicting) interests should not be underestimated.

Social Action Analysis

The social action perspective on industrial relations 'stresses that the individual retains at least some freedom of action and ability to influence events' in the manner they believe to be most appropriate or preferable (Jackson 1982). This theory emphasises the role players' or actors' definitions, perceptions and influences on reality. It is these definitions and perceptions that determine their relationships, behaviour and actions. Therefore, with this frame of reference social and industrial relations actions are best understood in terms of their subjectively intended meanings. Concentration on observed behaviour at the workplace restricts the value of any interpretation, as it would overlook the deeper intent of the actors. The actors' decisions are determined not just by the specific work situations they find themselves in, but by a plethora of wider and underlying influences, such as the attitudes, values, experiences and expectations developed over a lifetime both inside and outside the workplace. The central relevance of this particular perspective is that it attributes to the individual actors some prerogative or discretion to shape the actual workplace and society in which they exist along their desired lines. In this context, however, they are restricted by their own perception of reality. Thus, the social action analysis accords some control or priority to the individual over the structure or system in which they find themselves. It offers a frame of reference which concentrates on the range of industrial relations system outputs as being as much the end result of the actions of its constituent parts as of the structure of the system itself. The social action theory is in fact rooted in a well-developed sociological school of thought which argues that just as 'society makes man … man makes society' (Silverman 1970).

The impact on Irish industrial relations of individuals like James Larkin and William Martin Murphy arguably supports this perspective. However, this has to be balanced against the fact that unskilled unions gained a foothold in Ireland only twenty years after they had established themselves in the rest of the UK. To explain this one must look to system factors connected with the industrially underdeveloped nature of the Irish economy – the so-called 'beer and biscuits' nature of Irish industry. Furthermore, in the UK and many other countries, the conditions following the Industrial Revolution produced radical union leaders not dissimilar to Larkin, indicating that apparent social action effects may be due to underlying system factors.

Systems Analysis

The systems theory of industrial relations originated in the late 1950s in the United States when John Dunlop proposed that 'an industrial relations system at any one time in its development is regarded as comprised of certain actors, certain contexts, an ideology which binds the industrial relations system together, and a body of rules created to govern the actors at the workplace and work community' (Dunlop 1958). Dunlop's construction of an integrated model is based on a view of the industrial relations system as one which, though overlapping and interacting with the economic and political decision-making systems, is nevertheless a societal sub-system in its own right. This sub-system's output or product is comprised of a set of rules pertaining to the employment relationship, which spans their design, application and interpretation. Accordingly, the industrial relations system is primarily concerned with an output of rules covering all pay and condition matters, together with the installation of procedures for their administration and application. The systems theory of industrial relations is therefore based upon the standard input-process-output model, which Dunlop argues can be applied regardless of the economic or political system in place.

Under the input heading, Dunlop identifies three sets of influences: actors, environmental contexts and ideology, which combine in the bargaining, conciliation and legislative processes to yield a body, network or web of rules. The actors include the different worker categories (whether organised or unorganised), the various layers of management (together with their respective representatives) and the range of third-party agencies. The environmental context impinging on the state of the industrial relations system is comprised of technological, market/budgetary and societal power location and distribution variables. The technological impact is reflected in such factors as the size, skill and gender breakdown of the workforce, its concentration or distribution and the location and duration of the employment. The market or budgetary constraints, whether applied locally, nationally or internationally, affect all enterprise types, not just the entity's management but ultimately all of the system's role players. The 'power' input relates to the structural context of or degree of autonomy afforded to the industrial relations system by wider society. This will, of course, be significantly influenced by the distribution of power in that society. The ideological input recognises that while each group of actors in the system may have their own set of ideas, these are sufficiently congruent for a level of mutual tolerance, common belief or unifying ideological compatibility to prevail.

CONCLUSION AND CRITIQUE OF MODELS

As evidenced by their contrasting premises and prognoses, all of the models of industrial relations outlined above have been subjected to critical evaluation. Despite its prevalence and robustness, the pluralist analysis, for example, has been criticised for its ready acceptance of the social and political status quo and a fundamental conservatism which assumes an illusory balance of power between the various interest groups (Fox 1973; Goldthorpe 1974). Unlike both the unitary and Marxist theories, pluralism appears less value driven. Yet pluralism does not desist from prescriptions that favour the constant negotiation or renegotiation of conflicts based on compromise and tolerance for other views (Clegg 1975). This both enhances and detracts from its standing. Similarly, the unitary perspective is cautioned for its unrealistically utopian outlook, limited applicability, e.g. to non-union entities, and a paternalistic management orientation that assumes a generally accepted value system. Indeed, D'Art and Turner's (2002a) overview of Irish industrial relations serves as a sturdy challenge to this perspective. Their findings support the argument 'for the utility and continuing relevance of trade unions and collective bargaining'. The classic Marxist analysis is considered to be anachronistic given that, among other things, the nature of class conflict has substantially changed and contemporary society, with its mixed economy and welfare state, is now more open and socially mobile. The distribution of power, property and social status in society is more widely diffused today (at least in the developed world) than it was in the nineteenth century and consequently undermines the theory's simplistic classifications. Nonetheless, in drawing attention to the nature of power and control in the workplace and society, the neo-Marxist and radical analysis presents an intellectual challenge to unitarist and pluralist thinking.

In regard to social action theory critics point to its neglect of those structural features that influence the action of its actors. It is argued that this oversight really reflects the theory's own inability to explain the very nature of the wider system inside which these actions occur.

Systems theory has also been subjected to considerable critical evaluation, refinement and modification. For example, it is contended that the model's narrow focus omits the reality of and mechanisms for the distribution of wealth and power in society. In effect, its convenient unifying ideology cum status quo inclination, which takes society as given, merely accords the industrial relations system some functional role in the maintenance of stability and overlooks a range of issues, including industrial relations change, the source of conflict and the system's inter-relationship with the 'outside' political, economic and social scene. It is also argued that its structural emphasis leads to an output or rules focus at the expense of the actual decision or rule-making processes. Additionally, it fails to explain the important behavioural variables, i.e. why actors act as they do. It is also suggested that the system's model ought to accommodate the significant role of the owners of business, who warrant inclusion in both an actor's and contextual capacity. Wood (1978/1979) also recommends that a modifying distinction be made in the model 'between the system which "produces" rules, i.e. the industrial relations system, and the system which is governed by such rules, i.e. the production system'. Therefore, the revised approach recommends focusing upon both the narrower rule-making processes and the wider contextual influences, e.g. political, legal and social contexts.

In conclusion, far from being a descriptive subject based on common sense, a single analytical framework or a set of incontrovertible facts and statistics, political and theoretical controversy is inherent in the topic of industrial relations. There is a variety of ways of interpreting what is going on and a multitude of opinions about what should be happening in this subject area. However, the fact that there is no universally accepted global theory is unavoidable and should be accepted by the student as an attractive dimension of a topic that easily lends itself to contrasting perspectives, opinions and debate. It is for the student to make up his/her own mind on these matters, since this book endeavours to take a neutral line, presenting the different sides of the various theories, propositions and debates.

CHAPTER 2

Individual Employment Law

OVERVIEW

The principal purpose of labour law is to regulate, support and restrain the power of management and the power of organised labour (Kahn-Freund 1977). The process of legislative intervention in the employment relationship can be traced back as far as the 1349 Ordinance of Labourers. This initiative was designed to impose wage ceilings for both artisans and labourers in the Black Death era of severe labour shortages. It wasn't until the nineteenth century that a range of protective statutes were enacted covering such matters as health and safety and the form that wage payments should take. Since 1967 there have been significant developments, particularly in the area of individual employment law. These legislative initiatives may be viewed as a countervailing force attempting to redress the unequal bargaining power of the individual vis-à-vis the employing organisation.

Of course, at the root of the employment relationship is the common law contract of employment, with its power to command and duty to obey. Statute law was historically accorded a marginal role in its attempts to regulate and co-ordinate this relationship. However, though management still retain the power to hire and fire, this prerogative has been considerably restrained by a range of legislation, including unfair dismissal, notice, redundancy and employment equality, and recently by the trend of high-profile employees seeking injunctions in the courts to restrain or reverse dismissals in breach of contract or the rules of fair procedures. In an attempt to cover the more salient and relevant aspects of 'individual' employment law this chapter reviews the role of the employment contract, dismissal law, equality legislation and finally summarises other statutes of particular relevance to industrial relations at work. Accordingly, little attention is paid to those areas of the law that have had little usage or have not given rise to controversy of any magnitude in recent years. For students requiring further details there are a range of texts dealing with modern employment law, notably Meenan (1999), Fennell and Lynch (1993), Forde (2001) and von Prondzynski and McCarthy (1989).

As the contract of employment is the basis of much law, this is considered first. Second, we will discuss in detail the Unfair Dismissals Acts 1977–2001, followed by a review of the role and operation of the Employment Appeals Tribunal (EAT). We will then provide an overview of other employment legislation dealt with by the Tribunal. Finally, we will examine equality legislation and the state institutions for adjudication in that area. The Rights Commissioners have functions under both employment and industrial relations law and they are discussed in the next chapter.

THE CONTRACT OF EMPLOYMENT

The contract of employment is the legal basis of the employment relationship and is central to the interpretation and application of statutory rights. As with the basic law of contract it requires that there be an offer from the employer which is accepted by the employee, that there be consideration or remuneration from the employer for work done and that there be an intention to create a legal relationship. The contract may be concluded on an oral or written basis. However, the passing of the Terms of Employment (Information) Act 1994 should in effect have brought the completely oral contract to an end. Basically, any employee who has one month's service is entitled to a written statement of his/her basic terms and conditions of employment, including hours of work, rates of pay and provision in relation to overtime, sick pay, holidays, etc. The former requirement to work not less than eight hours per week to be entitled to the statement has been removed as a result of the Protection of Employees (Part-Time Work) Act 2001. This statement must be received within two months of taking up employment. Existing employees at the time the Act was passed, i.e. in May 1994, must request the statement. A complaint goes to a Rights Commissioner in the event of failure to comply with the Act.

Common law attempts to distinguish between a contract *of* service, i.e. with an employee, and a contract *for* service, i.e. with an independent contractor (see Table 2.1). This is of some relevance given that it is only an 'employee' who can avail of the protection afforded under labour law. Case law indicates that three tests may be applied to differentiate between these contract types.

Table 2.1
Key Differences between Contracts of Service and Contracts for Service

Of Service	For Service
Employer-employee relationship	Employer-independent contractor relationship
Usually a continuous relationship	A once-off piece of work relationship
Duty of care owed to employees	Duty of care arising from occupier's liability
Generally vicariously liable for the acts of employees	Generally not vicariously liable for the acts of independent contractors
Protective legislation applies to contract	Protective legislation does not apply (excluding Safety, Health and Welfare at Work Act 1989)
Wage/salary payment method	Fee payment method
Subject of contract is to carry on continuous work	Subject of contract is once-off job

Source: Gunnigle *et al.* (1992)

- **Control**: Can the employer tell the employee what to do and how to do it?
- **Integration**: Is the employee's work integrated into the business or is it a case of the independent contractor working for the business?
- **Multiple**: What is the nature of the entire arrangement between the employer and the worker? This would be reflected in answers to the following types of questions.
  - Are there wages, sick and holiday pay? Who pays them?
  - Are income tax and social security deducted under the PAYE and PRSI systems, respectively, by the employer?
  - Does the worker share in the profits/losses?
  - Who provides the tools and equipment for the job?
  - Are there specific provisions relating to termination?
  - Is the employer entitled to exclusive service?
  - Is it a genuine case of self-employment or is there an attempt to avoid protective legislation?

Lord Wedderburn (1986) has concluded that the variety of legal 'tests' have splintered in the hands of the judiciary and it is 'not practicable to lay down precise tests' or a 'hard and fast list'. Indeed, he suggested that most courts now appear to apply the 'elephant test' for the employee, i.e. an animal that is too difficult to define but easy to recognise when you see it. However, the Irish Supreme Court, in the landmark decision of *Henry Denny and Sons (Ireland)* v. *The Minister for Social Welfare (1998) I.R. 34* provided a measure of clarity on this issue and sent out a strong message to employers that despite the stated nature of the relationship, a court will look at the reality of the arrangement. The Denny case considered the social insurance status of a supermarket demonstrator whose contract clearly stated that she was providing her services as an independent contractor. The Court nonetheless found that she was an employee. Justice Keane (www.bailii.org/ie/cases/IESC/1997/9.html) stated:

> While each case must be determined in the light of its particular facts and circumstances, in general a person will be regarded as providing his or her services under a contract of service and not as an independent contractor where he or she is performing those services for another person and not for himself or herself.

DISMISSAL AND THE LAW

The Unfair Dismissals Acts 1977–2001 was an important development in Irish labour law, as it gave a remedy to employees for unfair dismissals. However, the Acts do not prevent an unfair dismissal, although employees may seek an injunction against unfair dismissal and there have been a number of developments in this regard in recent years.

Following a review of anomalies and difficulties with the Act, an amendment act was passed in 1993, with the changes principally favouring employees.

The Provisions of the Unfair Dismissals Acts 1977–2001

It is estimated that the Act applies to most employees in Ireland. Under its provisions, once an 'employee' has been continuously employed for one year (the former requirement to be normally expected to work not less than eight hours per week has been removed as a result of the Protection of Employees (Part-Time Work) Act 2001), he has a right to claim unfair dismissal. Prior to the passing of the 1991 Part-Time Employees legislation, an employee needed to have worked eighteen hours per week in order to claim. In the event of perceived unfair dismissal, a case may be brought before either a Rights Commissioner or the Employment Appeals Tribunal (EAT) within six months of the date of dismissal. Under the 1993 amending Act, however, either the Tribunal or the Rights Commissioner may extend this time limit by six months in exceptional circumstances. The option of going directly to the Tribunal only applies in the event of either party objecting to a Rights Commissioner hearing. Either party may appeal the Tribunal's decision to the Circuit Court within six weeks from the date on which the determination is communicated to the parties, and where an employer fails to carry out a determination an employee may also bring about enforcement proceedings in the Circuit Court. Of course, if the employee has taken the matter to the Labour Court or has instituted proceedings for damages at common law for wrongful dismissal, he would not also be entitled to redress under the Act.

The number of claims made has decreased slightly in recent years. For example, in 1996 the EAT dealt with 1,133 direct claims and appeals from Rights Commissioners, whereas the corresponding figures for 1999, 2000 and 2001 were 848, 808 and 957, respectively. This decline (up to 2000) may well be attributed to the more buoyant economy and the fact that compensation is only awarded under the Act for loss of earnings, while the economic uncertainty prevailing from 2001 prompted an increasing number of claims.

The Unfair Dismissals Act 2001 made certain amendments to the exclusions from the Acts of people working for close relatives and people undergoing full-time training or apprenticeship in FÁS establishments, who shall not apply where the dismissal results from:

- the employee's pregnancy, giving birth or breastfeeding (or any matters connected therewith); or
- the exercise or proposed exercise by the employee of rights under the Maternity Protection Act 1994; Adoptive Leave Act 1995; Parental Leave Act 1998; and Carer's Leave Act 2001.

A number of categories of employees are not covered under the Unfair Dismissals Acts 1977–2001. This includes:

- people with less than one year's continuous service with the same employer (unless the employee is alleging the dismissal took place on grounds of pregnancy (or related matters), trade union membership or activities or the exercise of rights in relation to maternity, adoptive, parental or *force majeure* leave);
- people over the normal retiring age;

- close relatives of the employer who are members of his/her household and work in a private dwelling house;
- people employed by the Defence Forces and the Garda Síochána;
- people employed by or under the state (excluding those provided for under Section 17 of the Industrial Relations Act 1969);
- people undergoing full-time training or apprenticeship in FÁS establishments;
- people engaged under a statutory apprenticeship during:
  - the six months after commencement of the apprenticeship; and
  - the period of one month following completion of the apprenticeship, provided the employee is not absent from work on protective leave.
- officers of local authorities or health boards (excluding temporary officers) and of vocational educational committees and committees of agriculture;
- people normally working outside the state; and
- replacement of an employee on carer's leave under the Carer's Leave Act 2001 where written notice is given in advance by the employer and the dismissal duly occurs for the purpose of facilitating the return to work of that other employee.

The Act provides that a dismissal will automatically be deemed to be unfair if it can be attributed to:

- trade union membership or activities (including industrial action);
- religious or political opinion;
- involvement in civil or criminal legal proceedings against the employer;
- race or colour;
- sexual orientation;
- age;
- being a member of the Travelling community;
- pregnancy or matters connected with pregnancy;
- the exercise of maternity, adoptive leave or holiday entitlements;
- the exercise of entitlements under the National Minimum Wage Act 2000 (one year's service not required); or
- the exercise of rights under the Carer's Leave Act 2001 (one year's service not required).

The burden of proof in dismissal cases normally resides with the employer, but the employee must show that he is actually covered by the Act's provisions and that a dismissal actually took place. In general, employers bear the brunt of the Act's regulatory force insofar as the onus of responsibility is on them to show that they have acted reasonably. The Tribunal then attempts to evaluate the employer's (re)action and sanction with a view to determining whether it lies within the range of responses which a 'reasonable' employer might make. A common determinant of the Tribunal's decisions on the status of a dismissal is whether the employer followed fair and proper procedures prior to the dismissal. This requirement of procedural fairness is rooted in the common law concept of natural justice and in the provisions of the 1937 Constitution. In addition, the Code of Practice on Grievance and Disciplinary Procedures (Statutory Instrument 146/2000) issued by the Labour Relations Commission, updating a similar code issued in 1996, provides a clear rationale for the adoption of such procedures. This code is admissible in proceedings before, amongst others, the EAT. The amendment Act of 1993 also provides that the existence or otherwise of a dismissal procedure is a factor the Tribunal can take into account in making its determinations.

The four basic obligations in regard to disciplinary procedural arrangements identified from case law by Fennell and Lynch (1993: 230–1) are:

- **Investigation**: An inadequate investigation of the situation on the part of the employer may give rise to a dismissal being deemed unfair. Accordingly, a reasonable and fair investigation of the matter should be undertaken by the employer.
- **Hearing**: The employer must put the relevant case before the employee, thus allowing him/her to respond. A refusal to allow trade union representation at such meetings is likely to render the dismissal unfair.
- **Warning**: Prior to dismissal for misconduct or poor performance the employee should generally be given a series of warnings, thus providing him/her with an opportunity to improve.
- **Proportionate penalties**: A dismissal will be judged to be unfair where the employer is seen to overreact, that is, if a lesser penalty would have been more appropriate in the circumstances.

The normal reaction of the EAT to a failure to follow fair procedures, especially those laid down in a collective agreement or written disciplinary procedure, is to judge the dismissal to be unfair. However, the extent of the contribution on the employee's part to the circumstances resulting in the dismissal will be taken into account when the Tribunal decides upon the appropriate remedy. Consequently, even if the Tribunal concludes, for whatever reason, that a dismissal was unfair, it might consider it appropriate to make a 100 per cent deduction from the compensation that the employee would otherwise be entitled to. It is also notable, however, that the Circuit Court has sometimes concluded that an otherwise 'fair dismissal' does not automatically become unfair due to its procedural defects. Nevertheless, a direct result of this 'procedural fairness' factor is that there have been widespread changes in companies' procedures, practices and decision-making processes, with disciplinary and dismissal procedures now commonplace (O'Connor 1982; Wallace 1989). This is discussed further in Chapter 10.

Fair Dismissal

Those areas where a dismissal may be justified can largely (but not exclusively) be categorised under the following headings: conduct, capability/competence/qualifications and redundancy.

Conduct

This may take the form of a single act of gross misconduct or a series of minor acts where the employee disregards relevant warnings. Dismissal arising out of alleged employee gross misconduct is one of the most common case types coming before a Rights Commissioner or the Tribunal. A fair dismissal under this heading normally occurs where the essential employer-employee relationship of trust is undermined. It generally applies to matters of abuse of sick leave, substance or alcohol abuse, criminal convictions, dishonesty, disobedience, breach of the duty of loyalty and fidelity and violence or intimidation (see Madden and Kerr 1996). The Tribunal has not, however, established any objective standard of 'unacceptable conduct' which justifies dismissal. Instead, it opts to evaluate the dismissal decision on the grounds of 'reasonableness' given the particular circumstances of each case. Consequently, one cannot construct a comprehensive and rigid checklist of conduct types that will be determined by the Tribunal to be unacceptable and warrant dismissal. The 'reasonableness' parameters inside which it will evaluate each case relate to the nature and extent of the investigation undertaken prior to the dismissal and the conclusion reached on the basis of the information yielded. Accordingly, an employer is obliged to carry out a fair and full investigation while adhering to the aforementioned principles of natural justice (see above). It is also relevant under this heading that 'off-duty' conduct, where it has implications for the employer, may be, and in instances has been, judged by both the Tribunal and the courts to constitute grounds for fair dismissal.

Capability/Competence/Qualifications

Dismissal pertaining to the capability, competence or qualifications of the employee relating to work of the kind which he was employed to do may be justified. Of course, these 'driven' dismissals often require the employer to advise the employee in advance of the relevant failure, thus enabling him/her to improve. Competence-related dismissals tend to arise where the employee is alleged to demonstrate a sub-standard work rate. Capability-related dismissals normally surface under the guise of attendance at work. Employees who are persistently late or fail to attend work regularly are commonly judged by the Tribunal to be incapable of performing the work they were employed to do. Indeed, even in those cases of persistent or extensive absence due to illness the furnishing of medical certification may not protect an employee from a dismissal where the employer has satisfied themselves that a return to work is not imminent.

Redundancy

Dismissals on the grounds of redundancy usually constitute fair dismissals. Accordingly, dismissal attributed to the employer ceasing business, reducing workforce size or no longer requiring the employee's kind of work is not unfair. The onus of proving that a genuine redundancy situation exists, however, resides with the employer and the claimant/employee can certainly question the validity of the redundancy. However, even if there is a genuine redundancy situation, an employee can argue that he was unfairly selected. This can arise if the employee can show:

- that they were in the same position as one or more other employees who were not made redundant;

- that an agreed redundancy procedure, e.g. last in first out (LIFO), was unjustifiably breached; or
- that the dismissal was for a reason defined as unfair under the Unfair Dismissals Acts 1977–2001.

Effectively, then, the employer is precluded from using arbitrary criteria when selecting staff for redundancy, though he may successfully plead special reasons for departing from an agreed or traditional procedure. He also needs to be careful that in carrying out the selection for redundancy, fair procedures are followed.

Any Other Substantial Reason

This has been a 'catch-all' category and can include issues such as damage to the employer's business or failure to conform to certain behavioural norms during one's private life, as in *Flynn* v. *Sister Mary Anne Power and The Sisters of the Holy Faith (1985)*.

Constructive Dismissal

The term 'constructive dismissal' relates to those cases where the employee terminates the contract on account of the employer's conduct. For example, an employee would be entitled to terminate the contract where the employer's conduct constitutes a significant breach going to the root of the contract or in the event of the employer indicating that he no longer intends to be bound by one or more of its essential terms, e.g. refusal to pay the employee's wages. Even in those cases where the employee is not legally entitled to terminate the contract, a constructive dismissal may be argued if the employer has acted unreasonably. The reasonableness of the employee in refusing to accept changes in the terms or conditions of employment will be considered by the Tribunal in light of the circumstances and of good industrial relations. However, the onus of proof that there was an act or omission on the employer's part constituting a breach of contract resides with the employee. Case law precedent, however, has led some authorities to conclude that this concept of constructive dismissal was somewhat meaningless and that the relevant criteria to be applied remain something of a mystery (von Prondzynski and McCarthy 1989). What is clear is that each case will turn on its own facts and that a hasty decision to resign on the employee's part without attempting in some way to resolve the problem may make it difficult to discharge the onus of proof that is upon them.

Unfair Dismissal Remedies

The Act provides for three remedial options in the event of a dismissal being deemed to have been unfair: reinstatement, re-engagement and compensation. However, it is interesting to note that of the 815 claims disposed of directly by the Tribunal in 1999, 400 were withdrawn during hearing, 151 were withdrawn prior to hearing, 113 were dismissed and 151 were allowed. This pattern is also evident in the 2001 figures, where

691 claims were disposed of, 301 withdrawn during hearing, 151 withdrawn prior to hearing, 108 dismissed and 124 allowed. A proportion of the withdrawals during hearing may be explained by parties negotiating settlements immediately before the hearing was about to get under way. However, the withdrawals prior to hearing, i.e. before the parties had even assembled, are more difficult to explain. The absence of state legal aid for claimants in these types of hearings may well be one contributory factor. Reinstatement enables the employee to resume in the same position on the same contractual terms as those applying prior to the dismissal event. A practical implication of this award is that the dismissal is effectively deemed never to have occurred. Accordingly, the relevant back-pay will be awarded, the employee's seniority maintained and pension rights restored. Furthermore, if there have been any changes in the interim in the terms and conditions of employment that would have been applicable to that employee they must also now be enforced, e.g. a pay rise. Reinstatement is only awarded where the employee is judged not to have contributed to the dismissal in any way. Of the 151 claims allowed by the Tribunal in 1999, reinstatement was ordered in just five cases. Likewise in 2002, reinstatement was ordered in just one out of the 135 cases allowed by the Tribunal (see website for summary details of outcomes of cases and awards since 1977).

Re-engagement entitles the employee to resume in the same or in a reasonably suitable different position on contractual terms that are deemed reasonable in light of prevailing circumstances. Such awards do not normally date back to the date of dismissal. As a result, though the unfairly dismissed employee's continuity of service is not affected, the period elapsing between the dismissal and the re-engagement effectively constitutes suspension without pay. Of the aforementioned 151 claims, re-engagement was ordered in seven instances. In 2002 it applied in three cases out of the 135 allowed. When deciding between a reinstatement or re-engagement, the Tribunal tends to take account of the extent, if any, to which the employee contributed to the unfair dismissal. However, over the years 1988–1991 it is estimated that out of 3,502 claimants only 202 (six per cent) were re-employed (Mulligan 1993). Compensation or payment is therefore the most common remedial option, but may only be awarded up to a maximum of 104 weeks' net remuneration (including bonus payments) in respect of the employment from which the employee was dismissed. Up to 1993, the size of payment was determined by taking into account the estimated future loss, pension loss and the present loss of remuneration (from the date of dismissal to the date of hearings) incurred by the employee, as reduced by tax rebates, social welfare payments and earnings since dismissal, where applicable.

Arising from the 1993 legislation, however, compensation calculations must disregard income tax rebates made by reason of the dismissal and unemployment, sickness and occupational injury payments to an employee under the Social Welfare Act 1981–1993. Deductions are also likely to be made from the compensation figure awarded where it is judged that the employee's conduct contributed to the dismissal or that the employee failed to take adequate steps to secure alternate employment. The practical consequence of these calculations is that, for example, over the four-year period 1988–1991 the average compensatory award was £3,149 (Mulligan 1993).

However, arising from the aforementioned compensation calculation changes, together with the other provision under the 1993 amendment whereby a basic award of up to four weeks' remuneration is payable to claimants held to be unfairly dismissed where no financial loss has been incurred, this average award level has increased. In fact, in 1996 the average compensation awarded by the Tribunal was £5,354.05. By 1999, however, due (it may be speculated) to greater employment opportunities with the knock-on effect on a claimant's loss, average compensation had again fallen to £3,068.86. By 2002 the figure stood at €5,317 (£4,187).

Of course, the Tribunal retains the prerogative to select whichever remedy it deems appropriate in the particular circumstances. Though the Tribunal elicits the views of the parties to the case, it may still choose to overlook same and issue an alternate remedy. According to Madden and Kerr (1996: 456), the factors which appear to drive this decision are 'the poor nature of the relationship between the parties, the fact that the employee has made serious allegations about the employer, the fact that the employee is not fit to return to work [and] the fact that changes in the work situation means that no suitable job is available'. Where the Tribunal issues a reinstatement or re-engagement award it would appear to assume that the relationship between the parties is not beyond repair. Fennell and Lynch's (1993) review indicates, however, that while the Pyrrhic victory of compensation is the preferred remedy, re-employment is ordered where the employer acted extremely badly or the claimant is in great hardship.

THE UNFAIR DISMISSALS ACTS 1977–2001 IN PERSPECTIVE

While in the past employer organisations have chided alleged impact on job creation initiatives, this allegation is strongly contested (Department of Labour 1986a). The Department of Labour view was strongly influenced by an authoritative study conducted by Williams and Whelan (1986), who surveyed employers in 694 companies employing under 40 employees, of which 360 completed the survey (a response rate of fifty-two per cent). When asked to identify the 'single greatest difficulty firms encountered in the last twelve months, no respondents specifically mentioned any aspect of labour legislation' (Williams and Whelan 1986: 12). Instead, uncertainty of demand, cash flow/bad debts and taxation (especially VAT) were to the fore. When asked about 'government measures, policies or legislation which caused problems for their business in the last year, only a small percentage (under three per cent) mentioned Unfair Dismissals' (Williams and Whelan 1986: 6). However, when asked specifically about reform of employment legislation, over half of the firms favoured amendments. Sixty per cent of those referred to the Unfair Dismissals Act 1977, but Williams and Whelan (1986: 35) note that 'firms would prefer a small reduction in PRSI or PAYE to amendment of this Act'. Williams and Whelan (1986: 36) conclude that 'the overall pattern of the survey responses seems to us to suggest that the extent to which employment levels are being damped by the existing legislation is somewhat limited'.

Some authors even argue that the Act has had major beneficial consequences for the conduct of industrial relations in the country. According to Murphy (1989):

The Act has been a considerable success and has contributed to more effective management in notoriously problematic areas of management decision making … in many areas of personnel administration and disciplinary control … [it] has strengthened collective bargaining at workplace level by creating a closer harmony between employer and trade union views of what constitutes a fair dismissal.

Browne (1994) paints a less optimistic view of the 1977 Act, with a number of negative findings for trade unions and workers emerging from her empirical research. She found an association between occupational status and success: 'claimants from higher occupational grades have a greater success rate at the Tribunal than claimants from lower occupational grades' (Browne 1994: 195). She found that unions coped poorly with the legalism of the EAT, while employers 'put trust and faith behind the law' (Browne 1994). Workers taking cases were also at a significant disadvantage because of the costs of legal representation and the advantages this conferred on employers. Browne (1994: 204) also argues the juridification of the employment relationship inherent in this process has 'individualised conflict, marginalised collective bargaining and made the role of the shop steward less relevant than previously'.

THE EMPLOYMENT APPEALS TRIBUNAL (EAT)

The EAT is the main institution for adjudicating on individual employment law. It was initially established under Section 39 of the Redundancy Payments Act 1967 as the Redundancy Appeals Tribunal. Its initial role was to adjudicate on claims for statutory redundancy payment. The Minimum Notice and Terms of Employment Act 1973 extended the Tribunal's functions to adjudicating on claims for statutory minimum notice. The Tribunal was renamed the EAT under the terms of the Unfair Dismissals Act 1977. Since then the EAT has been given further responsibility for adjudicating on a wide range of employment legislation, but interestingly, not cases under the equality legislation. The EAT also hears appeals from the decisions of Rights Commissioners under various individual employment legislation, but not from recommendations made under collective industrial relation legislation.

EAT Usage

The number of cases referred to the EAT has varied over time (see Figure 2.2). There was a major growth in cases in the 1980s associated with the burgeoning employment legislation and large-scale redundancies. The number of cases in the 1990s was substantially lower – 50,001 cases in total as against a total of 59,046 in the 1980s. With the slowdown in the economy in 2001 there has been an upturn in the number of cases, primarily caused by the growth in cases under Minimum Notice and Terms of Employment and Redundancy legislation. Figure 2.2 sets out the workload of the EAT for the period 2000–2002. Legislation under the EAT's responsibility, but excluded from Table 2.2, are the Carer's Leave Act 2001, the Adoptive Leave Act 1995, the Protection of Young Persons (Employment) Act 1996 and the Protections of Persons

Reporting Child Abuse Act 1998. The large number of cases referred under the Minimum Notice Act is due to a requirement for a determination from the Tribunal in order for receivers who have been appointed to insolvent companies to make payments to employees as preferred creditors. In the last two years, the bulk of the Tribunal's work has been accounted for by the minimum notice legislation and cases under the Unfair Dismissal Acts 1977–2001 and the Organisation of Working Time Act 1997. The small number of cases under the maternity and parental leave legislation is noteworthy and presumably is due to the implementation of the legislation and limited disputes as to its interpretation.

Figure 2.1
Outline Schema of State Institutions for Adjudicating on Employment Legislation

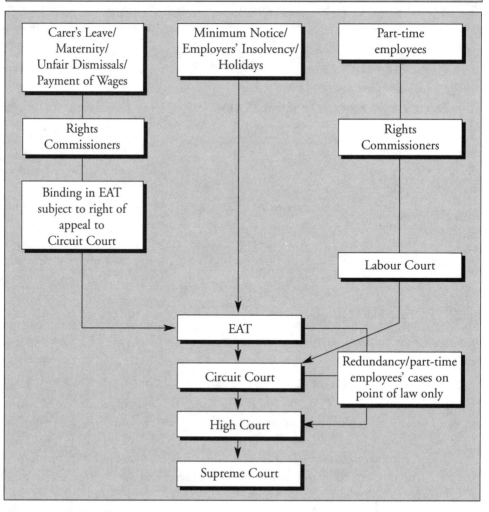

Figure 2.2
Number of EAT Referrals, 1978–2002

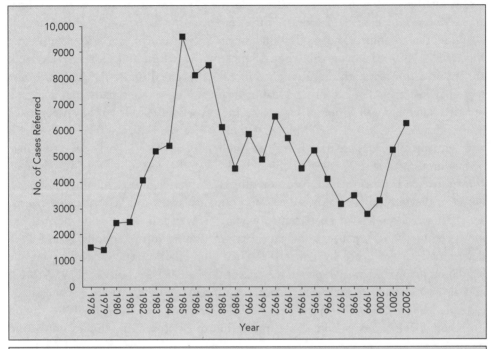

Source: EAT annual reports

Table 2.2
Claims and Appeals Referred to the EAT, 2000–2002

Legislation	2000	2001	2002
Minimum Notice and Terms of Employment Acts	1,749	3,216	3,966
Unfair Dismissals Acts	808	957	1,311
Redundancy Payments Acts	300	612	485
Protection of Employees (Employers' Insolvency) Acts	183	6	7
Worker Protection (Regular Part-Time Employees) Act	58	65	0
Maternity Acts	0	1	3
Payment of Wages Act	52	75	85
Terms of Employment (Information) Act	51	56	6
Organisation of Working Time Act	170	264	327
Parental Leave Act (appeals against RC decisions)	6	5	2
EC (Transfer of Undertakings) (Amendment) Regulations			2
EC (Protection of Employment) Regulations			65
Total	3,377	5,257	6,259

Source: EAT annual reports

Processing a Case at the EAT

Applications to the EAT are made on special forms available from the Tribunal or the Department of Enterprise, Trade and Employment. Claimants must give their names and addresses, the name and address of the employer, the Act(s) under which they are claiming, the grounds of the application and the redress sought (von Prondzynski and McCarthy 1989). Claimants should give representatives' name and address (if any) and are required to observe the application time limits specified under the Act, otherwise they may lose their right to bring a claim. In presenting a case a party may make an opening statement, call witnesses, cross-examine any witnesses called by any other party, give evidence and address the Tribunal at the close of the evidence (EAT 2002b: 17, www.entemp.ie). Cases are usually held in public, but at the Tribunal's discretion may be held in camera at the request of either party. Each division of the EAT is separately constituted and determinations are not subject to precedents set in other divisions; however, they are subject to precedents on points of law established in higher courts. The EAT's decision (called a determination) can be given at the close of the hearing but more commonly it is issued some time later in written form. Appeals against EAT determinations are heard by either the Circuit or High Court, depending on the legislation involved. For example, in the case of the Unfair Dismissals Acts 1977–2001, appeals may be made to the Circuit Court within six weeks. At the Circuit Court these cases are heard *de novo*, that is, there is a full rehearing of the case. Appeals in relation to the other acts, such as redundancy, protection of employees, minimum notice and part-time workers, are appealed to the High Court, and in these cases the EAT is the final arbiter of the 'facts of the case', as appeals are only on a 'point of law'.

Should an employer fail to carry out the terms of a determination, proceedings may be taken by the Minister for Enterprise, Trade and Employment to the Circuit Court in order to ensure compliance, an enforcement mechanism that can be cumbersome. Thus, in principle the Tribunal's decisions are legally binding, subject to any appeal on an employer. Claimants are not similarly bound by the outcome of an EAT decision and, in theory, could engage in industrial action despite being unsuccessful, if they have exhausted procedures as required by Section 9 of the Industrial Relations Act 1990 (see Chapter 3). There is little reality to this possibility, however, as by the time an EAT issues a decision the heat will typically have gone out of a dispute and the possibility of industrial action is extremely remote and unrealistic. Indeed, the same is the case even if the applicant is successful and there are difficulties getting an employer to abide by the determination.

The Operation of the EAT

By contrast with the Labour Court, the EAT is more legalistic in its composition and operation. The chairman of the Tribunal must, under statute, be a barrister of seven years' standing and, although not a requirement, the vice-chairmen tend to be legal practitioners. As of 2001 there were twenty-two vice-chairmen and sixty ordinary members, who are nominated by the ICTU and employer organisations and appointed by the Minister for Enterprise, Trade and Employment, usually for a three-year term (Meenan 1999; EAT 2001). The EAT operates in divisions consisting of a chairperson or vice-chairperson and one member from the trade union and employer sides. Browne (1994: 184–5) notes that EAT is a 'forum which had become highly legalistic'. Forde (1992) notes that EAT proceedings are subject to the principles of 'constitutional' or 'natural justice', and in the past it has come under criticism for being excessively legalistic. Fennell and Lynch (1993) describe the EAT's approach as 'legalistic, individualistic, rights based, heavily reliant on common law notions of fair procedure and assessment of reasonableness' (see also Butler 1997). The Tribunal would seem to be attempting to reduce the degree of legalism, as in recently published guidelines it has drawn attention to the fact that 'the Tribunal was established to provide a speedy and relatively informal means for the resolution of disputes under the various legislation that comes within the Tribunal's scope. All practitioners should bear this principle in mind when preparing and presenting cases and should avoid "legalisms"' (EAT 2002b: 1). In its new guidelines, the Tribunal (2002b: 2, www.entemp.ie) notes that while it 'is empowered to take evidence on oath, it is not essential to take sworn evidence, and evidence may be presented in a less formal manner. By and large, the Tribunal endeavours to limit the application of the oath to cases where it is necessary'.

Whether this reduction in legalism will be realised, however, is a matter for conjecture and future research. There are several factors militating against any great reduction in legalism. First, similar objectives were laid down in the context of the launch of the Unfair Dismissals Act in 1977 but these failed to transpire because of the common law basis of the legislation (von Prondzynski and McCarthy 1989; Browne 1994). Second, Browne (1994: 184) found that in cases under the Unfair Dismissal Acts, parties with legal representation have an advantage in terms of procedures and outcomes. If this effect persists it may continue to create a rational reason for availing of legal representation and relying on legal processes. As late as 2002 the evidence from the EAT itself indicates that legal representation continues to be the norm in unfair dismissals cases (see Table 2.3).

Table 2.3
Representation at Hearings Under Unfair Dismissal Acts, 1977–2001, in 2002

Employee Representation			Employer Representation		
Legal Rep.	Trade Union	Other	Legal. Rep.	Employer Organisation	Other
484	89	24	399	75	45
(81.1%)	(14.9%)	(4%)	(76.9%)	(14.5%)	(8.7%)

Note: The figures exclude cases where there was either self-representation or no representation.
Source: EAT (2001)

Any evaluation of the EAT needs to be considered against the reality of the move from voluntarism to legalism in the area of individual employment law. As Fennell and Lynch (1993: 9) note, the EAT's approach 'is one [more] concerned with the vindication of workers' rights than the conciliation of conflicts of interests'. These are also rights which extend to all employees, unionised and non-unionised. While unions have been found to cope poorly with the law in the case of dismissal disputes, however, unions do have the alternative of either referral to the Labour Court under the Industrial Relations Acts 1946–1990 or the EAT under the Unfair Dismissals Acts 1977–2001, but not both. While this provides a collective alternative to the EAT, there are reports of the Labour Court being reluctant to become involved in dismissal cases where workers have the twelve-month service requirement.

Maternity Law

As noted in the introduction to this section, the 1981 maternity legislation was replaced by the Maternity Protection Act 1994 in order to comply with the Pregnant Workers' Directive. Most of the provisions in the directive were already covered by the 1981 Act, but some additions, such as health and safety leave entitlements, were necessitated.

The Maternity Protection Act 1994 (as amended) entitles female employees to a period of paid maternity leave of at least eighteen weeks with an additional right to eight weeks' further unpaid leave. The employer concerned must be notified in writing at least four weeks prior to the expected 'confinement' and a medical certificate establishing the fact of pregnancy must be supplied. In addition to this leave period an important addition in the 1994 Act is the right to time off, without loss of pay, for ante- and post-natal medical visits. This entitlement is dependent on the provision of both medical evidence of pregnancy and the appropriate notification to the employer concerned. There is no qualifying service or minimum weekly working hours requirement to secure this right. The employee can choose the exact dates of the maternity leave, but the period must cover the four weeks prior to and post confinement. While on paid maternity leave the employee's employment rights are preserved. She is entitled to return to her job after the birth, provided she notifies the employer of her intentions in writing at least four working weeks in advance of the envisaged date of return. It is worth noting that the EAT had held in some unfair dismissal cases prior to the 1994 Act that written notification of return to work is a mandatory requirement. As a result, a new provision in the Act allowed the EAT or a Rights Commissioner to extend the time for giving the notification where there are 'reasonable grounds' for the failure or the delay in providing it. However, the procedural requirements for the exercise of the right to take maternity leave and the right to return to work have been judged to be 'unnecessarily complex' (Kerr 1987).

The 1994 Act also introduced a potential right to health and safety leave from work for pregnant workers, workers who are breastfeeding or who have recently given birth. This leave exists independently of maternity leave and can occur from the beginning of pregnancy up to twenty-six weeks after the birth. To be entitled, the worker must be at risk as a result of exposure to specific physical, chemical or biological agents that the employer is unable to eliminate and where suitable alternative work cannot be found. In addition, if a doctor certifies that nightwork is unsuitable and the worker cannot be moved to day work, she may become entitled to such leave.

An assessment as to whether a medical risk exists appears to be a matter for the Health and Safety Authority to decide. Disputes as to leave entitlements are heard by a Rights Commissioner with an appeal to the EAT. Dismissal-related disputes may be brought to either a Rights Commissioner or the EAT. Following the setting up of a Social Partners Working Group to review the 1994 Act (which reported in March 2001), the basic period of paid leave was introduced from fourteen to eighteen weeks and the period of unpaid leave from four to eight weeks. Other changes recommended by the group have been accepted in principle by government but still remain to be implemented. These are likely to include the right to paid time off for a complete set of ante-natal classes, a right to breastfeeding facilities or breaks and the right to postpone up to four weeks of paid maternity leave when a child is hospitalised.

HEALTH AND SAFETY AT WORK

The relevance of the health and safety topic is reflected by the fact that in 1996 a total of 4,805 accidents, of which fifty-nine were fatal, had been reported to the Health and Safety Authority. By 2001 this figure had risen to 8,576, of which sixty-four were fatal. In 1992, a survey conducted by the Federation of Irish Employers (FIE, now IBEC) indicated that on average member companies had thirty accidents per year, resulting in the loss of 139 working days per company. The total cost of claims in 1989 for the survey group was over £4.5 million (FIE 1991). Total employers' liability insurance, another indicator of the magnitude of the problem, is estimated to run at over £100 million per annum (Carroll and Byrne 1992). Over the 1991–1996 period, the Irish Insurance Federation allowed an average of 8,187 employers' liability claims per annum. Health and safety has been an important part of the European Community's social policy agenda since the late 1970s and by the end of 1995 – the European Year of Safety, Hygiene and Health Protection at Work – over thirty directives concerned with the subject had been adopted as Community law.

Legislation pertaining to health and safety at work is very complex, as in addition to common law principles it spans some twenty primary enactments together with hundreds of regulations, which are constantly increasing in number. For example, in 2001 alone thirteen new sets of regulations were passed to develop existing legislation or to implement European directives. Barrington (1982) has classified these provisions as follows.

- Legislation which deals exclusively with the health and safety of workers.
- Statutes concerned with the regulation of working hours (now superseded by the passing of the Organisation of Working Time Act 1997).
- Statutes not designed exclusively as worker protection measures, but nevertheless providing varying degrees of protection.
- Statutes on the borderline between issues of general environmental pollution and those of occupational health and safety.

Safety at work is the responsibility of everyone at the workplace, both employer and employee. The primary responsibility, however, rests with the employer. Most claims for personal injury following a work accident contend that the employer failed in one or more of his common law duties. Under common law the Irish courts have decided that employers are obliged to exercise reasonable care toward employees in relation to health and safety matters. Common law takes effect after the event and its primary function is to compensate staff for injuries received at work. The implications of common law are that employers must:

- provide a safe system of work;
- ensure the provision of competent fellow workers;
- provide safety equipment and effective supervision; and
- provide a safe place of work.

The provision of a safe system of work obliges the employer to show that the provision of the system provided is at least in accord with the general practice of that trade. Accordingly, an employer would not be responsible solely because an accident occurred in the course of the job – some element of negligence would have to be involved. The failure to provide competent fellow workers (including subordinates and supervisors) may, but rarely does, constitute the basis of a claim. According to Gunnigle *et al.* (1992) this duty obliges an employer to:

- clarify the personal qualities and skills required to do the particular job;
- ensure the existence of a systematic recruitment and selection procedure; and
- provide the necessary training to do the job and special remedial training where required.

Furthermore, the employer may be found to be liable for the careless action of one employee that causes injury to another employee, i.e. vicarious liability. The common law obligation to provide proper safety equipment for the purpose of avoiding staff exposure to risk and injury includes a requirement that management take reasonable steps, up to and including disciplinary action, to ensure the use of that equipment. The provision of a safe place of work demands that the workplace be organised in the interests of health and safety. This obligation also extends to a customer's premises. Consequently, if workers are injured while working on a customer's premises they may successfully claim against their own employer.

In recent years the employer's duty to provide a safe workplace, hitherto confined to reducing risks to the physical health of the employee, has been extended to his psychological well-being. Several court decisions in the UK have established employers' obligation to prevent foreseeable risk from stress in work and successful claims have also been brought in Ireland in relation to bullying and harassment as well as stress under the employers liability heading (McMahon 2001).

The most significant piece of legislation in this area is the Safety, Health and Welfare at Work Act 1989, the first Act to be applicable to all workplaces and acknowledged as a statutory reflection of the common law position. It sets down major principles which all employers and employees must observe. According to Gunnigle *et al.* (1992) it was the most significant piece of legislation within the employment sphere in the last ten years because:

- it was the first attempt to codify the law on safety, health and welfare in over twenty-five years;
- it established the National Authority for Occupational Safety and Health for the purpose of providing integrated co-ordination and monitoring of safety, health and welfare at work;
- it introduced flexibility in the area of employee representation and consultation;
- it emphasised the preparation of proactive safety, health and welfare policies within the organisation;
- it changed the emphasis of the inspectorate system from one with a punitive focus to a facilitative one. It also strengthened the powers of the inspectorate where companies refused to conform with the legislation; and
- it emphasised the formulation of voluntary codes of practice and regulations and it broadened the scope from one with a safety bias to consideration of occupational health and welfare issues.

In effect, it was essentially a 'framework act' with a guiding philosophy and direction to be supplemented by way of regulations and codes of practice. The National Authority, which develops these regulations and codes, is primarily responsible for enforcing, advising, promoting and undertaking research in the area. The Authority's inspectorate has wide-ranging enforcement powers that extend to the right to serve a prohibition notice – requiring that work should stop when there is a risk of imminent and serious injury to workers – and to prosecute employers. In 2000, for example, 13,738 inspections took place, rising to 14,929 visits in 2001. Eighty-one prosecutions were initiated in 2001, with seventy-three convictions resulting. The Authority has also issued guidelines on the formulation of a safety statement. Under the 1989 Act, a safety statement that details the manner in which the health, safety and welfare of staff will be ensured at the workplace is obligatory on all employers. However, a survey carried out by the Authority in 1991 revealed that only sixteen per cent of workplaces had satisfactory safety statements. Overall, the Act obliges employers 'insofar as is reasonably practicable' to:

- design and maintain a place of work which is safe and without risk to health;
- provide safe means of access to and egress from a place of work;
- provide and maintain plant and equipment which is safe and without risk to health;
- provide necessary information, instruction, training and supervision for safe and healthy working;
- provide and maintain suitable protective clothing or equipment where hazards cannot otherwise be controlled;
- prepare adequate emergency plans;
- prevent risks to health and safety in relation to use of articles or substances;
- provide welfare facilities; and
- acquire the services of a competent person when necessary to ensure the safety and health of employees at work.

From the employees' perspective there is an obligation that they:

- take reasonable care to ensure the safety of themselves and others;
- co-operate with their employer in relation to compliance with statutory requirements;
- use protective equipment, clothing or other means for securing safety, health and welfare; and
- report potential risks to the employer in the event of their becoming aware of any.

The Act also entitles staff to be consulted for the purpose of making arrangements for co-operation in promoting and developing health, safety and welfare at work. Furthermore, they have the right to make representations to their employer on such matters and their views must be taken into account 'insofar as is reasonably practicable'. If the workforce so decides, they may appoint a safety representative to act on their behalf. Amongst other entitlements, the safety representative may inspect the workplace at an agreed frequency and may accompany a Health and Safety Authority inspector on a tour of inspection.

As noted above, European influences in this area have been considerable. In 1989, the same year as the Safety, Health and Welfare at Work Act was enacted, the EC agreed the so-called 'Framework' Directive on Health and Safety and in some respects our domestic legislation was influenced by its passage. Indeed, the power to issue regulations to develop the 1989 Act was used to implement the framework and six other health and safety directives together by way of the Safety, Health and Welfare at Work (General Application) Regulations (SI 44/93). From 1980 on, health and safety directives have been implemented in Ireland on such diverse and technical subjects as safety signs, exposure to chemical, physical and biological agents, noise, manual handling of loads, visual display screens, lead, asbestos and protective equipment at work.

OTHER EMPLOYMENT LEGISLATION

Table 2.4
Summary of Other Employment Legislation in Ireland

Act	Scope
Organisation of Working Time Act 1997	Working hours, rest breaks, rest periods, annual leave, public holidays, Sunday working, zero hour contracts
Protection of Young Persons Act 1996 (Employment)	Working hours and age limits for young people at work
Minimum Notice Acts 1973–1991	Minimum notice periods on dismissal
Terms of Employment (Information) Act 1994	Written statement on terms and conditions of employment
Payment of Wages Acts 1991	Methods of payment and deductions from wages
Protection of Employees (Part-Time Work) Act 2001	Extends protection of employment legislation to all part-time workers and ensures equal treatment on a pro rata basis with full-time colleagues
Pensions Act 1990	Administration of pension schemes
Redundancy Payments Acts 1967–1991	Lump sum payment on redundancy
Protection of Employment Act 1977	Consultation prior to collective redundancies (as amended)
Transfer of Undertaking Regulations 1980	Protecting employees' rights in cases of change of ownership
Protection of Employees (Employers' Payments Due to Employees in Case of Insolvency) Acts 1984–1991	Employer insolvency
Adoptive Leave Act 1995	Rights to leave from work in the event of adoption
Data Protection Act 1988	Access to automated/computer data
Parental Leave Act 1998	Rights to leave from work for both parents from the birth or adoption of a child up to the child reaching five years of age
National Minimum Wage Act 2000	Introduces a minimum wage depending upon age and experience of employee
Carer's Leave Act 2001	Rights to leave from work to care for a person in need of full-time care and attention

Organisation of Working Time

Again, as a result of the necessity to implement an EU measure, the 'Working Time' Directive, the area of working hours and holidays is codified in one piece of legislation – the Organisation of Working Time Act 1997. In the process, a number of pieces of legislation were repealed, including the Conditions of Employment Acts 1936 and 1944 and the Holidays (Employees) Act 1973. In addition, the part-time workers legislation of 1991 (since repealed – see below) required amendment in the area of holiday entitlements.

This piece of legislation is long and complex, and like its predecessors, full of exemptions and exceptions in the area of working hours, rest periods and breaks. Some of its salient points are:

- a maximum working week of forty-eight hours, over a reference period of four, six or twelve months, depending on the category of worker;
- minimum rest breaks of fifteen minutes per 4.5 hours worked and thirty minutes per six hours worked;
- minimum rest period of eleven hours per twenty-four hours and twenty-four hours per week, i.e. a consecutive weekly rest period of thirty-five hours;
- minimum annual leave entitlements of four weeks for full-time workers and eight per cent of hours worked in the case of part-time or casual employees;
- entitlement to some form of compensation, whether by way of payment or time off in lieu of Sunday work;
- entitlement to a minimum payment should a worker be engaged on a zero-hour contract and not be provided with any or the requisite amount of work; and
- special restrictions on hours worked at night, especially night work involving particular hazards.

Complaints under this Act are made to a Rights Commissioner, with a right of appeal to the Labour Court.

Young People at Work

The Protection of Young Persons (Employment) Act 1996 prohibits the employment of children less than sixteen years of age. However, a child over fourteen years may be permitted to do light non-industrial work during school holidays, provided it is not harmful to health, development or schooling. The Act further provides for setting limits on the working hours of young people, for rest intervals and the prohibition of night work.

Minimum Notice Law

In the absence of a specific term in the contract of employment dealing with the issue of notice, the minimum notice legislation entitles employees to a minimum period (or to accept pay in lieu) of notice prior to dismissal. Employees with between thirteen weeks and two years of continuous service are entitled to one week's notice and thereafter entitlements increase on a gradual basis up to a maximum of eight weeks' notice where an employee has fifteen or more years of service. An employer is also entitled to at least one week's notice from an employee with thirteen or more weeks' service. A study of the Act by Gunnigle *et al.* (1992) reveals that the EAT has determined that:

- notice given must be sufficiently certain and precise, leaving no room for ambiguity or uncertainty;
- the precise expiry date must be specified; and
- employees to whom the notice provisions apply are entitled to the same rights during the minimum notice period as they would enjoy but for the notice.

The minimum notice right does not, however, preclude either side from terminating the contract without notice on account of what the EAT would adjudge to be 'severe misconduct' by the other party (von Prondzynski and McCarthy 1989). During 2002 the Tribunal disposed of 2,925 claims under the Minimum Notice and Terms of Employment Act 1973–2001. Of these 2,097 were allowed, 382 were dismissed, 284 were withdrawn during hearing and 162 were withdrawn prior to hearing.

Terms of Employment

As noted above, regarding the contract of employment an employer is obliged to furnish any employee who has one month's continuous service with a written statement outlining basic terms of employment. The minimum notice legislation referred to above used to be called the Minimum Notice and Terms of Employment Act 1973 and provided for a similar statement as the Terms of Employment (Information) Act 1994 now does.

The essential differences are, firstly, that the employee (if employed since May 1994) is automatically entitled to the statement and does not have to request it. Second, there is a direct method of complaint for an aggrieved employee to a Rights Commissioner, whereas under the 1973 Act it was up to the Department of Labour to take proceedings. This led to a widespread lack of compliance and there is some evidence that this lack of compliance is still common in some sectors. The information required in the statement includes:

- names of the employer and employee and the address of the employer in the state;
- the place of work and the employee's job title and nature of work;
- the date of commencement of employment;
- details of pay, including overtime, commission and bonus and the methods of calculating them;
- whether pay is to be weekly, monthly or otherwise;
- conditions about hours of work, including details of breaks and provision in relation to overtime;
- holiday entitlements;

- sick pay arrangements and pension schemes, if any; and
- periods of notice or, if the contract of employment is for a fixed time, the date when the contract expires.

Again, this legislation was introduced to comply with an EU directive. Complaints are made to a Rights Commissioner initially, with a right of appeal to the Tribunal. The number of appeals to the Tribunal has increased in recent years. For example, in 1996 there were just four cases dealt with by the Tribunal on appeal. However, by 2001 this figure had risen to fourteen, of which ten were upheld, one was upset, one was varied and two were withdrawn. In 2002 just six appeals or claims were referred to the Tribunal.

Wage Payment Law

Under the Payment of Wages Act, 1991 seven legal wage payment methods are provided for, including payment by cheque, bank draft, credit transfer or similar method, postal order and cash. Provision is also made for those situations in which financial institutions are affected by industrial action. Where the employee is paid on a non-cash basis and the cash is not readily available, subject to the employee's consent the employer must pay wages by another non-cash method. Should the employee not agree, the employer must pay the wages in cash. The circumstances in which deductions, in particular those relating to acts or omissions of the employee, can legally be made from wages and payments to be made by employers are also set down. Effectively, deductions must be provided for in the contract (or other written form), the employee must be made aware in advance that a deduction will be made and the deduction must be reasonable in relation to the employee's wages. In the even of a dispute, the initial claim is made to a Rights Commissioner with a right of appeal to the Tribunal. In 1999 the Tribunal dealt with twenty-seven appeals from Rights Commissioner decisions – eleven were upheld, five were upset and eleven were withdrawn. By 2002 this figure had risen to fifty-nine, with fifteen upheld, thirteen upset, one varied and thirty withdrawn.

Part-Time Workers' Law

Arising from the growth of the secondary labour market, or the 'peripheral' workforce, the Worker Protection (Regular Part-Time Employees) Act came into operation with effect from April 1991. All part-time workers were covered by the Act if they worked at least thirteen weeks with the same employer and were normally expected to work not less than eight hours a week for that employer. This Act was recently replaced by the Protection of Employees (Part-Time Work) Act 2001, which was introduced as a result of the EU framework directive on part-time work. This is a very important piece of legislation in that it extends the protection of employment legislation to all part-time workers, regardless of the number of hours worked per week. Perhaps more significantly, it also entitles part-time workers to pro rata treatment with their comparable full-time colleagues in relation to conditions of employment such as pay and annual leave.

Complaints under this Act are made to a Rights Commissioner with a right of appeal to the Tribunal. A further similar directive on the rights of fixed-term contract workers vis-à-vis their full-time counterparts was signed into Irish law in 2003.

Pensions Provisions

The Pensions Act of 1990, while not making occupational pension schemes compulsory, does attempt to regulate both those schemes already in existence before the Act was passed and those that came into operation after 1990. Effectively, the legislation (Gunnigle *et al.* 1992):

- establishes a Pensions Board to monitor and supervise the new requirements under the Act;
- provides for the compulsory preservation of pension entitlements for employees who change employments;
- introduces a minimum funding standard for certain funded schemes;
- provides for the disclosure of information to scheme members;
- clarifies the duties and responsibilities of scheme trustees; and
- implements the principle of equal treatment for men and women in occupational benefit schemes.

In 2002 the Pensions (Amendment) Act was passed. Amongst other provisions the Act provides for the introduction of a framework for Personal Retirement Savings Accounts (PRSAs), their associated tax reliefs and arrangements and the establishment of a Pensions Ombudsman.

Data Protection Law

The Data Protection Act 1988 entitles individuals to establish the existence of automated personal data, to have access to such data in relation to them and to have inaccurate data rectified or erased. The Act also obliges the data controller, i.e. the organisation that uses automated personal data, to adhere to a number of obligations, including the accuracy, relevance, use, etc. of such data. Furthermore, a Data Protection Commissioner is provided with a legal basis for intervening where an individual complains that the principles have not been observed. The relevant principles provided for in the Act are:

- that the data controller fairly obtains and processes the data;
- that the automated data be factually accurate and, where necessary, up to date;
- that the data is kept for one or more specified and lawful purposes;
- that the data shall not be used or disclosed in any manner incompatible with the specified and lawful purposes;
- that the data retained be attainable, relevant and not excessive in relation to the specified and lawful purposes;

- that the personal data shall not be kept for longer than is necessary for the specified and lawful purposes; and
- that appropriate security measures should be taken by data controllers and processors against unauthorised access to or attention, disclosure or destruction of the data and against its accidental destruction or loss.

A new Data Protection (Amendment) Act was enacted in 2003. This substantially amended and substituted many of the provisions of the Data Protection Act, 1988 and belatedly gave effect to the EU Direction 95/46 on data protection. The Act extends the employers' duties and employees' entitlements to cover information kept in manual as well as copmuterised form, such as personnel files.

REDUNDANCY AND OWNERSHIP CHANGES

Redundancy Payments Acts 1967–2003

The subject of statutory redundancy entitlements constitutes a fertile area for disputes, although the number of claims appears to have fallen in recent years, possibly reflecting economic trends. For example, during 1992, 687 cases under the Redundancy Payments Acts 1967–1991 were dealt with by the EAT, whereas in 1999 only 252 claims were disposed of. The volatile incidence of claims is evident from the fact that in 2000, 2001 and 2002, 300, 612 and 485 cases, respectively, were referred to the Tribunal. This legislation applies to workers with at least 104 weeks of continuous service and who have not reached retirement age. As a result of the negotiations on Sustaining Progress the entitlement to statutory provision has been revised and employees are now entitled to two weeks' pay per year of service plus one week's lump sum. A week's pay in such circumstances is currently subject to a statutory ceiling of €507.90 per week, though it is adjusted from time to time. Employers may reclaim sixty per cent of this redundancy pay from the Social Insurance Fund, into which they make regular payments themselves through PRSI contributions. Applications for these rebates are processed by the Redundancy Payments Section of the Department for Enterprise, Trade and Employment (www.entemp.ie/erir/redundancy.htm). Payment is subject to employers giving workers proper notice of being made redundant (at least two weeks). The Redundancy Payments Section processes applications for these rebates – see Forms RP1 (Notice), RP2 (Redundancy Certificate) and RP3 (for the rebate). In addition to statutory redundancy entitlements, in many cases in Ireland redundancy pay is enhanced through collective bargaining. Enhanced payments are also frequently made in non-union companies. The rebate does not apply to such additional payments.

Protection of Employment Act 1977

Where collective redundancies arise, the provisions of the Protection of Employment Act 1977 come into force. These require the employer to supply the employees' representatives with specific information regarding the proposed redundancies and to consult with those representatives at least thirty days before the first dismissal takes place to see if they can be lessened or avoided. The employer is also obliged to advise the Minister for Enterprise, Trade and Employment at least thirty days in advance of the first dismissal. Despite the apparent stringency of these requirements, however, the legislation is considered to be of limited value. A number of authors have pointed out that the wide exceptions provided for in the Act mean that its enforcement is least possible where it is most necessary (see von Prondzynski and McCarthy 1989; Gunnigle *et al.* 1992).

Protection of Employees (Employers' Insolvency) Acts 1984–2001

In the event of the employer becoming insolvent the Protection of Employees (Employers' Insolvency) Acts 1984–2001 comes into play. Subject to certain limits and conditions, monies due to workers by way of pay arrears (including holiday and sick pay), entitlements under the minimum notice, equal pay, unfair dismissals and employment equality enactments and monies due from court orders in respect of wages, sick pay, holiday pay or damages at common law for wrongful dismissal may be paid out of the Redundancy and Employers' Insolvency Fund. Outstanding employee contributions to an occupational pension scheme up to a year prior to the insolvency date, which the employer deducted but did not pay over, are also protected. In 1992 the EAT had to deal with 276 cases under this Act. By 1996 this had decreased to nineteen complaints, of which all were allowed. In 2001 only two complaints (against decisions of the Minister for Enterprise, Trade and Employment) were disposed of (and allowed) by the Tribunal.

The Transfer of Undertaking Regulations 1980

The Transfer of Undertaking Regulations 1980, again based on the EU 'Acquired Rights' Directive, are designed to protect employees' jobs in the event of a change in their employer's identity, where the business in question resumes its activities having been sold as a going concern. Subject to the employer's right to effectuate redundancies for economic, technical or organisational reasons involving changes in the workforce, employees are entitled to continue working under the same terms of employment with service and contractual rights maintained. Both the outgoing and incoming employer are also obliged to keep employees informed of developments, though this requirement is often ignored in practice.

These regulations have attracted criticism in recent years due to the increasing number of transactions in which the European Court of Justice has held them to apply, including contracting out or in and change of contractor situations. Ultimately, this led to a review and consolidation of the directive with the principal change being a requirement that the entity being transferred must be 'an organised grouping of resources'. These changes remain to be implemented in Irish law despite the deadline for transposition having passed. An employee whose rights are infringed under the legislation resulting in dismissal may bring an unfair dismissal claim to the EAT or

Rights Commissioner in the normal manner. There is some evidence at present of a slight row back at European level in the scope of this directive.

EMPLOYMENT EQUALITY AND THE LAW

As with many of the employment legislation initiatives taken in recent years, the introduction of equality legislation was primarily prompted by our membership of the European Community (EC) and the necessity to comply with its directives. Under this heading, legal provisions in relation to equal pay and equal treatment in employment, as well as maternity rights, are of particular relevance. Each of the original pieces of domestic legislation in this area has actually been repealed and amended. The Anti-Discrimination (Pay) Act 1974 and the Employment Equality Act 1977 were passed to implement the equal pay and equal treatment directives, respectively, in the 1970s. The subsequent consolidation of these two measures into one Act – the Employment Equality Act 1998 – has significantly altered and broadened the law in this area. Equally, The Maternity (Protection of Employees) Act 1981 gave way to the Maternity Protection Act 1994 in order to effectuate the so-called 'Pregnant Workers' Directive of 1992. The details of these initiatives are considered below.

Equal Pay

The Anti-Discrimination (Pay) Act 1974 entitled men and women to equal pay for equal work. As well as gender, the 1998 enactment also allows a claim to be made where the complainant is alleging he or she is performing equal work but is being paid less on grounds of marital status, family status, sexual orientation, religion, age, disability, race or membership of the Traveller community. For the purposes of an equal pay claim, pay is interpreted as basic wages together with all direct and indirect financial benefits and incentives (excluding pension benefits). The person or persons claiming – group claims are common – must compare themselves with an actual comparator. The comparator need not be a current employee, but can be someone employed in the three years prior to the complainant or, it would appear, three years after him or her. The complainant must also satisfy the following conditions:

- he or she must be working under a contract of service;
- he or she must be working for the same or an associated employer; a significant change here is that the requirement to work in the same 'place' was removed in the 1998 Act; and
- he or she must be performing 'like work' with the comparator, that is, either (a) his/her work is identical, (b) job differences are insignificant in relation to the job as a whole or (c) his/her work is 'equal in value' in terms of criteria like responsibility, skill, physical or mental effort.

If the complainant can establish these requirements, the onus shifts to the employer to show that there are grounds other than gender (or marital status, age, disability, etc.) for the difference in the respective rates of pay. Standard grounds in this respect include qualifications, experience, service or grading. (For details of methods of complaint see the section on remedy routes below.)

Undoubtedly the 1974 enactment contributed to the improved relative position of female workers in the national wage structure. For example, over the 1970–1980 period average hourly female earnings rose by eleven per cent against the equivalent male rate (McMahon 1987). However, with the average hourly female rate standing at seventy-three per cent of the male rate in 1997, it is apparent that there remains considerable scope for improvement. Yet specific definitions of indirect discrimination (see below) were introduced in this area for the first time. This does not appear to have led to any great increase in claims. Of the forty-two claims dealt with by the Director of Equality Investigations in 2001, only ten involved issues of equal pay.

Relative to other employment legislation, such as the Unfair Dismissals Acts, the cumulative number of cases heard under pre-1998 legislation is not large and this can give rise to two interpretations. First, that the legislation is being largely complied with, or second, that applicants may be reluctant to initiate cases. There is *prima facia* but not conclusive evidence to support the latter possibility. The much larger number of enquiries to the Employment Equality Authority by comparison with the relatively small number of cases that result in an Equality Officer investigation indicates that the number of cases being processed understates the extent to which equality issues are of concern to employees. The data in Table 2.5 indicates a higher success rate for employers when cases are taken. This may indicate that employers concede cases which have merit when first raised or alternately may indicate a difficulty for employees meeting the burden of proof (or a mix of both). According to Fennell and Lynch (1993), the 1974 Act was 'fraught with difficulties'. In their view, these included 'the failure to specifically guarantee a remedy for indirect pay discrimination' (see below), together with the 'requirement of a male comparator' when pursuing claims. Under the 1998 Act the latter requirement remains, despite calls for a 'hypothetical comparator' to be introduced.

Table 2.5 *Equality Officer Recommendations, 1978–2002*				
	Employment Equality Act 1977		Anti-Discrimination (Pay) Act 1974	
	No. of Cases	In Favour of Claimant	No. of Cases	In Favour of Claimant
Total	492	188*	563	233*

* These figures refer only to cases in the period 1978–2000.
Source: Employment Equality Agency, LRC and ODEI

Employment Equality

The Employment Equality Act 1977 was designed to protect against discrimination on grounds of gender or marital status in relation to access to employment, i.e. recruitment and selection, and terms and conditions of employment as well as access to promotion and training schemes, benefits, facilities and services and treatment in relation to dismissal. There were a limited number of situations where sex constituted an occupational qualification for a job – where the Act did not apply – such as physiology (excluding physical strength or stamina) or authenticity for the purpose of entertainment, e.g. sperm donor or model. These still apply with the passage of the Employment Equality Act 1998.

As with equal pay, a broader range of potentially discriminatory grounds has been introduced in the new legislation, including family status, sexual orientation, religion, age, disability, race (including colour, nationality, ethnic or national origins) and membership of the Traveller community. However, a number of detailed qualifications and exceptions exist that make it difficult to predict how an individual complainant will fare. The new Act also makes it unlawful to victimise an employee for exercising his or her rights under the legislation.

Unlawful discrimination can take place directly or indirectly. Direct discrimination occurs where a person is treated less favourably than a person with or without the relevant characteristic, i.e. gender, age, disability, etc., is or would be treated in similar circumstances. For example, claims in relation to discrimination at the recruitment and selection stage are quite common and often revolve around alleged discriminatory questions or treatment at the interview (McMahon 2002). This may take the form of asking only women questions in relation to child-minding responsibilities at an interview or refusing to interview a person because of their age, race or a disability. The definitions of indirect discrimination were reshaped in the 1998 Act to take into account both the decision of the Supreme Court in the 1996 *Nathan* v. *Bailey Gibson Ltd. Case (ELR, No. 2, 1996)* and European Union (EU) definitions. Basically, indirect discrimination involves an apparently neutral practice or requirement that effectively serves to discriminate against a particular category because fewer of its members are able to comply with it. The practice or requirement must not be objectively justifiable for the employment in question. For example, a minimum height requirement for a job where height was not a relevant factor might operate to indirectly discriminate against women as a group, as opposed to men.

Sexual Harassment

Successive Labour Court decisions since 1985 had determined that sexual harassment, though not specifically alluded to, was actually prohibited under the Employment Equality Act 1977 as less favourable treatment in relation to conditions of employment. The 1977 Act did not define sexual harassment and so it was a matter for the Labour Court to determine. The 1998 Act tackles this issue and defines sexual harassment as acts of physical intimacy, requests for sexual favours or other acts such as words, gestures or the display of pictures or other material that are unwelcome to the recipient and could reasonably be regarded as sexually offensive, humiliating or intimidating on grounds of gender. Included in the list of potential harassers are employers, fellow employees or clients, customers or other business contacts of the employer. Sexual harassment at the place where the recipient is employed or 'otherwise in the course of her/his employment' is covered by the Act. However, it is a defence for the employer to show that he took 'such steps as are reasonably practicable' to prevent or reverse the harassment. In practice, this will necessitate having the appropriate complaints procedure in place to deal with the problem and ensuring that it is implemented (McMahon 2001).

The Employment Equality Bill 2004

Further amendments to Irish equality legislation became necessary as a result of EU directives. The bill proposes extended protection from discrimination on a number of grounds and will amend the definition of indirect discrimination, with persons over sixty-five years of age and self-employed people now covered. A number of exclusions are due to be amended and the requirement on employers to adapt the workplace to facilitate employees with disabilities will be enhanced (see website for final details of the Act, which will be posted when passed).

Remedy Routes

Under the 1998 Act a new system of complaints has been introduced, although it retains many of the features of its predecessor. The Employment Equality Agency was renamed the Equality Authority to reflect its wider remit to promote an equality agenda. This agenda is summed up in the Authority's mission, which is to realise 'positive change in the situation of those experiencing inequality by:

- promoting and defending the rights established in the equality legislation;
- providing leadership in building a commitment to addressing equality issues in practice;
- creating a wider awareness of equality issues;
- celebrating diversity in Irish society;
- mainstreaming equality considerations across all sectors' (Equality Authority 2001: 10).

The Authority is still charged with providing information on the legislation and advising potential complainants as well as taking proceedings on someone's behalf where it is not reasonable to expect the person in question to take a case themselves. It is also empowered to conduct enquiries and to issue non-discrimination notices and ultimately to apply for an injunction in the Circuit or High Court to prevent discrimination continuing. An interesting new feature is the power to invite employers to carry out 'Equality Reviews' and/or 'prepare and implement equality action plans'. The Authority also 'can provide legal assistance to claimants taking cases under the Employment Equality Act 1998 and the Equal Status Act 2000 where cases have a strategic importance' (Equality Authority 2001: 21). The Authority reports a caseload of some 489 cases under the Employment Equality Act in 2002. This represented an increase of approximately 200 cases on the previous year. The Authority also published the first Code of Practice on Sexual Harassment and Harassment at Work in 2002 (available at www.equality.ie).

THE OFFICE OF THE DIRECTOR OF EQUALITY INVESTIGATIONS (ODEI) – THE
EQUALITY TRIBUNAL

Under the provisions of the Equality Act 1998, Equality Officers were transferred from
the Labour Relations Commission to a newly established Office of Director of Equality
Investigations (ODEI) (Langford 2001: 78). The ODEI was established in October
1999, is headed by a Director and operates under the auspices of the Department of
Justice, Equality and Law Reform. In 2002 the name of the ODEI was changed to
ODEI – Equality Tribunal so that it is now generally referred to as the Equality
Tribunal. The name was changed in an attempt 'to resolve the confusion that arose at
all levels about the relative identities and functions of the Equality Tribunal and other
equality organisations' (Office of Director of Equality Investigations (ODEI) – Equality
Tribunal 2002: 7). The Director of Equality Investigations may award up to three years'
arrears of equal pay or compensation of up to 104 weeks' remuneration in an equal
treatment case. The Labour Court has the same powers, with an additional power to
order reinstatement or re-engagement (with or without compensation) in a dismissal
case. Potential appeals lie from the Director to the Labour Court, and from the Labour
Court to the Circuit Court. The Circuit Court may also enforce decisions of the Director
or the Labour Court, and lastly, points of law may be referred to the High Court.

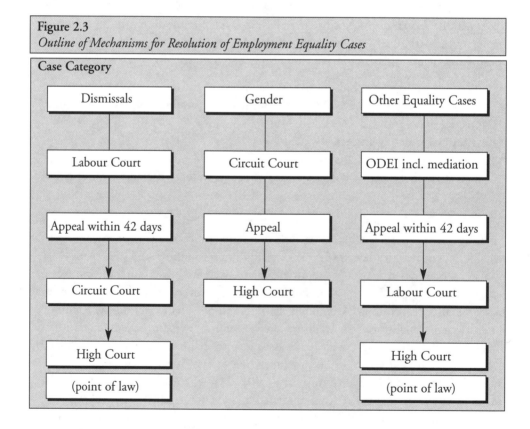

Figure 2.3
Outline of Mechanisms for Resolution of Employment Equality Cases

Case Category

Dismissals	Gender	Other Equality Cases
Labour Court	Circuit Court	ODEI incl. mediation
Appeal within 42 days	Appeal	Appeal within 42 days
Circuit Court	High Court	Labour Court
High Court (point of law)		High Court (point of law)

Cases may be referred to the Tribunal within six months of the act of alleged discrimination occurring. The Tribunal (www.odei.ie) notes that a case cannot be referred to it if a court has begun hearing a case by the complainant regarding the same issue. Conversely, a complainant who has referred a case to the Tribunal cannot recover damages through court proceedings regarding the same issue once the Tribunal has begun an investigation of their complaint or it has been settled by mediation.

The Process of Referring an Equality Case

The Tribunal likens the process of investigating cases to that of the EAT or the Labour Court rather than the civil courts (ODEI 2002: 8). Cases are heard by a Tribunal Equality Officer, who are described by ODEI (2002: 10) as 'sole member tribunals'. The Tribunal Equality Officer considers the evidence presented by the parties to the case and after the hearing he makes a written decision, which must be published. Should discrimination be found to have taken place the Equality Officer can make an order for redress, which can include compensation, equal pay, arrears for equal pay, equal treatment or an order for a particular course of action to be taken (ODEI 2002: 10). The decisions are binding and enforceable. Decisions of cases taken under the Employment Equality Act 1998 may be appealed to the Labour Court within forty-two days. Table 2.6 displays the number of referrals under each discriminatory ground to the Equality Tribunal for the years 2000–2002. ODEI reports the number of cases and the number of individual claims because some claimants may group their individual claims together into one case (2002: 14). Between 2000 and 2002 there was a substantial increase in individual claims (122 per cent) and cases (149 per cent). Race cases have shown a substantial jump since 2000, which is indicative of the growing multi-ethnic nature of the Irish labour force (Table 2.6).

Table 2.6
Employment Equality Referrals to ODEI – The Equality Tribunal, 2000–2002

Year	2002		2001		2000	
	Individual Claims	Cases	Individual Claims	Cases	Individual Claims	Cases
Gender	78	54	118	59	72	40
Age	39	34	23	22	19	16
Disability	44	42	26	26	10	10
Race	43	30	27	15	2	1
Traveller community	4	3	3	3	4	4
Marital status	2	2	1	1	3	3
Family status	5	5	2	2	2	2
Sexual orientation	5	4	5	4	1	1
Religion	1	1	1	1	1	1
No ground listed	13	10	11	8	0	0
Multiple grounds	75	69	43	41	25	24
Total	309	254	260	182	139	102

Source: ODEI (2002: 16)

Mediation

An alternative to investigation is mediation, which commenced in the Equality Tribunal in December 2000. If the Director of Equality Investigations feels a case could be resolved by mediation, she (as of 2003 the Director is Ms Melanie Pine) may request the parties involved to consider using it (www.odei.ie/Mediation). Alternatively, the Employment Equality Act allows the Labour Court to either conduct mediation itself (in cases referred to it) or to refer a case to the Director for mediation. The parties to a case must give their consent before it can be referred by the Director to a Tribunal Mediation Officer. If an agreement is reached at the end of the mediation process, the Mediation Officer draws up the terms of the agreement which, once signed by the parties, becomes legally binding and may be enforced through the Circuit Court (www.odei.ie/Mediation). Unlike Equality Officer decisions, mediation agreements are not published. Should a case remain unresolved after mediation, the complainant may resubmit the complaint to the Director for investigation. The option of mediation would seem to have a number of advantages, including that of being, on average, three times quicker than an investigation before an Equality Officer (ODEI/Equality Tribunal 2002b: 3). Indeed, the Director of Equality Investigations (Pine 2003: press release 17 October, www.odei.ie) recognised that the success of mediation was because 'this fast, confidential option, which is open to all parties until the end of the actual hearing, works to the mutual satisfaction of both parties'. In the two years 2001–2002, a total of eighty cases (involving 118 individual claims) have been referred to mediation.

The Equality Tribunal is not the only institution from which redress may be sought for employment equality cases. Alternatives are available depending on the grounds of a compliant. If a person claims to have been dismissed in circumstances amounting to discrimination or victimisation, then the case 'may be brought to the Labour Court and shall not be brought to the Director', i.e. the Equality Tribunal. In addition, gender-based complaints or claims in relation to the infringement of the equal pay or equal treatment directives may be brought to the Circuit Court. The Circuit Court is empowered to award unlimited compensation in this regard, although with an equal pay claim the period of compensation is limited to the six years before the date of referral (and any subsequent arrears). However, the number of direct referrals to the Labour Court or Circuit Court is much smaller than those to the Equality Tribunal, making it the main locus of redress for cases taken under employment equality legislation.

CHAPTER 3

Collective Industrial Relations Law

INTRODUCTION

This chapter sets out to examine the role of common law, legislation and the 1937 Irish Constitution (Bunreacht na hÉireann) on industrial relations. The legal implications of collective bargaining are dealt with in Chapter 9. In this chapter we deal with the evolution of collective industrial relations law in Ireland from pre-independence days to its present framework. It is not intended to provide a comprehensive treatment of industrial relations law, as this would be beyond the scope of the book. There are now a number of specialist law texts that address the technical aspects of industrial relations law (see Kerr and Whyte 1985; Kerr 1991a; Forde 1991; Fennell and Lynch 1993; Meenan 1999). Instead, the objective is to familiarise students with the approach of the law, some of the basic legal provisions and the manner in which social actors within the industrial relations system have regarded and interacted with the law. Particular emphasis is placed on understanding the evolution of the law in its historical and social context.

There are a number of reasons why a historical appreciation of labour law is essential for students of industrial relations. First, a number of laws enacted prior to the foundation of the state in 1922 remain on the statute books and continue in force unless repealed or found to be repugnant to the Constitution (von Prondzynski 1989; Kerr 1989). Second, much of recent legislation, especially the trade disputes provisions of the Industrial Relations Act 1990, is based on legislative principles developed prior to 1922. Third, the law cannot be understood in the absence of its social context. In this regard, the impact of social activism on the development of industrial relations legislation has been especially important. Historical experience can mark the boundaries of what is practicable and possible in legislating for industrial relations. Finally, an understanding of the evolution of collective legislation can inform contemporary debates on the role of the law in industrial relations.

OVERVIEW

While prior to 1824 the approach of both politics and the law to the early trade unions was one of trenchant opposition, during the nineteenth century the role of the law and politics diverged. From 1824 the political system often resulted in measures favourable to trade unions, which were subsequently frustrated or reversed by the legal system. In effect trade unions grew up with liberal democracy and were arguably a key part of that democracy.

The role adopted by the law has been ascribed to two factors. One is that the attitude of a judiciary, which was drawn from the ruling class, lacked any understanding or empathy with working men and was biased against working-class organisations. The second factor is that the legal judgments arose out of the logic of the individually based 'common law' system, which was at odds with the collective values trade unionism implied.

Common law is judge made law. A key principle of common law is that 'restraint of trade' is illegal. This means that interference with the right of individuals or businesses to pursue their own commercial ends is contrary to common law. As trade unions sought to *collectively* regulate the terms and conditions of employment (to restrain trade), this brought them into conflict with common law. Common law is itself based on the liberal principle of individuals being free to maximise their own welfare. An equal and, in the case of industrial relations, opposite principle of liberalism is that individuals should be free to combine to promote their own ends. This implies a right of association, which would vindicate the right of workers to organise to promote their collective interests through trade unions.

The evolution of state policy towards trade unions during the eighteenth century can be seen as conflict between the two liberal principles of 'restraint of trade' and 'freedom of association'. In this conflict, through legislation the political system tended to deliver greater liberties to trade unions while the common law legal system either restricted or rowed back on those liberties. The tension between the individually based common law system and collective industrial relations continues to be a feature of industrial relations to this day. This tension is much less than it was historically, due to extensive legislative provisions and the role of the Constitution. However, where legislation or the Constitution does not cover an aspect of collective industrial relations, then the common law takes effect. Also, within the Irish legal system, legislation and the Constitution tend to be interpreted in terms of common law individual liberal principles, rather than the collectivist principles applying in a number of European countries.

THE LAW AND POLITICS BEFORE 1825

The early approach of the state and legal system was one of open hostility to the emergent trade unions or combinations. This hostility dated back to the sixteenth century when 'combinations of workmen were made illegal' (Boyle 1988: 7). As the power of the medieval guilds weakened in the eighteenth century, skilled workers, or journeymen, increasingly relied on trade clubs for their protection. These trade clubs became known as combinations and later as trade unions. The response of the Irish Parliament was to pass a series of statutes (in 1715, 1729, 1743 and 1792) to regulate the work and wages of craftsmen. Some of these measures had a protective effect, requiring payment in 'coin of the realm', i.e. legal tender, or prohibiting payment in public houses; however, their major function was to set maximum wages. Boyle (1988: 9) writes that 'it would be tedious to list the successive anti-combinations acts passed by the Irish legislature'. These provided for increasingly stiffer penalties in Ireland than in the rest of the UK. Boyle (1988: 9) notes a 1757 act provided for imprisonment with hard labour for six months and whipping for an attempt to administer or take oaths or attempts by workers to set wages. In 1799 a new Combination Act was introduced and this was amended the following year with the passage of the General Combination Law of 1800 (see D'Arcy 1994; Pelling 1976). This law was applied to Ireland in 1803 but with provision for the maximum jail sentence of six months, whereas it was three months on the British mainland (see D'Arcy 1994: 9). While regarded as the first *systematic* attempt to suppress the early trade unions, Pelling (1976) notes the Combination Acts 1799–1800 were not as significant a departure from earlier legal practice, as is sometimes claimed. He suggests that the main difference from earlier legislation was that the Combination Acts provided for a summary sentence and conviction.

The various legal attempts to suppress combinations failed, as evidenced by the continued existence of combinations in the skilled trades (Boyle 1988; Boyd 1972). There are a number of reasons for the failure of legal suppression. The laws were difficult to enforce due to the secrecy of the combinations, social pressure was exerted on employers and employers were sometimes subject to intimidation. However, by far the most important reason was the scarce skills possessed by craftsmen, which made employers reluctant to use the law. There was no reluctance among employers in opposing unionisation among unskilled workers or semi-skilled workers threatened by new technology. Pelling (1976: 28) notes that 'in unskilled work ... or in skilled trades, where the skilled artisans were threatened by the introduction of machinery, combination was difficult to maintain and it readily degenerated into violence both against employers and against workmen willing to adhere to the combination'. However, replacing striking workers was often more effective for employers than resorting to the law.

In 1824 the Combination Acts 1799–1800 and other provisions banning combinations were repealed following the campaigning work of an employer, Francis Place (a master tailor), and David Hume, MP. Their repeal was aided by the fact that government had felt increasingly embarrassed because of the unbalanced implementation of the Acts. While they had been used against workers, provisions forbidding employer combination had not been put into effect (Pelling 1976: 26). Among the key arguments used to support the case for repeal was the ineffectiveness of the Acts and evidence that they worsened relations between master and workmen. Francis Place believed that repressive legislation merely encouraged combinations and that if removed, the combinations would die out (Boyle 1988: 26). This was, of course, a vain hope.

Boyle (1988: xi) notes that the repeal of the combination laws gave trade unions a legal existence and 'brought Irish trade union law into conformity with that prevailing in the rest of the UK'. However, for a number of reasons the repeal had only limited effect. First, subsequent to the repeal of the Combination Acts, a further piece of legislation was introduced – the Combination Laws Repeal Amendment Act 1825. This act created crimes of intimidation, obstruction and molestation, which 'frequently formed the basis of criminal prosecution of workers engaged in industrial action' (Kerr and Whyte 1985: 214). Second, trade unions were vulnerable to restrictions on taking oaths, which they frequently did in order to retain secrecy. This became apparent in

1834 when six Dorset farm labourers were transported to Australia for seven years for taking an illegal and seditious oath. The six, who became known as the Tolpuddle Martyrs, had joined the short-lived Grand National and Consolidated Union (a union for general workers) and taken an oath of secrecy. The establishment newspaper, the *Times* of London, objected to this sentence on the grounds that there was no evidence to substantiate the charge of sedition against the six. They were eventually pardoned and repatriated after a public campaign led by the *Times* newspaper.

Finally, the unions continued to fall foul of the common law doctrines of restraint of trade and criminal conspiracy. The doctrine of criminal conspiracy meant that an action that was otherwise not illegal was made illegal if two or more workers combined in that action. Kerr and Whyte (1985: 214) note that it was unlawful for persons to combine to peacefully persuade others to leave their employment with the object of forcing an employer to improve conditions of employment.

However, not all employers used the law. By the 1850s employers had begun to deal with the craft-based 'model unions', which had grown out of the new trades formed by the Industrial Revolution. The acceptance of the model unions saw Parliament move to allow a limited use of industrial action in the Molestation of Workmen Act 1859. This Act sought to remove the crimes of criminal conspiracy, molestation and obstruction from actions designed to fix wages or hours of work and also to give a measure of protection to peaceful industrial action (Kerr and Whyte 1985: 214). The intention of Parliament was frustrated by judicial interpretations, which found that the Act provided no protection for a breach of contract, which a strike involved.

CRIMINAL LAW AND COLLECTIVE INDUSTRIAL RELATIONS

Up until 1871 the underlying common law doctrine of criminal conspiracy was the commanding influence in regulating the employment relationship. By 1870, however, the growing acceptance of trade unions had set the ground for change. A Royal Commission (the Erle Commission) was established in 1867 which reported favourably on the influence of trade unions in 1869, recommending that they be granted legal recognition and be regulated. The union members on the Commission, however, merely wished unions to be legalised without obligation. Many members of the model unions now owned smallholdings and extensions of the franchise to owners of small property, which meant the model unions were able to harness their members' voting power to good effect. In return for their support in the 1870 elections, the Liberals, under Gladstone, delivered the reforming legislation the unions sought. The resulting Trade Union Act of 1871, as subsequently amended, still governs the legal status of trade unions in Ireland today. The Act legalised the existence of trade unions but carefully sought to refrain from giving them the status of corporate entities, that is, entities capable of suing and being sued in their own name. The Act declares that the mere fact that a trade union's aims are in restraint of trade is not sufficient to render any union member 'liable for criminal prosecution for conspiracy' (Kerr 1991a: 1). The Act encouraged trade unions to register with the Registrar of Friendly Societies but this was not mandatory. The general intention of the provisions was to allow trade unions to exist within the law but to prevent legal regulation of their affairs. This approach is the foundation of present-day voluntarism.

The 1871 Act, while legitimising the existence of unions, failed to provide sufficient protection for their actions in trade dispute situations. This arose because of the continuing influence of the underlying common law concept of criminal conspiracy. The 1871 Act had been carefully framed to exclude the threat of a strike from being a statutory offence. However, the judiciary found in *Regina* v. *Bunn (1872)* that in common law, the existence of a combination (two or more people acting together) converted an otherwise non-criminal act into a crime. It was found that the employer had a right to employ whoever he liked and any union interference with this was a criminal offence (O'Hara 1981: 16). It was 'unjustifiable annoyance and interference with the masters in the course of their business' (Kerr and Whyte 1985: 215). Furthermore, picketing was held to be a criminal offence and even minor expressions of opinion were sufficient to lead to a jail sentence. Sixteen women in South Wales were sentenced to eleven days in prison for calling out 'baaah' (indicating they considered them sheep) to substitute working miners during a strike. The effect of these decisions was to significantly frustrate the operation of trade unions.

In the election of 1874, the trade union movement switched its allegiance to the Conservative party, led by Disraeli, in return for a promise of legislation that would be favourable to them. As a result of this support, the Conservatives won the election and there followed a two-year period of legislative activity. The first Act introduced was the Conspiracy and Protection of Property Act 1875, which restricted the remit of the criminal law. This Act, which is also still on the statute books in Ireland, had the following provisions:

- that no one was liable for any act committed 'in contemplation or furtherance of a trade dispute' unless the act would also be a crime if committed by one person;
- a breach of contract by workers of gas or water supply was to remain a crime in certain circumstances;
- the Act gave a degree of immunity to peaceful picketing in connection with a trade dispute (that is, picketing that does not entail violence or intimidation); and
- a breach of contract by any person which endangered human life, risked serious bodily injury or exposed valuable property to destruction continued to be a crime.

The Employers and Workmen Act 1875 followed, which freed individual workers from criminal liability for breach of their employment contract by providing that a breach of such a contract by a worker was no longer held to be a criminal offence. The penalty was now limited to civil damages. A final Act, the Trade Union Amendment Act 1876, resolved a difficulty unions had experienced in protecting their funds by ensuring that trustees could be held accountable for funds.

The broad effect of these legislative changes was to establish a *voluntarist* system of industrial relations in which the law was designed to play a minor role. Trade unions were granted *immunities* from acts that would otherwise have been criminal offences, but they were not given rights. This met a demand of the model unions that 'they wanted nothing from the law other than that it leave them alone'. The net effect of the legislative provisions of this time is that the criminal law now applies to industrial relations only insofar as actions are in themselves criminal acts. Thus, the use of force, intimidation and trespass continues to be illegal in trade disputes because they are illegal acts if committed by one person.

THE CIVIL LAW

The legislation introduced by Parliament did not go unchallenged for long. Denied the use of criminal liabilities, employers challenged the legality of picketing and secondly had resort to the notion of civil conspiracy under the law of tort (Kerr and Whyte 1985). In *Lyons* v. *Wilkins (1896–1898)* it was found that even peaceful picketing to persuade workers not to work constituted 'watching and besetting'. This threatened to nullify the protection for picketing contained in the Conspiracy and Protection of Property Act 1875 (Saville 1967: 347). This decision seemed to conflict with the House of Lords' (the highest court of appeal in the UK) decision in *Allen* v. *Flood (1897)*, which seemed to allow peaceful picketing. This made the common law position on picketing unclear and this is still the case today. Costelloe (2003) suggests the decision in *Lyons* v. *Wilkins* is considered the most persuasive. However, the entitlement to strike seemed to be protected by a number of judgments, including that of *Allen* v. *Flood (1897)*, which indicated that a strike was lawful at common law (see Forde 1991: 12–15).

Two cases, however, were to throw this presumption into question. The first was the Belfast case of *Quinn* v. *Leathem (1901)*. In pursuit of enforcing a closed shop, the Belfast Journeymen Butchers' Association persuaded a supplier not to supply meat to a butcher. While no unlawful act had been committed by any of the defendants individually, they had conspired to induce a breach of a 'third-party' contract. This combination to injure was an unlawful conspiracy, entitling the plaintiff to recover civil damages. The Conspiracy and Protection of Property Act 1875 was found to offer no protection, since it gave immunity only from *criminal* conspiracy, while the actions of the Association involved the tort of conspiracy – a *civil* offence. The judgment meant that if two or more persons combine together without legal justification to injure another, they were liable for damages for conspiracy. Forde (1991: 15) writes the consequences of *Quinn* v. *Leathem* were 'to render the participation in many strikes tortuous and … to throw the entire area of the law into great confusion'. However, the judgment was against Quinn, who was treasurer of the Association, and not the Association itself. This limited the impact of the decision, as only minimal damages could be recovered from union officials.

From the trade union perspective, a far more disturbing development was the decision of the House of Lords in the case of *The Taff Vale Railway Company* v. *Amalgamated Society of Railway Servants (1901)*. The case arose as a result of a strike protesting the dismissal of a signalman on the Taff Vale Railway Company by members of the Amalgamated Society of Railway Servants. Richard Bell, the union's general secretary, had persuaded workers brought in to replace striking workers not to work. In legal terms, he induced them to breach their contract of employment (a third-party employment contract) with the Taff Vale Company. The company sought an injunction and damages against the union. Prior to 1901 it was believed that 'since trade unions were not legally constituted corporations they could not be sued for damages' (Saville 1967: 347). The decision reached by the law lords overturned this view. They found that a registered trade union was a legal entity, possessing sufficient attributes of corporate personality to enable it to be sued. The Taff Vale Company was awarded £23,000 damages and costs reported to be £13,000 – a huge sum at the time. This decision threatened to reduce unions to impotence. If they called a strike their funds were at risk, endangering their very capacity to exist. During the subsequent five years it has been estimated that unions lost £200,000 in similar actions. However, the use of the law was a tactical issue and not all employers faced with industrial action used it.

Yet again the trade union movement turned to the political process to overturn the precedents established by Taff Vale and other cases (Saville 1967; Boyle 1988: 226; Wallace 1988c). Following the 1906 elections, a Liberal government was able to assume office due to the support of fifty-four LIB-LAB deputies. These were MPs who supported the trade unions, some of whom were members of the Liberal Party and others members of the emergent Labour Party, the Labour Representation Committee, a forerunner of the UK Labour Party. In return for this support the government enacted the Trade Disputes Act 1906. This Act provided protection to trade unions and their members by granting them immunity from the tort of civil conspiracy. This reinforced the protection for peaceful picketing and granted immunities for actions that would otherwise have been actionable at common law. The immunities, which were conferred on union members and their agents (union officials), were restricted to where they were *acting in contemplation or furtherance of a trade dispute* – the so-called 'golden formula', a phrase coined by Wedderburn (1965: 222). Section 4 of the Act, however, provided *trade unions* with a *total* immunity from being sued under the law of tort, in effect reversing the Taff Vale decision. As von Prondzynski (1989: 214) notes, the Trade Disputes Act 1906 adopted a very simple technique – it identified the main judicial decisions which had disabled trade unions and gave unions immunities from legal action which might arise under these judicial precedents.

Known as a 'Bill of Rights for Workers', the 1906 Act actually provided no legal rights and did not confer a right to strike. Kerr and Whyte (1985) report that the trade unions opposed the enactment of a comprehensive labour law code with positive rights and obligations and opted for the pragmatic immunities approach. This contrasts with the approaches adopted by trade unions in a number of European countries. While arising from the demands of trade unions, it is important to stress that this voluntarism had advantages for employers. Legal abstentionism extended to the area of individual employment law, leaving employers with few obligations. The law did not impose any requirements on employers to recognise or negotiate with trade unions. It left management free to decide on a pragmatic basis if they would or would not deal with them. It is noteworthy that today voluntarism has given way to legalism in individual employment law and the adequacy of the voluntarist approach in matters of union recognition continues to be a matter of debate (see D'Art and Turner 2002b).

The final piece of collective legislation enacted prior to 1922 was the Trade Union

Act 1913. This Act's most important provision is to allow a trade union's funds to be applied for political purposes. The Act reversed the decision of the House of Lords in the case of *Osborne* v. *Amalgamated Society of Railway Servants (1911)*, which held that unions were not entitled to raise or expend funds for political purposes. The Act specified that, provided political purposes were included in the union's objects and a separate political fund was set up (from which members could easily opt out), a union could use its funds for political purposes. As a result of the Act, unions in Ireland may operate a political fund but must offer members an easy way of opting out of paying the political contribution. This is known as 'the contracting out' condition, which makes it easier for trade unions to maintain a political fund than if there were a 'contracting in' condition which required members to specifically opt to pay a political levy.

COLLECTIVE LEGISLATION AFTER 1922

Table 3.1 summarises the main legislative developments in Irish collective labour law since 1922. The eighteen years between 1922 and 1940 saw a period of legislative inaction with only one statute passed – the Trade Union Act of 1935, which enables trade unions to hold an unlimited amount of land. The main concern of trade union movement in the newly independent state was to preserve the legacy embodied in the acts of the UK Parliament (McGingley 1990). The first major piece of legislation post-1922 was the Trade Union Act of 1941. This was enacted against the backdrop of concern over the operation of British unions in the new state and the perceived structural defects in the trade union movement. Von Prondzynski (1989) notes the existence of a belief in government that the large number of trade unions, which were fragmented and unco-ordinated, and the substantial number of British-based unions operating here were hostile to the best interests of the state.

From 1936 to 1939 this concern was paralleled by a debate on reform within the trade union movement. This debate, however, emanated from the contradictory view that a united movement could more effectively 'take on employers'. In this debate, the ITGWU proposed restructuring Irish trade unions into ten industrial unions. However, the Irish Trade Union Congress (ITUC) failed to support the ITGWU proposal at its 1939 Annual Delegate Congress. Instead, it opted for the less radical policy of encouraging union amalgamations. Unhappy at that decision, the government decided to introduce its own measures in the Trade Union Act 1941. This Act established a requirement that in order to engage in collective bargaining, organisations had to possess a negotiating licence – any organisation granted such a licence, including an employer organisation, would then be an 'authorised trade union' (see Chapter 5). Among other provisions, the 1941 Act confined the immunities in the Trade Disputes Act 1906 to authorised trade unions. A more controversial provision of the Act provided for restrictions on negotiation rights, but this provision was struck down by the Supreme Court in a challenge in 1947 (see discussion on the Constitution below).

Following this decision, governments were reluctant to enter the area of industrial relations legislation. The need for consensus on legislation was driven home by the experience with the Trade Union Bill 1966. This bill proposed to legislate for secret ballots prior to industrial action and to remove the immunities in the 1906 Act from trade union members who engaged in unofficial action. Though the Irish Congress of Trade Unions (ICTU) had seemed prepared to accept the bill, when it was first mooted in 1965 it was subsequently strongly opposed by individual trade unions and trade union activists. The bill lapsed in 1969, at which time the Minister of Labour, Dr Paddy Hillery, TD, remarked, 'Whatever about the merits of these particular proposals, it was clear that it would have been futile to go ahead with them in light of the trade union reaction' (Dáil Debates 1969: 1,325). At the same time the Electricity (Special Provisions) Act 1966 was also repealed. This Act had forbidden industrial action in the ESB. Strikers were committed to Mountjoy Jail for contempt of court in 1968 after taking strike action. They were released following intensive late-night negotiations; however, they insisted that taxis be made available to take them home. These were provided at the government's instruction, which caused them embarrassment. The fate of the Trade Union Bill 1966 and the Electricity (Special Provisions) Act 1966 contrasted with the ready acceptance of the institutional provisions in the Industrial Relations Act 1946 and the Industrial Relations Act 1969. Both of these Acts are discussed in detail in the following chapter.

The Trade Union Act of 1971 discouraged the formation of new unions. It required a union to give eighteen months' advance notice to the Minister for Labour and the ICTU of its intention to apply for a negotiation licence, to have a minimum of £5,000 on deposit with the High Court and to have 500 members in the state at the date of application. There was provision to waive these requirements if 'the High Court, after hearing any evidence adduced by the applicant, the Minister, the Congress and any other trade union declare[d] that the granting of a negotiation licence to the applicant would not be against the public interest' (Section 3(2) of 1971 Act).

Obviously, these provisions did not affect established unions and as such would not have been opposed to their interests. The measures provided a degree of protection to existing unions from competition by new unions being founded. This was an issue that had arisen in a number of high-profile disputes in the 1960s, notably when the National Busmens' Union (NBU) was established in a breakaway from the ITGWU (McCarthy 1973). Section 4 of the Trade Union Act 1975 provides that the Oireachtas would meet the 'expenses incurred by the Minister in the administration of this Act' for those unions that successfully merge or amalgamate under Section 3(2). The Industrial Relations Act 1990 made a number of amendments designed to encourage mergers and to discourage formation of new or breakaway unions. The Act amended the Trade Union Act of 1975 by offering grants towards the expenses incurred in an attempted merger or transfer of engagement, even if the attempt fails. The expenses extend to a two-year period prior to the merger attempt. The Act also amends the Industrial Relations Act 1971 by increasing the minimum membership to 1,000 in order for a new union to qualify for the granting of a negotiating licence and alters the sum of money required to be held on deposit with the High Court. The amount required varies according to the size of the union but the minimum deposit of IR£20,000 is specified in the Act.

Table 3.1

Collective Labour Legislation Enacted by the Oireachtas, 1922–2003

Statute	Provisions
Trade Union Act 1935	Trade unions allowed to own unlimited amount of land
Trade Union Act 1941	Negotiation licences, sole representation rights
Trade Union Act 1942	Exemptions from negotiation licences, appeals in sole representation rights situations
Industrial Relations Act 1946	Establishment of the Labour Court
Trade Union Act 1947–1952	Six Acts extending power to reduce deposits to be maintained with Registrar of Friendly Societies Irish unions by seventy-five per cent
Industrial Relations Act 1969	Enlargement of the Labour Court, establishment of office of Rights Commissioners
Trade Union Act 1971	New negotiation licence rules: £5,000 deposit, 500 members, eighteen-month wait
Trade Union Act 1975	Encouraged the amalgamation of trade unions by providing funding for expenses for successful mergers
Industrial Relations Act 1976	Established a Joint Labour Committee (JLC) for agricultural workers and allowed them access to the Labour Court
Worker Participation (State Enterprises) Act 1977–1988	Provided for elected worker directors and sub-board-level participation
Trade Disputes (Amendment) Act 1982	Extended immunities of the 1906 Act to all except the Defence Forces and Gardaí
Industrial Relations Act 1990	Established the Labour Relations Commission, repealed 1906 and 1982 Trade Disputes Acts, provides for pre-strike secret ballots, immunities restricted, injunctions curbed, funding for trade union rationalisation even if unsuccessful
Industrial Relations (Amendment) Act 2001	Deals with disputes arising out of union recognition – allows for legal determination of terms and conditions of employment but not statutory recognition

Source: Adapted and extended from McGinley (1990)

VOLUNTARISM IN CONTEXT

In Britain the Trade Disputes Act 1906 was modified by the Conservative government in 1927 but reinstated by the Labour government in 1945. Again in 1971 the Conservatives introduced the legalistic, and ill-fated, Industrial Relations Act 1971 to replace the voluntarist 1906 Act. The Labour government elected in 1974 reinstated many of the principles of the 1906 Act in the Trade Union and Labour Relations Act 1975, but following the election of the Thatcher government in 1979, many of these immunities were systematically removed (Brown *et al.* 1997: 81).

This time, however, the Labour Party did not reverse the changes on assuming power. Trade disputes law in the UK is today highly restrictive and legalistic. The trade union movement in Britain has been unable to replicate the historic use of political action to achieve changes to trade disputes law, although they have achieved a measure to provide for statutory union recognition – the Employment Relations Act 1999. By contrast with the experience in the UK, in Ireland the provisions of the 1906 Act remained largely undisturbed up to 1990.

Voluntarism is not a widespread feature of industrial relations in other European Union (EU) countries, with only Denmark possessing a system described as voluntarist. Eaton (2000) notes that in Denmark

> what is generally known as a right to strike is in fact a freedom to strike, however, even the Danish system does not have the thoroughgoing legal abstentionism of Ireland. This is demonstrated by the distinction between *'disputes of rights'* and *'disputes of interest'*, made from the outset in Denmark [and Sweden] (Eaton 2000: 134).

Eaton (2000: 134) notes this distinction is also made in other countries such as New Zealand, Germany, Canada and Spain. A dispute of right exists where there is some pre-existing rule that can be applied to determine the rights and wrongs of a dispute (Commission of Enquiry on Industrial Relations 1981; McCarthy and von Prondzynski 1982). Thus, in legally based systems employment legislation defines the rights and wrongs of dismissals, equality, redundancy disputes, etc. The collective agreement is also a 'pre-existing rule' that can be used for adjudicating on terms and conditions of employment during the period of an agreement. Disputes of interests, on the other hand, are defined by the absence of any pre-existing rule that could be used to adjudicate on a dispute. For example, where, on the termination of a collective agreement, a trade union makes a pay claim of eight per cent and an employer offers two per cent, there is said to be no way of deciding between these two positions. In general, strikes involving disputes of interests are legal. By contrast, in disputes of rights, the right, or freedom, to strike is circumscribed by a requirement to have the dispute determined, often in specialist Labour Courts, by the application of the rule (Eaton 2000).

THE OPERATION OF VOLUNTARISM IN IRELAND

In the 1950s, trade dispute law was not the subject of major controversy. This was a manifestation of the low Irish strike levels in that decade. With the growth in strikes in the 1960s (see Chapter 8) it became common to find commentators decrying the imperfections of the Irish system, especially the Trade Disputes Act 1906. In the case *Goulding Chemicals Ltd* v. *Bolger (1977)*, Justice Parke commented:

> The Trade Disputes Act 1906 was a child of political expediency hastily conceived and prematurely delivered. It has now survived more than the allotted span of life with all its inbred imperfections still uncorrected. Indeed I suspect that apart from such of those imperfections as have already become apparent others may yet be discovered by those of agile and ingenious mind (quoted in Commission of Inquiry on Industrial Relations 1981: 222).

Among some of the readily identifiable defects of the Act from an employer perspective was the fact that the Act protected unofficial strikes and strikes by a minority of workers. Equally, strikes in breach of collective agreements were protected. In a dissenting decision in the *Becton Dickenson* v. *Lee and Others (1973)* case, Justice FitzGerald commented, 'The ultraliberal interpretation of the Trade Disputes Act 1906, coupled with the failure of the authorities to enforce the law has led to a public misconception and belief that a right to protest carries with it a right to picket. This is not the law'.

However, these views have not gone unchallenged. Far from being a rushed response to a political situation, Kidner (1982) notes that the 1906 Act was the subject of great care and consideration during the years following the Taff Vale decision. A number of authorities have noted that most of the imperfections discovered had been used to restrict the intended effect of the Act (see Kerr and Whyte 1985; von Prondzynski and McCarthy 1984). First, courts found that the definition of a worker as someone 'employed in trade or industry' excluded many public sector workers, such as civil servants. As a result such workers did not enjoy immunities in a trade dispute situation (Forde 1991: 16). Second, the immunities in the 1906 Act were found to be limited to breaches of *third-party employment* contracts, as demonstrated by the Supreme Court case of *Talbot (Ireland) Ltd* v. *Merrigan (1981)*. In that case it was found that breach of a *commercial* contract was not protected and an injunction was granted to prevent the *blacking* of goods, i.e. the refusal to handle goods. Third was the criteria used by the courts in granting injunctions, which are restraining orders preventing named individuals from engaging in certain actions. An injunction may be granted on an interim, interlocutory or permanent basis. An interim injunction is one granted pending a hearing on the application for an injunction. Employers could seek interim injunctions on an *ex-parte* basis, that is, without the union being present. An interlocutory injunction is one granted pending a full hearing of the case. A permanent injunction is one granted following a full hearing of a case. An interim or interlocutory injunction was available to an employer if they met the following two criteria:

• that there was a fair case that there was a legal problem with the union action; and
• if the balance of convenience was in favour of granting the injunction.

Once an employer could establish that there was a 'fair issue to be tried' the court would proceed to consider where the 'balance of convenience' lay. This was usually decided in favour of an employer. An employer could easily demonstrate they would incur financial loss, while the union could only show the industrial action would be delayed. The courts took no regard of the fact that delaying industrial action would nearly always effectively defeat that action (see Kerr and Whyte 1985).

The use of an injunction was not without its problems for employers, as many were reluctant to enforce injunctions if employees disregarded them. This arose because in order to enforce the injunction, an employer had to have employees cited for contempt of court. This could lead to the imprisonment of employees, a step many employers were reluctant to take. Justice Brian Walsh of the Supreme Court notes that injunctions were frequently flouted by employees and used as 'bargaining counters' by employers (Walsh 1985: viii).

Finally, it should also be noted that a number of legal decisions in Ireland have been more favourable to workers and unions than in the UK. For instance, while in the UK it was found that strike was a breach of an employment contract, in Ireland the *Becton Dickenson v. Lee (1973)* case would seem to have decided it was merely a suspension of the contract.

THE DEBATE ON LEGAL REFORM

Irrespective of the above illustrative difficulties which trade unions experienced with restrictive interpretations of the 1906 Act the main concern of public policymakers and employers was with the increasing level of strikes of the 1960s. Reform of Irish industrial relations and trade disputes law had been high on the agenda of the Department of Labour since its establishment in 1966 (Kerr 1991a: 179). Since the early 1970s, employers had advocated radical reform of the law applicable to trade disputes, with the Industrial Development Authority (IDA) also being associated with such demands (Duffy 1993). Kerr (1991a: 179) locates the persistence of the reform debate in the perceived state of industrial relations, which some considered throughout the 1960s and 1970s to be in serious disorder – unofficial strikes were widespread, there were frequent disruptions to essential services and there were a significant, if small, number of inter-union disputes.

The heightened level of strikes from the mid-1970s prompted the Fianna Fáil government to set up a Commission of Inquiry on Industrial Relations in 1978. The Commission, from which the ICTU withdrew shortly after it was established, reached a very different conclusion from that reached by the British Royal Commission of Inquiry 1965–1968 (the Donovan Commission). Donovan had supported the retention of the voluntarist system, but the Irish Commission argued that there was a 'failure of existing voluntary arrangements' and recommended the repeal of the legislation on trade disputes and its replacement by new consolidated legislation (Commission of Inquiry on Industrial Relations 1981: 205, 296). In essence, this new legislation would place procedural requirements on trade unions and would again make them liable to be sued in tort if the procedures were not observed. The Commission carefully avoided suggesting the reintroduction of criminal liability and favoured the retention of the immunities-based approach in the Conspiracy and Protection of Property Act 1875.

The Commission's report, while generally welcomed by employers, drew criticism from trade unionists and academics. The most thorough analysis of the report was undertaken by McCarthy and von Prondzynski (1982), who pointed out that the Commission's recommendations were not backed by any original research, the secondary research they had deployed had been used in a selective and misleading manner and the views of the leading expert on labour law, Otto Kahn-Freund, were used to support a position of which he would not have approved (McCarthy and von Prondzynski 1982: 221–2). Kelly and Roche (1983: 222) argued that the Commission's recommendations were not congruent with the voluntarist tradition of Irish industrial relations. Wallace (1988c) argued that at a conceptual level there was a major discontinuity in the Commission's analysis in that it identified the problems of Irish industrial relations as rooted in trade unions' structure, but the prescriptions were related to trade disputes. Subsequent to the Commission's report, a study by Wallace and O'Shea (1987) undermined the Commission's claim that unofficial strikes were associated with small unions. The Commission had suggested that 'the small size of many unions tends to make it difficult for them to provide an adequate level of service to members … inadequate levels of service lead to disaffection among members and frequently to unofficial action' (Commission of Inquiry on Industrial Relations 1981: 25). Wallace and O'Shea (1987: 94) found that in the period 1978 to 1986, unofficial action was extremely rare among members of small unions and was overwhelmingly associated with members of larger unions – the direct opposite of the Commission's assertion.

Government Proposals for Reform

The Fine Gael-Labour government's reaction appeared to be a rejection of the Commission's recommendations. In 1983 the Department of Labour published a discussion paper that appeared to endorse the reservations of academic commentators (Department of Labour 1983). In 1985 there seemed to be a complete rejection of the Commission's approach when the Department of Labour, with Ruairi Quinn as minister, published proposals for a 'positive right to strike' (Department of Labour 1985), which was followed by an elaboration of these proposals in 1986 (Department of Labour 1986b). Employers' groups such as the Federation of Irish Employers (FIE) expressed initial outrage while trade unionists, such as the then president of the ITGWU, John Carroll, gave a guarded welcome to the proposals. However, the tenor of these responses changed within months, with the employers seeking movement on the proposals but the unions becoming lukewarm. Unions had become concerned at restrictions to be placed on the positive rights (see Kerr 1986: 17). The rejection of the 'positive rights approach' means that, despite impressions to the contrary, there is not a right to strike in Irish legislation.

Revised proposals were advanced in 1988 by the Department of Labour. The immediate origin of these is to be found in the Programme for National Recovery

(PNR), which was signed in 1987. The 1988 proposals reverted to an immunities-based approach, with Bonner (1989) identifying the primary reason for this being the unenthusiastic response of ICTU to the positive rights approach. However, a number of the procedural requirements to be complied with in the event of industrial action replicated the proposed exceptions to the right to strike contained in the 1986 proposals. The new proposals were presented as an attempt to achieve a balance between the rights and responsibilities of employers and trade unions. It was argued that 'the law had become extraordinarily complex and its precise limits were vague and confusing. The usefulness of statute law in providing a guide to conduct had diminished and it was increasingly necessary to look to case law' (Department of Labour 1991a: 4). Thus, the explicit objectives of the trade disputes provisions were to provide clarity in the law, to keep case law out of industrial relations as far as possible and to mark off 'the boundaries of what is permissible in trade disputes situations' (Department of Labour 1991a: 4).

The proposals formed the basis of the Industrial Relations Bill, 1989. The bill was generally well received in the Dáil although Kerr (1991a: 181) notes some sharp disagreements on some of the details of the bill. Pat Rabbitte, TD and Eamonn Gilmore, TD, of the Workers Party, criticised the bill on a number of grounds, notably that the Section 9 requirements (see below) would make the position of shop stewards vulnerable and that it would lead to more intervention into industrial relations by the courts (Rabbitte and Gilmore 1990). These and a small number of other objections, however, did not impede the bill's passage.

The question arises as to why the Act was readily accepted by the trade union movement. It is likely that there were a number of factors in the acceptance. First, there was a threat of a constitutional challenge to the 1906 Act due to the total immunity trade unions enjoyed from being sued in tort. It was feared that the immunity would not survive a challenge based on Article 34, which guarantees access to the courts. The 1990 Act limits the immunity to situations when unions were *acting in contemplation or furtherance of a trade dispute*. Second, the 1990 Act restricts the ease with which the courts could grant injunctions, which was a response to trade union complaints in the area. Third, there may have been a trade union fear that even more onerous legislation could be introduced, as in the UK. Finally, it is possible that trade union leaders may have seen the new measures as strengthening trade union organisations at the expense of unofficial groupings. The greater centralisation of industrial relations in the 1980s, noted by von Prondzynski (1998), meant that leadership support was more influential than in 1966.

THE INDUSTRIAL RELATIONS ACT 1990

The Industrial Relations Act 1990, which passed into law on 18 July 1990, is the most significant piece of collective industrial relations legislation in Ireland. The stated purpose of the Act 'is to put in place an improved framework for the conduct of industrial relations and for the resolution of trade disputes (with) the overall aim ... to maintain a stable and orderly industrial relations climate' (Department of Labour 1991a: 1). It was recognised that a complete consensus 'as to what the legislative framework should contain would not be possible' and sought to address the major issues and 'devise arrangements which would be workable and which both sides could live with' (Department of Labour 1991a: 5).

The provisions of the Act can be broadly divided between provisions covering trade disputes, trade union law and institutional provisions. Only the first two are dealt with here, with the institutional provisions being dealt with in the following chapter.

Trade Disputes Provisions

The approach adopted in the area of trade disputes law was to repeal the Trade Disputes Act 1906 and the Trade Disputes (Amendment) Act 1982 and to reintroduce the main provisions of these Acts with a number of changes. The following is a summary of the main provisions.

1. Section 8 contains definitions of an employer, a trade dispute, a trade union, a worker, industrial action and a strike (for a list of the definitions and a discussion on them see Kerr 1991a: 183–6 and Meenan 1999: 167–76). Some key points from the definitions are as follows.
    *   A worker does not include a member of the Defence Forces or of the Garda Síochána. It is notable that this exclusion did not prevent the taking of industrial action in the 'blue flu' action in 1998.
    *   A trade dispute only covers disputes between employers and workers, which has the effect of withdrawing protection from worker versus worker (inter-union) disputes, but 'can include disputes involving former workers' (Meenan 1999: 169).
    *   The purpose of a strike must be to compel an employer to accept or not accept certain terms or conditions affecting employment. This excludes political strikes over such matters as taxation or a general strike (Meenan 1999: 175) or a protest at the imprisonment of an individual (Kerr 1991a: 186).
2. Section 9 withdraws immunities from any form of industrial action in individual disputes that are in breach of agreed procedures contained either in *writing* or in *custom or in practice*. However, the section requires employers to observe procedures. In the event of an employer not observing procedures employees may engage in industrial action without exhausting procedures.
3. Section 11 both clarifies and restricts the provisions for picketing.
    *   Picketing is lawful at a place where an employee works or where an employer carries on business or, where this is not practical, at the approaches to the place of work.
    *   Limitations are placed on where and who workers can picket. Specifically, workers may only picket their employer or, in the case of secondary action, picket another employer if that (secondary) employer is seeking to frustrate the industrial action by directly assisting the primary employer. Normal commercial activity does not meet the criterion for frustration of industrial action, nor does any sympathy action in support of workers by workers in other companies.

4. In Section 12, immunities previously available to union members under the Trades Disputes Act 1906 in relation to conspiracy and combination are re-enacted without amendment.

5. Under Section 13, the former total immunity from being sued in tort that trade unions enjoyed is restricted to situations where trade unions are 'acting in contemplation or furtherance of a trade dispute' – the so-called 'golden formula'.

6. Under Section 14, trade unions are required to incorporate provisions for a secret ballot into union rulebooks. These require that a secret ballot be conducted in the event of *any form of industrial action*. Immunities are withdrawn from any industrial action where a majority of workers vote against such action in a secret ballot. Unions that persistently disregard the secret balloting requirements may lose their negotiating licence. However, as a result of the decision in *Halligan and Others* v. *Nolan Transport (Oaklands) Limited (1998)*, they are not liable in tort.

7. Section 19 places limitations on the granting of *ex-parte* injunctions (those with only one party present). An injunction will not be granted provided the following applies:
    *   a secret ballot has been held;
    *   a majority has voted in favour of industrial action; and
    *   seven days' notice of such action has been given to an employer.
    Interlocutory injunctions (an injunction pending a full trial) are not available to an employer where in addition to the two previous requirements the union establishes a fair case that it was 'acting in contemplation or furtherance of a trade dispute' (adapted from Wallace and O'Sullivan 2002a).

As of 18 July 1992, union rules must contain provisions for the holding of secret ballots before any form of industrial action can be taken and all unions have complied with the requirement for the incorporation of the balloting provisions in their rules. It is sometimes wrongly suggested that the Act outlaws unofficial strikes, but Kerr (1991a) makes it clear that is not the case. An unofficial strike that complied with the balloting provisions and where employees served the required seven days' notice would be quite legal, as there is no requirement for union approval for industrial action. It is important to note that during the passage of the bill changes were made to the secret balloting provisions. These changes protected the position of ICTU-sanctioned all-out strikes and pickets by requiring that any secondary action be sanctioned by ICTU.

The Operation of the Industrial Relations Act 1990

The trade disputes provisions have been the most controversial part of the 1990 Act. As early as 1991, Wilkinson (1991: 21) argued that the Act had 'a restrictive rather than reformative effect' and that it 'acted to the detriment of trade unions'. Kerr (1991b), however, suggested that the Act was introduced against a background of consensus. Within a short period after its introduction, trade unions found themselves involved in a number of cases that clashed with the stated intention of the Act to remove the law from industrial relations and reinforce voluntarism (see Kerr 1991a: 194; Wallace 1991).

A number of these first cases led to initial disquiet in some unions. At its inaugural conference, the Irish Municipal, Public and Civil Trade Union (IMPACT) voted by an overwhelming majority to call on trade unions to campaign for changes to the Act (Kerr 1991a: 181). Two motions condemning the Act were put down at the 1991 ICTU Annual Delegate Conference. The motion, tabled by the Irish Distributive and Administrative Trade Union (IDATU), was only narrowly defeated. It had sought to commit ICTU to 'lobby extensively to have the Act amended so that an equitable balance between the interests of employees and trade unions is achieved' (Frawley 1991). In contrast, the assistant general secretary of the ICTU, Kevin Duffy (1993), defended the Act and claimed to be unaware of any situation in which a union had found it impossible to deal with a dispute because of the provisions of this legislation.

In the period since 1993, the Act would appear to have been influential in the outcome of at least a small number of disputes. A Ryanair dispute in March 1998 involving sympathy action in support of fewer than fifty SIPTU baggage handlers is the most notable example. SIPTU had sought negotiation rights, which Ryanair refused and a dispute ensued. In this dispute, workers employed in other companies (Aer Rianta and Aer Lingus) engaged in sympathetic industrial action in support of the baggage handlers. The industrial action quickly collapsed. Although legal action was not taken against the unions, the fact that the sympathy action would not have enjoyed immunity appears to have been instrumental in the collapse of the dispute (Sheehan 1998a).

The two most notable disputes in which the Act has been invoked are the series of cases involving *Nolan Transport (Oaklands) Ltd* v. *Halligan and Others (1993–1998)* (referred to as the Nolan Transport cases) and the case of *G&T Crampton* v. *Building and Allied Trade Union (BATU) (1997)*. Both of these cases have been crucial in the interpretation of the Act and because of this are discussed in some detail below.

The *G&T Crampton* v. *BATU* Case, 1997

The *G&T Crampton* v. *BATU* case involved a dispute over the termination of the employment of a number of bricklayers on a site on which G&T Crampton was the main contractor. When one subcontractor completed work they terminated the employment of the bricklayers and a new subcontractor commenced work on the next phase of the building, without re-employing the bricklayers. The bricklayers entered into dispute, claiming they were in fact employees of the main contractor – G&T Crampton. The company applied for an interlocutory injunction restraining the bricklayers and their union from engaging in industrial action and interfering with their business (see Meenan 1999: 177). The case revolved around the balloting provisions of the 1990 Act and whether the union had complied with these provisions. In the High Court, Justice Laffoy found for the company and the case was appealed by the union to the Supreme Court. The Supreme Court found that the onus lay on the party resisting an application for an interlocutory injunction (the union) to prove a number of requirements had been met. These requirements were:

- that a secret ballot had been held;
- that it had been properly conducted;
- that the outcome was in favour of the action taken; and
- that the required notice (a minimum of one week) had been given.

If these conditions were met, then the union needed 'to establish a fair case that it was acting in contemplation or furtherance of a trade dispute' in order for an injunction to be refused. In the event, the Supreme Court found that the requirements in relation to the secret ballot were not fulfilled and it upheld the injunction. Meenan (1999: 177) notes Justice Laffoy's comments in the High Court that 'there was no evidence before the Court as to the outcome of the secret ballot conducted by the union and, in particular, there is no evidence that the outcome favoured picketing the site'.

The Nolan Transport Cases, 1993–1998

This case involved the issue of union recognition in a small transport company, the alleged dismissal of two employees and a picket organised by SIPTU. The key issues in the case revolved around the conduct of the ballot for strike action and question of the existence of a trade dispute. At a full trial in the High Court in 1994, Justice Barron found no trade dispute existed and that the real reason for the dispute was an attempt by the union to gain recognition (which he found did not qualify as a trade dispute), not the alleged dismissals. The Court found that the ballot conducted was fraudulent and that this was sufficient for the immunities not to be available to SIPTU and the union members. The absence of a trade dispute also meant the immunities were unavailable. The union was fined IR£600,000 and costs – a figure which was reported to have reached in excess of IR£2 million by the time the decision on an appeal to the Supreme Court was heard in 1998.

Following the 1994 High Court decision in the Nolan Transport case, the 1990 Act was the subject of debate at a number of union conferences (see Wallace and O'Sullivan 2002a). In general, this debate focused around two key points: (a) the belief that political undertakings given prior to the introduction of the Act had not been honoured and (b) the attitude of the judiciary to trade unions. Jimmy Somers (general president, SIPTU) claimed the courts had interpreted and applied the Act in a manner inconsistent with assurances given to Congress (ICTU 1995: 60). Brian Anderson of MSF argued that the judges created law and 'such laws are invariably in favour of employers and opposed to the needs of workers' (ICTU 1995: 63). The latter comments echo the trade union views in the years prior to enactment of the Trade Disputes Act 1906 (see Saville 1967: 347). To some in the trade union movement there seemed to be parallels with Taff Vale. Evidence that these views were more widely held among trade union officials is provided by the results of a pilot survey of union officials by Wallace and Delany (1997). They found that seventy-three per cent of union officials surveyed thought 'the 1990 Act was a mistake which should not have been accepted in its current form and which needs major amendment or repeal' (Wallace and Delany 1997: 114).

Observations on the importance of judicial attitudes were not confined to trade unionists. Shortly after the passage of the Act in 1991, Tony Kerr had pointed to the likely importance of the attitude of the judicial interpretation for the Act (Kerr 1991a: 256). In the event, the judiciary's attitude was to prove crucial when the case was taken on appeal to the Supreme Court. The Supreme Court differed with a number of the views and decisions of Justice Barron and overturned the High Court decision. The Supreme Court found that the employees 'at the very least, had good grounds for thinking themselves dismissed', that a trade dispute did exist and that a recognition dispute qualified as a trade dispute. The Supreme Court rejected other grounds of appeal, including one that the Court should reject the findings of fact by Justice Barron in relation to the conduct of the ballot.

However, there seems to have been some difference in the Supreme Court on this point. Justice O'Flaherty commented that the ballot was a 'shambles', which seems to imply it was badly conducted rather than fraudulent, as found by Justice Barron in the High Court. Any variation in the judgment was not to prove important, however, as the Court found that liability in tort did not follow from an improperly conducted ballot. The prescribed penalty was the loss of a union's negotiating licence. The most important part of the judgment was that the workers had a reasonable belief they were acting in contemplation and furtherance of a trade dispute, and as a result they were covered by the immunities. However, both Nolan Transport and SIPTU were strongly criticised for the manner in which the dispute was conducted (see Wallace and O'Sullivan 2002a: 177). In this context SIPTU decided not to seek its costs and O'Keeffe (1998: 350) notes 'the Court prudently held that each side should bear its own costs'.

After Nolan Transport and G&T Crampton

O'Keeffe (1998) notes that the outcome of the appeal in the Nolan Transport (1998) case was generally greeted with a sigh of relief by trade unions. Wallace and O'Sullivan (2002a: 175) suggest that following that decision, an assertion of a judiciary hostile to trade unions seems difficult to sustain. In his judgment on the Nolan Transport case, Justice O'Flaherty even went so far as to assert that 'the whole point of the Industrial Relations Act 1990 was … to copper-fasten the special privileges of trade unions in many respects'. Wallace and O'Sullivan (2002a) note that while the decision has removed any discernable campaign for change, the decision leaves unaltered a number of union complaints. Based on assurances given in the Dáil and Seanad, unions had believed that there would be no right of action by an employer against a ballot and that only an aggrieved member of a trade union could take an action (ICTU 1995: 60). The Supreme Court rulings in the G&T Crampton and Nolan Transport cases make it clear that employers can use the conduct of a ballot by a union to seek an injunction. While unions had believed that an employer would have no right of action under the balloting provisions, as early as 1991 Francis Meenan had drawn attention to the potential for a challenge based on the balloting requirements. She had pointed to the 'complicated rules in respect of such ballots … the need for ballots for secondary action, the complex provisions for the aggregation of votes in a multi-union ballot' as among the multiplicity of factors that could be used to challenge the ballots (Meenan 1991: 11). It is now clear that this view was prescient and the precedents in the G&T Crampton and Nolan Transport cases provide criteria against which the courts will evaluate the conduct of ballots in the event of a challenge. The conduct of ballots will be reviewed against the rules that unions have been required to incorporate in their rulebooks since July 1992. These are as shown in Table 3.2.

Table 3.2

Balloting Requirements for Any Industrial Action

(1) the union shall not organise, participate in, sanction or support a strike or other industrial action without a secret ballot, entitlement to vote on which shall be accorded equally to all members whom it is reasonable to believe will be called upon to engage in the strike or other industrial action;

(2) the union shall take reasonable steps to ensure that every member entitled to vote in the ballot votes without interference from, or constraint imposed by, the union or any of its members, officials or employees and, so far as is reasonably possible, that such members shall be given a fair opportunity of voting;

(3) the committee or management or other controlling authority of a trade union shall have full discretion in relation to organising, participating in, sanctioning or supporting a strike or other industrial action notwithstanding that the majority of those voting in the ballot, including an aggregate ballot, favour such strike or industrial action;

(4) the committee or management or other controlling authority of a trade union shall have full discretion in relation to organising, participating in, sanctioning or supporting a strike or other industrial action against the wishes of a majority of those voting in a secret ballot, except where, in the case of ballots by more than one trade union, an aggregate majority of all votes cast favours such strike or other industrial action;

(5) where the outcome of a secret ballot conducted by a trade union which is affiliated to the Irish Congress of Trade Unions or, in the case of ballots by more than one such trade union, an aggregate majority of all the votes cast is in favour of supporting a strike organised by another trade union, a decision to take such supportive action shall not be implemented unless the action has been sanctioned by the Irish Congress of Trade Unions;

(6) as soon as practicable after the conduct of a secret ballot the trade union shall take reasonable steps to make known to its members entitled to vote in the ballot (i) the number of ballot papers issued, (ii) the number of votes cast, (iii) the number of votes in favour of the proposal, (iv) the number of votes cast against the proposal and (v) the number of spoilt votes.

Source: Industrial Relations Act 1990

A number of key features stand out from the above requirements and the criteria arising from the Nolan Transport and G&T Crampton judgments. Given the technical nature of the above rules there are many opportunities for unions to slip up in the conduct of ballots. Great care needs to be exercised in framing any wording of a ballot and the ballot must specify the action for which approval is sought. It is essential for a union to be able to prove that an appropriate secret ballot has been held in compliance with the Act (O'Keeffe 1998). It has been suggested by Justice Murphy in the Nolan Transport case that professional and independent guidance be put in place and that these requirements be incorporated into unions' rules. O'Keeffe (1998: 35) has supported such measures, arguing 'such a system is to be hoped for, if it would lay to rest the difficulties which emerged in Nolan and G&T Crampton, and check any such tendencies to accede to employers' requests to scrutinise the ballot in search of irregularities'. Wallace and O'Sullivan (2002a: 176) note that this would extend the law 'beyond the explicit provisions of the 1990 Act'. They also question whether this has happened in practice, noting the absence of empirical evidence on the extent to which unions have put such provisions in place.

It is clear that failure to hold a proper secret ballot will not affect the immunities available to a trade union but will enable an employer to make a case for an injunction. Kerr (1991a: 197) had correctly noted this, claiming 'the only consequences to union members taking "unofficial action" (i.e. without holding a ballot or by holding an invalid ballot) is that the restrictions … on the availability of interim and interlocutory injunctions will not apply'. There is not any systematic empirical evidence of the impact and operation of the 1990 Act following the two judgments, although it does seem that injunctions continue to be readily available to employers in the building trade due to challenges to union ballots.

Unions and their members will not be liable for damages in tort where:

- the immunities cover the particular tort (a corollary being if the tort is not covered they may be liable);
- if they can prove they had a reasonable belief they were acting in contemplation or furtherance of a trade dispute; and
- if the industrial action was sanctioned in a properly conducted secret ballot in compliance with Section 14 by a majority of the people who would be expected to participate in the action.

The technical nature of the decision in the Nolan Transport and G&T Crampton cases has not disposed of a number of the complaints made by trade unions of a failure to honour undertakings given to them prior to the introduction of the Act. Thus, it is still open to an employer – and not just union members, as unions understood – to query the conduct of a ballot. Despite this, there is no longer any discernible campaign for change from that quarter. Neither did employers react unfavourably to the finding that the immunities were available to trade unions. Wallace and O'Sullivan (2002a) have pointed to the paradox that the acceptance of the 1990 Act (after the Nolan Transport case) lies in a decision based on the general principle underlying the much-criticised Trade Disputes Act 1906. By contrast the challenge to the ballot caused difficulties for the union involved without any benefit to the employer in the case.

More recently, however, employers' representatives have raised the issue of union liability for unofficial action. Frawley (2004b: 13) quotes Bredan McGinty, director of industrial relations, IBEC, as saying, 'An inevitable consequence of the recent increase in unofficial industrial action is that greater penalties will have to be imposed on trade unions whose members take part in unofficial action'. He suggests that unions should be made vicariously liable for the unofficial action of their members, just as employers are held liable for bullying and harassment though they do not condone such behaviour (Frawley 2004b: 13). Thus, while it had seemed that the issue of union liability in tort had been settled following the 1998 judgment in the Nolan Transport case, the issue continues to raise its head over 100 years after the *Quinn* v. *Leathem* case.

THE CONSTITUTION AND INDUSTRIAL RELATIONS

The 1937 Constitution provides for a right of association in Article 40.6.1 (iii). This article guarantees liberty for 'the right of citizens to form associations and unions. Laws, however, may be enacted for the regulation and control in the public interest of the foregoing right'. In Article 40.6.2 it is specified that the laws regulating this right 'shall contain no political, religious or class discrimination'. Within a short time this article was tested in the case of *NUR* v. *Sullivan*. Part III of the Trade Union Act 1941 provided for the establishment of a tribunal that could grant 'a determination that a specified union (or unions) alone should have the sole right to organise workers of a particular class'. In effect, this was an exclusive organisation right, which although not formally providing for 'sole negotiating rights' encouraged that end (Forde 1991: 29). As the Act precluded a British union being granted the sole right to organise workers, this provision posed a major threat to British-based unions (O'Hara 1981: 38).

Prior to its enactment, part III of the bill had been the focus of trenchant opposition by the majority of the trade union movement. It also attracted much criticism in the Dáil, where its constitutionality was questioned. Following its enactment, some unions operated the provision and applied for sole negotiating rights. In 1945 the ITGWU applied to the tribunal for the sole right to organise workers in the road passenger service of CIE. The NUR and a number of workers initiated a constitutional challenge against Sullivan (the chairman of the tribunal). The High Court found the provision to be constitutional. The Court reasoned that it was merely a regulation of the right to form a union, which was explicitly provided for in the Constitution. The Supreme Court, however, overturned this decision, finding 'the denial of a person's choice of which union he can join is not a control of the exercise of freedom of association but denied it altogether' (Forde 1991: 18).

The right to join unions, however, does not automatically create a right to be accepted into membership by a trade union, as indicated in the case of *Tierney* v. *Amalgamated Society of Woodworkers (ASW) (1995)*. In this case Tierney had sought to join the ASW in pursuit of a right to work. His application was refused as he had not served an apprenticeship and the union did not accept he was a genuine carpenter. Tierney failed in both the High Court and the Supreme Court on a number of grounds, including that the Constitution provided no support for the case (Kerr and Whyte 1985: 5) and the union had acted fairly within their rules (Forde 1991: 140).

The right of association has been found to imply an equal and opposite right of disassociation. Two cases stand out in this regard. The first was the *Educational Company of Ireland* v. *Fitzpatrick (1960)* in which some thirty-six workers in the Irish Union of Distributive Workers and Clerks (IUDWC) went on strike and picketed in pursuit of enforcing a closed shop. A closed shop involves a situation in which all employees in a particular class of employees are required to be union members. In this case, the picket was found to be illegal. This arose because the picketing was only protected by the Trade Disputes Act 1906 and the immunity in that Act was subordinate to the constitutional right of disassociation of the non-unionists. The strike, of course, collapsed without the protection for picketing being available.

The existence of a right of disassociation was confirmed by the case of *Meskell* v. *CIE (1973)*. The case revolved around efforts to increase the levels of union membership in CIE and in particular to tackle the issue of some employees not remaining in benefit (not paying their union dues). This was a recurrent problem in the 1960s prior to the introduction of the 'check-off system' whereby union dues are deducted directly from wages ('deducted at source'). Management and four unions reached agreement on a proposal to dismiss all workers on a Friday and re-employ them on the following Monday with an additional condition in their contract of employment. This condition required employees to 'at all times' be a member of one of the four named unions. John Meskell, a bus conductor with fifteen years' service who was a paid-up member in good standing, refused to give this undertaking and was dismissed. He lost his appeal in the High Court but was successful in the Supreme Court. The company argued that they were entitled in common law to dismiss but this was found to provide no protection due to the superior position of the constitutional right of disassociation. Meskell was awarded £2,000 damages plus costs – a substantial sum for that time.

The above two cases, however, limit the right of employers to require workers to join specified unions prior to them commencing employment (Kerr and Whyte 1985: 13). Thus, while the post-entry closed shop is unconstitutional, the pre-entry closed shop may well be constitutional. This is because although the Constitution guarantees the right to work it does not guarantee a right to employment and generally employers can employ who they wish. However, even if such undertakings are extracted from employees prior to commencing employment, they may be able to simply change their mind and engage in industrial action in pursuit of their right to join a union of their choosing. In *Becton Dickinson & Co. Ltd* v. *Lee and Others (1973)*, five employees who had given a signed undertaking prior to taking up employment to join the National Engineering and Electrical Trade Union (NEETU) subsequently sought to stay with the trade union they had been members of in a previous employment, the Amalgamated Union of Engineering and Foundry Workers (AEF). The company refused to recognise the AEF and a strike ensued. The company sought an injunction but this was refused on the grounds that the employees could rely on the entitlement to picket guaranteed by the Trade Disputes Act 1906.

The right of association does not place any requirement on an employer to recognise or negotiate with any particular trade union. The leading case in this regard is that of *Abbott and Whelan* v. *the Southern Health Board and the ITGWU (1982)*. About half of a number of a particular category of workers in the Southern Health Board (SHB) left the ITGWU and joined the Amalgamated Transport and General Workers Union (ATGWU). They entered into dispute to try and force the SHB to recognise and negotiate with their new union. The SHB refused. Abbott and Whelan initiated a High Court case seeking certain reliefs. They sought to have the SHB recognise and negotiate with their new union, the ATGWU. They also sought to prevent the ITGWU from purporting to negotiate with the SHB on their behalf, as they were no longer members. They lost on both grounds. The High Court found that as the SHB was not required to recognise any union, the SHB did not have to recognise the ATGWU. Neither was there any constitutional right to negotiate with a union of one's choice and the SHB could not be prevented from negotiating with the ITGWU, as an employer was free to recognise or not recognise any union. The principles laid down in the Abbott and Whelan case have been subsequently confirmed in the more complex series of cases taken by the Irish Locomotive Drivers' Association (see Higgins 2000a). The implication of these judgments is that although the Constitution provides for a right to form unions, this does not have as a corollary the right to recognition, negotiation or representation. However, there may be a limited right of representation arising out of a series of international cases under the European Convention on Human Rights, as established in the *National Belgian Police Union* v. *Belgium (1975)*. However, Kerr and Whyte (1985: 18) suggest that this right is restricted to a right of representation in individual grievance and disciplinary cases and does not extend to a right of negotiation on terms and conditions of employment.

THE CONSTITUTION IN CONTEXT

A number of the above decisions have given rise to controversy. On the one hand, the *NUR* v. *Sullivan* decision has been criticised for restricting government's capacity to regulate trade unions. On the other hand, the decisions establishing an implied right of disassociation have been criticised for converting a collective right into an individual one. Kerr and Whyte (1985) write that 'the right to *form* unions is of its very nature a collective right, so it is difficult to see how its corollary can be a right not to *join* unions, which is an individual right'. Subsequent to the Educational Company of Ireland case there was strong criticism by the trade union movement of the decision in the case and many representations by the trade union movement to government to avoid the effects of the decision. However, in his foreword to Kerr and Whyte's *Irish Trade Union Law*, Justice Walsh of the Supreme Court strongly defends the decision. He points out that 'it is difficult to understand the shock and surprise which was created in Irish trade union circles' (Walsh 1985: vi). He notes that the decision was consistent with Article 20 of the United Nations Universal Declaration on Human Rights, which proclaimed that 'no one may be compelled to be a member of an association' and that the decision was consistent with the views taken by the European Court of Human Rights in their interpretation of the European Convention on Human Rights (Walsh 1985: vi).

While the Educational Company and the Meskell cases led to controversy, this has receded and petered out over time. The decision is no longer an issue of any major debate. Neither did the decision create difficulties for the wider trade union movement in gaining recognition, as evidenced by its continued growth in the twenty years following the decision (Wallace 2003). Closed shop disputes are no longer common and agreements to deal with the issue of union recognition in a different fashion have emerged in response to the constitutional prohibition on the closed shop. These make it a matter for the union involved to recruit employees if the employees wish to join and require the union to take into membership all such eligible employees. In the changed environment it appears that such provisions are broadly acceptable to unions.

In the area of trade disputes and industrial action, the Constitution has a number of implications and there are likely to be others yet to be discovered (Forde 1991: 210). While the 1990 Act was designed to limit the possibility of a constitutional challenge. Forde (1991: 191) notes that the possibility of a challenge is still open 'on account of the distinctive privileges it confers on trade union and employers' associations'. Furthermore, Costelloe (2003) notes the courts are bound to remedy strike action that interferes with the constitutional rights of individuals and the Constitution recognises a wide range of property, social and economic interests. This could give a right of action in industrial relations cases, with immunities being challenged on property or religious grounds (see *Crowley* v. *Ireland (1980)*). The interpretation of constitutional rights in light of legislative provisions is likely to be crucial in any future cases (see Forde 1991: 210). Justice O'Flaherty's comments in the Nolan Transport case that 'the whole point of the Industrial Relations Act 1990 was … to copper-fasten the special privileges of trade unions in many respects and to give them additional rights' may be regarded as a source of comfort for trade unions.

For many employers and unions there is a great reluctance to resort to constitutional rights in industrial disputes. Thus we have the paradox that the Constitution is hugely important, yet rarely used. In addition to the general disadvantages of resorting to the law, there are additional reasons why employers and unions are reluctant to resort to appealing to constitutional rights. First, cases can involve enormous costs, far outstripping any benefit if one wins and involving the potential for huge losses if one loses. Second, such cases take many years to come to trial, which conflicts with the frequent need to resolve industrial disputes speedily. Finally, the outcome of cases can be quite uncertain, as demonstrated by the frequent reversal of High Court decisions by the Supreme Court and by the differing opinions expressed by Supreme Court judges when deciding cases. Students may wish to view the Constitution like an old minefield. A good deal of the mines have been cleared (principles decided) and even if one steps on a mine the probability is it will not explode (closed shop provisions may often operate without being contested). However, sometimes a mine does explode (the potential for a major personal or organisational disaster is ever-present for the unwary industrial relations practitioner).

CHAPTER 4

The Institutional Framework
of Industrial Relations

OVERVIEW

The study of industrial relations has long been concerned with the role of institutions. Flanders (1965: 4) gave institutions a central role, defining the subject of industrial relations as the study of the 'institutions of job regulation'. Dunlop (1958) identified specialist government agencies as one of the institutional elements of his systems approach. While the institutional focus was subsequently subject to widespread criticism, notably by radical and Marxist writers who have seen industrial relations as being centrally concerned with the exercise of power and control (see Fox 1973; Hyman 1975; Edwards 2003). Nevertheless, there is general agreement that the study of institutions is an important part of industrial relations. State provision of third-party dispute resolution institutions is highly developed in Ireland, with Forde (1992: 35) noting that most other advanced industrial societies provide similar institutions.

There are a number of reasons for establishing specialist state institutions for dispute resolution. Traditionally, their provision has been seen as deriving from a need to promote social justice. Thus, Eaton (2000: 134) writes of a requirement for alternatives to the civil courts that can be accessed speedily, have a relative lack of formality and which deliver speedy decisions. However, there are questions about the extent to which these objectives are realised in practice. Eaton (2000: 134) notes that while they are generally more user friendly than ordinary courts, there are complaints that they have become too formal and legalistic.

In addition to the social justice imperative, the need for specialist agencies is driven by political and economic imperatives. Political pressure can arise from a need for the state to Act in the role of industrial peacemaker, especially in the case of disputes in essential services (Farnham and Pimlott 1990). The state will also be concerned with the costs of strikes and the potential impact on inward investment. This is especially important in the Irish case where foreign direct investment (FDI) accounts for some fifty per cent of manufacturing employment. This compares to an average of nineteen per cent for eleven other member states of the European Union for which the OECD presents data (F. Barry, 2002). While political and economic pressures exist for state action, governments will wish to limit their direct involvement, which is achieved through the provision of independent state agencies.

The idea of third-party provision for industrial relations had a long gestation period, dating back to at least the early 1800s in the UK. While the Combination Acts 1799–1800 sought to repress unions, they also allowed for the provision of third-party intervention, but this was not proceeded with. There was an early, but very limited, effort to provide for arbitration under the Arbitration Act of 1824 (Kerr and Whyte

1985: 337). Farnham and Pimlott (1990) note the ad hoc use of conciliation by the mid-1800s. The Conciliation Act of 1896 gave the Board of Trade discretionary powers to assist parties in industrial disputes with advice and to conciliate on the application of both parties (Kerr and Whyte 1985). As with other existing legislation, this provision was continued with the establishment of the Irish state in 1922. Kelly (1989a: 185) notes that 'during the 1920s and 1930s the Department of Industry and Commerce contained a small staff of conciliators whose purpose was to aid employers and trade unions who were in dispute with each other'. This arrangement was supplemented by 'courts of inquiry' that dealt with 'particularly difficult disputes' (Kelly 1989a: 185). In 1946, the new statutory provisions of the Industrial Relations Act overtook these arrangements. That Act established the Labour Court and, in so doing, reinforced the voluntarist nature of Irish industrial relations.

This voluntarism means that parties are generally free to attempt to resolve disputes through the process of collective bargaining. Irish law places no compulsion to engage in collective bargaining or to reach agreement. However, industrial action involves costs for the parties and as a result they will tend to seek alternatives to outright conflict. In unionised employments, direct negotiation is the chief method for the resolution of disputes, with referral to an independent third party for conciliation, adjudication, arbitration or other ruling being common where there is a failure to reach agreement.

Since 1946, institutional provision has grown substantially, with a diverse range of state institutions now existing. Some deal mainly with collective disputes while others are largely concerned with individual employment law. In the area of collective disputes, the Labour Relations Commission (LRC) and the Labour Court are the chief institutions. Not all state employees have the right of access to the LRC or Labour Court, rather there is a range of alternative statutory conciliation and arbitration schemes covering public sector workers. The main institutions in the individual employment law area are the Employment Appeals Tribunal (EAT) and the Office of the Director of Equality Investigations (ODEI) – The Equality Tribunal. Rights Commissioners have a range of functions covering both collective industrial relations issues and individual employment law. The Labour Court also deals with the area of individual employment law, most notably equality issues.

THE INSTITUTIONAL CHANGES IN THE INDUSTRIAL RELATIONS ACT 1990

The Industrial Relations Act 1990 marked the most significant change to the collective institutional arrangements in Ireland since the Industrial Relations Act of 1946. Nonetheless, the 1990 Act is best viewed as bringing evolutionary, rather than revolutionary, change to the institutional arrangements. This is evident if one compares the fundamental provisions of the 1990 Industrial Relations Act with those laid down in the 1946 Industrial Relations Act. The 1946 Act had established the Labour Court, which provided both a conciliation and non-binding adjudication service.

The terms under which the Labour Court was to operate established a number of important principles. First, use of either services of the Court was, in most instances, at the discretion of the parties involved – in other words, resort to the Court was optional.

Second, the use of conciliation did not lead to any legal obligations on the parties to reach agreement or, as in other jurisdictions such as the US, to 'bargain in good faith'. Third, in most cases the Labour Court delivered non-binding recommendations. These principles remain intact in the new institutional arrangements. The main change was the establishment of a new body, the Labour Relations Commission (LRC), and the continuation of the Labour Court with a revised and more limited role. The use of the LRC and Labour Court continues, in large measure, to be optional and no change has been made to the generally non-binding nature of Labour Court recommendations.

Rationales for the Institutional Reforms

Even prior to the enactment of the Industrial Relations Act 1990, the case for institutional reform had been advanced by a number of industrial relations academics (Sapsford *et al.* 1979; McCarthy 1982). Most notably, the Commission of Inquiry on Industrial Relations (1981: 136) had advocated the establishment of a separate Conciliation Service and a Labour Tribunal, with both institutions being attached to a new 'Labour Relations Board'. This proposal was not proceeded with and the 1990 Act separated the Labour Court from the Conciliation Service, with the latter being incorporated in the newly established LRC.

A number of rationales underlie the institutional changes. There was a desire to encourage local settlement of disputes, to promote 'best practice' industrial relations and restore the Labour Court to a 'court of last resort'. The then Minister for Labour, Mr Bertie Ahern, TD, noted that 'one the main reasons for establishing the commission is to have a body with primary responsibility for the promotion of better industrial relations' which would 'be able to highlight examples of good practice and encourage others to adopt similar practices' (Dáil Debates 1990: 747–8). Kevin Bonner (1989: 265), then secretary of the Department of Labour, argued that 'a body such as the Labour Court with responsibility for investigating and issuing recommendations is constrained from adopting a more forceful role in the promotion of good industrial relations'.

Part of the more forceful role envisaged by the Minister for Labour was 'to encourage and facilitate a more active approach to dispute prevention and resolution' and restoring 'the original purpose and status of the Labour Court to investigations and recommendations' (Dáil Debates 1990: 747). The Minister contended that 'it would appear that having developed the habit of referring matters to the Court for adjudication, that parties to disputes have found it difficult to revert back to settling their own problems' (Dáil Debates 1990: 749). Relatively trivial matters were being heard by the Court, which had assumed the mantle of 'court of first resort' (Dáil Debates 1990: 747). Kerr (1991a) notes that the 1990 Act envisaged that the Court would again become 'the final authoritative tribunal in industrial relations matters' whose recommendations would once again be documents 'with great moral authority with the main responsibility for dispute resolution being shifted back to the parties themselves'. In 1991, Kieran Mulvey, chief executive of the LRC, confirmed this objective for the newly established LRC, specifying the Commission had the clear intent of changing 'the almost automatic reference (of disputes) to the Court' (Mulvey 1991a).

The main opposition came from the Labour Court. Shortly after proposals were published for the establishment of a Labour Relations Commission in 1988 (Department of Labour 1988), the Court responded, expressing difficulty in understanding

> how the effectiveness of the conciliation service or the quality of its work could be better achieved under the proposed Labour Relations Commission than is possible under the Court. The same staff would be involved, their terms of reference would be the same and the outcome of their work would be unchanged – either the case would be resolved or referred to the Court (Labour Court 1989: 108).

The Court concluded that it could not 'envisage the setting up of a Labour Relations Commission as establishing an improved dispute-settling service to the constituents of the social partners on either qualitative or administrative grounds' (Labour Court 1988: 109). In fact, the Court asserted that the proposed Commission 'would profoundly diminish the effectiveness of the Court by divorcing from it the right to determine the cases it will hear and separating from it the conciliation service which has always been regarded as an integral part of the Court' (Labour Court 1989: 109).

In addition to the trenchant Labour Court critique, there were a number of more qualified academic reservations. Professor Brian Hillery, TD, expressed a concern that far from becoming a significant agent in the promotion of good industrial relations, the Commission might become 'just another layer of bureaucracy' (see Hourihan 1990). Among other observations, Wallace (1991) suggested that structural considerations could limit the impact and effectiveness of the institutional reforms, in particular where the establishment of an advisory service was concerned. He also speculated that should the LRC be successful in promoting high levels of settlement at local level (at conciliation or in the workplace), there was a possibility that cases coming to the Court could be those in which management were unwilling or unable to give concessions (Wallace 1991). This could lead to the Court having to deal with a large number of 'hopeless cases' and, in such an event, there was the possibility of the Court being unfavourably perceived among workers.

Despite the Labour Court's opposition, the establishment of the new institutional arrangements proceeded smoothly and the LRC commenced operation in January 1991. The evolutionary nature of the changes, exemplified by the retention of the existing voluntarist features, accounted in large part for the general acceptance of the Commission (see Wallace 1991). This approach ensured a lack of opposition from either the trade unions or employer organisations. Indeed, the changes appear to have been generally welcomed, reflecting a feeling among some industrial relations practitioners that the Labour Court needed some 'freshening up' (author interview with FIE official 1991).

This general welcome by trade unions and employer organisations was to prove more important than the Labour Court opposition. While the institutional measures are now established and well accepted, this general acceptance does not establish that the stated objectives of the 1990 Act have been achieved. The extent to which the objectives underlying the institutional provisions of the 1990 Act have been met needs to be subjected to detailed empirical investigation, which is discussed further below.

The New Institutional Arrangements and the Labour Relations Commission

The most significant change in the 1990 Industrial Relations Act was the provision for the establishment of the LRC and its separation from the Labour Court. The LRC, which commenced operation in January 1991, is a tripartite body with trade union, employer and independent representation (see www.lrc.ie for details). The Commission was given the overall responsibility for promoting good industrial relations and provides a range of services that are designed to both prevent and resolve disputes (see Table 4.1). The Rights Commissioners service was transferred to the LRC (from the Department of Labour – not the Labour Court), as was the function of monitoring industrial relations developments. In addition, the Commission was given a number of new functions concerned with the provision of an advisory service, the drafting and implementation of codes of practice, the conduct and commissioning of research and the provision of assistance to Joint Industrial Councils (JICs) and Joint Labour Committees (JLCs) (see Table 4.1).

Table 4.1
Summary of Functions of Labour Relations Commission

- To provide a conciliation service.
- To provide a Rights Commissioners service.
- To provide an industrial relations advisory, developmental and research service.
- To prepare codes of practice relevant to industrial relations matters.
- To offer guidance on codes of practice and help to resolve disputes concerning their implementation.
- To review and monitor developments in the area of industrial relations.
- To conduct or commission research into matters relevant to industrial relations.
- To assist JLCs and JICs in the exercise of their functions.

Source: LRC annual report 2002

The LRC is now the most significant state institution in Irish industrial relations. The range of functions and the large number of cases it deals with means that it has the widest impact on industrial relations. While not having the same coverage, the Labour Court's designation as 'court of last resort' gives it a very important role, especially in efforts to resolve major disputes. The EAT deals with a larger volume of cases than the LRC but these only involve individual workers, while the LRC will typically deal with issues covering large numbers of workers. The LRC also has a role in formulating rules for the conduct of industrial relations through codes of practice, while the EAT merely administers and interprets legislation. Thus, the LRC has a much greater impact on industrial relations than the EAT. The EAT does, however, have a wider coverage as it will regularly deal with cases from non-union as well as unionised employments, while the LRC usually deals with unionised employments.

The Conciliation Service

As noted above, a conciliation service was provided by the Department of Industry and Commerce from the foundation of the state. The Industrial Relations Act 1946 repealed the 1896 Conciliation Act and empowered the newly established Labour Court to appoint individuals as Conciliation Officers. The Industrial Relations Act of 1969 changed the name of Conciliation Officers to Industrial Relations Officers (IROs). The 1969 Act provided that IROs 'shall assist in the prevention and settlement of trade disputes and in the establishment and maintenance of means for conducting voluntary negotiations between employers and workers'. This provision was designed to establish a proactive role for IROs in heading off disputes, in effect an extension of their role to providing an advisory service. In the event, this expanded role did not develop for a number of reasons, including inadequate resources, the extensive demands on the service in the context of the increased industrial relations activity of the 1970s and possibly a reluctance among IROs to become involved in giving formal advice, lest that could damage their perceived independence.

Conciliation is the involvement of an independent third party in the negotiation of the settlement to a dispute with the purpose of aiding the parties to develop and agree a mutually acceptable solution (see Kerr and Whyte 1985; Salamon 1998). The process of conciliation is closely related to but subtly different from that of mediation. In mediation, 'the third party is more Active in assisting the parties going so far as to submit his [or her] proposals for settlement' (ILO 1980, cited in Salamon 1998: 421), while conciliation describes a process where the conciliator does not offer proposals for the settlement of a dispute. An IRO has no power to compel the parties to reach agreement and they retain control over the final outcome. While there are both advantages and disadvantages to conciliation (see Salamon 1998), it is this element of 'disputant control' that is the essential ingredient of conciliation that makes the process attractive to the parties. This is a control that the parties relinquish to a degree when a case is referred to adjudication in the Labour Court. The terms 'mediation' and 'conciliation' tend to be used interchangeably and there may be no real difference in practice.

The procedure at a conciliation conference is for an IRO to meet both parties jointly in order to allow each side to outline their views on a dispute. Having listened to both parties, the IRO will typically hold separate meetings (known as side conferences) with both parties to get a better idea of the basis for the dispute and what is required to resolve the issue. The IRO will generally seek to explore the room for movement and the parties' true positions. This will be done on the basis that the information is confidential to the IRO but may be used in order to explore potential solutions.

Not only is conciliation a long-standing state service, it is also the LRC's most important function (Mulvey 1991a, 1991b). This is evident from the extent of the demand for the service (see Table 4.2) but also because cases will typically be concerned with efforts to resolve disputes involving many workers. The widespread use of the institutional framework, including conciliation, indicates the degree to which the process has gained acceptance (see Wallace and McDonnell 2000: 185). As far back as the 1970s, Krislov (1972: 44) found that 'the vast majority of Irish management and labour officials ... are receptive to conciliation ... [and] overwhelmingly believe that conciliation averts strikes'. In 1998 a survey by Clarke and Murphy found that in general the LRC service was well respected, with respondents considering the independence of the service and staff's expertise and experience to be vital (cited in Sheehan 1998b: 18). The report recommended that the conciliation service would benefit greatly if it was to expand its traditional recruitment pool and move beyond the traditional recruitment methods of the civil service (cited in Sheehan 1998b: 18).

Table 4.2
Conciliation Service Case Load and Settlement Levels, 1946–2002

Year	Number of Disputes in which Conciliation Conferences were Held	Number and Percentage of Disputes Settled at Conciliation	
1946–1947	166	105	63%
1947–1948	228	153	67%
1949	135	81	60%
1950	102	66	65%
1951	157	111	71%
1952	169	134	79%
1953	143	94	66%
1954	166	110	66%
1955	188	135	72%
1956	173	116	67%
1957	191	119	62%
1958	226	136	60%
1959	191	125	65%
1960	197	122	62%
1961	211	151	72%
1962	300	214	71%
1963	337	238	71%
1964	388	282	73%
1965	450	289	64%
1966	429	300	70%
1967	532	377	71%
1968	546	408	75%
1969	414	327	79%
1970	564	451	80%
1971	628	429	68%
1972	713	443	62%
1973	855	487	57%

Table 4.2 (continued)
Conciliation Service Case Load and Settlement Levels, 1946–2002

Year	Number of Disputes in which Conciliation Conferences were Held	Number and Percentage of Disputes Settled at Conciliation	
1974	951	646	68%
1975	1,108	576	52%
1976	1,071	581	54%
1977	1,175	638	54%
1978	1,288	651	51%
1979	1,301	634	49%
1980	1,379	693	50%
1981	1,582	756	48%
1982	1,855	923	50%
1983	2,090	1,113	53%
1984	1,750	1,037	59%
1985	2,021	1,355	67%
1986	1,892	1,268	67%
1987	1,787	1,151	64%
1988	1,571	1,064	68%
1989	1,450	1,019	70%
1990	1,552	1,143	74%
1991	1,880	1,598	85%+ (85%)
1992	1,935	1,451	73%+ (75%)
1993	1,884	1,338*	69%+ (71%)
1994	1,551	1,028	66%+ (66%)
1995	1,692	1,184	67%+ (70%)
1996	1,487	1,204*	78%+ (81%)
1997	1,588	1,318*	82%+ (83%)
1998	1,563	1,286*	81%+ (82%)
1999	1,923	1,615*	83%+ (84%)
2000	1,899	1,614*	83%+ (85%)
2001	1,815	1,507*	81%+ (83%)
2002	1,693	1,371*	77%+ (81%)
2003	1,597	1,310*	n/a (82%)

+ For purposes of pre- and post-1991 comparisons these settlement figures are calculated using the number of cases referred to the Labour Court. This is the procedure employed by the Labour Court to report settlement levels up to 1990. Figures in brackets are LRC-reported settlement rates at conciliation and are based on cases heard at the Labour Court following a conciliation hearing. Not all cases referred to the Labour Court result in a hearing and as a result the LRC figures overstate the settlement level at conciliation in all except two years.

* These figures have been calculated from the rounded percentage figure and as such are approximations.

n/a = not available

Source: Various Labour Court and LRC annual reports

There seems to be some degree of tension between this recommendation and the general degree of satisfaction with the service under current recruitment mechanisms. Thus, the question arises that 'if the current service is so well regarded, why is there a need for change?' The possible impact that wider recruitment would have on the perceived independence of the service also needs to be considered. Krislov (1972: 47) found that over fifty per cent of respondents felt it important that Conciliation Officers should have no prior union or management background. The Commission of Inquiry on Industrial Relations (1981: 150) was also concerned with impartiality and as a result recommended that although recruitment should be extended beyond the Department of Labour to the wider civil service, IROs should not be recruited outside the civil service. Civil service recruitment, they noted, had the distinct advantage of allowing for easy relocation of those 'who prove to be ineffective as IROs or are dissatisfied with their work', a facility which would not exist for recruits outside the civil service (Commission of Inquiry on Industrial Relations 1981: 150).

Conciliation and the Industrial Relations Act 1990

In order to examine the extent to which the underlying objectives of the Industrial Relations Act 1990 have been achieved, we examine the changes associated with the usage and success rate of conciliation after 1990, when the LRC took over responsibility for the conciliation service. Unfortunately, this task is complicated by discontinuities between the way data is compiled and reported by the LRC and the way the same data was compiled and reported by the Labour Court prior to 1991. There are a number of problems in comparing pre-1991 figures with the figures since then. These require adjustments to the LRC published figures for success at conciliation (for a detailed discussion on this see Wallace and O'Sullivan 2002a: 182–4). Recalculating the conciliation settlement figures on the basis of *referrals to Labour Court following a conciliation hearing*, this reduces the overall settlement level for the years 1991 to 2000 by 1.5 percentage points. The effect for the years 2001 and 2002 is somewhat larger, averaging a reduction of three percentage points.

Despite the limitations and inconsistencies in the comparability of the data, the published figures indicate two firm conclusions arising from the institutional changes brought about by the Industrial Relations Act 1990. First, there is a continued high usage of conciliation, with the order of magnitude in the period 1991 to 2002 being similar to that pertaining in the 1980s. Using the published figures, any reduction in usage of conciliation is most noticeable in the period 1986 to 1990 – the last five-year period when the Labour Court had responsibility for conciliation (see Table 4.3). There is no evidence of a return to the lower levels of usage of conciliation of the 1970s, or indeed the much lower levels of the 1960s. Wallace and O'Sullivan (2002a: 183) note that the evidence provides 'no support for the hypothesis that the Industrial Relations Act 1990 has promoted any substantially greater settlement of issues at local level', i.e. without third-party involvement. In considering the reasons for this, Wallace and McDonnell (2000) suggest that the fundamental reason is the proceduralisation of industrial relations since the 1960s and they reject suggestions that it is due to a loss of the 'art of compromise', as suggested by Horgan (1989: 198). Indeed, the higher settlement level at conciliation, with current levels running at some twenty percentage points above that the 1970s, provides *prima facia*, if not conclusive, evidence of a greater willingness to compromise.

The higher settlement at conciliation is the second main conclusion that arises from the data. This conclusion holds up, despite the overstating of the settlement rate in LRC published figures. The average annual settlement rate at conciliation in the years 1971 to 1980 was 56.5 per cent, rising to an annual average of sixty-two per cent in the years 1981 to 1990 (see Table 4.4). Adjusting for the overstatement in the LRC figures would indicate a settlement rate of around seventy-five per cent, which is substantially higher than the pre-1990 figure (see Wallace and O'Sullivan 2002a: 183).

Table 4.3
Disputes at Conciliation

Time Period	Average Number of Conciliation Cases per Annum
1946–1950	146
1951–1960	180
1961–1970	417
1971–1980	1,047
1981–1990	1,755
(1981–1985)	1,860
(1986–1990)	1,650
1991–2000	1,740
2001–2002	1,754

Source: Labour Court and LRC annual reports, adapted from Wallace and O'Sullivan (2002a)

The higher settlement rate at conciliation indicates that the separation of the conciliation service from the Labour Court has not had the negative effect the Labour Court envisaged in 1989 – indeed, it appears to have been beneficial. Wallace and O'Sullivan (2002a) note that 'this greater level of settlement at conciliation is the single most significant change occurring since the LRC took over responsibility for the conciliation service'. Although not ruling out other reasons, they suggest 'there is a strong case that this improvement is due to the operation of the new institutional arrangements in the 1990 Act' (Wallace and O'Sullivan 2002a: 184).

However, a number of caveats need to be attached to this conclusion. First, the higher settlement level of the 1990s commenced in the early 1980s and might have continued without the changes of the 1990 Act. It is noteworthy that other developments, such as the fall in strikes (see Chapter 8), indicate less willingness of workers to engage in militant action, and the factors which have brought about this fall may also have contributed to the greater settlement level at conciliation. In this regard, Wallace and O'Sullivan (2002a: 148) caution that factors other than the changes to the 1990 Act, 'such as a weaker labour movement and greater social consensus/partnership, cannot be ruled out'.

The second caveat is the absence of rigorous research evidence as to how conciliation might have produced a higher settlement level. The techniques used at conciliation are not widely researched, although Duffy (1993) indicated that immediately after the establishment of the LRC, IROs were less willing than previously to allow unions or management to use the conciliation service as a stepping stone to a full Labour Court investigation. It is unclear whether this greater 'interventionist role' was merely an immediate response following the establishment of the LRC or if it has been sustained over time. While establishing this would require systematic research, informal contacts made with practitioners for this book do not suggest that this approach has been widely sustained beyond the initial period. It has been suggested to us that it is used on comparatively rare occasions, such as when the conciliation service becomes involved in a dispute (with the Court's approval) after a Court recommendation has failed to resolve a dispute. If this is the case it leaves open the question as to what mechanism brought about the higher settlement level. It may well be that a variety of factors have been at work, some internal to the conciliation process and others external to it.

Table 4.4
Annual Average Conciliation Settlement Levels, 1951–2002

Years	Percentage Annual Average Settlement Levels for Period
1951–1960	67.0
1961–1970	72.6
1971–1980	56.6
1981–1990	62.0
1991–2000	76.7* (78.2)
2001–2002	79* (82)

* This statistic is compiled using Labour Court reported figures for referrals to conciliation and is preferred to the LRC reported figures (in brackets), as they are more comparable to the figures prior to 1991.

Source: Derived from Labour Court and LRC annual reports

RIGHTS COMMISSIONERS

The office of Rights Commissioner was created under the Industrial Relations Act 1969 with their function being to intervene in and investigate industrial disputes with the view to promoting settlement. The service was designed to be speedy and informal and, as with all of the institutional arrangements in Ireland, there is no charge for its use. Initially the service operated from the Department of Labour, but since 1991 it has been attached to the LRC. The Minister for Enterprise, Trade and Employment appoints Rights Commissioners from a panel submitted by the LRC. The Commissioners, of which there are currently five, are independent in the performance of their functions.

There are a number of statutory restrictions on the types of cases that Rights Commissioners may hear. First, they may not investigate disputes connected with the rates of pay, hours or times of work or annual holidays of a body of workers. Second, the workers concerned must have access to the Labour Court, a requirement that excludes certain categories of state employees, such as civil servants. Third, the Labour Court must not have issued a recommendation about the dispute – this is to prevent a right of appeal from the Labour Court, which would undermine the Court's recommendations. Finally, a party to the dispute must not have objected *in writing* to an investigation. Parties have twenty-one days (from the date of notification by post that a dispute has been referred) to object in writing, and in the event of such an objection, an investigation may take place.

Rights Commissioners were primarily established to reduce the Labour Court's workload and to provide a 'prompt adjudication service for what may be regarded as the less major industrial relations issues' (Kelly 1989a: 186). Investigations are held in private, with Rights Commissioners obliged to issue a written recommendation. Under the Industrial Relations Acts 1969–1990, a recommendation by a Rights Commissioner is not legally binding and there is provision for an appeal to the Labour Court. Such appeals must be notified in writing to the Labour Court within six weeks from the date of the recommendation.

The focus on individual disputes delineates their role from that of IROs, although individual disputes may also be dealt with at conciliation. However, there is one vitally important distinction between the two services. When a Rights Commissioner's recommendation is appealed to the Labour Court, the decision is binding (see the section on the Labour Court for a further discussion). This does not apply when the case is referred to the Labour Court following conciliation, and the difference can be hugely important for either an employer or employee considering referring a case to a Rights Commissioner. Appeals against a Rights Commissioner's recommendation under individual employment legislation are made to the EAT and again all appeals must be made within six weeks.

Table 4.5 contains a full list of the relevant legislation for which Rights Commissioners now have responsibility. There has been a major growth in the usage of the Rights Commissioners' service in recent years, partly due to the extended functions they have been given under new employment legislation, but also due to increased usage under the Industrial Relations Acts 1969–1990. A breakdown of referrals in the years 1999 to 2002 indicates that employment legislation accounted for sixty-six per cent of all cases in the years 1999 to 2001. The addition of new functions, notably under the Protection of Part-Time Work Act 2001, saw this rise to seventy-seven per cent of all cases in 2002 (see Table 4.5). In the individual employment legislation area, the highest number of referrals occurs under the Payment of Wages Act 1991, the Protection of Employees (Part-Time Work) Act 2001, the Organisation of Working Time Act 1997 and the Unfair Dismissals Acts 1977–2001.

When established, the intention was that the Rights Commissioners' service would be a more informal avenue for dealing with industrial disputes than a full Labour Court investigation. When operating under the Industrial Relations Acts 1969–1990, they follow their own procedures and adopt their own practices, having no statutory guidelines to direct their activity (von Prondzynski and McCarthy 1989). When operating under employment legislation there is evidence of limitations on the discretion of Rights Commissioners because of the need to apply the criteria of the relevant legislation (Commission of Inquiry on Industrial Relations 1981: 159; O'Leary 2000).

Table 4.5
Activity of Rights Commissioner Service, 1999–2002

Legislation	1999	2000	2001	2002
Adoptive Leave Act 1995	1	0	1	0
Industrial Relations Acts 1969–1990	1,064	1,062	1,363	1,334
Maternity Protection Act 1994	18	9	9	21
Organisation of Working Time Act 1997	526	620	740	967
Parental Leave Act 1998	57	42	42	23
Payment of Wages Act 1991	739	907	1,125	1,177
Protection for Persons Reporting Child Abuse Act 1998	0	0	0	0
Protection of Young Persons (Employment) Act 1996	17	0	1	0
Terms of Employment (Information) Act 1994	199	83	141	150
Unfair Dismissals Acts 1977–2001	335	466	632	868
Protection of Employees (Part-Time Work) Act 2001	–	–	27	1092
National Minimum Wage Act 2000	–	17	59	48
EC Transfer of Undertakings (Amendment) Regs, 2000	–	0	13	11
Carer's Leave Act 2001	–	–	1	0
Protection of Employment Act 1977	0	0	28	3
EC (Protection of Employment) Regs, 2000	–	0	2	1
Totals	2,996	3,206	4,184	5,695

Source: LRC, various annual reports

The requirement for greater legalism implied by employment legislation appears to operate in quite a subtle way and seems to differ between individual Rights Commissioners (O'Leary 2000). O'Leary (2000: 31) interviewed four Commissioners, all of whom 'implied they would try to settle a case if possible before making a recommendation'. Individual Commissioners differed on how they said they would exercise this flexibility (O'Leary 2000: 31). One Commissioner said that while 'legislation only allowed him to adjudicate he acted as a conciliator in sixty per cent to eighty per cent of referrals'. Two Commissioners described the primary role in terms of adjudication, namely seeing mediation/conciliation as 'an optional extra' with the 'primary being to issue recommendations' (O'Leary 2000: 30). The fourth Commissioner indicated that under employment legislation he would operate in more of an adjudication role, implying a more mediation/conciliation approach when operating under the industrial relations legislation.

Previous research has indicated a general degree of satisfaction with the service by managers and shop stewards (Commission of Inquiry on Industrial Relations 1981; Connaughton 1982; Wallace 1982; Kelly 1989a). Kelly (1989a: 190) attributes the relative success of Rights Commissioners to the fact that the service is 'appropriate to the kind of issues dealt with'. In other words, they offer a mechanism for avoiding bruising and costly conflict over relatively small individual issues. From the Rights

Commissioners' point of view, the nature of the cases dealt with can affect the process. O'Leary (2000) reports that Commissioners themselves found disciplinary cases involving suspension and dismissal the most difficult to deal with because of their emotional connotations. O'Leary (2000: 36–7) also found continuing satisfaction among IBEC and SIPTU representatives with the level of assistance, attitude and fairness of Rights Commissioner hearings, but noted some difficulty in accessing the service in urgent cases, most notably outside Dublin.

Evaluation of the service by practitioners can also be affected by the perceived effectiveness of individual Commissioners. A recent development in the usage of the Rights Commissioners' service has been a dramatic growth in the years 1998 to 2000 (the latest years for which data has been published) in frequent user referrals (see Figure 4.1). This increase parallels an increase in frequent users of conciliation, which is discussed below. Overall, the level of usage of the Rights Commissioners' service is a further indication of the continued high, and in this case growing, reliance on third-party institutions.

Figure 4.1
Frequent User* Referrals to Rights Commissioner Service, 1993–2000

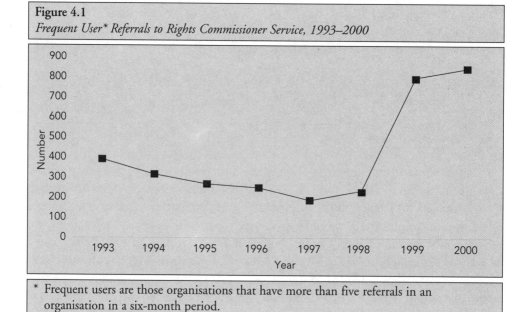

* Frequent users are those organisations that have more than five referrals in an organisation in a six-month period.

Source: LRC (2000: 66)

THE ADVISORY, DEVELOPMENTAL AND RESEARCH SERVICE (THE ADVISORY SERVICE)

The introduction of the advisory service of the LRC was a particularly innovative feature of the Industrial Relations Act 1990. The Act provides that 'the Commission may if it thinks fit, on request or on its own initiative, provide for employers, employers' associations, workers and trade unions such advice it thinks appropriate on any matter concerned with industrial relations'. According to the Minister for Labour, Bertie Ahern, TD, the reasoning behind the establishment of the advisory service was that there were some organisations using the Labour Court's conciliation service regularly and it was clear that there were underlying problems which needed to be addressed in a more fundamental manner (Dáil Debates 1990: 372). The underlying thesis was that a small number of employers were 'responsible for a disproportionate number of the difficulties which arise in the area of industrial relations' (Wallace 1991). The belief was that by focusing on these organisations and conducting industrial relations audits and providing expert advice, it should be possible to lower the incidence of industrial action at a national level.

Disputes may be merely a symptom of greater underlying problems in the workplace and such problems often remain after a dispute has been settled. The main focus of the conciliation service is to deal with the immediate dispute. The advisory service's brief, however, is to help identify the underlying problems giving rise to recurring industrial relations unrest where impartial advice from a third party acceptable to management and unions could help to resolve such issues (Department of Labour 1991a).

The Advisory Service in Operation

While the Commission of Inquiry on Industrial Relations (1981: 155) claimed that there would be insufficient demand to justify the establishment of an advisory-type service, this has not proven to be the case. The general demand for the advisory service has been on the increase since its creation, so much so that in 2000 it completed fifty-six interventions compared with forty-one in 1999. The advisory service notes that this 'represents an increase in activity of 200 per cent over the last two years' (LRC 2000: 53). This high level of usage is in line with the general high utilisation of other state third-party machinery in Ireland, which has already been noted.

In the early years of operation, much of the advisory service's work was focused on the 'problem cases', with the focus being reflected in the carrying out of diagnostic audits in situations where industrial relations were considered poor (information direct from Advisory Service 1999). Audits involve a review of an organisation's industrial relations procedures and practices by an advisory officer, followed by the issuing of a report containing recommendations for the parties involved and, if needed, by follow-up assistance (LRC 2000: 53). Such audits have been associated with the service's 'frequent users initiative', launched in 1992, and reported in the LRC annual reports until 2000, but not since then. This involved identifying those companies that had a disproportionate usage of the LRC's conciliation service. A frequent user was defined as 'an organisation with over five referrals to the conciliation service in a six-month period' (information direct from Advisory Service 1999). The aims of the frequent users initiative were to:

- identify those organisations – employers and trade unions – which use the Commission's services frequently;
- establish the reasons for such frequent use; and
- recommend measures for the improvement of industrial relations, if necessary (LRC 1996: 22).

Figure 4.2 charts an initial decline in frequent user referrals between 1993 and 1995. Since 1995, however, the numbers of frequent users have increased and surpassed the level of 1992 in the years 1997 to 2000. Thus, the early reduction in the incidence of frequent users was not maintained in the longer term and the service no longer concentrates on reducing frequent users. There are at least two reasons for this development. First, the service considers that the definition of a frequent user as 'five referrals to conciliation in a six-month period' was too blunt, as it did not allow for the wide range of size among users (information direct from Advisory Service 1999). The 'size effect' means that certain large organisations, such as health boards, might quite legitimately have five or more conciliation referrals in six months without this being excessive. Second, the failure to achieve a continued reduction in frequent users is considered within the advisory service to be due at least in part to underlying structural factors (information direct from Advisory Service 1999). O'Sullivan (2000) also highlights the importance of structural factors in two case studies of advisory service investigations.

Figure 4.2
Frequent User Referrals to Conciliation, 1993–2000

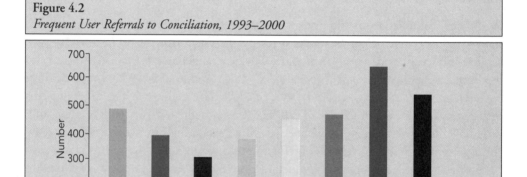

Source: LRC annual reports

Since 1995 there has been a shift in focus within the advisory service from frequent user referrals and diagnostic audits towards assisting employers and employees 'to implement effective problem-solving mechanisms' (LRC 1999: 24). The LRC claims that 'the resulting transformation from adversarial relations to those founded on principles of partnership and mutual benefit allows enterprises to concentrate on core objectives' (LRC 1999: 24). The change in focus has led to the advisory service shifting its attention from organisations with intractable structural problems towards those organisations where a mutual gains approach has greater prospects of success (information direct from Advisory Service 1999). Thus, some organisations that avail of the advisory service are closer to the 'exemplar organisational' category, rather than fitting into the problem 'frequent user' category envisaged in the Industrial Relations

Act 1990. The evolution in the approach of the advisory service may be linked to efforts to construct workplace partnership and the ICTU initiatives on New Forms of Work Organisation (ICTU 1993). These are initiatives that may owe much to the need for Irish trade unions and employers to grapple with the extremely open nature of the Irish economy and international competition in labour and product markets (see Chapter 12).

The question arises as to what extent this new focus can affect the general usage of third parties, which the 1990 Act sought to reduce. O'Sullivan (2000) suggests that the high demand on resources restricts the number of intensive investigations that can be undertaken. This, combined with the greater focus on exemplar organisations, limits the potential for an impact on the general usage of conciliation and the Labour Court.

Codes of Practice

One of the LRC's functions is to draft codes of practice in consultation with employer and trade union organisations and other interested parties. When approved by the Commission, the draft is then submitted to the Minister for Enterprise, Trade and Employment, who can make a statutory instrument declaring the code to be a code of practice for the purposes of the 1990 Act. While codes of practice are set in a statutory framework, they are not directly enforceable as a breach of the code will not attract any civil or criminal sanction. The Commission of Inquiry on Industrial Relations (1981) made the point 'that voluntary codes possess the serious disadvantage of being least likely to be adopted in the very circumstances where they are most needed'. The issue would then arise of how to enforce such codes, and it is interesting that provisions in the Conspiracy and Protection of Property Act 1875, which make industrial action in certain essential services a criminal offence, are unused. These restrictions were extended to strikes in the Electricity Supply Board (ESB) under the terms of the Electricity Supply Act 1927, but have also lain unused.

The codes of practice are intended to give guidance to employers and trade unions on particular issues and are intended to have strong moral authority. While that is the case, they are also 'admissible in evidence' and there is some confusion as to what is intended by this provision. Kerr (1991b) has likened this provision to the 'rules of the road' in that codes of practice can be taken into account by the courts or the dispute settlement agencies in determining any issue to which they may be relevant. The LRC has drafted seven codes of practice, which have all been promulgated (LRC 2002: 67). An eighth is likely to be added to the list in the form of a Code of Practice on Victimisation, arising from criticisms of the operation of the Industrial Relations (Amendment) Act 2001. The main objective of the code will be to prohibit the victimisation of employees who are members of trade unions or are engaged in trade union activity.

The full list is contained in Table 4.6 and includes one on employee representatives and one on disputes procedures. The former constitutes general guidelines and there is no requirement that the parties in any particular employment adopt them. The code of practice on dispute procedures, including disputes in essential services, is of a more fundamental nature. This code is designed to establish a template for procedures to be adopted in the event of a dispute, but before it can take effect it has to be adopted in individual employments.

There has been an extremely poor take-up rate of the codes of practice for disputes in essential services (Kelly 2000). According to Kelly (2000), the main difficulties are due to trade unions being unhappy with the interference in their entitlement to take strike or other industrial action and suspicions at the provisions for binding arbitration contained in the codes. The LRC (2000: 68) quotes Kelly as finding that 'none of the respondents felt that the current industrial relations climate in Ireland warranted the implementation of mandatory provisions for essential service providers'.

However, in late 2003, under the pressure to agree on industrial peace and the modernisation agenda under Section 19 of Sustaining Progress, codes on disputes in essential services were adopted in the civil service, health and local authorities (Dobbins 2003b). These codes were adopted after a twelve-year wait and were a precondition for the payment of benchmarking. Essential services include 'those whose cessation or interruption could endanger life, or cause major damage to the national economy, or widespread hardship to the Community", and particularly: health services, energy supplies, including gas and electricity, water and sewage services, fire, ambulance and rescue services and certain elements of public transport' (Dobbins 2003b: 16). The health or local authority codes require the exhaustion of extensive procedures but do not incorporate a 'no strike' clause. The codes do provide for 'maintenance of an emergency level of service within both of these essential services' in the event of industrial action (Dobbins 2003b).

Table 4.6
Codes of Practice Promulgated by the LRC

- Code of Practice on Dispute Procedures, including Procedures in Essential Services
- Code of Practice on Duties and Responsibilities of Employer Representatives and the Protection and Facilities to be Afforded Them by Their Employer
- Code of Practice on Grievance and Discipline Procedures
- Code of Practice on Compensatory Rest Periods
- Code of Practice on Sunday Working in the Retail Trade
- Code of Practice on Voluntary Dispute Resolution
- Code of Practice Detailing Procedures for Addressing Bullying in the Workplace

Source: LRC annual report (2002)

JOINT INDUSTRIAL COUNCILS (JICS)

A Joint Industrial Council is a voluntary negotiating body 'for an industry or part of an industry and is representative of employees and workers' (Labour Court 2001b: 16). They are designed to facilitate collective bargaining at industry level in certain industrial sectors (Gunnigle and Flood 1990). They generally cover industries with high levels of unionisation and are composed of representatives of employers and trade unions within the industry and are presided over by an independent chairperson. Joint Industrial Councils may be registered with the Labour Court. At present there are three JICs registered but only one of these is active – the Construction Industry JIC, which held five meetings in 2002. Of the two other registered JICs, the Joint Board of Conciliation and Arbitration for the Footwear Industry has been suspended since October 1983 and the JIC for the Dublin Wholesale Fruit and Vegetable Trade has not formally met since the early 1970s. Unregistered JICs include the following: bacon curing, chocolate and crumb factory, banks, electrical contracting, flour milling, grocery provision and allied trades, hosiery industry, printing and allied trades in Dublin, state industrial employees, woollen and worsted manufacture and telecom. Many of these JICs have not met in a number of years. The Labour Court identifies the state industrial employees and electrical contractors industry as meeting regularly, with the printing industry JIC meeting periodically. There are also a number of JICs in existence that never have contact with the Labour Court. They constitute industrial relations forums within companies. For example, the ESB has a JIC that Acts as an internal industrial relations tribunal but which has no contact with the Court.

While in 1992 approximately 83,000 workers were noted as being represented by JICs (LRC 1992), no current estimates are available from the LRC. Overall there has been a decline in the importance of industry-wide regulation of industrial relations since at least the early 1980s. For example, in banking, the four associated banks progressively withdrew from the banking JIC in favour of individual organisation negotiations in the late 1980s. The employer Banks Staff Relations Committee, which co-ordinated the employer side in negotiations with unions, was wound up in 1993, making the Banking JIC redundant (Wallace *et al.* 2001). The decreased relevance of national industry regulation of industrial relations, given the growth in the openness of the economy and the rise of global competition, is probably the main reason for the decline of the JICs.

The essential economic function of JICs is to take wages out of domestic competition, ensuring that industrial conflict was not driven by employers seeking to gain a competitive advantage over other employers by driving down wages. The mechanism for achieving this is registering agreements with the Labour Court, which are legally binding on all employers and unions in an industry. In an economy that has been described as the 'world's most globalised country for the third year in a row (*Irish Times* 2003: 13)' and where industries are open to external competition, merely taking wages out of domestic competition no longer makes any economic sense.

JOINT LABOUR COMMITTEES (JLCs)

Joint Labour Committees are 'statutory bodies established under the Industrial Relations Acts 1946 to 2001 to provide machinery for the fixing of minimum rates of pay and the regulation of conditions of employment' (Labour Court 2001b: 15). They are comprised of employer and trade union representatives and an independent chairperson. They typically exist in employments where collective bargaining is poorly established and are designed to protect vulnerable workers (Wallace and O'Sullivan 2002b). Their function is to set legally binding minimum wages and conditions of employment for those workers covered by the particular JLC.

The mechanism for this is making an Employment Regulation Order (ERO). This comes about by the JLC submitting proposals to the Labour Court for fixing minimum wage rates or for regulating conditions. If the Court accepts the proposals it makes an ERO, giving legal effect to the proposals. Inspectors attached to the Department of Enterprise, Trade and Employment are responsible for enforcing EROs, with cases being taken to the District Court and not the Labour Court or Employment Appeals Tribunal. In contrast with the decline in the JICs, there has been a major expansion in the coverage of workers by JLCs since the late 1980s. By 1998 over 160,000 workers were covered by JLCs in comparison with only 88,000 at the start of the 1990s (see Figure 4.3). This increased coverage has been driven by the massive expansion of the services sector that took place during the 1990s (Wallace *et al.* 2001; Wallace and O'Sullivan 2002c).

Figure 4.3
Number of Workers Covered by JLC System, 1926–1998

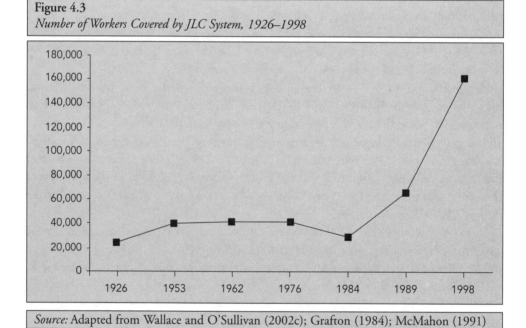

Source: Adapted from Wallace and O'Sullivan (2002c); Grafton (1984); McMahon (1991)

Wallace and O'Sullivan (2002c) record that while some JLCs seem a relic of a distant era, e.g. the 'Brush and Broom' JLC, others, such as those in retailing, catering, hotels and contract cleaning, are part of the modern economy and have seen some of the greatest expansion in recent years.

In the past the effectiveness of the JLC system in providing for wage equity was questioned by McMahon (1991). McMahon (1991: 307–8) noted the main limitation was that the system did not cover a significant proportion of workers on very low earnings, a situation that changed in 2000 with the adoption of a national hourly minimum wage. Justifying the hourly minimum wage, the Tanaiste, Mary Harney, TD, noted that it was introduced so that 'those sectors of the labour force, especially women and young persons currently on low pay, will get a better share of the fruits of economic growth of recent years' (see Wallace and O'Sullivan 2002c).

The existence of a national minimum wage raises significant questions as to the future of JLCs. The National Minimum Wage Commission (1998: 36) advocated a 'radical assessment of the role and functions of the JLC system' in light of the national minimum wage. However, JLCs do much more than determine minimum wage rates and are responsible for setting a wide range of minimum terms and conditions of employment for the employments they cover. In this regard, it is noteworthy that ICTU has favoured the retention of the JLC system, though in an extended role (National Minimum Wage Commission 1998: 34–5). Any study of the JLCs would need to address issues wider than those related to pay. Wallace and O'Sullivan (2002c: 9) note a number of areas requiring study, including the following:

> not all workers across a JLC sector are covered. For example, one of the Catering EROs excludes managers, assistant managers and trainee managers (Labour Court 2001). The fragmented nature of the system has led to confusion amongst employers and employees as to which of a multitude of wage rates apply to them. The inspection system is hampered by the small number of inspectors (approximately fifteen) who have responsibility for inspecting the premises of 162,000 workers and, as employers are not required to register their premises with the Inspectorate, accurate records of premises liable for inspection are not maintained.

THE LABOUR COURT

As noted previously, the Labour Court was established under the Industrial Relations Act of 1946. Subsequent amendments were introduced under the Industrial Relations Acts 1969, 1976 and 2001 but the major changes were contained in the Industrial Relations Act of 1990. The 1946 Act specified that the Court was established 'to make further and better provisions for promoting harmonious relations between workers and their employers and for this purpose to establish machinery ... for the prevention of trade disputes' (Industrial Relations Act 1946). The Labour Court's current mission statement is 'to find a basis for real and substantial agreement through the provision of fast, fair, informal and inexpensive arrangements for the adjudication and resolution of trade disputes' (Labour Court 2001b). The Court describes its functions as providing a 'comprehensive service for the resolution of disputes about industrial relations, equality, organisation of working time and national minimum wage matters' (Labour Court 2001b).

At present, the Court consists of three divisions, comprising a chairman, two deputy chairmen and six ordinary members. The Minister for Enterprise, Trade and Employment appoints the ordinary members of the Court on the basis of nominations made by IBEC and ICTU. The members of the Court are former industrial relations practitioners with no requirement for legal qualifications and the chairman and deputy chairmen have also traditionally been drawn from similar backgrounds. The chairman up to 2003, Mr Finbar Flood, was previously chief executive of Guinness Breweries and the current chairman, Kevin Duffy, was previously assistant general secretary of ICTU.

The Court normally sits in a division comprising three people – the chairman or a deputy chairman, an employer member and a workers member. While the respective employer or trade union body nominates these members, they are not representatives of these bodies and Act independently. In special circumstances, all of the members of the Court may sit on a case. Despite its title, the Labour Court is not a 'court of law'; in fact the title 'court' is misleading (von Prondzynski and McCarthy 1989; Finlay 1996: 18–19). While the Court has the power to summon witnesses and hear evidence on oath, it rarely does so.

The Labour Court has a wide range of functions in relation to industrial relations. Legislation provides for it to undertake the following:

- investigate trade disputes under the Industrial Relations Acts 1946–2001;
- investigate at the request of the Minister for Enterprise, Trade and Employment trade disputes affecting the public interest or conduct an enquiry into a trade dispute of special importance and report on its findings;
- hear appeals of Rights Commissioners' recommendations under the Industrial Relations Act;
- establish JLCs and decide on questions concerning their operation;
- register, vary and interpret employment agreements;
- register JICs;
- investigate complaints of breaches of registered employment agreements;
- investigate complaints of breaches of codes of practice made under the Industrial Relations Act 1990 (following consideration by the LRC);
- give its opinion as to the interpretation of a code of practice made under the Industrial Relations Act 1990; and
- investigate disputes (where negotiation arrangements are not in place) under the Industrial Relations (Amendment) Act 2001. (Labour Court 2001b, www.labourcourt.ie.)

Although it was initially solely an industrial relations body, the Labour Court now has an additional range of functions in the area of employment law, including legislation dealing with equality, the national minimum wage, organisation of working time and part-time work (see website for a comprehensive listing). Table 4.7 outlines the number of referrals received by the Court in the years 2000 to 2002. The vast bulk of the Court's work continues to be in the area of industrial relations, although the Court has noted that dealing with employment law issues, particularly under equality legislation, has been extremely time consuming (Labour Court 2002: 4).

Investigations Under the Industrial Relations Acts

Under the Industrial Relations Acts 1946–2001 the following are the prescribed circumstances in which the Labour Court may investigate disputes:

- where it receives a report from the Labour Relations Commission that no further efforts on its part will help resolve the dispute;

Table 4.7
Referrals Received by the Labour Court by Category of Dispute, 2000–2002

Section/Act/Application	2000	2001	2002
Breach or interpretation of registered employment agreement	68	111	121
Appeal against RC recommendation	147	133	144
Cases referred directly by the unions or workers under Industrial Relations Act 1969	127	127	92
Cases referred to the court by the LRC	315	344	386
Cases referred to court directly under Industrial Relations Act 1990 (exceptional circumstances)	0	0	4
Industrial Relations (Amendment) Act 2001	0	0	10
Sub-total industrial relations cases	**657**	**715**	**757**
Anti-Discrimination (Pay) Act 1974	4	4	3
Employment Equality Act 1977–1998	48	82	99
Organisation of Working Time Act 1997	66	75	78
National Minimum Wage Act 2000	0	7	3
Sub-total employment law	**118**	**168**	**183**
Other	4	1	0
Overall total	779	884	940

Source: Labour Court annual reports 2000–2002

- where it is notified by the chairperson of the Commission that the Commission has waived its function of conciliation in the dispute;
- where it is hearing an appeal in relation to a recommendation of a Rights Commissioner;
- where it decides after consultation with the Commission that exceptional circumstances of the case warrant a Labour Court investigation; and
- where it is referred to under Section 20(1) of the Industrial Relations Act 1969.

In addition, the Court has the function to 'investigate, at the request of the Minister for Enterprise, Trade and Employment, trade disputes affecting the public interest, or conduct an enquiry into a trade dispute of special importance and report on its findings' (Labour Court 2001: 4). Most cases are referred to the Court, but occasionally the Court will intervene in a dispute and invite the parties to a hearing. In practice, the foregoing means that there is a progressive and orderly mechanism for referrals, usually from conciliation or following Rights Commissioners' hearings, but there is sufficient flexibility for the Court to become involved in special circumstances. This tends to occur in high-profile cases of national importance, as typified by the nursing dispute of 1998.

Method of Investigation

The Court investigates disputes by requiring the parties to a dispute to provide it with written submissions of their positions on the dispute and holding hearings. While all parties to a dispute are entitled to attend, there is no compulsion to do so. The hearings are usually held in private, unless one of the parties concerned requests a public hearing (Labour Court 2001b). The court notes that the majority of hearings take place in Dublin, but hearings take place once a month in Cork and Limerick and elsewhere as necessary (www.labourcourt.ie). The written submissions should reach the Court three days in advance of a hearing. These hearings are generally informal and non-legalistic, with the written submissions being read to the Court by the main spokesperson for each side. The parties are free to make supplementary oral submissions and raise queries on each other's case. The members of the Court may also seek clarification or elaboration as they see fit. In standard industrial relations cases, the Court has indicated that it aims to issue a recommendation/determination/order within three weeks (Labour Court 2001b).

The Role of the Labour Court and its Recommendations

Section 19 of the Industrial Relations Act 1969 outlines that 'the Court having investigated a trade dispute may make a recommendation setting forth its opinions on the merits of the dispute and the terms on which it should be settled'. Prior to the enactment of this legislation the Court, under Section 68 of the 1946 Act, was obliged to have regard to a number of issues, including the public interest, the promotion of industrial peace, the fairness of the terms to the parties concerned and the prospect of the terms being acceptable to them. This section was repealed in 1969, as it was clear to the Court that it was almost impossible to reconcile all of the criteria specified in the 1946 Act (Kerr and Whyte 1985). R.J. Mortished, the first chairman of the Court, highlighted this in the Court's third annual report when he wrote that 'a settlement acceptable to the parties might be against the public interest and one which was not acceptable to the parties would not promote industrial peace' (Labour Court 1948).

There are a range of views among writers of the role and function of recommendations. They are described variously as 'having moral force', being 'designed to persuade' or being designed to 'promote accommodation'. Thus, Gavin P. Duffy described the Labour Court as being designed 'to bring about peace by *persuasion* instead of submission by coercion' (cited in Forde 1991: 30). Von Prondzynski (1998: 62) also emphasises the persuasive function, describing the Court as 'a body which uses its good offices to *persuade and cajole*'. McCarthy (1984: 37, 52) considers a Labour Court recommendation as 'essentially a third view' and that the Court was established 'as a body whose purpose was to *promote accommodation* … to Act as an honest broker, neither to apply law nor to create it'.

These normative descriptions of the Court and bases for recommendations give a useful sense of the 'alternative nature' of the body, but there are some tensions between them. If the Court is seen as bringing about accommodation (by issuing a recommendation based on compromise) rather than deciding on the merits of a dispute, it can be argued that a claim to moral authority is compromised. Equally, if the Court's recommendations are persuasive, it may be suggested the requirement for moral authority hardly arises. And a role that seeks accommodation suggests a focus on what is practical and acceptable, namely the statutory requirement that recommendations are made 'to resolve an industrial dispute'.

The above descriptions of the Court's role and its recommendations arise from normative values based on pluralism (see Chapter 7), and it is noteworthy that there has been little, if any, critique of the Court from a radical perspective. According to Forde (1991: 36), the Court 'has been the butt of considerable criticism, sometimes being accused of being anti-employer and on other occasions of being anti-union and indeed anti-government'. In practice, however, the criticisms advanced tend to be based on pragmatic dissatisfaction with the perceived effectiveness of the Court or the acceptability of its recommendations, not its role within the industrial relations institutional framework.

It would appear that, in common with settlement rates at conciliation, the rate of acceptance of Labour Court recommendations may have increased in recent years. Hourihan (1996: 16) notes, 'last year [1995], the Court conducted a survey of acceptance rates in regard to its recommendations between April and June and found that eighty-four per cent were accepted by both sides, a finding with which she [Evelyn Owens, former chair of the Labour Court] says she was pleased'. Though the survey relates to a short period of time, eighty-four per cent is in excess of the acceptance rate from 1947 to 1976 noted by the Commission of Inquiry on Industrial Relations (1981: 127). In contrast, Kevin Duffy, chairman of the Court, was reported in 2004 as saying, 'There is frustration at the top of the Court over the matter of acceptance of Court rulings. How widespread a problem is it? "It is very difficult to get reliable figures. We feel that around three quarters are accepted"' (*Industrial Relations News* 2004: 22). This relatively high acceptance rate has not, however, extended to union recognition disputes. Gunnigle *et al.* (2002b) note that of a total of eighty-one recommendations in union recognition cases covering the period 1990 to 1999, the Court recommended recognition in the vast majority of cases (ninety-three per cent). However, only thirty per cent of organisations actually recognised a union following the recommendation (Gunnigle *et al.* 2002b: 236). Many such cases were referred by trade unions under Section 20(1) of the Industrial Relations Act 1969 and employers have frequently not attended such hearings in case their attendance might confer *de facto* recognition on the union.

Even though the parties to a dispute are generally free to reject Labour Court recommendations, there can be significant constraints to doing this – negative publicity and even public opprobrium being possibilities. The most important constraint, however, probably arises if there is no prospect of further concessions by the other party. Even where rejected, a Labour Court recommendation may continue to have relevance, acting as an 'anchor' to which both parties may be drawn back. A practice adopted in some instances, where a Labour Court recommendation has not been acceptable, has been for the dissatisfied party to return to the Court to seek 'clarification' of the recommendation. The hope has been that such clarification would make the recommendation more palatable or introduce enough 'wriggle room' to gain acceptance. A recommendation normally takes the form of a summary of the case submitted by each party to the dispute followed by a rationale for recommended settlement. Occasionally the Court may issue an oral recommendation.

While Labour Court recommendations are generally not binding, there has been debate on whether they should be. More recently, the provisions of the National Agreement 'Sustaining Progress' obliged the parties to a dispute to accept that 'disputes about possible breaches of the agreement; claims of inability to pay; and disputes concerning normal ongoing change will be referred in the first instance to the Labour Relations Commission and, if unresolved there, referred to the Labour Court on the basis that the parties agree, in advance, to accept the Recommendations of the Court' (see Labour Court 2002: 5; Sustaining Progress 2003; see also Chapter 13).

The Adjudicative Functions of the Labour Court

In addition to recommendations, the Court may issue determinations, decisions or orders, depending on the relevant legislation under which an issue has been heard, and these can have binding effect. When issuing a decision on an appeal from a Rights Commissioner's recommendation in an industrial relations case, the decision is binding on the parties. A similar stipulation applies where workers or their trade unions refer a dispute on their own to the Court for investigation under Section 20(1) of the Industrial Relations Act 1969. In such cases, the union side has to agree in advance to accept the Court's recommendation. Such referrals have frequently been used in trade union recognition cases and employers are not bound by the recommendation. However, as von Prondzynski and McCarthy (1989) point out, there is no enforcement mechanism in either of these cases. The Labour Court (website) carefully notes that 'where the recommendation of a Rights Commissioner in an industrial relations case is appealed to the Labour Court, it is *expected* that the parties will abide by the Court's decision on the appeal'. This seems to accept that it is not *legally* binding. By contrast, the Court indicates that 'there are certain other categories of cases ... in which the decision of the Court (as expressed by a Determination, Order or Decision, depending on the legislation under which it is heard) is enforceable' (through the civil Courts) (www.labourcourt.ie). Such cases include:

- appeals of decisions of Rights Commissioners under the Organisation of Working Time or National Minimum Wage Acts;
- appeals of decisions of Equality Officers under equality legislation;
- dismissal cases under equality legislation;
- complaints of breaches of registered agreements; and
- employment Regulation Orders made by the Court (Labour Court, www.labourcourt.ie).

In other words, in these cases the Labour Court determinations, orders or decisions *are* legally binding. However, even here the issue of enforcement has given rise to difficulty. The then chairman of the court, Mr Finbar Flood, reported that 'the Court in 1998 was hampered by its lack of power to enforce awards; this often results in claimants, who believed that their award was automatically guaranteed, subsequently realising that they had to go to the civil courts for enforcement' (Labour Court 1998: 7).

Usage of the Labour Court and the Industrial Relations Act 1990

The number of cases dealt with by the Labour Court rose dramatically throughout the 1970s, reaching a peak in 1983 when it issued 1,045 recommendations (see Figure 4.4). This contrasts with the situation in the 1960s, when the Court heard on average 100 cases per year. There has been much comment on the growth in Labour Court usage, with a number of reasons being advanced to explain the increase. The Court complained about no longer being a 'court of last resort' due to a general overdependence on it and the failure of the parties to conduct full and meaningful negotiations at local level (Labour Court 1977).

Figure 4.4
Labour Court Cases Completed, 1973–2002

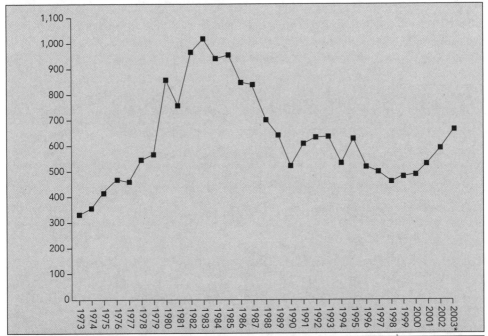

* Provisional figure supplied directly by the Labour Court.

Source: Labour Court annual reports

A fundamental objective of the Industrial Relations Act 1990 was to reduce the reliance on third parties, including the Labour Court. In order to see if there has been a reduction in Labour Court usage following the 1990 Act, it is necessary to exclude non-industrial relations cases, such as those dealing with equality issues. Figure 4.5 shows that there has indeed been a reduction in Labour Court usage, but it is clear that the reduction predated the introduction of the institutional changes of the 1990 Act in January 1991.

After 1991, the number of Labour Court referrals has oscillated between 400 and 600, which is on par with the levels pertaining when the Act was introduced. This raises the question of the extent to which the objective of returning the Court to being a 'court of last resort' has been achieved. Finbar Flood repeatedly indicated his concern with the Court being used as a staging post. In 2000, he commented:

> the use of the Court as a staging post on the negotiation highway continues to be of concern. Any diminution or dilution of the role of the Court in the industrial relations process as a Court of last resort can only be detrimental to the entire machinery on which the public and private sectors rely for the orderly resolution of disputes (Labour Court 2000: 6).

The high usage of the Labour Court parallels the high usage of conciliation and again emphasises the extent to which 'the Irish system of industrial relations continues to be categorised by a high degree of reliance on institutional usage' (Wallace and O'Sullivan 2002a: 185). Wallace and McDonnell (2000: 173) attribute this to 'the growth in proceduralisation' and the requirement in procedure agreements that parties in dispute refer an issue to the Labour Court prior to any strike, lockout or other form of industrial action (see also Wallace and O'Sullivan 2002a). While it may be

Figure 4.5
Numbers of Labour Court Cases Completed under Industrial Relations Legislation, 1985–2003

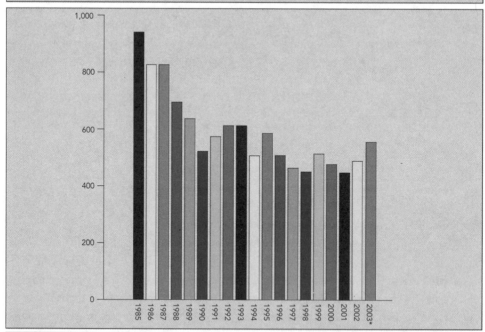

* Provisional figure supplied directly the Labour Court. The increase in 2003 is partly accounted for by the increased number of Section 32 cases under the Industrial Relations Act 1946 (such cases involve a complaint of a breach of an Employment Regulation Order and have been used by unions in the cases of agreements related to pensions).

Note: The figures exclude cases under the Anti-Discrimination (Pay) Act 1974, the Employment Equality Act 1977 and the Employment Equality Act 1998.

Source: Labour Court annual reports

understandable that third parties will decry this usage, it is arguable that it is an integral part of the industrial relations system, which has been constructed since the 1960s. It is also a system which the actors, at least as measured by their revealed preferences, appear content to utilise on a regular basis.

INSTITUTIONS AND ARRANGEMENTS FOR INDUSTRIAL RELATIONS IN THE PUBLIC SECTOR

The state is the main employer in the country, with some 299,000 public service employees and a further 36,800 employed in regional bodies (mostly in local authorities) as of December 2002. This comprises 19.2 per cent of the total employment in the state. The annual public sector pay and pensions bill in 2002 was €11,746 million, which accounted for 9.1 per cent of GDP and 11.1 per cent of GNP for that year (Department of Finance 2003c: 7). The state provides employment in a range of areas, including the civil service proper, education, local authorities and health boards, security forces and state-sponsored bodies.

The public sector is highly unionised, having a trade union density of approximately eighty per cent in contrast to under thirty per cent in the private sector (Wallace 2003). Since higher union density is found internationally across public sectors, it is likely that there is an underlying reason for this. The efficiencies of dealing with large groups of employees through collective, as distinct from individual, bargaining offers substantial advantages to state employers and governments. A notable characteristic of public sector industrial relations is the role of the Department of Finance. It acts as the government's advisor on matters relating to public sector pay and employment-related matters. It will critically review pay claims, lay down appropriate policy guidelines and oversee their implementation through direct and indirect negotiations.

While public sector industrial relations has been of particular concern since the foundation of the state (McGinley 1997: 235), the relative importance of public sector industrial relations has grown in recent years. Among the factors driving this are the diverging union density rates between public and private sectors, a concern with quality of the delivery of public services, the impact of benchmarking and privatisation.

Privatisation, which relative to developments in the UK was initially limited, has gathered pace in the last number of years with the privatisation of Telecom, Irish Steel (became Ispat – now closed) and Irish Sugar (now Greencore). Even where privatisation has not taken place, the commercial semi-state sector is facing greater competition, as exemplified by experience in the ESB, Voluntary Health Insurance (VHI), Aer Rianta, Dublin Bus and Aer Lingus. EU competition policy is driving this in some areas, such as electricity generation, while in other sectors, such as air transport, private sector initiatives are the driving force, as with Ryanair. It is notable that unionisation is low or non-existent in many of these companies competing with state or previous state companies, for example Ryanair and the telecom company O_2 (previously Esat Digifone).

McGinley (1997: 234) notes a number of other distinctive features to public sector employments, including a low level of part-time work and the fact that many public sector groups provide essential services. While recognising the differences between the public and private sectors, Cox and Hughes (1989: 99) suggest it would be inappropriate to view public sector industrial relations as inherently different. There is, however, one distinctive area – the provision for third-party institutions – embodied in a range of conciliation and arbitration schemes. This is a separate system to the LRC and Labour Court systems and covers approximately fifty per cent of the state's employees. A demand by public sector employees for such a scheme had gone back to the early 1930s, but despite government promises it proved extremely difficult to achieve agreement on the parameters of an acceptable scheme (McGinley 1997; Cox and Hughes 1989). The exclusion of civil servants and other employees from access to the Labour Court under the Industrial Relations Act 1946 gave an added incentive to the campaign for a civil service scheme. McCarthy (1984: 35) writes that their exclusion appeared to have been based on the grounds 'that their inclusion might lead them to take a view of their relationship with their employer, the government, which would be excessively and improperly adversarial in character'. McCarthy (1984: 35) notes that at the time, civil servants could not envisage taking industrial action and as a result they 'not uncommonly found themselves treated in a summary and very casual fashion by the Department of Finance, which had overall responsibility for personnel matters in the civil service'.

The government eventually conceded a conciliation and arbitration (C&A) for civil servants on a temporary basis in 1950, which was made permanent in 1955. Similar schemes were introduced for teachers in 1954–1955, Gardaí in 1962 and officers or local authorities in 1963. Schemes were also introduced covering health boards and the vocational educational committees. These schemes involve a system of conciliation which covers a wide range of issues. While the items covered vary across the individual schemes, the items typically covered include pay, allowances, overtime rates, hours, grading and principles governing recruitment, promotion, discipline, superannuation and annual leave (McGinley 1997: 244). The schemes generally allow items not specified to be discussed by agreement of both sides. Individual items are commonly excluded, which has been the subject of criticism.

The composition and specific role of conciliation councils differs between schemes, but they generally provide for a conciliation council, involving equal numbers of staff (employees) and official (employer) representatives. These are appointed in accordance with the terms of the individual schemes and the chief representative of the 'official' side chairs the conciliation council (McGinley 1997: 243). The Department of Finance is often involved in many of the conciliation and arbitration hearings, along with representatives from the relevant department. Another important actor on the management side in the public sector is the Local Government Staff Negotiations Board (LGSNB) and the Health Services Employers Association (HSEA). They assist local authorities and health boards, acting on behalf of management on the appropriate conciliation and arbitration scheme. In the civil service scheme, a network of staff panels rationalise claims from recognised unions or staff associations prior to conciliation. Reports are prepared of discussions on claims and agreed by both sides and these are submitted to the relevant minister (McGinley 1997: 244). These may record agreement, disagreement or merely record the discussion. Agreed recommendations are rarely rejected. Cox and Hughes (1989: 107) quote a high level of agreement (some eighty per cent) as having been the norm. Issues that are not resolved may proceed to arbitration, provided they are arbitrable under the terms of the particular scheme.

The system of arbitration covers a narrower range of issues, such as pay and allowances, overtime, total weekly hours of work, annual and sick leave, but excludes issues such as discipline, which are not arbitrable. McCarthy (1984: 35) writes that 'the arbitration process was seen as the centrepiece of the system'. All of the schemes provide for an arbitration board with representatives of the official and staff sides. The boards are chaired by a jointly agreed independent chairperson appointed by government, usually eminent senior counsels (McGinley 1997: 244). Both sides make detailed written submissions and these are supplemented by oral submissions as appropriate. The finding of the board is sent to the Minister for Finance and the other appropriate ministers, who have one month to approve the report or submit it to the government. Under the local authority and health board schemes, the management or staff side have the option of rejecting the decision at arbitration.

In the other schemes, an award can only be refused by moving a Dáil motion to reject or amend it – a course of action which, although exceptional, has happened on two notable occasions. The first occurred in 1953 under the trial civil service scheme, and the second in 1986 when a motion for the phased payment of a teacher's award was placed before the Dáil and passed. While strictly in accordance with the scheme, both of these actions were met by intense opposition and hostility (Cox and Hughes 1989: 107). Referring to the 1953 case, McCarthy (1984: 36) notes accusations of bad faith by civil servants, which derived from the civil servants' perception of 'their weakness as a bargaining partner' and their view that only binding arbitration could remedy that situation. It is noteworthy that this attitude in relation to the C&A schemes is quite different from the general attitude of unions, which have generally favoured non-binding Labour Court recommendations.

Initially, no group that had access to a C&A scheme had access to the Labour Court/LRC mechanisms, but this has changed as a result of the nursing dispute in 1998. Frawley (1998: 6) noted that the dispute 'was regarded as stark evidence of the inability of the scheme to cope with such complex and broad pay disputes'. During that dispute both public and some private sector hospitals were involved. Both employers and unions agreed that the dispute with the private sector hospitals would be referred to the Labour Court and the resulting recommendation, if accepted, would be extended to nurses in the health boards. This proved an innovative way of getting the Labour Court involved in adjudicating on a dispute where formally the employees (nurses) did not have access to the Court. The dispute was eventually resolved after the Labour Court issued two recommendations. As a result of this experience, 'employers and unions in the health service have decided to scrap their scheme altogether and instead use the LRC and Labour Court', which has been the case since 1998 (Frawley 1998: 6). The local authorities and Teachers Union Of Ireland (TUI) academic staff of institutes of technology followed the health services in abandoning their C&A scheme in favour of using the LRC and Labour Court in 1998 and 2002, respectively (Frawley 2002).

These developments are hardly surprising given what Frawley notes as the more active role of the LRC and Labour Court in the public sector. He comments that 'their greater flexibility and pragmatism has been used to resolve disputes that the inflexible C&A schemes could not hope to achieve' (Frawley 2002: 15). While other public sector groups have kept their C&A schemes, the schemes have not been retained unchanged. All the other public sector C&A schemes have been revised, except that for the Gardaí; however, a deadline date of March 2004 was set for a new Gardaí scheme (see Frawley 2003b; Higgins 2003). In addition to the specific grades in the public sector discussed above, employees in most state-sponsored bodies have access to the Labour Court.

A separate body makes recommendations to the government from time to time on the remuneration of higher grades in the civil service, local authorities, health boards and the Garda Síochána. This is known as the Review Body on Higher Remuneration in the Public Sector. This is a standing body that also advises on the remuneration of members of the government, the Oireachtas and the judiciary (Cox and Hughes 1989). The fact that the body's recommendations apply to politicians means that their recommendations tend to command headlines and be somewhat controversial. There is considerable tension between arguments for pay restraint, which underlie much of government policy, and arguments that in order to retain senior public servants it is necessary to match rates of senior private sector management. The review body conducts or commissions research on remuneration from time to time, although McGinley (2001: 23) notes a judgment as to the validity of its survey practice was not possible since the body never gave enough details of the manner in which the surveys were conducted. The sixth general review in 2000 'resulted in large increases for a number of grades – 33.3 per cent for the Secretary General, Department of Finance, 25.4 per cent for the nine Level 11 Secretaries, 15.8 per cent for Secretaries at Level 111 and 28.5 per cent for the Garda Commissioner' (B. Barry, 2002). Increases at lower levels received lower increases – Assistant Secretary, 14.8 per cent and 18.1 per cent for Assistant Garda Commissioner. The HAY method was used to rank jobs and it has been claimed that the review body 'virtually allowed its consultants to take over the process of pay setting' (McGinley 2001: 25). This exercise was influential in the subsequent benchmarking process but a recommendation for performance-related pay was not followed through in that review.

CHAPTER 5

Trade Unions

INTRODUCTION

This chapter considers the nature and role of trade unions in Irish industrial relations. The types of unions, their objectives and their governing structures are reviewed. The chapter subsequently examines the issues of trade union density, recognition and influence using recent research evidence. The pattern of trade union membership is normally evaluated through the utilisation of some measure of trade union density, that is, the actual level of trade union membership expressed as a percentage of the potential 'unionisable' workforce. The two common measures of union density are as follows: (i) workforce density: the percentage of the workforce (including the unemployed) who are trade union members and (ii) employment density: the percentage of employees who are trade union members. This chapter also reviews the changing pattern of union membership in Ireland and in so doing addresses some of the critical challenges facing the Irish trade union movement.

ROLE AND OBJECTIVES OF TRADE UNIONS

Trade unions have traditionally been seen as the most effective means of countering employer power and achieving satisfactory pay and working conditions for employees. As seen in Chapter 3, their role is well established in legislation dating back to the nineteenth century. In essence, trade unions are organisations that aim to unite workers with common interests while seeking to define those interests, express them, safeguard and advance them through their interactions (particularly collective bargaining) with individual employers, employer associations, government, government agencies and other parties. The basic strength of a union, therefore, lies in its ability to organise and unite workers.

By joining trade unions, employees provide themselves with the collective means to redress the imbalance in bargaining power that is often perceived to exist between individual workers and their employer. Sidney and Beatrice Webb (1920: 1), who wrote the first comprehensive history of trade unions and early collective bargaining, defined a trade union as 'a continuous association of wage earners with the objective of improving or maintaining conditions of employment'. While this description aptly describes the workplace collective bargaining role of trade unions, it fails to explicitly address the broader societal role of trade unions in advancing worker interests in the political arena. Salamon (1998: 85) provides a more comprehensive definition of a trade union as 'any organisation, whose membership consists of employees, which seeks to organise and represent their interests both in the workplace and society and, in particular, seeks to regulate the employment relationship through the direct process of collective bargaining with management'.

This description captures the essence of a trade union's role, namely as permanent associations of organised employees whose primary objectives are to:

- replace individual bargaining with collective bargaining, thereby redressing the balance of bargaining power in favour of employees and reducing management prerogative in employment-related matters;
- facilitate the development of a political system where worker interests have a greater degree of influence on political decisions and result in an economic and social framework which reflects the interests of wage earners and the working class; and
- achieve satisfactory levels of pay and conditions of employment and provide members with a range of services.

LEGAL POSITION

The main legislation dealing with the formation and operation of trade unions are the Trade Union Acts of 1941, 1971 and 1975, the Industrial Relations Act 1990 and the Industrial Relations (Amendment) Act 2001, with the 1990 Act being the most significant. Trade unions are defined under the 1941 Trade Union Act as bodies carrying on negotiations for fixing wages or other conditions of employment. This legal definition of trade unions is very broad and embraces employer organisations (see Kerr 1997). The legislation stipulates that, apart from certain 'excepted bodies', only 'authorised' trade unions holding a negotiating licence are permitted to engage in collective bargaining on pay and working conditions. This legislation also specifies the conditions which a union must fulfil before it can be issued with such a licence. Trade unions may only gain a negotiating licence when they register with the Registrar of Friendly Societies and meet specified criteria, particularly the following.

- **Notification**: Unions must notify the Minister for Enterprise, Trade and Employment and ICTU at least eighteen months before applying for a licence.
- **Membership**: A minimum of 1,000 members.
- **Financial deposit**: Ranging from €25,395 for up to 2,000 members to €55,869 for more than 20,000 members, together with €1,016 for each additional 1,000 members (or part of 1,000 members) in excess of 20,000 members to a maximum of €76,184.

It should be noted that financial deposits are not required where a new trade union is formed as a result of the amalgamation of two or more unions. Trade unions with headquarters outside the Republic of Ireland need not register as outlined. However, they must be legally recognised trade unions in their country of origin and meet prescribed guidelines in relation to their controlling authority. Otherwise such unions must meet the notification, membership and deposit requirements set out above.

The legislation also provides for the operation of a number of 'excepted' bodies. These 'excepted' bodies are not required to hold a negotiating licence to engage in collective bargaining (Kerr and Whyte 1985). Examples of excepted bodies include the Irish Hospital Consultants Association and the Irish Dental Association. A number of organisations that now hold a negotiation licence and operate as a trade union were originally 'excepted bodies', such as the Irish Nurses Organisation (von Prondzynski and Richards 1994).

Alternatives to Trade Union Organisation

While trade unions have historically been the most prominent means of representing worker interests to employers, government and other parties, there are a number of alternative approaches workers may use. For example, they may choose to deal with employers on an individual basis (individual bargaining). This may be attractive to workers who are in a strong bargaining position, such as those in possession of particular skills or knowledge that is highly valued by employers. This may be the case when particular categories of labour are in short supply (see Chapter 9). However, many workers might not join unions due to employer unwillingness to concede union recognition and grant negotiation rights. While workers may be free to join unions, there is a major disincentive when a union cannot negotiate on a worker's behalf (see Wallace 2003).

Structural alternatives to trade unions are 'staff associations', 'works committees' or other such groups. Staff associations have traditionally been comprised of white-collar employees, such as professional and managerial staff, who may prefer not to be members of a trade union. The officers of a staff association usually represent their members through consultation with the company's senior management on collective as well as individual issues. Some managers and employees have viewed them as an alternative to traditional trade unionism. Joining a staff association gives some of the benefits of collective organisation since by joining together workers can present a united front to employers and redress some of the bargaining imbalance. Another perceived advantage of staff associations is that they provide a collective voice for employees without the introduction of an 'outside' third party into management-employee relations. Some employees may prefer to join staff associations for particular reasons. For example, the traditional perception of trade unions as catering for blue-collar workers may create a 'snob' value that encourages employees to join/remain in staff associations.

From an employer perspective, staff associations may be perceived as less difficult to deal with and less likely to engage in confrontation or adversarial bargaining. However, work-based associations have been criticised because of their lack of independence. They may also be at a serious disadvantage due to the absence of an external organisation structure, inadequate resources and lack of access to bargaining expertise or legal advice. These factors may combine to limit the bargaining power of staff associations in their interactions with management. Traditional trade unionists have taken a cynical view of staff associations, viewing them as a poor apology for a real trade union and inhibiting collective solidarity. Some of the major contrasts between trade unions and staff associations are summarised in Table 5.1. It is important to note that these generalisations may not characterise all trade unions or staff associations.

Table 5.1
Contrasts between Trade Unions and Staff Associations

	Trade Unions	Staff Associations
Objectives	1. Replace individual bargaining with collective bargaining	1. Similar but with less ideological commitment
	2. Pay and employment conditions	2. Yes
	3. Political	3. No
Controlling authority	Union headquarters; normally a strong role for ICTU	No external authority
Rules/ procedures	Detailed constitution; often with strong political dimension	None or brief constitution; oriented to firm
External resources	Access to external expertise and resources; influence on national issues, e.g. centralised agreements on pay and other economic and social issues	None except by contracting in
Methods	Collective bargaining, often with adversarial orientation	More consultative orientation
Use of sanctions	Prepared to use strike weapon	Most unlikely
Services to members	May have range of services	Limited

A SUMMARY OVERVIEW OF THE DEVELOPMENT OF TRADE UNIONS

The early combinations were almost exclusively composed of skilled workers, or 'journeymen', as they were known. They were purely local bodies and their existence was often tenuous. The historical development of trade unions is inextricably linked to the development of industrial relations. The current nature of the trade union movement in Ireland has its origins in the dramatic changes brought about by the Industrial Revolution, beginning in Britain in the eighteenth century and later spreading to Europe and North America. Developments in technology, particularly the use of steam power, improved machinery and greater sources of raw materials allowed for the production of goods in larger quantities for wider consumer markets. These developments heralded a gradual change from a largely peasant society based on agriculture and craft production to an industry-based society with new social divisions where greater numbers of people worked in the 'factory system' and relied on wages for their existence. In this new order, people now worked together in much larger numbers and on much more tightly defined tasks. This scenario led to the emergence of modern management as a result of the need to plan, control, direct and organise the use of equipment, capital, materials and people in the factory system.

By and large the early factory owners adopted authoritarian approaches to workers. Working conditions were poor, hours of work long and 'sweated labour' common. Workers themselves could do little about this situation, as they had little or no economic or political power. However, it was only the skilled workers who were successful in establishing any large-scale permanent unionisation in Ireland up to the early twentieth century. Until 1850, even the trade unions of skilled workers were modest and local organisations. A new type of trade union was prompted by the foundation of the Amalgamated Society of Engineers (ASE) in the UK in 1850–1851. The members that this union represented were products of the Industrial Revolution – skilled workers in the engineering industry.

These unions extended their operation to Ireland and by the early 1900s the trade union movement had become well established in Ireland, mostly in the larger cities of Dublin, Belfast and Cork (McNamara *et al.* 1988; Boyle 1988). The growth in influence and power of the 'new unionism', which primarily sought to organise unskilled workers, was most obviously manifested in the leadership skills of Jim Larkin and the Irish Transport and General Workers Union. The festering conflict between employer and worker interests came to a head in the lockout of 1913 (see Yeates 2000). An important effect of this turbulent period was that it served to accelerate the organisation of employees into trade unions and employers into employer associations, thus placing an ever increasing emphasis on industrial relations.

After the difficulties and confrontation of 1913, labour relations slowly moved towards a more constructive approach based on negotiations and bargained agreement. The union movement had arrived and employers had to take steps to accommodate it. This was done through multi-employer bargaining via employer associations and through the employment of labour relations officers to deal with personnel and industrial relations matters at organisation level. Roche and Larragy (1986) estimate that union membership[1] rose from 110,000 in 1914 to 250,000 in 1920, leading Roche (1997a: 54) to label this period the 'first phase of rapid mass union membership growth in Ireland'.

The period from the early 1920s on saw a reversal in unions' fortunes. Membership fell in the face of economic recession and external competition as the government pursued an open economy policy. In Britain, the 1920s were characterised by a prolonged period of depression and industrial conflict. This unrest culminated in the General Strike of 1926 in Britain. During this period, workers and their trade unions became increasingly suspicious of management motives in introducing welfare initiatives in the workplace. The unions became particularly anti-welfare, as they saw it as a managerial strategy to prevent worker organisation. Now, with the demise of welfare, trade unions – particularly the new general unions – stepped up their organisation drives. Helped by the numerous grievances of industrial workers, union membership increased gradually throughout the 1930s. As unemployment began to fall, the unions' position was reinforced and collective bargaining became more

---

1   Based on figures for membership of trade unions affiliated to the Irish Trade Union Congress. For greater detail, see Roche and Larragy (1986); Roche (1997a).

widespread. In many organisations this period saw the establishment of a personnel function, with the emphasis on industrial relations rather than welfare. While the industrial relations aspect of management has its roots much farther back in the early attempts to organise workers in the new factories of eighteenth and nineteenth century Britain, it was not until the inter-war years that management-union relations became an established element of the managerial role. The position of the trade union movement as a significant actor in the industrial relations framework was firmly established in Britain by the end of World War II.

In Ireland, too, trade union membership rose steadily from the early 1930s. Between 1930 and 1940 trade union membership increased from 99,500 to 151,600, representing an increase in employment density from twenty per cent to twenty-six per cent over the decade (Roche 1997a). This trend reflected an acceleration in the level of industrialisation and economic activity. This was aided by the closed economy policy and promotion of infant industries pursued by the Fianna Fáil party in government from 1932 onwards.

The rate of growth in union membership slowed during World War II, a development which Roche (1997a) attributes to a cyclical downturn in economic activity (and employment) as a result of the war, combined with the effects of wage tribunals that controlled the level of wage rises and thus restricted union influence of wage movements over the period. This phase ended in 1946 and marked the start of a new era for Irish industrial relations with the establishment of the Labour Court under the terms of the Industrial Relations Act of that year. The removal of mandated restrictions on wage movements led to a rapid increase in trade union membership in the post-World War II period. Union membership rose from 172,000 in 1945 to over 449,000 in 1975. This represents more than a doubling of employment density over the thirty years: in 1945 the level of employment density was just under twenty-eight per cent but by 1975 this figure had risen to fifty-nine per cent (see Roche 1997a).

The period of fastest growth in union membership was during the immediate post-war years from 1945 until the early 1950s. Aggregate union membership increased from 172,000 in 1945 to 306,000 in 1955, representing an increase in employment density of fifty-seven per cent (from twenty-eight per cent in 1945 to forty-six per cent in 1955).

One reason for this growth was the greater cohesion of the union movement in negotiating increases in pay and improvements in employment conditions in the post-war period. The advent of the 'wage round' system became an important means by which the Irish trade union movement could exert its influence on Irish economic affairs (see Chapter 13). Roche (1997a: 56) notes the significance of a change in state strategy in helping the development of trade unions in Ireland, notably in establishing the Labour Court and a new framework for public sector industrial relations:

> The setting up of the Labour Court in 1946 symbolised the advent of a more tolerant or supportive approach to trade unions on the part of the Irish state. A similar change in state strategy was responsible for the granting of recognition to public service unions and the establishment of the civil service conciliation

and arbitration schemes between 1946 and the early 1950s. The Labour Court actively sought to encourage union recognition in sectors where it had hitherto been opposed by employers – adding further institutional support to the expansion of trade union membership.

The 1950s witnessed a continued, but much less rapid, increase in trade union density, although the economic recession of the 1950s slowed union growth. The economic climate of the 1960s was quite different and was marked by significant economic expansion and employment growth. The 1960s saw continued steady growth in union membership and density.

Behind this steady growth, a number of other developments in the nature of Irish trade unionism are significant. Shop stewards became established and helped develop and expand plant-level bargaining (see Marsh 1973; Wallace 1982; McPartlin 1997). Another important development of this period was the growth in white-collar trade unionisation (Bain 1970; Kelly 1975). Increasingly, workers in administrative, supervisory and other 'staff' categories joined trade unions and demanded bargaining rights with their employers. An important catalyst in this regard was the apparent success of craft and general unions in negotiating improvements in pay and working conditions. Many white-collar workers increasingly viewed unionisation as an important means of replicating or improving on the gains of their counterparts in general or skilled job categories. Of particular note here is the growth in union membership in areas such as insurance, finance and advertising.

The early 1970s saw a further slowing of the pace of unionisation, with only modest growth in levels of union membership. Roche attributes this to a saturation effect where there was almost full unionisation in those sectors of the economy where unionisation was easiest to achieve, namely in manufacturing industry other than small firms. After 1976 there was a further increase in unionisation due to the expansion of the public sector by the Fianna Fáil government elected in 1977. An important factor impacting on the role of Irish trade unions over this period was the national wage agreement 'era' of 1970 to 1982. National wage agreements involved centralised negotiations between trade unions and employers on pay and employment conditions which, once agreed, applied to all organised workers. Far from eliminating workplace bargaining, national agreements merely changed its focus. Various types of productivity deals were negotiated throughout the period. In fact, productivity became an important means for work groups to gain pay increases above the stated maxima in national wage agreements (McCarthy 1977; Wallace 1982; O'Brien 1981, 1989a). Indeed, the emphasis on industrial relations continued to expand throughout this era.

Another development in the post-World War II period that had a significant impact on the Irish trade union movement was the growth of investment by multinational companies (MNCs). Although Ireland had a multinational presence prior to the 1950s, the significant growth of MNC investment came about from a reversal of previous government policy of protectionism and movement towards an open market economy in the late 1950s. The increase in MNC investment took off in the 1960s and mushroomed for much of the 1970s. O'Malley (1983) estimated that the foreign industry sector grew at an average rate of 21.4 per cent per year in the 1960 to 1974 period compared with a rate of 5.6 per cent for all industry (O'Malley 1983).

For many of the newer MNCs operating here, especially those of US origin, the Irish industrial relations framework represented something of a new experience. High levels of unionisation and union recognition, reliance on voluntary collective agreements, non-binding arbitration, multi-unionism and differing employment legislation represented challenges for such organisations. Of particular concern was the question of unionisation. For many US companies in particular, the prospect of dealing with trade unions was a new departure. Many such organisations had a clear preference for non-union status (Murray 1984). Even companies that had dealt with unions before were often unhappy about the prospect of dealing with a number of unions representing different categories of workers. Thus, where unions were recognised, this was generally achieved through what became known as 'sweetheart deals', whereby newly established firms agreed to recognise a particular union or limited number of unions. Such agreements were based on closed shop arrangements where workers were required to become and remain members of a particular union while in that firm's employment (Wallace 1982; Enderwick 1986; Fennell and Lynch 1993). Up to the late 1970s, such so-called 'sweetheart deals' represented the conventional pattern of industrial relations among inward-investing foreign companies. Such agreements, however, came into some disrepute as a result of a number of disputes, notably the eleven-week strike in Ferenka, Limerick in 1977 (for a detailed discussion see Wallace 1982). This strike involved an attempt by a large body of workers to gain recognition for the Marine Port and General Workers' Union. The workers had become members of the ITGWU as part of a pre-production agreement signed between that union and the company but wished to leave that union. The strike was accompanied by the eventual closure of the plant, which had employed some 1,450 workers.

Employment density reached a record level of sixty-two per cent in 1980. However, the next seven years saw a steady decline in membership and density, so that by 1987 employment density had fallen to fifty-seven per cent. This figure represented a decrease in union membership of approximately 45,000 (from almost 528,000 in 1980 to over 483,000 in 1987). The major reasons posited for this decline were deep economic recession, a rapid increase in unemployment and changes in employment structure involving decline/stagnation of employment in traditionally highly unionised sectors, such as 'traditional' manufacturing and the public sector, and growth in sectors which have usually posed difficulties for union penetration, such as electronics/computing and private services (see Roche and Larragy 1989a; Roche 1992a, 1994b, 1997a).

The harsh economic climate of the early to mid-1980s dramatically changed the industrial relations environment. This period, which was characterised by widespread company rationalisations and redundancies, significantly altered the bargaining environment, with adverse consequences for unions. Employers increasingly sought to address issues such as payment structures and levels of wage increases, the extent of demarcation and the erosion of managerial prerogative by trade unions. There was also evidence internationally of the changed climate of the early 1980s. Restrictive trade union legislation in Britain and hard-line management approaches in many firms indicated a more offensive approach to dealings with trade unions. There were negative outcomes for unions in strikes by miners in Britain and air traffic controllers in the US. Trade union membership began to fall in many Western countries. Many of the newer, and apparently successful, companies had evolved a management style and a corporate culture that rejected collective dealings with trade unions. The term *employee relations* gradually gained acceptance in the management vocabulary, signifying the subtle but significant change from 'collectivist' management-union to 'individualist' management-employee interaction (see Gunnigle *et al.* 1997b).

Unions themselves moved to adapt to their changing environment. Merger activity increased dramatically throughout the 1980s as unions attempted to both rationalise their activities and improve services to members. The most significant merger in Ireland was that between the Federated Workers Union of Ireland (FWUI) and the Irish Transport and General Workers Union (ITGWU) to form the Services Industrial Professional and Technical Union (SIPTU). There is conclusive evidence of increased employer opposition to union recognition since the 1980s and of significant growth of non-union firms, especially among the US multinational sector (McGovern 1989a; Gunnigle 1995b). Overall, the 1980s saw a number of factors combine to create a very difficult environment for trade unions, which contributed to a decline in union penetration in Irish organisations.

The years from the late 1980s to the present have witnessed a reversal of fortunes in the levels of union membership. However, there is some emerging disagreement on this. On one hand, Wallace (2003: 4) reports that trade union membership rose from approximately 474,590 in 1990 to some 595,086 in 2001, rising again to 625,053 in 2002 according to Department of Enterprise, Trade and Employment figures. This increase seems largely related to the huge growth in the numbers of people at work in the Irish economy. However, in spite of this suggested growth in aggregate membership, union density continued to fall. It is estimated that employment density stood at approximately forty-three per cent in 2001 (Wallace 2003; see also Dobbins 2001a[2]).

Even if unions are gaining somewhat from increased employment, the rate of growth in union membership is less than the rate of employment growth, leading to a decline in union density. Other important trends noted by Roche and Ashmore (2001) are the increase in the proportion of women who are trade union members and the increasing proportion of union members employed in the public sector. Again, we return to many of these issues later in this chapter.

---

2   However, this figure is contested by D'Art and Turner (2004), since using the 2003 Quarterly National Household Survey for 2003 suggests that union membership is 546,800 and an employment density figure of only thirty-eight per cent overall. In addition they suggest a private sector unionisation figure of only twenty-three per cent. These figures are based on a working paper which was received shortly prior to this book's publication so it was not possible to address the issues raised by D'Art and Turner. The treatment in this chapter is based on the DUES data and the figures returned to the Department of Enterprise, Trade and Employment for union members. (Lecturers should consult the website for updates on the issues raised by D'Art and Turner.)

TYPES OF TRADE UNIONS

Irish trade unions have traditionally been organised on an occupational basis. This means that workers tend to join a specific union because of the particular job or trade in which they are employed. Trade unions in Ireland have traditionally been grouped into three broad categories, namely craft unions, general unions and white-collar unions. It should be noted that it is extremely difficult to categorise unions as 'pure' craft, general or white-collar since many unions deviate from a tight definition of their union category on some dimension. For example, general unions may have white-collar and craft workers in membership and not all 'craft' unions operate a recognised apprenticeship system. Thus, the categorisation of trade unions as craft, general or white-collar should be interpreted as broadly indicative of union types in Ireland. Other countries may be characterised by different union classifications. In Japan, for example, one finds a proliferation of so-called 'enterprise unions'. These are company-based unions comprised of different employee categories (manual, administrative, etc.) whose sole membership comes from the enterprise in which it operates. Even in the UK, which has a similar union classification to Ireland, Turner (1962) suggests that a more appropriate categorisation of union types is one based on whether union membership is 'open' to employees regardless of occupation or 'closed' to all employees except those working in a defined trade requiring a prescribed apprenticeship or training period. However, the craft, general and white-collar categorisation provides a convenient benchmark upon which to analyse Irish trade unions.

Craft Unions

Craft unions cater for workers who possess a particular skill in a trade where entry is restricted to workers who have completed a prescribed apprenticeship programme or equivalent. Prominent examples of occupational categories that are organised in craft unions are electricians and fitters.

   Craft unions represent the first form of union organisation and have their origins in the early unions that emerged in Britain at the start of the nineteenth century. These 'model' unions, as they became known, confined their membership to skilled categories such as printers and carpenters who had served a recognised apprenticeship in their particular trade. The first British craft union to organise in Ireland was the Amalgamated Society of Engineers (Boyd 1972). It established five Irish branches in 1851, shortly after its foundation, and by 1858 it had ten branches here with a membership of 1,300.

   These early craft unions represented a relatively small proportion of the labour force. In Ireland, it is estimated that by 1890 there were only about 17,500 trade union members in total, all of whom were skilled workers (Boyd 1972). However, the significance of the 'model' unions was that by becoming accepted as important actors in the industrial relations system they created a vital bridgehead in ensuring the acceptance of trade unions as part of the political and organisational framework.

   Craft unions have traditionally been protective of their trade by ensuring that only people holding union cards are permitted to carry out certain types of skilled work. By controlling entry to the craft, such unions have customarily held considerable negotiating power. This strategy is often criticised as being a source of restrictive work practices and demarcation disputes. The relative influence of craft unions has decreased over time, as reflected in the reduction of their share of union members from a high of seventeen per cent in 1940 to approximately ten per cent in 1995 (Roche and Ashmore 2001). Increased mechanisation and consequent de-skilling has had a detrimental impact on craft union membership, with some older craft unions having ceased to exist as their traditional craft was rendered obsolete by developments in technology and work practices.

However, craft unions remain an important part of Ireland's industrial relations system. Figures from the Irish Congress of Trade Unions suggest that in 2001 the two main engineering craft unions (the Technical, Electrical and Engineering Union (TEEU) and the National Union of Sheet Metal Workers of Ireland (NUSMWI)) accounted for approximately 6.5 per cent of ICTU members. A third engineering craft union, the Amalgamated Engineering and Electrical Union (AEEU), had approximately 11,000 members prior to merging with the Manufacturing, Science and Finance Union (MSF) to form AMICUS (see Frawley 2002). The major building unions (the Union of Construction and Allied Trades and Technicians (UCATT), the Building and Allied Trades Unions (BATU) and the Operative Plasterers and Allied Trades Society of Ireland (OPATSI)) account for approximately five per cent of total ICTU membership (ICTU 2002).

General Unions

Unlike the restrictive recruitment strategies of craft unions, general trade unions adopt an open approach, taking into membership all categories of workers, regardless of skill or industry. Despite this open recruitment approach, general unions have traditionally catered for semi-skilled and unskilled workers. In more recent years, some general unions have attracted white-collar and some craft categories into membership.

The origins of general trade unions are rooted in the increased number of unskilled or general workers employed in the large factories, transport companies and other large organisations that characterised late nineteenth and early twentieth century Britain, and to a lesser extent Ireland. These new unions tended to be more militant than the more traditional craft unions of the period. They initially organised categories such as general labourers and dock-workers and were noted for both their aggressive bargaining style in attempting to improve pay and working conditions of their members and for their greater political consciousness in attempting to advance working-class interests.

While there was a small number of local general unions catering for unskilled workers in Ireland from the 1860s, such as the Limerick Dock Labourers Society (Wallace 1982), unskilled unionisation only emerged as a force in the early 1900s. Their development is especially associated with the arrival of Jim Larkin in 1907. Boyd (1972: 74) notes:

the years 1907 and 1913 are outstanding in Irish trade union history for they are the years in which the unskilled labourers, at first in Belfast and then in

Dublin, asserted their right to belong to trade unions. In each city this right was bitterly contested by employers … on the workers side was Jim Larkin … He led the struggles for free trade unionism and will be remembered as long as there is a Labour movement in Ireland.

Jim Larkin was an organiser with the National Union of Dock Labourers (NUDL) in Liverpool and moved to Belfast as a union organiser in 1907. He subsequently extended his organising activities to Dublin and other Irish cities. After a dispute with the NUDL, Larkin left the union and established the Irish Transport and General Workers Union (ITGWU) in 1909. When James Connolly returned from the US in 1910, he soon became active in the labour movement and joined the ITGWU, becoming an organiser in Belfast. The ITGWU and other general unions catered for categories such as dockers, carters and railway workers. They became engaged in a series of strikes in 1911 and 1912, culminating in the Dublin lockout of 1913, which lasted some six months. The fallout from this bitter dispute initially dealt a severe blow to the ITGWU – their membership declined from 45,000 in 1913, prior to the lockout, to 5,000 afterwards. However, by 1919 membership had recovered to 100,000 (Boyd 1972; McNamara et al. 1988). Larkin left for the US in 1914, where he spent the war years and was jailed for opposition to the war. He was subsequently pardoned and on his return sought to resume his position as general secretary of the ITGWU. William O'Brien, who had taken over as general secretary of the union after the execution of James Connolly in 1916, resisted this. In 1924, while Jim Larkin was out of the country, his brother founded the Worker Union of Ireland (WUI) and Jim Larkin became general secretary on his return. There followed a period of intense bitterness between the two unions, which lasted into the 1950s. In 1990 both unions merged to form SIPTU, which is the largest union in the country with a financial membership of about 195,000.

General unions are common in all types of organisations and industrial sectors and account for approximately forty-seven per cent of trade union members within ICTU, with SIPTU itself accounting for around thirty-eight per cent of its membership (ICTU 2002).

White-Collar Unions

White-collar unions normally cater for professional, supervisory, technical, clerical and managerial grades. Such workers have long formed unions, although they often did not use the term 'union' to describe their organisations. The Irish Banks Officials Association (IBOA) had been formed in 1917 and already had high levels of density. Teachers' unions also had a long history, with the Irish National Teachers Union (INTO) being founded in the 1860s and the Teachers' Union of Ireland (TUI) in 1899 (see Logan 1999). White-collar unions experienced significant growth in membership, particularly in the period from the late 1960s until the early 1980s. The share of union members in white-collar unions increased from twenty-four per cent in 1940 to approximately forty-two per cent in the mid-1990s (Roche and Ashmore 2001). In the ten-year period 1966 to 1976, white-collar unions increased their membership by seventy-one per cent as compared to overall union membership growth of thirty per cent (Roche and Larragy 1989a).

The dramatic growth in the services sector, particularly in the public sector, was a significant factor facilitating the growth of white-collar unionisation. While some white-collar workers were generally reluctant to join trade unions, Kelly (1975) identified a number of factors that served to increase the propensity of white-collar workers to unionise. In particular, he noted the impact of negative circumstances at work, especially poor job design and general quality of working life, as important factors encouraging white-collar unionisation.

One can also point to changing attitudes of white-collar workers to trade unions, a development accelerated by the emergence of unions designed to cater for the specific needs of white-collar workers. The British-based Association of Scientific Technical and Managerial Staffs (ASTMS) attracted a large number of Irish insurance workers and other professional staffs into its membership. The ITGWU became the first general union to explicitly develop a white-collar section under the now TD Pat Rabbitte.

Another significant aspect in white-collar unionisation was the large advances in pay and conditions secured by blue-collar unions, which encouraged hitherto more conservative white-collar workers to unionise. White-collar categories thus represented a relative 'greenfield' opportunity for union membership drives in the 1960s and 1970s. The ASTMS was a product of this era of white-collar unionisation.

In evaluating union membership statistics it is difficult to differentiate between white-collar and blue-collar workers. However, the major areas of concentration of white-collar workers are the public sector and in financial/professional services. Recent figures from the Irish Congress of Trade Unions (ICTU) suggest that the five largest public sector unions – the Irish Municipal Public and Civil Trade Union (IMPACT), the Communications Workers Union (CWU), the Irish Nurses Organisation (INO), the Civil and Public Services Union (CPSU) and the Public Services Executive Union (PSEU) – account for over twenty-one per cent of ICTU members, while two of the three major teachers' unions – the INTO and the TUI – account for approximately seven per cent of ICTU members. The third teachers' union, the Association of Secondary Teachers of Ireland (ASTI), with a membership of almost 16,000, left ICTU in 2000 in a dispute over centralised agreements. Turning to the financial services sector, the two major unions there – the IBOA and AMICUS – account for almost six per cent of ICTU membership (ICTU 2002). As noted earlier, many white-collar workers are also members of general unions such as SIPTU.

Industrial Unions

Pure industrial unions, in the sense of unions catering for all workers in a particular industry, are not part of the Irish union structure. However, there are some trade unions whose membership is comprised only of workers in particular industries or industrial sectors. Many of these unions operate in the state or semi-state sectors, notably the National Bus and Rail Workers Union (NBRU), the Irish National Teachers

Organisation (INTO) and the ESB Officers Association (ESBOA). The Irish Bank Officials Association (IBOA), which recruits members at every level within the banking sector, is a union confined to one particular segment of the private sector. Some older unions, whose membership was confined to traditional industrial sectors, have been absorbed into the larger general unions, e.g. the Irish Shoe and Leather Workers Union.

TRADE UNION STRUCTURE AND GOVERNMENT

While it is always difficult to generalise about the structures of different organisations, it is possible to identify a number of common characteristics in the organisation structure of the majority of Irish trade unions. A basic characteristic of the governing structure is that ultimate decision-making authority is vested in the membership and executed through resolutions passed at the Delegate Conferences held on an annual or, in the case of SIPTU and other unions, biannual basis. It is then the job of the union executive to carry out the policy decided. The union officials' primary task is to carry out the operational aspects of the union's role, servicing the membership through assistance and advice.

The branch is the basic organisational unit in the union structure and it may be organised on either a geographic (catering for several enterprises) or individual enterprise basis. A typical union structure is outlined in Figure 5.1. The structure and personnel of trade unions in Ireland can be described at three levels, namely the workplace, branch and national level.

Workplace Level

At workplace level the *shop steward* is the key union representative. Their role is to represent employee interests on workplace issues, liaise with union officials and keep members *au fait* with union affairs. In practice, shop stewards may become involved in much workplace bargaining involving local grievances or disputes (Wallace 1982). On more major issues, their role is to support the trade union official and give feedback to the membership. Salamon (1998: 175) describes a shop steward as 'an employee who is accepted by management and union as a lay representative of the union and its members with responsibility to Act on their behalf in industrial relations matters at the organisational level'. An employee's first personal contact with a trade union will normally occur in the workplace. This usually happens when a shop steward invites a new employee to become a union member. Shop stewards are elected or appointed by fellow trade union members at elections, which normally take place once a year. A number of shop stewards may be elected to represent different sections/employment categories within an organisation.

Shop stewards are also employees of the organisation and as such must perform their normal job. It should be noted that the Code of Practice (under the Industrial Relations Act 1990), issued in 1993 in respect of employee representatives, states that such representatives should be afforded 'reasonable' time off to perform their representative duties. Equally, trade union representatives are charged with representing their members in a fair and equitable manner. It has become custom and practice in a number of organisations for shop stewards to be given time off to perform their union role and have access to requisite facilities, e.g. secretarial and telephone. However, these are often minimal and it is extremely rare for shop stewards to be given substantial leave to perform their union duties. This may be because the small scale of most Irish organisations does not facilitate such resources being afforded to shop stewards.

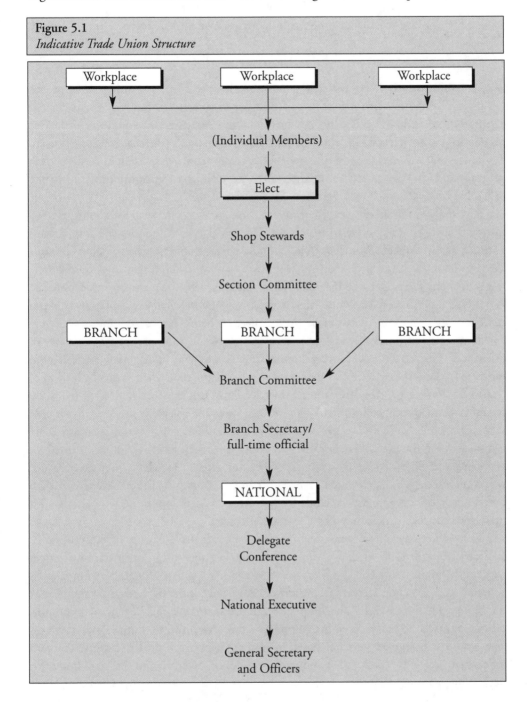

Figure 5.1
Indicative Trade Union Structure

In the context of the operation of trade unions, the shop steward performs a number of important tasks. These include:

- recruiting new members into the union;
- collecting union subscriptions from members in the absence of automatic 'check-off' arrangements;
- negotiating with management representatives on behalf of members;
- acting as a channel of communication between members and the union central office; and
- defending and advancing the interests of members.

The number of shop stewards grew considerably from the mid-1960s to the 1980s. This growth is probably due to a number of factors, particularly the increased acceptance of shop stewards by management; the increase in plant-level collective bargaining; the increase in employment legislation and consequent attention to 'policing' employee rights in the workplace; and the heavy demands on union officials and the associated reluctance of some unions to appoint more full-time officials.

It is suggested that the vast majority of shop stewards may spend about an hour during the working day on their union activities, paid by their employers, and perhaps as much again, unpaid. Research suggests that a considerable number of shop stewards take on the job because they feel they would be good at it, think it is important or feel it would help them 'get on' (Marsh 1973; Salamon 1987). A considerable number, however, are persuaded into it and undertake it reluctantly. Wallace (1982: 200) found the chief reason for this was the nature of the job, being seen as thankless and time consuming. Sometimes managers may perceive shop stewards as the source of grievances. However, the Donovan Commission found that managers who dealt with industrial relations saw them 'as being more a lubricant than an irritant' in industrial relations. Wallace (1982: 201) found that sixty-five per cent of managers felt shop stewards' contribution to industrial relations was positive, as against only eight per cent who saw them as making a negative contribution. The role of stewards is to articulate grievances felt by members. Because of their role, they may be more attuned to problems and likewise they may 'squash' or filter grievances which they feel are not worth progressing. Shop stewards have a difficult situation in that they have to maintain the support of their members while at the same time maintaining a position with management from which they can negotiate effectively.

The section committee is normally comprised of an elected group of shop stewards. It allows stewards representing various sections/groupings in the organisation to meet regularly, discuss common problems and decide on policy. Such a committee is generally called a shop stewards' committee. All of the shop stewards are members of the same trade union and if the shop stewards are members of different trade unions, the committee is called a joint shop stewards committee. Joint shop stewards committees can regulate conflict between unions, support and, if necessary, sanction individual stewards. They also constitute a more powerful and unified body for negotiating with management.

Branch Level

The branch is the fundamental element of trade union organisation and provides the means by which the ordinary 'rank and file' can participate directly in the affairs of the union (Salamon 1998; McPartlin 1997). The branch comprises a group of trade union members. Sometimes all the members of a branch work in one large organisation, but, as is more often the case in Ireland, a branch is made up of people from different organisations who work in a particular geographical area. Figure 5.1 above indicates how individual trade union members and their elected representatives are grouped together into a trade union branch. The union branch carries out two important functions:

- it manages the internal affairs of the union; and
- it strives for improvements of the terms and conditions of employment for branch members.

The branch is thus the basic unit of trade union organisation and is usually divided into several broad sections according to the grade or type of worker. McPartlin (1997: 82) suggests 'the branch plays a pivotal role in internal union affairs, as a channel of communication, disseminating policy and instructions downward and the views of the membership upwards'.

The branch decides policy at ordinary general meetings and at the branch annual general meeting (AGM). A branch committee manages the affairs of the branch, which normally operates on a part-time basis. This committee is elected or appointed at the AGM and also elects delegates to attend the union's annual delegate conference. The branch committee and all branch members are serviced by a branch secretary. In larger unions, the branch secretary will have assistance and they are all permanent employees of the union. If this is the case, then they are known as full-time branch officials whose primary functions are the administration of branch affairs and the negotiation of terms and conditions for all branch members with management representatives.

National Level

The election of union officers takes place at the annual or biannual delegate conference. Motions concerning the union and its policies are also discussed and voted upon. The motions are usually branch resolutions and a motion that is approved at the annual delegate conference (ADC) becomes a resolution of the conference and thus the union's policy. As illustrated in Figure 5.1, the ADC is comprised of branch delegates, the union's National Executive Council (NEC) and the union's General Council. As well as forming resolutions, a second function of the ADC is to Act as a controlling body to which the NEC and the general officers of the union are accountable. The delegate conference represents the lay membership of the union (McPartlin 1997: 82).

The National Executive Council is responsible for carrying out the decisions of the ADC. In particular, it appoints the union's full-time branch officials and appoints staff employed by the union. The general officers of a union are usually full-time employees of the union and they do not have another job. In some unions, they are appointed to their position by the National Executive Council, and in others they are elected at the delegate conference or by a ballot of union members. The general officers usually consist of a general president, a general secretary, a general vice-president and a general treasurer.

IRISH CONGRESS OF TRADE UNIONS (ICTU)

The Irish Congress of Trade Unions (ICTU) is the central co-ordinating body for the Irish trade union movement. Roche and Ashmore (2001) estimate that in the mid-1990s ninety-seven per cent of trade unionists were in membership of unions affiliated to Congress. The role of the ICTU is aptly summarised in a 1996 Incomes Data Services/Institute of Personnel and Development (IDS/IPD) publication as follows:

> the function of the ICTU is to 'represent the collective will and purpose of the Irish trade union movement'. Its main task is to co-ordinate trade union activity by representing unions in national collective bargaining, overseeing inter-union relations, representing the unions on various national agencies and to Act as the voice of the trade union movement internationally through membership of the European Trade Union Confederation and involvement in the work of other international institutions (IDS/IPD 1996: 162).

While the Congress Acts as a representative of the collective interests of the Irish trade union movement, individual unions retain a large degree of autonomy and the ICTU relies on the co-operation of affiliated unions in promoting its overall goals.

The Irish Congress of Trade Unions was established in 1959 as a result of a merger between the Irish Trade Union Congress (ITUC) and the Congress of Irish Unions (CIU). This merger served to heal a longstanding rift in the Irish union movement, which was partially related to personality differences but also embraced ideological differences between Irish and British-based unions (see IDS/IPD 1996). The CIU had primarily represented some ten Irish-based unions, notably the ITGWU, while the ITUC, which was founded in 1894, was composed of the remaining Irish and British-based unions (see McPartlin 1997). In 1958, the year prior to the merger, the CIU had unions with 188,969 affiliated members, while the figure for the ITUC was 226,333 (McCarthy 1977).

The ICTU is an all-Ireland body with the presidency and vice-presidency alternating in two-year terms between officials from the Republic and from Northern Ireland. The main governing authority of the ICTU lies in the biannual delegate conference, which establishes overall policy. Special delegate conferences are held to vote on the ratification of national agreements. The ICTU executive is responsible for policy execution as well as general administration. Ultimate decision-making power within the Congress is vested in the delegate conference. Here, delegates from affiliated unions consider various resolutions presented by union delegates and those adopted become ICTU policy. Both trade unions and trades councils (see below) are allowed to send delegates to these conferences and to vote on motions. Voting rights are based on membership size so that, for example, larger trade unions have greater voting rights than smaller unions. The ICTU Executive Council is elected at the delegate conference and is responsible for policy execution as well as general administration and management. The General Purposes Committee has responsibility for dealing with urgent matters between Executive Council meetings, while a system of subcommittees is used to deal with a range of particular issues, as discussed below.

The ICTU plays a particularly important role at national level, representing and articulating union views to government and other institutions. The ICTU role is particularly significant in centralised pay negotiations. Along with the other social partners (government, employer and farming representatives and representatives of the voluntary sector), it is party to national negotiations on pay and other aspects of social and economic policy. It is the vehicle through which trade unions decide on participation in centralised pay bargaining, approve any agreement thus concluded and ensure affiliated unions adhere to the terms of such agreements. The ICTU also represents trade unions on several national bodies and provides union nominees for conciliation and arbitration services.

Various committees operate under the auspices of the ICTU. As noted above, the General Purposes Committee deals with urgent business between Executive Council meetings. Other key committees include the Disputes Committee, the Industrial Relations Committee and the Demarcation Committee. The *Disputes Committee* deals with inter-union disputes, most of which tend to revolve around jurisdiction over membership (see McPartlin 1997). Much of this work concerns interpretation of Rule 47 of the ICTU Constitution, which regulates procedures for the transfer of members between unions. The *Demarcation Committee* deals with inter-union disputes in relation to the demarcation of work. Such disputes normally concern issues such as work boundaries and job content, e.g. disputes between different craft unions or between a craft union and a general union as to whose members should carry out certain tasks. The *Industrial Relations Committee* has the particularly important responsibility of dealing with applications for an 'all-out' picket in disputes. Such a picket obliges all union members employed in the organisation in dispute not to pass the picket. This does not impact on the right of an individual union to engage in strike activity and place a picket which requires its own members to obey, i.e. a single-union picket. A trade union requesting an all-out picket must apply to the Industrial Relations Committee, which must then meet with the striking union, other consenting and/or objecting unions and any other union which establishes its right to be consulted because of its members' involvement.

TRADES COUNCILS

These are voluntary groupings of unions on a regional or local basis. They are made up of officials and members of local unions who meet regularly to consider matters of common interest. They can be influential in determining union policy and are sometimes perceived to relate more closely to membership needs than the Congress.

Trades councils became particularly active in relation to certain political issues and were very much to the fore in the PAYE protests of the early 1980s. In 2002 there were some thirty-two trades councils affiliated to the ICTU.

In the remaining sections we consider patterns of trade union membership in Ireland, paying particular attention to changing membership trends and developments in the area of trade union recognition.

British and Irish Unions

A unique characteristic of Irish trade union structure is the fact that a number of British-based unions operate in the Republic of Ireland. Figures from ICTU suggest that there are approximately fifteen British-based unions operating in the Republic of Ireland. Roche and Ashmore (2001) estimate that in 1995 British-based unions accounted for almost twelve per cent of total trade union membership in Ireland. These include major unions, such as the Amalgamated Transport and General Workers Union (ATGWU) and the MSF (now AMICUS/MSF). Because trade unions rely primarily on current income from membership subscriptions, these unions are often in a strong financial position to service their Irish membership. On the other hand, major policy decisions in such unions are often taken in the UK and there has been some debate on the priority accorded to the concerns of the Irish membership in such decisions. Roche and Larragy (1989a) note the declining trend in the share of union members catered for by British unions, but attribute this to changes in the structural composition of the workforce rather than any factors deriving from their national base.

Trade Union Democracy

A common criticism of trade unions is that they fail to exercise adequate control over their membership or that militant minorities exercise undue influence over union affairs. These criticisms often refer to situations where it is alleged that a particular group of trade union members pursue a course of action that is at odds with the wishes of either the majority of the membership or the union officialdom. An implication of this line of thought is that unions can exert a type of autocratic control over the membership. This interpretation fails to appreciate the internal structure and operation of trade unions within our voluntary tradition. The very existence of trade unions is centred on meeting the needs of the membership. If they fail to do this, then their very *raison d'être* diminishes. Trade union discipline and control is based on a moral set of acceptable practices and the union hierarchy will be keen to ensure these are upheld through persuasion rather than compulsion in order to retain membership confidence (Brannick and Kelly 1987).

While it is true that unions do have power to decide on issues, it seems that control works in both directions (Marchington 1982). A union can exert a certain degree of control over their members in deciding on an appropriate line of action and it also has a disciplinary role in certain circumstances. However, the membership also has the right to decide on policy and they can exert control over the union to get it to serve the needs as perceived by that membership, e.g. by withholding subscriptions or threatening to join another union. In a multi-union environment, and with falling union density, trade unions must be very circumspect to meeting those needs lest it experience an exodus of membership.

TRADE UNION MEMBERSHIP IN IRELAND

In the previous sections we reviewed the nature, objectives, structure and government of trade unions. Clearly, such factors play a key role in influencing the extent to which workers join and remain in membership of trade unions. In this section we focus on the issue of trade union membership. We review in greater detail the pattern of trade union membership, with considerable emphasis on developments at the level of the enterprise, particularly regarding trade union recognition and influence.

As noted in the introduction to this chapter, the most widely used indicator of trade union penetration in a country is union density. The two commonly used measures of union density are:

- **Workforce density**: The percentage of the total civilian workforce, i.e. including those employed and those seeking employment, who are trade union members.
- **Employment density**: The percentage of civilian employees who are trade union members.

Employment density will always be greater than workforce density due to the fact that many unemployed members do not retain their membership in Ireland when they become unemployed.

The Republic of Ireland is characterised by relatively high, but falling, levels of trade union density. Employment density reached record levels in 1980 at sixty-two per cent but has since fallen, with the most dramatic decreases occurring since 1995. Table 5.2 illustrates that by 1990 employment density had dropped to fifty-seven per cent. Workforce density showed a steeper decline, from fifty-five per cent in 1980 to forty-five per cent in 1990.

As noted earlier, the decline in union density in the 1980s is principally attributed to macroeconomic factors, particularly economic depression, increased unemployment and changes in employment structure involving decline/stagnation of employment in traditionally highly unionised sectors and growth in sectors which have traditionally posed difficulties for union penetration (see Roche 1992a, 1994b, 1997a; Roche and Ashmore 2001). In addition to these factors, it is also likely that developments at enterprise level have also contributed to this decline, most notably changes in management approaches to industrial relations. Of particular significance in this respect was the growth in union avoidance strategies on the part of employers and the increased adoption of so-called 'individualist' human resource management (HRM) practices (see Beaumont 1995a; Gunnigle 1995a, 1995b; Gunnigle et al. 1997a; McGovern 1989b). This issue is discussed in greater depth in Chapters 14 and 15.

Table 5.2
Trade Union Membership and Density, 1925 –2003

Year	Membership	Employment Density (%)	Workforce Density (%)
1925	123,000	21.2	18.7
1930	99,450	20.0	20.0
1935	130,230	22.6	18.6
1940	151,630	26.2	23.0
1945	172,340	27.7	25.3
1955	305,620	45.7	41.6
1965	358,050	52.4	48.8
1975	449,520	60.0	53.2
1980	527,960	62.0	55.3
1985	485,040	61.3	47.5
1990	474,590	57.1	45.0
1995	504,450	53.1	41.1
2000*	586,944	43.2	38.8
2001*	595,086	44.2	38.3
2002**	644,400	44.7	40.6
2003**	641,633	43.6	39.0

* Workforce equals number of civilian employees plus those on the live register.

**Membership figures for 2000–2003 from the Department of Enterprise, Trade and Employment.

Note: Employment density figures are derived using the latest CSO figures for employment for 2000-2004 and as such there are slight differences to earlier published figures.

Source: Figures for 1925–1999 are derived from the UCD DUES Data Series (see Roche 1992a, 1997a; Dobbins 2001a).

Looking at trends in union membership in the 1990s, we find an overall increase in union membership but a significant downward trend in union density. The data presented in Table 5.2 indicates that union membership rose from over 485,000 in 1985 to over 500,000 in 1995, and more recent data from the Department of Enterprise, Trade and Employment suggests that membership grew to over 640,000 by 2003. Despite probable differences in reporting protocols between both sources of data, the overall picture is one of an increase in membership, which appears to reflect the large numbers of people at work, particularly from the mid-1990s.

However, if we consider trends in union density, the picture is not so sanguine for trade unions. While aggregate union membership has increased, levels of trade union density have fallen substantially. Employment density in 2003 stood at forty-four per cent, representing a fall of approximately eighteen percentage points since 1980 and over thirteen percentage points since 1990 (reasons for growth and decline in trade union membership are discussed later in this chapter). It is important to note that figures for Irish trade union membership do not include the estimated 25,000 members of the Garda and Army representative associations. Clearly the inclusion of these figures would increase the levels of trade union density in Ireland. Neither do these figures include a number of organisations with 'excepted body' status granted under the terms of the 1941 Trade Union Act.

In comparison to other countries, we find that levels of union density in Ireland are relatively high. Table 5.3 illustrates that while trade union density in Ireland is much lower than a number of Scandinavian countries, a more encouraging picture emerges when Ireland is compared with many other countries. Ireland's trade union density compares favourably with a union density of twenty-nine per cent in the UK and is considerably higher than in the US, where employment density as a proportion of the non-agricultural workforce is approximately 13.5 per cent and confined to a small number of industrial sectors.

Table 5.3
International Employment Density, 2001 (percentage)

Australia (a)	35.0	Japan	20.7
Austria	39.8	Luxembourg	50.0
Belgium	69.2	Netherlands	27.0
Canada (b)	30.1	New Zealand	20.0
Denmark	87.5	Norway (c)	54.9
Finland	79.0	Portugal	30.0
France	9.1	Spain	15.0
Germany	29.7	Sweden	79.0
Greece	32.5	United Kingdom	29.0
Italy	35.4	United States	13.5

Note: (a) 1995 figure (b) 1999 figure (c) 1998 figure.

Source: Carley (2003); Finlayson (2000); Lismoen (2000); Wilson (2000)

Turning to the distribution of trade union membership by size of union, we find considerable imbalance, as illustrated in Table 5.4. What we find is a small group of quite large unions that cater for the great majority of Irish trade union members. The remaining unions are small in membership terms. Indeed, taking a longer-term perspective, we see a trend whereby a few larger unions have come to dominate union membership in Ireland.

Table 5.4
Trade Union Membership in Ireland by Size of Union, 2001

Number of Members	Number of Unions	Percentage of Total Membership
Less than 1,000	15	1.0
1,000–4,999	13	5.6
5,000–9,999	3	3.4
10,000–19,999	8	19.4
20,000 or over	7	70.6

Note: This table only refers to trade unions holding negotiating licences under the Trade Union Acts and excludes a number of other representative bodies that do not hold such a licence but operate as trade unions.

Source: Registrar of Friendly Societies

A common criticism of Irish trade union structure has been that there are too many unions relative to total membership. It has been suggested that this causes problems for management, who have to deal with a number of unions and also leads to inter-union rivalry and conflict as unions compete with each other for membership. At an aggregate level, Ireland does have a large number of unions dealing with a small membership (in 2001, some forty-six unions catered for a total membership of almost 600,000 – see Table 5.4). However, a closer examination of aggregate union membership statistics indicates that the vast majority of trade unionists are members of a small number of quite large trade unions, leaving a large number of small unions which cater for a very small proportion of total union membership (see Table 5.4). Rationalisation of trade union structure in Ireland has been high on the agenda of successive governments. In addition, the promotion of union mergers has long been a trade union objective. The 1939 Annual Delegate Congress of the ITUC adopted a policy of amalgamations as official policy and this was translated into the objectives of the ICTU when it was founded in 1959. The aggregate number of trade unions has declined dramatically, falling from over 100 unions at the turn of the 1960s to some forty-six unions at the latest count (see Table 5.5). The merger of the two largest trade unions in the country, the ITGWU and FWUI, in 1990 to form SIPTU was the most significant trade union merger in Ireland.

Rationalisation can, however, take place in a number of ways other than mergers: 'unions can cease to operate, can cancel their registration with the Registrar of Friendly Societies (cease to exist), can de-merge or new unions can be formed' (Wallace *et al.* 2002: 8). Table 5.6 sets out the rationalisation activity from 1977 to 1998, with perhaps two of the most notable features being the contribution of cancellations (forty-five in total) and the large number of new unions formed without merger activity (twenty-four) (Wallace *et al.* 2000). McPartlin (1997) notes a major increase in the number of union mergers from 1985 onwards. Roche (1994b) documents a significant size effect in the rationalisation activity. Smaller unions are in decline, with growth in trade union membership occurring mostly among these larger unions. This may be seen as a vindication of government policy to encourage the reduction of small unions, although Roche (1994b: 19) has emphasised financial reasons for rationalisation rather than any legislative incentives. Also, it is not possible to view these developments in purely national terms. Union rationalisation has been a feature of many countries, notably the UK and Germany, since the 1980s and as such would seem to be driven by the broader global challenges facing unions.

The merger that led to the formation of SIPTU in 1990 heralded a wave of negotiations by trade unions on possible mergers and amalgamations. For example, a recent merging of MSF and the AEEU resulted in the formation of the fourth-largest trade union in the Republic of Ireland, AMICUS, with approximately 30,000 members. Thus, the number of trade unions in the Republic has declined dramatically in recent years (see Table 5.5), leading McPartlin (1997: 95) to conclude that 'Irish trade unionism is no longer the fragmented and conflicted movement that has so often been criticised in the past'.

Table 5.5
Number of Trade Unions in Ireland, 1980–2001

Year	Number of Unions	Year	Number of Unions
1980	86	1996	56
1985	77	1997	55
1990	67	1998	47
1991	62	1999	46
1992	59	2000	46
1993	59	2001	46
1994	56	2002	46
1995	56	2003	46

Note: Figures presented here are based only on trade unions holding negotiating licences.

Source: Figures for 1980–1999 from Labour Relations Commission Annual Report 2000, figures for 2000–2001 from Department of Enterprise, Trade and Employment

Union mergers clearly facilitate some rationalisation in the trade union movement but may also be a source of discontent due to the potential loss of identity and influence of individual trade unions, particularly where a small union merges with a much larger one. In addition, as Clegg (1980) has argued, single union representation of the workforce does not eliminate problems or issues, as grievances now have to be resolved within the single union.

The ten largest trade unions in terms of membership are outlined in Table 5.7. These ten unions have a combined membership of some 479,208 and account for approximately eighty per cent of all trade union members. From this table we can also see that SIPTU, the largest union in the state, caters for thirty-eight per cent of total trade union membership.

Table 5.6
Composite Figures for Union Rationalisation, 1977–1998

Time Period	Transfers of Engagements	Amalgama-tions	Cancellations with Merger Activity	Cancellations without Merger Activity	New Unions Registered as a Result of Mergers	New Unions Registered without Merger Activity
1977–1998	18	8 (involving 17 unions)	35	10*	8	24*

* These figures are only for the years 1981–1998 due to unavailability of information.

Source: Registrar of Friendly Societies

Table 5.7
Large Trade Unions in Ireland, 2001

Name of Union	Membership
1 SIPTU – Services, Industrial, Professional and Technical Union	248,938
2 Irish Municipal, Public and Civil Trade Union	38,200
3 MANDATE – The Union of Retail, Bar and Administrative Workers	37,979
4 Technical Engineering and Electrical Union	30,396
5 Irish Nurses Organisation	27,501
6 Irish National Teachers Organisation	21,469
7 AMICUS – Manufacturing, Science and Finance Union	21,000
8 Amalgamated Transport and General Workers Union	19,881
9 Communications Workers Union	18,024
10 Association of Secondary Teachers, Ireland	15,820

Source: ICTU (2002); Registrar of Friendly Societies (2002)

TRADE UNION DENSITY AT ORGANISATION LEVEL

While national statistics provide us with an overall picture of trade union density, it is necessary to look at union membership levels at organisation level to gain insights into the operational role and impact of trade unions. The levels of trade union membership and the extent of trade union recognition are key indicators of the nature of enterprise-level industrial relations.

In examining levels of trade union density at organisation level (the number of employees in a given organisation who are trade union members), the Cranfield-University of Limerick Study (CUL) provides a useful source of information.[3] This study is based on a postal survey of human resource management and industrial relations practice in Ireland's largest organisations and currently has data from 1992, 1995 and 1999 (see Brewster and Hegewisch 1994; Gunnigle *et al.* 1994; Gunnigle *et al.* 1997c; Morley *et al.* 2001). In this study, respondents were asked to indicate the proportion of the workforce in their organisation which was in membership of a trade union. These findings are summarised in Figure 5.2. As we can see, the level of trade union density among the organisations surveyed was quite high: in the most recent

---

3   The Cranfield-University of Limerick (CUL) Study of Human Resource Management in Ireland forms part of the Cranfield Network (*Cranet*) on International HRM, first established in 1989 and currently involving twenty-six participating countries. The Irish node of this study is located at the Employment Relations Research Unit, University of Limerick and is directed by Michael Morley, Patrick Gunnigle and Tom Turner. For a summary of data emanating from the international study see Brewster, C. and Hegewisch, A. (1994), *Policy and Practice in European Human Resource Management: The Price Waterhouse Cranfield Survey,* London: Routledge. For review of the 1992 Irish data see Gunnigle, P., Flood, P., Morley, M. and Turner, T. (1994), *Continuity and Change in Irish Employee Relations,* Dublin: Oak Tree Press, and for the 1995 data see Gunnigle, P., Morley, M., Clifford, N. and Turner, T. (1997), *Human Resource Management in Irish Organisations: Practice in Perspective,* Dublin: Oak Tree Press. Information from the most recent survey (1999/2000) is available from the University of Limerick (see Morley *et al.* 2001).

survey (1999/2000) just over half of the respondent organisations reported that fifty-one per cent or more of their employees were union members. These findings indicate that levels of trade union density in Irish organisations are reasonably high and consistent with the aggregate national statistics discussed earlier. However, as we shall see below in our discussion on union recognition, newer organisations appear to have significantly lower levels of union density and many are opting for a non-union approach.

Figure 5.2
Proportion of Workforce Members of a Trade Union

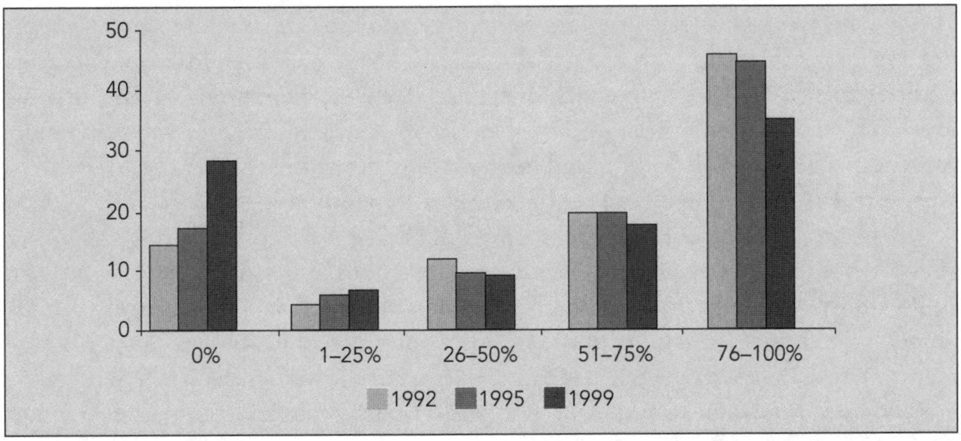

Source: Cranfield-University of Limerick (1992, 1995, 1999)

TRADE UNION RECOGNITION

A number of commentators have identified changes in the extent and nature of collective employee representation as a critical dimension of a shift in employer approaches to industrial relations (for example, see Kochan *et al.* 1986). Of particular significance in this regard is the trend in union recognition and the role of collective bargaining. Collectivism in industrial relations incorporates the extent to which management acknowledges employees' right to collective representation and the involvement of the collective in influencing management decision making (Purcell 1987; Gunnigle 1995b). Trade union recognition is a critical barometer of 'collectivism'. In Ireland, granting such recognition remains largely an issue of management prerogative. This is not to say that trade union action, or a decision of the Labour Court, may not convince employers to accede to union recognition, but rather to acknowledge the reality that currently the decision to concede recognition is largely an issue of management discretion.

Salamon (1998: 175) defines trade union recognition as 'the process by which management formally accepts one or more trade unions as the representative(s) of all, or a group, of its employees for the purpose of jointly determining terms and conditions of employment on a collective basis'. Salamon (1998: 175) goes on to suggest that trade union recognition is 'perhaps the most important stage in the development of an organisation's industrial relations system ... it confers legitimacy and determines the scope of the trade union's role'. By securing recognition, an employer acknowledges a trade union's right to represent and protect its members' interests in the workplace and to become jointly involved in regulating key aspects of the employment relationship. As Torrington and Hall (1991: 504) specifically comment, trade union recognition represents 'an almost irrevocable movement away from unilateral decision making by management'.

We have seen in Chapter 3 that in the Irish Constitution (1937) the state guarantees liberty for the exercise of the 'right of citizens to form associations or unions' but that this does not extend to a right to recognition or a right to negotiate. Historically, this lack of statutory provision in relation to trade union recognition was not a major problem in Irish industrial relations. Most medium and large employers traditionally recognised and concluded collective agreements with trade unions. However, trade union recognition has more recently become an extremely contentious issue, which is addressed below. Before doing this, however, it is useful to look at recent research evidence on trade union recognition in Ireland.

If we first look at evidence from the CUL study, we find a relatively high, but falling, percentage of companies recognising trade unions in Ireland. As we can see from Table 5.8, sixty-nine per cent of the organisations surveyed in 1999 recognised trade unions for collective bargaining purposes. This represented a fall of over ten percentage points since 1995, when eighty per cent of organisations recognised trade unions. As was the case in relation to union density, these findings illustrate an overall trend of relatively high, but falling, levels of trade union penetration.

Table 5.8
Trade Union Recognition, 1992–1999

Trade Union Recognition	1992	1995	1999
Yes	83% (186)	80% (205)	69.2% (296)
No	17% (38)	20% (50)	30.8% (132)

Note: Actual numbers in parentheses.

Source: Cranfield-University of Limerick (1992, 1995, 1999)

However, it should be noted that the CUL study draws on data from Ireland's largest organisations. Trade unions have clearly been successful in securing recognition in such organisations. However, the picture is not quite so positive when we look at more recently established firms. It is widely accepted that trade union penetration tends to be strongest in the public service and 'traditional' manufacturing (see Roche 1997a; Wallace 2003). Therefore, it is useful to look outside these sectors for a further indicator of the changing role of trade unions. The next section therefore considers empirical findings on industrial relations in newly established firms. The greenfield site study consisted of two phases: phase one covered fifty-three firms over the period 1987 to 1992 and the second phase covered twenty-three firms over the period 1992 to 1997 (see Gunnigle 1995a, 1995b; Gunnigle *et al.* 1997b; Gunnigle *et al.* 2001).

UNION RECOGNITION IN 'NEWER' ORGANISATIONS

Information on the industrial relations strategies and practices of 'greenfield' companies is a useful barometer of change in industrial relations and particularly trade union penetration. Greenfield companies are less constrained by established practice and thus possess greater scope to choose what they feel are 'appropriate' industrial relations approaches and to establish polices and practices which will develop and reinforce their chosen approach. It is therefore reasonable to suggest that if approaches to industrial relations are changing, the evidence of such change should be most evident in greenfield sites.

The study on greenfield site companies found a high incidence of non-unionism, with over sixty-five per cent of these new firms not recognising trade unions (as opposed to approximately thirty-one per cent in the CUL study). Examining the data by phase of study, we find a trend of increasing union avoidance. In the period 1987 to 1992, fifty-three per cent of firms were non-union while in the period 1992 to 1997, the corresponding figure was ninety-one per cent.

Further differences are evident between the two phases. For the period 1987 to 1992, non-unionism was predominantly confined to US-owned firms in 'high technology sectors'. No US-owned firm operating in a 'high technology' sector recognised trade unions, while most Irish and European companies recognised trade unions. However, data from the period 1992 to 1997 suggests that union avoidance pervades all greenfield companies and is not just confined to those of US origin (Gunnigle *et al.* 2001). These findings confirm evidence from an earlier study by Hourihan (1996) on union recognition trends among overseas firms. In a period when foreign direct investment in Ireland was at an all-time high, it is clear that these new companies have overwhelmingly chosen the non-union route.

FACTORS IMPACTING ON TRADE UNION DENSITY AND RECOGNITION

A number of variables have been advanced to account for variations in union membership and recognition between organisations (see Bain and Price 1983; Hirsch and Berger 1984). Turner *et al.* (1994) suggests that, in general, the factors they found to be determinants of inter-establishment variations in the level of union membership are similar to those that account for the presence, or absence, of union recognition in an organisation. Green (1991) distinguishes between the supply of an available union to each workplace and the demand for a union by workers. The presence of a union at a workplace acts as a 'gateway' enabling workers to become union members. On the supply side, the structural factors associated with the job itself determine whether there is a recognised union available, and on the demand side, individual characteristics also determine whether an employee joins an available union. His analysis pointed to the importance of such structural factors as industry, sector, occupation, firm size, gender and proportion of part-time workers in determining union status (Green 1991; Beaumont and Harris 1991). Roche (1997a) encapsulates these influences by identifying three sets of factors that impact on employee decisions on joining and remaining in membership of a trade union, namely cyclical, institutional and structural factors, as outlined in Table 5.9.

Cyclical factors relate to the general business cycle. For example, it might be expected that people will be less inclined to join trade unions when the economy is in recession and unemployment is high. Roche and Larragy (1989b) further argue that union membership will be positively associated with growth in wage levels ('credit effect') and the level of inflation ('threat effect').

Table 5.9
Influences on Trade Union Growth and Decline

Type of Influence	Examples	Nature of Effect on Union Growth
Cyclical	Rate of change in wages, prices, employees at work, unemployment, profits and productivity	Short-run change
Institutional	Legislative initiatives; changes in bargaining levels; political composition of governments; employer ideologies/ strategies	May accelerate or retard growth during particular periods (shorter term) or on a long-term basis
Structural	Changing sectoral/occupational/gender composition of workforce; level of employment concentration; general social attitudes towards trade unionism	Incremental and long-term effects

Source: Roche (1997a)

Institutional factors relate to the impact of various institutions (such as trade unions) on industrial relations. Key issues here include the role of government in regulating the operation of labour markets and industrial relations interactions through, for example, legislation (see Chapter 3) and the operation of specific industrial relations agencies/institutions, such as the Labour Court and the LRC. An issue of special importance is government approaches to trade unions, particularly trade union recognition. Clearly, such a factor can act as a spur or an impediment to trade union growth. Another important institutional influence is the nature and level of collective bargaining. Since the mid-1980s we have seen the development of broad-ranging centralised agreements between the 'social partners'. The model clearly facilitates a high level of union influence on major economic and social policy decisions. However, they may also result in the senior echelons of the union hierarchy being perceived as remote and out of touch by the 'grass roots' membership.

Structural factors relate to the changes in the structural composition and distribution of the workforce as well as to broader social divisions in society at large (see Roche 1997a: 45). Internationally, union membership tends to be higher in the public than the private sector. Within the private sector, certain industries or industrial segments have proved more receptive to union penetration than others. For example, traditional manufacturing sectors in Ireland, such as the food and drink sector, have much higher levels of unionisation than the computer/electronics sector, an area where unions have encountered severe difficulties in achieving membership and recognition. Employment category, gender and the nature of employment contracts are also influential. Blue-collar workers were traditionally more receptive to union membership than white-collar workers. Permanent employees are more likely to join than part-time or temporary workers. In addition, there was a higher level of union membership among men, although this may have been due to the types of jobs in which they worked, and some forty per cent of SIPTU members now are women. Some recent research evidence on the impact of these various factors on union membership, with particular focus on Ireland, is considered below.

Looking at the broader international literature we find that size, sector, industry and the proportion of white-collar, part-time and female workers have all figured prominently as significant explanatory variables in empirical studies on union penetration (Bain and Price 1983; Bain and Elsheikh 1979; Booth 1986; Deery and Cieri 1991). Variations in union membership levels are associated with shifts in the gender, occupational and industrial composition of potential union membership (particularly shifts in employment in the public/private and manufacturing/services sectors) and changes in industrial structure, such as employment concentration, single or multi-establishment status, product markets and capital intensity.

It has been suggested that *single independent establishments* are more likely to have a negative impact on unionisation than establishments that are owned or controlled by a large corporation (Bain and Elsheikh 1980). It is argued that a single establishment is more likely to relate to its employees in a paternalistic manner in how terms and conditions of employment are determined and in a personal and informal way, rather than by formal rules applied impersonally to all – an approach which may facilitate collective organisation. It has also been suggested that unionisation is affected by the *nature of the market* in which the product or service of the establishment is sold or delivered (Bain and Elsheikh 1979). In this regard, it is argued that union penetration is less likely among firms that operate in highly competitive product markets.

Turning specifically to the Irish context, Turner *et al.* (1994) found that the level of unionisation was positively related to establishment size (number of employees). Namely, larger organisations are more likely to recognise trade unions and tend to have a greater proportion of their workers in union membership. As the authors point out, this finding is consistently supported by most of the empirical research on the determinants of unionisation.

Evidence from the 1999 CUL study shows a strong sectoral impact. Here we find that the level of union density is highest in the public sector. Eight in ten public sector companies had union membership levels of between seventy-six to one hundred per cent, while the equivalent private sector level was two in ten. Hourihan (1996) estimated a union density in the public service of approximately eighty per cent but only around thirty-six per cent in the private sector. Wallace (2003) places the private sector density in 2003 at under thirty per cent (see also Sheehan 2003b). This decline indicates the scale of the challenge facing trade unions in private sector employment.

Within the private sector there are considerable variations, as noted by Turner *et al.* (1994). Their analysis identified three particular industrial sectors which were positively related to union density: 'traditional' manufacturing had the strongest effect, while the 'transport and communications' and 'banking' sectors were also positively associated with union penetration. Transport and communications is traditionally a highly unionised sector, while banking in the Republic of Ireland is also highly unionised, with the employees in the four largest banks covered by a single trade union, the IBOA. However, there was a significant decline in density following an unsuccessful bank strike in 1992.

A factor considered particularly influential in explaining variations in trade union membership is *country of ownership* (Beaumont 1985; Gunnigle 1995b). In particular, US-owned companies in the electronics industry are reputed to pursue an active strategy of union avoidance or union marginalisation through the use of human resource management (HRM) practices, such as individual employment contracts, direct employee communication and the prompt handling of grievances (Gunnigle 1995a, 1995b). The CUL study found that country of ownership had a significant impact on the proportion of an organisation's workforce that were trade union members. Irish and other European-owned organisations tend to have the highest levels of union membership, while US-owned organisations tended to have significantly lower levels of union recognition and density.

On the issue of trade union recognition, the CUL study also found a significant variation between different organisations. US-owned organisations were less likely to recognise trade unions: forty-nine per cent of US-owned organisations recognised trade unions while the corresponding figure for Irish and other foreign-owned organisations was seventy-five per cent and eighty per cent, respectively. We have seen earlier that recent studies of newly established firms in the manufacturing and internationally traded services sectors point to an even higher incidence of non-union approaches by US-owned firms (Gunnigle 1995a, 1995b; Hourihan 1996). Country of ownership is widely used as a proxy measure of the impact of managerial values on variations in the extent of trade union recognition. This approach is based on the assumption that decisions on trade union recognition will closely reflect underlying managerial values associated with country of ownership (Poole 1986; Guest and Rosenthal 1992). These findings bear out the suggestion that US-owned organisations are more likely to pursue a strategy of union avoidance (see also Beaumont 1985; Kochan *et al.* 1986).

In concluding our analysis of patterns of trade union density and recognition in Ireland, we can see that levels of union density appear relatively high when compared to levels internationally, but longitudinal data from some domestic sources illustrates recent difficulties faced by trade unions. The trend of falling union density since the early 1980s continued through the 1990s, even when the latter period was characterised by high employment (see Wallace 2003). Evidence from larger organisations over the period 1992 to 1999 illustrates the growth in the number of companies not recognising unions. This finding is supplemented by greenfield site data, which illustrates growing union avoidance across greenfield companies and not just limited to US-owned high-tech companies, though they do predominate in not recognising unions. This issue is considered further in subsequent chapters and in our consideration of recent developments in the area of union recognition, discussed later.

TRADE UNION INFLUENCE AND THE NATURE OF MANAGEMENT-UNION RELATIONS

While analyses of trade union density and recognition are relatively straightforward and objective, assessing trade union influence is an altogether more complex task. First, and unlike 'hard' measures such as membership and recognition, influence is largely perceptual. Second, influence can differ depending on the nature and type of influence that is being talked about. For example, it is generally accepted that the existence of centralised agreements on pay and related matters since 1987 has greatly facilitated high levels of union influence on national affairs, particularly in areas of economic and social policy. In attempting to more accurately assess union influence at enterprise level, trade union recognition and density are useful proxies for union influence, and that points to a decline in union representativeness. However, we have also noted that union penetration in Ireland remains comparatively high by international standards.

Alongside the 'hard' indicators of trade union penetration, the CUL study explored management perceptions of the changing influence of trade unions. Respondents were asked to indicate whether they felt the influence of trade unions had increased, decreased or remained stable in their organisation over 'the past three years'. The results are summarised in Figure 5.3 and provide some interesting insights on perceptions of union influence. Using the most recent data (1999/2000), we find that six in ten respondent organisations reported that trade union influence in their firm has remained stable in the recent past. Looking only at those organisations where respondents reported a change in union influence, we see slightly more organisations report a decrease than an increase in union influence.

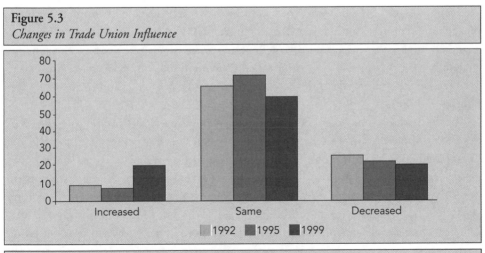

Figure 5.3
Changes in Trade Union Influence

Source: Cranfield-University of Limerick Study (1992, 1995, 1999)

CURRENT ISSUES AFFECTING TRADE UNIONS: THE DEBATE ON UNION RECOGNITION

A particular issue in the context of changing patterns of industrial relations concerns trade union recognition and the future role of collective bargaining. We have already seen that the 1980s and 1990s witnessed a serious decline in trade union density. In the 1980s, the decline was principally attributed to macroeconomic factors, notably economic depression and increased levels of unemployment. However, union density continued to decline during the period of exceptional economic prosperity and low unemployment that has existed from the mid-1990s to 2004. Thus, we must look at the evidence that is available regarding increased employer opposition to union recognition. Our earlier analyses of trends in trade union density and recognition have highlighted these developments, which are considered further in Chapters 14 and 15.

The decline in trade union penetration in new firms, particularly in 'high technology' sectors, is clearly an issue of concern for trade unions. Indeed, the Irish trade union movement, principally through the Irish Congress of Trade Unions (ICTU), has been to the fore in evaluating means of increasing union influence, legitimacy and representativeness at both enterprise and national level (see ICTU 1993, 1995; Beaumont 1995a; Sparrow and Hiltrop 1994). A critical part of this strategy involved raising the issue of union recognition in discussions on centralised agreements. Under the terms of Partnership 2000, it was agreed that a 'High Level Group' be established to consider the issue of trade union recognition disputes. This working group comprised a broad membership representative of government departments, the ICTU, Irish Business and Employers Confederation (IBEC) and IDA Ireland.

In evaluating the extent of union avoidance, the High Level Group's report identified two major areas where non-recognition of unions was particularly evident: small indigenous firms and the multinational sector. In the multinational sector, the report noted that non-union approaches are common among US-owned firms and are generally associated with the adoption of well-developed human resource management policies and systems. The report further suggested that because of the 'generally high value-added nature of the enterprises concerned' and the presence of 'generally good' terms and conditions of employment, employees in this sector do not usually seek to join trade unions to protect or advance their interests (quoted in Sheehan 1998c).

In the Irish context, there is contradictory evidence on this point. Toner's (1987) findings in the electronics sector pointed to the presence of good terms and conditions of employment among the non-union firms studied (see also Flood and Toner 1997). However, Gunnigle's (1995a and 1995b) study of greenfield firms does not support the thesis that non-union firms provide pay and benefits that are above either the regional or sectoral norms, or better than those provided by similar unionised firms.

The High Level Group submitted its final report in 1999, which resulted in the introduction of the Code of Practice on Voluntary Dispute Resolution and the Industrial Relations (Amendment) Act 2001 (see Figure 5.5). The general idea of the Code of Practice is that disputes in relation to union recognition should be dealt with within the context of the current system of voluntary collective bargaining. This means that disputes in relation to union recognition should be processed through a series of steps, involving the Labour Relations Commission and its Advisory Service, the use of a 'cooling off' period for intractable disputes and, ultimately, for a recommendation on the case by the Labour Court.

The Industrial Relations (Amendment) Act 2001 sidestepped the issue of recognition and provided a set of procedures to allow unions to seek to have pay, terms of conditions of employment and dispute resolution and disciplinary procedures addressed (D'Art 2002: 33). The provisions of the 2001 Act are used as a 'fallback' measure whereby a union or excepted body may request a further investigation by the Labour Court, which can issue a recommendation.

Should the dispute remain unresolved, the Labour Court has the power to issue a legally binding determination on pay and terms of employment for one year by making an employment regulation order (ERO) – it could not, however, grant union recognition (see Wallace 2003: 10). Should the dispute still remain unresolved after this time, the Labour Court may vacate, affirm or vary its determination. The Code of Practice and the Act explicitly exclude decisions to be made on 'arrangements for collective bargaining'. Rather, only disputes relating to pay and conditions, dispute resolution and disciplinary procedures may be processed.

From a trade union perspective, a critical element of the new arrangements is the lack of support for any mandatory system through which union recognition would be required of employers. The High Level Group clearly opposed this approach, apparently on the grounds of its incongruity with Ireland's tradition of voluntary collective bargaining: 'a requirement for mandatory trade union recognition would represent a shift from the current largely voluntary system of industrial relations which has demonstrated a capacity to adapt to changing circumstances and which is generally seen as very valuable' (quoted in Sheehan 1998c).

Looking at the broader context within which the new procedures were formulated, a number of issues should be borne in mind. Of primary significance is the fact that much of Ireland's economic growth since the 1980s has been fuelled by the multinational sector, a substantial proportion of which are non-union firms. In seeking to attract more foreign direct investment and encourage firms already here to increase investment, governments are acutely aware that imposition of mandatory union recognition mechanisms would act as a severe disincentive to such investment. D'Art and Turner (2002b), however, argue that the evidence from Scandinavian countries is that US companies are prepared to deal with unions when they are required to by law. IDA Ireland, as members of the High Level Group, would likely have articulated the implications of mandatory union recognition as a significant disadvantage in their efforts in selling Ireland as a site for foreign direct investment. From the employers' perspective, it is also likely that they sought to ensure that the report did not recommend approaches that would have a negative impact on multinational investment, such as any legally binding system of dealing with trade union recognition. Indeed, from an employer perspective, it was suggested that the new arrangements may represent a considerable improvement on the pre-existing situation, since they recommend that both parties become 'locked' into voluntary procedures until a Labour Court recommendation is issued (Sheehan 1998d).

Early assessments of the procedures have highlighted their weaknesses in regard to advancing the interests of unions in achieving greater recognition. The Code of Practice and the Act have been criticised for the absence of a statutory recognition provision, for a lack of time limits on the steps outlined and for the absence of a provision providing protection for trade union activists (see Gunnigle *et al.* 2002b; D'Art and Turner 2002b). The ICTU itself has recognised such obstacles for unions. In 2002 it established a Working Group, whose terms of reference included reviewing the operation of the new arrangements.

In its report, the Working Group concluded that the Code of Practice 'has completely failed to achieve its aim of voluntarily resolving disputes about union recognition' (*Industrial Relations News* 2002: 25). It also noted the low number of cases (two) that had been the subject of a Labour Court recommendation under the Industrial Relations (Amendment) Act since it came into effect. While the group did not recommend the repeal of the Act, it did recommend that the ICTU seek the introduction of new or amended legislation which would oblige employers to allow employees to be represented, if enough workers so requested (*Industrial Relations News* 2002). This suggests that the group did not consider the Act to have significantly aided the position of trade unions at increasing recognition. Indeed, D'Art and Turner (2002b: 21) go further in their examination of the Act by concluding that 'as an instrument or mechanism supporting the efforts of union members to gain recognition in non-union firms, the Industrial Relations Act may be at best ineffective or at worst damaging for unions'.

D'Art and Turner (2002b) have favoured mandatory legislative provisions, pointing to the early relative success of UK unions under the mandatory recognition provisions of the Employment Relations Act 1999. This provides for a voluntary recognition process with strict time limits and, failing agreement, a procedure to allow for a trade union to apply for compulsory recognition to the Conciliation and Arbitration Committee (CAC). This latter provision may lead to a ballot, where a vote in favour of recognition within a bargaining unit is required to gain recognition (see Wood and Moor 2002).

Wallace (2003), on the other hand, has pointed to difficulties with a mandatory union provision, based on experience in the US, and has suggested it may be good for neither employers nor trade unions. He has argued that it is unlikely that it would allow unions to address either of the two reasons behind the decline in trade unions density, which he identifies as the opposition by US companies and the expansion of the services sector, which has traditionally had lower unionisation rates. He suggests a preferred option for legislation could be the Scandinavian one. In this context Wallace (2003: 11) notes there is in essence 'a right to trade union recognition and representation rights as a matter of course – even where this is at the demand of only a small minority of employees. This approach would complement the right to join and form unions incorporated in Article 40.1.6(iii) of the 1937 Irish Constitution'.

Given the apparent dissatisfaction of trade unions, as expressed by ICTU's Working

Group, with the Code of Practice and 2001 Act, it was agreed by the social partners, under Sustaining Progress, that changes would be made to the legislation (see Sheehan 2003a; 2003c). The more prominent elements of the proposed amendments as contained in the subsequent Industrial Relations (Amendment) Bill 2003 are the following:

- An amended Code of Practice on Voluntary Dispute Resolution, with a time limit on the dispute resolution process of twenty-six weeks, up to a maximum of thirty-four weeks where necessary, to the point of issuance of a binding determination by the Labour Court.
- The Labour Court will be empowered to investigate cases where the timeframes set out in the amended Code have been breached or exhausted.
- A new Code of Practice on Victimisation that will define victimisation and victimisation practices in the context of a trade union recognition dispute.
- Complaints of victimisation from an employee or a trade union may be heard by a Rights Commissioner (Sheehan 2003e).

It remains to be seen whether these proposed changes will be finalised and if they will be sufficient to counter the highlighted inadequacies of the current arrangements and assist unions in their objective to increase union recognition.

CHAPTER 6

Employer Associations

INTRODUCTION

As with worker organisations, employers are also likely to combine for purposes associated with employment and labour matters (Smith 1970). This chapter considers the role of employer associations in Irish industrial relations. In particular, we examine the operation and structure of employer associations, the legal definition of employer associations in Ireland, employer association membership and the range of services provided by such associations. However, we begin by considering employers' objectives in industrial relations, which crystallises the reasons why employers join associations for industrial relations and other related purposes.

EMPLOYER OBJECTIVES IN INDUSTRIAL RELATIONS

The primary concern for organisations operating in a competitive environment is to maximise organisational effectiveness and generate satisfactory returns for the owners/stakeholders. Such returns are often expressed in terms of cost effectiveness and, for the commercial organisation, profitability. Management's primary role is to organise the factors of production, including labour, to achieve these objectives. Consequently, it makes decisions in a variety of areas to facilitate the achievement of corporate goals. Industrial relations is one such area where management must decide on optimal structures and practices.

It is difficult to assess the degree to which employers have specific industrial relations objectives or adopt related workplace strategies. Organisations vary so greatly in terms of structure and philosophy that it would be impractical to suggest a comprehensive set of industrial relations objectives. Indeed, it is clear that a particular organisation's industrial relations priorities and approach are heavily influenced by a combination of internal and external variables, such as product market conditions and business goals, which differ considerably between organisations. (This theme is further developed in Chapter 14. Nevertheless, it is worth considering some general beliefs common among employers. Thomason (1984) identifies a number of generic employer objectives in industrial relations as follows.

1. **Preservation and consolidation of the private enterprise system:** This has larger political overtones and relates to employer desires to develop and preserve a 'business-friendly' political and economic environment conducive to achieving business objectives at enterprise level. They will be particularly concerned that principles such as private ownership, the profit motive and preservation of authority and control in decision making are maintained and fostered.

2. **Achievement of satisfactory returns for the owners**: This relates directly to the organisation's primary business goals. For commercial organisations to survive in the long term, satisfactory profit levels must be achieved. Managerial approaches and strategies will always be influenced by this primary concern. Non-profit-making organisations will also be concerned with cost effectiveness and the quality of their product or service.

3. **Effective utilisation of human resources**: Human resources are a key management resource and their effective utilisation is central to the management process.

4. **Maintenance of control and authority in decision making**: Employers will strive to ensure effective control and authority in executing its management role, particularly in strategic decision making.

5. **Good employer-employee relations**: Employers will also strive to maintain good working relations with employees, but this must be achieved within the operational constraints of the organisation. The scope to agree attractive remuneration levels and conditions of employment, for example, will vary according to the organisation's market position and profitability, as well as its human resource philosophy. Good industrial relations will be a priority since they constitute an important ingredient in ensuring the organisation achieves its primary business goals (as well as being laudable in itself).

To help achieve such objectives, particular employers have found it beneficial to combine with other employers into permanent organisations. At the outset it is necessary to distinguish between *employer associations*, which are concerned with industrial relations issues, and *trade associations*, which are primarily concerned with trade or commercial matters. Oechslin (1985) defines employer associations as 'formal groups of employers set up to defend, represent or advise affiliated employers and to strengthen their position in society at large with respect to labour matters as distinct from commercial matters'.

This chapter considers the role of such employer associations, with particular emphasis on the Irish context.

THE HISTORICAL DEVELOPMENT OF EMPLOYER ASSOCIATIONS

Employer organisations undoubtedly existed before the emergence of modern trade unionism and some possibly had connections with the guilds of the Middle Ages. As Adam Smith observed as far back as 1776, employers were likely to combine into associations for purposes related with employment and labour matters generally.

However, the major impetus for the growth of employer associations was undoubtedly the perceived need to react to and deal with the 'new unionism' and counter growing union power. This helps distinguish between employer organisations whose precise *raison d'être* was to deal with labour matters (employer associations) from those where trade and commercial reasons were the main reason for their existence and development (trade associations). Another traditional reason why employers have formed representative associations is to prevent harmful economic competition with each other, particularly in relation to pay and working conditions. Other reasons for the growth of employer associations include the increased complexity of collective bargaining, the growth of employment legislation and the important role of employer associations in providing a forum for exchanging views between employers.

In their early attempts to grapple with organised labour and employment matters, employers, after initially dealing with such issues on an individual enterprise basis, soon found it opportune to combine either on an ad hoc or temporary basis or to form permanent associations. The reasons behind the formation of such associations were largely functional. Most of the early business enterprises were owner managed by the traditional entrepreneur/master. It has been argued that entrepreneurs have a weaker spirit of association than other social groupings and therefore any attempts at combination would need to have a solid rationale (Oechslin 1985). Consequently, many of the early employer associations were forums for exchanging views and opinions and this role later developed into one of joint strategy formulation. Such organisations mostly operated on a regional/industry-wide basis. Central umbrella associations were a later development. Thus, the early employer organisations were largely Masters' associations for particular industrial sectors and/or regions that had combined for a variety of reasons, not necessarily related to labour matters. While some of these exist today, the more important contemporary employer associations are those of corporate employers with specific employment-related objectives.

EMPLOYER ASSOCIATIONS IN IRELAND

As discussed above, employer organisations in Ireland are classified into two categories, employer associations and trade associations, both of which must register with the Registrar of Friendly Societies. Employer associations are involved in industrial relations and must hold a negotiating licence under the terms of the Trade Union Act 1941. This distinguishes them from trade associations, which are not required to hold such a licence. Employer associations are in effect trade unions of employers and fall within the same legal definition as a trade union. While this may not initially seem significant, it can have important implications for the role and membership of employer associations. In particular, it suggests an approach to industrial relations which emphasises the role of collectives or combinations as opposed to individuals. In 2001 there were eleven employer associations as defined above (shown in Table 6.1).

While the number of employer associations with negotiation licences is considerably less than their trade union counterparts, there is considerable diversity in membership composition. Within this listing one can find examples of traditional Masters' associations, industry-based associations and a general association that is national in scope. It is interesting that in evaluating the role of employer associations in European countries, Traxler (1998) identifies a trend whereby countries are characterised by single employer associations and suggests that there has been a gradual erosion of task-based employer associations. In the Irish context, over recent years the Irish Business and Employers Confederation (IBEC) has come to be the major employer force in both labour and trade matters. We now consider IBEC's role in Irish industrial relations.

Table 6.1
Employer Associations Holding Negotiation Licences, 2001

Name of Association	Membership
Construction Industry Federation	2,718
Cork Master Butchers Association	32
Dublin Master Victuallers Association	140
Irish Business And Employers Confederation	3,997
Irish Commercial Horticultural Association	334
Irish Hotels Federation	895
Irish Master Printers Association	38
Irish Pharmaceutical Union	1,380
Irish Printing Federation	69
Licensed Vintners Association	686
Society of Irish Motor Industry	1,664
Total	**11,953**

Source: Registrar of Friendly Societies (2002)

The Irish Business and Employers Confederation (IBEC)

The largest employer association in Ireland by far is the Irish Business and Employers Confederation (IBEC). IBEC was formed on 1 January 1993 as a result of the merger of the then largest employer association, the Federation of Irish Employers (FIE, formerly the Federated Union of Employers) and the then dominant trade/commercial association, the Confederation of Irish Industry (CII).

IBEC represents business and employers in all matters relating to industrial relations, labour and social affairs. IBEC claims to have over 3,500 firms in membership. These firms employ some 300,000 people, or approximately one-third of the country's total employment (excluding agriculture, the public service and the self-employed). As the country's major representative of business and employers, IBEC seeks to shape national policies and influence decision making in a manner which protects and promotes member employers' interests. In 1996 IBEC developed a strategic policy framework which outlined its mission and vision (see Table 6.2), its strategic objectives and its policy objectives up to the year 2005. The major strategic issues identified include competitiveness, enterprise, state involvement in industry, employee relations, social policy and income development, European Union, education and training, the environment, innovation, research and development and employment.

Unlike the old FIE, IBEC's role is not confined solely to industrial relations. IBEC represents industry in matters of trade, economics, finance, taxation, planning and development. IBEC develops and reviews policy on this wide range of topics through consultation with members, research and expert advice and opinion. A major role of IBEC is the representation of employer interests on these issues to government and to the public at large. It also maintains employer representation on various national and international bodies.

> **Table 6.2**
> *Mission Statement – Irish Business and Employers Confederation*
>
> To vigorously pursue the development of a competitive and innovative economy; and be valued by its members as enhancing, to a significant extent, the overall climate in which business operates. To promote the achievement of constructive management/industrial relations, building on the improvements already made in recent years.
>
> and
>
> To provide and market a portfolio of value for money services, available centrally through the confederation's regional and sectoral networks, that assist the efficiency and effectiveness of individual members and groups of members in a variety of ways and enhances the attractiveness of confederation membership.

In all, the Confederation represents business and employers on approximately seventy separate organisations, institutions and committees in Ireland. Representatives are chosen from the National Executive Committee elected by members, managers with particular experience and expertise and senior executives from the Confederation. IBEC also represents Irish employers on approximately forty-five bodies internationally, including UNICE – the European employer representative body, the International Organisation of Employers (IOE) and the International Labour Organization (ILO). In this role, IBEC evaluates European and international developments and their effect on its affiliated membership.

IBEC's industrial and employee relations advisory and consultation services are organised on a regional basis. Five regional offices operate independently with back-up facilities provided by the head office in Dublin. Designated executives are often assigned to deal with individual company needs. Particularly important among these services is IBEC's role in representing member firms at mediation, conciliation and arbitration hearings. IBEC also provides a range of specialist services in areas such as management training, health and safety and legal advice and representation.

The Small Firms Association (SFA) is an independent association within IBEC that represents and supports small business. The Association claims to have over 7,000 member companies and provides business, economic and regulatory advice to its membership.

Construction Industry Federation (CIF)

The Construction Industry Federation (CIF) is the second-largest employer association in Ireland. Unlike IBEC, which represents employers from a range of industrial sectors, the CIF is essentially an industry-based association dealing with both trade/commercial and industrial relations matters affecting the construction industry. In 2003 CIF claimed to represent over 3,000 members through a network of thirteen branches in three regions and through thirty-seven sectoral associations. Firms in membership of the CIF employ around seventy-five to eighty per cent of all workers in privately owned construction firms.

In the area of industrial relations, CIF's main role involves monitoring and handling industrial relations on all large sites, dealing with any matters referred to it by member organisations, negotiation of national registered agreements, representing members at conciliation and arbitration and providing information and advice to member firms (Pollock and O'Dwyer 1985).

Irish Small and Medium Enterprises Association (ISME)

ISME is an employer organisation that represents commercial small and medium-sized organisations. It was established in 1993 by a group of small and medium-sized enterprises (SMEs) that broke away when the FIE and CII amalgamated to form IBEC. While ISME does not hold a negotiating licence and thus does not meet the established definition of an employer association, it has been prominent in commenting on economic and social affairs, including industrial relations.

ISME's primary function is to represent the interests of its members to government, government bodies and other major organisations impacting on competitive business. ISME distinguishes itself from other larger employer organisations by highlighting the fact that its members are entrepreneurs and not professional managers. ISME notes that their main strength lies in the fact that small and medium enterprises employ up to seventy per cent of those employed in the private sector and they therefore aim to represent a significant force in Irish business. ISME aims at harnessing that political influence and using it for what it perceives as the betterment of competitive business. ISME points out that 'independence enables it to speak out fearlessly' on behalf of competitive and entrepreneur-driven business. It claims to maintain and strengthen that independence through a growing membership base (ISME 1997). Beyond seeking to influence opinion on broad policy-level issues, e.g. centralised agreements, ISME does not appear to have a strong industrial relations dimension, but rather appears to concentrate primarily on trade and commercial matters.

ISME has often been viewed as somewhat of a maverick employer organisation and has not been involved in centralised pay negotiation. This stance seems to have changed in recent years, with ISME accepting the place of centralised pay agreements in Irish business, though it has sometimes been highly critical of IBEC's role in the negotiation of these. The most recent evidence of this was in early 2003, in an ISME statement on the draft terms of a new national wage agreement:

> it is imperative that IBEC, as the unelected representative of employers, stand up once and for all for the business community, and does not capitulate to demands that will undermine the competitive base of Irish industry. Unfortunately, as past experiences have confirmed, ISME fears that this plea will fall on deaf ears, as inevitably the employers body will concede on the core issues in order to protect their vested interests in the Social Partnership process (ISME 2003).

Other Employer Associations in Ireland

Most of the other employer associations are primarily concerned with trade and commercial issues, although some are quite involved in industrial relations. The industrial relations role of the Irish Hotels Federation (IHF) is largely confined to representing employer interests on the Hotels Joint Labour Committee and Hotels (Dublin) Joint Labour Committee and providing general industrial relations advice to members. It does not involve itself in local bargaining. Similarly, the Society of the Irish Motor Industry (SIMI) is mostly concerned with trade and commercial issues but does provide personnel/industrial relations advice and assistance. The Licensed Vintners Association (LVA) provides a range of services to Dublin publicans, one of which involves labour relations. It conducts negotiations on pay and working conditions with MANDATE, the Union of Retail, Bar and Administrative Work, and also provides affiliated members with a personnel advisory service covering areas such as personnel policy, discipline/dismissal and redundancies. The involvement of the remaining employer associations in industrial relations is limited.

Other Employer Groupings

While this chapter is primarily concerned with formal employer associations operating in the area of industrial relations, it is also important to note, as discussed earlier, that employers may also establish and combine in less formal groupings. Such groups are generally used by employers as a forum for exchanging views and information on industrial relations matters and also as a mechanism for co-ordinating employer approaches to specific industrial relations issues. Such groupings have the advantage of informality and cohesiveness while conferring none of the obligations or costs attached to formal association membership. They may be formed on a regional or sectoral basis, e.g. the electronics sector, and may meet on either a semi-permanent basis or only when a significant issue arises. The Chartered Institute of Personnel and Development (CIPD) in Ireland, which is the major professional association for management practitioners in industrial relations, may also act as a forum for the exchange of opinions, debate and comment on industrial relations matters.

OBJECTIVES OF EMPLOYER ASSOCIATIONS

Some common employer objectives in industrial relations were outlined above and include:

- support for the private enterprise system;
- achievement of satisfactory returns for the owners of the organisation;
- effective utilisation of human resources; and
- maintenance of management prerogative in decision making and ensuring good employer-employee relations.

Most employers would subscribe, with varying degrees of commitment, to these general objectives and many have found that through combination they can provide a common front and more effectively achieve employer goals at both the micro and macro level.

However, beyond these common objectives, Windmuller (1984) argues that it is inappropriate to refer to the views and approaches of employer organisations as constituting a specific ideology and suggests that employer associations, unlike trade unions, do not subscribe to some ideal economic and social system and are not part of a quasi-political movement. While it may be valid to say that employer associations do not affiliate to a particular political party (as trade unions often do), employer associations do have broad economic, social and political objectives that they pursue and their role is not just confined to micro-level issues, but also to larger societal-level matters such as political control, economic and social policy. This is particularly the case with national-level associations. At enterprise level, employer associations will seek to provide members with a range of services to help them more effectively deal with industrial relations issues. A summary classification of broad employer association objectives is outlined in Table 6.3.

Table 6.3
Objectives of Employer Associations

1. **Political:** To effectively represent employer views to government, the general public and other appropriate bodies so as to preserve and develop a political, economic and social climate within which business objectives can be achieved.

2. **Economic:** To create an economic environment that supports the free enterprise system and ensures that managerial prerogative in decision making is protected.

3. **Social:** To ensure any social or legal changes best represent the interests of affiliated employers.

4. **Industrial relations:** To ensure a legislative and procedural environment that supports free collective bargaining, to co-ordinate employer views and approaches on industrial relations matters and provide assistance to affiliated employers.

In a political era where lobby groups are becoming increasingly important, employer associations have assumed a significant role in representing employer interests on national issues. They provide a mechanism through which governments can solicit employer views on areas such as employment and labour legislation and are important vehicles for influencing public opinion on more general political issues. This political role of employer associations is most clearly associated with their desire to influence broad economic decision making. Employer organisations will generally support what could be termed conservative economic policies, which serve to protect the interests of capital and minimise the extent of government intervention in business and economic matters. In the area of social policy, employer associations will generally attempt to prevent, or at least lessen, the effects of protective labour or social legislation, such as legal moves towards extending industrial democracy or information disclosure.

However, they may accept some degree of social and legislative reform, provided their perceived effects on the interests of capital are not adverse.

Turning to the specific industrial relations role of employer associations, these may be categorised into four broad areas.

1. **Exchange of views:** We have already suggested that many of the early employer organisations were traditional Masters' associations that had initially combined to discuss labour relations and related issues. Such associations provided a useful forum for exchanging opinions and discussion. As the impact of trade unions increased and the state became more active in economic and social affairs, the role of such associations became even more important. Employers came together not only to exchange information, but to agree common policies and strategies. This led to a greater formality in the organisational structure of employer associations. This role is still important today. However, it is practically difficult to get a wide input into any general discussions on policy issues of national significance, although such opportunities can possibly be afforded at regional level. Yet for larger associations, policies and positions are generally decided by a limited representative body of employer opinion.

2. **Representation of employer views to government and its agencies:** As the laissez-faire political philosophy receded and government became more active in economic and social affairs, employers saw a need for their views to be effectively represented to government. This development is seen most clearly in countries such as the UK as a result of the growth of the welfare state in the post-war era and increased social and employment legislation. As Munns (1967) remarked in his research paper on employers associations for the Donovan Commission:

> all of the national organisations regard the representation of members' views to government as an important and growing part of the function. The general importance arises from the fact that much legislation has a direct bearing on industrial affairs and associations take very seriously their responsibility to seek amendments to existing or proposed legislation which would have a harmful effect on their members, or to improve the practical execution of the Government's intentions.

Employer associations, particularly at central level, will therefore seek to influence the direction and nature of labour legislation, and government policy generally, so that the position of affiliated employers is adequately protected. Such efforts have been most obvious on issues such as industrial democracy and financial disclosure and have contributed to either the dropping or dilution of such legislation (see Chapter 11).

This representative role in Ireland is largely filled by IBEC. IBEC plays a particularly prominent role in representing business and employer views on bodies such as the National Economic and Social Council (NESC), which was established by the government as a forum for the discussion of the principles relating to the efficient development of the national economy; the National Economic and Social Forum (NESF), also set up by the government, to achieve consensus on as wide a basis as possible on major economic and social policy issues; FÁS, the training and employment authority; the National Authority for Occupational Safety and Health, known as the Health and Safety Authority (HSA), which controls the operation and enforcement of occupational health and safety legislation in Ireland; and the Equality Authority, which is the statutory authority with responsibility for the elimination of discrimination and promotion of equality of opportunity in employment.

This political representation role of employer organisations is now well established in many countries. Consequently, when government seeks employers' views, it will generally approach the appropriate employer association. As Oechslin (1985) suggests, such a practice is both a recognition of the technical expertise and representative character of the employer association. Thus, it is important that employer associations present a representative front so that governments can readily identify its source of advice and also identify representatives of employer interests for appropriate bipartite or tripartite bodies, such as arbitration councils, government commissions, international organisations, etc. In Ireland, IBEC plays the lead role in nominating employer representatives to such bodies as the Labour Court, the Labour Relations Commission and the Employment Appeals Tribunal.

3. **Representation of employer interests to the public**: Allied to the political representation role of employer associations is their role in representing employer views to the public at large on relevant issues. This will commonly be achieved through the general media or the associations' own fora and publications. It is increasingly considered important that employer opinion on issues be adequately represented, and this public relations function is particularly relevant for central employer organisations. Relations with the media are an important element of this role, as is a competent research and publications section.

4. **Provision of specialised services to members**: Employer associations will provide a range of specialised industrial relations and related services for their affiliated membership. Sisson (1983) suggests that the main industrial relations services provided by employer associations are negotiation of pay and conditions of employment, operation of disputes procedures, advisory and consultancy services and representation.

The issue of employer association membership is discussed below, while the nature and utilisation of the industrial relations services of employer associations is considered later in this chapter.

MEMBERSHIP OF EMPLOYER ASSOCIATIONS

While the distinction between trade associations and employer associations is useful, it does not fully cater for situations where some organisations play a dual role in dealing with both trade and labour issues. Also, some countries may have a central organisation that represents employer interests in both commercial and labour areas, for example, the

Irish Business and Employers Confederation in Ireland and the Confederation of British Industry in Britain. We noted earlier that an apparent European trend is that countries are characterised by single employer associations and a gradual erosion of task-based employer associations (Traxler 1998). In the Irish context, over recent years IBEC has become the major employer force in both labour and trade matters.

This section considers issues relating to membership and structure of employer associations. In particular, it focuses on factors influencing membership and structure, such as industry/regional issues, ownership and organisation scale, and then considers the governance of employer associations.

Employer associations are comprised of a regionally, industrially and structurally diverse membership. Such regional and industrial diversity was manifested in the establishment of traditional Masters' associations, which were particularly common in the building and butchering trades and whose objectives were largely confined to local trade and employment-related matters. While some such associations still exist today, many have amalgamated with larger national associations. While not a prerequisite for the representation of employer views at national level, the formation of a central representative confederation is an important mechanism for more effectively co-ordinating and articulating employer views. Of course, the role of such a confederation is dependent on numerous factors, not least the locus of collective bargaining. In countries dominated by industry-wide bargaining, such as Germany, the role of industry-wide associations may be dominant. However, a co-ordinated employer voice may also be necessary and this is generally provided by a central confederation. In Ireland, this role is provided by IBEC and is particularly prominent during periods of centralised pay agreements, which have now characterised Irish industrial relations for the better part of three decades.

Turning to the specifics of membership of employer associations, Thomason (1984) differentiates between *entrepreneurs*, who essentially own (at least partly) and run their businesses, and abstract *corporate entities* that are run by professional managements. He argues that the change in composition of employer association membership from entrepreneur owner-managers to corporate business forms run by professional management partly explains the changing role of employer associations. The corporate business firm has replaced the older entrepreneurial firm as the prevalent type of organisation in membership of employer associations. Thomason suggests that this mix partly explains the diverse philosophies and roles of different employer associations.

There are also some tentative indications that ownership may influence employer association membership (Brown 1981). In Ireland a study of newly established companies found that US-owned firms were less likely to join employer associations (Gunnigle 1995b). This may be related to the corporate approach to trade unions and collective bargaining. Where this involves a preference for non-union status, such organisations may be reluctant to join an employer association (see also Purcell and Sisson 1983; Oechslin 1985).

The issue of public sector organisations becoming members of an employer association is a relatively recent phenomenon. While initially it might seem incompatible for public sector organisations to join an employer association (traditionally a bastion of free enterprise), many have adopted a pragmatic approach by utilising employer association services in certain areas (Oechslin 1985). In Ireland, the Department of Finance and the Local Government Staff Negotiations Board fulfil the key advisory and assistance role for management in many parts of the public sector. However, some public sector organisations, particularly those in the semi-state sector, have taken up membership of employer associations as a result of high levels of unionisation in the public sector and the consequent need for expertise and advice on industrial relations issues.

As was the case in relation to trade union recognition, it is argued that organisation size is a key determinant of membership and utilisation of employer associations. For example, it has been suggested that small firms have more to gain by joining employer associations (ILO 1975). The major reasons are related to cost and resources. When a small organisation reaches the stage where it becomes involved in formalised collective bargaining it may be particularly attractive to join an employer association. Such firms are not generally in a position to employ personnel/HR specialists and owner/managers may not have either the necessary time or expertise to effectively handle such matters. Since the cost of joining an employer association is generally related to the size and/or profitability of the individual firm, it may be relatively inexpensive for small firms to join.

However, despite the plausability of this line of argument, there is no conclusive evidence to support the view that small firms are more likely to join employers associations (Government Social Survey, UK 1968). In fact, the research evidence on workplace industrial relations suggests that employer associations are not more frequently used by smaller organisations (Brown 1981; Daniel and Millward 1983). Brown (1981: 21) suggests that 'one theory that can be dismissed is that employers associations are primarily used by the smaller establishments who lack specialist resources'.

Thus, the available literature seems to indicate that larger firms are more likely to join and utilise the services of employer associations and that employer association membership is positively correlated with an organisation's size, recognition of a trade union and the presence of specialist personnel/HR function.

Advantages and Disadvantages of Employer Association Membership

We have already considered some of the factors influencing an organisation's decision to join an employer association for industrial relations purposes. Clearly, a key factor influencing employer association membership and utilisation is the desired managerial approach and philosophy towards workforce management. Contextual factors such as industry, size, market position and history/ownership also impact upon decisions on employer association membership. It is obviously a decision for the senior management of a particular enterprise to critically evaluate its own position and decide if membership of an employer association is appropriate to its own particular circumstances. However, at a general level it is useful to outline the main advantages and disadvantages of employer association membership for individual organisations. These are summarised in Table 6.4.

Table 6.4
Advantages and Disadvantages of Employer Association Membership

Advantages	Disadvantages
Collective approaches and uniform policy	Cost of membership
Advice on trade union matters	Loss of autonomy
Technical advice and information	Loss of flexibility
Skilled negotiators	Comparisons with other firms
Expert advisory and consultancy services	Greater acceptance of role for trade unions
Standardised pay and employment conditions	Greater formalisation in industrial relations
On par with regional/industry norms	
Assistance in industrial relations difficulties	
Influence on government/national affairs	

The next section reviews the services provided by employer associations, which correlate closely with the advantages of employer association membership. Some of the reasons why organisations may choose not to join an employer association are now considered.

One of the disadvantages of employer association membership is a potential reduction of *autonomy* in decision making for the individual organisation. Employer associations will be keen that members maintain a standard line in negotiations on pay and conditions of employment through the development of agreed policy guidelines, e.g. member firms will be expected to keep pay increases within the terms of centrally negotiated agreements. These guidelines will reflect the needs of a diverse membership (in terms of organisation size, profitability, etc.). The individual organisation must decide if such norms are appropriate to its particular needs. For example, an organisation may wish to award a pay increase which breaches the guidelines laid down by an employer association.

Comparability is also an important factor. By virtue of association membership, a particular organisation's pay and conditions will generally be compared to that pertaining in other member firms. Trade unions will use the terms of collective agreements struck with some member firms as leverage to secure similar terms with other organisations.

The issues of autonomy and comparability reflect the difficulties employer associations face in developing common policies for a diverse membership. They also highlight the difficulties employer associations face in enforcing policy guidelines and raise the issue of control over affiliates. Breaches of agreed policy guidelines by individual member organisations can detrimentally affect the credibility of such guidelines and may incur the wrath of sections of the affiliated membership. This has occasionally resulted in firms withdrawing from membership or being disaffiliated by the association. Such breaches of discipline are almost inescapable in associations where membership is voluntary and general policies are laid down for a diverse membership. Like trade unions, employer associations will strive to ensure maximum organisation of its potential members and, in practice, exercise a more informal authority over members, relying on persuasion and peer pressure to secure adherence to common policies. Employer associations are generally reluctant to punish non-conforming members and particularly so where expulsion is considered.

Should a large number of enterprises, or even a few significant employers, not join an employer association, its representativeness is clearly called into question. Sisson (1983) notes some important British organisations which have either withdrawn from membership or never joined employer associations, e.g. Esso, *Daily Mirror*, British Leyland and Ford. In Ireland, too, there is some evidence of notable enterprises not in association membership. These are often major employers and exert considerable influence on local pay trends and general industrial relations matters. An important factor in such decisions seems to be related to the degree of influence such organisations believe they might have on association policy and the restrictions that membership would place on their capacity for manoeuvre.

It is also important to evaluate how association membership fits in with the *corporate personnel/HR philosophy*. This issue is also discussed below in assessing employer association membership and utilisation in new ('greenfield') companies. Employer associations are in effect trade unions of employers and have traditionally sought to deal with their employee counterparts through collective bargaining. However, some firms have a clear preference for a non-union status. In recent years, Ireland has seen considerable growth in the high technology sector. This has largely been the result of foreign (mostly American) firms establishing subsidiaries here. Non-union US companies such as Intel, Dell, Motorola and Microsoft are now an integral part of the industrial scene. Some of these firms have brought with them a particular corporate approach to industrial relations that places emphasis on dealing with employees on an individual basis rather than through trade unions. For some such firms, membership of an employer association, i.e. a trade union of employers, is seen as incompatible with a management approach based on direct contact with individual workers.

IBEC seems acutely aware of the need to attract into membership employers who have an explicit preference for greater individualism in management-industrial relations. Consequently, we have seen the creation of special-status membership categories which allow affiliated firms considerable flexibility in decision making while retaining association membership and engaging in less formal policy co-ordination. Employee Relations Services Limited (ERS) is a fully owned subsidiary of IBEC, which seems in part designed to attract into its membership companies which might not otherwise become members of IBEC. ERS provides a range of specialist services in areas such as management strategies and payment systems, e.g. performance-related pay. It also provides an industrial relations auditing service designed to furnish senior managers with an evaluation of industrial relations in their enterprise. ERS members pay a similar joining fee to IBEC and have free access to IBEC's other services (see Tables 6.5 and 6.6 for IBEC and ERS subscription rates). IBEC members may use ERS services at a preferential rate. Many non-union companies may be more comfortable with membership of ERS as it maintains their 'non-union' stance. Such special-status arrangements avoid the apparent stigma of joining a 'trade union of employers' and are clearly perceived as an important mechanism in attracting such companies, which are often US owned and non-union, into membership.

Table 6.5
IBEC Subscription Rates, 2002

Subscription Based on Total Salaries & Wages* (Euro)		Subscription Based on Turnover (Euro)	
Total Salaries and Wages	Subscription	Turnover Scale	Subscription
0–826,600	1,505	13,000,000 –31,999,999	2,879
10,740,101– 11,814,300	23,809	32,000,000– 63,999,999	7,223
20,929,501– 23,022,400	46,390	64,000,000– 129,999,999	14,433
40,448,501– 44,857,400	80,711	130,000,000– 189,999,999	18,038
67,846,901– 101,770,400	110,317	190,000,000– 253,999,999	21,644
Over 228,977,101	137,058	Over 254,000,000	28,854

* These are just some of the rates taken from a comprehensive scale of subscription rates available. Subscriptions are rounded to the nearest euro.

Source: Supplied directly by IBEC

A more pragmatic reason for non-membership is related to *cost* (see Tables 6.5 and 6.6). An important issue here may be that firms pay the full cost of membership regardless of services used. By contrast, an organisation which uses management consultants normally pays on the basis of services rendered. Most employer association subscriptions are related to the size of the firm (number of employees) or, as in the case of IBEC, to the companies' total salaries and wages or turnover in a financial year. Subscription costs can be substantial for larger organisations (Ridgely 1988).

Related to the issue of costs may be the perception among firms with a highly developed and well-resourced human resource (HR) function that they do not need the services provided by employer associations. This is based on the premise that such services can be adequately provided by the company's own HR function and as such the

Table 6.6
IBEC Subscription Rates in Respect of Employee Relations Services, 2002

First year minimum payment	€1,000
Minimum subscription per annum	€759
and/or	
For each of: first 200 employees	€31.49
next 800 employees	€30.05
next 1,000 employees	€15.12
remaining employees	€7.46

Note: IBEC's subscription rates are normally based on a company's total salaries and wages paid in the latest financial year, but the turnover scale may apply in respect of companies with high turnover to labour costs. The subscription paid is the higher of the two scales (supplied directly by IBEC).

Source: Supplied directly by IBEC

subscription paid for employer association membership does not represent good value for money. The suggestion that larger firms with well-developed HR functions may not need many of the services provided by employer associations is alluded to in Reynaud's (1978) suggestion that employer associations may become 'an organisation of services for the small undertakings paid for by the big ones'. We have seen above that the research evidence does not support this view and it seems that large firms use employer associations as much, and often more, than small ones (Brown 1981; Daniel and Millward 1983).

THE GOVERNING STRUCTURE OF EMPLOYER ASSOCIATIONS

In general, employer associations are organised so that ultimate decision-making power resides with the affiliated membership. However, there is a high degree of complexity in the structural arrangements of employer associations, with various models of internal government in evidence, and we can merely generalise on common themes with respect to governing structures. Windmuller (1984) suggests that the governing structures of the major employers associations will be composed of three to four levels:

1. Assembly or general meetings.
2. General or executive council.
3. Executive board or management committee.
4. Presiding officer (president/general secretary/chairman).

Windmuller (1984) suggests that this structure attempts to cater for membership participation while allowing day-to-day management to be carried out by full-time staff. He argues that because of their large and unwieldy nature, general assemblies or meetings rarely occur more than once year and are largely a vehicle through which the membership influence and communicate with the central administration of the association. They help decide upon general policy issues and elect the various committees. In commenting on their role, Windmuller (1984) suggests that 'hardly anywhere do general meetings exercise real power beyond the election of executive bodies'.

In contrast, the executive or general council tends to be much smaller. It is normally comprised of elected representatives and some office holders, will often be representative of various industrial, regional or sectional interests and will meet with greater frequency (possibly four to five times per year). The executive or general council is usually responsible for the appointment of the various committees and monitors their work and the general running of the association. Again, Windmuller comments that 'councils carry some weight but still lack the continuity and compactness to be the decisive element in policy formulation'.

Perhaps the most important layer in the governing structure of employer associations is the management or executive committee/board. This is normally much smaller and meets regularly (possibly on a monthly basis). Its membership consists of representatives usually elected on a regional basis from the various branch/industrial divisions from the major enterprises and some office holders of the association. Such bodies may also elect the various standing committees (finance, industrial relations, law, etc.) depending on whether there is a general council or not. Such committees often have the power to co-opt members, which is often used to bring in prestigious and influential people from the business community who can make a valuable contribution to committee work. The executive board or general council exerts considerable influence on association policies and approaches and, together with the association president and the senior staff, is primarily responsible for policy formulation and execution.

For many associations, the position of chairman or general secretary is a part-time position held by a senior manager from an affiliated enterprise. However, with the increasing demands of association work, this often creates a dilemma for the incumbent as this job requires considerable time away from their employer. Depending on the demands of the position, the relationship between the president and full-time senior manager of the association (director general/managing director) can be a crucial one. The director general is normally expected to administer all the association's affairs according to the policy guidelines laid down by the general assembly, the general council and/or the executive committee. The post-holder is expected to work closely with the association president and take their advice on general policy matters. A primary role for the director general will be to manage the professional staff of the association. The numbers of staff working in employer associations, particularly national 'peak' associations, has increased considerably over recent years, both in scale and areas of specialisation, and now cover areas such as labour law, health and safety, negotiations, research and administration.

It appears that while employer association structure presents an image of active participatory democracy, this may be somewhat misleading. For pragmatic purposes, control and direction of association affairs is generally vested in the hands of a small number of affiliated members who together with the president and full-time staff oversee the general running of the association. That is not to say that employer association affairs take little account of the wishes of the membership. On the contrary, since affiliation to employer associations is voluntary and because associations continually strive to be the authentic representative voice of their constituency, such associations must be very circumspect to take on board the needs and wishes of their membership.

Like trade unions, the primary source of revenue for employer associations is membership subscriptions. These subscriptions are used to cover the main costs of running the association, principally wages and salaries. We have mentioned that the membership subscriptions of member firms are usually related to some measure of turnover or company size. Other sources of revenue are training programmes, publications and payments for specialist services. However, given the general lack of information on employer association finances it is difficult to estimate the value of such sources or the breakdown of association expenditure.

The Governing Structure of the Irish Business and Employers Confederation (IBEC)

Within the organisational structure of IBEC, the role of the general membership of affiliated organisations is to elect a General Council comprising 250 representatives who then determine general policy and appoint the National Executive Council. The Council itself is comprised of office holders and nominees from the various regions and branches, totalling seventy in all. It is primarily responsible for overseeing policy formulation and implementation, appointing the key specialist committees and the permanent secretariat in conjunction with the director general and confederation secretary. The director general and the full-time staff are responsible for carrying out the primary activities and services of the association (see Figure 6.1).

EMPLOYER ASSOCIATION MEMBERSHIP AND MANAGEMENT APPROACHES TO INDUSTRIAL RELATIONS

Membership of employer associations is seen as a useful indicator of preferred management approaches to industrial relations (see also Chapter 15). Membership of employer associations has traditionally been associated with the pluralist industrial relations model. A recent study of industrial relations in new 'greenfield' companies in the manufacturing and traded services sectors found that the majority of firms (seventy per cent) surveyed were employer association members (see Table 6.7) (Gunnigle *et al.* 2001). This represents an increase of eight percentage points on the 1987–1992 figure (see Gunnigle 1995a, 1995b).

It is worth noting that most of those companies that indicated membership of an employer association in the 1992–1997 study used the association for industrial relations and general human resources advice rather than by way of direct involvement at establishment level (see Gunnigle *et al.* 2001). Indeed, Table 6.8 shows a trend of a reduction in the involvement of an employer association by the greenfield member companies studied in establishment-level industrial relations. This may be indicative of a change in the role of collectivism in enterprise-level industrial relations in Ireland (see Gunnigle *et al.* 2001).

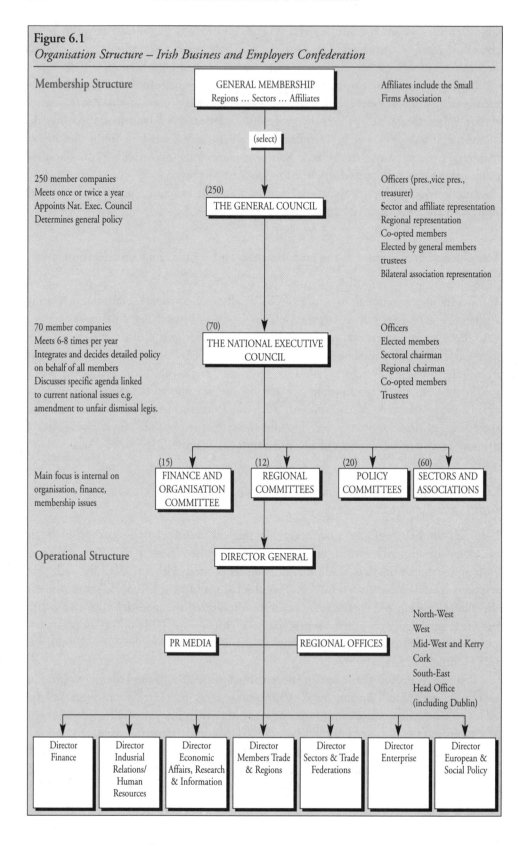

Figure 6.1
Organisation Structure – Irish Business and Employers Confederation

Employer associations have traditionally been integral to the pluralist industrial relations model. However, growth of the non-union sector, particularly in greenfield sites, and a related expansion of individualistic human resource management (HRM) policies means that for such companies, membership of an employer association (in essence a trade union of employers) is often perceived as incompatible with a management approach based on individual dealings with employees. We have seen how Ireland's foremost employer association has responded to this development, in part by establishing an advisory and consultancy service (ERS, discussed above) that provides particular services but does not confer the normal status of employer association membership.

Table 6.7
Membership of Employer Associations

Membership of Employer Associations	1987–1992	1992–1997
Yes	62% (33)	70% (16)
No	38% (20)	30% (7)

Note: Actual numbers in parentheses.

Source: Gunnigle *et al.* (2001)

Table 6.8
Employer Association Membership and Utilisation of Services

	Direct Involvement in Establishment-Level Industrial Relations	Industrial Relations Advice	General HR Advice
1987–1992 (n=33)	36% (12)	97% (32)	97% (32)
1992–1997 (n=16)	12.5% (2)	50% (8)	87.5% (14)

Source: Gunnigle *et al.* (2001)

We have already noted that the extant literature indicates that employer associations are most relevant in the private sector and that membership is positively related to trade union recognition, increased company size and the presence of a specialist HR function (Brown 1981; Daniel and Millward 1983). Indeed, trade union recognition appears to be a key factor. Formalised collective bargaining arrangements, procedural agreements and a developed shop steward system (all characteristics of the traditional pluralist industrial relations model) appear to be positively related to employer association membership and extensive utilisation of employer association services (Brown 1981). Even in smaller organisations the prospect of employer association membership may become increasingly attractive when such firms reach a stage of development where trade union recognition has been granted and there is a move towards formalising the company's approach to industrial relations management (Gunnigle and Brady 1984; Gunnigle 1989). The evidence from greenfield firms sheds further light on the role of employer associations in Irish industrial relations. Here we find the more general pattern of utilisation was for firms to use the employer association primarily as a source of information and advice across a range of personnel/HR issues, including industrial relations.

EMPLOYER ASSOCIATION SERVICES

It was suggested earlier that employer associations provide a range of industrial relations services for their affiliated membership, particularly in the area of negotiations, research and advice and representation. These various services are discussed below.

Research and Advisory Services

In reviewing the UK context, Sisson (1983) suggests that the major expansion in the work of employer associations has been in the provision of various advisory and consultancy services (see also Commission on Industrial Relations 1972; Gladstone 1984). These advisory and consultancy services fall into three broad categories, namely legal, pay and specialist consultancy.

The growth of both collective industrial relations legislation and protective employment legislation since the early 1970s has led to a significant increase in employer demand for specialist legal advice on these matters. Employer associations are expected to provide specialist legal advice and assistance to members in areas such as dismissal, redundancy, employment conditions, employment equality and industrial disputes. It is now usual for larger employer associations to have a specialist legal section that provides such advice and assistance in addition to information guidelines on legislation for the general membership. In Ireland, we find that IBEC publishes a range of material on a wide variety of topics to keep its members abreast of legislative developments in industrial relations.

A more traditional employer association service concerns the provision of information and advice on both basic wage rates and levels of pay increases to member firms. Most employer associations carry out surveys and analyses of wage rates and fringe benefits for differing occupations, regions and sizes of organisation. Consequently, they are able to provide member firms with up-to-date information on local, regional and national pay trends and advise such firms on reward issues. IBEC's research and information service gathers data on all aspects of work and employment, e.g. annualised hours, absence figures, etc. It interprets information it collects through, for example, the IBEC/Economic and Social Research Institute (ESRI) monthly industrial survey, and also provides opinions on the likely impact of particular findings or initiatives for employers, e.g. the likely impact of European works council legislation (see Chapter 11).

In addition to legal and pay advice, many employer organisations will also provide members with specialist advice and assistance on particular issues. This role is a general one and varies between associations. However, areas of specialist assistance include job evaluation, productivity schemes, work study, bonus schemes and recruitment. An Irish pilot study by Butler in 1986 found that advisory and consultancy services were seen by members as the most useful function of employer associations and that those services dealing with legislation, pay and redundancy were the most widely utilised (Butler 1986).

Representation

Apart from providing member firms with information and advice, employer associations may directly assist members by acting on their behalf in industrial relations negotiations. This role can be important at several levels. Employer associations can represent members in workplace-level negotiations on, for example, the introduction of new technology. They can also play a more extensive role in representing their affiliates in either industry-level or national-level bargaining. This function of representation will also apply to mediation and arbitration, where employer associations can represent affiliates at tribunal hearings, conciliation meetings and arbitration hearings. Given the growth in employment legislation and the greater complexity of industrial relations negotiations, this role is likely to increase in significance.

The representational role of employer associations involves both a political dimension and third-party representation. Representing employer views to government, state institutions, trade unions, the general public and other interested parties is a key role of employer associations. In general, one often finds a clear distinction between employer representation on trade/commercial issues and employer representation on industrial relations matters. Indeed, this was clearly the case in Ireland until 1993. Up to this time, the Confederation of Irish Industry (CII) operated as the national organisation representing employer interests in matters of trade, economics, finance, taxation, planning and development. However, the CII did not involve itself in industrial relations. This latter role was primarily executed by the then Federation of Irish Employers (FIE) (previously the FUE). The merger of the CII and FIE in 1993 consolidated these dual roles into one employer body, namely IBEC, which is consulted by and makes representations to government on both industrial relations and general business/commercial matters. Apart from IBEC, industry-based associations, such as the Construction Industry Federation (CIF), also carry out representative functions related to their own sector.

An equally important representational function of employer associations occurs at conciliation and arbitration fora. Representing member firms at the Labour Relations Commission, Labour Court, Employment Appeals Tribunal and other third-party hearings is a valued and important service of employer associations (see Table 6.9 for the frequency of IBEC representation at third-party dispute resolution institutions and trade union negotiations). Affiliated firms will normally call on the services of their employer association if involved in third-party proceedings, although the extent of such utilisation may only involve obtaining advice and direction. At Labour Court hearings in particular it is common for the employer case to be presented by an employer association official. This may also occur at Employment Appeals Tribunal hearings, although there is an increasing tendency for employers to opt for legal representation at these fora.

The industrial relations arm of IBEC is involved in providing industrial relations advice and assistance to members. The provision of such advice/assistance may involve direct IBEC participation in negotiations with trade unions and would also cover research and specialist advisory services as well as assistance with the preparation of employment agreements, consultation on particular HR issues and the provision of premises and facilities for consultation and negotiation. The industrial relations functions of IBEC essentially encapsulate the previous roles of the FIE. IBEC staff provide advice in response to membership enquiries and also engage in direct consultation with members on all aspects of employment, such as pay, contracts, conditions of employment, recruitment, discipline and dismissal. This includes direct negotiation and bargaining on behalf of members and representation before hearings of the Labour Court, the Labour Relations Commission, Rights Commissioners and the Employment Appeals Tribunal.

Table 6.9
FIE/IBEC Mediation, Arbitration and Negotiations

	1986	1987	1988	1989*	1992*	1995	1996	1997*
Labour Court investigation	538	488	386	394	217	159	169	170
Labour Court/Labour Relations Commission conciliation	1,470	1,146	874	1,014	684	486	556	546
Employment Appeals Tribunal	396	190	n/a*	216	258	165	159	225
Rights Commissioner	586	429	n/a*	346	266	204	173	247
Equality Officer	28	35	n/a*	72	18	11	6	28
Consultation with members	6,400	6,919	6,726	5,864	4,804	4,218	4,048	3,917
Trade union negotiations	2,928	2,842	2,702	2,540	1,286	797	764	1,040

* Figures for the following years not available in IBEC annual reports: 1990, 1991, 1993, 1994 and since 1997.
Source: IBEC annual reports

Education and Training

It is common for larger employer associations to provide training and development programmes for their membership. Particular emphasis is often placed on training HR/industrial relations specialists. Associations generally attempt to keep the membership up to date on current developments in areas such as employment law, working conditions and EU matters. Employer associations may also run joint training and development programmes with national or regional management training centres, which eases the demand on resources while meeting the needs of the membership. An example here is IBEC's joint training initiatives with the Irish Management Institute (IMI).

Collective Bargaining

By far the most obvious service provided by employer associations for their affiliated membership is in the actual conduct of collective bargaining. The role of employer associations in representing members in collective bargaining is important at two levels: multi-employer bargaining at industrial, regional or national level and enterprise-level bargaining (see also Chapter 9). The issue of bargaining levels is significant in determining the role of employer associations in collective bargaining. Traditionally, the major role of employer associations has been in the conduct of multi-employer bargaining, especially at industry or national level. In the UK context, the Donovan Commission (1968: 20) remarked that 'the practice of industry wide bargaining is closely bound up with the existence of employers' associations'.

It went on to conclude that a major reason why firms continued to remain members of employer associations was their support for multi-employer bargaining:

> … membership of employers' associations is a consequence of unquestioning commitment to maintain the formal system of industrial relations. The system provides for industry-wide bargaining; employers' associations are essential for this; therefore companies belong to employers associations (Donovan Commission 1968: 22).

While this argument has some foundation, it is clear that where the focus of bargaining has shifted upwards to national level or downwards to enterprise level, the role and importance of employer associations in collective bargaining has remained prominent. Multi-employer bargaining on an industry-wide basis has traditionally meant a key role for the appropriate employer association in conducting negotiations over pay and related issues on behalf of their affiliated membership. This form of bargaining was particularly common in Britain up to the 1980s but seems to have waned since then, with greater emphasis on enterprise-level bargaining. It still remains a common format for collective bargaining in other countries, such as Germany, and is practised in some industrial sectors in Ireland. The CIF, for example, continues to play an important role in collective bargaining in the general building sector.

The apex of multi-employer bargaining involves negotiations at national level involving central employer association(s), trade unions and possibly government. This form of collective bargaining gives a very prominent role to 'peak-level' employer associations. During periods of centralised pay agreements in Ireland (1970–1982, 1987 to date), employer associations, particularly IBEC, play a pivotal role in representing employer opinion to the other social partners. In effect, this means that individual affiliated members delegate bargaining responsibilities to their employer associations, thus making the employer association and not the individual employer the main actor on the employer side in industrial relations negotiations on pay and associated issues.

As we shall see in Chapter 13, collective bargaining in Ireland in the post-World War II period was initially characterised by the wage round system and later by a series of national agreements. Between 1946 and 1970 we had twelve wage rounds, five of which were negotiated centrally between employer representatives and trade unions, giving a prominent role to employer associations. The remainder were characterised by periods of intensive collective bargaining at either industry or enterprise level, with wage increases permeating through to most organised employees (see Roche 1997b).

In the 1970–1982 period, employer associations, largely through the Irish Employers Confederation and the Federated Union of Employers (now IBEC), played a major role in the negotiation of a series of centralised pay agreements. When this system ended in 1982, there was a return to so-called 'free' collective bargaining in the private sector. This changed the role of employer associations from being the key employer actor in pay negotiations to a more supportive role in providing advice and assistance to individual enterprises and co-ordinating approaches to pay negotiations. The pattern of centralised national agreements on pay and related issues was re-established through the Programme for National Recovery (PNR), negotiated by the 'social partners' in 1986, and helped restore the then FUE (now IBEC) and, to a lesser extent, other employer associations such as the CIF to their pivotal position in national pay bargaining. Since then, we have had five further centrally negotiated agreements, some of which made for provision for some degree of local (enterprise-level) bargaining, which also facilitated a significant role for employer association involvement in the conduct of enterprise-level industrial relations on pay and related matters.

It is therefore apparent that while enterprise-level collective bargaining was sometimes thought to leave little for employer associations, this is demonstrably not the case in the Irish context. Where the focus of pay bargaining has shifted to enterprise level, as in the 1982–1986 period, there was little evidence of a dramatic reduction in the role of employer associations. Indeed, it appears that employer associations have an important role to play in single-employer bargaining. This role incorporates the co-ordination of policy on pay- and employment-related issues, formulating general guidelines for affiliated employers, supplying research data and information for use in negotiations and providing expert personnel to either conduct the negotiations or advise and assist local management. This supportive and co-ordinating role at enterprise level is an important one from an employer viewpoint. By giving advice on pay trends and related issues, employer associations provide the basic information with which the individual organisation enters the bargaining process. By co-ordinating employer approaches, it establishes a framework for the conduct of such negotiations and by providing negotiating personnel, it may either conduct the negotiations or advise/assist management in such negotiations.

Disputes Procedures and Adjustment

Closely associated with the prevalence of multi-employer bargaining is employer association involvement in the operation of disputes procedures. This role seems particularly important in some sectors of industry in the UK, but is a significantly less prominent function of employer associations in Ireland. However, employer associations do tend to actively promote the use of workplace grievance and disputes procedures that cater for dispute referral to third-party conciliation and arbitration. Unlike the UK, however, the operation of external disputes procedures at industry or national level by employer associations never played a significant role in the Irish industrial relations framework. Here, disputes procedures are normally negotiated at enterprise level. The role of employer associations is primarily to assist and advise members on the formulation and operation of such procedures.

The provision of strike insurance or other types of mutual defence schemes for employers involved in an industrial dispute has been a traditional function of employer associations. Again, practice varies widely, from informal commitments of support, through mutual aid agreements to standard insurance schemes.

CHAPTER 7

The Nature of Industrial Action

INTRODUCTION

Industrial conflict is one of the most emotive aspects of industrial relations and a major reason why the field often makes headlines in the media. One has only to think of the disputes over recognition and working conditions between Dunnes Stores and the MANDATE trade union in 1995 and 1996, the nurses' dispute with the Health Board and Voluntary Hospitals in 1997, the Garda 'blue flu' in 1998 or the pay dispute between the Association of Secondary Teachers of Ireland (ASTI) and the Department of Education in 2000–2002. Inevitably, media commentary is driven by immediate concerns of those involved – management, workers, government and consumers – with the causes of the dispute being rehearsed from differing perspectives. The media also frequently pronounce on the 'rights' and 'wrongs' of the dispute. Thus, the nurses and Dunnes Stores disputes received overall media support while the secondary teachers' actions were generally condemned. Such support or condemnation is almost invariably based on underlying, but unidentified, value judgments.

While it is easy to highlight the inadequacies of media and popular commentaries, academic analysis is also categorised by differences and contradictions that reflect varying industrial relations paradigms and their underlying assumptions. Two broad conflicting assumptions as to the nature of industrial conflict can be identified. The first proceeds on the implicit assumption that such conflict is frictional and is not a fundamental aspect of the employment relationship. The second explicitly sees industrial conflict as being inherent in the employment relationship and/or the nature of society.

At first glance industrial conflict appears to be something that should be easily identifiable. Actions such as strikes, lockouts, go slows and work to rules are manifest forms of industrial action and obviously constitute conflict. Less obvious forms of conflict are absenteeism, labour turnover and dismissals. Even actions such as sabotage, industrial espionage and passive non-co-operation can be expressions of conflict. Hebdon and Stern (1998: 204) note that arbitration and strikes can be direct substitutes. This view of conflict is a variation on the notion that diplomacy is war conducted by another means.

Some influential social scientists even consider competition in business as a form of conflict. Dahrendorf (1959: 209) writes, 'I can see no reason why a conceptual distinction between competition and conflict should be necessary or, indeed, desirable'. In support of this view one can point to the regulation of competition, which sees some of the most bruising conflicts in business that can far exceed the importance and size of industrial relations disputes. The dispute between the American federal government and Microsoft, resolved in 2002, is a case in point.

Conflict, then, is capable of taking a wide variety of forms, which is difficult to encapsulate in a single definition and which may not even be immediately recognisable as conflict. Given the difficulties in defining conflict, industrial relations scholars have drawn attention to the diverse forms that conflict can take and the way in which it is organised. Thus, it is well accepted that conflict can be collective or individual, organised or unorganised (spontaneous), expressed or latent and may occur between workers and management, between workers and workers or between managers and managers (see Jackson 1991). These are distinctions which are explored further in this chapter.

APPROACHES TO THE STUDY OF CONFLICT

A standard starting point for analysing conflict is the unitarist-pluralist dichotomy introduced into the study of industrial relations by Alan Fox (1966) in his work for the UK Donovan Commission 1965–1968. The analysis arose from the Oxford School of Industrial Relations and was an effort to redress the lack of theoretical analysis in the subject. This work must be viewed against the historical context from which it emerged. The key features of this context were rising and high levels of trade union membership and the apparent failure, at least in advanced economies, of traditional management policies of opposition to unionisation (see Chapter 5). Fox (1966) presented unitarism and pluralism under two headings: as competing conceptual frameworks for viewing the industrial enterprise and as alternate employer approaches to the management of industrial relations. He categorised unitarism as a view of the industrial enterprise in which there is one source of authority and one focus of loyalty. Unitarism proceeds on the implicit premise that organisations are essentially cohesive and harmonious units and that all members of the organisation (management and employees) have common interests and share common goals (Fox 1966, 1974, 1977; Marchington 1982).

In essence, unitarism views the industrial enterprise as a team. Implicit in the team view is the acceptance of a common goal, that there is no place for factions and that people accept their places. Conflict is viewed as dysfunctional, occurring only as a result of misunderstandings, the action of troublemakers, a breakdown in communications or other non-fundamental reasons – namely frictional factors. In this perspective, industrial conflict is not seen as inevitable and a need for institutional arrangements to deal with conflict hardly arises. Appropriate management initiatives, such as effective communication, proper recruitment and selection and leadership, should be capable of either preventing conflict or resolving it when it arises.

Within the unitarist framework unions are contradictorily viewed as either too powerful or no longer necessary. They either 'achieve too much for their members in that they block change and inhibit efficiency or, conversely, as being irrelevant in that management is much more able than trade unions to identify and satisfy employees' needs' (Marchington 1982: 38).

Fox (1966) contrasted this unitarism with a pluralist conceptual framework that he considered offered a more realistic view of the industrial enterprise and which also held out the prospect of more effective management of industrial relations. He argued that pluralism accepts the reality that there are different interests at the heart of the employment relationship and as a result there is the potential for conflict. Insofar as there are shared goals within an organisation these are instrumental – workers need to earn a living and the employers need workers to produce output.

Pluralism implies that factions and different groups are likely to emerge in organisations and these cannot be eliminated or integrated fully into the organisation. Management's job is to balance the competing interests. This perspective, Fox (1966) argued, allows for the development of a more realistic approach to channelling and limiting any conflict that may arise. Fox (1966) categorises the team view inherent in unitarism as unrealistic and dysfunctional, as it limits the development of effective policies to manage and channel conflict. In resisting unionisation, long-term damage may be caused to industrial relations as union recognition may only be achieved after a trial of strength, involving attempted dismissal of union activists (troublemakers), strikes or other industrial action. By contrast, a pluralist view allows for the reality of trade union recognition by the development of appropriate procedures and including relevant actors, such as shop stewards, in the processes of conflict resolution. In effect, management regain power by sharing it.

PERSPECTIVES ON CONFLICT

The unitarist-pluralist dichotomy has been used to shed light on the actions and behaviour of individuals and groups who are involved in conflict situations. Of particular significance in industrial relations is the impact of differing conflict perspectives on the actions and behaviour of managers and their representatives in supervision in dealing with industrial conflict. Adopting a unitarist or pluralist perspective may lead to differing responses to the management of conflict, as illustrated in Table 7.1. This outlines ideal responses to conflict and, as Marchington (1982) points out, managers may behave in a unitarist fashion in one situation and be pluralist in other circumstances. Furthermore, as Fox (1974) and Purcell and Sisson (1983) have shown, the unitarist-pluralist distinction does not exhaust the range of options open to management (see Chapters 14 and 15). Nonetheless, the classification is useful as a starting point and indeed has formed the foundation for much subsequent analysis.

DEVELOPMENTS IN CONFLICT ANALYSIS POST-DONOVAN

Goldthorpe (1974) notes that politicians and public policy-makers in the UK largely disregarded the recommendations of the Donovan Commission, introducing instead the ill-fated Industrial Relations Act 1971. In contrast to its fate among public policy-makers, the unitarist-pluralist analysis had a major impact on industrial relations practitioners and on subsequent academic analysis. At the practitioner level, personnel managers responded by introducing pluralist policies and procedures in the late 1960s and 1970s (see Marchington 1982). This change was arguably driven more by pragmatism than any ideological commitment to pluralism. Low unemployment, arising from Keynesian post-war demand management, had changed the balance of power between capital and labour and meant that employers had to accommodate this reality. Thus, acceptability of the Donovan procedural prescriptions was assisted by the fact that they were gently leading people in the direction in which they were going anyway.

The influence of the Donovan prescriptions extended to Ireland, with personnel managers moving to negotiate workplace-level procedural agreements. The widespread proceduralisation of Irish workplace industrial relations, which exists today in unionised companies, is a direct result of this development (see Murray 1984; Wallace 1989). For industrial relations academics, the unitarist-pluralist classification has become a standard tool of classification and analysis. Conceptual approaches that start from the implicit assumption that conflict is frictional and/or dysfunctional are classified as unitarist. Those that see conflict as being inherent in the employment relationship are categorised as pluralist. We now consider these in greater detail.

Unitarism Developed

The various unitarist approaches have an underlying assumption that industrial conflict is frictional, not fundamental and its elimination is within management control. Unitarism allows that differences of interest may arise at an individual or group level, but 'class' as a unit of analysis is not deployed and the possibility of class conflict is simply not recognised (see Dahrendorf 1959).

Implicit examples of unitarist ideology are found in the various human relations approaches, which originate with the work of Mayo in the 1920s (Mayo 1949; Rose 1977). Human relations was paradoxically a reaction to the class conflicts associated with the growth of mass production and the introduction of scientific management in the US in the early decades of the twentieth century. However, as Coser (1956: 24) points out, Mayo 'never considers the possibility that an industrial relations system might contain conflicting interests, as distinct from different attitudes or "logics"'. To Mayo, management embodied the central purposes of society and all of his research was conducted to help management solve its problems (Coser 1956: 24).

In the human relations school, conflict is variously seen as a failure to meet the social needs of workers, incompatible personalities, overly strict supervision, the action of troublemakers or deviants, inadequate management or breakdown in communications (Mayo 1949; Scott and Homans 1947; Whyte 1951; Rose 1977). According to Mayo (1949: 128), the elimination of conflict and different interests is merely a matter of 'intelligent organisation that takes careful account of all the group interests involved'. Mayo (1949: 23, 191) envisages this being done by management deploying certain 'social skills' to ensure good communication and mutual understanding. Dahrendorf (1959: 111) points out that popular writers on management echo and adopt this implicit unitarist view that the individual must understand the goals and functions of the industrial enterprise as their goals and functions (see Drucker 1950: 156–65).

Arguably, the most significant omission in the human relations treatment of conflict arises not from *a priori* theoretical considerations, but the systematic suppression of the evidence of both individual and collective conflict observed during the Hawthorne studies. Bramel and Friend (1981), writing in *American Psychologist*, document these lapses: 'worker resistance to management was commonplace at Hawthorne (despite absence of a union), yet tended to be covered up in the popular writings of Mayo and Roethlisberger' (Bramel and Friend 1981: 874). They note that management employed dismissals, threats, the removal of breaks and increased hours of work. Restrictions of output among workers and a concern for the job security of fellow workers were also observed by the investigators but written off by them as irrational (Bramel and Friend, 1981: 875). Thus, Bramel and Friend (1981: 867) go on to note that the very evidence uncovered in the Hawthorne studies contradicts the conflict-free view of the capitalist firm.

The Depression of the 1930s was not a fertile ground for the 'soft' policies advocated by the human relations school. Indeed, Rose (1977: 170) notes 'the rapid decay of the approach with the spread, and relative failure, of human relations training for supervisors'. The growing unionisation in the US following the introduction of Roosevelt's New Deal and the 1935 Wagner Act saw a move away from human relations (Rose 1977).

Finally, the approach was subject to devastating critical assaults. Rose (1977: 171) writes that 'between 1946 and 1950 nearly all the conventional charges against the school were systematically pressed: neglect of unions; managerial bias; acceptance of manipulation; *inadequate treatment of industrial conflict*; failure to relate the factory to the wider social structure and fear of anomie'. The attacks culminated in exposure of fatal methodological flaws in the Hawthorne studies and criticism of its neglect of economic factors (Rose 1977: 172) The development of the neo-human relations school post-World War II can also be seen as a reaction to the limitations of the earlier approach, particularly the neglect of financial rewards (Rose 1977).

Maslow (1945) provided an explanation for conflict arising at an individual level. He identified a hierarchy of needs, with the implication that failure to meet the needs at any level could lead to conflict (Maslow 1954). Thus, when basic needs were met, employees were identified as possessing a need for personal growth, or self-actualisation. Meeting these needs could avoid conflict and lead to more productive and happier workers (Huczynski and Buchanan 1991). Herzberg (1968) introduced the distinction between satisfiers and dissatisifiers; poor pay may create dissatisfaction (and conflict) but good pay will not necessarily create satisfaction (absence of conflict). While the neo-human relations approach was influential in management circles in the 1960s and 1970s, it had little impact on the practise of industrial relations, not least because like the earlier human relations approach, it sought to deal with conflict in a totally managerial framework, excluding collective actors (see Rose 1977).

The human resource management (HRM) approach to conflict is conceptually like its human relations predecessors, i.e. an implicitly unitarist framework (see Walton 1985). However, it is much more sophisticated than simple unitarism. It does not imply an absence of conflict, merely that it can be handled via appropriate human resource policies, thus retaining the key feature of the earlier human relations approaches. The greater sophistication is inherent in the panoply of policies measures that HRM can deploy. Teamworking, team briefings, merit pay, performance appraisal and a host of other techniques are indicative of an awareness of a highly developed need for planning to avoid conflict and ensuring employees are motivated – a possibility absent in Fox's (1966) sketch of unitarism.

It may be argued that HRM has had greater impact in tackling conflict than its conceptual predecessors. There is indeed evidence to support a substantial decrease in conflict (as measured by strikes and changes in workplace relations) since the early 1980s; however, the contribution of HRM to such a decrease is uncertain. Globalisation, the failure of state socialism as an alternative to capitalism, social partnership, neo-liberal economic policies and the decreased power of labour vis-à-vis capital are just some of a number of alternative causal variables for any reduction in conflict. Even if HRM has worked to reduce overt conflict, such as strikes and effort bargaining, Edwards (1992: 363) argues it 'has not dissolved the bases of conflict' and it is crucial to understand where lines of tension remain.

Pluralism Developed

As with the unitarist-based academic explanations of conflict, there is a range of approaches to the analysis of conflict that can be classified under the banner of pluralism. Defined in this broad sense, pluralism means that the employment relationship is viewed as being based on a 'plurality of interests'. All approaches share the proposition that to a greater or lesser degree, conflict is inherent in the employment relationship. It is not hard to sketch out *a priori* reasons why conflict might be a fundamental part of the employment relationship. Employer needs for productivity, cost effectiveness and change can be at odds with workers' needs for job security, 'good pay' and rewarding work (for example, see Allen 1971; Jackson 1987; Hyman 1989; Huczynski and Buchanan 1991).

Indeed, such conflicts of interest are not just confined to the 'financial exchange' dimension but, in terms of pluralist analysis, are potentially inherent in other aspects of the employment relationship. The management of organisations requires the exercise of employer/managerial authority over employees on dimensions such as working time, work flow and task allocation (see Reed 1989; Morley *et al.* 1998). Furthermore, the contract of employment is unlike most commercial contracts, specific on rewards but not on effort. Any and all of these factors hold the potential for conflict and are emphasised to a greater or lesser degree by differing pluralist approaches. These are institutional-pluralist, Marxist and radical approaches. Each of these brings insights into the nature of industrial conflict and, by provoking debate, provides a greater degree of sophistication to researching and analysing conflict. As with the unitarist approaches, they do not provide definitive answers as to the cause of conflict, as there are fundamental differences between the various pluralist approaches.

Institutional Pluralism

Fox's original 1966 contribution is classified under the heading of institutional pluralism and is just one of a number of approaches which emphasise the role of institutions. Among other early writers in the institutional tradition were Flanders, W.E.J. McCarthy and Clegg in the UK and John T. Dunlop, Clark Kerr, A. Ross and P. Hartman in the US. Institutional approaches are considered functionalist in nature, since although they see conflict as normal and inherent in the employment relationship, they regard it as being capable of being accommodated and controlled by institutional mechanisms (see Goldthorpe 1974). In effect, institutional explanations of conflict focus on the organisations into which the differing interest tend to form and on the rules that regulate their relations (see Dunlop 1958).

An early approach in the institutional tradition was that of Ross and Hartman (1960: 49–54), who saw the development of industrial relations institutions, especially the growth of multi-employer bargaining and state intervention to assist dispute resolution, as having moderated 'primitive attitudes' to industrial action. These and other factors led them to predict the 'withering away of the strike', a prediction which was confounded by the resurgence of class conflict in Europe in the 1960s and 1970s (see Crouch and Pizzorno 1978).

The UK Donovan Commission recommendations for institutional reform were grounded in an institutional-pluralist perspective. This approach was also based on the tradition of voluntarism and aimed at developing workplace systems for channelling and resolving conflict. Jackson (1991) points out that there are options other than voluntarism arising from an institutional-pluralist approach. In Germany, the systems of co-determination at works council and board level constitute a set of institutional arrangements designed to prevent rather than channel or resolve conflict (Jackson 1991). In the 1950s and 1960s, these worked effectively to allow the rationalisation of the coal industry in Germany without major conflict, something which stands in stark contrast to the UK experience in the 1970s and 1980s. Other European countries, such as the Netherlands, France and Sweden, have also evolved employee participation institutional arrangements of a less developed nature designed to prevent conflict (see Ferner and Hyman 1998). Apart from limited provision for worker democracy in the state sector and European works councils in some companies, such co-determination provisions have not been a significant feature of the Irish system of industrial relations.

Marxism

The Marxist perspective sees conflict as being rooted in two factors – the nature of capitalist societies and the nature of work under capitalism. Capitalist society is divided into two classes – the propertied (bourgeoisie) and labouring or working class (proletariat), with the former expropriating the latter through the extraction of surplus value from their labour. The hierarchical nature of society and the unequal nature of rewards, combined with the unrewarding and alienating nature of work under capitalism, causes conflict (Hyman 1975; Braverman 1974). These factors lead (or may lead) to the development of class consciousness among workers, with industrial conflict taking place along class lines between the proletariat and the bourgeoisie. In essence, Marx's class analysis is concerned with exploring the effects of common economic conditions leading to organised action (see Dahrendorf 1959: 76). Marxism sees conflict as not just being inherent in the employment relationship but also as irreconcilable. Classical Marxism predicted that as capitalism matured, a growing and ever-impoverished working class would create the conditions for a working-class revolution. Industrial conflict is therefore part of a broader class-based conflict with the potential to overthrow capitalism.

Radicals

There is substantial crossover between Marxist and modern radical industrial relations academics, with the term being used interchangeably by some writers (see Salamon 2000). However, there are significant differences between classical Marxists and radicals, and it is necessary to highlight some of these differences. The radical perspective is focused on the basic premise of an inequality in the employment relationship – capital is considered more powerful than labour (see Fox 1974; Goldthorpe 1974). As with Marxism, there is a focus on the hierarchical nature of society, the unequal rewards and unrewarding work. The key difference is that the radical view does not approach the comprehensiveness or extremities of classical Marxist explanations. In fact, the term 'radical' is an elastic one, stretching from Social Democrats through the so-called radical-pluralism of Alan Fox (1974) to neo-Marxists who seek to analyse contemporary society using Marxist concepts in a non-doctrinaire way. This diverse group is united by an effort to understand the fundamental *root causes* of industrial conflict in a societal as well as an organisational context. The development of a radical critique in the 1970s can in part be seen as a response to the growth in industrial conflict post-Donovan and the failure of the pluralist prescriptions to stem the tide of strikes, especially unofficial ones.

The notion of a radical approach owes much to the work of Alan Fox, who revised his pluralist analysis in a series of publications from 1973 onwards. Fox (1974) focuses on the issues of power and control in the workplace. While continuing to assert the superiority of pluralism over unitarism, he pointed to limitations in the pluralist approach and a radical alternative. 'Like the pluralist approach it [the radical approach] emphasises the gross disparity of power between the employer and the individual employee' (Fox 1977: 141). He continues, 'unlike the pluralist, however, the radical does not see the collective organisation of employees as restoring the balance of power (or anything as yet approaching it) between the propertied and propertyless' (Fox 1977: 141). The need in pluralism to bind workers ever closer in procedures is evidence of a low trust relationship between those who manage and are managed. In essence, radicals point to the limits of institutional provisions where these are not underpinned by some degree of value consensus (Goldthorpe 1974).

Unlike classical Marxists, Fox (1974) does not anticipate any revolutionary change. He argues that the approach of many rank-and-file employees probably consists of a low-key acceptance of the organisation's essential characteristics, accepting it without 'enthusiasm and commitment' (Fox 1977: 143). In essence, the industrial enterprise is divided into a 'them and us' mentality and involves control, not commitment (see D'Art and Turner 2002c; Whelan 1982). In this scenario, conflict is institutionalised through collective bargaining but agreements may only be observed on the basis of expediency.

Instead of advancing the proposition that revolution is inherent or even inevitable in the employment relationship, radical writers have been concerned to explain the limited extent of industrial conflict. Fox (1977: 142) argues that if workers go too far in challenging management power, privilege, values and objectives, they would face the combined power of employer and government, which 'would soon reveal where ultimate power lay'. Challenges are acceptable on a limited range of issues and the concessions workers achieve mean they have a stake in the system and have much to lose from going too far. Thus, the differences of interests in the employment relationship may not even be 'synonymous with the use of overt collective industrial action' (Salamon 1998: 397). Later radical writers, such as Edwards (1986), note that while the 'actors' involved in industrial relation have 'divergent wants', they also depend on each other and so need to co-operate across a range of issues. Thus, conflict and co-operation are integral parts of the employment relationship.

A Perspective on Differing Conceptual Frameworks

The analysis above merely sketches the main elements of the various approaches, which require wider reading in order to explore them in greater depth. Neither has it been possible to explore all schools of thought. For instance, Weber saw the growth of bureaucracy as having a major role in promoting conflict. Also, some human relations writers have given attention to systems factors, notably the role of technology on the management of employees. In this view certain technology promotes repetitive, unrewarding work, which is geared towards Taylorist work organisation (Woodward 1958). Such analysis was particularly identified with work in the automotive industry. However, outside of such classic examples it is not easy to identify a unidirectional link between conflict and technology. Blauner (1964) suggested that technology might initially lead to less rewarding work and increased conflict, but over time it would have a liberating effect and decrease conflict. Furthermore, Marxists have challenged the notion that technology is an independent variable. They point out that technology that dehumanises work is introduced to lower the costs of labour and to increase profits.

While the various methods are at odds with one another, the debate surrounding the approaches and modern empirical research has led to a more nuanced understanding of conflict. It is now clear that unitarism has many more strings to its bow in informing managerial policies than in the 'straw man' model advanced by Fox in 1966. However, unitarism has no capacity to explain the difference in conflict between countries and across time periods.

Whatever its limitations, Fox's (1966) contribution remains one of the most insightful and influential works in industrial relations theorising. The prescriptions have been largely adopted and implemented in many unionised organisations, albeit there are significant limitations, as with all institutional approaches, on their ability to contain conflict. Following the radical critique, it is now understood that pluralist analysis is based on the premise 'that institutional arrangements can influence behaviour, regardless of the distribution of power, personality factors, or the particular product or market conditions of the firm' (Wallace and O'Shea 1987). Clearly, such factors have the potential to limit or enhance pluralist prescriptions. That institutional arrangements can influence behaviour is not in doubt, but what is in question is the degree of institutional influence, the limitations on such influence and the precise effect of institutional arrangements relative to other factors, including economic and political ones. Furthermore, there is no guarantee that institutional arrangements, which in the past worked to prevent or resolve conflict, will continue to do so, or even if they do that they will continue to be highly regarded. It is salutary to note that the German system of strong unions, protective labour legislation and co-determination, which was praised for so long, has now come under sustained criticism as being at the root of that country's current economic malaise.

Contemporary Marxists have grappled with the failure of many of Marx's predictions to materialise. Some point to the extent to which capitalist societies reformed after the Great Depression of the 1930s, with Keynesian demand management policies and the welfare state ensuring the stability of such societies. Some claim that Marx predicted the *relative* not *absolute* impoverishment of the working class, while others suggest that impoverishment has been staved off in the developed world due to the extension of capitalism to the developing world. Writing from a classical Marxist perspective, Arrighi (1990:54) writes 'that in the past the tensions of capitalism could be eased by expansion of the system into new regions and that capitalism now operates on a truly global scale'. The extensive strikes in Korea in the 1980s and 1990s are seen as evidence of the extension of traditional capital-labour conflicts to the newer economies in the developing world (Cho, 1985; Edwards, 1992; Salamon, 2000). The Irish trade unions have taken an interest in the working conditions and trade union rights in developing countries, as demonstrated by the following extract from *The Irish Times*.

Abuse of Sportswear Workers Highlighted

Irish Olympic athletes, sportspeople and parents buying children's runners have been urged to back an international campaign aimed at stopping abuse of workers in the sportswear industry. Factories in developing countries are 'breaking all the rules' to meet the unreasonable demands of massive sports corporations. These companies will reap particularly large profits during this Olympic year, Ms Kanjai Kaewchoo, president of the Thai Textile Garment and Leather Workers' Federation, told the ICTU women's conference in Galway yesterday. Speaking through an interpreter, Ms Kaewchoo said that more than a million women in Thailand were employed in the sportswear industry and many are paid six cents a piece. Employees were regularly paid $3 a day to make $93 runners and could be forced to work up to forty-five extra hours a week – at the risk of losing their jobs. Apart from poor pay, sportswear manufacturing staff encountered backache and eye strain, while access to trade union membership was denied, she said. The Olympic Council of Ireland has been urged to back the Play Fair at the Olympics campaign, supported by ICTU, SIPTU and Oxfam Ireland (the website is www.fairolympics.org).

Source: Siggins (2004)

While a number of classical Marxist predictions have not been realised, the notion that industrial conflict arises from inherent antagonism between capital and labour remains a powerful hypothesis to explain the permanence of such conflict, its underlying causes and periodic resurgence despite pluralist or managerial efforts at containment. Many industrial relations writers, neo-Marxists included, now regard the organisation of work in a capitalist society as a complex mix of conflict and co-operation. The simple zero-sum game inherent in classical Marxist analysis is mediated by the interdependence of employers and workers. Controlling workers is only one way of achieving effective work organisation (see Grint 1991). Edwards (1992) notes that 'there are aspects of new employment systems which benefit workers, and critical analysis does not imply that workers' and managers' interests are totally opposed'. The possibility of worker resistance to the introduction of new information technology, which was of much concern to the European Commission in the 1980s, now seem misplaced as workers willingly embraced such technology. Indeed, workers have an interest in effective management and management have an interest in tapping their workforce's initiative and creativity. Thus, while there may be difference of interests underling the employment relationship, there are also strong imperatives which limit conflict and promote co-operation. Globalisation and international competition can heighten the need for collaborative arrangements to protect employment, although such collaboration may be less than total (see Chapter 12). This interdependence is evidenced by findings that workers and their representatives (shop stewards) prefer competent managers (Sturdy *et al.* 1992; Edwards 1992). This interdependence is also emphasised by the generally positive perceptions that studies reveal management have of the role played by shop stewards, findings which are at odds with the militant image in which they are sometimes portrayed (Donovan 1968; Wallace 1982; Ackers and Black 1992).

Table 7.1
Perspectives on Industrial Conflict

The Unitarist Perspective
The unitarist perspective on conflict in organisations essentially views conflict as an aberration that occurs because 'something has gone wrong'. Harmony and unity are seen as the natural state, with conflict an abnormal phenomenon that occurs as a result of some failure in the normal functioning of the organisations, such as poor communications, poor management or the work of 'troublemakers'. While viewing conflict as abnormal, the unitarist perspective also sees conflict as essentially negative and damaging to the normal harmonious, productive state of the organisation. Thus, conflict is viewed as something that

can and should be avoided. Where it does occur, management should take appropriate steps to eradicate it, probably by addressing the alleged source, i.e. improve communications or organisational design, training managers or getting rid of troublemakers.

The Pluralist Perspective

The pluralist perspective views conflict as a naturally occurring phenomenon in organisations. It is accepted as an inherent characteristic of organisations arising from the differing perspectives and interests of all the groups and individuals who make up the organisation. Since conflict is seen as inevitable, management should expect it to occur and plan for its eventuality so that it can be handled successfully and not endanger the achievement of the organisation's primary objectives. This pluralist perspective is consistent with the view that conflict is not necessarily negative but can have beneficial effects. Efforts should therefore be concentrated on channelling conflict to realise such organisational benefits. The emphasis is therefore on the management of conflict as opposed to its elimination.

The Classical Marxist Perspective

Conflict in capitalist societies is seen as a symptom of the structural enmity that exists between capital and labour, employer and employee. Such enmity arises from the organisation of work in capitalist societies and the unequal distribution of power between the dominant establishment group that owns the means of production (employers, shareholders) and those whose labour is required to produce goods and services (workers). Therefore, conflict in organisations is simply a manifestation of broader class conflict in relation to the distribution of power in society, and organisations themselves are simply a microcosm of a broader class conflict between the bourgeoisie (who control economic resources and political power) and the proletariat, with managers representing the interests of capital. In the Marxist perspective conflict is seen as instigating revolutionary change designed to dismantle the capitalist system, redistribute power in favour of workers and the working class and ultimately achieve a classless society.

The Radical Perspective

The radical perspective overlaps with Marxist analysis – it sees conflict as endemic in industrial societies, with a major cause being the unequal power distribution both in society and in organisations. Efforts by employers to organise work lead to a need for control, which tends to lead to compliance rather than commitment. Revolution or radical social change is not to be expected, as workers generally accept the system and their place in it. However, there are limitations to any efforts to contain conflict through institutions or procedural regulation. Workers may observe agreements on the basis of expedience. More recently, the complex interaction between conflict and co-operation and the mutual interdependence of managers and workers is emphasised. HRM is seen as another form of control, leading to work intensification, stress and long working hours – the new forms of social conflict.

Source: Adapted and extended from Morley *et al.* (1998: 263–4)

Functions of Conflict

While conflict may pose problems for society, organisations and workers, there is a strong tradition in social science that argues that conflict is functional. Coser (1956) has been an advocate for viewing conflict in a functional light and a strong critic of those who regard it as dysfunctional. Writing on American industrial relations, he notes that union organisation has frequently been accompanied by the organisation of employers into employer organisations, even to the extent that sometimes the employers have organised at the suggestion and with the help of the union (Coser 1956: 131). However, he is careful to note limitations to this functionality, with conservative employers seeing no need for an accommodation with unions and wishing to 'smash' them (Coser 1956: 130–1). This is arguably the dominant trend in the US since the 1960s.

Those who see conflict as functional oppose its suppression and warn of the dangers inherent in such a utopian venture. For example, Dahrendorf (1959: 224), a noted critic of Marxism, declares the notion of the suppression of social conflict as meaningless. He asserts 'that effective suppression of conflict is in the long run impossible' (Dahrendorf 1959: 224). At a societal level, it is not hard to think of examples of failed attempts to contain, suppress or eliminate conflict. In former Communist countries such as Poland and the Soviet Union, free trade unions were not allowed and the primary function of those unions that did exist was to serve the needs of the state. This suppression of industrial conflict only led to greater upheavals eventually. Right-wing dictatorships have experienced similar developments, as exemplified by the collapse of apartheid in South Africa and the overthrow of the Fascism of Franco in Spain, the Salazar in Portugal and the fall of the Pinochet regime in Chile.

In accepting the social reality of conflict, Dahrendorf (1959: 207) has suggested that Coser 'was too preoccupied with what he himself tends to call the "positive" or "integrative" functions of conflict'. For instance, Coser (1956) considered that conflict needed to be contained within communal bounds (trade unions and employer organisations being classical examples) and he disapproved of non-communal conflict. However, the requirement that conflict be conducted within a communal framework represents a contentious value judgment that is at odds with social reality. Specific conflicts can, and do, take their own course and, as Hyman (1989: 108) contends, are not necessarily capable of being contained within 'the social structures which give rise to them'. The many recent demonstrations against globalisation, sometimes involving violence, is indicative of a resurgent conflict against capitalism and a response by capitalism not contained within communal or institutional boundaries. This conflict is also much more intense and violent than industrial conflict in most developed countries.

In an organisational context, Morley et al. (1998) note a number of positive aspects of conflict, including the capacity to facilitate articulation of individual or group grievances, the identification and review of discriminatory or unfair employment practices, positive changes in work arrangements or management regulation and as a 'pressure release' mechanism that allows parties to vent opinions and positions that are a source of concern. Within the discipline of organisational behaviour, the interactionist perspective argues that it is necessary to ensure a 'prescribed' level of industrial conflict and means for its resolution in organisations, since the absence of conflict inhibits initiative and innovation (Robbins 1983; van de Vliert 1985; de Dreu and van de Vliert 1997).

Viewed from an industrial relations perspective, many aspects of our current employment practice and regulation derive from former conflicts. The general provision for a forty-hour working week was established in the early to mid-1960s in a series of groundbreaking industrial disputes – this was subsequently reduced, without overt conflict, to thirty-nine hours as part of the Programme for National Recovery (PNR), 1987–1991. The claim for an increase in the statutory redundancy provisions to two weeks' pay per year, introduced in 2003 as part of the Sustaining Progress agreement, first arose out of a sit-in at Peerless Rugs in Athy and a strike in the Irish Glass Bottle Company in Dublin during 2002. Irish equality legislation of the 1970s arose in large part from European Community requirements, but its introduction was also a result of campaigning by the women's movement and the trade unions, which brought them into conflict with government and employers.

It is not just on the workers' side that one can identify examples of conflict being functional, as it has benefited both employers and government. In the 1980s, a series of disputes in which unions were relatively unsuccessful led to greater flexibility in the Irish labour market, the reduction of traditional effort bargaining and union givebacks or concession bargaining (Wallace and Clifford 1998). Equally, the willingness of union members to accept the modest terms of the PNR in 1987 cannot be separated from these developments and the concern that Irish trade unions had at the negative strike outcomes for UK trade unions under Thatcherism (see Chapter 13).

The Dual Face of Conflict

While drawing attention to the functional nature of conflict, it is also the case that parties to industrial relations can suffer substantial damage from conflict, both personal and organisational. This can arise from factors such as inadequate measures to handle conflict, inadequate negotiating skills or, as economists point out, through imperfect information as to where each side is prepared to settle in a dispute. More fundamentally, it may be inherent in the nature of the particular conflict situation. Indeed, in many situations conflict may have a *dual nature*, having both positive and negative aspects to it. When company closures occur, there are frequently harrowing interviews with employees who are traumatised by the immediate impact and express great anxiety for their future. The negative personal aspects of this conflict are manifest, yet the alternative for an economy as a whole is the stagnation of state Socialism. Faced with competition from low-cost countries, employers advocate 'moving up the value chain' (RTÉ interview with Brendan Butler, IBEC, September 2003). This is a functional strategic choice for an economy if that can indeed be achieved. However, industrial restructuring sees workers pay a heavy price, because they have sunk costs in their employment.

Principled opposition to this restructuring, such as occurred with the many factory occupations in the 1970s in Ireland, has been replaced with the negotiation of redundancy payments in excess of the minimum provided under the Redundancy Payments Acts. In other words, redundancies and restructuring are now generally accepted; the only substantive issue is often the terms on which the redundancies will take place. The Peerless Rugs and Irish Glass Bottle disputes of 2002 were settled following enhanced redundancy payments. Indeed, it is not uncommon for practitioners to claim that when companies seek redundancies these are oversubscribed where the severance terms are generous. This is a classic instance of the institutionalisation of conflict through collective bargaining.

However, the influence of this institutionalisation is confined to the unionised sector. In contrast to the practice in their home country, many US non-union multinationals pay redundancy terms well above the statutory minimum, for example, in Digital, eight weeks' pay per year of service. In this way employees in non-union companies enjoy benefits first negotiated by unionised employees – in effect, these companies might be considered to be, in part, 'crypto-unionised'.

NATURE AND FORMS OF INDUSTRIAL ACTION

As noted in the introduction to this chapter, the concept of industrial conflict is a broad one and includes latent conflict. Latent conflict is conflict that may be inherent in the employment relationship but not expressed; industrial action, on the other hand, is the manifest expression of conflict. The fact that conflict may be latent implies that an absence of conflict cannot automatically be considered a 'good thing'. Workers may be unable to express conflict because they have insufficient power, resources or, alternatively, management may buy out conflict to the long-run detriment of the organisation – what practitioners refer to as 'cheque book' industrial relations.

While it is difficult to define conflict, industrial action can be defined as 'any temporary suspension of normal working arrangements which is initiated unilaterally by either employees (whether through their union or not), or management, with the aim of exerting pressure within the collective bargaining process (Salamon 2000: 411). At a general level, industrial action is generally divided into two broad categories: explicit and organised collective industrial action and unorganised and implicit individual industrial action (see Salamon 1998). Organised, collective action encompasses systematic, collective efforts in pursuing a conscious strategy through co-ordinated action designed to achieve specified objectives. Table 7.3 contains examples of the main forms of both individual and collective industrial action.

The most common examples of organised industrial action arising from workers are strikes, go slows, overtime bans and the withdrawal of co-operation. Lockouts and plant closures are less recognised management-initiated conflict. Unorganised or individual action tends to represent spontaneous, reactive and random responses to the employment relationship, which does not form part of a conscious strategy on behalf of its proponents. Unorganised or individual conflict can include absenteeism, turnover, theft, passive non-co-operation and industrial sabotage on the employee side. Overly strict supervision, bullying, victimisation, speed-ups, industrial accidents and unauthorised deductions of wages constitute examples of management-initiated conflict. The conceptual difference between the two forms of action is that individual unorganised action represents a 'withdrawal from the source of discontent' by individuals, while organised collective action is more likely to be a conscious strategy to change the situation that is the source of the discontent (Hyman 1989: 56). In terms of conducting research, Edwards (1992) has argued 'that the key question is not whether a given form of behaviour is a type of conflict but how the conflictual aspects of work are organised, expressed and regulated'.

Individual Unorganised Conflict

While absenteeism and high labour turnover can be indicators of individual conflict, this is not necessarily the case. An inability to attend work due to illness or other factors is not an indication of conflict. Absenteeism is determined by a range of factors, including the ability to attend work (affected by illness, sex role responsibilities, age and transportation difficulties) and the motivation to attend (see Gunnigle *et al.* 1997a). Absenteeism rates are influenced by the generosity or otherwise of social welfare systems (Edwards 1992). For example, the US has lower levels of absenteeism than Sweden, due mainly, if not exclusively, to the lower levels of social security in the US. Thus, absenteeism in the US may under-express the extent of individual conflict (as workers may find it too expensive to be absent), and over-express it in Sweden (where workers are not under such pressure to attend work). Equally, employees may persist working in what they consider unrewarding jobs because of high unemployment and the lack of an alternative choice. These reservations aside, absenteeism and turnover rates can be affected by the nature of the job – a job which has low discretion and is unrewarding may lead to higher absenteeism.

There are major difficulties in measuring absenteeism and accounting for its causes (O'Muircheartaigh 1975), but working days lost due to absenteeism are many multiples of working days lost due to strikes. According to the Small Firms Association (SFA), in 2002, the national average for absenteeism was 3.4 per cent, or 7.8 working days. For larger firms this rose to 4.6 per cent, or 10.5 working days, while for small firms the average fell to 2.6 per cent, or 5.9 working days.

Absenteeism rates also vary across sectors. As Table 7.2 shows, in 2002 the electronics industry had the highest average absence rate, followed by other manufacturing industries. Service industries such as food/drink/tobacco and wholesale distribution occupied the lower end of the average absence rate scale for 2002.

Labour turnover refers to the number of persons who leave an organisation within a specified time period. Clearly, employees leave organisations for a variety of reasons, many of which have little to do with industrial relations. Bowey (1974) classifies the factors generating wastage into 'pull' and 'push' factors. 'Pull' factors are those that attract employees to another organisation, while 'push' factors cause employees to leave involuntarily. 'Pull' factors identified include moving for higher earnings, moving to further one's career and the attraction of alternative job opportunities. 'Push' factors identified include leaving to avoid strains arising from interpersonal or other forms of conflict at work, 'running down' (reducing headcount) of an organisation and problems in relation to the induction/socialisation of new employees.

However, high turnover is more likely to be associated with the nature of work organisation as established by management. For instance, Royle and Towers (2002) note high levels of absenteeism in McDonald's as an expression of unorganised individual conflict against the McDonald's work system. Other individual forms of conflict can be subtle and virtually impossible to detect or measure. Employees may engage in passive non-co-operation, may under-perform in a number of ways or may exhibit low-trust behaviour. Such individual action may not even be conscious and can have long-term effects on the employment relationship.

Table 7.2
Average Absence Rate by Industry, 2002

Industry	Average Percentage Absence Rate
Electronics	4.61
Textiles/Clothing/Footwear	4.23
Non-metallic mineral products	3.92
Rubber/Plastics	3.91
Metals/Engineering	3.78
Chemical/Pharmaceutical/Healthcare	3.28
Food/Drink/Tobacco	3.23
Paper/Printing/Publishing	3.19
Wholesale distribution	2.18
Other	3.34

Source: SFA (2002)

It is important to note that individual action can emanate from management as well as workers. For instance, Salamon (2000: 424) notes that speed-ups, disciplinary action and unilateral changes to agreed working arrangements can be viewed as management-initiated conflict. Hyman (1989: 226), however, considers these to be 'part of the normal repressive reality of work'. This argument presumes that work is 'normally' repressive, whereas discipline and agreed work arrangements have a regulatory function and it is the *breach* of the regulatory function that constitutes management-initiated conflict.

Of course, the extent to which management engage in such breaches can largely be a matter of perception. In a study of forty-nine unofficial strikes, Wallace and O'Shea (1987: 140) note that only one manager saw himself as breaking procedures, while shop stewards and union officials reported a much higher level of managerial breaches. Beynon's (1973) study of the Ford motor plant in Halewood paints a vivid picture of the reality of speed-ups as management-initiated conflict. He notes that 'production managers out to make a name for themselves' engaged in speed-ups, resulting in 'unofficial walkouts'. 'We just said no and if they pushed it we went home … this was naked aggression being met with violent defiance' (Beynon 1973: 138–9). The eventual result was an agreement by management that 'conceded to stewards the right to hold the key that locked the assembly line' (Beynon 1973: 139).

Individual conflict may be directly or inversely related to collective forms of actions such as strikes. Wallace (1982) reported a direct relationship with turnover and strikes in the Limerick Ferenka plant – a highly strike-prone organisation which also had high turnover, with forty-four per cent of employees leaving in one year. On the other hand, in the UK coal industry, Handy (1968) reported an inverse relationship between strikes and individual forms of conflict, e.g. absenteeism, labour wastage and industrial accidents. Thus, when strikes fell in the coal mines, accidents rose. This is explicable by the fact that a significant proportion of strikes in mining were over safety. Where workers felt they could not undertake strikes against dangerous conditions, this led to increased accidents. Where accidents substitute for strikes in this way they are a manifestation of the costs of latent (unexpressed) industrial conflict. Thus, high employee discontent and high strikes can, depending on circumstances, be complements or substitutes for one another (see Jackson 1991: 216).

Collective Organised Conflict

As noted earlier, the various industrial relations traditions share a common view that conflict is inherent in the antagonism within the employment relationship. The 'fact' that the employment relationship may be characterised by conflict rarely gives rise to any public concern or comment, yet collective industrial action is commonly perceived as extremely negative and damaging. Rollinson (1993) identifies three principal reasons why industrial action is seen in such negative terms:

1. Industrial action (as initiated by workers) is normally vertical in nature and therefore challenges the legitimacy of management authority/prerogative in decision making.
2. Industrial action tends to be highly visible, both within and outside the organisation, and can often involve large numbers of workers.
3. The objective of industrial action tends to be misunderstood: such action is commonly seen as 'irrational' and/or dysfunctional, with most conflict situations viewed as being capable of resolution by discussions and negotiation and therefore should not result in industrial action.

Rollinson (1993) suggests that the argument that industrial action is irrational/dysfunctional is a fundamentally flawed perspective. While negotiation and compromise are capable of resolving much industrial conflict, it is inevitable that at some stage, and in some organisations, either party will not modify its position, but rather utilise some form of industrial action to achieve its aims. Thus, as Rollinson (1993: 252) specifically comments, industrial conflict is 'simply a rational extension of the negotiation process' (see also Morley *et al.* 1998). Indeed, collective bargaining requires the possibility of industrial action, since without that possibility there would be only a limited incentive for either party to reach agreement during negotiations. This is especially true of distributive bargaining – typically those negotiations over pay and other substantive terms of employment. Thus, the costs that industrial action may impose on both parties brings a reality to negotiations.

Organised collective conflict is generally associated solely with the existence of trade unions, a view that, while largely correct, is not fully accurate. The resistance of the 'luddites' to the new lace machines and factory production in the period 1811 to 1813 was notable for the fact that the opposition came from groups of workers who were not organised in the early trade unions, or combinations, as they were then called (Darvall 1964). Furthermore, pre-existing collective conflict among unorganised workers can be a trigger for unionisation. While collective conflict is not necessarily synonymous with trade unions, it is uncommon to find unorganised workers engaging in formal collective action. Indeed, the Industrial Relations Act 1990 only grants immunity for industrial action to trade unions and their members from being sued in common law. Thus, strikes are associated in the overwhelming majority of cases with the existence of a union. In essence, trade unions provide a mechanism for the expression of conflict in structured forms, such as strikes and go slows. They also provide an ordered mechanism for resolution of that conflict through collective bargaining.

While unions are the main initiators of collective conflict, this is almost invariably a reaction to management action or inaction. Salamon (2000: 424) notes that by passively resisting union demands or by unilaterally initiating change, it can 'place the onus on the employees or union to take direct industrial action'. Conceptually, then, all collective industrial action should be viewed as joint industrial action, in that both union and management will have decided to allow the action to proceed by making too few concessions to meet the demands of the other side or by demanding too much.

As Edwards (1992) correctly notes, a major defect in much theorising about the causes of industrial action has been an insufficient attention to the role of employers and managers. While trade unions are the most frequent initiators of collective conflict, employers also initiate conflict in the form of plant closures, lay-offs or lockouts. Salamon (2000: 421) notes that because of its permanency, plant closures or a threat of closure 'may be considered a more powerful sanction than the employees' temporary stoppage of work through strike action'. Lay-offs, on the other hand, have an implied temporary nature to them and indeed it is common for employers to give 'protective notice' to employees where they may be affected by industrial action but not part of that action themselves.

Published strike statistics do not distinguish between lockouts and strikes. Lockouts are rare in Ireland, in part due to the historical connotations arising from the 1913 lockout (see Yeates 2000). In some countries, the lockout may be more socially acceptable, such as in Germany, but even there it is seldom used (Fuerstenberg 1987: 170). Stokke and Thörnqvist (2001) note that a 'pure', or what they term '*active*' lockout – one initiated solely by the employer – is uncommon.

Table 7.3
Forms of Industrial Action

- **Strike:** Collective in nature, involving temporary withdrawal of labour.

- **Lockout:** The most conspicuous form of organised industrial action instigated by employers, which involves preventing the workforce, or a proportion thereof, from attending work.

- **Withdrawal of co-opération:** Collective in nature, involving the withdrawal of representatives from joint institutions; strict interpretation of and rigorous adherence to procedures, absence of flexibility.

- **Work to rule:** Collective in nature, involving working only in accordance with the strict interpretation of written terms and conditions of employment, job description or other rules, such as those concerning safety or hygiene.

- **Overtime ban:** Collective in nature, involving refusal to work outside normal contractual hours of work.

- **Go slow:** Collective in nature, involving working at a lower-than-average level of performance.

- **Work-in/sit-in:** Occupation of the workplace or section thereof; denial of access to management. This approach is often used to prevent movement of plant and equipment (often associated with plant closures).

- **Blacking of goods/services:** Refusing to handle goods or co-operate with services from a particular employer(s).

- **Unilateral management changes:** Changes to the agreed speed of work; work intensification; job insecurity; unilateral changes to terms of contract of employment by employer – if considered unreasonable by EAT, may constitute grounds for constructive dismissal.

- **Other management action:** Blacklisting of workers; harassment and intimidation; industrial accidents due to improper safety, speed-ups, etc.

- **Sabotage and industrial espionage:** Individual or collective in nature, involving conscious action to damage goods or equipment; illegitimate leaking of commercial information to competitors; distributing false, damaging information about an organisation.

- **Whistleblowing:** Generally individual but may be collective. Providing information on company malpractice, for example, in commercial area or health and safety matters.

- **Pilfering and theft:** Individual in nature, involving stealing by employees, either from the organisation or customers, and unauthorised deductions of wages by management.

- **Absenteeism:** Generically defined as all absences from work other than authorised leave. It is estimated that only a small proportion of absenteeism may represent a form of industrial action. Where it does, it can represent an individualised response to perceived problems in the workplace.

- **Labour turnover:** Only a proportion of labour turnover in organisations may represent a form of industrial action.

- **Motivational withdrawal:** Lack of trust; passive non-co-operation; low productivity.

OTHER FORMS OF COLLECTIVE INDUSTRIAL ACTION: AN OVERVIEW

Other forms of industrial action by employees include a ban on overtime, work to rule, go slow, withdrawal of co-operation and 'blacking' goods. In Ireland, any such action by workers is now subject to the notice and balloting provisions of the Industrial Relations Act 1990 if workers are to enjoy the immunities under that Act. In the past, UK workers in railways, mining and printing have used other forms of industrial action with considerable success (Clegg 1980: 259–60). The use of other forms of industrial action may be a warning to management of employees' opposition to a proposed course of action and a signal of their resolve to oppose it. In such instances, the action may be designed to prevent or limit the possibility of full-scale strike action but not to exclude it. Clegg (1980: 259) notes a strike may be 'too powerful a weapon to use', as it would be disproportionate in the disruption it would cause. Other forms of industrial action may be used as a cut-price substitute for all-out strike action, with the chief aim being to reduce the costs of industrial action to the union members.

As with individual conflict, collective forms of industrial action can be directly or inversely related to the incidents of strikes, with empirical evidence suggesting that a direct link is the most common. Clegg (1980: 260) notes 'that where one sanction is used within a plant the other is likely to be used as well'. Stoke and Thörnqvist (2001: 251) suggest 'that the relation between strikes and other forms of industrial conflict is complementary; high levels of strikes are associated with high levels of non-strike action, and vice versa'.

Statistics on the incidence of other forms of industrial action are not collected in Ireland and there is limited research on their occurrence. Wallace (1982) found that employers surveyed estimated such action was four to five times more frequent than strikes. However, that research is dated and there is no data to show how recent efforts to develop workplace partnership have affected their incidence. The strong likelihood is that, like strikes, the absolute incidence of such actions has declined, but changes in their incidence relative to strikes is more uncertain. In the UK, there was an increase in both strikes and non-strikes from 1980 to 1984 (Edwards 1992). Subsequently, strikes and other forms of industrial action fell but the relative popularity of non-strike action, such as overtime bans, seemed to rise (Edwards 1992: 378).

However, as with strikes, the use of other forms of action has the potential to be a double-edged sword. The ASTI's refusal to co-operate with the Leaving and Junior Certificate examinations in 2001 led to a public backlash that caused the union to back down on the threat (Frawley 2001a). Other forms of industrial action can also be more difficult to co-ordinate and ensure solidarity than a strike. They are also open to a range of cut-price employer responses, such as withholding pay – the Department of Education's response to the ASTI withdrawal of voluntary supervision of break times in 2000. In this case, the result was that the monies deducted were repaid to the ASTI teachers after the Data Protection Commissioner concluded that 'the Department had breached data protection law by using the [teachers'] trade union membership data as it had' (Frawley 2001b). Thus, as with strikes, the effectiveness of other forms of industrial action is contingent on a range of factors, including organisational, societal and legal ones.

Limitations on the Collective/Individual Classification of Conflict

The conceptual distinction between organised collective industrial action and unorganised individual industrial action is not clear-cut in real-world industrial relations. Some conflicts, such as absenteeism, speed-ups, theft and sabotage, may straddle the individual/collective and organised/unorganised divide. Speed-ups may arise not just from the individual ambition of a manager but may be driven by general company policy (see Beynon 1973). In cases where industrial action is illegal, groups of workers may resort to individual action in an organised way. Thus, in May 1998 the non-union Garda Representative Association (GRA) organised a 'blue flu' protest, despite the fact that the Gardaí are barred by law from being members of a trade union and from taking industrial action. This involved individual members of the GRA 'calling in sick' and not reporting for duty on a particular day – in effect, individual action that was organised. This phenomenon is not new, with Blyton and Turnbull (1994) noting its use previously in the New York Police Department. While the Garda 'blue flu' day was highly visible, much individual organised conflict at the level of work groups may go unnoticed and unrecorded. It may simply be impossible to distinguish passive non-co-operation from normal working.

In addition to the potential for individual action to be organised, apparently organised collective action can be reactive and spontaneous in nature. The American term 'wildcat strikes', implying a spontaneous reaction to a particular incident, captures the frequently reactive and spontaneous nature of such unofficial industrial action, which may not be part of any broader conflict strategy (see Hyman 1989). Absenteeism may be 'arranged' by groups of workers in order to artificially create overtime and supervisors may even acquiesce in such arrangements. This typically occurs where workers have a high degree of discretion over their work, as in the case of maintenance craft workers. The introduction of annualised hours has been used in attempts to decrease the extent of such overtime in a number of Irish companies. There is evidence for considerable success for such efforts where the overtime was truly discretionary (for example, Irish Cement). Efforts in other companies have been unsuccessful, notably Coca Cola, where large-scale expansion of demand led to the company having to buy out the Annual Hours arrangement, having initially paid for its introduction (see Darcy 1998).

Individuals may engage in theft but so may work groups. The definition of what constitutes theft may be socially defined; behaviour found in one group of workers may be regarded as theft while among other employees equivalent behaviour may not be defined as theft. On occasions, employees may see activities that management consider to be theft as informal compensation or a 'perk'. This is an issue that sometimes raises its head at the Employment Appeals Tribunal (EAT) in dismissal cases. Nonetheless, in formal industrial relations, the general unacceptability of theft is reflected in the standard penalty of summary dismissal often found in agreed disciplinary procedures. No more than any other form of conflict, theft is not confined to employees, as indicated by the necessity for statutory protection in the form of the Truck Acts 1831–1896. These Acts prevented payment in kind and restricted unauthorised deductions from wages by employers (von Prondzynski and McCarthy 1984: 66–8). These provisions still exist in the Payment of Wages Act 1991. Theft is not confined to manual workers, as indicated by the existence of white-collar crime, although this may be less visible, often because organisations may wish to avoid undesirable publicity.

Industrial espionage is mainly an individual form of conflict, although on occasion groups of employees, notably managerial or administrative employees, may combine in acts of industrial sabotage. Kelleher (2003: 14) asserts that 'industrial espionage cases are on the rise in Ireland' due to the greater use of computers and e-mail. This assertion seems to be based on anecdotal information rather than any systematic research, but nonetheless it emphasises the potential for such forms of conflict arising with information technology. It also draws attention to the fact that such conflict in the employment relationship is not confined to the 'cloth cap' era of industrial relations.

Whistleblowing is only distinguished from industrial espionage by the motivation of the individual and the legal legitimacy of disclosing such information. That whistle blowing is a form of individual conflict that can have significant effects on organisations is demonstrated by the release of information by a whistleblower in Allied Irish Banks (AIB) in May/June 2004. It is commonly believed that this information was released by a disgruntled AIB employee. The position of the whistleblower can be very vulnerable and in Ireland whistleblowers are not protected by legislation, even where they disclose wrongdoing which would be in the public interest. The vulnerability of whistleblowers is demonstrated by one of the most celebrated cases of whistleblowing, that involving Karen Silkwood. Karen Silkwood, was a union shop steward, who exposed major safety abuses at the Kerr McGee Corporation's Nuclear plant in Oklahoma in the late 1970s. As a result, the Nuclear Regulatoratory Authority of America closed the plant. Karen was killed in suspicious circumstances, shortly after providing the information detailing the abuse to her union official. Karen's parents were subsequently awarded $10,000,000 damages in a court case taken against the company, for company harassment of Silkwood during her employment (these events formed the basis of the film *Karen Silkwood* starring Meryl Streep).

Industrial sabotage is described as the 'deliberate disruption of work flows within an organisation or the undermining of the conditions whereby dominant management purposes are readily achieved' (Watson 1987: 306). Beynon (1973: 139) notes that before the introduction of negotiated agreements on the control of work in the Ford plant in Halewood, 'individual acts of sabotage were also common at this time. Men pulled the safety wire and stopped the line'. However, such acts of individually motivated sabotage could backfire on individuals if they did not have tacit collective approval. 'Unless you were sure of the support of your steward and workmates, to miss a job on the line at this time meant you took on the whole world' (Beynon 1973: 132–4). In organised industrial relations, industrial sabotage occurs but it is comparatively little used (Brown 1977). Rigby and Aledo (2001: 291) note industrial sabotage in Spain during strikes in 1999, including 'the cutting of electrical cables during a rail strike, engine drivers destroying the safety mechanisms in their cabs and striking shipyard workers immobilizing the bridge giving access to the Bay of Cadiz'. Macfarlane (1981: 60) suggests that 'when sabotage takes place it is normally in the context of a bitter industrial dispute and is carried out by individual strikers, without the authority of the strike organisers'. Sabotage is so unacceptable that its occurrence is seldom even contemplated in procedural agreements. Indeed, in Ireland it is normal for strikers and management to agree on an orderly rundown of plants prior to strike action and to provide for emergency maintenance, if necessary, during strike action.

Case Study: Collective Conflict over Flexibility in Dunnes Stores

Dunnes Stores is an Irish-owned company involved in the retailing of foodstuffs, drapery and hardware/household goods. Founded in 1944, by the mid-1990s the company had developed to become Ireland's largest retailer, with 62 outlets nationwide employing approximately 9,000 workers. In 1995 Dunnes Stores considered it vital that it place itself in a position to respond to the customer's changing and growing demands and to the greater competitive challenge (source: LCR14816). The company had traditionally resisted the unions' influence and had been reluctant to utilise state third parties, refusing on occasion to attend Labour Court hearings. In 1995 a strike occurred over issues arising from atypical working, with the company seeking maximum flexibility, including some innovative methods such as zero hours contracts. Zero hours contracts represent a situation where workers are not guaranteed any minimum number of hours of work per week. These can be seen as a response to the Worker Protection (Regular Part-Time Employees) Act 1991, which required employees to normally work a regular eight hours per week in order to be covered by the legislation. Details of the lead-up to the dispute are contained in Table 7.4.

Table 7.4
Timeline of Lead-up to Strike in 1995

November 1993	MANDATE served claim for local bargaining clause (flexible) of PESP. Claim subsequently declined by company.
January 1994	MANDATE claims Dunnes workers treated less favourably than other workers in comparable employment. Union makes further efforts for payment of PESP.
Late summer 1994	Dunnes commence Sunday trading. Union not consulted. Strike results and pickets placed.
September 1994 to April 1995	Meeting held between management and union. No agreement reached. Union referred dispute to LRC, company declined invitation to attend. Ballot for industrial action held with eighty-six per cent in favour. Strike resulted, which closed outlets of company.
June to July 1995	Labour Court invited parties to a hearing and issued recommendation on 4 July.

Source: Labour Court recommendation 14816

The national strike closed down all Dunnes Stores outlets in the Republic of Ireland. As a result of the strike, a Labour Court hearing attended by both sides led to the strike being called off.

Following MANDATE's acceptance of the Labour Court's recommendation there followed a period of uncertainty. The chairman of the tribunal that had been set up to attempt to improve industrial relations, Mr Paddy Moriarty, resigned, blaming Dunnes Stores. There was disagreement between Dunnes and MANDATE over the implementation of the local bargaining clause of the PESP. In addition the 200 full-time jobs did not materialise, the 15-hour minimum working week was not implemented and hours of work were not being notified to workers in advance. This led to a further all-out strike, which took effect on 2 September 1996 and lasted until 14 September, resulting in the agreed settlement terms outlined in Table 7.5.

Table 7.5
Settlement Terms of 1996 Strike in Dunnes Stores

Issue	Settlement Terms	Comparison with 1995 Labour Court Recommendation
Payment of three per cent PESP exceptional clause.	Agreed, with back-pay to 4 September 1995, within three weeks of work resuming. Full union co-operation with new technology and associated work practices. Company to provide training.	Direct discussions to take place.
Pension	Meeting to take place within two weeks of return to work on the introduction of new scheme for all full-time and part-time staff.	Could be progressed at a later date.
Procedural agreement	Company guidelines on management union business replaced by problem resolution agreement (copy in Appendix 2). No reference to a tribunal.	Establishment of internal industrial tribunal.
Staffing levels	400 new jobs to be created on a **seven-day** roster. Company maintained six-day roster (excluding Sunday work) not viable. Extra 200 jobs created as a *quid pro quo*.	200 new full-time jobs to be created on a six-day (excluding Sunday from normal working) roster.

Source: Letter from Andrew Street, director of Dunnes Stores, to Mr Owen Nulty, general secretary of MANDATE, 9 September 1996.

The eventual settlement terms can be seen as residing within the spirit of the Labour Court recommendation despite the earlier unwillingness of Dunnes Stores to implement the Court's recommendations. That settlement was not, however, a permanent one, as there were continuing issues, notably over Sunday working. The Labour Court issued a recommendation on the issue following a hearing by the Court held on 8 December 1996, which the company did not attend. The Labour Court on this occasion recommended payment of double time plus one day's leave as part of its recommendation to solve a dispute over Sunday working in the pre-Christmas period.

Exercise
1. Discuss the use of strike action and the role of the state institutions.
2. What model of management strategy (see Chapters 14 and 15) does Dunnes seem best to fit?
3. How does the Dunnes approach compare to that used by other supermarkets, such as Superquinn, Tesco, Aldi and Lidl?

Source: Adapted from Wallace and Clifford (1998)

CHAPTER 8

Strikes

OVERVIEW

A strike can be defined as 'a temporary stoppage of work by a group of employees in order to express a grievance or enforce a demand' (Griffin 1939: 20). This long-standing definition emphasises that strikes are a temporary interruption in normal working. It also embodies an inherent implication, at odds with unitarist thinking, that strikes are rational actions undertaken to remedy a grievance or achieve a demand. Strike action is the most visible form of industrial action and a significant means through which trade unions have sought and secured improvements in pay and conditions of employment. As Salamon (1998: 402) notes:

> the strike is often depicted as the ultimate and most favoured form of collective action in that, by stopping work and leaving the workplace, the employees clearly demonstrate both the importance of the issue in dispute and their solidarity.

Despite their headline-grabbing status, strikes are relatively rare and many Irish organisations have never experienced strike action. Strike action can involve considerable hardship for strikers through lost income and the risk of job loss. For trade unions, strike action also represents a major dilemma: the prospects of success/failure must be weighed up together with implications for union membership, status and finances. Thus, there will always be a dilemma for strikers on when to end a strike and on what terms (see Crouch 1982). In addition to strikes against employers, strikes can take place because of disputes between unions (inter-union disputes) or because of disputes internal to the union (intra-union disputes).

Historically, the establishment of trade union representation and recognition in many countries was only achieved after successful strike action. In 1888, the successful strike in Bryant and May by twenty-two Match Girls in the UK, and the subsequent rash of strike action over the following two years, led to the first widespread unionisation of unskilled workers (Pelling 1976: 97). In Ireland, the establishment of unionisation of unskilled workers, following the founding of the Irish Transport and General Workers Union (ITGWU), was achieved by a similar wave of strikes and lockouts from 1909 to 1913 (see Chapter 5). Employers had previously been implacably opposed to accepting the unionisation of the unskilled, despite rhetoric to the contrary that they were not opposed to unions, only 'Mr Larkin's union'.

In addition to achieving industrial aims, strikes can mobilise collective interests in the broader social and political sphere. In France, strikes in 1936 and in 1968 led to major social and industrial changes. Political strikes have also occurred in Ireland. In the early 1980s there were a series of mass strikes against the disproportionate burden of taxation on PAYE workers, but these were largely unsuccessful. Eventual tax reform since 1987 has concentrated on reducing the tax burden rather than its redistribution. Strikes may be used as expressions of popular will, designed to bring about greater democracy; however, it is unusual for strikes to lead to revolutionary social change. An arguable exception is the case of Poland, where the strike activity of the Solidarnosc trade union in Gdansk, and elsewhere in Poland, indirectly contributed to the overthrow of communism and its eventual replacement with capitalism and a liberal parliamentary democracy. This (replacing communism with capitalism) contrasts with the role for industrial conflict as predicted by Marx.

Strikes can be a double-edged sword for trade unions. If successful, strikes can strengthen the union's position, but defeats in major strikes can lead to decreased union membership and their marginalisation. Following the 1913 lockout, which was a response to action, membership of the ITGWU fell from some 40,000 members to around 5,000, while in 1992, the Irish Bank Officials Association (IBOA) lost thirty per cent of their membership in an unsuccessful strike. Adams (1998) captures the broader political and social dimensions of strike activity in the following quote.

> Some industrial disputes rock the world. A shipyard strike in Poland in 1980 was the match that lit the fire that eventually consumed communism and led to the phoenix of democratic institutions rising from the ashes. An air traffic controllers strike in the US and a coal miners strike in the UK produced massive union defeats which dramatically altered the social climate. Subsequent to those setbacks union membership and influence receded like ice cubes in a hothouse.

EXPLANATIONS FOR STRIKES

The general approaches to the analysis of conflict discussed earlier provide no explanation for the expression of specific forms of conflict such as strikes. Strikes do not occur in a homogenous fashion. There are wide variations across countries, over time periods and between industries. As with theories of conflict there is no theory of strikes that can fully account for their incidence; nonetheless, there is a substantial body of research providing insights into the variables influencing strike activity.

Analysts have identified a multitude of factors that can influence the level and nature of strike activity (for example, see Hyman 1989; Edwards 1986, 1992; Brannick et al. 1997). It is beyond the scope of this text to review all such approaches, so instead we will focus on four particularly influential ones. These are the role of industrialisation and the effect of institutions and workplace collective bargaining; economic factors as expressed by both the short-run business cycle and long waves; industrial sector effects; and finally, the impact of political economy, including the role of centralised collective bargaining. The aim is to give an insight into a number of leading theoretical and empirical approaches to explaining strike incidence as a prelude to examining Irish strikes in detail.

It is a truism that the movement of workers into large-scale production is the cause of the emergence of strike action. Early craft unions used strikes as a method to defend their craft, while unskilled workers used the strike weapon to gain union recognition and improve pay and conditions of employment. Battles for recognition were frequently bruising contests, with employers making frequent use of the lockout, especially where unskilled workers were involved. Ross and Hartman (1960) and Kerr *et al.* (1962) drew on these historical factors to construct an institutionalist explanation for strikes and their variation over time and between countries. They suggested that conflicts were especially intense between labour and capital in the early twentieth century under the influence of syndicalist union policies and trenchant employer opposition to unionisation. As societies matured, these conflicts decreased; employers and unions came to accept each other, collective bargaining became established and more sophisticated and the state provided dispute resolution policies and procedures (Ross and Hartman 1960).

Within mature economies there remain differences, with strike incidence of differing countries being affected by a number of factors. Among key factors Ross and Hartman identified are the nature of union movements, with Communist-dominated and fragmented trade unions leading to higher strikes, and the existence of Labour/Social Democratic parties in power decreasing their incidence (Ross and Hartman 1960). In time they suggested the strike withers away in certain societies, notably Northern Europe. This prediction was confounded not just by the growth in strikes in the 1960s and 1970s, but also the broadening of strikes to many more groups than had traditionally been involved in strikes, such as white-collar workers. Yet it is salutary to note that, even in the UK, 'working days lost due to strikes remained at historically low levels from 1927 through to 1970' (Smith 2003: 206). Furthermore, the intensity of conflicts, as measured by violence on the part of the state, workers or employers, experienced prior to 1922 was generally not exceeded in the 1970s, although strikes in mining, printing and docking in the UK in the 1980s were accompanied by unusual levels of violence for a Northern European state (see Kelly 1998).

In contrast to the institutional thesis of the withering away of the strike are models which suggest that strike action is cyclical. There are two variants of the cyclical approach – one based on the link between strikes and the *short-run* (or Keynesian) business cycle and the second based on variation in strikes over *long-run waves* (or Kondratieff cycles) (Edwards 1992; Kelly 1998). Analysis of the link between the short-run business cycle and strikes has heavily influenced economists' approach to the analysis of strikes. The study of such links dates back to at least the early 1920s (Jackson 1991). The key idea underlying the existence of such a link is that in good times, the prospects for successful strikes are greater than when economic conditions are bad. Brannick *et al.* (1997: 299) write, 'obviously, unions are most likely to maximise their gains when business conditions are favourable'. It has also been suggested that revolt is most likely not when conditions of extreme misery exist, but when conditions are improving (see Brannick *et al.* 1997: 300).

In seeking to test the link between strikes and short-run business cycles, economists have linked strike action to the key macroeconomic variables, notably the rate of unemployment, changes in real or nominal wages, the rate of inflation and change in the profit ratio of organisations (see Edwards 1992; Brannick *et al.* 1997). Thus, strikes should decrease as unemployment rises, and rise in line with inflation or profits. Brannick *et al.* (1997: 300–1) write, 'an increase in prices will have an impact on the purchasing power of workers and is likely to lead to a trade union demand for a cost of living increase'.

While the economic analysis of strikes has a degree of utility in explaining strike incidence, there are a number of limitations. While a link between low unemployment and higher strikes is the most common economic variable to be tested, Brannick *et al.* (1997: 301) note that 'there is little consistent agreement as to the economic variables that influence strikes across countries'. Market forces are only one of a number of determinants of strike action and these can be counteracted by other factors, such as the nature and extent of unionisation (Shalev 1992) and the nature of collective bargaining (Clegg 1976). A further consideration is that certain sectors of the economy may be in a growth phase, even though the overall economy can be in decline, thus any macroeconomic analysis needs to be supplemented with sectoral studies.

The link between unemployment and low strikes may only hold where unions forego corporatism for purely industrial goals (Hibbs 1978). Most critical for the economic approach is Paldam and Pedersons's (1982) finding that the relationship between unemployment and strikes held in only one-third of seventeen countries examined for the period 1948–1975. This instability in the relationship of unemployment is graphically illustrated by recent Spanish experience. Rigby and Aledo (2001: 298) note that 'during the last two decades, unemployment has normally been double the European average yet Spain has experienced the highest strike rate in Europe while the decline in strike activity since 1994 has coincided with a decline in unemployment'. They also note 'a similar lack of fit occurs if the strike rate is tracked against the rate of economic growth' (Rigby and Aledo 2001: 298).

Kondratieff cycles, or long wave theory as it is now known (see Kelly 1998), implies the periodic resurgence of strikes over historical time periods – not their withering away. Kondratieff waves are based on the claimed existence in capitalist economies of long-run business cycles of boom and depression, which occur across approximately fifty-year cycles. Strike incidence and intensity increase at the upswing of long waves, reach their highest point before or at the peak of the waves and continue at a lower level during the downswings, as workers seek to protect and retain any gains achieved during the upswings (see Edwards 1992: 364; Kelly 1998: 86–9). At the bottom of the cycle (during extended recessions), strikes continue but at a lower level due to the poor prospects for their success.

In a seminal piece of work, Kelly (1998) claims to identify a number of strike waves coinciding with the peaks and downswings of Kondratieff cycles. Reviewing a range of international empirical studies, he writes, 'overall it can be argued that there are major strike waves towards the end of Kondratieff upswings (1860–1875, 1910–1920, 1968–1974) and minor strike waves towards Kondratieff downswings (1889–1893, 1935–1948)' (Kelly 1998: 89). Thus, the Kondratieff hypothesis enjoys a degree of empirical support, although there are difficulties with empirical testing.

The fifty-year cycle means that there is only a limited timeframe in which to test for long-run cycles and empirical testing also throws up anomalies (see Edwards 1992). Obviously, within long-run cycles there will be variations caused by short-run business cycles, which can and do vary across countries. More fundamentally, there is the general failure of strikes internationally to increase with the economic upswing of the 1990s, which has led to even neo-Marxists re-examining the withering away of the strike hypothesis (see Edwards 1992: 365). Among the factors that Edwards (1992) suggests might account for the non-return to high strikes are economic restructuring, the greater power of capital, the extension of conflicts to the developing world and the expression of conflict in forms other than strikes outside the industrial relations arena (Edwards 1992).

Just as strikes do not occur evenly through time, they vary across industries. Kerr and Siegel (1954) explain the inter-industry propensity to strike based on the characteristics of the job and the nature of the workers. They examined the relative strike rankings of industries in eleven countries and posited a two-factor explanation to account for the common rankings they found. Industries characterised by hard jobs that attract tough, combative workers living in isolated communities have high strike proneness, such as mining and docking. Industries characterised by easy or skilled work performed in pleasant surroundings, whose workers are integrated into the community, will attract more submissive men or women and have low strike proneness, such as railroad and agriculture.

While giving an insight into extremes of strike occurrence in some industries, the theory has been criticised on a number of grounds, not least that there are contradictory experiences in the same industries in different countries. Jackson (1991: 289) notes that Kerr and Siegel initially examined the steel industry but excluded it because there was substantial variation across countries, notably being high strike prone in some countries, such as the US, but low in the UK. The low strike proneness of certain industries, e.g. agriculture, can ignore short-lived counterexamples. In Ireland, agriculture experienced widespread strikes and agitation from 1917 to 1923, a period documented by the labour historian Emmet O'Connor (see O'Connor 1988). The portrayal of agricultural work by Kerr and Siegel (1954) seems oddly romantic, as not everyone shares the view that farm work is easy. Their analysis begs the questions whether men are made hard and combative by the job or if they are this way to begin with, and why women did not strike given the evident relative discrimination in pay and other opportunities in the labour markets at the time. It is not credible to argue that there were not potential grievances. The question arises as to what it was that limited these grievances from resulting in conflict. Most pointedly, the theory pays inadequate attention to management action, which has to be a key part of any theory of conflict (Edwards 1992). This theory has gained little attention in Ireland, probably because of the extremely limited amount of large-scale heavy industry such as mining and steel work.

Political economy explanations of strikes came to the fore in the 1970s with the development of neo-corporatist theories. Edwards (1992: 366) notes this approach sought to address why strike rates have been particularly low in Scandinavia and

Germany and high in the US, Australia and France, for example, as well as in Britain. These had been presaged by the institutionalist explanation of Ross and Hartman (1960), who had drawn attention to the mitigating effect of Labour and Social Democratic parties on strike levels. However, there is an important difference between their explanation and the later political economy explanations. The latter focused not only on the institutional aspects of such parties, but the political exchange dimension between capital and labour where labour parties gain power. It was observed that certain countries, Sweden being the archetype, experienced generally low strike levels despite the existence of high levels of unionisation. Strike levels had been high in Sweden prior to the accession to power of the Social Democratic government in 1932. Subsequently, strikes declined as unions sought 'to secure their end in the political and not the economic sphere' (Edwards 1992: 366). In France, by contrast, Shorter and Tilly (1974: 281) noted strikes remained high where Labour did not accede to power and in the US where the government did not interfere in workplace conflicts on the side of labour. The reasoning behind the political economy approaches is that strikes impose high costs on workers and trade unions and they can better achieve their aims through a Social Democratic or Labour Party that they control or is sympathetic to them.

It is suggested that neo-corporatist countries are more governable and stable in their industrial relations for a number of reasons. For instance, trade unions and employer organisations are given a monopoly position in representing the interests of workers and employers. Because of their capacity to affect state policies, trade unions exchange industrial action for political action and pursue a higher social wage instead of using their industrial muscle to achieve higher money wages. Employer-initiated conflict is reduced by the capacity of employer organisations to bind members in collective agreements or by the legal or general applicability of such agreements (see Kelly 2003).

The political economy approach has been particularly useful in drawing attention to the contrasts in strikes between differing countries and the need to be aware of the wider political and social context. However, it has a number of limitations (Edwards 1992: 368). Françoise (1989) notes that political economic theories are 'labour movement theories' and focus on the role of labour, paying insufficient attention to the role of employers or the state. Taking the latter point, there are limits to which even Labour governments can meet the expectations of labour, a case in point being France in the 1980s, when the Mitterand government had to abandon expansionist Keynesian policies because of their negative effect on the public finances and balance of payments.

Furthermore, the accession of Labour or Social Democratic parties to power does not necessarily lead to lower strikes, as there are quite a number of counterfactual examples, for instance, Australia (late 1940s and early 1970s), the UK (1978–1979, the winter of discontent) and Switzerland, where low strike levels have not been accompanied by labour parties holding power (see Jackson 1991). More pointedly, since the 1980s neo-liberal policies have been associated with dramatic reductions in strike levels, notably from 1985 onwards, during the period of the Conservative Thatcher government in the UK, but also in other countries. Such reductions in strikes have involved government exclusion of unions rather than any involvement in political trade-offs.

The foregoing review draws attention to the crucial role played by institutional, economic, structural and political factors that affect the occurrence of strikes and of which the actors in industrial relations may not even be aware. Because of the multiplicity of factors that influence strikes, no single approach can hope to provide a comprehensive explanation for them. The approaches reviewed are most useful in drawing attention to structural underpinnings of strikes, which unitarist explanations cannot account for. Thus, diagnoses based on unitarist notions, such as bad communications, troublemakers or bad management (the conceptual equivalent of troublemakers), provide no explanation of why strikes should vary across countries, industries and time. It is not credible to argue that high strike-prone industries or countries have worse communications and attract more troublemakers or bad managers. Undoubtedly such factors may be present, but they are more properly regarded as symptoms rather than causes of industrial conflict.

MEASUREMENT OF STRIKES

Information on strikes is the only data collected internationally on industrial conflict. It is standard practice to collect information on the number of strikes, the number of workers involved, the duration of the strike, working days lost and the cause of the strike. Two problems arise in relation to the compilation of strike statistics – their *completeness* and their *reliability. Completeness* relates to the extent to which statistics include all strikes. Different countries have adopted differing definitions of the strike for inclusion in their statistics. In Ireland, there is a low threshold for recording strikes. All strikes are counted which last at least a half day or involve a minimum of ten working days lost. In contrast, some countries have much higher thresholds for their figures. Most notable is the US, which only counts strikes involving more than 1,000 workers, an extremely high threshold which has caused some writers to question the utility of the information. Gall (1999) notes that comparatively recent changes in the compilation of strike data, notably the exclusion of public sector strikes in Belgium, France, Greece and Portugal, raises serious doubts about the validity of the data.

The second problem with strike statistics is one of *reliability.* The reliability of strike statistics is determined by the extent to which the number of strikes, the number of workers involved, the strike duration and working days lost are accurately recorded over time. Not only will strikes be excluded by the criteria used but within the criteria laid down there may be underreporting or overreporting (Brannick and Kelly 1982). While overreporting is not unknown (see Wallace and O'Shea 1987: 81), underreporting is the main problem and is likely to affect small strikes of shorter duration to a greater extent than larger and longer disputes (Kelly and Brannick 1989: 151). In the UK, the Department of Employment estimated in the 1980s that 'within the definitions set, only sixty-five per cent of all strikes in manufacturing are counted' (Wallace and O'Shea 1987: 80). In addition to quantitative information, the Central Statistics Office (CSO) in Ireland requests from employers the cause(s) of the strike. Apart from the undercounting of the number of strikes, the number of workers involved may vary, making it difficult to determine accurate numbers of working days lost. However, this is unlikely to have a major effect on the magnitude of working days lost.

Table 8.1	
Minimum Criteria for Inclusion in Statistics in Selected Countries	
Duration	**Country**
No minimum	Australia, Italy, Netherlands, Portugal[1], Turkey[2], Belgium[3]
Longer than 1 hour	Sweden, Spain, Finland
Longer than 4 hours ($^1/_2$ day)	Japan[4], Canada[5]
1 day or longer	Belgium, Germany[6,7], Switzerland, UK[8], US[9], France[10], Norway, Sweden
10 days or more lost	Australia, Ireland[11], New Zealand
100 days or more lost	Denmark

Notes: (1) Excludes general strikes at national level and public administration. (2) Excludes general strikes and most public sector strikes. (3) Excludes public sector strikes. (4) Excludes unofficial disputes. (5) And ten days not worked. (6) Unless 100 or more working days lost. (7) And more than ten workers involved. (8) And more than ten workers involved, unless 100 or more working days are lost. (9) And more than 1,000 employees involved. (10) Excludes agricultural workers. (11) Or more than one day's duration.

Source: Adapted from Office for National Statistics (2003: 188–9)

The primary agency for collecting data on strikes is the Central Statistics Office (CSO). Much of the information they receive on the occurrence of strikes comes from the Monitoring Unit of the Department of Enterprise, Trade and Employment, a function previously carried out by the employment exchanges. Based on the information supplied by the Monitoring Unit, the CSO contacts companies, or occasionally unions, for information and this forms the basis of the quarterly strike statistics. In recent years there is reason to believe that Irish strike statistics may now be more complete and accurate than is generally the case internationally. Wallace and O'Shea (1987: 80) identify the small size of the country and the high media profile of strikes as contributing to their accuracy. In addition, the number of strikes has declined since the 1980s and the visibility of the remaining ones is likely to have increased as a result. It may well be that strike statistics overstate the Irish strike experience relative to at least some other countries, thereby biasing international comparisons on strike incidence. It is unlikely, however, to significantly affect comparisons of working days lost.

Strike Indices

Four key measures are normally used in evaluating the extent and pattern of strike activity:

- strike frequency;
- strike breadth;
- strike duration; and
- working days lost.

Strike frequency is simply the number of stoppages in a defined time period. The number of strikes is a measure used in many economic studies of strikes and has been espoused as giving an indication of the general impact of strikes on management and the economy (see Kelly and Brannick 1989: 154–5). Turner (1969), however, has criticised it because it gives equal weight to large and small strikes (Turner 1969). It is also the index with the greatest reliability problems due to two factors – the different criteria used by different countries for the inclusion of strikes and the likelihood that many smaller strikes that meet the definition for inclusion may not be counted.

The second measure is the *strike breadth*, which is the number of workers involved in strikes. It gives an indication of the size of strikes but has a number of deficiencies, chiefly the number of workers involved may decline but there may be an increase in working days lost (Kelly and Brannick 1989).

The third index is *strike duration*, which refers to the length of strikes in days and can reflect differing strike 'cultures' across countries. For instance, French strikes have traditionally been short due to the absence of strike pay in trade unions and the fact that strikes can be demonstration strikes with a political purpose.

The final measure of strikes is *working days lost* (WDL), which is calculated by multiplying the number of workers involved by the strike duration. As this is a measure of the impact of strikes, if not actual costs, it is considered the most informative indicator of the pattern of strike activity. Kelly and Brannick (1989) consider 'it is probably safest to use all available indices' when judging the strike position of countries or sectors. When comparing strikes across countries, working days lost per thousand employees is the most frequently used statistic. However, even this is affected by the exclusion of strikes involving less than a thousand employees from the US data. When comparing across time within a country, Kelly and Brannick (1989) note the importance of standardising for the number of employees. Others have argued that the level of unionisation should be taken into account, although this is seldom done.

STRIKE ACTIVITY IN IRELAND

The Level of Strike Activity

A number of items stand out from a cursory inspection of the data. First, only a small proportion of all employments engage in strike action in any one year. It is not uncommon for those approaching the study of industrial relations for the first time to greatly overestimate the number of strikes per year. The number of recorded strikes has exceeded 200 in only one year, 1974, with 219 strikes. The number of strikes has only exceeded 100 in thirty of the years since 1922. On the other hand, the number of strikes has been under fifty in only fourteen years, twelve of which have occurred since the current round of national agreements recommenced in 1987. Thus, in the majority of years since the founding of the state, the number of strikes has been grouped between fifty and 100 per year.

A second feature of Irish strikes should be emphasised, which is not captured in the statistics. Irish strikes are generally conducted within understood rules of engagement. The levels of violence that pertained during the early decades of the twentieth century, and which are still found in some other countries, are notably absent from Irish strikes.

Turning to the indices for workers involved and working days lost, Kelly and Brannick (1983) have established that, in any one year, a few large strikes, which Wallace and O'Shea (1987) note are almost exclusively official strikes, exercise a disproportionate effect on those indices. Kelly and Brannick (1983: 69) show that over the period 1960–1979, forty-three strikes (only two per cent of all strikes in the period) accounted for 5.7 million working days lost, or fifty-seven per cent of the total working days lost. They make the apposite comment that 'the Irish strike pattern is extremely sensitive to this comparatively small number of large strikes and it has been an enduring feature over the twenty year period. Indeed, should these be removed from the Irish strike quantum, the result would be a record which would show a comparatively strike-free nation in terms of workers involved and total [working] days lost' (Kelly and Brannick 1983: 69). They point out that if this effect is not highlighted, it 'can lead to an unrepresentative and inaccurate portrayal of the Irish strike record' (Kelly and Brannick 1983: 69).

More recent data points to the enduring impact of large strikes on the pattern of strike activity in Ireland. In the years 1995–2002, the top two strikes accounted for 6.3 per cent of all strikes but accounted for 74.6 per cent of all working days lost and 77.9 per cent of workers involved in strikes. Thus, the phenomenon of a small number of strikes determining the Irish strike record continues into the period of social partnership.

Trends in Irish Strike Statistics

In looking at the variation over time, the evidence from the three strike indices in Figures 8.1, 8.2 and 8.3 indicate certain periods of higher and lower strike activity, combined with a large degree of fluctuation from year to year. In commenting on the pattern of strike activity in Ireland over the period 1922–1995, Brannick *et al.* (1997: 310) emphasise that all three indices of strike activity are 'broadly pro cyclical with respect to economic changes'. The years 1922–1924 mark the end of a particularly high strike-prone period of the 1913 lockout and the War of Independence. However, it would be incorrect to see that high strike-prone period as a purely national phenomenon, as it also marked the end of the Kondratieff wave of 1910–1920, identified by Kelly (1998). Brannick *et al.* (1997: 310) write that 'the decline in strike activity experienced in the 1920s is associated with recession and stagnation in the economic environment during the decade. This was followed by an increase in strike levels during the 1930s corresponding to a period of union growth and industrialisation'. Industrialisation followed the imposition of tariff barriers and quotas by the Fianna Fáil government elected in 1932, which provided an incentive for Irish and UK firms to set up production in Ireland.

Figure 8.1
Strike Frequency, 1922–2003

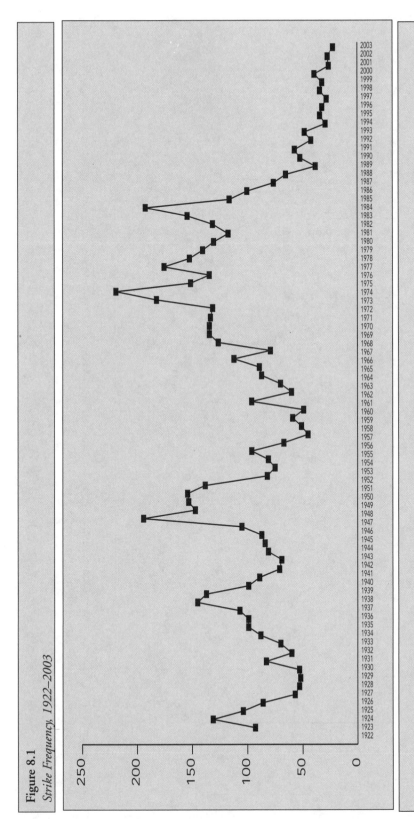

Note: Figures from the CSO are subject to minor fluctuations due to factors such as the carry-over of strikes from one year to another and variations in the numbers of workers participating in strike activity over the period of a particular strike. However, these minor variations do not affect overall trends in the pattern of strike activity.

Source: UCD Database of Strike Statistics, CSO; Wallace and O'Shea (1987)

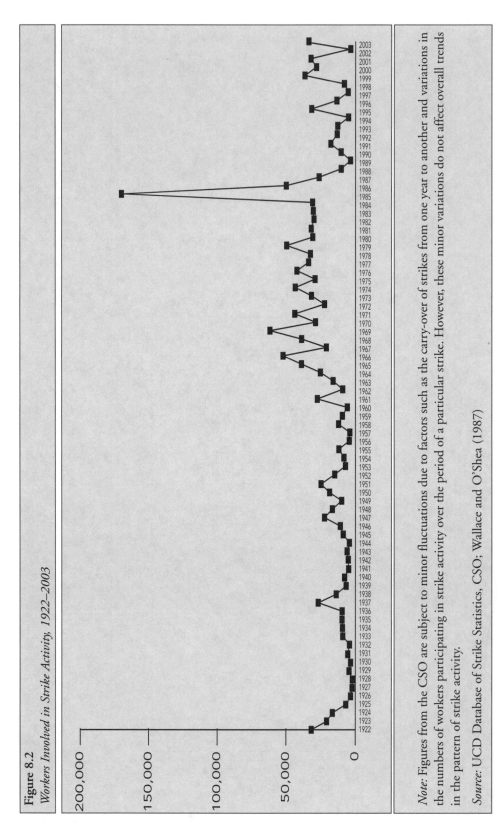

Figure 8.2
Workers Involved in Strike Activity, 1922–2003

Note: Figures from the CSO are subject to minor fluctuations due to factors such as the carry-over of strikes from one year to another and variations in the numbers of workers participating in strike activity over the period of a particular strike. However, these minor variations do not affect overall trends in the pattern of strike activity.

Source: UCD Database of Strike Statistics, CSO; Wallace and O'Shea (1987)

Figure 8.3
Working Days Lost through Strike Activity, 1922–2003

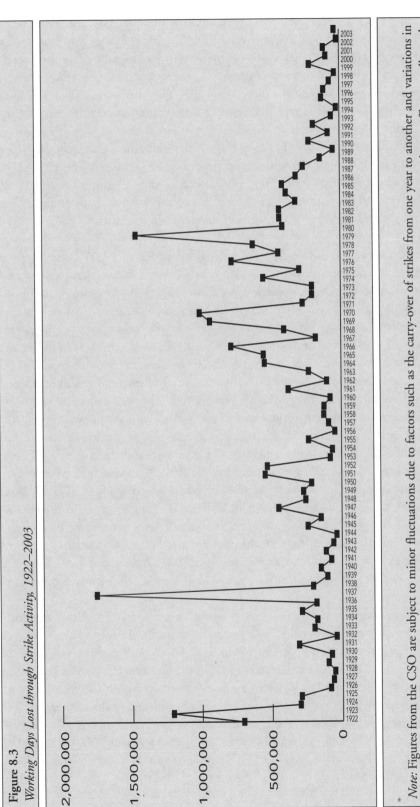

Note: Figures from the CSO are subject to minor fluctuations due to factors such as the carry-over of strikes from one year to another and variations in the numbers of workers participating in strike activity over the period of a particular strike. However, these minor variations do not affect overall trends in the pattern of strike activity.

Source: UCD Database of Strike Statistics, CSO; Wallace and O'Shea (1987)

Following 1937, the year with the largest number of work days lost, there was a decline in strike activity, coinciding with World War II and the Wages Standstill Order. Roche and Larragy (1989a: 27) have drawn attention to the negative effect this had on unionisation, and it is likely to have similarly affected strikes, as it would have greatly reduced the prospects of successful strikes over wages. The increase in the indices from 1945 to 1952 coincided again with a growth in unionisation and the removal of the Standstill Order and can be seen as an effort by workers to restore losses in earnings, which had declined since 1939. Following 1952 the strikes indices declined, which coincided with the economic depression and large-scale emigration of the 1950s. The growth in economic activity in the 1960s was accompanied by a return to a higher level of strike activity, which reached a peak in the late 1970s and then declined, but remained at relatively high levels by historical standards up to the mid-1980s.

The rise in strikes in Ireland in the 1960s should be viewed in an international context, being part of the Kondratieff wave identified by Kelly (1998) as lasting from 1968–1974. However, the Irish strike wave starts well before 1968 and lasts well beyond 1974. It is possible to suggest special reasons for this departure with a simplified narrative reading, as follows. After the 1950s depression wages were low and the increase in economic activity led to increases in strike activity as workers sought to gain improvements in their terms and conditions of employment. In the 1960s, the nature of decentralised collective bargaining based on comparability with open-ended agreements (see Chapter 13), combined with a low level of unemployment and rising inflation, led to increased strike activity (as measured by the three indices). The successes achieved emboldened workers and this coincided with the international strike wave starting in 1968. Efforts at reforming collective bargaining, with the introduction of national wage agreements, led to some fall-off in the strike indices in the early 1970s, but this was only temporary. The second half of the 1970s saw the strike indices increase, partly in response to the constraints of centralised bargaining. This increase coincided with the oil crisis and historically high levels of inflation but relatively low levels of unemployment. The early to mid-1980s saw a severe downturn in the Irish economy, with employers seeking concessions from employees. This led to a series of defensive strikes, a number of which were unsuccessful. Following this lack of success, strike activity declined. It subsequently remained low following the return to centralised bargaining in 1987.

Up to this point the narrative is consistent with a procyclical hypothesis, but post-1993 the story changes. Following the economic expansion post-1993 there was no return to the high strike levels of the 1960s and 1970s and the procyclical trend breaks down. The reduction in strike activity raises the question if we are at last seeing a withering away of the strike. Reviewing the evidence up to 1995, Brannick *et al.* (1997: 310) commented that 'there is no compelling evidence of the withering away of industrial action'. Nor has the strike withered away since Brannick *et al'.s* analysis. However, there is emerging evidence from the low strike levels of 2002 and 2003 of a disjuncture in Irish strike activity. The key question is whether this will be sustained.

Public/Private Sector

The relative strike activity in the public and private sectors over the period 1960–2002 is illustrated in Table 8.2. This data indicates that the private sector was the source of most strike activity as measured by all three indices during the decades of the 1960s and 1970s. Since then the indices have diverged. There has been a reduction in the proportion of strikes accounted for by the private sector, down from eighty per cent in the 1970s to an average of fifty-four per cent in the 1990s. There has also been a substantial drop in the relative proportion of workers involved in strike activity in the private sector, down from seventy-six per cent in the 1970s to an average of thirty-two per cent in the 1990s.

The larger number of workers involved is the main contributor to the public sector strike record and is reflective of the larger size of public organisations. When the average length of strikes (strike duration) is examined, a different pattern emerges – strike duration is much longer in the private sector. In the period 1990–1995, the average length of public sector strikes was 6.5 days while in the private sector the equivalent figure was twenty-one days. Brannick *et al.* (1997: 114) conclude that 'the public sector continued to experience higher levels of worker involvement into the 1990s. However, the average strike duration was only one-third that of the private sector. These different characteristics balance each other out resulting in both sectors having similar work-days lost rates'. The fact that private sector strikes are longer indicates a greater level of intransigence/difficulty in resolving such disputes.

Table 8.2
Proportionate Strike Activity in the Public and Private Sector, 1960–2002

Year	Strike Frequency (%)		Workers Involved (%)		Working Days Lost (%)	
	Public Sector	Private Sector	Public Sector	Private Sector	Public Sector	Private Sector
1960–1969	17.9	82.1	36.3	63.7	23.3	76.7
1970–1979	18.3	81.7	32.5	67.5	37.8	60.2
1980–1989	29.1	70.9	68.9	31.1	37.7	62.3
1990–1995	47.0	53.0	61.0	39.0	27.0	73.0
1996–2002	45.1	54.9	75.0	25.0	58.7	41.3

Source: 1960–1995 data from Brannick *et al.* (1997); 1996–2002 data supplied directly by the CSO

The commentary so far has not taken account of the differing numbers employed in the public and private sectors. Standardising for the level of employment confirms a decline in strike frequency, workers involved and working days lost over the period 1960–1995 in both the public and private sectors. The decline in strike frequency and workers involved is greatest in the private sector. Over the period 1990–1995, the public sector accounted for seven strikes per 100,000 workers, while the equivalent figure in the private sector was two strikes. Brannick *et al.* (1997: 313) conclude that 'in the 1990s public sector workers were three times as likely to strike than their counterparts in the private sector'. However, it is the higher level of workers involved per 100 employees that makes the greatest contribution to public sector strikes – twenty-seven employees per 100 employees in the public sector as against five per 100 employees in the private sector.

One must not conclude that the public sector has become more strike prone since the 1980s – it has not. The standardised strike frequency and working days lost have all declined in the public sector since the 1970s, and the number of workers involved and strike duration both declined in the 1990s. It is noteworthy that a relatively small number of public sector organisations have in the past been found to account for the bulk of strike activity in that sector (Kelly and Brannick 1985, 1986). Kelly and Brannick (1985, 1986) identified nine organisations that accounted for sixty-two per cent of all strikes, eighty-five per cent of workers involved and eighty-six per cent of working days lost in the public sector during 1960–1984.

In summary, the following are some of the key trends and developments.

- A reduction in the number of strikes in both public and private sectors since the 1980s, with the fall greatest in the private sector.
- An increase in the proportion of strikes accounted for by the public sector since the 1970s.
- A reduction in working days lost per 100 employees in both the public and private sector.
- A reduction in workers involved per 100 employees in the public sector, which is much greater than in the private sector.
- A reduction in average strike duration in the 1990s in the public sector.
- An increase in average strike duration in the private sector since the 1970s.
- A dramatic reduction in the proportion of workers involved in strikes in the private sector.
- An increase in the proportion of working days lost in the private sector since the 1970s.

Sectoral Considerations

At a sectoral level one finds that the high strike proneness of mining and low strike proneness of agriculture documented by Kerr and Siegel (1954) is replicated in the Irish figures. Brannick et al. (1997: 315) note that from 1922–1992 'the mining and turf sector has produced more strikes and work-days lost per employee than any other sector [and] the agriculture forestry and fishing sector ... rarely experiences strike activity'. However, the level of strikes and working days lost have not remained constant in mining and turf, with Brannick et al. (1997: 314) drawing attention to the fact that 'strike rates have declined by 300 per cent over the seventy year period'. Transport and communications and electricity, gas and water (sectors with high public ownership) have also had higher levels of strike frequency and working days lost in the period 1922–1992 (Brannick et al. 1997: 314). In commenting on the sharp decline in strike activity in the building and construction sector, Brannick *et al.* (1997) draw attention to the slump in the industry in the period 1981–1986. It may also be the case that the incidence of strike action in that industry has been affected by the growth of subcontracting, which changes a proportion of the workforce from employees to self-employed.

Industrial Development Policy and Strike Levels

In addition to the macro factors discussed earlier, it is apparent from a number of papers by Kelly and Brannick (1988a, 1991) that Irish industrial development policy has had a profound effect on the strike record. In particular, a seminal paper published in 1988 disentangles the strike record of British, Irish and US companies in three separate time periods: 1960–1969, 1970–1979 and 1980–1984. In the period 1961–1969, British companies in Ireland had the lowest strike record of the three groups, with US companies having the highest strike record. This changed dramatically with British companies becoming the most strike prone in the period 1970–1977. Kelly and Brannick (1988a: 40) write that 'the average length of the strike in the British-controlled company exceeded that in both other sectors, and each strike on average resulted in a greater level of worker involvement and man-days lost'. Any explanation for the increase in strikes based on cultural factors is rejected, as it cannot account for the early period of quiescence when satisfactory industrial relations had been established with workers. Kelly and Brannick (1988a: 45) instead draw attention to the '*disjunctive impact*' of industrial policy, which opened up the country's economy. They point especially to the effect of the Anglo Irish Free Trade Area Agreement (AIFTA) of 1965, which required a progressive reduction in protective tariffs of ten per cent per annum up to 1975.

Two groups of British companies are identified as having been affected. The first group was set up in the 1930s to avoid tariff barriers and quotas, and the second in the 1950s to take advantage of grant aid. Both groups concentrated on supplying the Irish market, with little of their production being exported. The increased competition caused by the progressive removal of the trade barriers led to 'a sharp disjuncture in the traditional relationship between the companies and their employees' and higher levels of strike activity (Kelly and Brannick 1988a: 52). These pressures led to 'slimming down policies' and 'new tougher stances by managements', and for workers, the deterioration in both 'economic and employment stability ... brought many stresses and strains' (Kelly and Brannick 1988a: 52).

It is clear from this analysis that the increased strike activity in British companies over the period are *symptoms* of industrial change and the dislocation this causes. This research destroys the notion that the industrial conflict experienced by these companies was caused by 'troublemakers', or indeed by 'bad managers'. The picture that emerges from this well-founded research is one of individual employees and managers bearing the price of industrial adaptation.

The role of management appears different in US multinational companies (MNCs). Kelly and Brannick found that US companies were the most strike prone in the multinational sector during the 1960s, but that strike activity has declined since the 1970s to a stage where US MNCs now have a low incidence of strike activity. Kelly and Brannick suggest this is due to the fact the US companies operate in newer industrial sectors and pursue sophisticated HR policies (see Chapters 14 and 15).

Two cautionary points need to be made when considering the above findings. First, HRM policies do not take place in a vacuum. Market demand, product life cycle and the age and size of the establishment can be important factors influencing the possibility of choosing a certain management style. In the last twenty years, the electronics sector has experienced high levels of market volatility, most notably in personal computer manufacture. In addressing such developments, strikes are a limited indicator of industrial conflict and one needs to have regard to other factors, such as plant closures and turnover (see Edwards 1992). Thus, companies pursuing 'soft' HRM policies, such as Wang and Digital, closed the bulk of their operations in Ireland while Dell, which is considered to have operated a more 'hard' HRM policy, has grown in size and scale.

OFFICIAL AND UNOFFICIAL STRIKES

Strikes may be official or unofficial, with an official strike being defined as 'a strike which is sanctioned by the relevant union authority' and an unofficial strike being a strike which does not have such sanction (Wallace and O'Shea 1987: 2). Official strikes normally take place after negotiations have failed to resolve the issue and when all due procedures, including resort to third parties, have been exhausted.

The utility of the distinction between official and unofficial has long been questioned. Brannick and Kelly (1983: 10) found that among union officials there was substantial variation in what was considered an unofficial strike. In some instances a strike may not be made official because the union did not know of the strike, because it would involve payment of strike pay, which the union cannot afford, or may be official at one level of the union but not at another level (see Jackson 1982: 197). In addition, strikes that start as unofficial may subsequently be made official. Unofficial strikes are distinguished from *unconstitutional* strikes, which are strikes in breach of procedures, not a strike in breach of the Constitution. Although there will obviously be a major overlap between the two categories, they are not necessarily identical. An organisation may not possess a procedural agreement and a union may sanction a strike that management claims is in breach of procedures, but which the union considers is not.

Unofficial strikes are generally of shorter duration and involve fewer workers than official strikes (Wallace and O'Shea 1987; Wallace 1988a, 1988b). As a result of these factors, working days lost in unofficial strikes have been less than those in official strikes in each year since data was first collected in 1976 (see Figures 8.4 and 8.5). There has been a dramatic reduction in unofficial strikes commencing in the early 1980s and this development has continued since then. During the years 1976–1979, the percentage of strikes that were unofficial was 66.8 per cent (Wallace and O'Shea 1987). This fell in the 1980s to forty-two per cent, twenty-seven per cent in the 1990s and an all-time low of twenty-three per cent for the years 2000–2002 (see Figure 8.3).

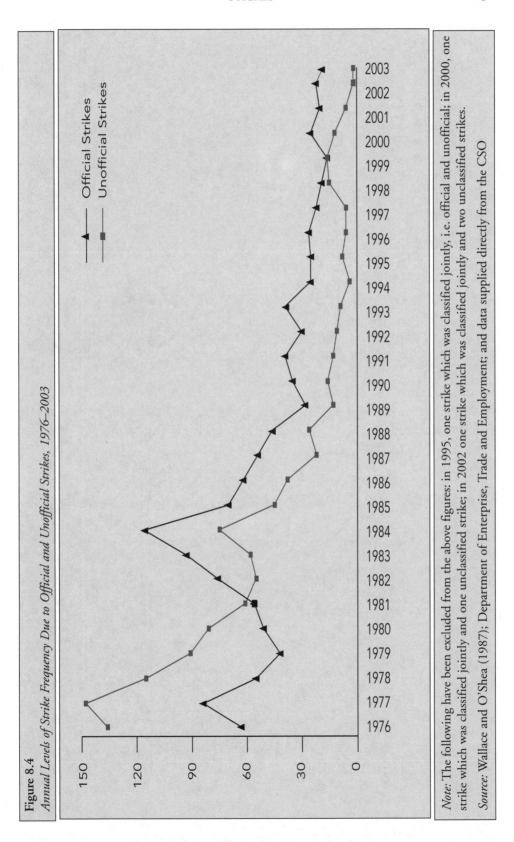

Figure 8.4

Annual Levels of Strike Frequency Due to Official and Unofficial Strikes, 1976–2003

Note: The following have been excluded from the above figures: in 1995, one strike which was classified jointly, i.e. official and unofficial; in 2000, one strike which was classified jointly and one unclassified strike; in 2002 one strike which was classified jointly and two unclassified strikes.

Source: Wallace and O'Shea (1987); Department of Enterprise, Trade and Employment; and data supplied directly from the CSO

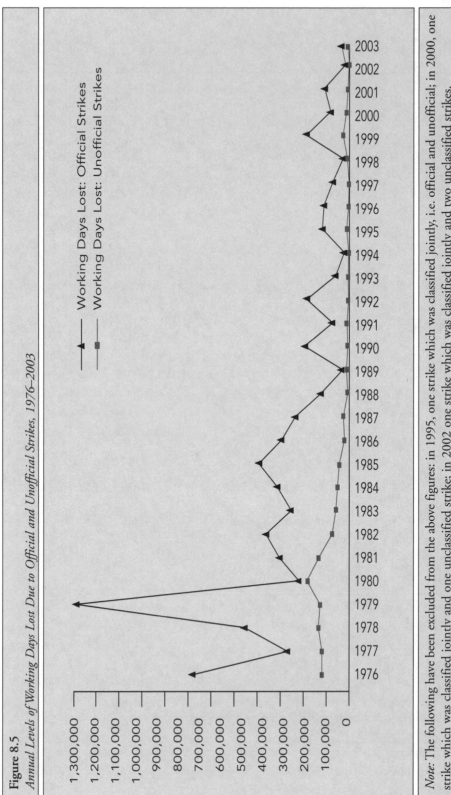

Figure 8.5
Annual Levels of Working Days Lost Due to Official and Unofficial Strikes, 1976–2003

Note: The following have been excluded from the above figures: in 1995, one strike which was classified jointly, i.e. official and unofficial; in 2000, one strike which was classified jointly and one unclassified strike; in 2002 one strike which was classified jointly and two unclassified strikes.

Source: Wallace and O'Shea (1987); Department of Enterprise, Trade and Employment; and data supplied directly from the CSO

Looking at the distribution of working days lost, we see an equally dramatic decrease in the impact of unofficial strikes. In the late 1970s, unofficial strikes accounted for almost sixteen per cent of total working days lost. This percentage increased to nineteen per cent in the 1980s but has since remained below ten per cent. Unofficial strikes are normally of shorter duration and involve less employees, so that unofficial strikes now account for quite a small proportion of working days lost due to strike activity (see Wallace and O'Shea 1987; Wallace 1988a, 1988b).

In Ireland, unofficial strikes tend to be subject to greater opprobrium than official strikes. The state institutions have a policy of refusing to involve themselves in unofficial strikes until workers return to work. Such policies have not excluded Industrial Relations Officers and Rights Commissioners from using 'creative measures' to become involved in resolving disputes (Wallace and O'Shea 1987: 183), for example, by trying to resolve a strike over a weekend when pickets were not placed but neither was the strike called off, the understanding being that if agreement was reached the strike would not resume on the Monday. Strikers themselves may view unofficial action as less extreme than an official strike and, as unofficial strikes are shorter, there may be rational reasons for workers to prefer unofficial to official action. However, this has to be weighed against the likely prospects of success and Wallace and O'Shea (1987) note that unofficial strikes are generally a weak weapon for workers.

Wallace and O'Shea (1987: 199) note that the majority, but not all, of unofficial strikes they studied were considered by respondents to be reactive in nature, sparked off by a particular event or incident at workplace level. Typical reactive events included the dismissal or suspension of a worker, unilateral changes in work practices or alleged management breach of procedures. However, twenty-nine per cent of unofficial strikes in the years 1978–1986 involved disputes over wages (Wallace and O'Shea 1987: 108). Indeed, the prevalence of unofficial strikes in the 1970s has been associated with the centralised agreements of that period (see Schregle 1975; O'Brien 1981; Brannick *et al.* 1997). The essential argument was that centralised agreements prescribed the levels of pay increases attainable in a given period. Since the great majority of trade unions (through the ICTU) are committed to these provisions, workers wishing to secure terms above those prescribed in national agreements were highly unlikely to get official union sanction for industrial action.

However, this claimed link between unofficial strikes and centralised agreements was based on anecdotal information. For example, Schregle (1975: 353) argues that 'under the National Wage Agreements there is a recognisable tendency for union members to take unofficial action where such action, if taken officially by the union, would contravene the National Agreement'. This is not strong evidence, and even if there was a link, it only applied in a minority of cases (see O'Brien 1981). The absence of any resurgence of unofficial strikes since 1987 means that any link that may have existed was of a transitory nature.

The greater reduction in unofficial as distinct from official strikes is one of the significant developments in Irish industrial relations in the last twenty years and one that awaits an explanation. A number of possible explanations can be advanced that might account for the development. A non-exhaustive list might include:

- the weakness of unofficial strikes and the weakened position of labour generally;
- workers' unwillingness to undertake unofficial strikes because of financial commitments;
- the eventual success of pluralist proceduralisation of industrial relations;
- the greater involvement of the law in regulating the employment relationship;
- greater central control by the union movement with less tolerance of unofficial action;
- the role of consensus/partnership industrial relations;
- international competition, including the greater openness of the economy;
- more sophisticated management of employment relations; and
- an international reduction in strikes.

Some of these are competing explanations and some are complementary or overlapping, but until further research is conducted they must remain conjectural. It is notable that the reduction in unofficial strikes and their contribution to the total working days lost long precedes the passage of the Industrial Relations Act 1990, which, along with other considerations, has led Wallace and O'Sullivan (2002a) to reject suggestions that the 1990 Act contributed to the decline.

Table 8.3
Summary of Official/Unofficial Strike Activity, 1976–2002

Time Period	Percentage of All Strikes that were Unofficial	WDL in Unofficial Strikes as a Percentage of the Total
1976–1979	66.8	15.5
1980–1989	42.1	19.3
1990–1999	27.4	6.8
2000–2002	23.0	8.3

Source: Wallace and O'Shea (1987); Department of Enterprise, Trade and Employment; and data supplied directly from the CSO

A final area of interest in relation to strike activity is the causes of strikes (see Table 8.4). Brannick *et al.* (1997) note that pay has traditionally been the source of high levels of strike activity but that its significance has declined in importance, particularly since the 1980s. They associate the decline in pay as a source of strike activity with the revival of centralised pay agreements in 1987 (Brannick *et al.* 1997). However, Table 8.4 shows the continued importance of pay as a cause of strike activity. While on average pay accounted for a quarter of strikes in the period 1995–2002, it accounted for almost half of all workers on strike and over half of total working days lost. The figures in Table 8.4 also point to the contribution of engagement/ dismissal/ redundancy and reorganisation/ demarcation/transfer issues as important causes of strike frequency, but not of great significance in contributing to the number of workers involved or working days lost.

Table 8.4

Strike Activity by Reported Cause of Strikes, 1995–2002

	Number of Strikes	Workers Involved	Percentage WDL
Wages	25.7	46.5	57.4
Engagement, dismissal, redundancy, etc.	18.7	6.7	7.5
Reorganisation, demarcation, transfers	16.2	7.0	5.0
Union representation, recognition	3.8	4.3	2.7
Re: Agreements	3.7	2.4	2.0
Re: Labour Court recommendation	5.0	2.0	8.3
Failed negotiations	2.4	10.5	7.2
Other matters	19.5	17.2*	8.8*
Unknown causes	3.7	3.4	1.9

* Over half of the figures for workers involved and WDL, in the 'other matters' category, are accounted for by one strike in 1995, the cause of which was a retirement issue.

Source: Data supplied directly by the CSO

A Consideration of Current Strike Levels

The reduction in strikes since the mid-1980s begs the question as to why they have declined. However, it is insufficient to focus on the decline without having regard to the recent break in the procyclical nature of Irish strike activity. The economy has experienced an economic boom since 1994 without the previous upswing in strike activity. Thus, it is not just the decline in strike activity which must be considered, but the non-appearance of an increase in strike activity. As with unofficial strikes, there is no shortage of factors that might account for the current reduced strike activity. One can point to greater competition, especially the greater openness of the economy; being linked to a hard currency post-1978; sophisticated management HRM policies; the proceduralisation of industrial relations; individual employment law; consensus/partnership industrial relations; and the general reduction in strikes internationally. Here we consider two points: the impact of consensus/partnership industrial relations and the experience of a number of other developed countries.

As indicated earlier, there has been a change in Irish strike levels since the mid-1980s. The fact that there have been less than sixty strikes in each year since 1988 provides *prima facia* evidence for what Thomas *et al.* (2003: 36) identify as 'a peace dividend' attaching to Irish centralised agreements since 1987. They see this as being driven by union leaders who have sought to move away from 'an overtly adversarial style of industrial relations which had contributed little to the wider political objectives of the movement particularly in relation to achieving a more equitable and just society' (Thomas *et al.* 2003: 36). However, attaining a peace dividend has not been an unproblematic exercise. Thomas *et al.* (2003: 36) point out that the relatively low level of conflict has only been secured and sustained by the social partners' continual striving 'through a series of dense personalised networks and an array of informal, formal and ad hoc institutions'.

Standardising for the substantial growth in employment indicates an even greater level of reduction in strike activity than the absolute figures (Thomas *et al.* 2003). In particular, the days lost per employee indicates a major reduction since 1986 (see Table 8.5). Standardising for the number of employees, however, overstates any peace dividend from centralised agreements, as many of the new jobs are non-union and days lost per union member (as the legal immunities are confined to union members) gives a lower reduction. Equally, many of the new jobs are in private services, a sector in which union density and strikes have traditionally been lower. As such, there is clear evidence of a structural contribution to the lowered strike activity from the shift to a services-based economy. Thus, even within an Irish context it is necessary to have regard to a multiplicity of factors that have may have contributed to the reduction in strike activity.

Table 8.5
Standardised Annual Average Strike Indices, 1982–2001

Period	Number of Strikes per 1,000,000 Employees	Breadth Involved per 1,000 Employees	Days Lost per Employee	Days Lost per Union Member
1982–1986	144.5	64.6	0.4	.74
1987–1991	49.3	12.4	0.1	.32
1992–1996	29.7	10.4	0.09	.21
1997–2001	n/a	n/a	n/a	.19

Source: Thomas *et al.* (2003); Roche (1997a); and data supplied directly by the CSO

Turning to the international evidence, Thomas *et al.* (2003: 42) claim that 'while there has been an overall decline in strike activity within the EU, the decline in industrial action within Ireland has been one of the sharpest'. However, looking at the rank order of twenty developed countries gives a different picture (see Table 8.6). While working days lost per 1,000 employees has declined considerably since the early 1980s, the Irish position only fell from fifth highest in 1981–1985 to seventh highest in the period 1991–1995, and has since returned to fifth highest in the period 1996–2000. Wallace and O'Sullivan (2002a: 190) express surprise at the limited evidence that such international comparisons provide for any reduction arising from Irish consensus industrial relations/social partnership. This suggests that Irish experience has to be considered in an international context and raises issues such as globalisation and greater international competition as drivers of the reduced Irish strike activity.

A complex interaction between centralised agreements and such international activity is probable. Thomas *et al.* (2003: 45) note 'the shared understanding of the interdependent mechanism within Ireland's small open economy allied to the "cold wind" of reality generated by the intensification of international competition'. This, they suggest, has 'changed the terrain in which the labour market parties operate, particularly in relation to the private sector', making a wave of industrial militancy reminiscent of the period 1965–1985 unlikely (Thomas *et al.* 2003: 45).

The continuing decline in private sector union density and the growth of services sector employment are also domestic factors that may act as a brake on increased strike activity, irrespective of the fate of centralised agreements. However, no more than in Ross and Hartman's time, there are dangers in speculating about the future course of strike action.

Table 8.6
International Comparison of Annual Average Working Days Lost per 1,000 Employees, 1981–2000

Country	1981–1985	1986–1990	1991–1995	1996–2000
Australia	386	224	130	85
Austria	2	2	6	1
Belgium	n/a	(48)	32	21
Canada	532	429	159	215
Denmark	306	41	45	296
Finland	326	410	218	56
France	78	111	94	68
Germany	52	5	17	2
Greece	516	6316	1148	29 (1996–1998)
Ireland	474 (5th highest)	242 (6th highest)	109 (7th highest)	91 (5th highest)
Italy	774	315	183	76
Japan	10	5	(3)	1
Netherlands	24	13	33	4
Norway	58	142	62	134
Portugal	176	82	34	20
United Kingdom	440	137	24	21
Spain	584	602	469	182
Sweden	40	134	50	9
Switzerland	n/s	n/s	1	2
United States	128	82	42	61

Notes: Brackets indicate averages based on incomplete data; n/s = not available; n/s = less than five days lost per 1,000. Some figures have been estimated.

Source: 1981–1995 data from Brown *et al.* (1997: 78); 1996–2000 data from Office for National Statistics (January 2003)

CHAPTER 9

Collective Bargaining

WHAT IS COLLECTIVE BARGAINING?

The process of collective bargaining is a mechanism to reconcile the divergent interests in the employment relationship. The principal feature of collective bargaining is that terms and conditions of employment are determined collectively, not individually. A number of prerequisites must be fulfilled for collective bargaining to become established. On the employee side there is a requirement that 'employees identify a commonality of purpose, organise and act in concert' (Salamon 2000: 326). In order to be able to do this effectively, workers must have the freedom to associate, thereby enabling them to join trade unions. On the employers' side, they must be prepared to recognise and negotiate with independent trade unions and accept the constraints placed upon their ability to deal with employees on an individual basis. As noted in Chapter 3, while the right of association is incorporated in Article 40.1.6 (iii) of the Irish Constitution, this does not impose a requirement on employers that they recognise or negotiate with unions. Thus, engaging in collective bargaining is a voluntary activity for Irish employers.

There is a further requirement that the trade unions be independent, namely that they should not be under the control or influence of employers. The extent to which the requirement for independence is fulfilled varies substantially across differing countries. For instance, company unions are prohibited under US law but the Japanese and Korean industrial relations systems are built on enterprise unions (Delany 1996; Dalzell *et al.* 1997). In the case of Japan, company personnel (especially managers) spend part of their time working for the union before returning to management. Trade unions in Western Europe developed within an adversarial framework and as a result trade union independence has not generally been an issue. The issue of independence has recently arisen in a case involving SIPTU and Ashford Castle. EIRI Associates (2004c: 15) note that in this instance the Labour Court effectively ruled that only trade unions can engage in 'collective bargaining'. The Court ruled in that case that 'it is clear to the Court that the employee forum is not an independent body representative of workers. It was established by the employer and the employer determined the parameters within which it could operate' (see Ashford Castle Limited and SIPTU, CD/03/658 decision no.17675).

In Ireland, management have on occasion promoted works committees as company-based alternatives to trade unions; in effect they were intended to vaccinate the company against unionisation. Although used in the 1960s these became uncommon thereafter, probably due to works committees acting as vehicles for a union organisation, rather than preventing unionisation. In the 1990s there was a limited resurrection of the use of works committees, associated with union recognition disputes. A notable example was Pat the Baker in 1993 (see Frawley 1993: 6 and Chapter 10).

The term 'collective bargaining' was coined by Sidney and Beatrice Webb (Webb and Webb 1897), but the practice had existed well before this, with the earlier forms of collective bargaining erroneously (as no independent third party was involved) being referred to as 'arbitration' or 'conciliation' (Jensen 1956). There are a number of definitions of collective bargaining that emphasise different aspect of the process. Gunnigle and Flood (1990: 227) refer to it as 'the process through which agreement on pay, working conditions, procedures and other negotiable issues are reached between organised employees and management representatives'.

Pluralists are the main advocates of collective bargaining. Clegg (1975: 314) emphatically writes that 'for the pluralist, collective bargaining is the right way to handle industrial relations'. Pluralism provides an alternative to the atomistic competition of free and equal contract in classical liberalism (notably neo-classical economics) and the 'engineered social integration of totalitarian (unitary) societies' (Fox 1974: 269). In effect, pluralist collective bargaining is an industrial equivalent to political democracy (see Clegg 1975). Thus, collective bargaining redresses a power imbalance between individual employees and employers. It allows workers to participate in setting the terms of employment and as a result aims to elicit the consent of those who live under the terms of any agreement. It allows the development of means for airing grievances and for the resolution of contentious issues through negotiation. The ensuing consent has the potential to produce greater stability between the parties to industrial relations. Collective bargaining arrangements can be seen as a means of airing grievances and differences of opinions on contentious issues through orderly negotiation aimed at securing eventual agreement. At the heart of collective bargaining is its potential for solving problems arising from conflicts of interests over the distribution of scarce resources. In this regard collective bargaining has the potential to ensure more equitable outcomes. This is the 'sword of justice' effect discussed further below.

The notion of consensus, or agreement, is found in many of the definitions of collective bargaining. The International Labour Organization (ILO) has referred to collective bargaining as 'negotiations about working conditions and terms of employment between an employer, a group of employers, or one or more employer organisations on one hand, or one or more employee organisations on the other with a view to reaching agreement' (ILO 1960). Green (1991: 76) discusses collective bargaining as fundamentally consisting 'of an employer, or a group of employers negotiating the terms and conditions of employees with the representatives of one or several worker organisations and reaching agreement on these issues'. Chamberlain and Kuhn (1965) argue that collective bargaining requires 'that some agreement be reached … some agreement must ultimately be forthcoming if collective bargaining continues. Thus neither party is independent under collective bargaining and neither can perform its function without the other'.

Hawkins (1979) offers possibly the best-known definition of collective bargaining, describing it as 'the resolution of conflict through compromise'. This definition, however, emphasises the distributive aspects of the process, seeming to exclude the resolution of conflict through 'collaboration' or 'co-operation'. These possibilities, identified by Walton and McKiersy (1965), have been emphasised by a number of authors since the 1970s (Fisher and Ury 1997; Lewicki *et al.* 2001; Hiltrop and Udall 1995), and are of particular interest given the contemporary efforts to develop 'partnership approaches' to industrial relations. While collaboration or co-operation may be part of collective bargaining, the process in Ireland has traditionally been a largely adversarial one.

That collective bargaining is generally conducted with a view to reaching agreement does not exclude the possibility of the use of coercive action, such as a strike or lockout. Clegg (1976) contends that this element of pressure is vital to collective bargaining, a view which contrasts with that advanced by Fox (1974). Fox (1974: 264) has taken issue with the 'basic procedural consensus', which presumes agreements must be reached – a requirement identified by many pluralists. As part of a vigorous debate, Clegg (1975) rejected this assertion, arguing to the contrary that an essential requirement of pluralism is that 'an acceptable compromise is not always and readily available'. He wrote that 'without the risk that agreement will not be reached, collective bargaining is a sham, and the pluralist doctrine is meaningless and not worthy of discussion' (Clegg 1975: 312). He advanced this view on the grounds that pluralism implies tolerance for opposing views, including those who reject pluralist arrangements. Clegg's (1975) response is a useful statement of a rigorous pluralist position, yet given the views of pluralists noted in the previous paragraph, the extent to which pluralists in general rigorously restrain from prescriptions which require agreement is questionable.

Irrespective of the validity of the philosophical differences between radicals (such as Fox) and pluralists (such as Clegg), at a practical level the possibility of breakdown is essential to collective bargaining. The desire to avoid the costs associated with industrial conflict, especially those associated with total breakdown, increases the likelihood of agreement in collective bargaining. Thus, Clegg (1975: 311–12) argues that the great advantage of collective bargaining is that compromise and agreement is the norm, despite the absence of any assurance that compromise and agreement will result from every negotiation.

ALTERNATIVES TO COLLECTIVE BARGAINING

Collective bargaining is by no means the only method of determining conditions of employment or regulating industrial relations. Even in countries where collective bargaining is dominant it exists side by side with other mechanisms, including individual bargaining and regulation by the government (legislation). Many aspects of the employment relationship will also be determined unilaterally, most notably by management. Although historically important, unilateral determination of terms and conditions by trade unions is now uncommon. In some countries, industrial democracy and employee involvement are important joint mechanisms for determining terms and conditions of employment, although these usually supplement the collective bargaining process.

While there are many suggestions that collective bargaining is being replaced by individual bargaining, this is highly questionable. Much of what is presented as 'individual bargaining' masks a high degree of co-ordination by employers at central or local level, leading to unilateral employer determination (not bargaining) of terms and conditions of employment. Brown *et al.* (2003: 204), summarising the results of the 1998 Workplace Employment Relations (WERS) survey in Britain, write: 'despite the considerable rhetoric and attention devoted to the individualisation of the employment relationship … negotiation of pay with individual employees was a rarity, accounting for less than five per cent of employees in the private sector'. It is likely that this situation is replicated in Ireland. Many employees in a non-union situation will be faced with unilaterally determined terms and conditions of employment, with only middle- and senior-ranking employees likely to negotiate their terms and conditions of employment. Of course, the unilateral terms may have been influenced by the terms laid down in collective agreements, but the extent of such influence is uncertain and worthy of empirical research.

THE NATURE OF COLLECTIVE BARGAINING

The Webbs were the first to attempt to develop a comprehensive theory of collective bargaining in their seminal work *Industrial Democracy*, first published in 1897. They saw collective bargaining as one of the means utilised by trade unions in pursuing their objective of 'maintaining and improving the conditions of their members' working lives' (Webb and Webb, 1897). As Flanders (1968a: 3) later commented, 'for the Webbs collective bargaining was exactly what the words implied: a collective equivalent and alternative to individual bargaining'. The Webbs saw collective bargaining as a fundamentally an *economic activity* by which the individual contract is replaced by a collective agreement. They saw the purpose of collective bargaining as being to determine under what terms labour will continue to be supplied to a company by its existing and future employees.

Flanders (1968a) has challenged the Webbs' view that collective bargaining is primarily an economic activity and an alternative to individual bargaining. He argues that collective bargaining is essentially a rule-making activity that has no proper counterpart in individual bargaining. He argues its function is to regulate, but not replace, individual bargaining. In other words, the end product of the individual bargain is a contract while the outcome of collective bargaining is a set of rules (Flanders 1968a: 4). Other authorities share this description of collective bargaining as a rule-making process. The ILO sees collective bargaining as being 'the negotiation of an agreed set of rules to govern the terms of the employment relationship, as well as the relationship between the bargaining parties themselves' (ILO 1973: 7). Flanders (1968a: 6) concedes that collective bargaining often replaces individual bargaining yet suggests that they are not complete alternatives (that is, mutually exclusive) as the Webbs inferred, and he suggests that collective bargaining and individual bargaining can co-exist.

In contradiction of the Webbs' view of collective bargaining as primarily an economic process, Flanders (1968a: 5) claims that collective bargaining is primarily an economic activity and suggests it is a political activity. He concurs with Harbison (1966), who proposed that an essential characteristic of collective bargaining is that it is 'a power relationship between organisations' and that it is best described 'as a diplomatic use of power'. In Flanders's eyes, there is no equivalent in the individual bargaining situation.

Alan Fox (1975) has attempted to rehabilitate the Webbs' perspective, arguing that individual bargaining can also embody a 'diplomatic use of power', that collective bargaining is not unique in its rule-making function and finally challenging the claim that the focus of collective bargaining is essentially a political activity. He points out that in individual bargaining, employers or employees may, for reasons of expediency, choose not to take advantage of a temporary superiority in bargaining power – a diplomatic use of power (Fox 1975: 156). Fox (1975) points out that individual bargaining defines the rules which will be observed by both parties if the contract is entered into and these are reviewed during the course of the continuing relationship (Fox 1975: 155). Thus, he claims 'the assertion that individual bargaining is not, as collective bargaining is, a rule-making process cannot be sustained' (Fox 1975: 155). Finally, Fox (1975) argues that the major bargaining preoccupations of trade unions is to secure increased financial reward and improved conditions and that trade unions find their major justification in the eyes of their members through this activity.

While the distinction between individual and collective bargaining has been hotly contested, the practical implications of the debate seem limited. Farnham and Pimlott (1990) claim that the theoretical distinction between collective bargaining as an economic or political activity has little conceptual or empirical validity. It is clear that irrespective of the distinctions between individual and collective bargaining, the latter involves the application of power. Furthermore, collective bargaining is intimately tied to the pursuit of political objectives at national level, albeit that the primary objective may be to improve the economic conditions of union members. The view of collective bargaining as being concerned with a power relationship between organisations predates Flanders's analysis. Perlman (1936: 154) highlighted the power struggle inherent in collective bargaining, seeing it as 'above all a technique whereby an inferior social class or group carries on a never slackening pressure for a bigger share in the social sovereignty'. Indeed, Perlman (1936: 154) did not see collective bargaining as being confined to the industrial arena but saw it manifesting itself 'equally in politics, legislation, Court litigation, government administration, religion, and education'.

Finally, collective bargaining also has an important rule-making function, with many of the rules now incorporated in individual employment legislation having been developed within a collective bargaining framework. The Webbs (1897) explicitly recognised that trade unions sought to impose a 'common rule', namely that they sought to limit arbitrary treatment of employees. As an example of this, collective bargaining imposed restrictions on employers' rights to dismiss employees long before the introduction of the Unfair Dismissals Act 1977. Collective agreements often allowed for representation of employees when faced with disciplinary action. In dismissals situations such agreements generally specified that employees be informed of the nature of the reason for any dismissal, required that employers justify any dismissal, allowed for disciplinary action to be proportionate to any offence and specified a right to appeal to a third party, such as a Rights Commissioner or the Labour Court. These limitations, negotiated by unions, contrast strongly with the common law entitlement that employers were entitled to dismiss 'for any reason or none'.

THREE THEORIES OF COLLECTIVE BARGAINING

The extensive debate on the nature of collective bargaining is useful in drawing attention to the multifaceted nature of the process. This is emphasised by Chamberlain and Kuhn (1965), who conclude that collective bargaining has three functions. It is a means of contracting for the sale of labour, a form of industrial government and a method of management. They classify these categories under the headings of a *marketing theory*, a *governmental theory* and a *managerial theory* of collective bargaining.

The *marketing theory* is essentially similar to the Webbs' classical view, which sees the individual contract as being replaced by the collective agreement. Collective bargaining's purpose is to determine the terms and conditions under which employees will supply labour to an organisation. In this view, the purpose of collective bargaining is to redress the inequity of bargaining power inherent in the employment relationship.

The *governmental theory* views collective bargaining as a form of industrial government. This view dates back to Leiserson (1922: 61), who argued that collective bargaining's principal function 'is to set up organs of government, define and limit them, provide agencies for making, executing and interpreting laws for industry and means for enforcement'.

The *managerial theory* stresses the functional relationship between a union and a company, suggesting that they combine 'in reaching decisions on matters in which both have vital interests' (Chamberlain and Kuhn 1965). The theory emphasises 'mutuality', namely that those who are integral to the conduct of an enterprise should have a voice in the decisions that affect them. Thus, collective bargaining is viewed as a method of management serving the interests of both parties. Collective bargaining serves employer interests of controlling labour and facilitating greater managerial control, which was especially important in the smokestack industries of steel, shipbuilding, etc., which employed large numbers of workers. Individualism is not really an option in such situations, while collective bargaining has huge economies of scale for the management of people.

From the trade union perspective, collective bargaining serves the interests of union members by regulating or checking the making of managerial decisions. This latter view suggests that collective bargaining will only persist so long as it continues to be seen to meet the needs of both parties. The management of labour in large-scale operations, associated with smokestack industries, meant that collective bargaining served both a strong governmental and managerial function. With the decline of such industries both of these functional imperatives have arguably been lessened, allowing for more individually based methods of management, which challenges the existence of collective bargaining.

Chamberlain and Kuhn (1965) see the three theories as reflecting different stages in the development of collective bargaining. Initially there was the fixing of the terms for sale of labour, later there emerged a need for procedures to settle disputes on pay and other matters, and finally came involvement in internal decision-making processes of a business. The view that collective bargaining is a dynamic process opens up the question of the future direction it will take. The Webbs suggested that collective bargaining would give way to legal regulation (see Flanders 1967: 75–6; Salamon 2000: 331). The growth of individual employment law in recent years would seem to provide an element of support for this prediction (see Browne 1994).

CRITIQUES OF COLLECTIVE BARGAINING

Whatever its potential advantages, the process of collective bargaining has been criticised from varying perspectives. Beaumont (1990: 106–10) has highlighted some of these negative commentaries. For example, those viewing industrial relations from the unitarist frame of reference have long contended that collective bargaining arrangements are unnecessary, as they emerge from an employer's failure to satisfy their employees' job needs. Those with a unitarist frame of reference see collective bargaining as resulting in undesirable conflict and introducing an external agency, namely a trade union, which acts as a competing focus of loyalty for employees within the workplace (see Fox 1966). More fundamentally, neo-classical economists question the efficiency effects of collective bargaining on resource allocation. In terms of contemporary developments there has been a major retreat from collective bargaining by employers in favour of unilateral regulation of the employment relationship.

A major debate took place during the 1970s in relation to the effect of the power balance in industrial relations. This debate was sparked off by Fox (1974: 267–9), who argued that pluralism assumed a rough balance of power between capital and labour and that no such balance existed, as well as claiming that capital was in reality more powerful and any appearance to the contrary was illusory. This analysis drew a strong rejoinder from Clegg (1975). While acknowledging that 'Fox had assembled an impressive number of statements by pluralists to the effect that under collective bargaining there ought to be a balance of power between the parties', he rejected the conclusion that this proved them 'to be true' (Clegg 1975: 313). He argues that no such requirement is in fact inherent in pluralism and that 'it is extremely difficult to measure bargaining power' (Clegg 1975: 313). He notes that Fox's exposition is conducted at a highly abstract level, using terms such as 'capital' and 'labour' that are inherently difficult to measure and that he (Fox) 'makes little or no use of empirical evidence'.

While this is the case, the problems of the measurement of power in social science is a common one (see Russell 1960; Lukes 1974) and the inability to measure it can lead to it being ignored. Thus, the pluralists who suggest that there is a rough balance of power are also measuring power (implicitly they are giving it a value around fifty per cent) without presenting empirical evidence (which Clegg identifies as the weakness in Fox's analysis). Pluralists, such as Clegg, who argue that a rough balance of power is not a feature of pluralist analysis are open to the charge that they ignore power (they are also measuring it by giving it a value close to zero). These issues go the heart of social science analysis and, irrespective of the merits of the differing positions, it is arguable that the fate of the British trade unions in the 1980s can be seen as vindication of Fox's assertion of the illusory nature of the power of trade unions.

Radical and Marxist writers have projected collective bargaining as being inherently conservative in its promotion of consensus. This discourages social change and operates to reinforce the status quo, thereby limiting challenges to the structures of ownership and control in society. According to Beaumont (1990), the radical and Marxist views suggest that collective bargaining has the effect of:

- producing only marginal improvements in the terms and conditions of employees;
- lowering union members' expectations with regard to what is realistically negotiable;
- making industrial conflict more manageable through the process of procedural regulation; and
- constraining the development of a cohesive working-class consciousness orientated towards larger political and economic change.

Writing from a Marxist perspective, Hyman (1975) argues that collective bargaining is a means of social control and an institutionalised expression of the class struggle between those owning capital and those selling labour in industry. While the critiques of collective bargaining provide insights into the fundamental nature of the process, there is a sense in which they are strongly influenced by the tenor of the times. The resurgence of industrial conflict in the 1960s redirected scholars' attention to Marxist analysis in seeking to explain the persistence of that conflict, despite the operation of pluralist institutions. Today the reality is that collective bargaining takes place under widely differing power balances within organisations and society. The issues at stake are different to those of the 1970s, with the relevance of collective bargaining being questioned by the growth of liberalism. Faced with this development, radical and Marxist writers have now raised queries as to the capacity of collective bargaining to meet these new challenges and have advanced a more sympathetic view of the process (see Kelly 2003; Edwards 2003).

COLLECTIVE BARGAINING AND ECONOMIC CONSIDERATIONS

Neo-classical economists see collective bargaining as increasing the cost of labour (wage rate) above the market rate and as a result labour becomes overpriced, causing unemployment. However, this view has long been subject to criticism by industrial relations scholars who note that wage rates within local labour markets, where there are no barriers to mobility, do not accord with such simple economic models (Lester 1952). Brown et al. (2003: 190) note that 'within local labour markets ... it is common to find a range of earnings across firms for workers in similar occupational categories at a given point in time'. Neo-classical writers have tried to explain this by claiming that workers in companies with a degree of product market power can, through collective bargaining, gain a share of the excess charges which are passed on to consumers (Brown et al. 2003:

193). However, this analysis is not shared by neo-Keynesians and institutional writers who point to the existence in large companies of internal labour markets, which can exist for efficiency reasons (Doeringer and Piore 1971).

There is considerable debate on these and other theories of pay determination, but from an industrial relations point of view, wages can be an important element in securing productive efficiency as distinct to the resource allocation role stressed by economists. Emphasising this point, Brown *et al.* (2003: 194) write: 'pay should be seen to play a part not only as a market price for labour, but also as a means by which managements can elicit productive effort from their workforce'. In this regard, since the 1964 Fawley productivity agreement, the role of collective bargaining in promoting productivity has been a central concern in industrial relations (see Flanders 1968b: 142). These issues are still to the fore in contemporary partnership approaches to collective bargaining.

Where employers are able to exercise strong control over local labour markets they may be able to reduce the returns to labour below the rate that would otherwise exist. This is known as having monopsonistic power. Even where alternatives exist in a local labour market, employees may be reluctant to leave employments even where they have grievances or are paid below the market rates because of the costs and uncertainty of moving employment. Moving employment means a loss of seniority and the uncertainty that one will be able to adapt to a new employment. In such a situation, collective bargaining can provide employees with a voice alternative to exit, being the only effective option for most employees in non-union situations.

It is important to note that neo-classical economists generally claim collective bargaining raises wages above the market rate and leads to unemployment, not inflation. In their view, inflation is caused by facilitative increases in the money supply. If central banks and governments control the money supply, then companies that agree to too high wage increases will eventually go out of business. This view contrasts with a Keynesian analysis that sees excess aggregate demand as a root cause of inflation and neo-Keynesian analysis which suggests a role for 'wage' inflation caused through collective bargaining. Phelps Brown (1971) argues that wages under collective bargaining may be twenty to twenty-five per cent higher than they otherwise would be and that this is achieved at the consumer's expense (other workers) through increased prices.

One of the key features of collective bargaining has been the 'sword of justice' aspect. Thus, 'wage inequalities are smallest in highly unionised countries' (see *The Economist* 1994: 19). This is paradoxical because the origin of trade unions in the skilled trades is founded on sectional interest, yet in action, they result in greater social equity.

While there is continuing evidence for a union mark-up this may be directly related to the size of the company, the size of the parent company and their power in the product market (Brown *et al.* 2003: 1991. While unskilled and semi-skilled employees have been found to enjoy higher wages in unionised plants, Stewart (1990) found that this effect disappeared when he controlled for the product market power of the employing company. Such a finding suggests wage rates may be less dependent on union organisation and on the outcomes from collective bargaining than on employer circumstances (see Brown *et al.* 2003: 193). This would also provide an explanation for the higher pay and conditions in those companies that practise sophisticated modern strategies. The capacity to earn supernormal profits may allow such companies to adopt the soft HRM-style strategies. Companies may seek to engage in policies that satisfy various stakeholders, employees included, rather than seek to employ labour at the market rate.

However, there is no guarantee that a high degree of labour market power (say, a quasi-monopoly position) will result in higher wages. Brown *et al.* (2003: 195) note American studies that show that where there are relatively few employers in a product market, 'they have found it relatively easy to combine to resist union demands'. Neither is there any guarantee that such soft HR policies will persist, as existing companies may be vulnerable to new companies that enter the market and lower their costs by hiring labour at the market rate.

The Development of Collective Bargaining and Public Policy

Collective bargaining struggled to establish itself, but by the time of World War II it was receiving strong support as a preferred mechanism for regulating the employment relationship. This was driven by the experiences of the Depression of the 1930s and the need, identified by Keynesian economic theory, to ensure sufficient aggregate demand. Cutting wage rates in the 1920s, as advocated by prevailing neo-classical economic theory, had led to the General Strike in the UK in 1926 and exacerbated the effects of the Great Depression of the 1930s, as workers were unable to purchase the outputs of the increasingly productive modern industries.

Strengthening the position of unions was seen as desirable. In the US, this was the policy underlying the 'New Deal' of Franklin D. Roosevelt, president from 1933 to 1945. Section 7 (a) of the US National Industrial Recovery Act (1933) granted employees 'the right to organise and bargain collectively through representatives of their own choosing' (see Millis and Brown 1950: 21–2). This right was strengthened further in the National Labour Relations Act (1935) and collective bargaining became widely established by 1937.

During World War II collective bargaining was used by the Allied powers to harness workers' contribution in the war effort. In the years after World War II, collective bargaining was advanced as a preferred mechanism for the conduct of industrial relations and an essential component of democratic societies (see Millis and Brown 1950: 677). In a wide-ranging study of US industrial relations, Golden and Parker (1955) identify collective bargaining as one of the fundamental causes of industrial peace. Myers (1955: 46) saw a basic cause of industrial peace as 'full acceptance by management of the collective bargaining process and of unionism as an institution'.

By the 1960s the industrial relations systems of many Western industrialised countries were based on collective bargaining arrangements. The Donovan Commission claimed that 'collective bargaining is the best method of conducting industrial relations' (Donovan 1968). The ILO (1973: 12–15) argued that collective bargaining offers a number of advantages, which explains its prevalence and broad acceptance in many countries. They note collective bargaining may be adopted to cope with the varying requirements of many different organisations and industrial sectors. They claimed it facilitates a diversity of agreements and as a result is far more flexible than other methods of industrial relations government, such as statutory control. Currently, the European Union strongly favours collective bargaining as a mechanism for delivering the 'social agenda'. Engagement in social dialogue by the representatives of employers and workers is seen as counterbalancing the union's economic agenda.

While widely advocated even in Western countries, collective bargaining was far from universal and was more developed in some countries than others. Under the Fascist dictatorships in Spain and Portugal, collective bargaining was undeveloped because of the restrictions on free trade unions. In France, collective bargaining was less developed due to a union preference for periodic political action to advance workers' interests and the small size of many French companies, which restricted collective organisation. Because of the political nature of French trade unions, when negotiations took place they led to 'understandings' rather than agreements. The unions, especially the largest trade union confederation, the Communist Confédération Générale du Travaile (CGT), opposed collective bargaining as a mechanism for conducting industrial relations, although for pragmatic reasons they did engage in bargaining. The resultant vacuum led to French industrial relations being widely regulated by law in the *code du travaile*. The nature of collective bargaining also differed from country to country, with national, industry and establishment bargaining being to the fore in differing countries and even varying within countries over time.

Despite the historical public policy support for collective bargaining, it has been under threat in more recent times. This has been most manifest in the UK and the US since the 1980s. Brown *et al.* (2003: 203) note that the 1998 UK Workplace Employment Relations Survey (WERS) found collective bargaining coverage dropped from seventy-five per cent in 1980 to forty per cent in 1998, with some sixty per cent of workers in 1998 without any collective bargaining coverage, compared to a figure of only twenty-five per cent in 1980. 'Collective bargaining covered sixty-one per cent of the public sector workforce but only twenty-four per cent of the private sector' (Brown *et al.* 2003: 199). They conclude that 'the reality for the vast majority of employees who work in the private sector in Britain is that management, not trade unions, now determine their pay' (Brown *et al.* 2003: 204). The coverage of collective bargaining is even lower in the US due to the much lower union density and the absence of employer organisations and industry-wide agreements. In addition to the reduction of coverage in the UK, Brown *et al.* (2003: 199) found the scope of bargaining diminished, meaning that the number of issues covered by negotiations was fewer. This represents a reversal from the previous historical trend, where the scope of bargaining had grown to cover ever-wider issues.

Kelly (2003: 14–15) has challenged the extent to which this represents a generalised trend as distinct from being an Anglo-American phenomenon. In the Countess Markievicz memorial lecture in 2003 he argued as follows.

Union decline in Britain and the USA is sometimes measured by reference to bargaining coverage and as Figure [9.1] (below) shows the proportion of workers covered by collective agreements fell dramatically in Britain after 1980 and to a lesser degree in the USA. What it also shows however is that the average level of bargaining coverage actually rose across the rest of Europe over the same period. This is a remarkable trend for a number of reasons. First, coverage was already high even in 1980 at just a little under eighty per cent so there seemed to be far more scope for decline rather than growth. Second, average union density levels across Europe fell through the 1980s and 1990s and in some countries are now extremely low. In France for instance density was less than ten per cent in 1998 and yet bargaining coverage was almost ninety per cent. In Spain the 1998 figures were sixteen per cent for union density but eighty-five per cent for coverage (see Kelly 2003, www.ul.ie/iair/).

Figure 9.1
Bargaining Coverage, 1980–1998

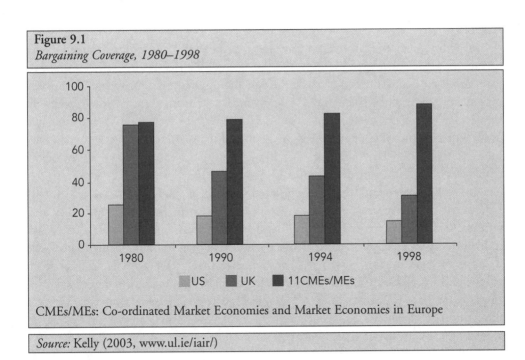

CMEs/MEs: Co-ordinated Market Economies and Market Economies in Europe

Source: Kelly (2003, www.ul.ie/iair/)

In Ireland the main developments have been a marked reluctance of multinational companies to recognise unions in recent years, thereby reducing bargaining coverage significantly in the private sector. The degree to which non-union employees can be considered to be covered by collective agreements as a result of national agreements is uncertain. There is no automatic extension of the terms of these agreements to non-union employees except insofar as the terms are incorporated into legislation for minimum pay, redundancy entitlements, etc. or where they influence making employment regulation orders made by the Joint Labour Committees (JLCs).

THE LAW AND COLLECTIVE BARGAINING

In relation to the role of the law and the outputs from collective bargaining there are two alternative models. Countries such as the US, Germany and Sweden have a system in which collective agreements are considered legally binding, while in the UK and Ireland they are 'binding in honour'. The Commission of Inquiry on Industrial Relations (1981: 214) noted that the Irish system reflects the view that collective bargaining, not the law, should be the primary source of regulation in the employment relationship. It was based on the presumption by all parties that recourse to the law will be avoided. Von Prondzynski (1998: 56) remarks that the voluntarist nature of the Irish system not only led trade unions to avoid the law but also persuaded successive governments to avoid legal intervention where possible. Most employers were willing to embrace an alternative regulatory framework based on collective bargaining. This voluntarism means that collective agreements are not generally legally binding because it is held that there is generally no intention on the part of the parties to create legal relations.

In addition, in the normal course of events neither trade unions nor employer organisations are considered to have a right of agency (Wallace 1989: 166). This follows from the legal requirement that someone concluding a contract on behalf of another person must have been given the authority, by that person, to act as their agent. In limited circumstances agency can exist. Kerr and Whyte (1985: 161) note this can occur where the number of employees 'is small and the matters dealt with are confined solely to that group'. In such cases, a trade union official can be a legal agent of the employees being represented (Kerr and Whyte 1985: 161).

Collective agreements that are registered with the Labour Court are also legally enforceable. Many such agreements are concerned with pension entitlements, which creates a strong imperative to give them legal effect as they concern the entitlements of individuals. While collective agreements are not legally enforceable of themselves, the terms of any agreement become a legal entitlement when actually applied to individual employees. In this way, a pay increase becomes incorporated into the contract of employment once paid by an employer. Similarly, where employees voluntarily accept a diminution in the terms and conditions of employment this can have the effect of amending the contract of employment.

THE STRUCTURE OF COLLECTIVE BARGAINING

Bargaining structure refers to the stable features that help to distinguish the collective bargaining process in any particular system (Parker *et al.* 1971). It refers to the framework in which negotiations between employers and organised workers take place. Parker *et al.* (1971) claim that variations in the bargaining structure of industrial relations systems can be accounted for by the differences which arise in respect of four aspects: *bargaining levels, bargaining units, bargaining forms* and *bargaining scope.* Bargaining structure in any particular system is dynamic and variations in one or more of these dimensions will alter the structure of collective bargaining from time to time.

Bargaining may take place at the *levels* of the workplace/enterprise, industry or nationally. It is normal for the application of agreements reached at a higher level, e.g. nationally, to be the subject of negotiation at the level of the workplace.

A *bargaining unit* refers to the group of workers to be covered by a particular bargained agreement. A bargaining unit may cover a narrow or wide group of workers. A bargaining unit could cover all fitters in a single company, all manual employees in an industry or all qualifying public sector workers, as in the case of the benchmarking process. A bargaining unit may also involve a single union, a group of unions or, for that matter, an association of unions that acts as bargaining agents at the negotiating table for employees. Bargaining units will vary according to the bargaining level at which the negotiation takes place. For example, a single union may negotiate at establishment level, whereas an association or federation of unions is more likely to negotiate at national level.

Bargaining form describes the degree of formality of an agreement. This may vary from an informal approach, which relies on unwritten agreements on the one hand, to a very formal approach, which utilises comprehensive written agreements. In general, the higher the bargaining level within an organisation, industry or country, the more likely it is that the degree of formality will be higher.

Bargaining scope relates to the range of issues to be covered, such as basic pay, shift premiums, overtime rates, holidays, hours of work, disciplinary procedures, etc. and may be comprehensive or restrictive in its range. A comprehensive scope implies that the scope of bargaining covers the entire range of employment issues affecting employees, while a restrictive scope suggests a focus on particular or problematic issues.

The end product of the collective bargaining process is the collective agreement. Collective agreements cover two different kinds of terms: *substantive* and *procedural*. Substantive terms cover issues such as pay, work quantity and quality, hours of work, overtime premiums, shift allowances, holiday entitlements, sick benefits and allowances. Procedural terms define the way in which substantive terms are made and how disputes over the application of agreed terms and conditions are to be dealt with (Anthony 1980). Such procedural terms may deal with discipline, grievances, disputes procedures, rule changes, how wage claims are to be processed and other such matters (Wallace 1989: 165).

BARGAINING LEVELS

While collective bargaining requires collective action on the part of employees, this is not a requirement of employers. Individual employers as well as employer associations may form a bargaining group with trade unions. Trade unions may bargain with one employer, a group of employers or with an employer association. Hence, collective bargaining may take place with a single employer or with a number of employers, the latter referred to as multi-employer bargaining. Single-employer bargaining can take place at a number of levels. The individual employer can be involved in both bargaining at establishment level (largely referred to as workplace bargaining) and at a multi-establishment level (if the organisation is a multi-site operation). In addition, collective bargaining at the level of the single employer might involve negotiations either with an individual union or a number of unions.

While in recent years there has been a growth in single union representation, multi-union negotiations are quite common in larger organisations in Ireland, such as the Health Boards, Coras Iompar Éireann (CIE) and the Electricity Supply Board (ESB). Multi-employer bargaining can take place at national, regional or industry level and an employer may be involved in both single- and multi-employer-level bargaining. In such instances, the issue of setting a precedent has particular importance, as a concession made by one employer can lead to claims on others in the bargaining group. We now set out to review three levels of bargaining.

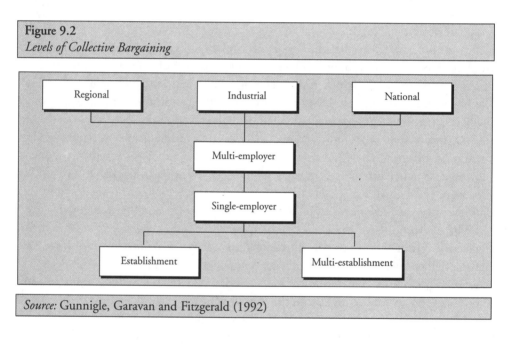

Figure 9.2
Levels of Collective Bargaining

Source: Gunnigle, Garavan and Fitzgerald (1992)

Multi-employer Bargaining

Multi-employer bargaining, especially bargaining within an industry, has a number of potential advantages, which historically saw it as a favoured form of bargaining in many situations. For unions, it provides an industry rate for the job, encourages wider labour market collective interests and offers protection to employees in weaker bargaining positions (see Gunnigle and Flood 1990; Brown *et al.* 2003: 199). For employers, it protects them from being picked off separately and limits the influence of the union at workplace level and their impact on detailed job control. In some countries the capacity of employer organisations to legally bind all employers in an industry limits 'good employers' from being undercut by those who seek to cut wages and costs by, for example, not providing training (Brown *et al.* 2003: 199). Gunnigle and Flood (1990) suggest that for organisations in comfortable trading positions, multi-employer bargaining is a relatively painless way of dealing with industrial relations. In effect, the most important advantage is the standardising of rates of pay and conditions by 'taking wages out of competition' (Brown *et al.* 2003).

Multi-employer bargaining can also have disadvantages. While standardising rates of pay can be beneficial, it may cause organisations to miss out on competitive opportunities. It limits the capacity for single-employer bargaining to allow management negotiators to more closely relate wage rates to establishment-level issues like productivity and cost reductions. In addition, it may remove the possibility of greater commitment to observe the terms of any agreements reached if employees have not been directly involved in the negotiations. However, this disadvantage may be overcome by allowing for agreements to be fine tuned and applied at the workplace level, a common practice in countries with industry-wide bargaining.

Industrial structure has been found to exercise an effect on the existence or otherwise of multi-employer bargaining in the US (see Pierson 1961). In a British study, Deaton and Beaumont (1980: 210) found that multi-employer bargaining was associated with high regional concentration of organisations operating within a similar labour market. Single-employer bargaining, on the other hand, was associated with larger establishments, multi-site organisations, foreign ownership, organisations operating within non-competitive product markets and the existence of specialist industrial relations managers at a senior level. It seems, then, that the determining factor in relation to the existence or otherwise of multi-employer bargaining has in recent years been determined less by industrial structure than the balance of advantage. That is, the balance of advantages has in many instances swung decisively against multi-employer bargaining in the UK and Ireland.

In the UK employer desire for workplace bargaining saw a decline in industry-wide agreements in the 1960s, which was a major factor after World War II (Donovan 1968). Brown *et al.* (2003) note that employer solidarity 'had shallower roots in Britain than most European countries', a situation mirrored in Ireland. The main reason they identify for the decline, however, is the limited extent to which 'wages can be taken out of competition'. In Ireland the balance of advantage has similarly swung from multi-employer bargaining due to the openness of the economy. This factor has been accentuated by the growth of private sector services. Both factors make it difficult, if not meaningless, to attempt to take wages out of competition through multi-employer bargaining in many industries. Thus, industry-wide bargaining, though widespread in the 1960s, is no longer a major factor in Irish industrial relations, as many of the industry-wide bargaining groups have since disbanded (O'Brien 1989a: 138).

Enterprise-Level Bargaining

Mirroring the decreased attractiveness of multi-employer bargaining have been growing pressures for enterprise-level bargaining. Brown *et al.* (2003) argue that these pressures come less from wage factors than productivity considerations, which allow employers to cultivate internal labour markets. They write: 'when much skill acquisition is on the job, and when technological change is constant and incremental, there are advantages in having fluid job titles, predictable career trajectories, and stable internal salary structures'. Kinnie (1986) suggests that in responding to these pressures, corporate management may on the one hand seek greater centralisation in order to exert central control over costs and work practices. On the other hand, they may wish to decentralise control so as to create individual cost centres and delegate responsibility for increased efficiency. Kinnie (1986) argues that the trend is for greater centralisation in combination with an element of establishment bargaining. He suggests that organisations are seeking to co-ordinate strategic decision making at corporate level while allowing greater operational discretion at local level. However, it is likely that there will be considerable variation within individual enterprises.

While national-level bargaining has been dominant in Ireland since 1987 (see Chapter 13), these agreements are often applied through collective negotiations at company level. The function of the national agreements is to set out agreed national-level guidelines for wage increases and other related issues. The national agreement may also allow scope for supplementary productivity bargaining at establishment level. However, these guidelines are always subject to the outcome of negotiations at company level.

National-Level Bargaining

Centralised bargaining essentially describes institutionalised negotiation between representatives of trade union confederations (in Ireland, the Irish Congress of Trade Unions [ICTU]) and employer associations (in Ireland, primarily the Irish Business and Employers Confederation [IBEC]) about wages and other issues. Since 1922 there have been significant changes in the levels at which bargaining has taken place. Bargaining has oscillated between national, industrial and enterprise levels. Centralised bargaining has been typified by attempts to adopt a corporatist approach to collective bargaining. Corporatist arrangements are distinguished from centralised bargaining in that corporatism attempts the following:

- integrates government intervention in collective bargaining so that negotiations become tripartite;
- promotes a debate over broader issues, such as macroeconomic concerns; and
- seeks a consensus on economic and social issues in pursuit of a 'national interest'.

Since 1970 (except for the period between 1982 and 1987), pay agreements have been negotiated through centralised bargaining. This has involved varying degrees of government involvement, first as a large employer and subsequently as government. Thus, national-level bargaining is inextricably bound up with a greater involvement by government in the industrial relations process than a simple voluntarist model implies. We now turn to examine corporatist theory on the role of the state.

NATIONAL-LEVEL BARGAINING AND THE ROLE OF THE STATE

National-level bargaining needs to be understood in the context of differing models for the management of industrial relations. Here we examine different state strategies to pay determination.

Liberal Collectivism

While collective bargaining may take place at differing levels of the economy, a major factor determining which level dominates is the role governments decide to adopt in relation to collective bargaining (Schmitter and Lehmbruch 1979; Crouch 1982; Roche 1989; Rollinson 1993). Into the 1960s Irish governments adopted an approach that is loosely referred to as voluntarism. Strictly speaking, the term 'voluntarism' is more correctly applied to role of the law, with the term *liberal collectivism* describing governmental non-involvement in collective bargaining (Palmer 1983; Rollinson 1993). Practitioners refer to such a situation as 'free collective bargaining'. Roche (1989: 116) refers to it as an 'auxiliary' approach, highlighting the fact that governments do not abstain from involvement in efforts to influence bargaining. Liberal collectivism involves a democratic state, autonomous trade unions and employer organisations, with 'attempts to intervene in pay determination regarded as invalid' (Roche 1989: 115).

However, governments may seek to indirectly influence the process by what Roche (1989) terms exhortation – essentially, appealing to the parties to take a particular course of action. This usually involves governments appealing to trade unions to exercise wage restraint, although it may also involve pleadings to employers to restrain prices. The state may also provide for third-party dispute resolution institutions and inducements to reform, such as grants for union amalgamations. Minimum protective legislation, typically in the area of health and safety and working conditions, may also be specified. These provide employees with a 'floor of rights', or minimum standards, which may be improved upon through the collective bargaining process. In addition, governments have the instrument of devaluation, which affects the value of pay awards by effectively reducing their value. The use of devaluation, however, is not exclusive to liberal collectivism.

Liberal collectivism came under pressure throughout Europe as a result of the success of Keynesian demand management policies employed in the aftermath of World War II. These policies were designed to prevent a recurrence of the economic dislocation that had been experienced in some countries after World War I and during the Great Depression, which commenced in 1929. Keynesian policies in the 1950s and 1960s led to unprecedented levels of 'full employment', which increased the power of organised labour. Employers could no longer rely on what Marx called the 'reserve army of the unemployed' to constrain the growth of wage rates. Roche (1989) notes that governments faced with the problems of 'inflation and economic survival' had two alternatives to liberal collectivism. These were 'to move in the direction of greater state intervention in collective bargaining or to jettison the commitment to full employment' (Roche 1989: 116).

Market Liberalism

Jettisoning the commitment to full employment, which had been part of the post-World War II consensus, meant 'discipline' would be restored to labour markets. This involved the adoption of an approach varyingly described in the industrial relations literature as individual liberalism (Palmer 1983), market liberalism (Rollinson 1993) or market control (Roche 1989). The dominant economic philosophy in market individualism/individual liberalism is one of laissez-faire and is the underlying principle in modern neo-classical economic theories, notably the monetarism of Milton Friedman.

In the neo-classical view, supply and demand is the ultimate arbitrator of the competing interests of capital and labour. Labour is a commodity, as any other, to be bought or sold. Wage rates and terms and conditions of employment are to be determined by the market. Trade unions and collective bargaining are seen as distorting the operation of the market and governments should move to limit their influence. In keeping with the laissez-faire doctrine, direct involvement by the state in industrial relations matters is to be avoided. Instead, indirect policies are applied, especially a tight monetary policy. From 1979 UK governments, under the Conservatives, pursued a tight monetary policy and industrial restructuring as part of their strategy of enforcing labour market discipline. Unemployment constrained the unions' power and strict control of the money supply ensured that companies that reached too-generous wage agreements with their workers risked going out of business (Roche 1989: 117).

The economic restrictions were augmented by legislation rolling back the trade disputes immunities enjoyed by trade unions and placing legal obligations on them. Crouch (1982) points out that market individualism subordinates employees to the control and authority of the owner and the relationship between them is at best paternalistic and at worst exploitative.

While to date no Irish government has deployed a strategy of thoroughgoing market liberalism (see Roche 1989), it would be a mistake to suggest that market forces have not affected the nature of Irish industrial relations. The open nature of the Irish economy, globalisation and EU competition policy are powerful forces shaping the nature of collective bargaining. Growing privatisation, management opposition to union recognition, a low tax regime and restrictions on government spending augment these influences. Taken together, these factors mean that collective bargaining and traditional industrial relations are under intense pressure to adapt. This process of adaptation can be seen in the union 'give backs' and the push for a flexible workforce in the 1980s and the union-management engagement with new forms of work organisation, attempts to develop workplace partnership and responses to market liberalisation and privatisation in the 1990s (see Hastings 2003).

Corporatism

The alternative to collective liberalism or individual liberalism is a system of industrial relations based on corporatism, which involves governments becoming more involved in collective bargaining (Roche 1989: 116). The origins of corporatism can be traced back to diverse sources, most notably the Social Christian tradition in the papal encyclical *Rerum Novarum* issued by Pope Leo XIII in 1893. Corporatist ideas were opposed to notions of atomistic individual competition inherent in laissez-faire economic theories and the class conflict models inherent in Marxism. Corporatism preached social harmony under organised and representative structures of workers and employers, co-ordinated by the state. In contrast to classical economic theories, it recognised the legitimacy of collective organisations representing workers (and employers).

The mass unemployment of the 1930s threatened the stability of the liberal democracies and led to the emergence of Fascism in a number of European countries, notably Italy, Germany, Spain and Portugal. Fascist countries turned to a form of corporatism where labour markets were regulated by the state in order to produce 'social harmony'. In this corporatism, free trade unions were abolished or severely restricted and the state acted as the controlling influence in regulating labour-management relations. Panitch (1979: 120) notes that 'the fascist states, gave a rude answer to the question of how the social harmony trumpeted in theory would in fact come to replace the competition and class conflict of capitalist society'. The associations with Fascist authoritarianism led to the concept of corporatism being viewed in overwhelmingly negative and pejorative terms post-World War II (Panitch 1979: 120; Schmitter 1979: 9). It was no surprise that after 1945 there was a new appreciation of the merits of free trade unions and collective bargaining as a brake on the power of capital.

Neo-corporatism

While the term 'corporatism' was in disfavour after 1945, by the 1970s political scientists and industrial relations scholars had begun to resurrect the ideas under the term of 'neo-corporatism' (or new corporatism) (Schmitter 1979). The re-examination of corporatist ideas was driven by the examples of a number of European states in the 1950s and 1960s, most notably Sweden. Sweden had strong trade unions and employer organisations and the economy had enjoyed remarkable economic success and modernisation. Collective bargaining played a major role in the Swedish economic model and there was none of the dire predictions inherent in classical or neo-classical economic theory. Sweden also seemed to finesse the problems of inflation and stagnation (so-called stagflation) that afflicted other European countries, notably the UK. The unions exercised restraint on their ability to push up wages in return for trade-offs in the political arena. Thus, in return for wage restraint, governments were committed to full employment and a high level of welfare provision. In order to deliver this high level of welfare, taxation levels were high, allowing the state to deliver high standards of education, health, pension, housing and other entitlements, producing a high 'social wage'.

Co-operation by the trade unions in the use of new technology and modernisation of the economy led to high labour productivity, ensuring that wage restraint did not mean low wages. In fact, wages were high by international standards, as the productivity of labour was high. Wage solidarity policies, in which manual workers received higher percentage wage increases than professional and white-collar workers, ensured a relatively narrow variance in the distribution of wages. This contributed to a low variation in income distribution and ensured a high degree of social solidarity. The neo-corporatism in Sweden was intimately bound up with the dominant role of the Swedish Social Democratic Party, which continuously held power from 1932 to 1976. Thus, there was a strong political aspect to the neo-corporatism of Sweden.

Other countries, however, exhibited examples of corporatist arrangements without the dominant role of a Social Democratic Party, for example, the Netherlands, the Federal Republic of Germany and Austria (Lehmbruch 1979). These were identified as exhibiting a degree of social consensus that allowed for strong central co-ordination of industrial relations and were termed corporatism based on social consensus, or what Lehmbruch (1979: 53) has termed 'consociational corporatism'. Corporatist arrangements were held together by what Roche (1989) has termed a 'virtuous circle' of full employment and high welfare provisions, which had the effect of legitimating and reinforcing the unions' wage restraint policies.

Differing Forms of Neo-corporatism

Pekkarinen *et al.* (1992) describe the Scandinavian neo-corporatism as *social corporatism*. Social corporatism involves restraining the industrial wage in return for a higher 'social wage' through a strongly redistributive taxation policy and, in the Swedish case, wage solidarity. Social corporatism is based on a political and ideological analysis that perceives conflict as endemic to capital-labour relations and where compromise arises from a position of power on both sides. Corporatism acts to institutionalise conflict as part of a democratic class struggle (Korpi 1983).

Pekkarinen *et al.* (1992) contrast this social corporatism with liberal corporatism. Liberal corporatism is based on the view that there is essentially a commonality of interests between capital and labour. Over time there is a gradual institutionalisation of a consensus, particularly between leaders rather than members of organisations. The management of economic adjustment and the sharing of burdens and rewards are controlled by the elites at the top of hierarchies of interest organisations. The gains go chiefly to insiders, reflecting the relative power of peak-level federations and their member organisations. There is an absence or only weak commitment to egalitarianism, resulting in the preservation of existing disparities in wealth and life chances. According to Pekkarinen *et al.* (1992), examples of this liberal corporatist approach are to be found in Austria and the Netherlands.

The distinctions made between liberal and social corporatism reflect ideal types, and real-life examples tend to fall somewhere between the two types. For example, it is now recognised that Swedish neo-corporatism prior to the 1980s paid considerable attention to international competitiveness. Moene and Wallerstein (1999: 234) note that 'the Nordic variety of corporatism was associated not with protectionism and monopolistic pricing, but with free trade and the subsequent need to remain competitive'. In evaluating any real-world corporatist system, the key question is not whether the example matches either of the ideal types, but which version the particular example most approximates. In this regard, the differences in taxation policy are crucial, with liberal corporatism being based on low taxation, which limits the redistributive capability of centralised agreements in such cases.

Corporatism and Empirical Evidence

The central tenet of neo-corporatist theory is that neo-corporatist systems are more governable and deliver superior economic outcomes. Research had initially posited that corporatist systems enjoyed superior economic performance to others. Empirical research by Calmfors and Driffill (1988) suggested a more complex U-shaped relationship between the degree of neo-corporatism and levels of economic performance rather than the linear relationship previously suggested. Calmfors and Driffill (1988) divided the countries they studied into centralised, intermediate and decentralised categories and compared employment and inflation levels for the period 1974 to 1985. First, their evidence indicated that the most centralised (or corporatist) economies had fared best in this period. Second, the economies with decentralised arrangements for bargaining fared better than intermediate countries possessing industry-level bargaining, with lower unemployment. However, this appears to have been at the expense of higher inflation.   Third, it appears that the intermediate economies, characterised by industry-level bargaining, had responded least well to the economic crisis of the 1970s.

The U-shaped relationship implies that highly centralised neo-corporatist arrangements as well as highly decentralised systems are conducive to economic success, and the ability of an economy to provide employment and the poorer performers are those countries with intermediate levels of centralisation, for example those with industry-wide bargaining. Dell'Aringa and Lodovici (1990) suggest that higher levels of corporatism performed better than lower levels during the period 1974 to 1987. In contrast, weak corporatist countries tended to perform the poorest. Crepaz (1992), studying the same period, found again that increasing levels of corporatism significantly depressed inflation and lowered unemployment for both the 1970s and 1980s. However, the presence of a Social Democratic party in power had a negative impact on economic growth. According to Crepaz (1992: 159), Social Democratic parties might not provide as many incentives to invest as do Conservative governments and have to 'maintain tax levels that have reached magnitudes that could plausibly be detrimental to capitalist expansion'.

Testing the effects of differing systems of bargaining on macroeconomic outcomes is sensitive to the time period chosen. Using data from the 1986 to 1996 period to test the validity of the Calmfors and Driffill model, the Organisation for Economic Co-operation and Development (OECD) (1997: 64) claims that the evidence from this time period 'does not point to many statistically significant relationships between most measures of economic performance and collective bargaining'. If this conclusion is correct, it raises questions about the causal relationship between social partnership and the performance of the Irish economy in recent years, namely why the Irish experience should be atypical.

Contemporary Corporatist Developments

Baccaro (2002: 6) distinguishes between

> two dimensions of corporatism: as a particular structure of the interest representation system, characterised by monopolistic, centralised and internally non-democratic associations, and as a particular policy-making process, also known as 'concertation' or 'social partnership'.

He sees the Irish system as falling into the latter category and being representative of what is alive in corporatism. While the former dimension of corporatism is more or less dead, having exhausted its predictive and explanatory capacities, the latter is very much alive and captures much of what is going on in various countries, mostly (but not exclusively) European. Thus, the highly redistributive and solidaristic policies of neo-corporatism came under threat following the 1970s. In Sweden the employers broke from the system, which had previously been lauded. By the mid-1980s it appeared that social corporatism as a specific political and economic approach to economic management had declined in many European countries (Golden et al. 1999: 194–8). However, by the 1990s corporatism had 'undergone an astonishingly lively and broad-based revival' with the emergence and re-emergence of social pacts at national level in a number of countries (Pochet and Fajertag 2000: 9).

These social pacts were described under the term '*competitive corporatism*'. The emergence of competitive corporatism has been attributed to increasing competition in a global market (including internal EU competition resulting from enlargement), a shift in the balance of power away from unions to capital and the crisis in employment in many EU countries in the 1990s (Goetschy 2000; Ferner and Hyman 1998). It was chiefly associated with the election of Social Democratic parties, which in conjunction with trade unions searched for an alternative or 'third way' to the neo-liberal prescription of deregulated labour markets and reduced welfare systems (Rhodes 1998: 200).

Thus, competitive corporatism is an attempt to meet the demands for economic efficiency while promoting some equity, or at least defending existing social protection systems (see Rhodes 1998: 179). For example, the alliance for the 'jobs pact' pursued in Germany rests on three pillars: the creation of a subsidised low wage sector to encourage employment growth; increased training to make companies more competitive; and lower personal taxation for employees and lower corporate taxes on company profits to attract more foreign direct investment (Bispinck and Schulten 2000).

Turner and Wallace (2000: 3) suggest that this competitive corporatism is remarkably similar to *liberal corporatism* and can be analysed under that heading. Competitive corporatism involves agreements between the social partners based on greater flexibility in the labour market, which in turn means increased wage flexibility and wage dispersion. Social security systems and social intervention are tailored more closely with the imperatives of competition. Labour market reforms are used to promote employment rather than through government demand management (Goetschy 2000). Turner and Wallace (2000: 4) write: 'in the new social pacts, economic efficiency takes precedence over equity issues. Indeed, the very policies of competitive corporatism, for example, labour market deregulation and a reduction in corporate taxation, promotes increased inequality'. As Rhodes (1998: 200) observes, competitive corporatism prioritises competitiveness and employment creation, but 'downplays the equity function of more traditional golden age forms of corporatism'.

CHAPTER 10

Negotiations

INTRODUCTION

The study of industrial relations negotiations developed in relative isolation from other areas in the field of conflict resolution theory. This study of negotiations typically involved the observation and description of formal negotiating situations between managers and trade unions. Publications involved prescriptive negotiation manuals based on the experience of 'expert' negotiators rather than on research. Valuable as these were, they had limitations. In recent decades an interdisciplinary approach to conflict resolution has emerged, resulting in a rich body of negotiation theory with contributions from disciplines such as psychology, sociology, anthropology, political science, industrial relations, economics and mathematics (see Thompson 2001). The benefit for the modern industrial relations negotiator in having an appreciation of negotiating theory is that prescriptions are now grounded in more robust research. These prescriptions are also more versatile and embrace a range of negotiating styles and approaches, rather than being confined to a single style or approach. Nonetheless, there remains much research to be done on negotiations and different approaches can work equally well for individual negotiators. This means negotiation theory and research needs to be adapted by individual negotiators to suit their style and preferences. There are also limitations to the contribution negotiation theory can make to the outcome of negotiations, which will be determined by structural factors, the nature of the case and underlying dynamics.

No more than becoming skilled in any other activity, negotiation requires study and practice. A common myth is the frequently encountered assertion that negotiation cannot be learned. Even an introduction can provide substantial benefits for industrial relations practitioners who engage in negotiations, just as an introductory chess book can greatly improve chess-playing ability. Students (and practitioners) who fail to acquaint themselves with the basic elements of negotiation risk placing themselves at a substantial disadvantage in the negotiation process. Naturally, exposure to a chapter in a single text is insufficient to make someone a skilled negotiator, but even a basic understanding can have significant benefits. However, one of the difficulties of modern negotiations textbooks is that it is difficult to assimilate and apply the exhaustive prescriptions contained in them. Thus, a short review has its own merits in that it can simplify and highlight key points.

The aim of this chapter is to introduce students to some of the basic ideas, their application and their limitations. The aim is to provide a rounded introduction to negotiations in an industrial relations setting. This discussion takes place in the context of key conflict resolution mechanisms at organisational level, namely industrial relations negotiations, grievance handling and disciplinary administration. Employee participation and partnership developments are discussed in following chapters. Although the material referred to here draws on extensive research, in order to aid the flow of the chapter references are kept to a minimum.

CONFLICT AND NEGOTIATION

Negotiation takes place to resolve conflict. In a negotiation context, Lewicki *et al.* (1999: 16) defines conflict as 'the perceived divergence of interest or a belief that the current parties' aspirations cannot be achieved simultaneously'. It is important to note that conflict can take place at a number of levels. It can be intra-personal (conflict within an individual), inter-personal (between individuals), intra-organisational (within an organisation) or inter-organisational (between organisations). Intra-personal conflicts commonly arise because individuals are undecided as to what they want. Inter-personal conflict can arise for a large number of reasons. Some conflicts may be personality based, but more often they are a manifestation of underlying differences of interests or may be concerned with power relations. In the previous chapter it was noted that social theorists have convincingly written on the functionality of conflict, thereby challenging the notion that conflict is necessarily bad or dysfunctional. However, an individual faced with an industrial relations conflict may find it difficult to identify the functional aspects of conflict.

Not infrequently, people, be they managers or employees, may be angry, emotional and upset. When asked what conflict means to them, people tend to describe it with words such as 'fight', 'aggro', 'trouble' and even more colourful images such as those noted by the ILO (1997) as being like a 'tornado', a 'fireball' or a 'faceless monster'. Yet if people are asked to reflect on potentially positive aspects of conflict, they generally have no difficulty identifying some. Typical positive images are illustrated by the following selection: conflict can be a 'thrill', an 'opportunity to perfect', a 'challenge', an 'adventure', an 'opportunity to know each other', 'growth', a 'reality focus' and 'spring' (ILO 1997).

Research indicates that the extent to which images of conflict will dominate in reality is likely to be determined by underlying structural factors and the dynamics of the situation. The presence or absence of skill in a negotiation can most likely only make a modest contribution to whether conflict will have a positive or negative outcome for the parties. Nonetheless, that modest contribution can be vital. While a high level of negotiation skill may not prevail over underlying structural factors, ineffective negotiations can cause needless breakdown and more negative outcomes for the parties involved.

NEGOTIATION: CONCEPTS AND THEORY

There are a number of definitions of negotiations, but in essence it is a complex social process aimed at resolving differences through discussion and *exchange*. Kennedy (1998) emphasises these aspects of negotiation, defining it as 'the process by which we search for the terms to obtain what we want from somebody who wants something from us'. The advantage of this definition is that it emphasises that negotiation is fundamentally an act of 'exchange' and reached by a process of 'searching'. Thus, it is not essentially about persuasion or communication, although these may be part of the process.

In emphasising the exchange aspect of negotiations, he draws attention to the idea that a negotiator can only attain some, or all, of *their* needs by being prepared to take into account some or all of the needs of the *other* party. This means that an ability to uncover the other party's needs is essential in the skilled negotiator's repertoire. Unskilled negotiators tend to focus excessively, and sometimes even exclusively, on their own needs and are less skilled at discovering the needs of the other party. Exchange also suggests that movement is an essential part of the negotiation process and this implies that it is necessary to be prepared to concede on certain items.

Strategic Choice

Parties can pursue a number of strategic options in any negotiation. These options are often discussed under the heading of negotiation styles but are best understood as choices which have to be made (see Figure 10.1). Parties can choose to either negotiate or not negotiate (that is, engaging in avoidance behaviour). They can choose to *compete*, which means that each party seeks to maximise their own outcomes; they can *accommodate*, which implies giving priority to the other party's outcomes; they can attempt *collaboration*, which involves an attempt to simultaneously meet both party's needs fully; or finally, they can *compromise*. Compromise arises where each side is concerned about their own outcomes but neither side can achieve those ends without the involvement of the other.

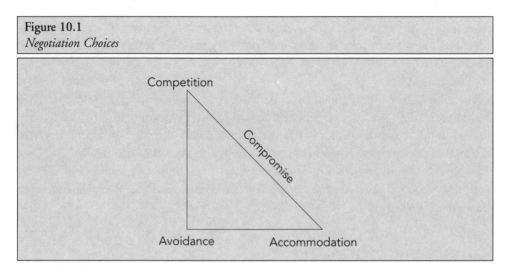

Figure 10.1
Negotiation Choices

It is not uncommon for parties to adopt one of these approaches by default and without conscious thought. This has the potential to be a serious mistake. Using a compromise strategy in a potential win-win situation risks 'leaving substantial value undiscovered'. A party that uses an accommodation approach when the outcomes are important to them will end up dissatisfied. For instance, a company that is in financial difficulty and that ignores this and grants a too-high wage increase may further damage the company and cause the loss of employment. A union official who concedes to a company without adequately attempting to meet members' needs may see the union lose support of its members and, in some cases, they may seek to join another union.

Avoidance

From a rational point of view, it is not always correct to negotiate. Entering into a negotiation process is justified in the following circumstances:

- when we need something from someone or need someone's consent;
- when the time and effort of negotiating are justified by the potential outcome; and
- when the outcome is uncertain.

It would make no sense for a parent faced with a child who is about to run across a busy road to start to negotiate over the child's intention. The only rational option is to grab them to prevent an accident, in other words, to exercise their greater power. Thus, in certain industrial relations situations, the favoured option may be unilateral action, such as when crucial action is necessary in relation to delivering an order, etc. Equally for employees, refusal to undertake an order that has safety implications may be preferable to entering into negotiations. The standard industrial relations prescription is to 'work under protest', but if this were to expose an employee to potential injury or loss of life, the risk may be considered too high.

Accommodation

This is indicated when one is more concerned about the other's outcomes than one's own. An accommodation approach was widely used by employers during the Irish World Cup campaign. Production stopped in many companies and widespread arrangements were made for employees to watch games. It was not the case that employers were unconcerned about their own situation, as pronouncements by IBEC at the time indicate. However, they placed the 'relationship' aspect ahead of their legal entitlements under contract law to insist on 'performance'. All negotiations are in fact a balancing of a range of factors, with relationships being particularly important in those interactions that are not 'one-off'. Sebenius (2001) notes that the intangibles of negotiation can be vitally important and that it is an error to ignore intangibles such as relationships. He calls this the error of focusing solely on price in negotiations. He suggests that 'most deals are fifty per cent emotion and fifty per cent economics' and argues that hard bargaining, focusing solely on price, 'often leaves potential joint gains unrealised'. This does not mean that negotiators can neglect the *hard* elements of negotiation, such as price; this is seldom sufficient in any complex negotiation.

Case Study: The 'Logic' of Accommodation

One party is given €100 to divide with another party as she/he likes; the second party can agree or disagree to any proposed arrangement. If the second party agrees, the €100 is divided in line with the first side's proposal; if not, neither party gets anything. Price logic would suggest the first party should propose something like '€99 for me and €1 for you'. Although this is an extreme allocation, it still represents a position in which the second party gets something rather that nothing. Pure price negotiators confidently predict the other side will agree to the split. It's like them finding a euro on the street – who wouldn't pick it up?

In laboratory experiments, however, most players turn down proposals that don't let them share in at least thirty-five to forty per cent of the €100. This also holds true in laboratory-based experiments, even when much larger stakes are involved and the amount forfeited is significant. While these rejections are 'irrational' on a pure price basis, studies show that when people feel a split is too unequal they reject the offer as unfair, are offended by the process and perhaps try to teach the 'greedy' person a lesson.

Source: Adapted from Sebenius (2001)

Competing

A competing strategy may be indicated when a party has high concerns about their own outcomes and the other party has high concerns about theirs. This is typically the case over items such as pay, hours of work, pensions and other such *substantive* aspects of industrial relations negotiations. Competitive negotiations are common in adversarial industrial relations negotiations (see Glanbia case study, Chapter 12). Competition is especially encountered in distributive bargaining, but an excessively competitive approach may prove counterproductive. Kennedy (1998) divides negotiation styles into two general approaches – red and blue styles. A red style is excessively competitive and uses aggressive tactics. He points out that the great disadvantage of this approach is the party one is negotiating against is very likely to respond in kind. This leads to a destructive spiral of attack and defence, limits the possibility for building relationships and excludes the capacity for problem solving.

Collaboration

A collaboration strategy is indicated where there are mutual gains to be generated, which is illustrated in Figure 10.2. In this approach both sides try to assist each other in gaining their desired outcome. A traditional aspect of collaborative bargaining was the productivity agreements of the 1960s and 1970s. Currently, annual hours agreements embody a number of elements of mutual gains bargaining (see Chapter 12). A collaborative strategy is associated with a problem-solving approach. This is essential, as mutual gains are frequently not obvious and may require considerable ingenuity to generate or discover. Collaboration can be understood as an attempt to 'grow the size of the pie'.

It is important to stress that no single approach to negotiation is correct. Students who are new to negotiation theory tend to suggest that collaboration is superior, but that is not necessarily the case. However, if resources are fixed, collaboration may involve a long and costly search for a non-existent solution (see Glanbia case study, Chapter 12). However, adding an extra dimension to the negotiation greatly increases the options for collaboration, provided that each party's needs differ somewhat. The following example illustrates this. If an apple pie is of a fixed size and if both parties like apple pies equally, then collaboration or accommodation does not yield a superior outcome to simply cutting up the cake on a fifty-fifty basis (a distributive approach). Adding an additional dimension to the negotiation mix can be the appropriate strategy. If one party has an apple pie and the other a rhubarb pie preference, then the possibility for mutually beneficial exchange arises (see Sweet Reason case on the website for a ten-minute demonstration of this principle, which can be used in class), provided both sides' preferences differ. Paradoxically, in integrative bargaining, it is identifying differences and exploiting them which leads to superior outcomes for both parties (Thompson 2001).

New negotiators also tend to find collaboration very difficult to *implement in practice* while maintaining that it is the approach they would use. We have already seen that entering negotiations is not always desirable and that the exercise of power may be justified rather than negotiation. In fact, some authors refer to competitive bargaining as 'controlling' or 'power'-centred bargaining (see Hiltrop and Udall 1995; Lewicki *et al.* 1999).

Figure 10.2
Negotiation Choices Expanded

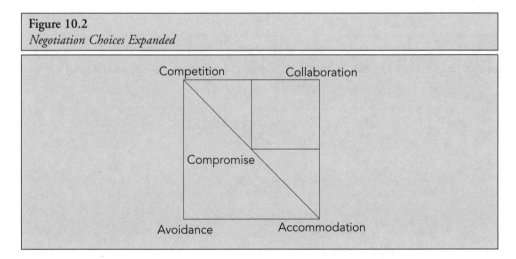

Distributive Bargaining

Distributive bargaining is typified by an exaggerated low or high opening position and misrepresentation of one's position. This is not necessarily a bad thing, as a high/low opening position provides room for movement. The main disadvantage to a too high or too low initial position can lead to one of the parties deciding it is not worth their while negotiating. If parties are confronted with an extreme opening offer, it may be necessary to get the other party to reframe their position, for which there are various techniques (see Lewicki *et al.* 2001; Thompson 2001).

The difference between the opening positions of both parties sets the bargaining range. Parties then may establish intermediate position(s) that they are prepared to move to during negotiations. If that proves insufficient to gain agreement, then they will have a fallback position, which is the least favourable offer they will agree to from the other side in order to avoid breakdown and referral to a third party (see Figure 10.3). Skilled negotiation should ensure a settlement if *at least the fallback positions* of the parties overlap. If they do not, then non-agreement is the correct outcome from a negotiation. Of course, parties may be unrealistic in setting a fallback position – it may be set too high (on the union side) or too low (on the management side) – and fallback positions established at the commencement of negotiations should be kept under review in light of new information discovered during negotiations.

The essence of distributive negotiation is to maximise the 'negotiator's surplus', that is, the portion of the overlap between the two parties, as shown in Figure 10.3. This can be illustrated by the following example: ICTU claims a fourteen per cent increase in pay over three years in national negotiations and the employers offer six per cent. If the employers are prepared as a fallback to offer eleven per cent and ICTU to accept nine per cent, then there is an overlap in their positions and, with sufficiently skilled negotiation, an agreement can be arrived at. If the settlement is for 9.5 per cent then the employers will have achieved seventy-five per cent of the negotiator's surplus, whereas if the agreement is for 10.5 per cent the union will have gained seventy-five per cent of the surplus.

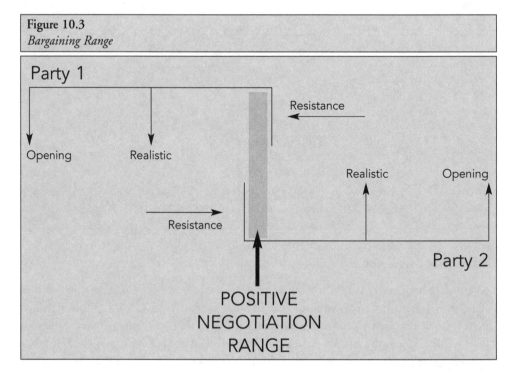

Figure 10.3
Bargaining Range

Even where bargaining ranges overlap, there can be incentives for the parties not to reach agreement. For instance, in workplace negotiations, if management are of the view that any agreement reached with a union risks not being endorsed by the membership, they may keep offers in reserve and make them at conciliation. They may even prefer not to move to a fallback position at conciliation, leaving room for an increased award at Labour Court adjudication. As noted in Chapter 4, there is evidence from the existence of such an effect in Irish industrial relations, with a criticism of the parties' failure to engage in meaningful negotiations attracting comment from the Labour Court chairmen. Of course, if union negotiators suspect that management are keeping concessions in reserve, this creates an incentive to refer issues to the Labour Court.

POWER IN NEGOTIATIONS

Bargaining power may be interpreted as the degree to which one party can achieve its negotiating goals despite the opposition of the other side. Relative bargaining power significantly influences the outcome of negotiations, with agreements normally favouring the party with the greatest bargaining power. The bargaining power of a party depends on a range of factors. Typically both external and internal to the negotiations process. Some factors will be set, such as economic factors, the business environment within an industry and levels of unemployment. While it is not always easy to obtain an accurate picture of another party's resistance point or fallback position, negotiators need to be aware that this information is important. A party that is able to evaluate the level of commitment of the other party and its constituents to achieving its stated objectives will, everything else being equal, be at an advantage. The negotiation process can involve much bluff and rhetoric aimed at convincing the other side that one's resistance (fallback position) is higher than it actually is to encourage the other party to make concessions. An accurate perception of actual fallback positions indicates how far a party can go without risking breakdown in negotiations. For negotiators in distributive negotiations, the opposite holds true, namely that it is important not to inadvertently reveal one's fallback position.

   While much power will be determined independently of negotiators, there are measures that negotiators can influence. The most important action that negotiators can take to increase their bargaining power is to identify a strong BATNA (best alternative to a negotiated agreement), which should not be confused with a fallback position. For someone considering negotiating to buy a house, a fallback position is the highest price that person is prepared to pay. A BATNA, however, could be any one of the following: buying another house, renting, sharing accommodation or waiting for prices to fall. The better a party's BATNA, the more negotiation power and leverage they have. Disclosing one's fallback position, or reservation price, is never a good idea in distributive bargaining, but disclosing one's BATNA may be very helpful if it is both strong and credible.

Trust in Negotiations

Commentators frequently ascribe difficulties in industrial relations negotiations to a breakdown of trust. However, the issue of trust is not clear-cut in a negotiation context.

The presence of a high level of trust may facilitate integrative negotiations, yet Fisher and Ury (1997) suggest that it can be a mistake to either trust or not trust another party in a negotiation. It is simply wrong to suggest that it is not possible to negotiate with a party one does not trust – for example, police forces regularly negotiate with criminals who it would be difficult to trust. Fisher and Ury (1997) offer negotiators a way out of the trust dilemma, suggesting that negotiators should go ahead independent of trust. Thus, a party can proceed on the basis of revealed behaviour of the other party or objective protection can be built into any proposed agreement (see also Kennedy 1998). Such measures are common; for example, a legally binding guarantee on a second-hand car is a practical example of objective protection. A negotiator is also entitled to and should test the propositions advanced by the other party. Principled negotiation does not imply a negotiator should abandon their critical faculties.

Case Study: To Trust or Not to Trust?
TEX Engineering employs 500 employees, but due to competition it is forced to lay off 250 employees. A negotiating meeting is arranged at which the personnel director announces to the union representing the workers that he wants to handle this in a constructive way and get away from the adversarial high ball/low ball approach. He says the company wishes to deal with its employees in a fair way but there is a limit to what they will pay. Instead of starting low then haggling and eventually going to the Labour Court, he is prepared to tell the union what is on offer. Pointing to his briefcase he says there is three weeks 'in the bag' and the union can take this but 'that is all there is'. The personnel director has a reputation for being a tough but honest negotiator.

Topic for class discussion
What kind of issues should the union consider in evaluating the offer on the table? (This case study is abstracted from a real-life case and pointers for class discussion are available for lecturers on the website.)

Types of Bargaining

Integrative Bargaining

Integrative bargaining is characterised by an effort to address interests rather than positions in negotiations. Integrative bargaining involves efforts to simultaneously meet the interests (or needs, see below) of both parties. Lewicki *et al.* (1999) identify a number of key steps in the integrative negotiation process, including the following.

- Identify and define the problem in a mutually acceptable way.
- Keep the statement of the problem to be addressed simple.
- State the problem as a goal and identify the obstacles to reaching that goal.
- Depersonalise the problem.
- Identity the needs of the other party.

A key feature of integrative negotiations is the free sharing of all relevant information and an open exchange of ideas. A free flow of information is essential, as are concerted efforts by both sides to understand the needs of the other party and a concern for meeting those needs when identified. One method for developing ideas is 'brainstorming', where ideas are generated and then evaluated with reference to pre-established and mutually agreed criteria. Such criteria are usually of a broad nature, such as acceptability to both parties, workability and fairness. In the brainstorming processes, all ideas are noted down and only those that meet the criteria are retained for further discussion and negotiation.

True integrative negotiations do not involve the parties setting ideal, realistic and fallback positions, as these are characteristics of distributive bargaining. Nor does it involve concealing any information that is material to the negotiations. Some negotiators may claim to be negotiating on a win-win basis, but are actually attempting to manipulate the other party. A test of a party's true intentions is to see if the party making the claim of engaging in a win-win negotiation is sharing all relevant information and if adequate concern is being shown for the other party's needs. A negative answer to either of these questions indicates that a distributive approach is really being adopted.

Interest-Based Bargaining

A particular form of integrative bargaining termed 'principled bargaining' or 'interest-based bargaining' has been popularised by Fisher and Ury (1997). According to Lewicki *et al.* (1999), interests are 'the underlying concerns, needs, desires or fears that motivate a negotiator to take a particular position'. The notion of interests can sometimes cause difficulty for students and it may be easier to think in terms of 'needs-based' bargaining and distinguish it from 'positional' bargaining. The central proposition in 'interest-based bargaining' is that by focusing on interests rather than positions, better outcomes can be achieved for both parties. By contrast, focusing on positions (bargaining demands) can make it more difficult to gain agreement.

This is somewhat paradoxical, as industrial relations theorists have identified differing interests as being at the root of employment conflict. However, an example demonstrates how a focus on interests can work in a common Irish industrial relations situation involving restructuring. In a negotiation, a union's position might be no redundancies and no dis-improvement in terms and conditions of employment, but their interests might be a need for job security. However, it may only be possible to achieve *job security* (the need) by improving competitiveness (meeting the employer's need), which may necessitate agreement to new work methods and a reduction in employee numbers through redundancies. The *position* of no dis-improvement in terms and conditions of employment and no redundancies must then give way in order to meet the underlying primary *need* of job security.

Case Study: Partnership and Relationship Change – WILO Pumps

WILO Pumps Ltd (WPL) is a Limerick-based Irish subsidiary of the German based WILO-SALMSON Group, which specialises in the manufacture and marketing of central heating pumps, primarily for the European market. Since 1996 WPL endured intense competition from sister plants to produce and supply its motors at very competitive prices, thereby forcing it to adopt a highly focused approach on cost reduction within an environment demanding high-quality standards. WPL's management expended much effort in focusing on many improvement initiatives over a five-year period. While definite progress was made, the results, as perceived by management, did not give the return for the effort expended. Consequently, it was agreed that relationships between the maintenance team and management, which were extremely adversarial, would need to be drastically developed to ensure the long-term future of the plant. Discussions took place with the assistant general secretary of the Technical Electrical Engineering Union (TEEU) in Limerick, a critical outcome of which was the acceptance of each other's bona fides and the mutual acceptance of the principle of achieving a win-win outcome for all parties. With the assistance of an independent facilitator, it was agreed that the extended management team and the entire maintenance department would meet off-site to explore the possibility of a way forward. This joint session became the major turning point for the plant, as both parties realised they had far more common interests than the differences that divided them.

The group agreed to meet on a monthly basis over an eight-month period to develop their relationships, improve communication channels and work on improvement initiatives in partnership. As a result, management became much more attuned to the underlying needs of its employees in bringing about change, which were respect, involvement and trust, the real drivers of sustainable change. On the union side, a keen appreciation of the business needs of the company developed. These ultimately led to negotiated reductions in labour headcount (reductions of approximately twenty-five per cent), increased employee efficiencies of sixty per cent and 110 per cent in its two key departments and a dramatically changed working environment where much greater levels of mutual respect and trust prevailed that facilitated these improvements. The key to achieving these solutions was the systematic use of problem solving and mutual gains bargaining, with employees being an integral part of defining and producing mutually agreed solutions.

Within twelve months of these successful changes, the core motor manufacturing business of WPL was closed, resulting in a reduction of eight-five per cent of the workforce. This was done for Group strategic reasons that were outside the Limerick facility's control. In another six months an increase in production from eighteen pieces per paid hour to twenty-four pieces per paid hour would have been achievable. Despite the trauma of the closure, the development of relationships within the plant had dramatically changed attitudes on both sides and these survived the closure decision and thus created a supportive environment for everyone in dealing with the closure. Subsequently, members of management, union officials and shop stewards have made presentations to the partnership network on their experiences in effecting a change in relationships.

Case study contributed by Brendan Lyons, former managing director, WILO Pumps (see www.partnershiplearningnetwork.com for class discussion questions).

Mixed Motive Negotiations

In industrial relations, many negotiations involve a mix of distributive and integrative elements. Lewicki *et al.* (2001) refer to this as '*mixed motive bargaining*', and the capacity to manage the complexities involved is the key of a skilled negotiator. In the 1980s it became common among writers to categorise distributive negotiations in somewhat garish terms and label it unfavourably compared to integrative negotiations. There has been a reaction to this and as Thompson (2001) points out, even if one is successful in growing the pie, there is still a pie to be cut up and this is best addressed through distributive bargaining.

A useful way to handle mixed motive negotiations is to separate the two phases. The integrative element can be dealt with first, using problem-solving techniques and sharing information, and the distributive element (agreeing on the distribution of the gains) can then be subsequently dealt with. Such an approach was used in the cost and competitiveness review (CCR) in the Electricity Supply Board case outlined in Chapter 12. Even within the distributive phase, the use of creative and integrative techniques has the capacity to ensure a greater prospect of success and to solidify the relationship between the parties. Thus, some of the key techniques that are described as integrative are also used during distributive bargaining by skilled negotiators. It must be emphasised again that this does not include disclosing one's fallback position. A party that does this is unlikely to achieve any more than their fallback as a result, thereby foregoing any *negotiator's surplus* that is available. We will now discuss the negotiation process in typical distributive and mixed motive bargaining, which is often characteristic of industrial relations negotiations.

DISTRIBUTIVE AND MIXED MOTIVE NEGOTIATIONS: A FURTHER CONSIDERATION OF THE PROCESSES

Industrial relations negotiations tend to be highly ritualistic processes in which both parties engage in an elaborate game. Normally, the formal initiation of industrial relations negotiations begins with one party presenting a claim to the other. It is a convention of normal industrial relations that a claim once served will be the subject of negotiation. Many, if not all, disputes procedure agreements make a provision for direct discussion between the parties prior to any form of trade union or employer-initiated industrial action (Wallace 1989). In addition, the Industrial Relations Act of 1990 has encouraged the resolution of issues at local level, and the conciliation service of the LRC may wish to see efforts at local discussion before they agree to intervene in a dispute (see Chapter 4).

The negotiating process itself will generally follow a number of predictable phases. These may be categorised as (1) preparation for negotiations (2) bargaining and (3) follow-up action, as outlined in Table 10.1.

PREPARATION FOR NEGOTIATIONS

Administrative Arrangements

Advance attention to the 'boring' administrative details is essential. An agenda should be agreed; the physical facilities should be appropriate; the venue should be spacious, free from interruptions, convenient, have appropriate seating and adjournment arrangements (non-intimidating caucus rooms) and back-up facilities (phone, fax, typing, etc.). Most industrial relations negotiations take place within an organisation. There may be occasions when it is appropriate to move off-site to provide a more neutral atmosphere or to avoid on-the-job interruptions or leaks from the negotiations. Conscious consideration should be given to all these matters. Many of the administrative details will be undertaken as a matter of course but it may be necessary 'to negotiate the negotiations'. This shows concern for the other party and demonstrates good faith in checking that they are comfortable with any proposed arrangements that are being made. If one party is unhappy about an arrangement, the time to raise that is in advance. If one becomes uncomfortable during the negotiations, it is best to address such an issue as soon as possible. For example, if an off-site venue proves unsatisfactory due, say, to noise, it is best to suggest a change of venue.

Table 10.1
Stages and Phases of Industrial Relations Negotiations

1. PREPARATION
- Conduct relevant research.
- Agree negotiating objectives.
- Check mandate.
- Assess relative bargaining power.
- Choose negotiating team.
- Make appropriate administrative arrangements.

2. BARGAINING
- Opening Phase
    - Parties outline their case (expectation structuring).
    - Exploring the other side's case.
- Trading Phase
    - Movement and solution building.
    - Exchange.
    - Compromise.
- Closing Phase
    - Final movements.
    - Ensure clarity on agreement.
    - Recording agreement.
  or
    - Noting areas of disagreement.
    - Noting subsequent action.
        - Referral to appropriate third party.
        - Option for industrial action.

3. POST-NEGOTIATION
- Document agreement/disagreement.
- Agree action plans.
- Communicate.
- Implement action plans.
- Review.

Research

Many authors have stressed the importance of preparation for negotiations (Lewicki *et al.* 2001; Hiltrop and Udall 1995; Hawkins 1979). Adequate research helps to focus negotiations on facts rather than discussing opinions or value judgments (Fisher and Ury 1997). Preparatory research might also incorporate an evaluation of the repercussions of likely settlement options and knock-on effects of different potential outcomes of negotiations. While preparation is important, research has found that skilled negotiators do not spend more time in preparation than average negotiators but they do spend more time considering how to use information (www.huthwaite.co.uk/articles). All negotiators will be faced with a situation where they have not been able to prepare and Hiltrop and Udall (1995) strongly advise that in such situations, negotiators should listen, ask questions for information and adjourn at an early opportunity. Such an approach is particularly recommended in grievance interviews, as it prevents possible ill-considered responses by management to employee grievances.

Research is an essential prerequisite for negotiations and there are many sources of information. Trade unions maintain research departments, as do employers' organisations. The LRC maintains an informative website and the Labour Court (www.labourcourt.ie) has a search facility enabling parties to search previous cases. The EAT also publishes a summary of unfair dismissal cases and the decisions in such cases.

Setting Objectives

Having conducted adequate research, the most important decision in preparing for negotiation is for a party to identify *what* they want to achieve. If a negotiation involves a number of items in the bargaining mix, identifying what one wants is only part of the task – it is essential to then prioritise objectives. This is in order to identify those items that can be traded. Negotiation conventions require that parties be prepared to move during negotiations and that trading is superior to compromise (see below).

There are two conventional ways of prioritising. Parties can attach labels to items identifying them in decreasing order of importance, as follows:

* items they must get;
* items they intend to get;
* items they would like to get.

Alternatively, it is possible to label items one, two, three and so on in decreasing order of priority. Using the first method there is a great temptation to allot a large number of items to the 'must get' category. However, Kennedy (1998) points out that the more items one has to achieve from a bargaining mix, the lower one's power position is. This arises because one has fewer items to trade in return for concessions from the other party. Many negotiators, however, think the opposite is the case and that the more they have to get the higher their power position. This is a serious mistake that can impede agreement being reached, even where the real interests of the parties lie in reaching a settlement (see Kennedy 1998).

Establishing bargaining objectives relative to one's interests is preferable to deciding on emotional or other grounds. This requires a critical examination of a case's strengths and weaknesses. Research shows that negotiators tend to be better able to evaluate weaknesses in the other party's case than the weaknesses in their own. A technique to address this is to engage in role reversal, where some members of one's negotiation team take on the role of the other party. It is important to bear in mind that a party is more likely to achieve its objectives if it can make exchanges that enable the other party to meet its interests. Ignoring the other party's interests and thinking (cognition) is a serious mistake (Lewicki *et al.* 2001).

Objectives can be tangible, e.g. wage costs not to increase more than three per cent in twelve months, or intangible. The intangibles can be vitally important, and for managers might include issues such as ensuring good relations with employees and their representatives. Bargaining objectives will vary according to the issue at hand. While parties should be clear on their walk-away position (fallback), flexible objectives are generally preferable to rigid ones, as information uncovered during negotiations can alter the perception of one's interests. It is important that each party's objectives are clearly articulated and approved by constituents, particularly top management on the managerial side and trade union members/representatives on the union side. This helps to ensure that each negotiating team has a clear mandate. It is also vital that objectives be agreed and communicated within the negotiating team to ensure the commitment of all members to their achievement.

Team Organisation

Conscious consideration should be given to the choice of a negotiating team in advance. The size and composition of the negotiating team largely depends on the issue for negotiation. In industrial relations it is inadvisable to enter negotiations with less than two people. Having at least two people provides a witness as to what was said and can increase objectivity. Above two, the question arises as to the optimum size. Increased numbers can give solidarity, ensure greater technical knowledge and improved planning and judgment. A greater number also allows the allocation of responsibilities in presenting the case, analysis of verbal and non-verbal responses, recordkeeping and consideration of the consequences of various settlement options and management responses (Nierenberg 1968). Yet greater numbers can increase the possibility of internal disagreement and the inclusion of less skilled/unskilled negotiators who may be more prone to make errors or who may be picked off by the other party. For trade unions, large numbers of shop stewards may attend negotiations as observers to ensure that the various constituents are fairly represented by the lead negotiator(s). In such situations, strict rules for making contributions should be laid out in advance to prevent someone making a point that would undermine a case.

Dealing specifically with the composition of management teams in industrial relations negotiations, Canning (1979) identifies three main tasks that need to be provided for.

- **Spokesman/team leader:** The role of the chief management representative is to present arguments, control strategy and tactics and make major on-the-spot decisions.

- **Observer/analyst:** Here the role is to evaluate progress relative to objectives, spot key reactions, identify changes in approach and advise the chief negotiator.
- **Recorder:** This involves recording key points in negotiations and documenting the final agreement.

In forming a negotiation team, both unions and management should ensure that these functions are fully provided for. For instance, if a recorder is omitted, then that team may have no option but to accept the other party's contemporaneous record of the event. If neither party provides for this function, then the capacity for confusion and disagreement over what was agreed is enormous.

More vital than any allocation of roles, however, is the way in which a team gels. During the negotiation process, team members should support the lead spokesperson without supplanting her/him. Team members should display empathy and be mutually supportive. A clarification or digression can be of enormous benefit to a team member under pressure or who has made an error. There are few situations in a negotiation that cannot be retrieved with an appropriate and *prompt* 'clarification' or 'amplification'. A team should have unanimously agreed the objectives and the approach to be used in negotiation. This will involve considerable intra-team negotiation prior to the commencement of negotiations. Any disagreements or differences should be aired and resolved in advance, otherwise they risk raising their head during negotiations with the other party. This resolution can only take place through intra-organisational negotiations and the difficulties of this should not be ignored. However, the same principles apply here as apply to general negotiation theory, with an even stronger emphasis on the benefits of an open, integrative approach. Yet not all elements within an organisation will have the same objectives and this can be particularly true of a trade union representing a disparate group of workers.

OPENING PHASE

The opening phase will concentrate on each side setting out their case and seeking clarification from the other side. It is vitally important to be clear on all the items in the bargaining mix. The subsequent introduction of new demands is generally considered to be outside accepted negotiation conventions, but highly integrative negotiation may focus on identifying and exploring previously unidentified options. Following the opening phase, each side may adjourn to consider any new information and to consult with their principals – the board or head office of a company on the management side and the membership or senior official on the union side. In particular, unions need to keep in touch with their members.

A key activity noted by Walton and McKiersie (1965) in the opening phase is *attitudinal structuring*. This involves attempts to define the negotiation in terms favourable to either side. This is done through the deployment of so-called '*key commitments*'. These are underlying arguments that aim at concentrating negotiations on one party's side of the case. Management might justify the need for a pay pause by citing the need to remain competitive and contain costs. A union may argue for a five per cent pay increase to compensate for inflation and to reward employees above this for increased productivity.

Key commitments are not bargaining objectives. In the above example, the bargaining objective for management is the pay pause and for the union it is the claim for a five per cent increase. Bargaining objectives are concrete and can be traded, whereas key commitments are merely underlying arguments and can only be argued. It is vital in the opening phase of distributive negotiations not to be fazed by an apparent rejection of one's concerns/key commitments. Industrial relations negotiations can be long, drawn-out affairs and early movement may merely fuel a belief that further unrealisable concessions are possible.

TRADING PHASE

The second phase involves further testing the arguments advanced and exploring possible solutions. Identifying areas for movement and solution building is a critical aspect of this process. In particular, the identification of possible trade-offs is a key skill helping to produce potentially superior outcomes to compromise. Nonetheless, in some situations simple compromise, if acceptable to both parties, may be preferable to artificial efforts to generate non-existent mutual gains. Many of the key skills in negotiations, such as active listening and conditional offers, are concentrated in this phase and these are discussed in detail below.

CLOSING PHASE

This phase carries many traps for the unwary and can lead to major difficulties in implementation. Three tasks normally have to be undertaken in this phase: finalising the agreement, noting issues for further negotiation or details of breakdown. Offers and counteroffers may come rapidly after little happening in the earlier phase. This is especially the case where parties have *unwisely* used a 'chicken tactic' (see below). In this situation, it is all too easy to lose sight of the cost or value of proposals – careful costing of proposals in advance will limit the prospect of errors. A further danger is for both parties to have different beliefs as to what *has* been agreed. It is essential to slow down and proceed in a deliberate, considered manner. Each party should be clear on the substance and interpretation of any agreement. Active listening, involving paraphrasing and asking questions to ensure identical understanding, are essential. Leading and closed questions are used at this part of the negotiation. It is useful to agree details of future meetings. Any review of procedures should be clearly specified and agreed before the parties leave the negotiating table. If negotiations do break down, then it may be advisable for channels of communication to be kept open. If this is felt useful, parties should be clear as to how communication will be reinitiated and by whom. The idea that long-term relations may be more important than the issues at hand is an important principle for both parties to keep in mind. The Huthwaite research indicates that skilled negotiators were more than twice as likely to refer to long-term consideration during negotiations (www.huthwaite.co.uk/articles).

POST-NEGOTIATION

Post-negotiation, the key consideration is the implementation of the agreement as understood. If an agreement is not implemented or is implemented in a way other than that understood by the party one has negotiated with, this is likely to lead to deteriorated relations and will almost certainly damage the credibility of the negotiator that has allowed this to happen. Problems can arise in the post-negotiation situation not only in delivering to the other party what has been agreed, but in implementing all of the concessions agreed by the other party. This can particularly affect management. For example, in a number of cases in the 1980s, work change measures agreed by unions and paid for by management were not subsequently fully implemented. The problem in such situations can be traced back to the preparation stage, in the identification of what one wants. Once the negotiations have reached an end, the parties involved will normally report back on the outcome. This post-negotiation stage will normally review the implementation of the agreement(s) and the overall implications of the outcome for relations generally. The way in which the agreement is communicated to employees should also be agreed upon, as well as decisions on any administrative obligations. It is useful to carefully document all aspects of the negotiations for future reference. Details of implementation should be worked out and responsibilities allocated. Equally, both parties may be keen to review and assess the lessons learned from the negotiations experience. Skilled negotiators claim they do this more frequently than average negotiators.

KEY COMMUNICATION SKILLS

Outlining Your Case

As we have seen, key commitments are the underlying arguments on which a side bases its case. One should only use the strong key commitments and not be tempted to substitute weaker ones, as the deployment of weak arguments undermines one's case. It can be tempting in the early phase of a negotiation to become disheartened if one's points do not seem to gain acceptance. This leads to the temptation to deploy other, less strong arguments, which is a mistake and is known as 'argument dilution'. Research by the Huthwaite group notes that skilled negotiators use 'fewer not more arguments (key commitments)' to support their case, whereas 'average negotiators use more and so dilute their case' (www.huthwaite.co.uk/articles).

Questioning

The art of questioning is essential in negotiations and more important than making statements. Making statements conveys information to the other party, whereas asking questions is designed to acquire information. The types of questions that should be asked tend to vary as negotiations proceed. During the opening phase questions should generally be exploratory and invite the other party to explain and develop their case. Questions which facilitate this start with what/how/can/are/why. A union negotiator involved in an annual hours negotiation might ask the following: Can you develop your reason for proposing an annual hours system? What specific concessions are management looking for? Are there any other concessions being asked of workers? Are management prepared to quantify the total savings? How is it proposed the mutual gains will be distributed?

Mirror questions are very useful in the early stage of negotiation. A mirror question involves repeating one or two words that the other party has just said, with an inflexion in one's voice to indicate it is a question. For example, an employee with a grievance might make a statement as follows: 'I am finding it difficult at work'. A mirror question in this case could be, 'Difficult at work?' This invites the person to develop and amplify the point they were making. Mirror questions have the advantage of being non-directive (they do not lead the other person), they are friendly to the other party and encourage the other person to develop and amplify their points in a less adversarial way. As such, they hold out the option of achieving maximum information. Mirror questions are especially useful in grievance and disciplinary interviews.

As negotiations progress, questions that are designed to check and confirm information should be used more. They are more specific and direct. For example: 'Let me see if we have understood you correctly – is the union asking that only twenty per cent of reserve hours be worked in any year?', 'So the union would reduce its demand to only work twenty per cent of reserve hours if the company introduces a pension scheme based on the enhanced annual hours salary?' This latter question also demonstrates the use of linkage and potential trading.

Questions that 'lead with your chin' are to be avoided at all times, yet it is surprising how often they are encountered. Such questions take the following form: 'So the union is not prepared to agree to increase productivity?' 'So annual hours are not acceptable to the union?' It is very difficult for the other party to do anything other than confirm questions such as these. This can lead to breakdown or to concessions from the party asking the question.

Multiple and complex questions should never be used. They create confusion and give the other party the opportunity to focus only on the part of the question they are happiest to address.

Depersonalising Issues

Allowing personalities to enter negotiations is a dangerous ploy. The problems involved must be defined in a way that is mutually acceptable to both parties. Both parties must try to 'depersonalise' the problem by accepting that there are legitimate differences of viewpoint on the problem. This can only be done if both parties understand each other's real interests, as opposed to just seeing each other's negotiating positions (Fisher and Ury 1997).

Good negotiators are polite but firm. Politeness is achieved by allowing others to speak and not interrupting. Kennedy (1998) advises never interrupting, since if the point the other person making is wrong, it will collapse of its own weight through careful probing after the person is finished speaking. On the other hand, if the other party is correct, then one is acquiring valuable information. Obviously, politeness in negotiations must be balanced with firmness. Misrepresentations should be immediately corrected and dominating and bullying behaviour have to be dealt with when it occurs.

Avoiding Blaming by Reframing Points

Blaming is particularly destructive in negotiations and skilled negotiators tend to avoid it. A simple technique to avoid blaming while still expressing the strength of one's feelings is to frame points in terms of 'I/we' messages rather than 'you' messages. Messages which begin, 'We feel …', 'I think …', 'It seems to us …' are found to be less threatening to the receiver but are not less assertive. The following two examples illustrate blaming behaviour on the part of management and the union in negotiations: 'Management do not listen' or 'You should control your members, otherwise we cannot deal with you'. These statements can be changed to deliver the same message without the negative effect. For example: 'By listening carefully management could avoid many of its difficulties' or 'If we had a coherent union approach it would make it easier for management to consider addressing employees' needs'.

Parties need to be able to respond to blaming behaviour when it occurs. The above statements can also be changed around to create the potential for movement. Management could respond to the union complaints of not listening as follows: 'So the difficulties can be resolved if we listen more carefully?' The union could respond by saying, 'So if we have a united and coherent approach, management will address our concerns?'

Labelling Behaviour

Labelling behaviour is linked to the previous point and involves offering a signpost to what one is about to do and the reasons behind any suggestions, points, etc., for example, 'Can I ask you a question – what is the maximum number of reserve hours which any employee will have to work?', 'The reason I am making the following proposal is … '. Among the benefits of labelling are that it slows down negotiations, adds a degree of formality, takes away from the 'cut and trust' and draws attention to what is being said, thereby improving communication and decreasing ambiguity (www.huthwaite.co.uk/articles).

Active Listening and Signalling

Active listening is not merely listening intently – it involves listening to what another person has said, paraphrasing your understanding of what has been said and checking with the other person if your understanding is correct. It is only when the other person agrees with your paraphrased version that you have understood fully. Active listening also involves listening for what is *not* said. Signalling and picking up on signals are key skills in negotiations. Negotiators also need to listen for shifts in emphasis during a negotiation. If a party changes from saying 'We could not agree to that proposal' to 'Agreeing to that proposal is not possible in the present circumstances', this may indicate movement. In any event it invites the response, 'In what circumstances could you agree to our proposal?'

TRADING

Making Offers

Making offers is the most vital point in a negotiation and this needs knowledge of the appropriate way in which they should be made and also requires considerable practice to execute properly. Remember, once an offer is put on the table it cannot be removed unless the other party rejects it. For this reason a team should agree in advance on who will make offers or indicate movement. Generally, they should only be made through the lead spokesperson unless otherwise agreed explicitly in advance. Even then, this should only happen for a good reason, such as a member of the team possessing specialist knowledge. Less skilled negotiators tend to blurt out offers without adequate preparation and without linking them to any requirement for concession by the other party.

There is often an expectation that having made a concession, the other side are then under an obligation to respond with a concession. This expectation is frequently disappointed. In fact, the other party may immediately indicate the offer is inadequate and demand further concessions without being prepared to make any movement. This happens because the person making the concession has made a fundamental mistake. They have sent an inadvertent signal that their negotiation style is one of accommodation. Furthermore, they have not given sufficient attention to emphasising their needs to the other party. It is therefore rational for the other party to expect further concessions without the need for movement on their part. That party is not being unreasonable, they are just responding rationally to the inadvertent signals they have received.

Dressing Up the Offer

Skilled negotiators tend to talk in terms of 'proposals', not offers. They talk about their proposal and show how it is designed to respond to the needs of the other party. For example: 'The reason we are making this proposal is because we have listened carefully to a number of points you've made, we feel a number of them have merit and we want to try to meet them within the limits of our mandate. In order to do this we are proposing the following … '. It is not a good idea to describe one's own proposals as 'fair', 'good', 'generous', etc., as such descriptions act as irritants to the other side, i.e. if they do not accept an offer described as fair, the implication is that *they* are not being fair. However, offers can be justified by comparison to objective standards, such as the going rate in the industry, provisions in national agreements, previous Labour Court recommendations, etc.

Size of Offers

It is common for the initial movements to be large and for later movements to decrease in size. This is contrary to hardball tactics that suggest small concessions be made initially. However, this invites the obvious response of small movements from the other side. The benefit of larger movements followed by subsequent decreasing ones is that it signals decreasing room for movement to the other party without in any way having to disclose one's fallback position. More importantly, one can require greater concessions in return.

Conditional Offers

When making a proposal it should be framed so as to incorporate something you want from the other party. This should be linked *directly* to any concession you intend making to the other party and the concession should be made conditional on the other party agreeing to this with phrases such as: 'If you were prepared to consider movement on X and Y, that would enable us to reconsider our position on A and B'. Initial proposals should be tentative and designed to see if the linkages being made between issues are likely to be reciprocated by the other side. If they are not, then they need not be pursued further. If they are, then they can be made more specific. 'If the union was prepared to agree to a ten per cent increase in productivity and to agree to work reserve hours as required, then that would be sufficient for us to consider a significant move on the pension scheme and to make improvements to the sick pay scheme'. In this case, the offer made by management is still less specific than the request from the other party. If the union is interested they can ask: 'By how much do you propose to increase the pension and the sick pay scheme?' If the other party does not agree to the required concession, then there is no obligation on the person making a proposal to *leave their offer on the table*. Making offers/proposals conditional has the dual advantage of identifying what a party wants in exchange and allowing a withdrawal of an offer if that exchange is not agreed. This is why making proposals conditional is so important.

Responding to Proposals/Offers

In responding to offers, it is generally not a good idea to talk down or make little of an offer, even if that offer is inadequate. A much better strategy is to welcome the fact that an offer has been made and then to indicate how it would need to be improved in order to enable progress to be made. Put simply, effective negotiation involves opening doors rather than closing them. If a proposal is unacceptable, it may be possible to incorporate some element of the other party's offer in a counterproposal. However, care should be taken in making counterproposals, as the Huthwaite research notes that skilled negotiators use much 'fewer counterproposals than average negotiators'. Immediate and numerous counterproposals are often weak because they tend to arrive at a time when the other party is concerned with *its* proposals and can be perceived as designed to block the other party's proposals.

Adjournments

Adjournments should not be made to release pressure and 'blow off steam'. Proper preparation can ensure that is not necessary. Remember, the other party will be alert for non-verbal behaviour and inappropriate adjournments can inadvertently reveal a lot about one's position. It is a very good idea when adjourning to ask the other party to consider/reflect on key issues you have raised. Of course, this should be immediately followed up on resumption by asking if the other party has considered the points and what proposals they have to respond to them. Using adjournments in this way can prevent negotiations getting stuck in a rut or going around in circles.

DEVELOPING INTEGRATIVE OPTIONS

It is often thought that integrative negotiations are 'soft', but Fisher and Ury (1997) suggest that interest-based negotiations involve real toughness. While the inter-personal interaction may be easier in integrative negotiations, they place considerable demands on the skill of the negotiator. As noted, most negotiations are neither fully distributive nor integrative. In such mixed motive negotiations, theory suggests a number of techniques for moving the negotiations towards the integrative end of the spectrum. The deployment of such approaches has been demonstrated to increase the prospects for a successful outcome and to leave both parties feeling more satisfied with the process.

Enlarge the Pie

The most obvious integrative technique is to enlarge the 'pie'. This may be easier said than done, yet ingenuity can lead to one identifying ways in which this can be achieved. For instance, in the ESB and Aer Lingus cases, discussed in Chapter 12, management was able to achieve their objectives by making employees part-owners of the company through an employee share ownership plan (ESOP). The following industrial relations case study is designed to allow students to identify options to break an apparent deadlock in negotiations over redundancies. By developing options it should be possible to make a proposal that meets the needs of the employees while remaining within the mandate established by head office.

Case Study: Redundancies in MSC Engineering Plc – Developing Options
Due to a fall in orders, MSC Engineering Plc decide to make twenty-five of their sixty clerical/administrative/sales staff redundant. They consult their employees, as required under EU legislation. The employees take the news very badly and threaten strike action. Previous to this the union was not active, although some twenty per cent of the employees were members. All except five now join and the union agrees to represent them. Faced with this difficulty, the company agrees to negotiate on the terms of the redundancy subject to the withdrawal of the threat of strike action. The union agrees to suspend any consideration of

strike action pending the outcome of negotiations.

There is a good atmosphere to the negotiations at first and a series of issues are resolved, including workloads following the restructuring, outplacement assistance and pension arrangements that will maximise the value of any settlement by minimising tax liability. The issue of whether redundancies should be voluntary, on a basis of LIFO (last in first out) or FIFO (first in first out) is not addressed prior to moving on to the major issue of enhanced redundancy payments. As a result of the positive progress, you (as local) managers are anxious that the union committee will accept and endorse any package in order to maintain a good working relationship following the restructuring and ensure that there are limited negative 'survivor effects'.

Following this positive phase, the negotiations on the terms of the redundancy compensation become difficult and face breakdown. The company offers three weeks pay per year of service (including statutory entitlement), with a cap on payments of €15,000. The union looks for eight weeks per year of service (plus statutory) and rejects the company cap as 'derisory', suggesting a cap of €60,000 at most. They point out that when three people left in 1996, the company paid four weeks per year of service (plus statutory) without any union involvement.

The union demand is reduced to six weeks (including the statutory entitlement of two weeks) during negotiations, but the union negotiator indicates to you in an 'off the record' briefing that a settlement of five weeks (including statutory) would be acceptable. However, she adds that nothing less will be acceptable, although it is unimportant how this figure is made up. She also indicates that special provision will have to be made for employees with less than two years' service.

Your French headquarters have given you an absolute instruction that you may not pay more than four weeks per year of service, as the company cannot afford any more. However, they add that if local management can find other ways of 'squaring the circle' they will not object. They leave it to you to finalise the negotiations with this in mind. The company pays VHI on an annual subscription basis starting in January of each year. All employees are entitled to a minimum of a month's notice, with those having ten years' service having higher entitlements in line with legislation. There are no company cars.

Service of staff

Number of years of service	Number of staff	Average salary for group (€)
15	2	40,000
12	4	37,000
10	6	35,500
8	6	33,000
5	4	32,500
3	4	30,000
2	5	27,000
Less than 2	12	25,000
Less than 1	17	22,500

Task
Break into groups of four or five, appoint a *rapporteur* and spend twenty minutes discussing the case and come up with options to break the deadlock. Record these and report back.

> **For Discussion**
> Are there any integrative options available and to what extent is the company addressing the correct (in their interests) negotiating question?
>   Lecturer guidelines are available on the website for this case. The issue of selecting on the basis of suitability has been excluded from the case for reasons of simplicity.

Negotiate on a Package Basis

Less effective negotiators negotiate on an item-by-item basis, especially when they are making 'offers'. They treat each item in a bargaining mix separately, moving through an agenda each item at a time. This is a mistake, as it reduces negotiation on each item to a win-lose situation. While it may be somewhat more difficult to deal with a number of issues at a time, the prospects of a successful outcome are greatly increased by negotiating on a package basis. The reason for this is that it increases the possibilities for exchanges. It also reduces the need for compromise, which is a win-lose outcome. Thompson (2001) notes that parties should search for trade-offs and not compromises. Lewicki *et al.* (2001) refer to this technique as 'logrolling'. One word of caution in relation to the use of trade-offs or logrolling techniques: it can disintegrate into a typical distributive bargaining situation, with parties focusing on who's winning more. In such situations, the point made earlier about distributive justice can be vital. Both parties need to perceive not just that they are better off than if they did not reach agreement, but that the share of the spoils is fair.

Prioritise and then Trade

Trade-offs work best where a team prioritises their objectives in advance (see above). If a team has prioritised in advance, then appropriate trade-offs are easier to identify and agree. This tactic is typically an iterative process of trial and error and may require the parties to redefine problems by separating or 'unbundling' issues in order to come up with a mutually acceptable package. The best possible situation is where a party has identified an item as a low priority and can exchange that with the other party for a high priority to them. For example, in the ESB case in Chapter 12, management had prioritised the need to shed 2,000 jobs and the union prioritised adequate compensation for this and an acceptable mechanism for agreeing the redundancies. There was then the need of the remaining employees. Management prioritised changed work arrangements to enable it to operate with the reduced manning levels. Employees, while not necessarily welcoming such changes, prioritised financial rewards, including profit sharing and an ESOP.

Thompson (2001) points out that trade-offs work not because they build common ground, but because they exploit differences. It is somewhat counterintuitive to think that differences can promote agreement, but this *is* the case. The most quoted example in negotiation texts is the peace agreement between Israel and Egypt. Israel sought security while Egypt wanted the return of the west bank. The peace agreement between Egypt and Israel was built on these differences.

Non-specific Compensation

Another integrative tactic is for one party to offer non-specific compensation in return for movement on a particular item. This is regularly used when management is attempting to attract a job applicant but cannot meet their salary demand without affecting their wage profile, so they may offer generous relocation expenses, pay for educational courses or make a company car available.

Cutting the Cost of Compliance

This involves decreasing the cost of the other party to agreeing to your proposals. Cutting the costs for one party is a staple of industrial relations. For example, the use of productivity deals in the 1960s and 1970s was designed to decrease the costs of wage increases for employers. As with all integrative techniques they need to be evaluated against rigorous criteria. For example, by the early 1980s management had become disenchanted with some productivity bargaining, which failed to deliver any real productivity gains (see Chapter 13).

Finding a Bridge Solution

When using this tactic, both sides aim to invent novel options that satisfy their interests. A classic example of this occurred during negotiations on the Partnership 2000 agreement. The employer negotiators said the most they would pay on the basis increase (excluding the local bargaining clause) was seven per cent, while ICTU said it would not accept less than eight per cent – an apparent impasse. Yet agreement was reached on an overall eight per cent increase through the novel use of phasing, which meant that management would only have to pay seven per cent over the period of the agreement – the circle was squared!

Hardball Tactics

Research indicates that some negotiation tactics are outside the accepted norm, while others are regarded as 'part of the game'. Deliberate lying, refusing to accept reality and failure to implement agreements are examples of the former and are referred to as 'bad faith' tactics. Such tactics are commonly viewed as unethical (Lewicki *et al.* 1999). A party that employs bad faith tactics risks loosing their credibility as a negotiator and damaging the long-term relationship. This can be the worst possible outcome where there is an ongoing relationship between the parties and can be much more costly than any temporary gain.

In addition to bad faith tactics, hardball tactics can be viewed as ethically 'questionable' because they coerce/trick opponents into submission. However, as numerous writers have noted, the acceptability of hardball tactics is blurred and may be viewed as 'part of the game' (see Lewicki *et al.* 1999; Fisher and Ury 1997; Ury 1992). The perceptions of what is acceptable/unacceptable may be culturally influenced and a whole genre of research has been spawned by the need to discover cross-national differences in preferences for negotiating tactics. As a general rule of thumb, though, hardball tactics are not widely recommended. This is because they hold the risk of being ineffective, especially where negotiating parties are faced with the prospect of a long-term relationship. Typically, risky hardball tactics are the use of chicken (waiting until the very end to make movement), intimidation or *fait accompli* (introduction of unilateral change).

However, such tactics may be encountered and how to deal with difficult negotiators tends to be the most-asked question at negotiation courses. Although many people are fazed by hardball tactics, a number of relatively simple techniques can be used to cope with them (Lewicki *et al.* 2001; Fisher and Ury 1997). The simplest response may be to ignore hardball tactics, either by switching topics or by calling an adjournment. Sidestepping a hardball tactic can give the *thrower* the impression that it will not be tolerated or that it is not going to work. A second option is 'talks about talks', i.e. discussing the ways in which the negotiations are to be conducted before the true negotiations begin. Doing this helps to concentrate the negotiations on issues rather than on the personalities of the individuals involved. Finally, befriending the opposition or co-opting them makes it more difficult for them to engage in hardball tactics. While responding in kind is an option, there is a danger of descending into a negative spiral. Indicating that one will cease this behaviour if the other party also does so is a potential way out of this dilemma.

NEGOTIATION: A SUMMARY

The negotiation process involves interactions between people of varying personalities in different organisational contexts. Therefore, it is often impossible to predict the ways in which such negotiations will be carried out, or indeed, the kinds of outcomes to which they will give rise. Persistent problems in negotiations may arise for numerous reasons, such as inflexibility, abrasive approach, poor preparation and inadequate knowledge. Such problems may be tackled by improving the negotiating team's competence. It is always worthwhile to ensure that the members of the negotiating team have been carefully selected, are experienced and are appropriately trained. Writers have consistently emphasised the importance of negotiating skills as a means of achieving success in negotiations (Nierenberg 1968; Scott 1981; Atkinson 1977). Other writers suggest that incompetent negotiators do not cause problems in negotiation so much as by inherent flaws in the process itself.

It has been proposed that the entire negotiation process needs to undergo re-evaluation (Fisher and Ury 1997). A general criticism has been the perceived dominance of distributive bargaining, with its emphasis on dividing limited resources. It is argued that this approach encourages both parties to develop adversarial positions, believing that any gains can only be made by inflicting losses on the other party. Distributive bargaining reflects the very essence of the traditional pluralist industrial relations model: claims, offers, bluff, threats, compromise, movement, agreement or conflict. Approaches based on more integrative/co-operative bargaining (also known as the joint problem-solving approach) are often seen as a more attractive alternative (particularly from a managerial perspective), with their emphasis on a collaborative approach, exploring common ground and seeking solutions of mutual benefit to both parties.

Fisher and Ury's (1986) work on developing an alternative approach to negotiations has been one of the most influential contributions to the negotiation literature, but nonetheless it is only a partial theory of negotiation. There is also a lack of evidence of a widespread take-up of principled negotiations and no evidence of it supplanting distributive negotiations. Indeed, those who would wish to suggest this might be the case would need strong evidence, not just some well-publicised exemplar cases, such as Aughinish Alumina in Ireland (see Chapter 12). This is because integrative bargaining is not new and has long been part of the negotiator's armoury. Even in national partnership, there is clear evidence of co-existing adversarial distributive bargaining and integrative bargaining. Prior to each bargaining round, it is normal for each party to adopt widely differing positions. The parties have strong disagreements over issues such as mandatory union recognition and how to address low pay (see Chapter 13). These have all the marks of distributive bargaining, but there are also examples of integrative techniques, as already discussed – in essence, mixed motive negotiations.

Both the conventional, adversarial approach and the more collaborative, problem-solving alternatives tend to be appropriate in different circumstances (see Chapter 12). Given the structure of organisations and the inherent potential for conflict in the employment relationship, adversarial bargaining is likely to continue. Research evidence suggests that the pluralist approach to industrial relations continues to characterise industrial relations practice in many Irish organisations (D'Art and Turner 2002c).

GRIEVANCE AND DISCIPLINARY ISSUES

Both grievance and discipline represent a form of explicit expression of conflict in the employment relationship. Just like all other conflict, one of the options for attempting to resolve such conflict is to negotiate over the issues involved. The parameters are normally determined by the contract of employment, legislation and either written procedures or custom and practice. As with all conflict situations, there is the option to negotiate or not negotiate. However, in both grievance and disciplinary situations, refusing to engage with one another has the potential to prejudice a case in the event of an appeal to a third party. It is important to note that grievance procedures can serve to give employers advance warning and an opportunity to resolve issues internally. For example, there can be an obligation on employees to utilise the internal grievance procedures prior to referring equality cases to a third party for adjudication.

Grievance and disciplinary procedures are now common in Irish workplaces and can be found in both unionised and non-union workplaces (see Wallace 1989). In unionised workplaces these will normally be jointly agreed between union and management, while in non-union companies they will be designed by management. Wallace (1989) has termed procedures in non-union companies 'parallel procedures', as they are modelled on or are 'parallel' to procedures developed originally in unionised workplaces.

There are two general types of procedures: one for dealing with grievances or disputes (initiated by employees) and one for handling disciplinary matters (initiated by management). Complaints initiated by employees are dealt with through a grievance procedure, which is designed to allow individuals (or small groups) to process grievances in a structured way. In contrast, the term 'dispute procedure' refers to collective grievances based on claims of a group of workers. In practice, both terms can be used interchangeably (Wallace 1989). It can also be difficult to distinguish between collective and individual grievances, as sometimes a grievance may be initiated by an individual but may have significance for a larger group of workers. Such cases can be especially emotional and difficult to resolve and it is questionable if it is appropriate to deal with such issues through a disciplinary procedure.

Salamon (1998: 533) defines a grievance procedure as 'an operational mechanism which defines, and may limit, the exercise of managerial authority and power through establishing a formal regulatory framework for handling specified issues'. Discipline, on the other hand, is defined as 'that element of the system concerned with formal action taken by management against an individual who fails to conform to the rules established by management within the organisation' (Salamon 1998: 545). Prescriptive management texts claim that grievance procedures have a number of benefits. They can provide an opportunity for an employee to 'voice' concerns, provide feedback to management, limit misunderstandings and disputes over what is appropriate, provide an avenue of communication and increase fairness and consistency (see Hawkins 1979; Thomason 1984; Gunnigle et al. 1997a). It is an empirical question as to whether such claims are realised in practice. While grievance procedures provide a mechanism for employee voice, it is not clear that employees will always be comfortable using such procedures, as they may feel it would get them into difficulties with management.

There has been a major growth in attention to the bullying and harassment aspects of inter-personal conflicts in recent years, with codes of practice on how to handle such issues now published by a number of bodies (the Health and Safety Authority, the LRC and the Equality Authority). Such issues are sensitive. At one end of a continuum, it may be suggested that the investigation of bullying and harassment presents management with an 'impossible dilemma' and it is certain that negotiations to resolve complaints can be extremely difficult for a manager. Procedures often provide for mediation or an adjudication process in the event that the issue is unresolved through inter-personal negotiations (see Task Force on the Prevention of Workplace Bullying 2001). On the other hand, there are strong suggestions in the literature that bullying takes place largely by those in superior power positions (Field 1996; Murray and Keane 1998) and that employees who complain about bullying tend to leave organisations. In quite a number of instances, this will involve the negotiation of a voluntary severance package with the company. The Hirem Recruitment case study below represents such an example.

Case Study: Hirem Recruitment plc

Mary has been working for a non-union recruitment agency called Hirem for four years. She has become very experienced and has direct contact with a wide range of clients. The company has had a high labour turnover and Mary is in fact the longest-serving employee.

Realising her value, Mary negotiates a substantial salary increase, hinting that if it were not forthcoming, she would leave. She also gets agreement for the employment of an assistant, as she has been working extremely long hours. One day Mary comes across a note in the handwriting of the general manager to Mary's direct manager. This note indicates that he (the general manager) considers she has become too independent in her work, has too many direct contacts with clients and there is a risk she will leave and take clients with her. The note also says that her recent salary increase (she now earns €28,000 per annum) has made it too expensive to continue to employ her. The note indicates it is not possible to replace her at present but that the new assistant will take over her job in six months and that preparations can then be made for her dismissal.

Mary is shocked at this note and decides to photocopy it. She continues to work and after four months her immediate manager makes a number of complaints over a two-month period about her work. At the end of this period, the manager sends for her and indicates that her work is not satisfactory and she is to be made redundant. Mary informs the company that she has joined a trade union and that she has proof that the real reason for her dismissal is quite different. She hands the manager a copy of the general manager's note. Finally, Mary informs the company that she feels she has been 'bullied and harassed' and that this has caused her substantial stress and that she can not continue to work with the company but expects a 'handsome package' to leave. The manager informs Mary that that note was private and that copying any confidential material was a matter for disciplinary action.

Following further discussion, the manager indicates that she will accept Mary's resignation and will make a goodwill payment of €2,000 to 'dispose of the matter'. Mary rejects this 'as totally inadequate' and indicates that 'she will sue' and 'take a case for unfair dismissal'. Following consideration of the situation, the company indicates they are prepared to *negotiate* but not with a trade union, as they have a policy of 'not dealing with unions'. Mary proposes they negotiate with her solicitor but the company say they would prefer 'to keep the law out of it at this stage'. They indicate that Mary can have a fellow employee to represent her. Mary rejects this, as she indicates that a fellow employee would not have sufficient expertise. Mary has anticipated the manager's response and proposes that an expert negotiator from Alternative Disputes Resolution (ADR Ltd.) negotiate on her behalf. The general manager agrees and a negotiating meeting is set up. Due to prior commitments of both parties, it is agreed that this meeting will last no longer than an hour and that if agreement is not reached, the parties 'will go their separate ways'.

(Guidelines and briefs for using this case for analysis and discussion or for role-play negotiation are available for lecturers on the website.)

In relation to discipline, prescriptive texts suggest that a 'positive' or 'corrective' approach be used, with the aim of improving employee performance (see Torrington and Hall 1998). However, while the advocated 'positive' approaches to grievance and disciplinary issues are to be lauded, they need to be critically considered. Salamon (1998: 547) notes that disciplinary action has both a punitive and corrective aspect to it. In addition, disciplinary action involves the potential exercise of superior power by management, and this can make such action problematic. In some instances, management may back off from consistently implementing disciplinary action because this might create or accentuate a 'them and us' divide. Managers may also find dealing with disciplinary action distasteful and avoid it for that reason.

The implementation of a positive approach to grievance and disciplinary administration may also be clouded by two factors. First, there may be a desire to meet legal requirements rather than enact a corrective approach. Second, line managers, who have responsibility for dealing with disciplinary issues, may not see a positive approach as appropriate. Finally, managers may not possess the necessary skills or training to implement such an approach. Looking at the implementation of disciplinary action, Salamon (1998: 547) suggests that the positive (corrective) approach tends to be adopted only in minor transgressions. The 'ultimate sanction of dismissal is retributive or … a deterrent to others' (Salamon 1998: 547). Neither is there any guarantee that disciplinary procedures will lead to 'positive' effects. Thus, employees 'may play the system', being late or absent and work the 'warning system'. They may take their warnings up to the final warning stage and then wait for the step-back function to kick in, which will see warnings move back to the previous warning stage after a period. Salamon (1998: 547) suggests that while some employees (such as those whose reward or career progression is linked to formal performance or appraisal reviews) might not like to receive a formal reprimand because of the possible effect on their career, this does not mean that other employees will place as much emphasis on such warnings, particularly those in manual or lower clerical groups for whom there may be little, if any, career prospects.

Finally, it should be noted that the notion of the appropriateness of disciplinary action is based on the assumption that factors connected with the individual are at fault. However, changing the underlying nature of work organisation can have dramatic effects on absence rates, lateness, performance, etc. Salamon (1998: 547) suggests that the adoption of management approaches based on 'responsible autonomy' can serve to reduce management's need to use 'ad hoc direct formal disciplinary action'. In this approach, regular performance management is used to develop a more positive corrective approach, which emphasises team and self-discipline and reduces the need for managerial discipline. It has been reported, for instance, that the use of grievance and disciplinary action decreased substantially in Aughinish Alumina when they introduced annual hours working in the 1990s (see also Irish Cement case, Chapter 12). Edwards (1994) argues that newer forms of self-discipline do not necessarily reflect increased employee commitment and conformity, but rather may reflect greater management capacity to control employees. He argues that even where advanced forms of delegative participation and teamworking exist, employees and work teams may be reluctant to engage in disciplinary measures against co-workers. This leaves managers to rely on traditional forms of disciplinary action in situations where breaches of rules or standards occur (see also Salamon 1998: 547).

A further issue is that despite the elaborate procedural norms that characterise disciplinary administration, many of the underlying concepts are quite subjective. Of particular note are concepts such as 'reasonableness', 'fairness' and 'consistency'. As far back as the 1950s, Gouldner (1954) noted that workers had indulgency expectations, believing that procedures would be implemented in 'an indulgent' way, namely that the full force of procedures would not be used. Similarly, Wallace and O'Shea (1987) note that employees often have expectations that management will act leniently in disciplinary matters and that a reversal of a previously 'flexible' approach can cause conflict. The need for consistency in disciplinary matters is highlighted by many texts.

However, this contrasts with the need to take account of the unique circumstances surrounding any particular transgression. Balancing these competing demands requires skill and attention to detail. The above reservations should be borne in mind when considering the remainder of this chapter, which deals with the general prescriptive norms and practices for handling grievances and discipline in the workplace.

GRIEVANCE HANDLING

The term 'grievance' is used to describe a formal expression of employee dissatisfaction, initiated by an individual employee or small group of employees. Given the nature of people and their workplaces, it is inevitable that grievances will arise from time to time. At some stage most employees will encounter issues which cause them concern and which, as a result, may be voiced as a grievance. Line management and employees/employee representatives handle the vast majority of workplace grievances and disputes at workplace level. It is particularly important that managers are aware of the importance of appropriate grievance handling. It is generally recommended that grievances should be handled promptly, and grievance procedures normally specify short time limits for each phase of the process. Some summary guidelines for managers involved in grievance handling are outlined in Table 10.2.

Table 10.2
Management Checklist for Grievance Handling

✓ Management should make every effort to understand the nature of and the reasons for disputes and grievances.

✓ All levels of management should be aware of the potentially significant influence that grievance handling has on industrial relations and company performance generally.

✓ Management should establish a policy that sets out an orderly and effective framework for handling employee grievances.

✓ Line management, particularly first-level supervision, should be aware of their key role in effective grievance handling.

GRIEVANCE PROCEDURES

The main aim of grievance procedures is to ensure that issues raised by employees are adequately handled and settled fairly at or as near as possible to their point of origin. Such aims are based on the premise that, operated effectively, grievance procedures embrace a strong preventative dimension in helping thwart the escalation of grievance issues into more serious disputes. Ideally, the immediate supervisor should handle most problems or complaints raised by employees without recourse to a formal grievance procedure. However, issues that warrant more thorough consideration may be more appropriately handled through a formal written and agreed procedure.

Thus, an important dimension in grievance handling is the establishment and application of grievance procedures (Thomason 1984). Such a procedure normally outlines the stages and approaches to be followed in handling grievances in the workplace. Grievance and disputes procedures in industrial relations usually incorporate a number of common features, of which the features shown in Table 10.3 are particularly important.

GRIEVANCE AND DISCIPLINARY INTERVIEWS

The vast majority of grievance issues arise at employee-supervisor level. Prescriptive texts suggest the importance of authority being delegated to enable supervisors and team leaders to handle issues raised at this level. Equally, it is stressed that supervisors must be willing and able to make decisions and act upon them at this level, thus minimising the number of cases being progressed to a higher level. The recommended approach to conducting grievance and disciplinary interviews is the 'problem-solving' approach. This approach is based on the ideas of a 'principled' approach to negotiation and on the presumption that collaboration (joint problem solving) is a superior way of addressing problems. For instance, in the past the Institute of Personnel Management has advocated such an approach and there are undoubted advantages to its use. It holds out the best prospect for successful resolution of grievance and disciplinary issues. The conceptual basis for joint problem solving is that it attempts to remove the 'power' dimension from the grievance and disciplinary process. As with all integrative approaches, the reliance is on collaboration rather than the exercise of power. However, it is arguable that power cannot be removed, because even if problem solving fails to give a satisfactory outcome, either party may resort to alternatives. The employer will have the option to decide the issue based on their superior power position, while the employee may only seek a remedy for any unsatisfactory outcome from their point of view. That said, supervisors and line managers may resent the apparent diminution in power implied by the joint problem-solving approach.

The problem for grievance and disciplinary interviews is that alternative approaches to interviewing are held to be inferior (see Table 10.5). A frank and friendly manner may work in straightforward situations, but will not address more fundamental issues; in effect, it is an accommodation approach and depends on the other party placing a low priority on their concerns and a high priority on the company's concerns. The 'tell and listen' course may work, but it places no obligations on the other party to come up with solutions and an avoidance strategy may result. The 'tell and sell' approach is inherently employee unfriendly, does not require the employee to be part of generating solutions and may result in them having little commitment to any 'selling' in which the supervisor/manager has engaged. It may also create resentment in the employee. The 'sweet and sour' style is generally considered unethical and can land a company in legal difficulties if, as is likely, it creates a contradictory approach within management to the issue. Intimidation is unethical and can lead to accusations of bullying and harassment.

Given the challenges of the joint problem-solving approach, many organisations may fall back on satisfying legal requirements. The key issue in satisfying the legal requirements is for management to investigate the issue to obtain full facts and document the procedures adopted. Such a procedure falls short of the positive approach to discipline. It is a matter for further workplace-based research to investigate how grievance and disciplinary matters are operated in practice. However, such research would be difficult to conduct given the sensitivity involved in such issues, which would rule out direct observation.

Table 10.3
Contents of a Typical Grievance Procedure

- The procedure should be in writing for purposes of clarity.
- The grievance should be raised at the appropriate level. Usually the grievance is first discussed between employees and their immediate manager or supervisor.
- There should be an appeal mechanism to the various levels of management.
- The procedure should be simple and quick in operation.
- Time limits should be specified for each stage of the procedure.
- If an issue is not dealt with in the specified time, the next stage of the procedure may be invoked.
- Employees have the right to be represented by their trade union or an employee of their choice at the various stages of the procedure.
- There should be provision for issues to be referred to a third party if agreement cannot be reached 'in house'. This may be absent in non-union procedures.
- The procedure should or usually does contain a 'peace clause', with both parties foregoing the use of industrial action prior to all stages of the agreed procedures being exhausted.

Table 10.4
Grievance and Disciplinary Interviews: Joint Problem Solving

Requires non-directive, open-minded interviewing.
- Questioning and active listening.

Establish the issue from the employee perspective.
- Address employee's interests.

State the issue from the employer perspective.
- Requires assertiveness.

Problem solving.

- Allow employee to suggest solutions.

- Evaluate solution with reference to objective, mutually agreed standards.

Implementing.
- Requires employee to meet company needs and company to address employee needs.

Dangers
Manager may not engage with the process.
- May be considered to concede too much power.

Employee may not engage with the process.
- Employee may regard it as mere manipulation on manager's part.

HANDLING DISCIPLINARY ISSUES

The nature of industrial organisation creates the need for disciplinary measures. Employees have to attend on time, conform to certain behaviour, meet standards of performance and so on. Management will normally determine what are seen as acceptable rules and standards in areas such as employee performance, attendance and conduct at work. However, these are nowadays circumscribed by extensive employment legislation (see Chapter 2). In addition, they may be the subject of joint regulation through collective agreements or, most importantly, the unwritten *expectations* of employees and work groups. Inevitably, situations will arise where employees fail to meet expectations. Such disciplinary action may range from relatively minor and informal rebukes to more serious forms, such as formal warnings, suspension or dismissal. Such action is often not straightforward and can be contested by employees.

The following case study is designed to illustrate some of the intricacies of disciplinary action in practice.

Table 10.5
Possible Approaches to Grievance and Disciplinary Interviewing

Frank and friendly
Inform the person of the problem in an open and friendly way.

Tell and listen
Inform the person of the problem and then listen sympathetically.

Tell and sell
Inform the person of the problem and tell them of the consequences if they do not take a particular course of action.

Joint problem solving
Both sides explore the problem from their differing perspectives, search for mutually agreeable solutions, agree a solution and implementation and action plan.

Sweet and sour
Issue dealt with by more than two people form the one side; one adopts a hard approach and the other a 'softer' approach. Aim is to manipulate the other party into agreeing to the 'softer' settlement.

Intimidation
Use of threats.

Disciplinary Case Study: Furnworks Ltd
Bill Brennan has recently been appointed general manager of Furnworks Ltd, a small to medium-sized furniture company employing fifty people, located in the northwest. The company is unionised but the union is not particularly active and neither is the company a member of an employers' organisation. In the past the company has had a number of negative experiences with employment legislation. On taking up the position, the directors made it clear to Bill that a major improvement was expected in this area. Bill's predecessor had left

unexpectedly and he heard on the grapevine that one of the reasons why his predecessor 'was encouraged to leave' was because of the negative publicity associated with the loss of employment law cases. He heard that the directors had been embarrassed by local press coverage.

Three months after taking up employment the plant manager, Tom Joyce, approaches Bill in connection with a problem that has arisen with an employee named Peter Turner. Peter has been with the company for eight years and Tom informs Bill that he 'has a history'. About a year ago he was seen in a pub during working hours, being absent from his job without the permission of his supervisor. However, the person who informed the company was not prepared to give evidence and when Turner point-blank denied he had been in the pub on the day in question, the plant manager (Tom Joyce) felt he could not take any action.

About four weeks ago Peter Turner was involved in a lifting incident after which he complained he had hurt his back. Subsequently, he went on sick leave and submitted several sick certificates from his local GP to the effect that he was unable to work due to a back injury. The company has a sick pay scheme. In the written procedure agreement with the union there is a stipulation that 'any abuse of the sick pay scheme will lead to instant dismissal'.

Last week Tom Joyce received information that Peter Turner was on a sun holiday in the Canary Islands. This alerted Tom Joyce, as Peter Turner is known as a 'sun worshipper' because he takes so many sun holidays and always seems to have a suntan (in fact, his nickname is 'Ra' after the Egyptian sun god). Concerned that Turner would deny he had been on holiday, Tom Joyce found out when Turner was due to return, waited in Knock Airport and secretly took a video of him coming out of the arrivals area. He was suitably dressed in colourful holiday gear and accompanied by his wife and three children.

Tom Joyce informs Bill that he has had enough of Turner's antics and that 'he has slipped up this time and either he goes or I go'. He goes on to indicate that as per normal company practice he is holding a disciplinary hearing in the morning and 'will deal with the issue' if that is okay with Bill.

Bill is a personal friend of yours and he knows you are doing a course in industrial relations. Immediately after Tom Joyce has left the office Bill rings you and asks for advice on the matter because he says 'he's worried in case the thing goes wrong'.

Exercise for class discussion or written analysis
Advise Bill using the following format:

1. strengths of the case for the company;
2. weaknesses of the case for the company;
3. action which you would recommend Bill to take in his role as general manager; and
4. outline the range of *all possible* options available to Peter Turner in the event that he is dismissed.

(Guidelines to this case are available for lecturers on the website.)

Disciplinary Procedures

Disciplinary procedures serve to bring alleged offences to the notice of employees, indicate how they can respond to such charges and the disciplinary action that may be taken. Salamon (1998: 557) describes the purpose of a disciplinary procedure as being 'to provide an acceptable mechanism within which management may exercise its control over employees when their performance or behaviour does not reach the required standards'. Disciplinary procedures generally provide for lesser sanctions, such as oral or written warnings for lesser offences and for suspension/dismissal/reallocation for more serious acts. Case law arising under the Unfair Dismissals Acts 1997–2001 has a high degree of emphasis on procedural justice. While the absence of a disciplinary procedure will not automatically lead to an employer losing a case, it can make it more difficult to establish that a dismissal was fair. In almost all circumstances, instant dismissal will be found to be unfair.

Referral to the EAT is not the only option for an employee or a trade union, and depending on the circumstances, cases may be referred to Rights Commissioners, the Labour Court or industrial action may be initiated. In individual disputes, industrial action may follow after seven days' notice, if there are no procedures (either in writing or custom and practice) or if management do not utilise procedures.

Table 10.6
Outline Contents of a Disciplinary Procedure

- Indication of conduct and other issues which may lead to disciplinary action.
- Provision for a formal pre-disciplinary counselling phase in the case of lesser issues.
- Employee is entitled to know the complaint.
- Entitlement of employee to representation by shop steward, union official or other appropriate person.
- Person hearing case on management should not have a conflict of interest.
- Employee is entitled to challenge any evidence/allegations.
- Provision of graded penalties for lesser issues, such as conduct, performance. Usually oral and written.
- Provision for support action by management to assist improved performance/conduct, e.g. training, use of employee assistance programme.
- For removal of warnings following a set period.
- Provision in case of alleged gross misconduct, for suspension with pay to allow for an investigation.
- Provision for suspension/dismissal/ reassignment of duties for a first offence for major issues of gross misconduct or persistent failure to address lesser issues.
- An appeal to senior management.
- Provision for referral to third party in the event that disciplinary action is challenged.

Nature of Offences

There are certain offences where dismissal will invariably be justified. Theft is the most obvious, although the employer must be able to establish that the theft took place and that the employee was involved. This is not always unproblematic, especially where white-collar managerial employees are involved. They may have wide discretion in their jobs and be entitled to a broad range of perks. The offences that warrant dismissal for a first offence in one organisation may not merit dismissal in another. This is especially the case in the 'grey area' of fighting and substance abuse, for example. A fight on a building site can be viewed in a different light to one in an educational institution.

Company Rules and Standards

Not all grievance and disputes procedures will indicate specific disciplinary offences. Instead these may be outlined in company rules. This may especially be the case in non-union companies where norms are determined unilaterally by management and are not the subject of joint management-union agreement. The establishment of explicit workplace rules can help ensure consistency in the treatment of employees. Such an outline of rules and standards should indicate: (1) those rules and standards where breaches may lead to dismissal in the first instance, e.g. theft or violence at work, and (2) those rules and standards where breaches would lead to the operation of a standard disciplinary procedure, e.g. lateness. It would be impossible to cover all the possible transgressions of rules that might occur. Stated rules and standards can only outline general areas or deal with specific transgressions that occur frequently.

An integral part of managerial work involves the coaching and counselling of employees. This may involve informally reprimanding employees. In the event of the facts of a case pointing to the need for formal disciplinary action, management should adhere to the disciplinary procedure and, where appropriate, issue a formal disciplinary warning. In issuing formal warnings it is suggested that the approach should be remedial rather than penal, except in the most extreme circumstances (for example, see Salamon 1998). Managers should encourage improvements in individual conduct rather than simply impose sanctions. Again, clarity is very important. The warning should specify the way in which the employee's behaviour or performance was unsatisfactory, how performance can be improved, what the expected standard is and what the consequences of not improving are. Management are obliged to take any reasonable measures that might facilitate improvement, such as extra training.

Recordkeeping: Administrative and Legal Considerations

As with the outcome of all negotiations, keeping accurate records on grievance and disciplinary matters is essential. Since the unfair dismissals legislation places the burden of proof primarily on the employer, companies must be able to back up reasons for discipline with adequate documentary evidence. In equality cases, the onus of proof is on employees. However, an employer will need records if they wish to rebut evidence given by an employee. While recordkeeping is an important dimension of grievance handling, it should not be allowed to distract from the primary purpose of grievance administration. An overemphasis may create excessive red tape and cause frustration among employees. The details which need to be retained will vary according to the level a grievance or disciplinary process has reached.

At counselling interview stage, a brief note of the issue, the individual concerned, the date and the nature of the discussion will suffice. Procedures that allow for reprimands or verbal warnings at the counselling stage defeat the purpose of a counselling stage, which should be solely focused on identifying mutually acceptable solutions to the issues(s) raised. At verbal, written and all subsequent stages, records should be more elaborate. Some organisations require that grievances entering the procedure after the first stage must be served in writing with details of the issue and the employee(s) concerned. This is designed to help clarify the exact nature of the claim or grievance and helps avoid misunderstandings. This is particularly important at and after final warning stage, where it should be clearly documented that the employee was informed of the seriousness of the issue and the fact that future offences may lead to dismissal. A copy that has been signed by the employee (as evidence that they received and understood the letter) should be placed on their personal file. A copy should also be given to the employee's representative, the trade union (if appropriate) and to the manager(s) involved. Such records also provide management with useful information on the extent and nature of grievances in the organisation.

CHAPTER 11

Employee Involvement and Participation

INTRODUCTION

The terms 'employee participation' and 'involvement' may be interpreted as incorporating any mechanisms designed to increase employee input into managerial decision making. They are terms that are frequently used interchangeably, but there are considerable distinctions that can be made (see below). The concept of employee participation is based on the premise that people who work in an organisation should be entitled to influence decisions affecting them. It is sometimes seen as the political democratisation of the workplace, as it facilitates the redistribution of decision-making power away from management and towards employees (see Chamberlain 1948; Schregle 1974; Thomason 1984).

In Chapter 6, it was noted that the structure of industrial organisations, with the support of the legal and business systems, has traditionally placed decision-making power in the hands of employers. Notwithstanding the primacy accorded employers' position, employee participation in organisational decision making has a long history and various initiatives have been taken to promote this end. These range from information giving, to consultation with employees, to joint decision making and even worker control. These initiatives may result in a variety of institutional arrangements to facilitate employee participation/involvement at workplace level. Examples range across suggestion schemes, quality circles, empowerment, joint consultative committees, works councils or board-level participation.

In analysing the subject of employee participation it is customary to make two major distinctions: the first is between *direct* and *indirect* participation and the second is between *task*-centred and *power*-centred participation. Direct employee involvement encompasses any initiatives that provide for personal employee influence on decisions affecting their work and immediate work environment. Employees are directly involved themselves. Direct involvement is usually introduced at management's behest and may take a variety of forms, such as briefing groups, quality circles, consultative meetings and teamworking. From the 1980s it was frequently introduced as part of change initiatives whereby management transferred responsibility to employees for a limited range of job-related decisions, such as working methods, recruitment of team members and task allocation.

One particular initiative that has been around for some time is the *suggestion scheme*. Many Irish organisations have operated suggestion schemes with apparently varying degrees of success. A technique that appears to be increasing in popularity is the *attitude survey*. Gunnigle (1995a) found in newly established ('greenfield') companies that a number of non-union organisations periodically administered attitude surveys among employees. Opinion or attitude surveys normally involve management seeking to ascertain employees' views on the organisation, the effectiveness of communications, areas for improvement, skills and employee benefits, etc. This is normally done using structured questionnaires, sometimes complimented by interviews, focus groups and the like. Such surveys may often be independently administered and/or validated by external consultants or institutions (such as universities). A common feature of the above direct participation mechanisms is that they tend to be task centred and concentrated on the more effective execution of work.

In contrast, indirect participation is power centred and is often referred to as *representative participation*. It is an indirect form of employee influence, insofar as employee views and input are articulated through the use of some form of collective employee representatives on company boards or works councils. Such employee representatives are usually elected or nominated by the workforce and thus carry a mandate to represent the interests and views of those workers. They do not act in a personal capacity but as a conduit through which the broader mass of workers can influence organisational decision making. Indirect participation is considered power centred because it is largely concerned with redistributing decision-making power. It seeks to reduce the extent of management prerogative and bring about greater employee influence in areas that have traditionally been the remit of senior management.

The distinction between task-based indirect participation and power-centred indirect participation tends to mark off the respective positions of employer and trade union positions. Employers tend to favour task-centred participation while trade unions have generally sought to extend power-centred participation. However, not all trade unionists favour direct participation and an ambiguity has often been noted in trade union positions. For example, certain trade unionists may oppose the appointment of worker directors (a form of indirect participation), fearing it may undermine the enterprise-level role of trade unions and collective bargaining. They may be especially concerned at the capacity of unions to take an independent position to oppose company policy if workers have been involved in the formulation of that policy. Others view the appointment of worker directors as a positive development that introduces joint regulation in the enterprise, particularly in relation to higher-level strategic decisions.

THE DYNAMICS OF EMPLOYEE INVOLVEMENT AND PARTICIPATION

Many descriptions of employee participation tend to be 'elastic' in character and it is necessary to be more precise in outlining the principal components. Marchington and Wilkinson's (2000) analysis highlights the dynamic nature of employee involvement and participation and also 'deconstructs' its various components according to *degree, form, level* and *range* of subject matter. The degree of involvement and participation addresses the extent to which employees can influence management decisions, namely whether they are simply informed of changes, consulted or actually make decisions. This is demonstrated in Figure 11.1, which marks out a progression in the degree of participation rather than 'simply a move from zero participation to workers control' (Marchington and Wilkinson 2000: 342–3).

Figure 11.1
Ladder of Involvement and Participation

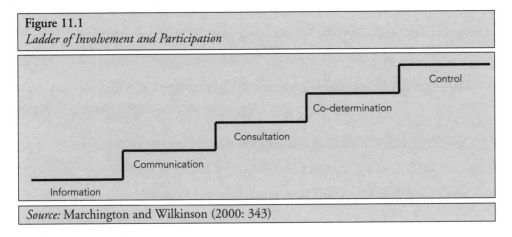

Source: Marchington and Wilkinson (2000: 343)

Second, there is the level at which such employee influence is exercised. This may occur at task, departmental, establishment or corporate level. Many of the current developments at enterprise level in Ireland focus on increasing direct employee involvement at *task level*, namely in decisions which affect their immediate work role. However, we also find employee influence exercised at higher levels in the organisational hierarchy, such as at business unit level (through collective bargaining) or corporate level (through worker directors).

Third, we have the scope or range of subject matter. This dimension addresses the type and number of issues over which employees have the opportunity to influence decisions. The most commonly used categorisation in this respect is to differentiate between influence at the operational level and strategic level. Influence at the strategic level implies a capacity for employee input on the future nature and role of the organisation.

Fourth, there are variations in the form of participation, thus one may have involvement in structures or *'financial'* or *'equity' participation*. Financial involvement involves profit-sharing or gainsharing schemes, whereby employees participate directly in the commercial success or failure of the organisation. Such schemes may allow workers to secure an equity share in their organisations. They usually link the financial rewards to employees to some measure of corporate or establishment performance.

While the terms 'industrial democracy', 'participation' and 'employee involvement' have been used interchangeably, it is possible to distinguish between these categories.

Industrial Democracy

Industrial democracy is generally understood to involve situations where workers exert primary control over organisational decision making. Salamon (2000: 370) describes industrial democracy as follows:

> Its central objective is the establishment of employee self-management within an organisation, whose ownership is vested in either the employees or the state and whose managerial function is exercised ultimately through a group, elected

by the employees themselves, which has the authority over all decisions of the organisation, including the allocation of 'profits' between extra wages and reinvestment.

This approach is sometimes seen as the ultimate form of employee influence, involving a fundamental restructuring of control and power in industrial organisations towards employees.

Employee Participation

Salamon (2000: 371) argues that employee participation denotes a 'distinct evolutionary development', which is aimed at extending collective employee influence beyond the traditional remit of collective bargaining into 'much wider areas of organisational planning and decision making at both the operational and, more importantly, strategic level'. The collectivist element is a critical distinguishing characteristic of employee participation. This approach involves employee influence working through representative structures such as trade unions, works councils or other forms of elected employee representation. Salamon (2000: 371) further notes the importance of power equality between capital and labour in giving effect to what he terms 'real' employee participation (see also Pateman 1970):

> ... 'real' participation ideally requires both sides to have 'equal power to determine the outcome of decisions'. In the absence of such power equality, employees can only rely on management goodwill, i.e. its acceptance of and commitment to a participative philosophy or style of organisational management. There must be more than just the provision of information to employees or their representatives; there must be a genuine opportunity for employees to influence major strategic organisational decisions.

Employee Involvement

Employee involvement embraces any means of increasing the direct involvement of workers in decisions affecting their work situation, such as work scheduling or quality monitoring. Salamon (2000: 372) notes that some of the more common mechanisms used to operationalise employee involvement (EI) include empowerment, teamworking, briefing groups and quality circles. He goes on to argue that employee involvement is generally introduced as a means of advancing management objectives:

> These measures have been introduced by management in order to optimise the utilisation of labour (in particular, to improve organisational quality and flexibility) and at the same time to secure the employee's identification with and commitment to the aims and needs of the organisation. Such measures may allow employees greater influence and control over decision making, but only

in relation to their immediate work operations; hence the phrase sometimes used of 'task participation'.

The suggestion that employee involvement tends to be management driven is also evident from Marchington and Wilkinson's (2000: 340) conclusion that 'more recent EI initiatives have been management sponsored and, not surprisingly, have reflected a management agenda concerned primarily with employee motivation and commitment to organisational objectives'. Similarly, Wilkinson's (1998: 1,720) analysis of the concept of employee 'empowerment' found that it largely focused on 'task-based involvement and attitudinal change' and did not incorporate any acknowledgement of 'workers having a right to a say'. Rather, it remained an employer (managerial) decision whether and how to empower employees. Wilkinson (1998: 1,720) also notes the potential variation in the extent of power that employees may be afforded under such schemes:

> Most [empowerment initiatives] are purposefully designed not to give workers a very significant role in decision making but rather to secure an enhanced employee contribution to the organisation with 'empowerment' taking place within the context of a strict management agenda. Empowerment schemes tend to be direct and based on individuals or small groups (usually the work group), a clear contrast with industrial democracy and participative schemes such as consultative committees which are collectivist and representative in nature.

The above distinctions emphasise that the various approaches differ in regard to the extent of employee influence on decision making and the level of institutional 'sophistication' of the differing forms of employee influence. Initial interest in employee influence revolved around worker participation and industrial democracy. However, over the past two decades there has been a significant shift in the employee influence debate towards more management-sponsored forms of employee influence. This has been accompanied by a move away from representative forms of participation and towards a greater focus on the direct involvement of individual employees in decisions of immediate work relevance. We now proceed to review that debate and developments.

INDIRECT EMPLOYEE INFLUENCE: DEBATE AND DEVELOPMENTS

The movement for worker influence in organisational decision making has its roots in early attempts to achieve worker control dating from the Industrial Revolution in the UK (see Coates and Topham 1968). These initiatives were based on a rejection of an economic order rooted in capitalism and wage labour. The movement for workers' control and self-management highlights an important question – whether employee involvement should aim at achieving a changed economic order through redrawing the decision-making mechanisms within organisations or whether it should try to bring about greater employee participation within the current structure of industrial organisations. It is clear that most, if not all, recent developments follow the latter route. Hyman and Mason (1995: 8) write that 'industrial democracy has little currency in contemporary market-driven economies where any worker or activist concern for industrial control has been fragmented and displaced by defensive struggles to retain individual employment and to protect employment rights'.

A further issue is whether promoting employee participation contributes to increasing employee influence. Salamon (1998: 377) argues that the appointment of worker directors is 'unlikely to affect significantly the power and decision making of senior management'. The Bullock Committee Report (1977: 72) noted that many organisations had 'developed a de facto two-tier system, delegating responsibility for the formulation and implementation of policy from the main board perhaps to a management committee'. Salamon (1998) identifies a number of other factors that serve to limit the extent to which worker directors can impact on management decision making. These are:

- the infrequency of board meetings;
- the exclusion of worker directors from other director and senior management meetings;
- the fact that the main role of the board of directors is to formally endorse senior management proposals/decisions; and
- the fact that board-level decisions rely heavily on senior management for information.

A Comparative Perspective

Developments to extend employee influence in organisational decision making have taken varying directions in different countries. With the demise of the early movements for workers' control, participation achieved its most concrete form through the extension of collective bargaining. More far-reaching developments took place in the post-World War II era, with various institutional arrangements developed to further employee participation, particularly in a number of European countries. While these developments fall considerably short of full industrial democracy, they entail institutional arrangements that provide for a degree of democratic input. This occurs within what Salamon (2000: 370) terms 'only a limited modification of the capitalist managerial authority system rather than a fundamental restructuring'. A classic example is the German system of co-determination involving the appointment of worker directors to the boards of firms employing more than 500 employees.

In the 1970s an extensive debate emerged on the desirability of extending representative participation, with a preference for a system along the German lines. West Germany had a strong tradition of representative participation dating back to the restructuring of the economy after World War II. This involves two pillars – co-determination and works councils. In structural terms *co-determination* entails the appointment of worker directors to the main (supervisory) board of companies. Germany, like a number of other European countries, has a two-tier board structure – a supervisory board to deal with policy issues and a management board to deal with operational affairs. At workplace level, works councils provide for formal employee representation to facilitate consultation, discussion and information exchange between workers and management. In the German system, works councils are required to co-operate with management but are composed solely of workers. Management do have a right to address meetings.

The Debate in the UK

In the 1970s an extensive debate also took place in the UK. Like Ireland, the UK does not have any established tradition of worker directors and its company structure is based around a single (unitary) board of directors, as opposed to European two-tier systems. As the European Economic Community (EEC) debate intensified in the 1970s, the UK government established a parliamentary Committee of Inquiry on Industrial Democracy to investigate the area of employee participation, with special reference to the issue of worker directors. Chaired by Lord Bullock, the committee included representatives of employers and trade unions (see Bullock 1977). The report considered whether worker directors should be 'an integral part of the normal management of the organisation' or whether their role should be confined to 'broad policy issues and the general overseeing of management' (Salamon 1988: 376). This debate focused on the relative advantages of retaining the unitary board structure or establishing a two-tier board structure (management and supervisory boards) with worker directors on the supervisory board only. This latter approach would have the effect of limiting worker director input to broad policy decisions, with general organisational decision making remaining a management remit through their exclusive representation on management boards.

The final report contained a majority proposal favouring the retention of the existing single, or unitary, board structure (Bullock 1977). This report proposed that boards of directors should be comprised of equal numbers of shareholder and employee representatives, together with a smaller number of co-opted independent directors (the so-called '2x + y' formula). However, employer representatives on the Bullock Committee vehemently opposed the idea of worker directors on the main board and produced a minority report that proposed a two-tier board structure with minority worker representation on supervisory boards only.

These conflicting positions are broadly representative of employer and labour positions in relation to worker representation at board level. Salamon (2000: 397) notes the different perceptions between management and trade unions of the role of worker directors. Management tend to view the role of worker directors in terms of developing 'a "coalition" between employers and management'. This is to be done by employee representatives making a positive contribution to the board and can involve articulating employee views, ensuring employee commitment to board-level decisions and by increasing employee awareness of the rationale for board-level decisions. We have already noted that while trade unions may favour worker directors, their attachment can be equivocal, as they may welcome the input into decision making but may fear the effect on collective bargaining.

The majority report of the Bullock Committee met with widespread employer opposition and was not acted upon. The election of a Conservative Government led by Margaret Thatcher in 1979 effectively ended any government-sponsored initiatives in relation to worker directors.

The EU Perspective

During the 1970s and into the 1980s, much of the focus of the employee participation and involvement debate took place at the level of the European Economic Community, as the European Union (EU) was then known. In 1972 the EEC Commission launched the so-called Draft Fifth Directive, which was designed to apply to all public limited companies employing 500 or more workers. The directive gave member countries an option of a number of systems but favoured a two-tier board system along German lines, involving the appointment of employee worker directors to the supervisory boards of companies. The Directive met with extensive employer opposition and made little progress.

The European Commission (1975) subsequently produced a Green Paper on Employee Participation and Company Structure, which took a more flexible approach. While still favouring a two-tier board system with worker directors on the supervisory board, the paper suggested that this was only one option for extending employee participation. The first draft of the European Company Statute (1976) also proposed a two-tier board system along similar lines. It further proposed that companies establish works councils and provide for the disclosure of certain types of company information. The Vredling Directive (1980) on employee rights to information disclosure recommended that multinational companies must consult and inform employees in subsidiaries in relation to strategic issues. Additionally, other proposals have demanded the provision of financial information through consolidated accounts.

These proposed measures did not come into effect on any widespread basis. Recently, however, concrete, if modest, developments at the EU level have emerged. First was the adoption by the EU of the European Works Councils Directive (EWC)(1994), second was the adoption of the directive on the European Company Statute in 2000 and third was the directive on Information Disclosure and Consultation finally adopted in 2002.

Biagi *et al.* (2002: 37) note that the directive on EWCs is 'considered as an extremely important model which has made it possible to get the enactment of the European Company Statute firstly and later on the directive on information and consultation rights in national undertakings'. In contrast to some other authors, Biagi *et al.* (2002: 37) take an essentially optimistic view of these new directives, suggesting they 'have re-opened an intensive debate on corporate governance, on employee involvement, on workers' participation'.

Although the EWC directive preceded the other two directives, we will consider the directive on the ECS first, followed by the information and consultation directive. The developments in relation to works councils are dealt with later in the section on works councils below.

PROSPECTS FOR PARTICIPATION ARISING FROM THE EUROPEAN COMPANY STATUTE (ECS) 2001

The European Company Statute (or *Societas Europaea* (SE) in Latin) was agreed by the European Council in Nice in December 2000 and subsequently formally adopted by the EU's Council of Ministers on 8 October 2001. Keller (2002: 424) notes that the essential idea of an ECS is to enable the establishment of 'a unified management structure and reporting system to be governed by Community law instead of a large number of widely differing national laws'. A decision of a company to incorporate itself as a European company is entirely voluntary. A European company can be created in any of four ways:

1. by merger of national companies from different member states;
2. by the creation of a joint venture between companies (or other entities) in different member states;
3. by the creation of a SE subsidiary of a national company; or
4. by the conversion of a national company into an SE (http://en.wikipedia.org/wiki/European_Company_Statute).

The directive comes into effect on 8 October 2004. Should a company decide to become a European company, this will remove the necessity for separate registration in all member states. The directive provides for the involvement of workers' representatives on the company's supervisory board. EIRI Associates (2004a: 15) note that:

> The participation arrangements only become activated if the company, before becoming a European company, already had participation arrangements in place under relevant national law. This also applies if a European company comes into existence through a merger or takeover if one of the merger partners or the company [being taken over] had participation arrangements in place.

Negotiations on the terms of the SE were especially difficult due to this factor. Member states with strong legislative provisions for worker participation feared that if there was no measure for employee participation present in the statute, 'many firms would use the new legislation to avoid stricter national rules on worker participation' (Higgins 2000b: 16). Furthermore, in member states without worker involvement provisions, there were concerns that the SE would lead to having such provisions being imposed on companies. In particular the UK, Ireland and especially Spain were slow to agree to provisions for workers' board-level involvement. Under the statute, management and employees of the European company must jointly agree provisions for worker involvement: 'if an SE is being established, a special negotiating body (SNB) is to be set up, to agree the form of participation to apply' (Higgins 2001: 13). If no agreement can be reached, the standards set in the annex to the directive must be applied.

While the EWC directive is concerned with employee representation at a lower/plant level, covering 'tactical and operational issues of company management', the SE addresses employee involvement at strategic decision-making levels (Keller 2002:

425). Because this is where the 'real' control lies, there have been lengthy debates about the statute's contents and introduction. For Ireland, the ECSs provisions uphold the voluntarist nature of industrial relations because employee involvement in SEs is 'established by voluntary negotiations between social partners at the level of the individual company, instead of binding legislative action at EU level' (Keller 2002: 439). The consequence for employee representatives in SEs is that 'their negotiated rights of information and consultation will be rather weak – and their number limited in contrast to shareholders' (Keller 2002: 441).

Taking a more pessimistic view to that of Biagi *et al.* (2002), Keller believes that such involvement (as defined in the statute) will hardly reach the level of '"co-management" by co-decision in the strict sense of the term, which includes the option to make use of existing veto power in order to block unilateral decision by management' (Keller 2002: 442). Furthermore, Baglioni (2003: 344) points out that 'member states are assigned a major role and functions in applying the Directive'. Keller (2002: 434) argues that as a result the 'ECS will most likely lead to at least fifteen different (and in the future, after the so-called "eastern-enlargement", even considerably more), nationally modelled SEs – rather than to a single, relatively unified and standardised "European" model'. Thus, he claims, 'it is quite clear that the onetime goal of genuine "Europeanisation" of industrial relations will not be achieved' (Keller 2002: 441).

This pessimistic view is contrasted with that of Biagi *et al.* (2002), who see merit in the flexibility for applying the three directives. They write: 'after the EWC story we finally learnt that it is not possible to identify one single road in promoting employee involvement in various countries … In this context the old idea of harmonisation has been, if not dropped, at least reconsidered deeply'.

The prospects for the success of the ECS is bound up with a range of factors, of which the provision for board-level worker representation is but one, arguably minor, element. Among other factors, Keller (2002: 435) identifies the potential disincentives which might arise from a common European tax policy (not yet created) against what the European Commission has argued are the 'huge' savings in transaction costs (administrative and legal costs, among others).

The EU Directive on Information and Consultation 2002

The final text of the Employee Information and Consultation Directive (2002/14/EC) was formally adopted in February 2002 and EU member states have until March 2005 to comply with its requirements, or by March 2008 in states with no existing permanent framework for information and consultation (Hall 2002). The directive is designed 'to establish a general framework setting out minimum requirements for the right to information and consultation of employees in undertakings or establishments within the European Community' (Hall 2001). Information and consultation is defined as taking place between the employer and employee representatives. Dr Tony Dundon of NUI Galway has pointed out that as a result, 'Irish companies will be required to establish some form of works council along lines similar to those in other EU countries' (see O'Regan 2003).

The following rights are specified in the directive:

- information on the recent and probable development of the undertakings or the establishment's activities and economic situation;
- information and consultation on the situation, structure and probable development of employment within the undertaking and on any anticipatory measures envisaged;
- in particular where there is a threat to employment; and
- information and consultation, with a view to reaching an agreement, on decisions likely to lead to substantial changes in work organisation or in contractual relations (Dobbins 2003d).

Member states have the option to apply the directive at either the level of undertakings or establishments, as follows:

- undertakings employing at least fifty employees in any one member state; or
- establishments employing at least twenty employees in any one member state.

Dobbins notes that in the Irish case there are arguments favouring both levels. He writes that 'in a small organisation with relatively simple structures it might make more sense to introduce a single information and consultation body, while in a larger more complex organisation, several information and consultation bodies could be required' (Dobbins 2003d). O'Regan (2003: 11) notes that depending on the decision on size, 'between fifty and seventy per cent of Irish workers will be legally entitled to an open and active employee information and consultation policy on the part of their employers'.

A further key issue in applying the directive to Ireland is whether to adopt an 'opt in' or 'opt out' approach. 'Opt in' would require employees to formally request the establishment of an information and consultation structure, whereas an 'opt out' approach would require the employer to establish a structure unless employees specified they did not want one. According to Tom Hayes of European Industrial Relations Intelligence (EIRI) Associates, the 'opt out' approach is likely to be less susceptible to legal challenge (Dobbins 2003d). The UK, however, has already chosen the 'opt in' approach, with a requirement for a formal written request from at least ten per cent of the undertaking's workforce in order for an employer to be required to open negotiations on the establishment of a structure. However, Hayes claims that this may well be found to be in breach of the directive by the European Court of Justice, because it may be judged to undermine employee access to information and consultation rights (Dobbins 2003d).

The directive goes beyond the current provisions for information and consultation in the case of redundancies, which require consultation after a decision has been made. There is provision for management and labour to agree on arrangements different from those laid down in the directive. The directive allows the parties to industrial relations to agree local arrangements on a voluntary basis. Dobbins (2003d) argues that 'commentators in Ireland believe that this looseness could create uncertainty and generate differing interpretations by management and trade unions/workers – for instance, in drawing the boundaries between information, consultation and joint decision making, individual and collective rights and direct and indirect (through employee representatives) channels'.

Government Response

As part of a consultation exercise the Department of Enterprise, Trade and Employment has published a discussion paper on the directive which notes that in order to comply with the directive, Irish legislation will need to ensure the following:

- the arrangements must be effective;
- they must take due account of the interests of both the enterprise and the employees;
- they must have due regard to the rights and obligations of both parties;
- they must be negotiated and operated in a spirit of co-operation;
- where the agreement is for an arrangement of direct involvement, i.e. where there is direct interaction between the employer and the employees, employees must be free at any later stage to exercise their right through representatives of their choosing (Industrial Relations Unit, Department of Enterprise, Trade and Employment 2003: 5–6).

The discussion paper notes that the Second Schedule of the Transnational Information and Consultation of Employees Act 1996 – which implemented the EU EWCs Directive (94/45/EC) in Ireland – could serve as a template for the employees' forum (www.entemp.ie/erir/constrans03.pdf).

Trade Union and Employer Perspectives

IBEC is lobbying for what the trade unions would call a 'minimalist' interpretation of the directive, primarily due to a concern to protect the prerogative to manage. In view of this, employers want to maintain and promote existing forms of direct interaction between management and employees. To a large degree, employer opposition to indirect representative structures has been based on the concern that they could frighten away foreign inward investment by multinationals, many of which are opposed to collective employee representation. Dobbins (2001b) summarises IBEC's position as being:

> opposed to the introduction of statutory-based mandatory employee representation structures such as works councils, instead preferring a voluntarist system that reflects the competitive situation of individual companies. It prefers the concept of direct communication between management and employees to collective representation. There is a perception within IBEC that works councils are rooted in the past and that the pace of change today requires companies to communicate with employees directly ... We don't have a problem with the idea of consultation in principle but we would oppose

anything that would interfere with a company's right to manage (www.eiro.eurofound.ie/2001/06/feature/ie0106168f.html).

Dobbins (2003d) notes that the US Chamber of Commerce has also been a vocal opponent of the directive. Dundon indicates as well that

> recent research at NUI, Galway found that 'a strong ideology and general distaste for consulting workers' continues to exist in the mindset of many Irish managers [and] ... many organisations have rather shallow communication arrangements that fall short of the requirements on the directive (O'Regan 2003: 11).

While this indicates a strong tension between unions and management, Dundon argues that the requirement for employee consultation and information procedures 'could prove highly beneficial for businesses operating in the Irish marketplace' (O'Regan 2003: 11). He quotes Watson Wyatt's 2002 Human Capital Index Survey: 'companies that successfully engage with their employees through representative structures, such as unions and works councils, can add as much as seven per cent to shareholder value' (O'Regan 2003: 11).

In contrast to IBEC, ICTU has expressed strong support for the directive. Dobbins (2001b) writes that 'it believes that the Directive could play a vital part in improving worker information and consultation rights relating to workplace change and restructuring'. Moreover, there is a perception within ICTU that the directive could potentially facilitate an increase in the diffusion of enterprise-level 'partnership' between employers and employee representatives. On the trade union side, a key concern is to ensure that representation is 'through trade unions alone'. Dobbins (2003d) suggests that 'in practice, however, they could face some difficulty in this regard, given that the Directive itself does not give trade unions an automatic guarantee that they will be the sole employee representative channel'.

IRISH WORKER PARTICIPATION: DEBATE AND LEGISLATION

Irish industrial relations came late to the participation debate. Kelly and Hourihan (1997: 405) note that 'the only opportunity to participate in Ireland was through the collective bargaining process'. However, by the mid-1960s, with the manifest success of the Germany experience and the prospect of entry into the 'Common Market', interest had been aroused in the concept. In 1967, ICTU held a conference on the topic and as a result adopted a position in favour of promoting industrial democracy. The conference instructed the Executive Council of ICTU to investigate the best means of implementing the principle of industrial democracy in Ireland, with particular regard to the experience of worker participation in other countries and the context of industrial, commercial and economic life in Ireland.

This was followed by a resolution adopted by the Annual Delegate Congress of ICTU in 1968, which called for government action to recognise the principle and application of industrial democracy in consultation with trade unions and the state sector.

In 1969 a study on industrial democracy by a joint committee of the Federated Union of Employers and the Confederation of Irish Industry led to the *Mulvey Report*. Surprisingly, this report, having examined industrial democracy in terms of employees sharing directly in the management of the enterprise, concluded that even in Germany there was no evidence to suggest that co-determination had in fact 'made any direct contribution to the sharing of managerial authority' (cited in Department of Labour 1986c: 32–3). Mulvey (1969) maintained that the best way for employees to influence managerial decisions is through the collective bargaining process and furthermore that this system is the most effective way of promoting a system of industrial democracy (cited in Department of Labour 1986c: 33). In 1972 a subcommittee was formed by the Employer-Labour Committee and they published a report in 1974 on works councils. It found that both 'inadequate resources of the trade union movement and the low priority given by senior management to personnel management' acted as a barrier to the development of employee participation in Ireland (Department of Labour 1986c: 35). Furthermore, they maintained that the best way of promoting works councils was through a national agreement.

The European Commission's (1972) draft Fifth Directive on the harmonisation of company structure and the EEC's on 'Employee Participation and Company Structure' (1975) raised the possibility of the extension of European-type participation in Ireland. The subsequent Department of Labour's Discussion Paper on Worker Participation (1980) examined in detail the implications of worker participation for Ireland. Among the items considered in the discussion document and also examined in this study were:

- access to company information;
- the state of present participative structures;
- management/trade union attitudes to participation; and
- the suitability, or otherwise, of EEC-type participative structures for Ireland.

Little resulted from these initiatives, however, and in 1985 the Minister for Labour, Mr Ruairi Quinn, appointed the Advisory Committee on Worker Participation. Its report supported increased levels of employee participation in Ireland. It was of the view that in the public sector sub-board levels should be developed. Also, the majority of the committee recommended the introduction of enabling legislation in the *private sector* for organisations with more than 100 employees. It was suggested that this should provide for participation structures at sub-board level, 'to be activated either by agreement between management and representatives of the workforce, or by a ballot of employees' (Department of Labour 1986c: 106). The employee representatives were to be 'selected/elected through trade union structures, where they exist' (Department of Labour 1986c: 106).

A minority of members of the Advisory Committee dissented from the recommendation for legislation mandating such participation in the private sector. In particular, the Federated Union of Employers (FUE) – the forerunner of IBEC – favoured a voluntary approach instead and did not support 'the concept of enabling legislation for works councils or similar kinds of participative bodies' (Department of Labour 1986c: 66). In the event, no such legislation was introduced. However, the committee unanimously endorsed direct forms of participation, the development of quality circles and of financial participation.

Worker Participation Legislation

Legislative provision for participation has been confined to the state sector. In 1977, the Worker Participation (State Enterprises) Act was passed and this was subsequently augmented by the Worker Participation (State Enterprises) Act (1988). In Ireland the appointment of worker directors has been restricted to the semi-state companies covered by this legislation. The 1977 Act provided for the appointment of worker directors to the boards of seven semi-state companies and did this within the existing unitary board structure of Irish business. These companies were Bord na Móna, CIE, ESB, Aer Lingus, B&I Shipping, Nitrigin Éireann Teoranta (NET) and Comhlucht Siuicre Éireann Teoranta (CSE). The 1988 Act extended board-level participation to include Irish Steel, Bord Gáis, VHI, An Post, Bord Telecom, Aer Rianta and the National Rehabilitation Board. The 1988 Act also provided that board-level participation could be extended to other organisations without the need for further primary legislation.

Provision for the establishment of sub-board-level participation structures was also introduced under the 1988 Act, which identifies thirty-nine state enterprises as being suitable for the introduction of sub-board structures. The legislation entails three basic requirements:

- the exchange of views and clear and reliable information between the enterprise and employees;
- the communication in good time of information likely to have a significant effect on employees; and
- the distribution of views and information arising from the participatory process to all employees.

Apart from these specific provisions, the legislation is largely of an 'enabling' variety. It is left to management and employee representatives in state organisations to develop mutually acceptable arrangements for employee participation following a request from the majority of employees. This reflects a voluntarist approach, with management and employee representatives being free to identify and implement the mode of sub-board-level participation. A wide range of participative options is provided for in the legislation, including representative and direct participatory forms.

The level of representation in non-commercial state companies is to be determined by the need to retain a balance of representative interests and to ensure the board operates as an effective body (IDS/IPD 1996). Now each case is to be considered on its merits by the Minister for Enterprise, Trade and Employment, who can prescribe the number of worker directors below one-third of the total board.

The legislation requires that candidates for election as worker director must be nominated by a trade union or other body, such as a staff association or equivalent, that is recognised for collective bargaining purposes in the organisation concerned. The electorate comprises full-time and regular part-time employees of the organisation (and subsidiaries in particular circumstances). Once elected, worker directors hold office for a four-year term and have equal status to other directors. As of 2003 there were fifty-four employee representatives on twenty boards in the public sector, together with a few worker directors on the boards of state companies which have been privatised. The number of representatives varies substantially between organisations, from five worker directors in An Post to only one representative on more recently established state-sponsored companies, such as An Coillte and the Railway Procurement Agency (O'Kelly and Compton 2003: 6).

The Operation of the Worker Participation Legislation

In an initial review of the operation of worker directors under the terms of the 1977 Act, Kelly (1989b) found that the experience had been broadly successful and concluded that employees have positive attitudes to board-level participation. He notes that management, though harbouring some reservations as to the role and contribution of worker directors, subsequently largely accepted their role (see also Murphy and Walsh 1980; Galvin 1980). In a later evaluation, Kelly and Hourihan (1997) noted that the new worker directors quickly settled into their roles and encountered little difficulty in becoming involved in board-level activities. Kelly's (1989b) analysis did not find any major conflict between the role of worker directors and the operation of collective bargaining/trade unions in the organisations studied. He found that trade unions had largely dominated the participatory process. He notes:

> For all practical purposes the principal trade unions ... control the worker director initiative. In the various elections the successful candidates have been trade union activists ... Furthermore, the great majority of worker directors continue to hold some form of union office, which turned out to be an important linkpin in the maintenance of satisfactory relationships between the two power centres. Thus, from the outset the prospect of an alternative, parallel and possibly competing employee voice dissolved into insignificance, and to date there is no evidence that it is ever likely to become a divisive issue (Kelly 1989b: 309).

Costello's (1983) study of the experience of worker directors in the seven state enterprises covered by the 1977 Act found that the exclusion of worker directors from more operational issues served to limit their influence. His analysis suggested that the impact of worker directors was primarily concentrated on broader corporate objectives, which effectively 'precluded worker directors from raising many of the issues which were of concern to the employees who had elected them' (Costello 1983: 57). 'Most of these issues were seen to fall within management's responsibility and attempts to raise them in the boardroom were invariably ruled out of order' (Costello 1983: 57).

Murphy and Walsh's (1980) study considered the views of trade union officials and shop stewards on the role and effectiveness of worker directors. Shop stewards saw benefits in the role of worker directors but were generally sceptical of the capacity of worker directors to influence board-level decisions because of their minority position. Stewards generally saw themselves as a more effective means of resolving employee problems. While seeing benefits in the role of worker directors, shop stewards also noted certain problems, particularly in relation to the extent of feedback from worker directors. In contrast, worker directors saw themselves as placing considerable weight on the need to maintain strong links between their representative role and the collective bargaining system in the organisation (Murphy and Walsh 1980).

The views of trade union officials were somewhat more critical than shop stewards. Officials were particularly sceptical of the capacity of worker directors to contribute to significant improvements in industrial relations. In reviewing these study findings, Kelly and Hourihan (1997: 429) note that trade union officials were 'quick to mark a boundary separating collective bargaining issues from those concerning company policies'. Kelly and Hourihan (1997: 429) also note there was no evidence of worker directors attempting to 'compete with, or compromise, the established workplace union organisation'.

Possibly the most difficult issues for worker directors to address are those decisions which, from an employee perspective, are particularly unpalatable, such as redundancies or closures. In such circumstances, worker directors unsurprisingly 'adopt the expected trade union stance and register their opposition' (Kelly and Hourihan 1997: 429). Although this may generally be the case, there have, in fact, been differences between unions and worker directors, most notably in 1999, when the ESB worker director, Joe LaCumbre, challenged both management and unions in the ESB to address the sort of radical change which he argued was required due to the pending deregulation of the electricity market. Sheehan (1999: 14) notes LaCumbre 'warned that some inefficient power stations could face closure if action is not taken and suggested that recent unofficial disputes had damaged the company. This received a frosty response from the chairman of the Group of Unions, Denis Rohan of the ATGWU' (Sheehan 1999: 14). Rohan pointed out:

> Mr LaCumbre's position was not that of his union, the staff or the other worker directors. He said it was 'ludicrous' to suggest that any of the older power stations may be inefficient and could face closure, as public service obligations could allow such concerns to be addressed. And he rejected the notion that the two unofficial disputes in Tarbert and Moneypoint were indicative of wider industrial relations problems (Sheehan 1999: 14).

A 1996 survey carried out by the Worker Directors' Group highlighted concerns among worker directors on privatisation; the confidentiality restrictions and the consequential limits on communicating relevant information to the workforce; a lack of knowledge in technical issues, such as finance; and exclusion from key board sub-committees (quoted in O'Kelly and Compton 2003: 9). The LRC carried out a survey of the worker directors in 2002, which although not published has been quoted by O'Kelly and Compton (2003: 9) as giving the following results:

- ninety-six per cent of the respondents had a positive experience as worker directors and the role gave them greater insights into the operations of their companies;
- seventy-six per cent felt the system had helped to improve industrial relations;
- eighty-three per cent felt their involvement had helped to improve communications;
- sixty-two per cent believed the process has helped the development of partnership; and
- sixty-two per cent said it had helped the change process in their organisations.

While this portrays a generally positive experience by the worker directors, it is notable that they 'were split 50-50 on the attitudes of management to the process, between "only tolerated by management" and "fully accepted by management"' (O'Kelly and Compton 2003: 9).

LEGISLATION FOR SUB-BOARD-LEVEL STRUCTURES IN THE PUBLIC SECTOR

Employer bodies have generally favoured the extension of participation at sub-board level on a voluntary basis and have advocated flexibility in allowing organisations to develop their own participative arrangements. IBEC has had a strong preference for dealing either with a system of collective bargaining or representative participation, but not both. As collective bargaining is established, this has meant that they have been opposed to legislation to extend representative participation in the private sector. They have, however, been supportive of individual companies' efforts, especially in promoting direct task-centred involvement as distinct from power-centred forms of participation. The Institute of Personnel Management[1] has adopted a broadly similar position, suggesting that employee participation may be 'attained through a wide variety of means depending on the characteristics of the organisation and the nature of its activities, structure, technology and history' (Industrial Participation Association (IPA)/Institute of Personnel Management (IPM) 1983).

Kelly and Hourihan (1997) consider the extent to which the legislation providing for worker directors in the Irish state sector has impacted on the development of sub-board participative structures in these organisations. They conclude that the legislation has had a 'catalytic effect' in progressing sub-board-level participation. In evaluating developments in the aftermath of the election of the first worker directors, Kelly and Hourihan (1997: 430) argue that these new directors found themselves 'structurally expressionless'. Over time, however, a variety of sub-structure forms emerged, which Kelly and Hourihan (1997) divide into two groups.

First, they identify organisations with a long tradition of management-employee participation. In these organisations, pre-existing sub-board-level mechanisms helped the new worker directors to 'connect' with trade unions and workers, which helped to promote a 'developing doctrine of participation' within these organisations (Kelly and Hourihan 1997: 431). Two examples illustrate this trend. In B&I the existing works

---

1   Now the Chartered Institute of Personnel and Development (CIPD).

council (established in 1972) became the mechanism for integrating worker directors into that organisation's participatory process:

> Following the first election of worker directors in 1978, the works council structure at B&I was adjusted to accommodate the worker directors. A superior sub-board participation body, known as the Policy Group, included the four worker directors and the other employee and management representatives ... At the Policy Group the worker directors discuss board policy issues and all relevant information is channelled through a network of subcommittees. Thus, the established sub-board mechanism, while retaining an independent purpose, became the primary back-up service and linking structure for the worker directors (Kelly and Hourihan 1997: 431).

The second example occurred in Aer Lingus, where the pre-existing Central Representative Council (CRC) played a similar role. Worker directors attended CRC meetings and its deliberations included consideration of the nature and implications of board-level decisions. The CRC also became the main mechanism for the articulation and representation of employee opinion to the board.

Kelly and Hourihan (1997) also identified a second group of organisations with no pre-existing sub-board participatory mechanisms. In this group two broad trends are evident. First, in some organisations the appointment of worker directors acted as a stimulus for the development of sub-board structures. Examples here include the ESB, Telecom Éireann and Bord Gáis. In the remainder, little progress has been achieved in this area. Coras Iompar Éireann (CIE) is seen as the most prominent example of a situation where little progress has been made in the area of sub-board-level participative structures.

Worker Directors Privatisation and Other Recent Developments

Privatisation has had serious consequences for Irish worker directors, with four companies having been privatised to date: B&I Shipping, Nitrigin Éireann Teoranta (NET), Comhlucht Siuicre Éireann Teoranta (CSE) and Telecom Éireann. B&I immediately abolished the system of worker directors. In the case of NET and CSE, the worker directors were retained on a consultative board, but 'all commercial, operational and policy decisions are taken by a second board' (O'Kelly and Compton 2003: 7). In Telecom Éireann (now Eircom), the government removed all the worker directors in preparation for privatisation. Worker representation is now through the Employee Share Ownership Trust (ESOT), which has three members on Eircom's board.

There was a negative reaction to the removal of the worker directors in Eircom and following union lobbying a review of the operation, effectiveness and coverage of the mechanisms under the Acts was included in the Programme for Prosperity and Fairness. This report has not been published at the time of writing; however, O'Kelly and Compton (2003: 9–10) have viewed draft report and indicate that there are wide divergences in the attitude to worker representatives by those making submissions. They write:

> As would be expected, the unions and employers hold opposing views on how the system has functioned and what changes would be necessary in the future. The unions believe that the statutory rights of employees should be further extended and strengthened, while the employers, on the other hand, oppose any further legislation for any form of employee involvement and any future changes should be within the framework of voluntary partnership agreements.

> Most tellingly, the government sees no argument for amending or repealing the legislation but also is not convinced there is a case for extending it to other State enterprises. The submission states that the Department's preference is for the informal nomination of an employee representative to a board, rather than going through a formal elective process' (O'Kelly and Compton 2003: 10).

The government submission indicates that future privatisations should be dealt with on a case-by-case basis.

O'Kelly and Compton (2003: 10) argue that within the context of developments such as the establishment of the National Centre for Partnership and Performance and the focus which that body has to promote greater employee involvement and enterprise-level partnership, 'the system of worker directors has been, to some extent, sidelined and put under pressure'. They argue:

> In the light of the experiences of worker directors, the future of board-level participation in the policy formation and decision-making process of any SE is not very encouraging. There is an underlying suspicion and opposition to any form of employee representation on boards of companies and the political climate is not as supportive as previously, seeing other forms of employee involvement, such as direct participation, as more relevant.

Works Councils

Works councils have a long-established tradition in many European countries, often enjoying legislative support and exerting considerable influence on the organisations in which they operate. Works councils are particularly associated with initiatives to extend employee participation in Germany and some other European countries since the end of World War II. As noted earlier, they represent a method of providing formal employee representation at workplace level to facilitate consultation and discussion of enterprise-related issues between workers and management. Their role is seen as primarily consultative and representing a broader range of employee opinion than trade unions alone.

This consultative role operates alongside collective bargaining, with works councils providing a mechanism for management-worker interaction on non-distributive issues.

This approach incorporates a division between collective bargaining and works councils. This division was facilitated in countries such as Germany by the fact that collective bargaining on pay and related matters normally took place at industry level, allowing works councils to become involved in 'non-pay' issues at workplace level. Salamon (1998: 380) comments that this

> apparent division allowed for the development of a more co-operative (integrative) relationship between management and employees within the organisation, with the more conflictual (distributive) wage bargaining being conducted between unions and employer associations outside the organisation. However, in Germany, the trend toward decentralisation in collective bargaining has led some organisations to negotiate works agreements with their works councils, with the inevitable potential for change in the relationship between management and the works council.

In assessing the advantages of works councils, Salamon (2000: 402) points to three main strengths.

1. Works councils provide a mechanism through which management and employee representatives can jointly consider issues of mutual concern and thus have the potential to facilitate more co-operative management-employee relations within the enterprise.
2. Works councils are representative of the entire workforce, not just unionised employees, and may be particularly appropriate in non-union firms (see discussion below).
3. Works councils provide a forum through which management and employees can address both strategic and operational issues.

Works councils in Europe are generally underpinned by statutes (such as the 1959 Works Council Act in Holland or the 1972 Works Constitution Act in Germany) which generally prescribe their specific role and nature. In reviewing developments in Europe (particularly Germany), Mills (1989) identifies four types of powers of works councils. First, there is *the right to be informed* on certain issues, such as the current state and future prospects of the enterprise. Second, there is the *right to be consulted* on particular matters, such as restructuring or collective redundancies. Third, there is the *right to independently investigate* certain matters, which generally involves a reciprocal obligation on management to co-operate in such investigation. Finally, there is the *right of co-determination*, which means that decisions cannot be made without the agreement of the works councils. Such issues might include working hours, pay and health and safety.

The rights of works councils will vary somewhat between countries, depending on the specific legislation. We also find considerable variation in national requirements for the establishment of works councils, ranging from the establishment of works councils in organisations employing six or more workers (Germany) to organisations employing 100 or more workers (Belgium). Based on the German experience, Mills (1989) categorises the issues over which works councils may have rights into economic and social issues. Economic issues relate to mergers/acquisitions, transfers, closure, expansion/contraction of operations, relocation, organisation structure, business trends and financial decisions. Social issues include redundancy/lay-offs, pay systems, training and development, pensions, profit distribution, holidays and health, safety and welfare.

European Works Councils

Increasing employee participation over workplace issues represents a 'key tenet' of the Community Charter of Fundamental Social Rights, generally known as the 'Social Charter' (Blyton and Turnbull 1994). As a result of the Social Charter, the EU published a draft directive in 1991 that proposed that companies with over 1,000 workers that operated in two or more member states must establish a *European Works Council* (EWC). The role of EWCs is to supplement national structures to secure information and consultation rights for workers on transnational company matters. In Ireland, this was given effect with the enactment of the Transnational Information and Consultation Act 1996. This Act provides for the establishment of a works council, or employee forum, in companies employing at least 1,000 workers across the EU and at least 150 workers in two EU member states.

In addressing the establishment of works councils, the Act outlines three ways in which 'transnational information and consultation' arrangements can be established (see Kelly and Hourihan 1997).

1. Through pre-directive agreements on information and consultation, concluded before the EU directive came into force (September 1996).
2. After the Act came into force, moves to establish works councils may be initiated by employers or by 100 employees or their representatives. This approach requires the establishment of a 'special negotiating body' of employee representatives. This body then negotiates the establishment of a European employees' forum or works council with management.
3. If agreement is not reached, then employers must establish an EWC in line with the requirements of the 1996 Act. These requirements deal with a number of aspects of the EWC:
   - composition – a minimum of three and a maximum of thirty members, with membership proportional to the number of employees in each state;
   - frequency of EWC meetings (meeting with central management at least once a year); and
   - issues for consideration at such meetings. Issues specified include the state of enterprise, business plans, employment and financial trends, organisation structure and organisation change/new working methods, transfers of production, mergers, cutbacks/closures and redundancy.

The legislation also provides for special meetings with management in 'exceptional circumstances' (such as closure, relocation or collective redundancies). The expenses of EWCs, or their equivalent, are to be borne by management. Employees who are members of works councils are entitled to reasonable paid time off to perform their works council functions and cannot be dismissed for performing their representative duties. The legislation deals with numerous other aspects relating to EWCs, such as voting and arbitration. An important employer concern in relation to works councils relates to the disclosure of commercially sensitive information. On this issue, the Irish legal context provides for the appointment of an independent arbitrator to deal with disputes over whether information being passed on or requested is commercially sensitive. Employees who disclose commercially sensitive information are subject to criminal sanctions.

Waddington and Kerckhofs (2003: 351–2) indicate that as of October 2002, 739 EWCs had been established in 639 multinational companies. The estimated number of companies falling within the scope of the directive was 1,865, giving an 'overall compliance rate of 34.3 per cent' (Waddington and Kerckhofs 2003: 352). In assessing progress, Kelly and Hourihan (1997) highlight a number of developments. They note that the Act's provision for the establishment of a 'European Employee's Forum' is a unique feature of the Irish legislation. They suggest one possible reason for this is that it is a less 'collectivist' term, which may find particular favour in the non-union sector.

An issue of particular interest is the role of trade unions in both the establishment and operation of EWCs. The 1996 Act provides that trade union officials can act as nominees to the 'special negotiating bodies' that may negotiate the establishment and ground rules for works councils. Kelly and Hourihan (1997: 423) point out that since the EU directive did not prescribe who might act as employee representatives on special negotiation bodies, the Irish Act 'must be seen as affording trade unions a central role in the overall process'. The legislation also provides that trade union officials may be appointed as 'expert advisors' to these special negotiating bodies if requested by workers. The Act provides that union officials may sit as expert advisors on special negotiation bodies but only employees of the company may sit on the works council.

Overall, Kelly and Hourihan's (1997) evaluation concludes that the Irish legislation effectively complies with the EU directive. While cautioning that it is too early to reach any firm conclusions on the implications of this legislation, they suggest that despite significant lobbying by trade unions, the general thrust of the legislation and the directive itself is 'widely seen as having better reflected employer priorities'. As a number of prominent multinationals initially indicated a preference for basing their EWC in Ireland, there have been suggestions that the Irish pro-employer approach has encouraged such a response (Kelly and Hourihan 1997). However, Kelly and Hourihan (1997: 425) write that 'the fact that English is the everyday language here must also be seen as a factor explaining any such decisions'.

More recent research indicates that the company's country of origin has a significant effect on satisfaction of members of EWCs with those councils. Reporting on a survey of EWC members with 472 respondents, Waddington and Kerckhofs (2003: 351–2) report that 'an EWC representative from continental Europe is less likely to be satisfied with his/her EWC if it is based in an Anglo Saxon country (and an Anglo Saxon EWC representative is likely to be more satisfied if s/he works for a company based in continental Europe)'.

Dundon (2002: 19) suggests that 'schemes such as works councils may deter inward multinational investment as well as overburden management'. However, he notes that due to EU directives, 'further regulation is likely to be the start of the story rather than the end' (2002: 19). He notes, however, that 'it is unclear how far European Social Policy will go towards reshaping management choice' (Dundon 2002: 22). Waddington (2003: 321) indicates that there is 'considerable variation in the agenda and role of EWCs', with the differences in the content of EWC agreements and the country of origin of MNCs having been found to be a key influence on EWC practice. Waddington (2003: 321) also notes that 'the flexibility inherent in the Directive has allowed Anglo-Saxon managements the opportunity to narrow the agenda and to offer low-quality information and consultation'. This has led to trade union discontent with the directive and campaign for changes. EIRI Associates (2004b: 19) record that in March 2004 the European Commission had a paper on the EWC directive ready for publication. It is understood that the key issues dealt with in the review are union demands to ensure that consultation takes place when policy options are being considered and not just when they are being implemented, and the dropping of the threshold from 1,000 employees to 500.

NON-UNION CONSULTATIVE BODIES

Works councils are not confined to unionised companies or unionised workers. In Chapter 5 the possibility of works committees to be used as a substitution for unions or collective bargaining was noted. Roche and Turner (1998: 72–3) describe this development thus:

> A more direct substitute for union voice is a company-based representation structure such as a staff association or works council sponsored by the company itself. How independent such structures are is often difficult to assess … However, a number of cases have occurred in recent years where a staff association or works council have taken a company to the Labour Court in disputes over pay and conditions indicating some degree of independence from management control. A notable feature of each of the cases is that the development of the representative structure occurred as a measure to block union recognition.

The structure and role of works councils, which are part of a union substitution strategy, is difficult to establish. Indeed, the whole concept of formal employee representation in the non-union sector remains somewhat of a 'black hole', with little available research evidence in the area. One key question, as noted by Roche and Turner (1998), is the extent to which works councils are independent. Some critics suggest that they are creations of management with little capacity for independent action and are in effect merely staff associations (see discussion on the role of staff associations in Chapter 5). The case examples in Table 11.1 from Roche and Turner's (1998) paper illustrate the variation and ambiguity which exists in relation to such councils.

Table 11.1
Enterprise-Level Work/Employee Councils and Associations: Some Examples

Case 1

When Saehan Media in Sligo was originally established in 1991, many of the employees joined SIPTU, but management refused recognition. Strike notice was served at one point, although it was later withdrawn, and the issue was the subject of a Labour Court recommendation in 1993, in which the Court took the traditional pro-recognition stance.

The employee council was formed to deal with negotiations on pay and conditions and took the company to the Court on a pay claim for terms above the PCW (LCR 14866). In 1994 it negotiated one per cent more than the PCW increase. The following year it claimed 14.5 per cent for a one-year agreement, although the company offered 10.5 per cent over three years. At the hearing, the council showed its confidence about criticising the company, when referring to its 'paltry wage policy', which had 'increased in-house pressure from staff for trade union membership and recognition'.

Case 2

In 1996 the works committee at Pat the Baker took the company to the Labour Court on the issue of van drivers' commission payments. The committee has also been involved in a Rights Commissioner's hearing in the past on the same issue of drivers' commission.

The Longford bakery firm's works committee had a significant role to play in the bitter nine-month recognition dispute of 1993 – it was in meetings between SIPTU and the works committee that the basis for a final resolution was worked out, and even though the company met SIPTU directly at the very end of the process, the works committee retains sole negotiating rights. The committee has about a dozen members, one representing each of the six departments in the Granard plant, one for each of the depots around the country and a chairperson. There are no management members on the committee, even from the supervisory staff. The committee meets with management once a month and discusses matters such as changes in procedures, individual grievances and so on.

Case 3

Elan corporation's 'Representative Council' was formed about twelve months ago, a few months before a Labour Court hearing on union recognition. It has twenty-two members, four of which are management representatives. Each department or area across the plant (and a number of R&D staff based in Trinity College) elects the employee members, and the chairperson is elected by this group of eighteen. The chair rotates on a six-month basis, and council members are elected for a term of two years by secret ballot. Fifty per cent of the council members retire each year, so elections will be held each year in the first week of December. Each member represents a constituency of forty to fifty people. A spokesman for Elan said that the council had discussed issues such as career progression, paternity leave, productivity bonuses and a new share option scheme. It has also been used by management as a means of communicating product and business updates. He added that the council was not seen as a body with which to negotiate agreements as much as a way for employees to have 'an input into decisions'.

Source: Roche and Turner (1998: 73–4), based on an article on staff associations in Higgins (1996)

DIRECT FORMS OF INVOLVEMENT AND PARTICIPATION: DEVELOPMENT AND DIFFUSION

Direct employee influence encompasses any initiatives designed to provide for personal involvement by employees, individually or as part of groups, in decisions affecting their jobs and/or immediate work environment. Such employee involvement (EI) may take a variety of forms, such as empowerment, briefing groups and teamworking. As noted earlier, direct involvement is generally instigated by management and is driven by managerial needs and objectives. Salamon (2000: 374) emphasises this point as follows:

> This strategy may be referred to as descending involvement, in so far as management invariably initiates the development for its own purposes (involvement is offered) and, as part of the change, may transfer authority and responsibility from itself to the employees for a limited range of work-related decisions (methods of working, allocation of tasks, maintenance of quality, etc.). However, the content of the process is confined largely to the implementation phase of operational decisions already made by management. This approach is intended to motivate the individual employee directly, to increase job satisfaction and to enhance the employee's sense of identification with the aims, objectives and decisions of the organisation (all of which have been determined by management).

Direct involvement tends to be quite an amorphous concept that may be used in organisations to describe a wide range of activities that vary considerably in their scope and impact on industrial relations practice. Direct involvement initiatives are principally confined to efforts at improving upward and downward communications, with little provision for employee influence on the decision-making process. However, some direct involvement initiatives do impact on the decision-making process and it is this dimension of direct employee involvement that is of most interest from an industrial relations perspective. The terms most widely used to describe this approach are *task involvement* or *task participation*. Geary (1994: 637) notes:

> Task participation is defined as opportunities which management provides at workplace level for consultation with and/or delegation of responsibilities and authority for decision making to its subordinates either as individuals or as groups of employees relating to the immediate work task and/or working conditions.

Thus, task participation involves the devolution of greater control over work-related decisions to employees. Employees are encouraged to become more actively involved in influencing decisions, contributing their opinions and in solving problems at the workplace level. Workers are required to assume greater responsibility for the general organisation and execution of work, while also being expected to concern themselves with broader enterprise objectives, such as improving productivity, controlling costs and general organisational efficiency:

With TP [task participation], then, employees are granted more control over their immediate work situation and are invited to participate in decisions that relate to the organisation of work at the point of production. Thus, workers may influence the manner in which work is allocated, the scheduling of work and when to take breaks. They are also actively encouraged to seek solutions to problems and to make suggestions that will improve the organisation's efficiency (Geary 1998: 3).

Sisson (1994) identifies two key forms of task participation. The first is *consultative participation*, whereby workers are given the opportunity to become involved in decisions and make their views known but are not involved in joint decision making. The second is *delegative participation*, whereby workers are empowered to make key decisions without the need for management approval. Delegative participation means that individual workers assume greater autonomy in their work.

Teamworking

Within the broad parameters of the debate on task participation, the growth of interest in *teamworking* emerges as a major theme with significant implications for industrial relations. The concept of teamworking has its traditional roots in movements designed to improve the quality of working life (see Morley *et al.* 1998). While these early developments met with some support in countries such as the US and Scandinavia, they had little impact in Ireland (Geary 1996, 1999). In Scandinavia these developments had a strong collectivist emphasis to them.

In recent years there has been a significant increase in teamworking, with employers now the key instigators, often in pursuit of organisational change (Beaumont 1995a). This contrasts with earlier initiatives that were worker/trade union driven and were designed to improve the quality of employees' working life. Teamworking is presented as an advanced form of delegative task participation, whereby workers make key decisions such as those concerning the selection of team members, the selection of team leaders, team members, team roles and task allocation (Geary 1994, 1995, 1996, 1999).

Geary (1996) argues that teamworking initiatives in Ireland have been few in number and largely efficiency driven rather than quality of work life/people driven. He further notes that Irish developments have largely involved 'tinkering at the margins' of existing work practices and are confined to a handful of foreign-owned companies. Although teamworking is somewhat more developed in some European countries, even there the developments seem modest, with some of the more significant progress being in the automotive sector, especially in Germany (Roth 1993; Womack *et al.* 1990). In evaluating the European experience of teamworking, Geary (1996) identifies five important issues.

1. **The regulation of teamwork**: The introduction of teamworking in Europe has been achieved more through agreement with employee representatives rather than via

unilateral imposition. This is attributed to the strength of collective employee representation (especially works councils and trade union involvement in industry-wide bargaining) in countries such as Germany and Sweden, which have led the way in its introduction.

2. **The objectives of teamwork**: Achieving a balance between managerial goals of improved efficiency and worker goals of improved quality of work life is a critical issue in facilitating the successful introduction of teamworking. In particular, it appears that trade unions are more willing to engage in teamworking when it is not used solely, or primarily, to achieve managerial aims.

3. **Impact on working lives**: Teamworking has favoured skilled workers and the 'gender divide' has been left relatively untouched, i.e. a major divide remains with limited opportunities for women. However, some specialist categories of staff, such as engineers and accountants, have been transferred to line positions. Employers have not solely relied on persuasion to introduce teamworking, but rather 'more traditional forms' of management control have also been utilised, such as increased employee surveillance and more intense work schedules. Overall, increased skill and effort levels have been a common outcome of teamworking. Geary also identifies positive changes associated with teamworking, such as improved working conditions and job security, which can lead to productive efficiencies and encourage worker acceptance of teamworking.

4. **Teamwork and management support**: The European experience indicates that management commitment and support is an absolute prerequisite for the effective introduction of teamworking. He suggests that if teamworking is introduced as an 'island solution' it has little chance of success and identifies line management 'indifference and resistance' as a key impediment to the effective introduction of teamworking.

5. **Integrating teamworking with HRM**: Geary suggests that the evidence from Europe indicates that teamworking is likely to be more successful where it is integrated with complementary changes in other aspects of personnel/HR policy. In particular, a number of key policy changes are identified:
   * shift from individual-based pay to team-based pay;
   * significant investment in training and development; and
   * maintenance of job security commitments.

TASK PARTICIPATION IN PRACTICE

The most important source of information on the extent and nature of the diffusion of task participation is the survey conducted by the European Foundation for the Improvement of Living and Working Conditions (EFILWC) in ten EU member states (see EFILWC 1997). Known as the EPOC (employee direct participation in organisational change) project, this study examined both the incidence of task participation and the nature of such participation. In particular it examined the scope and extent of autonomy afforded to employees. In Ireland the EPOC study surveyed a sample of Irish companies, excluding those with less than twenty-five employees. The study achieved a response rate of nearly thirty-nine per cent (382 organisations), which represented the highest response rate among all the countries involved in the study (EFIWLC 1997; also see Geary 1998, 1999).

Looking first at the diffusion of consultative participation, the EPOC study found that what Geary (1998: 12) labels 'temporary groups', particularly project groups or task forces, were found in thirty-six per cent of firms, while 'permanent groups', such as quality circles, were present in twenty-eight per cent of firms. Turning to delegative participation, the EPOC study found that team-based structures were present in forty-two per cent of respondent firms. Based on these findings, it was estimated that task participation was present in around one-third of Irish workplaces. Newly established firms were more likely to use task participation than their longer-established counterparts.

In addition to examining the incidence of task participation, the EPOC study considered the nature and intensity of such participation, particularly delegative participation (incorporating teamworking). The EPOC study utilised two measures in this regard. First, the scope of teamworking, which measured the extent of employees' rights to solely make decisions in relation to their work. Second, the extent of autonomy afforded to employees to select team members and to decide on which issues the team should tackle. The EPOC findings indicate that just seventeen per cent of Irish firms that used teamworking were characterised by a high-level team or group delegation.

In a further and more sophisticated attempt to identify the depth and scope of task participation, the EPOC study distinguished between the Japanese 'Toyota' model and the Scandinavian 'Volvo' model of teamworking and then considered which was the most prevalent model among respondent organisations. In this conceptualisation, the 'Toyota', or lean production, model is seen as one that places strict limits on team autonomy and where employee skills are largely of a generalist or routine kind. The 'Volvo' model is seen as being present where teams and team members possess greater levels of autonomy, where teams are comprised of workers with a variety of skill groupings and where there is considerable emphasis on training and development (Fröhlich and Pekruhl 1996; Geary 1998, 1999). The EPOC findings suggest that where teamworking is used, it most closely approximates to the 'Toyota' model, with less than one per cent of Irish firms utilising the 'Volvo' model. These findings suggest that while task participation is reasonably well diffused in Ireland, most organisations predominantly rely on traditional forms of work organisation within the team structures. Of particular note is the fact that the uptake of modes of work organisation, which devolve a high level of autonomy to workers and work teams, is very low. It thus appears that advanced forms of task participation are not common in Ireland.

A critical concern for organisations is how they can positively facilitate change. Geary's analysis identifies the effective 'managing of managers' as the key to successful teamworking (Geary 1994, 1995, 1999; Roche and Geary 2002). He argues that employers must move beyond their traditional concern of 'getting the goods out the door and reducing costs'. Rather, he suggests that there is a need to reconcile the management of managers with the objectives of employee involvement. In particular, he argues that the reward and appraisal system for managers should reward those managers who facilitate effective teamworking. Finally, it should be noted that if there is increased employee involvement and teamworking, it will not necessarily mean an end to 'adversarial' collective bargaining. As several commentators have noted, issues such as pay, workplace change and employment conditions may still be channelled through traditional collective bargaining.

FINANCIAL PARTICIPATION

'Financial participation' is a generic term to describe mechanisms through which employees can gain some form of financial or equity share in their organisations through various profit-sharing, share-ownership or similar schemes. Financial participation is often seen as developing a sense of ownership among workers by giving them a stake in their organisation while also integrating employees more fully into the market economy. Indeed, increasing employee loyalty, commitment and morale through the closer identification of employee interests with those of the organisation is a key objective of many schemes. However, financial participation of itself will not normally allow for any significant increase in employee influence, as employees will generally represent a minority of the shareholders. Organisations such as the John Lewis Partnership in the UK and Donnelly Mirrors in Ireland have long been known for their policy of sharing profits with employees, and other companies now offer share options or some other form of profit-sharing, such as Irish Cement, Dell and Abbott Laboratories.

Salamon (2000) identifies two major reasons for the developing interest in financial participation. First is an equity argument that workers should receive a share of the profits or other positive outcomes which they have helped to create. Second, such schemes encourage employee co-operation with management strategies to improve performance. Two broad forms of financial participation exist: the first is gain sharing or profit sharing and the second is employee share ownership.

Gain-sharing or *profit-sharing* arrangements essentially reward employees for improvements in organisation performance. While profit sharing is self-explanatory, gain sharing refers to arrangements where payments to workers are contingent on some measure of improvement in organisation performance other than profits. Commonly used measures are changes in levels of output or value added. However, gain-sharing arrangements may also be based on less obvious measures of performance, such as lower accident rates or scrap/rework levels. Gain-sharing arrangements are commonly linked to management attempts to instigate particular organisational change initiatives, often embracing attempts to increase employee involvement and commitment. We can identify a number of general objectives underlying such schemes (see Armstrong and Murliss 1994):

- to encourage all employees to identify themselves more closely with the company by developing a common concern for its progress;
- to stimulate a greater interest among employees in the affairs of the company as a whole;

- to encourage better co-operation between management and employees;
- to recognise that employees of the company have a moral right to share in the profits they helped to produce;
- to demonstrate in practical terms the goodwill of the company to its employees; and
- to reward success in businesses where profitability is cyclical.

Such schemes have become particularly popular in the UK and the US and have been linked to corporate successes using such criteria as market share, profitability and quality (see Hourihan 1995; Gunnigle *et al.* 2002a).

The second form of financial participation is an *employee share ownership plan* (ESOP). ESOPs involve the allocation of a proportion of company shares to employees according to some agreed formula. In Ireland, the utilisation of employee share ownership has traditionally been quite low (Long 1988; Gunnigle *et al.* 2002). However, some growth was initially stimulated by the Finance Acts of 1982–1984, which provided a number of incentives to organisations and employees with respect to ESOPs. Subsequent government measures reduced the tax incentive value of such schemes and this inhibited the development of share ownership in Ireland. However, the 1995 budget raised the tax exemption limit for buying company shares from €2,540 to €12,698. Hourihan (1995) noted an early response in the substantial share allocation initiatives by Guinness Ireland and Intel.

However, despite some growth in ESOPs in recent years, the overall scale remains quite modest. Table 11.2 indicates that employee share ownership is confined to a relatively small number of organisations. Furthermore, it is most common at executive levels within these organisations. The CUL survey also found that American and British companies were more likely to adopt share ownership schemes for all grades in the organisation than their Irish or other European-owned counterparts (Gunnigle *et al.* 1997d).

Table 11.2
Percentage of Organisations with Employee Share Options and Profit Sharing

	Management			Professional/ Technical			Clerical			Manual		
	1992	1995	1999	1992	1995	1999	1992	1995	1999	1992	1995	1999
Share options	22.8	23.0	21.5	13.6	13.8	13.9	9.2	11.5	11.2	8.8	9.6	9.0
Profit sharing	15.8	19.2	17.9	12.3	13.4	13.9	10.5	12.6	12.1	10.1	10.0	10.5

Source: Cranfield-University of Limerick Surveys (1992, 1995, 1999)

The CUL findings on the incidence of profit-sharing arrangements are broadly similar. Such arrangements are present in only a minority of organisations, with approximately eighteen per cent of managerial employees, fourteen per cent of both professional/technical, twelve per cent of clerical employees and 10.5 per cent of manual workers covered by such schemes. Unionisation would seem to be negatively associated with the presence of a profit-sharing scheme. A higher percentage of non-union firms (for all levels in the hierarchy) report the implementation of such a scheme, but the difference decreases as one descends the organisational hierarchy. As was the case with share option schemes, foreign-owned organisations were more likely to have profit-sharing arrangements.

In 1998 trade unions and management at Eircom (then Telecom Éireann), together with government representatives, established a major ESOP that provided for a 14.9 per cent employee shareholding linked to union/employee approval of a partnership initiative involving changes in work practices, a voluntary severance plan and other changes in industrial relations:

> Telecom Éireann requires major price reductions and consequential cost adjustments in order to meet the challenges posed by powerful international competitors and market deregulation. The union coalition (which involves the five unions representing Telecom Éireann staff) is prepared to participate actively in the speedy transformation of the company in return for a 14.9 per cent employee shareholding with a real voice for the staff in the future of Telecom Éireann (C. Scanlon, general secretary, CWU – see Sheehan 1998e: 9).

MANAGEMENT–EMPLOYEE COMMUNICATIONS

An important theme in the contemporary literature on industrial relations is the suggestion that employers have shifted the focus of their communications with employees away from representative fora (especially trade unions) and towards direct communications with individual employees (for example, see Salamon 1998; Bacon and Storey 1993). Salamon (2000: 382) suggests that 'since the early 1980s there has been a shift in the emphasis of organisational communication away from "disclosure" of information to *trade unions* in support of the collective bargaining process, and towards "dissemination" of information to *employees* in order to secure their greater involvement in and identification with the organisation's interests and objectives'. This shift is viewed by some as an attempt by management to adopt a more individualist employee relations orientation, which attempts to bypass or marginalise trade unions (Kochan *et al.* 1986; Blyton and Turnbull 1994; Gunnigle *et al.* 1997b).

Differences in organisational approaches to communications tend to focus on the nature and content of management-employee communications and the range of mechanisms used to facilitate such communications. The CUL surveys, carried out in 1992, 1995 and 1999, focused on two key aspects of the debate on management-employee communications: the fora used by management in communicating with employees and the type of information communicated to employees using such fora (see Gunnigle *et al.* 1997c).

Communications Fora

A particular area of interest is the extent to which the relative emphasis is on collectivist as against individualist fora (McLoughlin and Gourlay 1992; Blyton and Turnbull 1994). Summary findings from the CUL surveys on the pattern of utilisation of three communications modes are presented in Table 11.3. These findings indicate a substantial increase in direct written and verbal communication with employees. In relation to the use of representative staff bodies, there was some overall increase. However, the main picture is one of relative stability, with the great majority of respondent organisations reporting no change in the utilisation of representative staff bodies for communications. There is emphatic evidence of increased levels of utilisation of direct communications with employees. Surprisingly, in general this does not appear to be occurring at the expense of traditional collective lines of communication through representative bodies (generally trade unions). While larger organisations were more likely to increase all mechanisms, private sector companies were more likely to have increased direct communications when compared with their public sector counterparts (Gunnigle *et al.* 1997b). Furthermore, the increase in direct communication mechanisms appears to be occurring at a faster pace among the unionised private sector organisations.

In reviewing the content of management-employee communications, the CUL study explored the extent to which senior management communicated formally with employees on business strategy and financial performance (see Table 11.4). With respect to communications on business strategy, the findings indicate a high level of communications on strategy with management and professional/technical grades but a much lower level of communications with clerical and manual grades. In the 1999 survey, just over a quarter (twenty-seven per cent) of organisations reported that they communicate on strategy with manual grades. A similar picture emerges when one looks at the pattern of communications on financial performance. Again one finds significantly lower levels of communications on financial issues with clerical and manual grades. These figures are quite low given that, as is seen above, an apparent general trend of organisations increasing direct communications with their workforce exists. It seems that such direct communications are predominantly concerned with operational matters and not strategic or broader financial issues (see Gunnigle *et al.* 1997c).

Table 11.3

Changes in Management-Employee Communications

	Increased			Same			Decreased		
	1992	1995	1999	1992	1995	1999	1992	1995	1999
Rep. staff bodies	16%	13%	19%	48%	51%	38%	12%	7%	7%
Verbal direct	55%	51%	56%	34%	42%	42%	1%	2%	1%
Written direct	39%	46%	49%	42%	43%	45%	4%	1%	3%

Source: Cranfield-University of Limerick Surveys (1992, 1995, 1999)

Table 11.4

Formal Communications on Business Strategy and Financial Performance

Employee Category	Formal Communications On:					
	Strategy			Financial Performance		
	1992	1995	1999	1992	1995	1999
Management	94%	95%	92%	93%	94%	90%
Prof/Tech	66%	72%	59%	60%	64%	59%
Clerical	42%	50%	39%	41%	50%	42%
Manual	39%	38%	27%	36%	39%	30%

Source: Cranfield-University of Limerick Study (1997)

In evaluating these developments we can posit two broad factors which underpin management attempts to increase the extent and scope of management-employee communications. First, we can point to the perceived need to inform employees of developments in relation to the business and its environment. Second, increased and better communications are seen as an important means of eliciting employee support for organisation change initiatives. Our earlier evidence indicates that many organisations are placing a greater emphasis on direct communications with employees.

In a study of greenfield sites, Gunnigle (1995a) found a pronounced management focus on more direct communications with individual employees. This study found that a significant proportion of non-union firms (generally larger US-owned firms in high-technology sectors) emphasised extensive management-employee communications. This was undertaken as a means of developing a more individualist approach to employee relations and maintaining non-union status. Much of this communication focused on keeping employees informed of the company's product market performance. Such information was used to emphasise issues such as market volatility, intensity of competition and requirements for high-quality and low-cost production/service. In effect, the provision of such information was used to inform employees on 'market realities' as perceived by management. Direct communications was also seen as a means of increasing employees' sense of ownership and involvement in the organisation, which, it was hoped, would contribute to employee support for any management change initiatives.

Gunnigle's (1995a) findings suggest that, at least in greenfield firms, the motive for increased communications derives more from a commercial imperative than from any widespread desire to increase employee involvement. Thus, it appears that communications on business strategy and financial information were often used to condition employee attitudes and expectations by, for example, emphasising the need to maintain flexibility, to improve productivity and, more generally, to accept 'market imperatives' (see examples in Table 11.5).

> **Table 11.5**
> *Management-Employee Communications in Greenfield Sites*
>
> 'We place a heavy emphasis on communications but with a purpose: we emphasise volatility of the business sector and need to keep costs low. The absolute need for complete flexibility is reinforced by the use of temporary workers. At quality meetings I go through quarterly results with all employees. There is a monthly plant meeting between myself and all staff and I also meet regularly with groups of four to five employees. Another element is what we call "fireside chats": here the personnel manager takes around fourteen people into a "conference" to talk generally about any issue over coffee. All of these have a purpose: it keeps people in tune with reality and on their toes' (chief executive: data processing equipment).
>
> 'Strong communications is a key device in seeking to avoid union recognition. We are very keen to communicate on business strategy – it keeps employees in the picture. The MD gives regular communication briefings in small groups and the (US) president gets together with all employees at least once a year' (financial controller: electrical and instrument engineering).
>
> *Source:* Gunnigle (1995a: 206)

HIGH-PERFORMANCE WORK SYSTEMS, DIRECT INVOLVEMENT AND THE QUALITY OF WORK LIFE

The concept of high-performance work systems (HPWS) is closely associated with the new high-tech companies of the 1980s and especially those that located at greenfield sites. The essence of HPWS appears to lie in efforts to adopt a culture of continuous improvement and innovation at all levels in the organisation. This is to be achieved by a range of work organisation and human resource practices to sustain and develop this culture, particularly teamworking, quality consciousness and flexibility. It is argued that a specific characteristic of HPWS is a reliance on high levels of direct employee involvement in decision making (Lawler 1978, 1982).

In evaluating the impact of HPWS, an issue of noteworthy significance is their effect on employees' work experience. It is particularly important to address the coupling of initiatives for direct employee involvement with the application of management techniques designed to improve quality and productivity, especially just in time (JIT) and statistical process control (SPC) systems. The introduction of these initiatives is generally rooted in the premise that increased direct employee involvement and autonomy is *consistent* with the use of JIT, SPC or related techniques. Indeed, the argument that direct employee involvement/autonomy complements the use of SPC and JIT is often a key selling point in encouraging employees (and trade unions where these exist) to co-operate in the introduction of such approaches.

However, such a complementary relationship may not necessarily exist. In her incisive review of the implications of techniques such as JIT and SPC for employees, Klein (1989: 60) argues that such changes in production systems do not necessarily make for a more empowered workforce:

> In Japan ... where JIT and SPC have been used most comprehensively, employees are routinely organised into teams, but their involvement in workplace reform is

typically restricted to suggestions for process improvement through structured quality control circles or *kaizen* groups. Individual Japanese workers have unprecedented responsibility. Yet it is hard to think of them exercising genuine autonomy, that is, in the sense of independent self-management.

Using examples from both the US and Japan, Klein argues that increased pressures and constraints on workers are a common by-product of such manufacturing reforms. While allowing for greater employee involvement and autonomy than traditional assembly line systems, they are not conducive to the high levels of employee empowerment often thought to accompany a shift towards high-performance work systems. She writes:

> True, under JIT and SPC, employees become more self-managing than in a command and control factory. They investigate process improvements and monitor quality themselves; they consequently enjoy immediate, impartial feedback regarding their own performance ... They also gain a better understanding of all elements of the manufacturing process. On the other hand, the reform process that ushers in JIT and SPC is meant to *eliminate all variations within production* and therefore requires strict adherence to rigid methods and procedures. Within JIT, workers must meet set cycle times; with SPC, they must follow prescribed problem-solving methods. In their pure forms, then, JIT and SPC can turn workers into extensions of a system no less demanding than a busy assembly line. These systems can be very demanding on employees (Klein 1989: 61).

This analysis challenges the thesis that high-performance work systems necessarily contribute to an improved work experience for employees. In particular, Klein points to important aspects of the work experience which may regress or be lost as a result of reforms using SPC and JIT, namely:

- *individual autonomy* may be reduced due to the elimination of inventories under JIT, resulting in less slack or idle time which in turn limits the opportunity for workers to discuss issues, evaluate changes and make suggestions;
- *team autonomy* may be reduced because of the greater interdependency between groups due to the absence of buffer inventories, with resulting work pressures reducing the time available to consider broader changes in the work system; and
- *ability to influence work methods* may be reduced because SPC sets strict guidelines for working methods and procedures.

However, this analysis does not necessarily mean that high-performance work systems incorporating JIT and SPC cannot positively impact on workers' job experience. Rather, it points to the fact that these techniques and systems may be applied in differing ways. Thus, the issue of *management choice* is important. Equally important can be the role of workers and trade unions in influencing management choice as to the nature of deployment of these new systems. It is plausible to argue that unfettered management prerogative in introducing so-called high-performance work systems can contribute to a regression in employment conditions and employees' work experience. Klein (1989) argues that the key to improving employee involvement and autonomy when instigating high-performance work systems is to provide for *greater collaboration between teams* and to allow *greater opportunity for teams and individuals to propose and evaluate suggestions* for changes in the work process and in the conduct of different jobs. In other words, the application of new work systems is best facilitated through some combination of direct and indirect forms of employee involvement and participation.

This echoes Geary's analysis based on the European collectivist experience. In such settings, he suggests that a critical issue in teamworking is the development of strategies for dealing with employee representatives/trade unions (Geary 1994, 1996, 1999). Employers commonly object to the involvement of trade unions in work reorganisation and teamworking on the grounds that it is too time consuming and slows the process of organisational change. However, Geary points to the off-setting benefits of union involvement based on the European experience. First, trade unions/employee representatives have expertise that can benefit the process. Second, they can legitimise the 'necessity of proposed change' to their membership. An additional benefit is that such involvement forces management to integrate personnel/industrial relations considerations more centrally than might otherwise be the case.

Geary raises the critical question of how to involve employee representatives/trade unions in the introduction of work reorganisation initiatives such as teamworking. Since in the Irish and British context such changes are normally discussed in the traditional collective bargaining arena, he questions whether new institutional arrangements need to be developed. In many of the European countries that have experimented with teamwork, there is an institutional separation between collective bargaining and the workplace. In collective bargaining issues are frequently the remit of union-employer bargaining at industry level while working arrangements tend to be dealt with through representative structures, such as works councils in Germany and enterprise committees (*Comité d'enterprise*) in France. Turning specifically to the Irish context Geary poses a series of questions on this dilemma:

- Can the introduction of teamworking be productively discussed through traditional 'adversarial' collective bargaining arrangements?
- Is there a need for works council-type arrangements?
- Are Irish managers ready for this type of joint regulation?
- Is it better if the structures used to inform employees are employee based and not strictly union based?

Similar considerations can apply to the introduction of workplace change generally and in some instances temporary structures have been evolved to separate distributive industrial relations issues from the problem-solving phase. In the ESB cost and competitiveness review (CCR), a special tripartite body benchmarked the ESB against other energy producers internationally, and although this process was controversial it laid the groundwork for the eventual CCR agreement (Hastings 2003: 50; see also Chapter 12).

Partnership and Other Developments in Collective Workplace Industrial Relations

INTRODUCTION

Negotiation theory draws our attention to a different form of bargaining, with the main distinction made between distributive and integrative negotiations. The most significant development in Irish industrial relations in recent years has been the sequence of social partnership agreements between trade unions, employers and government at national level (see O'Donnell and O'Reardon 1996; Roche 1997b; Teague 1995; Turner 2002). It is arguable that these agreements represent a move towards the integrative end of the negotiation spectrum at national level (see Chapter 13). While these agreements were well established by the mid-1990s, there was a failure to replicate the consensus/partnership model at workplace level. This led to an emergent criticism of a failure to extend the partnership approach below national-level interactions.

Roche (1995) observed that the Irish model of social partnership is somewhat narrow, involving only the top levels of the union and employer bodies, and has not significantly impacted on developments in enterprise-level industrial relations. He described the Irish model as 'truncated' social partnership, inferring that employer-union relations at enterprise level continued to be characterised by adversarialism despite the existence of national-level partnership (Roche 1995: 28).

This gap came to be identified as an important issue, particularly for the trade unions, with ICTU arguing that enterprise-level partnership had the capacity to contribute to improvements in both industrial relations and business performance. IBEC has emphasised the importance of the competitiveness requirement in partnership agreements: 'partnership has to operate in the context of competitive requirements and has to facilitate those requirements' (IBEC 1999: vii). The national agreement Partnership 2000, signed in 1997, provided for the development of partnership at enterprise level and tied an option for a two per cent profit-sharing increase to such a development. Enterprise-level partnership has also been of interest to other bodies and organisations, notably the European Commission, and in Ireland, FORFÁS and NESC (see Gunnigle 1998a; Sheehan 2002). In 1997 the European Commission published a green paper, Partnership for a New Organisation of Work, which argued that improvements in competitiveness and employment could be stimulated through 'a better organisation of work at the workplace, based on high skills, high trust and high quality' (European Commission, 1997: 5). It goes on to invite the social partners to 'build a partnership for the development of a new framework for the modernisation of work'.

In addition to these explicit partnership developments, a number of collective agreements were negotiated during the late 1980s and the 1990s that were designed to protect employment and promote competitiveness. Although these are not necessarily called partnership agreements, they fall partly within a partnership-type framework. At workplace level, these agreements mirror the *social pacts* that emerged in a number of EU member states in the 1990s (see Chapter 9). Such agreements were termed '*employment pacts*' or pacts for employment and competitiveness by the European Foundation for the Improvement of Living and Working Conditions (Freyssinet *et al.* 1999). The term 'employment pacts' has not been used to any great extent in Ireland, but a small number of agreements equating to the term are readily identifiable. Such progress can be seen as an intermediate development between employee participation and collective bargaining, as they incorporate elements of both. In the case of employment pacts, negotiation is central but access to detailed company financial information and involvement in collaborative decision making complement this. The latter feature can sometimes be limited, but on other occasions has been found to be extensive (see Wallace 1999; Hastings 2003). This chapter sets out to explore the development and extent of these workplace developments in industrial relations.

PRESSURE FOR COLLABORATION

A key question is why pressure for various forms of enterprise-level partnerships emerged at this time in both Irish and European industrial history. In general, it is possible to suggest a number of stimuli. First, the decline in trade union penetration has prompted the union movement to seek mechanisms to increase their legitimacy and representativeness at both enterprise and national level (Beaumont 1995a; Sheehan 2002; Sparrow and Hiltrop 1994; Sparrow 2002). Second, we have the increasingly competitive environment facing organisations. This has placed pressure on organisations to reconfigure their industrial relations policies to facilitate improved performance and productivity. Third, companies have promoted competition between branches and plants in differing countries as a corporate policy.

Finally, there is the pressure of industrial restructuring. This arises from at least two sources: technological change, involving the rundown of older industries and social dumping, involving the relocation of processes and even services (such as computer technological support) to low-cost locations. In addressing these challenges workers and management have on occasion been thrown together to jointly try to stave off threats by increasing efficiency and containing or reducing labour costs. One way for unions to respond to these challenges is to seek to have an input in these changes, rather than opposing them; in other words, to engage in collaborative bargaining. The same holds for management – they can attempt to force through unilateral change but this may be resisted and be destructive. It can also lead to the parties having to subsequently engage in negotiations, with the risk that the climate for such negotiations is damaged.

THE CENTRALISED AGREEMENTS AND WORKPLACE PARTNERSHIP

Workplace partnership is a recent addition to Irish industrial relations. The Programme for Economic and Social Progress (PESP) focused on the traditional need to promote worker *participation*, not *partnership*. It claimed that 'it is important that the consensus at national level is translated into industrial relations practices and procedures at company level' (PESP 1991). The development of these, however, was left to a voluntary process to involve discussions under the aegis of the Employer Labour Conference, which did not lead to any institutional developments.

By the time the Programme for Competitiveness and Work (PCW) was agreed in 1994, there was a greater explicit focus on the issues of employment and competitiveness. The PCW emphasised that 'the central focus of this Programme is on the growth of employment and the competitiveness on which it must rest' (PCW 1994: 57). The agreement went on to add that 'at the level of the industry and the enterprise the pursuit of competitiveness must also address the implications of the changed environment for business and for employment' (PCW 1994: 58). As part of the PCW process, a Joint Declaration was issued by IBEC and the ICTU that recognised the importance of increased employee involvement in addition to greater competitiveness for the effective development of the enterprise, increased job satisfaction, closer identification of employees with the organisation and a safe and healthy work environment. Despite this strong endorsement, there were few concrete proposals within PCW for advancing such involvement beyond encouragement and a commitment by the social partners to support the use of the Irish Productivity Centre as 'a provider of information, expert assistance and advice and support for pilot initiatives' (PCW 1994: 59).

Partnership 2000

The union movement placed the development of workplace-level partnership to the fore in the next agreement, Partnership 2000, which contains the following provision: 'An objective of this Partnership is to extend partnership arrangements at enterprise level' (Partnership 2000 1997). It defined partnership as:

> an active relationship based on recognition of a common interest to secure the competitiveness, viability and prosperity of the enterprise. It involves a continuing commitment by employees to improvements in quality and efficiency; and the acceptance by employers of employees as stake holders with rights and interests to be considered in the context of major decisions affecting their employment (Partnership 2000 1997: 52).

It went on to suggest that the key to providing this encouragement lies in understanding that successful workplace innovation occurs 'in ways which support competitive strategy in an ever-changing market environment ... and crisis adjustment' (Partnership 2000 1997: 51). It identified that 'topics appropriate for discussion at enterprise level may include the following':

- employee involvement for competitiveness (opportunities for employees to be involved in and contribute to meeting the challenge of global competition);
- training, personal development and support;

- equality of opportunities;
- representational arrangements;
- forms of financial involvement;
- occupational health and safety and the work environment;
- composition of the workforce;
- co-operation with change, including new forms of work organisation; and
- adaptability, flexibility and innovation (Partnership 2000 1997: 53).

In order to support these developments, a National Centre for Partnership, based in the Department of An Taoiseach, was established.

Programme for Prosperity and Fairness (PPF)

The PPF specified the key objectives for the development of partnership at the level of the enterprise as being:

- to enhance organisational capability to contribute to competitive advantage;
- to improve the environment for work in tandem with the achievement of production and service excellence; and
- to build on existing workplace relationships through the establishment or deepening of the partnership process at enterprise level (PPF 2000: 14).

IBEC and ICTU committed themselves 'to work together to develop guidelines to assist companies in embarking on and successfully putting in place partnership arrangements', including 'financial participation measures' (PPF 2000: 15–16). The agreement enhanced the role of the National Centre for Partnership, which was renamed the National Centre for Partnership and Performance (NCPP). The agreement specified that the centre 'will be located within the Office for National Economic and Social Development alongside NESC and NESF' (PPF 2000: 132). The PPF agreement specified that:

> the National Centre for Partnership has an important role to play in this process. Maintaining our competitive strength and an environment conducive to innovation requires a new focus on improving the capability of enterprises, whether public or private. This leads to a greater emphasis on the quality of jobs and on performance. In this regard, the growing importance of new forms of work organisation, adaptation to change and lifelong learning need to be recognised (PPF 2000: 132).

The PPF (2000: 132) requires the Centre to 'work with IBEC and ICTU in supporting the deepening of partnership, including:

- deliberation, consensus-building and dissemination;
- monitoring;
- research and analysis; and
- training and facilitation'.

Sustaining Progress

Sustaining Progress reaffirmed the 'commitments under previous national agreements' and declared 'that the National Centre for Partnership and Performance will play an increasing role in supporting this process' (Sustaining Progress 2003: 77). It was to do this in conjunction with ICTU and IBEC, with the following activities being specified:

- the establishment of a Forum on the Workplace of the Future to foster in-depth discussion of how workplaces can best adapt to competitive pressures, improve the delivery of services and respond to the changing needs and preferences of employees;
- a joint action project with FÁS to promote a learning culture in Irish organisations;
- the development and dissemination of case studies of best practice in the area of partnership and performance;
- the development of a national training strategy to assist those involved in organisational change through partnership;
- the preparation of guidelines on the different forms of employee financial involvement;
- a project aimed at improving practices and procedures in relation to information, consultation and participation rights in the context of the Information and Consultation Directive; and
- the promotion of existing joint partnership training materials as developed with IBEC and ICTU (Sustaining Progress 2003: 77–8).

The above provisions in the centralised agreements represent a concerted attempt to promote partnership. However, none of the agreements provided for any legislative requirement for partnership, which differs from countries where employee participation has taken root. As such, there is a question as to whether a system of partnership can be brought about through voluntary [centralised] agreements, or whether legislation is required.

THE ESSENCE OF PARTNERSHIP-BASED INDUSTRIAL RELATIONS ARRANGEMENTS

We noted earlier that the proponents of partnership often point to deficiencies in the adversarial industrial relations model, in particular the apparent dominance of distributive bargaining on short-term issues and its emphasis on dividing limited resources. It is suggested that this approach leads the parties to develop adversarial positions, believing that any gains can only be made by inflicting losses on the other party (Fisher and Ury 1997). Indeed, distributive bargaining reflects the very essence of the traditional pluralist-adversarial model: claims, offers, bluffs, threats, compromise, movement, agreement or conflict.

In contrast, advocates of partnership at enterprise level posit that integrative/collaborative approaches represent a more attractive alternative, with their emphasis on exploring common ground and seeking solutions of mutual benefit for both employers and workers (Kochan and Osterman 1994; Roche and Kochan 1996).

It is further argued that this new model allows both sides to break out of the traditional adversarial relationship through the adoption of a partnership model based on 'mutual gains' principles, as follows:

- employers recognise and facilitate worker and trade union involvement in strategic decision making;
- workers/trade unions commit themselves actively to productivity improvements;
- the gains of productivity improvements are shared between employers and workers; and
- productivity improvements do not result in redundancies, but rather employers actively seek new markets to keep workers gainfully employed.

The essence of this partnership thesis is that, *with* management, workers and trade unions actively pursue solutions to business problems and appropriate work reorganisation in return for greater involvement in business decisions and in the process of work reorganisation (Gunnigle 1998a). It is characterised by a strong emphasis on consensual decision making using integrative rather than distributive approaches in management-union interactions and negotiations.

While this model, based on voluntary employer-union interaction, is the most widely understood form of enterprise partnership, it is not the only one. Cutcher-Gershenfeld and Verma (1994) identified three modes of shared decision making at enterprise level:

- non-union high commitment system;
- legislated works councils; and
- voluntary union-management joint governance.

The non-union high commitment approach has its roots in the US and places the primary focus on facilitating direct employee involvement in operational decision making at workplace level. In contrast, we have seen earlier that works councils normally reflect a legislated form of representative participation. In this system elected worker representatives have a right to shared decision making in prescribed areas of work organisation. Voluntary union-management self-governance arrangements equate to management-union partnership-based industrial relations arrangements. In analysing the characteristics of partnership-based industrial relations arrangements at enterprise level, Gunnigle (1998a) identifies three core dimensions:

- strategic impact;
- role of trade unions; and
- institutional sophistication.

Strategic impact: Employee and/or trade union involvement in the strategic decision-making process is probably the key element that characterises a highly developed 'strategic partnership' approach within organisations. The focus on high-level strategic decisions is important and serves to differentiate 'strategic partnerships' from lower-level workplace partnerships that focus on operational-level decisions, such as those related to work organisation or quality. That is not to say that operational workplace issues cannot be a focus of strategic partnership arrangements, but rather to indicate that the 'strategic' element refers to partnership in making long-term strategic decisions that impact on the future nature and direction of the enterprise as a whole. As McKersie (2002: 111) notes, a critical feature of strategic partnership is union or employee involvement in key corporate decisions. He writes that 'a key feature of partnerships is that the trade union has an opportunity to challenge or confront management before a decision is made' (McKersie 2002: 111).

Role of trade unions: Given the critical role played by the Irish trade union movement in the six centralised agreements negotiated since 1987, the debate on partnership generally sees trade unions as integral to the development of enterprise partnerships. They promote the idea and provide the institutional stimulus for the introduction of partnership agreements. However, much of Ireland's industrial development has been led by foreign-owned firms, which are predominantly non-union. In the Irish non-union sector there are many organisations that claim to have well-developed management-employee partnerships. However, there is an inherent difficulty involved in establishing the existence and nature of such partnerships, since most accounts are based solely on a managerial perspective. As such, these cases present difficulties in evaluating the nature and extent of partnership.

Institutional sophistication: This dimension refers to the extent to which there are well-developed institutional arrangements to facilitate a partnership approach at organisation and workplace level. The non-union high commitment system relies primarily on direct employee involvement through teamworking and problem-solving groups – it does not normally involve formal representative structures (Cutcher-Gershenfeld and Verma 1994). However, in high-level partnership, which provides for employee involvement in decision making, one would expect to find formal structures. In unionised firms these structures normally exist in addition to established collective bargaining arrangements. For strategic partnership one would expect to see provisions for union or worker representation at board level. An extract from a joint union/employer task force paper (1993) between Communications, Energy and Paper (CEP) Union and Bell (Canada) illustrates this point.

> [Union-management partnerships need to] involve, through the corporate steering committee and other exchanges of information, appropriate union executives in planning, strategy, training, and policy formulation in areas such as quality, human resources planning, new technology, major product development and market changes, and strategic alliances with other telecommunications companies. Another key distinction is that *these partnerships are at the corporate level where key business decisions are made that affect the viability of the enterprise.*

To support well-developed partnership arrangements at the operational level, one might also expect to see the development of management-employee/union institutions to facilitate joint decision making. However, partnership arrangements, particularly those of an operational nature, need not necessarily be underpinned by institutional arrangements.

One can point to arrangements for periodic management-employee briefings where the focus is on information sharing and consultation. Such approaches do not normally provide for joint decision making. Management informs employees, discusses issues, considers employee or union opinion but retains prerogative in decision making.

It is possible to identify two important components that may form part of industrial relations partnerships. These are *gainsharing* and *job security commitments*. Gainsharing broadly incorporates arrangements that reward workers for improvements in enterprise performance via profit sharing, share ownership or some other reward mechanism. Such schemes are critical in giving effect to an underlying principle of partnership, namely that the gains from improved performance are shared between employers and workers. In 1998 John O'Dowd, director of the National Centre for Partnership, suggested one of the key elements for successful workplace partnership is reasonable assurances of employment security so that employees will not be constrained by a sense of insecurity from making a significant contribution to organisational improvement.

Although job security commitments are said to form part of the partnership equation (see Sheehan 1998f: 20), there is little evidence of these being widespread (McCartney and Teague 2004; Wallace 1999). McCartney and Teague (2004) note that 'despite the use of innovative work practices, neither employer-volunteered job security pledges nor, more surprisingly, union-negotiated job ownership rights are particularly common'. The issue of job guarantees seems to have fallen into disrepute in the early 1980s when, faced with the downturn in the economy, such agreements proved illusory. Wallace (1999: 14) quotes Turlough O'Sullivan, IBEC director general, as saying,

> Management in companies have a clear view of optimum employment levels, and optimum manning levels, and therefore, they would not generally get into a negotiation where something other than optimum manning levels might ensue … The concept of building in an excess of fat, or whatever else you want to call it … to be fair, it's not something that trade unions here would push for.

MODELS OF ENTERPRISE-LEVEL PARTNERSHIP

Using the three core dimensions of enterprise-level partnerships, Gunnigle (1998a) describes two potential models of partnership. The first can be termed '*strategic partnerships*' that provide for union and/or employee involvement in top-level corporate decisions. In this respect one would expect to find two variants. First, we might have *union-management partnerships*. Such arrangements are characterised by institutional arrangements that allow for union involvement in strategic decision making and also give them a strong role in operational decision making at workplace level. In practice this means union representation at board level or equivalent, together with union representation in sub-board-level bodies to engage in shared decision making. A second variant is *employee-management partnerships*, whereby employees (not through unions) are represented in the highest levels of corporate decision making. We consider the strategic partnership arrangements later in this chapter. However, we can say that there is limited evidence of strategic partnerships in Ireland outside of the state sector.

The second partnership model can be termed 'operational partnerships'. Again, we can point to two possible variants. Operational union-management partnerships are normally characterised by union acceptance of change in work practices in return for participation in operational management decisions, such as those involving work organisation. In essence, the union provides a commitment to greater task flexibility and acceptance of change in exchange for greater union involvement in day-to-day decisions. Such arrangements often entail some job security commitments and the introduction of gainsharing. The second variant is operational employee-management partnerships. These partnership arrangements are to be found in some non-union, usually US high-tech companies. They bear the hallmarks of operational union-management partnerships but do not normally provide for representative participation. As noted, such arrangements present a difficulty in evaluating the extent of employee involvement.

It is important to point out that the extent of employee or union influence in operational partnership arrangements can vary considerably. Highly developed operational partnerships are likely to be based on joint decision-making principles whereby union/employee agreement is a requisite element of the decision-making process. Consensus is therefore a prerequisite and both parties' approval is necessary before proposals under consideration can be proceeded with. Less well-developed arrangements tend to have a more consultative focus. In this scenario, management agree to discuss upcoming decisions with employees/union(s) and share related information. Thus, employees or unions have the opportunity to influence decisions before implementation. However, there is no commitment to joint decision making and management may or may not take on board the opinions proffered.

Scope of Partnership Agreements

A survey by IBEC (1999: 6) reports that the most extensive new form of work organisation was teamworking (sixty-three per cent). Continuous improvement (thirty-seven per cent) and world-class manufacturing (WCM) (thirty-seven per cent) were next followed by just in time (JIT) (thirty-three per cent). IBEC considers the working methods in Table 12.1 to be 'methods which engage employees in the solution of challenges, and give teams more scope in operational functions' (IBEC 1999: 6). However, as the IBEC report notes, these items may or may not be linked to a formal partnership agreement (1999: vi). Indeed, the report questioned the extent of union involvement in 'partnership activities and arrangements' (IBEC 1999: vii). The study notes the following:

> The percentage of enterprises (thirty per cent) which have or are considering a formal partnership agreement with a trade union confirms that, while such arrangements may be necessary or desirable in some circumstances, partnership activities and arrangements, as evidenced by the survey results, take place without such formal agreements as part of the dynamic of a changing relationship within enterprises (IBEC 1999: vii).

This finding has serious implications for the role of trade unions in the partnership process, as it indicates that they are involved in only a minority of cases. This discovery is similar to those in Chapter 11 and again suggests that task-based employee involvement is the dominant form of employee involvement.

Table 12.1	
Companies with Particular Working Methods/Organisation of Work	
Working method	%
Annualised hours	11
Continuous improvement	43
World-class manufacturing	37
Total quality management	37
Just in time	33
Teamworking	63
Source: IBEC Partnership at Enterprise Level Survey Results (1999: 6)	

Further evidence on the scope of partnership agreements is available from a SIPTU survey. SIPTU's research unit reports that 484 partnership agreements have been recorded, covering 294 employments and over 80,700 members as of the end of January 2004 (information direct from SIPTU). This indicates that a substantial number of SIPTU members have been involved in one or more partnership agreements since 1997. Table 12.2 indicates that the spread of individual items dealt with in these agreements is very wide. Consistent with the IBEC 1999 results, there is evidence in the SIPTU agreements for significant adoption of new forms of work organisation. Ninety-three of the partnership agreements in the SIPTU survey contained provisions relating to co-operation with new forms of work organisation, while a further forty-two involved adaptability, flexibility and innovation. The most common provision was for some form of financial involvement, present in 131 of all agreements, since Partnership 2000. While it is not possible to definitely say that there is a direct connection between the high incidence of financial participation and the work organisation, the likelihood is that, in many cases, the trade-off was agreement to the new working methods/flexibility in return for employer concession on financial involvement.

DIFFUSION OF PARTNERSHIP: THE EVIDENCE TO DATE

There is a limited but growing body of empirical research that, either directly or indirectly, explores developments in enterprise-level industrial relations in Ireland. Some studies look specifically at the issue of partnership while others entail more general reviews. We now consider some of this evidence.

In 1997 the Irish Management Institute (IMI) conducted a pilot survey of participants who attended a Department of Enterprise, Trade and Employment/IMI conference on the theme 'Workplace 2000' (Hannigan 1997). Inevitably, this survey represents a biased sample, as participants at such a conference would be expected to have some positive interest in developing or promoting workplace partnerships. One would anticipate that the survey would reveal a positive picture on partnership. Interestingly, this was not the case (see Table 12.3). The IMI survey explored a number of dimensions of partnership. Respondents were asked to indicate the presence of these dimensions in their organisation on a one to five scale (low to high). The mean scores are outlined in Table 12.3.

Table 12.2
Areas Dealt with in Agreements under Partnership

	No. of Partnership Agreements under:			
Partnership Deals	P.2000	PPF	SP	ALL
Employee Involvement for Competitiveness Opportunities for employees to be involved in and contribute to meeting the challenge of global competition. Includes: • Staff briefings; participative training for reps; joint problem-solving taskforces; enterprise councils; self-directed teamworking.	5	1	0	6
Training, Personal Development & Support Enhancing competence, flexibility and innovation through skills development, professional training and assistance. • Training for career development; protection against bullying or unfair treatment; rights to personal privacy and data disclosure; Employee Assistance Programme; family support measures; apprenticeship quotas; educational leave.	32	14	2	48
Equality of Opportunity Consideration of equal opportunities and reconciliation of family and work responsibilities. • Positive Action Programmes; workplace childcare facilities; voluntary quota of employees with disabilities; flexi-time; Code of Practice on compassionate leave arrangements.	40	12	3	55
Representational Arrangements The role of the union and employee representatives and facilities for effective representation. • Adaptation to the LRC Code of Practice on employee representatives; improved management/union liaison; union DAS if not already provided for; 'fast track' negotiations to avoid damaging delays; economic literacy training for representatives; union input to induction training.	39	5	0	44

Table 12.2 (continued)
Areas Dealt with in Agreements under Partnership

Partnership Deals	No. of Partnership Agreements under:			
	P.2000	PPF	SP	ALL
Forms of Financial Involvement Profit sharing, employee share participation or other agreed forms of gainsharing that permit workers to share in the benefits of the company's success. • Free shares; profit-related bonus; option of converting bonus to shares based on approved plan to provide tax benefits; group performance-related incentive bonus schemes.	86	42	3	131
Composition of Workforce Issues relating to the employment of atypical workers, taking account of such factors as competitive pressures, flexibility and security of employment; conversion of temporary to permanent positions; improved benefits package for part-time, temporary and fixed-term contract staff.	8	10	1	19
Co-Operation with New Forms of Work Organisation The mechanisms by which employees and managers can be continuously innovative and accept the need for change to remain competitive. • Total quality management; world-class manufacturing; autonomous teamworking; suggestion schemes; joint taskforces.	59	32	2	93
Occupational Health & Safety Making work safer, cleaner, human centred and friendlier. • Survey of attitudes to work and conditions; risk analysis and accident prevention; non-adversarial settlement of injury claims; human-centred work design; health promotion activities; safety reps to be afforded necessary status and resources to be proactive in preventing accidents or to be involved in strategic decisions concerning safety and improvement to the working environment generally.	15	9	1	25
Problem Solving & Conflict Avoidance Developing a co-operative culture that facilitates a non-adversarial approach to problems. • Improved communication; structured resolution of disputes; problem-solving training; greater openness and trust.	7	10	1	18

Table 12.2 (continued)
Areas Dealt with in Agreements under Partnership

Partnership Deals	No. of Partnership Agreements under:			
	P.2000	PPF	SP	ALL
Adaptability, Flexibility & Innovation The means by which the organisation can be made more flexible, innovative and adapt to changing market requirements. • Job enhancement; multi-skilling; lower costs; new products/services.	26	16	0	42
Tax Breaks Tax-free lump sums for major restructuring. Paragraph 3.16	2	1	0	3
Total number of agreements recorded	319	152	13	484
Total number of employments recorded	192	94	8	294
Total number of members affected	70,266	16,546	745	87,557

Source: Information supplied directly by Research Department, SIPTU 2004

Table 12.3
The Diffusion of Partnership-Based Industrial Relations: Some Initial Findings

	Mean scores (range 1–5)
Direct Indicators of Partnership	
To what extent do you believe that partnership exists in your organisation?	2.79
Sharing in rewards of success	2.50
Employee involvement in strategic decision making	2.10
Existence of formal partnership agreement	2.05
Indirect Indicators of Partnership	
Open two-way communications	3.33
Employee involvement in decision making in work units	3.21
Top management commitment to partnership	3.07
Single status for all employees	2.95
Efficiency/Performance Indicators	
Employee responsiveness to customer requirements	3.81
Employee flexibility	3.67

Source: Hannigan (1997)

In evaluating these findings, a reasonably clear picture emerges. First, the direct indicators of partnership-based industrial relations approaches all score below the median value of three. Therefore, we can conclude that partnership-based approaches were not seen by respondents to be well developed in the respondent firms. Hannigan (1997: 1–2) writes that 'the key features of a partnership agreement, for example, employee involvement in strategic decision making and sharing in the rewards of success, are not present to any degree in this sample'. A second discernible finding is that the variables that score highest are those for employee flexibility and responsiveness to customer requirements – indicators of employee performance/efficiency and not partnership. We also find that management perceptions of their commitment to partnership score higher than their evaluation of the extent to which partnership actually exists in their organisations. The study also explored the impact of ownership by Irish private sector, public sector and foreign sector on variations in the uptake of partnership. Hannigan (1997: 4) concludes that the 'relative strength of each of the features of partnership do not differ greatly depending on the ownership structure of the respondent'. However, he notes the term 'partnership' was more likely to be used in public sector organisations and other Irish firms as compared to foreign-owned companies.

Arguably, the most comprehensive source of information on the diffusion of partnership approaches is the UCD/ESRI workplace survey (Roche and Geary 2002). This study investigated twelve key areas of workplace change and, where change had occurred, examined the predominant approach used by establishments to handle workplace change. This study looked at four optional approaches to handling change:

- management prerogative: change decisions made solely by management;
- traditional collective bargaining;
- partnership: engaging with trade unions to introduce change by consensus; and
- direct involvement: decided by management with the direct involvement of employees.

The data on workplace change in unionised establishments is summarised in Table 12.4, which indicates that partnership approaches are very much the exception rather than the rule. It also appears that where partnership is used, this occurs more in relation to operational rather than strategic issues. In contrast, we find much higher levels of utilisation of direct involvement in handling workplace change, both in relation to operational and strategic issues.

Looking at non-union establishments (Table 12.5), we find even greater use of direct employee involvement, which occurs in relation to both strategic and operational issues. Nevertheless, management prerogative remains the most widely practised means of introducing workplace change and particularly so in regard to strategic issues. The study also looked at how employers hoped to handle future workplace change. Respondents in unionised establishments indicated a clear preference for partnership approaches or direct employee involvement rather than collective bargaining. This was especially strong with regard to operational matters. Respondents in non-union establishments revealed a strong preference for greater use of direct employee involvement.

Table 12.4

Handling Workplace Change in Unionised Establishments

	How Change is Handled (%)			
	Management Prerogative	Collective Bargaining	Partnership	Direct Involvement
Operational Issues				
Pay levels	17	62	11	10
Payment systems	21	40	18	22
New plant and technology	48	13	11	27
Working time	8	38	16	38
Work practices	13	25	20	41
Numbers employed	65	13	14	8
Employee involvement	26	14	14	46
Promotion structures and criteria	77	8	11	5
Strategic Issues				
New products/services	62	2	8	29
Setting business targets	71	3	3	23
Identifying ways of realising targets	47	4	8	41
Plans regarding mergers, acquisitions or divestments	92	1	2	6

Source: Roche and Geary (2002: 75)

Table 12.5

Handling Workplace Change in Non-union Establishments

	How Change is Handled (%)	
	Management Prerogative	Direct Involvement
Operational Issues		
Pay levels	62	38
Payment systems	51	49
New plant and technology	52	48
Working time	20	80
Work practices	32	68
Numbers employed	33	67
Employee involvement	81	19
Promotion structures and criteria	76	24
Strategic Issues		
New products/services	56	44
Setting business targets	68	32
Identifying ways of realising targets	38	62
Plans regarding mergers, acquisitions or divestments	97	3

Source: Roche and Geary (1998)

An IBEC study in 2002 found that twenty-two per cent of companies surveyed operate a formal partnership arrangement (information direct from IBEC). Thirty-seven per cent of formal partnership arrangements are in unionised companies and thirty-four per cent occur in larger companies. They report that partnership is more likely to be found in the traditional manufacturing sector and least likely in the financial services sector. It is slightly more common in indigenous companies (twenty-six per cent) than in foreign-owned companies (twenty-one per cent). IBEC suggests that these figures 'mask the high incidence of informal employee involvement arrangements, particularly in the private sector'. There is a close correspondence with a 2003 summary of NCPP/ESRI Surveys on Attitudes and Experiences in the Workplace, where twenty-three per cent of respondents stated that partnership was in operation.

There is a strong consistency between the above findings and the CUL study findings discussed in Chapter 11. This study did not attempt to explicitly examine the incidence of partnership, but some inferences can be made from proxy measures. In 1999 just twenty-seven per cent of participating organisations reported that they communicate on strategy with manual grades. The CUL study also suggested a limited existence of consultative committees or works councils. The great majority of organisations with a works council or joint consultative committee were unionised (fifty-three of the sixty-three organisations). Overall, these studies provide evidence of limited trade union involvement in strategic decision making. They also point to the restricted impact of direct employee involvement – the predominant focus is on issues of immediate work relevance, not strategic issues. These initiatives seem to be primarily concerned with encouraging greater employee 'voice' on issues of immediate job-related interest rather than employee 'influence' on higher-level management decision making.

THE TRADE UNION STANDPOINT

A significant aspect of the debate on employee participation and involvement in Ireland concerns the role of trade unions. Traditionally, the Irish trade union movement did not seem particularly committed to initiatives to increase employee participation and involvement (Morrissey 1989). Indeed, apart from support for greater disclosure of information, the conventional trade union approach to employee participation was marked by a considerable degree of apathy. Such apathy has strong links to the doubts many trade unionists harbour about the implications of employee participation and involvement for the union's role in collective bargaining. Salamon (2000) identifies a number of factors which may explain trade union opposition to employee participation and involvement initiatives, particularly direct participation:

- management's tendency to emphasise the intrinsic rewards (such as increased job satisfaction) emanating from organisation change initiatives and to 'play down' the significance of extrinsic rewards;
- a suspicion that the primary objectives of organisation change initiatives are productivity improvement and cost reduction rather than increasing employee participation and involvement, and concern that such moves may lead to downsizing;

- a fear that organisational change initiatives may lead to a dilution or removal of traditional demarcation lines between groups of workers; and
- a feeling that direct participation represents a management desire to undermine existing representative arrangements, with a consequent diminution in the role of trade unions in workplace industrial relations.

Our earlier discussion provides some support for such union reservations. For example, Gunnigle's (1995a) greenfield site study indicated that management's objectives in increasing direct communications with employees were primarily aimed at conditioning employee attitudes and expectations to appreciate 'market realities' and accept the need for high levels of flexibility and productivity.

In spite of such reservations, recent years have seen a marked change in trade union approaches to employee participation and involvement. The ICTU policy documents, *New Forms of Work Organisation* (1993) and *Managing Change* (1995), posit that trade unions need to take a more proactive role in influencing the planning and implementation of new workforce management strategies (ICTU 1993, 1995). These reports place a particular focus on task participation at enterprise level and note the importance for trade unions of developing and actively participating in employee involvement initiatives at workplace level. 'Involvement with management in the implementation of ... initiatives will be the key to ensuring that the interests of ... members are met' (ICTU 1993). They also identify key aspects of employee participation and involvement that trade unions need to address, particularly the joint monitoring of participation initiatives at workplace level, involvement of trade unions in the internal communications processes of organisations, access to and understanding of business information and union involvement in high-level business decision making.

A RANK-AND-FILE PERSPECTIVE

Looking beyond the policy level and the 'official' trade union line, there is a dearth of independent research evidence on the role and reactions of trade union members to involvement and participation initiatives. D'Art and Turner (2002c) provide the most contemporary insight on the perception of this key constituency. Their work draws on a survey of members of a large general union in Ireland. A total of just over 2,000 members were surveyed in forty-three organisations and the survey achieved a response rate of twenty-nine per cent.

The Partnership 2000 agreement provides for considerable flexibility with regard to the nature of partnership arrangements. It does not 'impose any single structure or model of partnership' and recognises the need to 'tailor the approach to fit different employment settings' (Partnership 2000 1997: 63). However, the agreement does identify a number of issues that partnership at workplace level might embrace, notably employee co-operation in organisation change, changing forms of work organisation and financial participation.

D'Art and Turner's (2002c) study considered the diffusion of six specific workplace initiatives and union members' perceptions of their impact in fostering partnership with management. The six elements investigated were union management committees, teamworking, profit sharing, share schemes, schemes to give employees more control and schemes to give employees more financial information. Overall, the level of diffusion of these new workplace initiatives was not extensive: thirty-nine per cent reported that none of the six initiatives had been introduced in their workplace and only twenty-nine per cent reported that more than two of these initiatives were present. Initiatives to give employees greater control over their work were experienced by the lowest number of respondents (eleven per cent), while the number of respondents who experienced the other five initiatives averaged around thirty per cent.

As can be seen from Table 12.6, D'Art and Turner's (2002c) findings indicate that such new initiatives have had a mixed impact on levels of co-operation between workers and management. With the exception of teamworking, over half of the respondents reported no change in the levels of management-employee co-operation as a result of any of these initiatives. With regard to union-management committees, profit sharing and initiatives to give employees greater control over their work, the proportion of respondents reporting increased management-employee co-operation was similar to the proportion indicating decreased levels of co-operation. Financial information disclosure schemes were perceived to have the most positive impact on management-employee co-operation: thirty-two per cent of respondents reported an increase in co-operation, compared to thirteen per cent who reported that co-operation had decreased. In the case of teamworking and share schemes, thirty-two per cent and twenty-four per cent, respectively, reported increased levels of co-operation compared to nineteen per cent and fourteen per cent indicating decreased levels.

Table 12.6

Impact of New Workplace Initiatives on Levels of Co-operation with Management

	Union management committees	Team-working*	Profit sharing	Shares available to employees	Greater control over your work*	More financial information
Co-operation decreased greatly	10%	6%	8%	9%	12%	8%
Co-operation decreased	12%	13%	9%	5%	9%	5%
No change	52%	48%	64%	62%	57%	55%
Co-operation increased	24%	28%	17%	22%	20%	27%
Co-operation increased greatly	2%	4%	2%	2%	1%	5%
N =	100%	100%	100%	100%	100%	100%
	(316)	(300)	(253)	(301)	(226)	(293)

* These figures do not add up to 100 per cent due to rounding.

Source: Adapted from D'Art and Turner (2002c)

An important theme in the arguments put forward by union leaders in support of partnership-based arrangements at enterprise level is that such initiatives will have beneficial outcomes for rank-and-file trade union members in terms of their experience of work and will foster greater partnership between management and employees (ICTU 1993, 1995). It is also argued that partnership will serve to strengthen union organisation in the workplace and give workers a fairer share of a company's economic success (see D'Art and Turner 2002c). Table 12.7 summarises D'Art and Turner's main findings on trade union members' perceptions of the outcomes of new workplace initiatives.

Table 12.7
Worker Perceptions of Outcomes of New Workplace Initiatives

	Job-Related Outcomes		Institutional Outcomes		Rewards
	Influence in deciding how your job is done	Amount of work you have to do	Feelings of a 'them and us' divide	Influence of trade union in your workplace	Fairer share of profits to workers in your firm
Decreased	24%	3%	17%	38%	22%
No change	60%	32%	53%	47%	63%
Increased	16%	65%	30%	15%	15%
N=	100%	100%	100%	100%	100%
	(470)	(469)	(473)	(476)	(459)

Source: D'Art and Turner (2002c)

This information is revealing, as it provides insights into the outcomes of changes in work organisation for both individual workers and trade unions. Looking first at individual worker autonomy, the great majority of respondents (sixty per cent) felt that the influence they had over how to do their job remained unchanged. However, almost a quarter (twenty-four per cent) felt their level of influence had actually decreased and only sixteen per cent felt it had increased. There is considerable evidence of a perception of an increased work burden. A full sixty-five per cent of respondents reported that their work burden had increased, with only three per cent indicating it had decreased.

A basic premise of the partnership argument is that it serves to reduce or eliminate 'them and us' attitudes and moves the industrial relations agenda from adversarialism to co-operation (Kochan and Osterman 1994; Roche and Kochan 1996). D'Art and Turner's (2002c) evidence does not support this premise. While just over half the respondents (fifty-three per cent) reported no change, almost one-third (thirty per cent) felt that the 'them and us' divide had increased, as against almost one-fifth (seventeen per cent) reporting it had decreased.

Turning to the perceived impact on the role of trade unions at enterprise level, no change was reported by just less than half of the respondents (forty-seven per cent). However, where respondents felt that the union role had changed, this was more likely to result in a decrease (thirty-eight per cent) rather than an increase (fifteen per cent) in trade union influence. Finally, with regard to the share of profits going to workers, while most (sixty-three per cent) felt the situation had not changed, a decrease was reported by twenty-two per cent of respondents as against the fifteen per cent reporting an increase.

Taken together, the evidence suggests that the experience of new workplace initiatives by these union members has largely been neutral or negative. Of course, as D'Art and Turner (2002c) point out, it is plausible to argue that this (perceived) decline in union influence at enterprise level is unrelated to new workplace initiatives and may be traced to broader economic and social change. Nevertheless, these findings give some support to arguments that new workplace initiatives can serve to undermine and marginalise trade union influence at workplace level.

In evaluating their findings, D'Art and Turner (2002c: 268) conclude that in the companies surveyed, the development of a 'genuine sense of partnership at firm level has not occurred to any significant degree'. This finding is confirmed in Table 12.8, which indicates that the majority of respondents either believe that co-operation has declined (thirty-seven per cent) or remained unchanged (forty per cent) as against the companies citing co-operation had increased.

Table 12.8
Partnership and Co-operation between Management and Workers at Firm Level

Co-operation between management has declined to a great extent	14%
There is less co-operation in this workplace than before	23%
Nothing has changed here	40%
Co-operation has increased to some extent	22%
Co-operation has increased greatly	1%

Source: D'Art and Turner (2002c)

Having looked at general agreements on partnership, we now go on to examine the use of partnership-type methods, such as integrative bargaining, in restructuring situations. There is evidence from Europe of innovative agreements emerging during the 1990s that involved workers in collaborative measures to address challenges to employment and competitiveness. We examine the extent of the diffusion of these types of agreements in Ireland and the way in which they operate.

COMPETITIVENESS AND EMPLOYMENT: CONCESSION BARGAINING, EMPLOYMENT PACTS, RESTRUCTURING AGREEMENTS AND PRIVATISATION

The term 'employment pact' has been used to describe the agreements that emerged in the EU during the 1990s that were designed to protect employment and competitiveness. A 'pure' employment pact can be categorised by a trade-off of job maintenance in return for wage reductions, a wage freeze or alteration to some other terms and conditions of employment designed to achieve productivity increases. A classic example was the Volkswagen agreement on the reduction of hours of work to twenty-eight hours and a corresponding reduction in wages to maintain employment levels. This agreement was credited with turning around the Volkswagen group at a time of impending difficulty (see case study below).

The key element of an employment pact is the effort to protect employment, through agreements, to increase productivity, efficiency, flexibility or involving wage reductions (Freyssinet *et al.* 1999). Such agreements involve a collaborative approach to restructuring (http://www.eurofound.ie/industrial/pecs 2004). Freyssinet *et al.* (1999) indicate agreements may contain varying provisions relating to competitiveness and employment. Employment preservation can incorporate items such as minimum employment guarantees, non-compulsory redundancies or even employment creation. While employment pacts are distinguished from union giveback agreements, the categories are not fully separable, as union givebacks may incorporate an element of job protection measures.

Case Study: The Volkswagen Employment Pact

The 28.8-hour working week agreement reached at Volkswagen AG (VW) in late 1993 took the public by surprise. In spite of opposition from employers and politicians to union proposals for reductions in working hours, VW radically reduced its hours and successfully overcame a severe corporate crisis. The agreement's explicit aim of saving thousands of jobs was also met.

A number of factors were central to the agreement's acceptance and success. First, the consensual and pragmatic relationship between VW and the works council was a prerequisite for the speed and ease with which the agreement was reached. Second, the average annual income per employee at VW (DM60,500, or approximately €30,000, gross in 1994) exceeded average German earnings by some twelve per cent, making a cut in earnings more palatable. Third, workers were not averse to the reduction in hours, which saw them working substantially less than the general collectively agreed 38 hours. Finally, the level of company- and industry-specific skills meant employees would have had difficulties in gaining alternative employment in similar work; this made them more amenable to accepting the agreement. Subsequently, VW added several new elements to its working time system to fine tune and fit it to changing circumstances.

Source: Schulten *et al.* (1999) (The full text of this case is available at www.eurofound.ie/industrial/pecscstudies/germany.htm.)

Such collaborative agreements are far from being the only way in which organisational retrenchment takes place. Agreements related to competitiveness and employment can arise under a number of guises, ranging from union givebacks to partnership agreements providing for mutual gains. Equally, the negotiations involved may be distributive or integrative in nature or, more likely, a mix of both. The following typology is used to classify the range of agreements for discussion.

- Concession bargaining to sustain employment or to limit job losses. This involves union givebacks in pay and conditions of employment.
- Rationalisation agreements based on distributive bargaining providing for job losses, changes in work organisation and providing some security guarantees and/or negotiations on manning levels for the remaining employees.
- Rationalisation where there are attempts to engage in mutual gains bargaining.
- Explicit partnership agreements designed to maintain or expand employment.

Prior to the early 1980s, some collective agreements contained measures to protect employment, but as noted previously, these fell into disrepute among unions when they proved ineffectual in the conditions of the 1980s. As the 1980s progressed, a significant development in workplace industrial relations was the growth of concession bargaining, or 'union givebacks'.

CONCESSION BARGAINING

The term 'concession bargaining' arose in the US in the early 1980s and involves 'union givebacks'. By the mid- to late 1980s, the concept had made its way to Ireland, where it was not so much associated with US companies, but with Irish and other foreign-owned companies that would previously have had superior pay and conditions of employment. Examples of such companies are Aer Lingus, De Beers (diamond manufacturers), Krups, Waterford Crystal and Irish Steel. In some instances, companies introduced redundancies unilaterally, as in the first round of redundancies in Waterford Crystal in 1987. While there are a few examples of 'take it or leave it demands for concessions', they are very much in the minority. Employers who found it necessary to seek such concessions normally did so through the collective bargaining process. Even companies that have tried the 'take it or leave it' approach reverted to collective bargaining, presumably to gain legitimacy for their proposed measures.

Examples of cases of negotiations leading to union givebacks (concession bargaining) in the semi-state sector occurred in Aer Lingus in 1993 and in Irish Steel in 1995. The Aer Lingus agreement involved a plan for shedding 900 jobs, work reorganisation, changes to shift working, use of part-time workers and wage reductions in return for a government investment package in the state-owned airline and an equity stake of five per cent in the company for workers. The investment was to be of a once-off nature and was subject to approval by the European Commission. The combination of this investment and the equity stake granted to workers demonstrates an effort to preserve the company in a difficult situation following the first Gulf War and to enable the company to meet the challenge of market liberalisation. While the Irish Steel situation involved union givebacks it did have job protection measures, giving it an element of an employment pact, although this measure proved unsuccessful as the company subsequently closed.

Within the private sector there were a considerable number of examples of concession bargaining designed to meet the challenges of competitiveness in the 1980s. A notable example was the Plan for Competitiveness agreed in 1998 between the Bank of Ireland and the Irish Bank Officials Association (IBOA), which provided for the introduction of a two-tier employment structure in the Bank of Ireland. Thus, new employees were classified as 'bank assistants' to distinguish them from the established 'bank officials' grade. The bank assistants had lower starting salaries and a separate and lower salary scale. A variant of this arrangement, called the Competitive Strategy for the 1990s, was agreed between the IBOA and Allied Irish Banks in 1989. In this instance, the salary for new entrants was lowered and the scale lengthened, but a separate salary scale was not introduced. In 1995 Packard Electric, which manufactured equipment for the automobile industry and was located in an employment black spot in Dublin, reached an agreement for an increase in working hours from thirty-nine to forty-one hours per week together with concessions in work organisation. This was a highly controversial example of concession bargaining and was only narrowly accepted by employees in a ballot. The agreement proved a major failure as it did not avert the closure of the company in 1996 with a loss of the total number of 389 jobs.

Concession bargaining became quite rare after 1995, when workers were less likely to accept major concessions that reduced their pay and conditions, preferring to opt for a simple redundancy deal instead. However, concession bargaining has since reappeared in Aer Lingus in 2001 (www.eiro.eurofound.ie/2001/11/inbrief/ie0111203n.html) as that company moved to meet the competitive challenges from Ryanair by establishing itself as a low-cost airline.

RATIONALISATION AGREEMENTS

Downsizing and work restructuring are standard responses to commercial difficulties for companies. The question arises as to the extent to which these are accomplished through 'old-fashioned' distributive bargaining or the collaborative agreements of employment pacts/partnership. Rationalisation agreements involve employer-introduced redundancies with subsequently reduced manning levels. Employers may also negotiate the introduction of new methods of work organisation. Within Irish industrial relations there a number of well-established conventions on the way for handling redundancies, as follows.

- Redundancy is normally on the basis of voluntary severance, i.e. it is the employee's choice to leave, except where a company is closing.
- The employer is likely to have the right to select from those applying for redundancy, taking account of skills and business needs.
- Enhanced redundancy pay is paid in addition to the statutory entitlements. This can be extremely generous in some instances. Four to six weeks' pay per year of service is not uncommon in the private sector.

The level of compensation varies according to the industry and sometimes the location. Compensation levels can be at or close to the statutory norm in some instances, which is now two weeks' pay per year of service for employees with a minimum of 104 weeks' service.

Wallace (1999, 2000a, 2000b) has undertaken a comparison of the number of restructuring agreements that involved collaborative efforts to retain/grow jobs as against the number based largely on distributive-type bargaining. A distributive approach was defined as one that involved management agreeing on job losses in return for enhanced redundancy compensation above the level of the Redundancy Payments Acts. There were a total of 311 severance agreements for the years 1994–1998 as against only twenty-six additional agreements that met the criteria for a collaborative approach to restructuring and job protection. The twenty-six included agreements such as those in Aer Lingus and Irish Steel, which involved concession bargaining and union givebacks. Thus, concession bargaining can involve collaborative elements and where this was present (even at low levels) such agreements were included (an employment pacts approach). Hence, the dominant method for resolving restructuring appears to be a distributive one. Turlough O'Sullivan, director general of IBEC, summarises this position as follows.

> The vast majority of rationalisations in this country would be sorted out on a voluntary basis where a package is made available which will include redundancy pay, statutory redundancy pay, minimum notice, etc., which would be, in most cases, designed to attract people to take the opportunity to leave and perhaps find alternative employment. That process has been made easier in the last number of years because of the buoyancy in the labour market because there are so many jobs available. It's even easier now to persuade people to accept a voluntary redundancy package. In very few cases have we had to rely on involuntary redundancy, very, very few (quoted in Wallace 1999: 20–1).

The question arises as to why distributive or adversarial approaches are most used in restructuring despite the claimed advantages of a collaborative approach. The answer seems to be that distributive bargaining may suit the parties better. First, as noted by Turlough O'Sullivan above, a voluntary severance package combined with an enhanced redundancy payment will often be attractive to a sufficient number of employees to enable management to achieve the required job losses. Second, the reduction in costs associated with shedding jobs are definite, whereas proposals for innovative measures, such as new product development, are speculative and may not deliver the desired benefits. Third, if employees agree to increased efficiencies to protect jobs, this paradoxically creates a need for job reductions. Finally, in many situations the time required for the extensive information sharing and development of alternative solutions that collaborative bargaining relies on is not available. This was exactly the situation in the merger between Waterford Foods and Avonmore (see case study).

Case Study: The Glanbia (Avonmore-Waterford Group) Merger

The case followed a merger between Avonmore Foods Plc. and Waterford Foods Plc., which threatened substantial redundancies. An attempt was made by the general unions involved to have a collaborative arrangement, which would see the merged company maintaining jobs through efforts to expand its business – in other words, from the perspective of an employment pact. The company rejected this, as its main concern was to reap the organisational benefits of reduced operating costs through a rationalisation of production facilities and a reduction in the number of employees. The employment pact approach would not have yielded these improvements within any realistic timeframe.

The negotiations on the redundancies were conducted within the traditional framework in Ireland, with a requirement that redundancies be on a voluntary basis and that enhanced redundancy compensation be paid. The unions achieved an overall compensation of six weeks' pay per year of service in addition to the statutory requirements. There were, however, some minor elements of an employment pact to the agreement: the company provided for a local support fund of some IR£2.0 million to enable the funding of jobs locally, but the unions merely saw this as a public relations exercise. The company also agreed to the retention of some jobs and to the consolidation of temporary jobs, which gives the case a minor element of an employment pact.

Source: Wallace (1999) (The full text of the case is available at www.eurofound.ie/industrial/pecscstudies/ireland.htm.)

The key consideration for management in the Glanbia case was their desire to take advantage of the synergies of the merger by shedding jobs. Thus, they rejected union proposals for maintaining jobs through the development of new products, etc. Wallace (1999: 38) quotes a member of the human resources division as saying, 'This was not an option for the management negotiating team'. In this case the union achieved none of its job preservation objectives nor its attempts to influence the business strategy of the company. Equally, the union dropped this latter demand in favour of an increase in redundancy pay from four to six weeks' per year of service and an agreement on manning levels and working conditions following the rationalisation (Wallace 1999).

Thus, collaborative bargaining may best operate where there is a significant amount of time for the parties to work through issues and also where there is a mutual gain to be realised. In other words, one can only sensibly engage in mutual gains bargaining if such a gain is a reasonable prospect. There was no such prospect in the Glanbia case from the management point of view. Furthermore, in management's view, engaging in collaborative efforts to save jobs would have seriously damaged the company. This message that collaborative/partnership approaches are not always appropriate, and that distributive approaches can work better in common restructuring situations, may be unappealing to some, but it is difficult to see how the data can otherwise be interpreted.

EMPLOYMENT PACT AGREEMENTS

The above finding suggests that in restructuring situations, collaborative bargaining is not widespread, but agreements embodying collaborative bargaining have been hugely important in a minority of cases. Wallace (1999: 5) notes that 'the term employment pact is not one used in Irish industrial relations, however bargaining of an "employment pact" nature does take place'. He goes on to say that 'there are only a small number of "high level employment pact" type collective agreements' (Wallace 1999: 6), noting that a number of these agreements have 'a high degree of sophistication and are specific and detailed in their provisions' (Wallace 1999: 6). Examples include Telecom Éireann (now renamed Eircom), Irish Cement Ltd, Aughinish Alumina, Irish Steel (became Ispat, which has since closed), Analog Devices, GE Superabrasives, Aer Lingus, Aer Rianta, Guinness, Tesco, Boots, the Electricity Supply Board (ESB), Tara Mines and Team Aer Lingus.

As noted above, partnership/collaborative approaches may not always be appropriate due to the greater time involved and the costs this could impose on a business, which may be greater in the private sector than in the public sector. However, there is a class of collaborative agreements that have become more common in the private sector. These are agreements providing for the introduction of annual hours (Table 12.9) and seem to be most common in the unionised sector, particularly among craft workers (see Darcy 1998).

Table 12.9	
Selected Companies with Annualised Hours Agreements	
Aughinish Alumina, Limerick	Avonmore Foods Plc. (some craft workers only)
Becton Dickenson Insulin Syringe Ltd	GE Superabrasives, Ireland
Coca Cola, Drogheda	Irish Biscuits Ltd
Fruit of the Loom International Ltd	Irish Cement Ltd
Organon Ireland Ltd	Shannon Aerospace Ltd
Source: Darcy (1998)	

In Ireland, annualised hours agreements set out the average hours employees are expected to work at normal rates of pay over the period of a year. In an annualised hours system, a total number of working hours is set and these can then vary within agreed upper and lower limits. Actual hours worked are determined by production demands, levels of absenteeism and efficiency of working. The European Foundation (2004) suggests that 'on balance, the introduction of annualised hours has tended to reflect an employers' agenda geared towards cost reduction and productivity improvements, more so than a trade union/employee agenda'. They propose that 'to a large extent this is a reflection of the balance of power in the face of competitive pressures' and maintain that 'trade unions have sometimes pragmatically viewed annualised hours agreements as a means of achieving pay stability for their members, and providing scope for control over changes in working time' (European Foundation 2004). Wallace (1999), however, suggests that unions, notably the Technical, Electrical and Engineering Union (TEEU), may actively seek and embrace annualised hours as a means of mutual gains.

The mutual gains arise in the following way: workers are usually paid for a number of reserve hours, with the general expectation that not all such hours will be worked – this encourages efficiency and lowers absenteeism, as employees have a rational incentive to ensure that fellow team members do not take advantage of the situation. An enhanced annual salary is paid and this usually incorporates a proportion of overtime that employees would normally have worked. This enhanced salary can mean an enhanced pension if the company pension scheme is based on the new enhanced salary. In summary, employers can gain greater efficiency, lower overtime payments and decreased absenteeism, while employees have more leisure time, predictable high earnings and an enhanced pension. In addition, the working atmosphere may be improved (see Irish Cement case study) with a lowering of adversarialism and an increase in collaborative problem solving. Most notably, employees no longer have an incentive to resist contractors being employed to undertake maintenance work, as they do not lose overtime and the employment of contractors can reduce the need for employees to work reserve hours.

Case Study: Annualised Hours in Irish Cement Ltd.

This case study involves Irish Cement Ltd, which holds a dominant position in the supply of cement in Ireland. The main focus of the agreement was the negotiation of an annualised hours arrangement. The negotiations took place on a phased basis from 1994 to 1999 in the company's two plants and across different grades of employees. The nature of the industry, involving seasonal working, made annual hours especially appropriate for the business.

The outcomes of the various agreements seem positive, with management reporting significant improvement in the working environment. The unions achieved an income free from the fluctuations of overtime working and a reduction in working hours as part of the agreement. The company, on the other hand, was able to address their cost base and achieve the early retirement of some workers, with new workers being hired on different terms.

A major effect of the introduction of annual hours was a substantial reduction in employee absenteeism due to employees policing themselves in the newly introduced work teams. This came about from the fact that employees did not have to work all their reserve hours, however, if employees were absent this meant other workers had to turn up for work to take their place and this resulted in reserve hours having to be worked.

Source: Adapted from Wallace (1999) (Full text of case available at www.eurofound.ie/industrial/pecscstudies/ireland.htm.)

Wallace (1999) notes that while the Irish Cement Ltd agreement was rated as highly satisfactory by both union and management, not all situations are appropriate for annual hours and there have been notable failures. Annual hours seem most appropriate where there is significant seasonality in work and where there is substantial overtime worked, but it is possible to operate without that level of overtime. Coca Cola abandoned its annual hours due to an inability to operate without significant levels of overtime due to unanticipated increase in demand for its product. Nor have all annual hours been introduced in an obviously collaborative way. The European Foundation (2004) notes that efforts at 'the introduction of annualised hours has been more problematic in the public sector'. This was evidenced by the Prison Officers Association's (POA) reaction in 2003 to the Minister for Justice's proposal for a new annualised hours agreement 'to replace the then high levels of overtime' (European Foundation 2004). It is also notable that Blue Circle Cement in the UK, where annual hours originated, has subsequently abandoned that system of working. This raises questions about the permanency of the gains for annual hours, something which was widely remarked on in relation to the productivity agreements of the 1960s and 1970s.

Some of the highest-level collaborative 'employment pact'-type agreements have arisen in the public sector as responses to market liberalisation. The ESB is a major example (see case study). Hastings (2003) has conducted a major study of company restructuring in four semi-state companies: the ESB, Aer Lingus, An Post and Eircom. He considers political factors to have been crucial in these restructurings, but notes the nature of political influence differed in each case. Thus, he argues that the 'role that politics plays appears to be influenced by company-specific factors' (Hastings 2003: 192). He maintains that under the CCR change programme, management and unions together were more influential than the government department and notes that they made it a common cause to bypass government and departmental involvement as part of the process to prepare the company for marketisation. In Aer Lingus, Hastings (2003) notes the unions were in a much weaker position.

Case Study: Electricity Liberalisation and the ESB – A High-Level Employment Pact-Type Agreement

The ESB was a monopoly state-owned electrical utility which faced competition as a result of an EU directive and a government decision to liberalise the market for electricity. In order to prepare for competition, the company entered into a cost and competitiveness review (CCR) with its eleven representative trade unions.

The review was broken down into two parts. The first stage involved a review of relationships to examine underlying problems with industrial and employee relations combined with a fact-finding joint union-management tour of selected foreign electricity utilities. These tours sought to study the most efficient plants operating under a variety of different conditions. This fact-finding stage also involved defining the problems faced by the ESB, from a multi-actor perspective, and was combined with a problem-solving approach to addressing those issues.

When the broad parameters of what was necessary had been defined, the parties resumed their traditional collective bargaining roles. However, these negotiations were not purely distributive nor were they win-win types of negotiations. In essence, they were what Lewicki *et al.* (1994) termed 'mixed motive bargaining' in which both distributive and integrative elements were present (see Chapter 10).

The ESB settlement is extremely detailed and complex and cannot be adequately summarised in a short case study. However, the key settlement issues involved trade-offs, which are typical of the traditional method of dealing with restructuring noted earlier. These were voluntary redundancies of 2,000 jobs, involving early retirement with enhanced pension provisions and redundancy compensation of nine weeks' pay per year of service. To allow the ESB to operate with the reduced workforce, new work arrangements were agreed. The ESB case also involved new elements: an annual profit-sharing payment (index linked) and the establishment of a five per cent employee shareholding scheme. In addition, the government, with the approval of the European Commission, provided substantial capital investment.

Despite this positive experience the commitment to continued use of a collaborative approach to organisational change in the ESB was put in doubt when a company-wide ballot on industrial action was mooted 'in order to "force" the government to sanction talks on a new tripartite "partnership" agreement next year' (Sheehan 2003f).

Source: Adapted from Wallace (1999); see also
www.eurofound.ie/industrial/pecscstudies/ireland.htm

Extract from *Politics, Management and Industrial Relations: Four Semi-State Companies and the Challenges of Marketization*

The Personnel Function
The personnel/HR function was either sidelined or key personnel replaced as part of the restructuring process in all four cases. In the ESB Hastings notes the personnel function was

marginalised, being sidelined from strategic decision making. This had the effect of transforming ESB's adversarial climate into a 'more open partnership style'. In the Aer Lingus case, he notes that the act of employing an external consultant sidelined the personnel department. In Eircom and similar to the three cases previously mentioned, the personnel director was sourced from outside the company. In An Post, an external appointee replaced the personnel department as 'the incumbent figures in personnel were to some extent "gatekeepers" of the old regime' (Hastings 2003: 205). Hastings (2003) suggests that the human resources department was seen as part of the problem rather than part of the solution for the organisation.

Informality
The importance of informal contacts in managing the industrial relations process is stressed throughout. Hastings notes that in the ESB, although formal channels of bargaining set the basis for change, informality was crucial at national and local level. Informal bargaining was seen as necessary to lay the ground for more formal talks and also to ensure the survival of ESB as a single entity.

Forcing and Fostering
Hastings (2003) identifies two opposite approaches to restructuring, which are important in the context of our previous discussions on employee participation and partnership in Chapter 11. The first he terms *'fostering'* and the second *'forcing'*. He identifies fostering as involving either collective/national partnership and/or direct employee involvement. Interestingly, Hastings notes that having a fostering culture of bargaining present at the top of the organisation does not necessarily assume replication at all levels within the organisation, with adversarialism also continuing to exist. Partnership does not exclude a forcing approach – in the ESB management used *parallel fostering* and *forcing*. A fostering approach underpinned by partnership was facilitated by the commercial opportunities in Eircom. Strong union power was a key factor in this choice. Sequential forcing and fostering was used in Aer Lingus and An Post, which reflected the financial difficulties in both organisations. In An Post this took the form of a viability plan involving job losses and the introduction of atypical forms of work (both forcing). This resulted in an adversarial climate for a period, until there was a move towards partnership and ESOPs (fostering).

Source: Hastings (2003)

While collaborative employment pact arrangements involving what Hastings describes as fostering have been presented as a superior way to address restructuring issues, in the public sector they have also been the subject of recent criticism. Frawley (2004c: 14) quotes the general secretary of ICTU as admitting 'that the privatisation of Eircom has turned out to be "a major mistake and contrary to the public interest"'. Part of the 'fostering' during that privatisation was the granting of a 14.9 per cent shareholding in the company to employees. During the subsequent takeover by Tony O'Reilly's Valentia, workers doubled their stake to just under thirty per cent; however, Frawley (2004b) notes that there was strong criticism of proposed large-scale payments to the directors and members of management as part of a new flotation of the company on the stock market. Frawley (2004c: 14) quotes David Begg as saying: 'Most people think in terms of the loss suffered by investors ... but the worst part of it was to end up turning a public monopoly into a private monopoly'. However, on *Prime Time* on 16 March 2004, Begg pointed out that the union at the time had a difficult task and would have been criticised had they stood in the way of privatisation.

THE PROSPECTS FOR PARTNERSHIP AT ENTERPRISE LEVEL

McKersie (2002: 122) suggests that Ireland is an ideal location to test the premise that 'strategic partnerships, coupled with modern human resource systems' could be the basis for a new and successful model of industrial relations. The evidence to date suggests limited development (see Gunnigle 1998a). Turning to the prospects for partnership-based industrial relations arrangements, it appears that there are a number of difficulties to strategic management-union partnerships, particularly the following. Employers have traditionally been extremely reluctant to share decision-making power, especially in relation to strategic decisions, fearing that it will inhibit quick and decisive decision making and consequently reduce the organisation's capacity to respond to changes in the business environment. Stock markets tend to favour 'strong' executive control and thus the development of strategic partnerships may not be viewed positively, which is particularly the case among high-technology stocks. An issue with special resonance in Ireland is the great difficulty likely to be encountered in developing partnership arrangements in foreign-owned companies. In the majority of such firms, strategic decisions are made at corporate level, far removed from the Irish subsidiary. As such it may be particularly difficult for Irish trade unions to develop strategic partnerships in such situations.

The indigenous sector, particularly the public sector, is somewhat different. Here we have seen some of the most substantial developments and these have been linked to the agreement on benchmarking. Regarding development of partnership in the public sector, Sheehan (2004b: 23) claims that progress 'has been painfully slow', though the report of the Civil Service Performance Verification Group 'records "some progress"'. He goes on to indicate that the report says a number of factors 'are contributing towards developing the capacity of the partnership process to help secure the delivery of change and modernisation' (Sheehan 2004b: 23).

There has also been noteworthy experimentation with partnership-type arrangements in private sector companies, such as Aughinish Alumina and Dairygold. However, while the Aughinish example seems well established, when Dairygold experienced difficulties at the end of 2003 they responded with a distributive, not a partnership, approach to make 500 workers redundant, and the union with a twenty-four-hour strike in February 2004.

In evaluating the merits of recent developments in relation to partnership-based arrangements between employers and trade unions, it appears that both sides face a fundamental choice on the nature of workplace industrial relations: should worker/trade union involvement be confined to joint consultation or extended to joint regulation? From a worker/trade union perspective, joint consultation initiatives run the risk of remaining essentially 'symbolic'. Trade unions and workers may have no real influence and become associated with decisions where they possess no real input. Employers may be equally reticent to enter into joint regulation initiatives because it may lead to a slowing of the decision-making process.

In spite of these findings on the low uptake of workplace partnership, there is evidence of substantial experimentation. As noted above, it would certainly appear that longer-established organisations may provide a potentially fertile ground for experimentation with management-union partnerships. A critical area of concern for many such organisations is that of facilitating improved levels of performance on dimensions of quality and productivity. For many older, established organisations this requires extensive change in industrial relations, specifically on aspects such as (less) demarcation, (increased) task flexibility, (increased) responsibilities for workers and (reduced) staffing levels. Such changes must normally be achieved through negotiations with trade unions. Traditionally this would be achieved through adversarial bargaining and it is likely that this will remain the case in many organisations. However, it also likely that some companies will try to adopt a partnership approach. We have already seen evidence of such initiatives in companies such as the ESB, Auginish Alumina and Irish Cement Ltd.

Wallace (1999) has suggested that partnership developments are part of a continuing historical sedimentary process. To date, there are elements surviving in Irish industrial relations from the conservatism of the model unions, the revolutionary aspects of syndicalism, the nationalism of the post-independence period and the radicalism of the 1960s and 1970s. The depths of these strata differ considerably and developments that seemed overpowering at the time (such as the radicalism of the 1960s and 1970s) are now much diminished. At this stage it is unclear how permanent and influential the strata left by workplace partnership will be.

CHAPTER 13

The Process of Collective Bargaining in Ireland

THE DEVELOPMENT OF COLLECTIVE BARGAINING AND PAY DETERMINATION IN IRELAND

Collective bargaining in Ireland arose out of the economic, political and social developments of the nineteenth century. Industrial developments led to a major growth in trade unionism and, often consequentially, employer associations. Craft unions, which were the main workers' organisations in Ireland up to the early 1900s, were the first to establish a degree of collective regulation of work. This involved efforts to regulate their wages and conditions by unilateral action. They would devise union standard wage rates, so-called 'price lists', and present them to employers as a demand. The craft union would then oblige its members not to work for less than the going union rate. Faced with unilateral determination of rates, employers could either accept the union rates or employ non-union labour, with the ensuing possibility of industrial action, such as lockouts or strikes.

It was not just wage rates that were determined by the unions – they also regulated a limited number of terms and conditions of employment. For example, in order to prevent the 'dilution of the trade' they commonly sought to limit the ratio of apprentices to tradesmen. Some employers chose to negotiate with the trade unions and conclude collective agreements. By the 1860s some employers were arguing for the superiority of such arrangements (MacFarlane 1981; Pelling 1976). By the 1890s negotiated agreements arising from collective bargaining were being used, for example, to domesticate or tame the militant new unionism in the engineering industry in the UK after a lockout in 1896–1897 (Pelling 1976).

This early collective bargaining was dependent on the vagaries of the business cycle or the employer's goodwill (ILO 1960). In times of depression or competitive pressures employers frequently resorted to unilateral wage reductions, in effect ultimatums, which frequently resulted in strikes or lockouts. It was such wage reductions in mining that precipitated the general strike in the UK in 1926 (see McCord 1980).

Much higher levels of conflict accompanied the establishment of the 'new unions' representing semi-skilled and unskilled workers. While the Dublin employers prevailed in the 1913 lockout, as noted previously it was a Pyrrhic victory. These clashes and the costs associated with them heralded the gradual abandonment of resistance to unionisation. The new unions also moved away from syndicalism, which had the stated aim of overthrowing capitalism. Collective bargaining became the preferred alternative to all-out conflict for both parties. Yet despite this, the period between the two world wars saw collective bargaining still in its infancy in this country. Wages and conditions were still generally fixed by individual bargaining. O'Brien (1989a: 133) writes that 'while collective bargaining was extensive, it covered only a minority of all workers and it was unco-ordinated and rather haphazard'. Bargaining was mostly at the level of the individual firm or organisation, with only limited development of multi-employer bargaining via employer associations. The multi-employer bargaining that did exist was largely locally based until after the formation of the Federated Union of Employers (FUE) in 1942 (O'Brien 1989c: 73).

The onset of World War II brought a temporary cessation to much collective bargaining in Ireland. Wage determination was governed by the Wages Standstill Order (No. 83) of 1941, which was issued under the Emergency Powers Act of 1939. Prices rose steadily during the war period, which, combined with restriction on collective bargaining, led to a decline in purchasing power and a substantial erosion of living standards.

The suspension of the Wages Standstill Order after the end of the war led to widespread claims for wage increases and to the emergence of the wage round system in 1946. Since then wage bargaining has oscillated between decentralised and centralised bargaining. There have been two periods of largely decentralised bargaining (1946–1970 and 1982–1987), although during the first period there was a degree of co-ordination in four of the rounds (see below). There have also been two periods of centralised bargaining, involving either the employers and unions – the early national wage agreements of the 1970s – or involving the employers, unions and government (1970–1981 and 1982–1987) (see Table 13.1).

Table 13.1
Profile of Wage Bargaining, 1922–2004

	Level of Bargaining	Number of Agreements	Name
Pre-1941	Haphazard and sporadic bargaining	No systematic number of agreements	None
1941–1946	National legal regulation	Bargaining restricted by law	Wages Standstill Order
1946–1970	Industry and local – some national element in four of them	Twelve in total	Wage rounds
1970–1981	National, supplemented by local	Seven	National wage agreements
		Two	National understandings
1982–1987	Local and general public agreements	Varied in organisations – generally five (max six)	Decentralised wage agreements
1987–2004	Centralised	Six	Consensus /partnership agreements

THE WAGE ROUNDS, 1946–1970

Hillery (1989) records that wage rounds became institutionalised into the Irish model of collective bargaining despite being unsynchronised and largely unplanned. Wage rounds involved a general upward movement of wages and salaries over a period of time which recurred at intervals (see McCarthy *et al.* 1975: 30). In the US the term '*pattern bargaining*' is used to describe the type of process at work in the wage rounds, whereby a wage norm is established by one group and then extended throughout the economy. In the wage rounds the process worked like this: a bargaining group whose wages had been eroded by inflation and which felt that they had sufficient power would submit a claim on their employer. A strike might ensue and the settlement reached would then form a basis for other groups to restore their earnings relative to that settlement, which might be achieved with or without a strike. The terms of wage rounds were usually accepted relatively quickly by industry, particularly if the Labour Court issued a recommendation upholding the level of the wage round increase. Agreements up to the mid-1960s were open ended, but starting in 1966, 'fixed-term agreements became standard' (Hardiman 1988: 45). The actual duration of the open-ended rounds was largely dependent on economic conditions, particularly inflation. The cumulative effect of the open-ended nature and varying termination dates of most agreements resulted in a complex overlapping structure to the wage rounds.

Craft workers were to the fore in the initiation of new wage rounds, although a group that initiated a round once rarely sought to lead one a second time. The maintenance craftsmen were a notable exception, leading the 1966 and 1969 rounds. Eight of the twelve agreements were decentralised examples of free collective bargaining and were negotiated either 'at industry and trade or company level' (O'Brien 1989a: 134). The remaining four were bipartite agreements negotiated between the Federated Union of Employers (FUE) and ICTU at national level. O'Brien (1989b: 3) has described the earlier wage rounds of the 1940s and 1950s as 'sprawling untidy affairs, typical teenagers'. Hardiman (1988: 45), however, notes that negotiations during the depressed years of the 1950s 'displayed a certain "orderliness"'.

The first three of the centralised agreements were negotiated in 1948, 1952 and 1957 and were little more than 'ad hoc responses to particular economic circumstances' (O'Brien 1981: 9). Hardiman (1988: 45) describes the four 'centralised' agreements of the wage rounds as 'quite rudimentary and unsophisticated'. However, they were indicative of a pressure for co-ordination and for governments to become involved in the process of wage determination, pressure McCarthy (1977) traces back to the second wage round in 1948. These pressures were to increase with the growing strike activity of the 1960s and the heightened level of wage demands. As with other European countries, it was relative prosperity that heightened government concern at the impact of collective bargaining on the economy. During the 1960s, 'the annual average rate of economic growth was over four per cent, a marked contrast with the 1950s [which] led to an intensification of distributive bargaining' (Hardiman 1988: 45). While Roche (1989: 116) notes that from the late 1950s 'free collective bargaining secured the delivery of remarkable improvements in real income', by the end of the 1960s the system of wage rounds was under severe pressure. Roche (1989: 116) argues that 'it came to be identified by successive Irish governments as a significant contributor to economic problems, especially inflation'.

Critics of the wage rounds focused on wage competition between bargaining groups, with self-interest and sectional interest being pushed to the fore at the expense of the national interest (O'Brien 1989a). Sectional wage bargaining was particularly prevalent in the craft sector, where the protection of relativities and differentials was deeply entrenched. The end of the decade culminated with the maintenance craftsmen's dispute in 1969. The dispute between the FUE and the maintenance craft unions centred on efforts to establish a national-level multi-employer agreement covering craft workers, with the FUE seeking to break the relationship between contract craft and maintenance craft workers. The strike lasted for six weeks and ended in defeat for the FUE, but also left a left a legacy of bitterness on the part of some general unions to craft workers over the picketing policy employed by the craft workers during the strike. Breen *et al.* (1990: 169) argue that 'the dispute caused widespread disruption of industry and seriously threatened the solidarity of the trade union movement'. It is arguable, however, that much of this angst was concentrated at the level of union officialdom (see Allen 1997). Also, the disagreements tended to be over tactics rather than the outcome, whereas for employers and government the high wage increases were the paramount concern. Finally, any initial critical reaction at workplace level was mollified by the high wage increases achieved by other workers as a result of the maintenance craftsmen's headline settlement.

While the wage round system has been the subject of much criticism, these need to be placed in context. The argument that the wage rounds caused inflation is unproven and, although frequently asserted to exist in the 1960s, by the late 1970s a consensus emerged among economists that the trade-off was between real wages and employment (Hardiman 1988: 44). This consensus indicated that in a fixed exchange rate system (Ireland had a common currency with the UK), wages set at too high a level cause unemployment, not inflation. However, employment had grown appreciably during the 1960s and unemployment in 1969 was only four per cent. In terms of unemployment, therefore, there is little evidence that the outcomes from wage rounds were not out of line with the underlying growth of the economy. This can be explained by the fact that the wage increases of the wage rounds were on a low base, as Ireland still enjoyed a competitive advantage in terms of wage costs relative to the UK and many European countries.

The criticism of wage rounds based on protecting differentials is counterbalanced by the fact that the agreements generally provided for minimum increases. These were usually defined in absolute money terms, as opposed to percentage increases, and the effect of this was to compress the overall wage structure. 'Thus, in 1959 the highest paid bargaining group received approximately four times as much as did the lowest, but by 1970 this ratio had been cut in half' (OECD 1979: 40). It is also arguably unfair to criticise the wage round system on the basis of differentials and relativities, as centralised bargaining, both in the 1970s and since 1987, has also had to grapple with these issues and these agreements have not delivered greater wage equity (Turner 2002). Benchmarking in the public sector is the most recent example of the capacity for wage differentials and relativities issues to cause controversy.

CENTRALISED WAGE AGREEMENTS, 1970–1981

The outcome of the maintenance craftsmen's dispute and the level of claims being served for a new wage round in 1970 prompted the government to take action to change the system of wage determination. At the government's behest, the NIEC produced what was to prove to be a controversial report, *Income and Prices Policy*, in April 1970, which proposed that the NIEC would draft guidelines on pay increases, to be refined by a joint employer-labour body. The government responded quickly and reconstituted the Employer Labour Conference (ELC), which had previously enjoyed a brief existence from 1962 to 1963. When established, the ELC comprised forty-two members: twenty-one ICTU members, twelve from the Irish Employers' Confederation (IEC), five senior civil servants (representing the government as an employer) and four from state-sponsored bodies (Hardiman 1988: 51). In 1972 it was extended to twenty-five representatives from employer and union sides.

The ELC was to have a key role in the wage formation process up to 1981. At its inaugural meeting a working committee was appointed to draft proposals for national-level negotiations. Although the executive of ICTU approved the terms of reference for the reactivated ELC, a following ICTU annual delegate conference rejected the controversial NIEC proposals while leaving the way open for a voluntary prices policy (see Hardiman 1988: 51). Negotiations were entered into under the aegis of the ELC, but these broke down in October and the government responded by threatening to legislate. A Prices and Incomes Bill was published that proposed a statutory control of all incomes, limiting wage increases to six per cent, or IR£1.80, per week until the end of 1971. In announcing the bill, the then Minister for Finance, Mr George Colley, referred to the 'truly staggering' claims already submitted at industry level. He cited claims for thirty per cent for maintenance craftsmen, forty per cent for builders and sixty-six per cent and ninety-three per cent from competing electricians' unions (Dáil Debates 1970).

The trade unions opposed the Prices and Incomes Bill, with public sector unions being especially concerned as the government could have applied the measure directly to them. Employers, too, were not anxious to embrace a system of statutory wage determination and it is also doubtful if government really wished to take on this role. Allen (1997: 144) claims the bill 'was mainly a device by the Fianna Fáil Government to pressurise the union leaders into standing up against their own militants'. The threat was effective. Allen (1997: 145) notes that, although opposed to the bill, there was a refusal 'to call any stoppages against the measure, and it quickly became clear that the ICTU was looking for an accommodation with Fianna Fáil'. ICTU entered negotiations under the auspices of the ELC and following difficult negotiations concluded the first of what was to be a series of national wage agreements (NWAs). This provided for wage increases well in excess of those envisaged under the bill. An agreement specifying a ten per cent wage increase for twelve months, plus four per cent for a further six months, was accepted and as a result the government withdrew the Prices and Incomes Bill (Breen *et al.* 1990).

The initial agreements (1970–1976) were bipartite employer-union agreements with the government represented only in its capacity as a public sector employer. As the decade progressed the government, in its role as a government, became more directly involved in the negotiation of agreements. Seven national wage agreements were negotiated between 1970 and 1978, followed by two national understandings agreed in 1979 and 1980. The national understandings differed from the national wage agreements in that in addition to a union-employer pay agreement they included an agreement between the unions and government on a wide range of non-pay issues. As such, they can be considered to represent a more highly developed form of neo-corporatism than the NWAs. The agreements set wage increases for unionised workers across the economy and also became a standard for wage increases in non-union employments. The principle clauses in each agreement covered the basic norm for pay increases and the phasing of the implementation of the agreement. The substantive terms varied from agreement to agreement, with the basic pay increases being subject to the greatest variation (see Table 13.2). Fogarty *et al.* (1981: 19) commented that the national wage agreements were viewed as 'an award from Heaven or Dublin' and it became common for workers to seek to improve on the basic terms. Thus, free collective bargaining continued to operate in many instances at local level. This was possible through the operation of clauses, which provided for above the norm (ATN) increases. NWA norms were biased in favour of the lower paid by the specification of minimum absolute level of increases. However, as noted below, due to tax developments no lasting improvements were made in the position of the lower paid over the course of the agreements.

All the centralised agreements of the 1970s were negotiated under the guidance of the Employer Labour Conference, which also monitored the implementation and was involved in the interpretation of the agreements. The Labour Court, however, was given the central role in evaluating the admissibility of claims under the agreement. Each agreement, with the exception of the 1978 agreement, prohibited taking industrial action in pursuance of above the norm claims. The agreements were also maintained by moral persuasion and the threat of legislation. However, the threat of legal restriction was only put into effect against one group, members of the Irish Bank Officials Association (IBOA). Legislation was introduced in 1973, 1975 and 1976 to prevent the banks from paying increases above the terms of the NWAs to their employees (McCarthy 1977: 121; Kerr and Whyte 1985).

KEY ELEMENTS IN THE EVOLUTION OF THE NATIONAL WAGE AGREEMENTS

In the following subsections a number of key features of centralised bargaining from 1970 to 1981 are reviewed.

General Terms

The national wage agreements provided for flat-level increases in wages, which was a form of 'wage solidarity' designed to benefit the lower paid, combined with percentage increases which aimed the differentials between differing groups of workers by giving higher overall absolute increases to higher-paid workers (see Table 13.2).

Table 13.2 *Principal Pay Terms of the National Agreements*			
Year	Round No.	Phase	Details
1970	13	1	£2 a week for men, IR£1.70 for women.
		2	4% plus cost of living escalator of IR£33 a year.
1972	14	1	9% on first IR£30 a week, IR£2.50 minimum for men, £2.25 for women; 7.5% on next IR£10 a week and 4% on the remainder.
		2	4% plus cost of living escalator supplement of 16p for each 1% increase in the CPI.
1974	15	1	9% on first IR£30 a week; 7% on next IR£10 a week; 6% on next IR£10 a week - minimum IR£2.40 a week.
		2	4% plus 60p a week; cost of living escalator 10%.
1975	16	1	8% – minimum of IR£2 a week plus a quarter of 2nd phase of 14th round.
		2	5% – minimum increase of IR£1 a week.
		3	No increase except one quarter of 2nd phase of 14th round.
		4	2.8%.
1976	17	1	3% of basic pay plus IR£2 a week, subject to a maximum of IR£5 a week or IR£3 a week if greater.
1977	18	1	2.5% plus IR£1 a week, minimum increase of IR£2 a week, maximum increase IR£5 a week.
		2	2.5% plus IR£1 a week, minimum increase of IR£2, maximum increase of IR£4.23 a week.
1979	19	1	8% minimum increase IR£3.50 a week.
		2	2%.

Pay Terms and Conditions of the National Understandings			
Year	Round No.	Phase	Details
1979	20	1	9% minimum increase of IR£5.50 a week
		2	2% plus amount related to CPI movement, minimum increase IR£3.30 a week.
1980	21	1	8% plus IR£1 a week.
		2	7%.

Source: Adapted from OECD (1979); McGinley (1989a)

Gender Aspects of Pay Provisions

The agreements made provision for lower increases for women workers, but these were greater than had generally been achieved by women workers under the wage round system, where increases of only sixty per cent of the adult male rate were common. The higher increases for women workers were part of a process of gradually moving to an equal pay regime, which would have been required by entry into the EEC. The government had refused demands in the late 1960s to bring forward equal pay for equal work in anticipation of EEC entry (see Allen 1997).

Spread of Commencement Dates

The third agreement successfully narrowed the spread of termination dates, which had varied since the wage round system, reducing the termination dates from twenty-one months to about three months.

Duration of the Agreements and Indexation

Considerable difficulties emerged on the duration of agreements, with individual agreements varying in length. The most extreme example of this occurred in the fifth agreement in 1977, which was an interim one lasting only seven months. A central reason for the repeated difficulties over duration was the unpredictability of inflation. The 1970s were marked by extremely high levels of inflation, driven chiefly by external factors (notably the first and second oil crises in 1973–1974 and 1979–1980). A number of agreements contained escalator clauses, which indexed wage increases to the rate of inflation (as measured by the Consumer Price Index). The third agreement in 1974 contained such a clause, and when inflation rose from 11.4 per cent in 1973 to seventeen per cent in 1974, this triggered 'pay rises in the order of thirty per cent – the cost of living rose by approximately twenty-four per cent over the [twelve-month] period of the agreement' (OECD 1979: 50–1).

Pay, Tax and Other Benefits

The escalator provision in the fourth agreement was renegotiated as a result of government intervention to reduce value added tax (VAT) from certain items and the introduction of price subsidies as a package aimed at breaking the inflationary spiral. Hardiman (1988) suggests this 'created a degree of expectation that NWAs and budgets might be closely linked again in the future'. Subsequent agreements, up to the national understandings, did in fact have such linkages and they played a central role in gaining acceptance for the agreements. For example, it was generally accepted that the tax concessions were integral to its acceptance (Breen *et al.* 1990). However, linking tax and other budgetary considerations was most pronounced under the national understandings.

Ratification of Agreements

Each agreement was subject to ratification by a special delegate conference of ICTU. The third and fifth NWA and the first national understanding were rejected by special delegate conferences of the ICTU and agreement was only reached after the employers/government increased their offers. This process ensured that there was a strong input into the agreements from individual unions and from the members of unions who were balloted on agreements. Such ratification procedures have continued to be used during the centralised agreements since 1987.

Above and Below the Norm Provisions

Each NWA set out provisions for above the norm (ATN) claims, which essentially related to claims based on anomalies, productivity-based claims and claims for improvements in the conditions of employment. O'Brien (1989b: 9) suggests that these anomaly and productivity clauses 'were tried and tested to the point of exhaustion'. However, it was not just worker ingenuity that drove the ATN claims. Increases were not infrequently paid on management initiative and could be paid for business reasons, such as to 'retain quality labour' and to 'maintain or increase productivity' (see Wallace 1982). Thus, on occasion employers signed so-called 'sweetheart productivity deals', which specified productivity increases, but where no increases ensued (or were sought). These were signed in order to get around the restrictive clauses of the national agreements. The second and subsequent agreements introduced a below the norm clause, which allowed employers to claim inability to pay. The criteria for the use of this clause were restrictive and little use was made of it, particularly because Labour Court recommendations for inability to pay usually came with a provision for eventual payment of the increase and retrospection (O'Brien 1989a: 136).

The ATN claims led to a high level of wage drift, with claims under the ATN clauses being particularly prevalent in the public sector. The government were concerned that anomaly awards had outrun the costs of the agreement norms. The agreement was accepted at a delegate conference of the ICTU by a slender margin. Hardiman (1988) suggests that the unions were generally unhappy with the ATN clauses, which were stricter than before, at a time when most sectors were doing quite well. As a concession to the unions, the agreement allowed for up to two per cent extra to be negotiated at local level. For the first time it also permitted industrial action in certain circumstances in pursuance of ATN claims.

THE END OF NATIONAL AGREEMENTS, 1970–1981

The national understandings were ambitious attempts to integrate collective bargaining and government budgetary policy, but both agreements were only concluded after considerable difficulty. The first agreement was only accepted by the trade unions after an improved offer from the employers. By the time of the second national understanding, employers had become disenchanted with the process of centralised agreements and only accepted the agreement after direct government intervention. Although an agreement was concluded there was residual resentment within the FUE at 'undue political pressure' that they felt was brought to bear on them (Roche 1989: 124). Although formal talks opened on a new understanding, an impasse was soon reached on pay terms. At breakdown ICTU was claiming fifteen per cent while the FUE was only prepared to offer twelve per cent. Employer reluctance to enter a new agreement was heightened by ATN-fed wage drift, the high level of industrial action and the cost of the non-pay elements of the agreements (Fogarty *et al.* 1981). The expiry of the second national understanding heralded the suspension of centralised bargaining in Ireland. The newly elected Fine Gael-Labour Coalition Government was not as committed as Fianna Fáil had been to the process of centralised bargaining and did not intervene to avert a breakdown, and there followed a return to decentralised bargaining.

THE PERFORMANCE OF CENTRALISED BARGAINING, 1970–1981

The centralised agreements were a much more structured system than the pay rounds. Pay was set in specific terms, the duration of the agreements was fixed and machinery was provided to deal with disputes arising out of the terms of the agreements and any anomalies. In terms of process 'they had basically stabilised what had become a chaotic picture' (von Prondzynski 1992: 79). However, they can be viewed as failing to deliver on the objectives set for them and left unions, employers and government dissatisfied. McCarthy (1977) identified the following objectives for centralised bargaining:

- control inflation;
- moderate income increases;
- reduce industrial unrest;
- promote full employment; and
- deliver relatively higher increases to lower-paid workers.

International developments meant that any attempts to control inflation were stillborn and inflation actually rose precipitously during the 1970s, reaching twenty per cent by 1981. The impact of the two oil crises of 1973–1974 and 1979–1980 are dramatically illustrated in Figure 13.1. Only wage increases were initially subject to any control, which led to resentment from workers. Even wage increases, however, could not be contained as the ATN increases fed wage drift. Although there was some decline in working days lost in the early 1970s, there was a substantial increase after that and many strikes were unofficial (see Chapter 8). In spite of government attempts to promote full employment, unemployment rose over the duration of the agreements, from four per cent in 1969 to 10.7 per cent by 1982 (Conniffe and Kennedy 1984). This is not surprising, since at most the centralised agreements could influence only one variable – the wage rate. Thus, while employment grew over the period of the agreements, the labour force expanded at a greater rate (Hardiman 1988: 104).

In addition to these failures, the government experienced difficulty in honouring the wider social and welfare commitments in the national understandings. This was evidenced by the chairman of the Labour Court's reference to the national understandings as 'Notional Understandings' (Horgan 1989: 195). Some practitioners even referred to them ironically as 'national misunderstandings'.

Figure 13.1
Inflation, 1970–1987

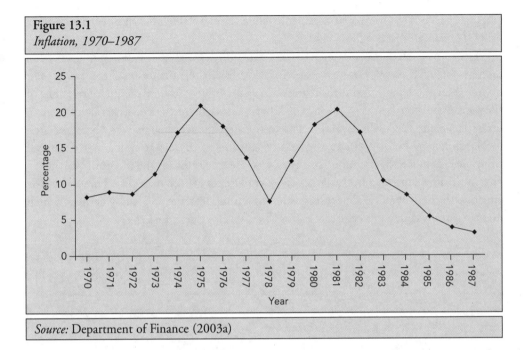

Source: Department of Finance (2003a)

The decentralised character of the Irish trade union movement and the inability of the FUE to stand firm against 'union pressure on national pay norms' have been pointed to as causing difficulties for the national agreements. However, it is not just in Ireland that a relatively buoyant labour market has led to pressure on corporatist arrangements, as Germany experienced a similar lack of employer solidarity during its post-war boom. Faced with a buoyant labour market, there is a natural incentive for employers to offer higher pay in order to attract, keep and motivate labour. Arguably, a more telling defect of the Irish experiment was that it represented an attempt to transplant an egalitarian model into a country with an inegalitarian taxation system. The extensive welfare and social provisions associated with the agreements had to be paid from out of a narrow tax base. The Irish political system was quite different from that in Sweden, where neo-corporatism had developed. In particular, there was no large Socialist or Labour party competing for or holding power, a feature which political scientists have suggested facilitates neo-corporatism. Irish governments were reluctant to take action to extend the tax base to include effective taxation of groups such as the self-employed and farmers, despite the fact that 'by the late 1970s almost ninety per cent of income tax came from the PAYE sector' (Hardiman 1988: 102).

This situation was compounded by the removal of rates, property taxes and car tax after the election of the Fianna Fáil Government in 1977. The proportion of the total tax take from personal income rose from only seven per cent in the mid-1960s to twelve per cent in 1974 and over fifteen per cent in 1976 (Conniffe and Kennedy 1984). This development meant that while pre-tax real incomes rose sharply through the 1970s, the post-tax wage increases over the duration of the agreements were much smaller. In 1970 the average tax take from wage earners was 18.3 per cent, but this had risen to thirty-two per cent by 1980 (see Figure 13.2). Thus, there existed a tax wedge where employers saw 'labour costs rising steeply while the net value of earnings increased but little' (Hardiman 1988: 99).

The result was that over time the pay terms of the agreements worked against the interests of both employers and workers. In effect, the operation of the tax system militated against pay restraint. Bristow (1982) argued 'the inadequate revision of allowances and rate bands in the face of inflation has caused the effective rate of income tax applicable to any given level of wages to rise steadily over many years' (Bristow, cited in Hardiman 1988: 102–3). In the case of employers, these factors led to withdrawal from the centralised agreements. In the case of the trade unions the inequities in the tax system became expressed in the large-scale tax marches (Sheehan 1983). These had little effect, with the overall burden of taxation remaining on wage and salary earners, which had risen from thirty per cent in 1979 to forty-five per cent in 1981.

Figure 13.2
Proportion of Personal Income Tax (Including Employee and Employer Social Security Contributions), 1970 and 1980 Compared

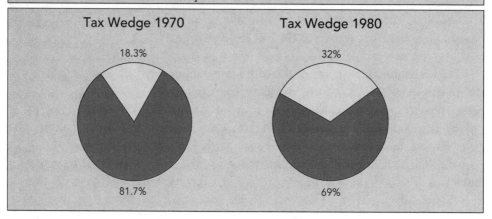

While noting the limitations of the national agreements to meet the objectives set for them, it would be wrong to suggest that they caused the economic dislocation of the 1980s. There are many contributory causes to that, some of which are external. In addition to the already noted oil crises, job losses occurred due to industrial restructuring consequent on entry to the EEC. Arguably more important was government economic policy, which had been pro-cyclical. Thus, governments had tended to increase spending when the economy was buoyant in the late 1970s, which forced cutbacks in the 1980s, accentuating the slump. Fitz Gerald (2000: 42) writes:

eight out of ten budgets over the course of the period 1980 to 1989 were deflationary. This was necessary to correct the huge imbalance in the public finances and it represented a strongly pro-cyclical fiscal stance at a time of very low growth. Over the ten years, the cumulative deflationary impetus imparted by fiscal policy amounted to around eight per cent of GNP. It is not surprising that the Irish economy did not shine over that period!

Allen (1997) notes that the problems arising from the borrowing in the late 1970s was accentuated by the high interest rates of the 1980s.

DECENTRALISED BARGAINING, 1982–1987

The decentralised collective bargaining that emerged in 1982 was quite different in both structure and outcomes to the earlier wage rounds, which can be ascribed to two main factors. First was the increased openness of the Irish economy, and second the severe recession. The economic uncertainty meant that agreements tended to be short, with agreements spanning one year and incorporating a single phase becoming more common as time went on (O'Brien 1989a: 140). Industry bargaining fell into disuse, and in the private sector the focus of bargaining activity moved to the level of the individual firm. During the 1960s there were sixty industrial bargaining groups, which determined not just pay increases, but also wage rates. O'Brien (1989a: 138) records that under economic pressures, most of these groupings 'were formally disbanded or fell into disuse' (see Chapters 4 and 9). There was a reduction in the totals at work due to redundancies in excess of 20,000 per annum. Unemployment rocketed from 8.9 per cent in 1981 to 18.1 per cent in 1986 (see Figure 13.3). The deteriorating economic circumstances introduced a 'new realism' into employer-employee relationships that transcended all facets of organisational activities, including collective bargaining (Gunnigle *et al.* 1994: 61). Irish wage costs per unit rose by only seven per cent between 1980 and 1985, compared with an average thirty-seven per cent increase in competing countries (Hardiman 1988: 220).

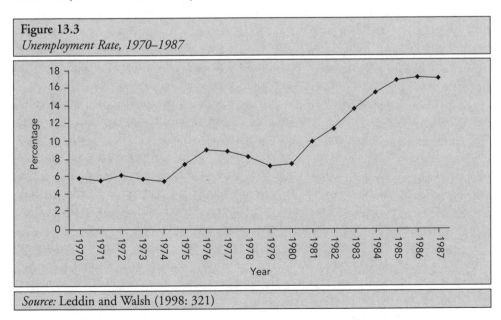

Figure 13.3
Unemployment Rate, 1970–1987

Source: Leddin and Walsh (1998: 321)

The 1980s saw a number of developments in workplace bargaining in Ireland that are now well understood, at least in their general outline. These developments straddled the period of decentralised bargaining from 1982 to 1987 and continued on into the resumption of centralised bargaining in late 1987. Gunnigle *et al.* (1994: 62) note that viability and economic performance became the key criteria shaping wage increases. The 'sweetheart' productivity deals of the 1970s were replaced by assertive employer demands that all or some wage increases now had to be earned through better company or individual performance (O'Brien 1989a: 139). The most visible aspect of this greater employer assertiveness involved organisational retrenchment, and in a significant number of cases, concession bargaining. Concession bargaining involved 'union givebacks' such as wage cuts, reductions in terms and conditions of employment and accompanying productivity concessions. Such concession bargaining was especially noticeable in companies that were leaders in terms of pay and conditions, such as Waterford Crystal, Aer Lingus, Krups, the Associated Banks and De Beers. These were introduced in a highly adversarial way in some instances, for example Packard Electrical Ltd, but in other instances were done partly through union involvement, as in the case of Aer Lingus. Waterford Crystal initially used a unilateral approach but when further retrenchment was necessary they reverted to involving the trade union (see Chapter 12).

As a result, settlements varied widely across industries, with no wage round norm being established. Indeed, some commentators questioned the existence of the wage round concept in the private sector between 1982 and 1987 (McGinley 1989b). The FUE sought to shift collective bargaining away from the notion of a specific norm in each wage round and from the idea that wage rounds ought to follow each other automatically. Their position was that pay increases should be closely tied to what the individual firm could bear (Hardiman 1988). As can be seen from Table 13.3, the level of wage increases decreased greatly over the duration of the period, in line with a reduction in the rate of inflation. At times the government attempted to impose a norm through pay guidelines, but these were largely ignored by private sector negotiators and, as von Prondzynski (1985) argues, were best seen as the government's opening position in the public sector pay negotiations. Table 13.3 records the estimated average increases achieved in the private sector over the period.

While the adverse economic circumstances led to a much-weakened trade union movement, there was some lengthening of the union negotiating agenda. Non-wage issues took on a greater significance than before, with issues such as hours of work, bonuses, leave and general working conditions becoming part of the agenda (Income Data Service 1992). Employers countered with demands for changes in working practices and methods, to which there seemed amongst trade union ranks 'to be a growing willingness to accept the need for changes' (FUE 1987). Many of the changes at workplace level were designed to achieve increased flexibility.

The changes in working conditions, however, were achieved not just through collective bargaining. Turlough O'Sullivan, director general of IBEC, emphasises that there was a lot of 'work done at enterprise level in the early to mid-1980s, by employers who had related to their employees, not just through trade unions, but through increased *direct communications with employees outside the collective bargaining system*' (Wallace and Clifford 1998). While acknowledging the role played by collective bargaining in the introduction of flexibility, Wallace and Clifford (1998) point out that collective bargaining has been used not so much as a means of *introducing flexibility*, but

Table 13.3
Private Sector Pay Increases, 1981–1987

Round	Average Cumulative Increase (%)	Average Length (months)
22	16.4	14.9
23	10.9	13.5
24	9.3	12.75
25	6.8	12
26	6.0	12
27	6.5*	15.4*

* Figures of around 4.5–6.5 per cent per annum were being agreed, but there were only a small number of agreements and events were overtaken by the PNR agreement.

Note: These figures may mask large disparities within and between rounds.

Source: McGinley (1989a)

as a way of seeking to regulate and constrain it. While the introduction of greater flexibility was the major development of the 1980s, this did not amount to an adoption of the Atkinson (1984) flexible firm model, but was characterised by partial adoption of elements of flexibility, or 'cherry picking'. Employers tended to implement those elements of flexibility which suited their circumstances but did not adopt a thoroughgoing approach. In some instances flexibility even decreased. For example, in redundancy situations it was common for companies to lay off temporary workers first, thereby reducing numerical flexibility.

Wallace (1999: 1) notes that

the negotiation of multi-skilling among craft workers appears to have been uncommon with add-skilling most evident. Substantial numeric flexibility was introduced in the services sector whereas functional flexibility was significantly extended in the 1980s in manufacturing. Functional flexibility was not a major issue in much of the services sector as such flexibility was normal in much of that sector.

THE RETURN TO CENTRALISED AGREEMENTS, 1987

While employers had enjoyed significant success in advancing their agenda during the period of decentralised bargaining, there were severe economic difficulties, with a growing crisis in the public finances being especially marked. The three principal elements in current government expenditure are foreign debt service, social welfare and the public sector payroll. At the end of 1986 the national debt of IR£24 billion was three times larger than it had been in 1980. The massive growth in unemployment saw expenditure in social services increase from 28.9 per cent of GNP in 1980 to 35.6 per cent in 1985 (NESC 1986).

Because of the perceived difficulties in tackling debt service and social welfare, the public sector payroll became the central focus of government action. *A Strategy for Development 1986–1990* report, issued by the NESC, emphasised the need for cogent action to address the 'twin problems of mass unemployment and chronic fiscal imbalance' (NESC 1986). The NESC report did not make any explicit recommendations on pay because the employer representatives on the council expressed the view that negotiations at the level of the firm was the most appropriate means of determining pay. Nonetheless, the report was to greatly influence future government thinking on national bargaining and income policy.

Interest in returning to a national agreement was expressed by a number of prominent trade union leaders throughout 1986, such as John Carroll of the ITGWU and Bill Attley of the Federated Workers Union of Ireland (FWUI). A number of factors help to explain the trade unions' interest in a return to centralised bargaining. Even with the abandonment of centralised bargaining in the early 1980s, there was a substantial body of union opinion that favoured centralised agreements. Issues such as employment, tax reform and social welfare were now central to the ICTU's agenda, as it would appear that the political and economic objectives of trade unions had converged. Congress expressed particular concern for the plight of low-paid employees, who were suffering most in the decentralised bargaining in the 1980s because of their weak bargaining position. The decision of the trade unions to participate in the negotiation of the Programme for National Recovery (PNR) must be seen in light of falling membership levels between 1980 and 1987 (Dineen and Wallace 1991). Union leaders also looked to the situation in Britain, where British unions had suffered major setbacks under the premiership of Margaret Thatcher.

Bill Attley, the then general secretary of the FWUI, warned that the trade union movement was in serious danger of being marginalised (ICTU 1987). The trade unions looked to the prospect of a new national agreement to 'beef up' their role and status in Irish society. ICTU was also concerned by the state of the public finances and government's need to control the public sector payroll. This could only be achieved by a combination of cutting numbers employed or freezing public sector pay. The prospect of having a pay freeze in the public sector while the private sector locally negotiated increases (even modest ones) posed a threat to the unity of the trade union movement. That this was a real prospect was illustrated by the government decision to refuse to implement a teachers' arbitration award.

Early 1987 brought the election of a Fianna Fáil Government whose economic strategy was to be broadly guided by the principles and priorities established in the NESC (1986) report. In April of 1987, ICTU proposed to government that there should be discussions about a national plan for growth and economic recovery, public finances and social services. There was no private sector employer push for a return to national agreements. Indeed, as a result of the bargaining advantages enjoyed by employers, they had considerable doubts about such a course of action (O'Brien 1989b). The FUE was especially concerned about the proposed reduction in working hours and that a national agreement would be too rigid. They were, however, 'gradually wooed into support of the government's wider economic policies in general … the cuts in public spending were the kind the private sector employers have been urging for years' (*Business and Finance* 1987).

The negotiations that followed were concluded in October 1987 and resulted in the Programme for National Recovery (PNR), the first of six such agreements. The programme was to cover the period up to January 1991. Employer support in the final analysis rested on the extremely modest terms of the agreement, particularly the fact that the pay terms were substantially lower than the emerging trend of 4.5 per cent to 6.5 per cent in the 27th round, which had just commenced in the autumn of 1987. In contrast with these figures, the average of 2.5 per cent in the PNR, even combined with a one-hour reduction in the working week (for those on forty hours per week), was irresistible. In addition to the pay terms of the agreement, a number of broad objectives were set out, as follows.

- The creation of a fiscal, exchange and monetary climate conducive to economic growth, including a commitment that the ratio of debt to GNP should be reduced.
- Movement towards greater equity and fairness in the tax system.
- Measures to generate employment opportunities. Notably, no extra expenditure was to be committed to this.
- A reduction of social inequalities.

In terms of its provisions, O'Brien (1989b: 23) argues that 'a whole host of old conventions were ditched and new conventions forged'. The first time around these included a thirty-nine-month agreement, a pay increase at or even slightly below the rate of inflation and a national commitment to pursue the reduction of working hours. There were also some absences from the agreement, notably, there was no provision for institutional monitoring of the agreement (as the ELC had in the 1970s). The pay terms were not fixed norms but guidelines, which in the private sector had to be agreed through local-level bargaining. The PNR also differed from agreements of the 1970s in that the terms concerning economic and social policy were expressed as specific targets and not as binding commitments.

KEY FEATURES OF THE CENTRALISED AGREEMENTS, 1987–2004

In the following subsections a number of key features of centralised bargaining from 1970 to 1981 are reviewed.

Wage Terms

The agreements can be divided into two broad groups. Four of the agreements had provision for more modest wage rises, while two, the Programme for Economic and Social Progress (PESP) and the Programme for Prosperity and Fairness (PPF), contained wage increases of a higher order of magnitude. The issue of ATN or BTN increases were not a feature of the agreements. There is evidence, however, of wage drift. Under the PNR, payments were reported to have averaged in the region of four per cent, rather than the two to three per cent provided for. There were a substantial number of agreements in excess of the national agreements negotiated in certain sectors, such as retailing (Wallace *et al.* 2001). Frawley (2000b: 4) reported that 'almost all of the major retail multiples, including Dunnes Stores, Tesco, Superquinn and Pennys, have now concluded wage deals fifteen per cent to twenty per cent in excess of the national agreement [Partnership 2000]'. Referring to growth and profit-driven increases above the terms of the PPF, Sheehan (2004a: 17) writes that 'the effective role of the national deal in those sort of circumstances was often to act as a sort of floor, with the LRC and the Labour Court effectively "policing" cases where conflict threatened'.

Wage Tax Trade-Offs

The central feature of the agreements was the trade union movement's exercise of wage restraint in return for reductions in personal income tax. This meant that real take-home pay increased at a rate greater than the nominal increases under the agreement. For example, the pay increase of the PNR was balanced with a provision for a IR£225 million reduction in the tax take. This commitment was actually oversubscribed, with tax reductions of IR£750 million being delivered over the course of the agreement. The employers also achieved substantial tax reductions on the corporate tax take, which was designed to encourage companies to locate in Ireland and to reward enterprise. Table 13.4 contains outline details of the wage and tax elements of the six agreements to date.

Table 13.4
Wage and Tax Elements of NWAs, 1987–2004

Programme	Years	Duration (months)	Tax Provisions	Pay Terms
Programme for National Recovery (PNR)	1987–1991	39 months (6-month pay pause to apply to the public sector)	Reduction of IR£225 million, including increases in the PAYE allowance costing IR£70 million. Widening of tax band and cut in tax rates to 30% and 53%.	3% on the first IR£120 per week. 2% on the remaining weekly pay. Minimum IR£4 increase per week.
Programme for Economic and Social Progress (PESP)	1991–1994	36 months	Reduce bottom rate to 25% – only 27% achieved plus 1% income levy added; also the marginal relief rate of taxation was reduced from 48% to 40%.	Year 1: 4% increase. Year 2: 3% increase* (+ 3% local (exceptional) bargaining clause). Year 3: 3.75%.
Programme for Competitiveness and Work (PCW)	1994–1997	36 months	IR£900 million tax cuts, reduction from 27% to 26% on standard	Year 1: 2.5% increase. Year 2: 2.5% increase.

Table 13.4 (continued)

Wage and Tax Elements of NWAs, 1987–2004

Programme	Years	Duration (months)	Tax Provisions	Pay Terms
Programme for Competitiveness and Work (PCW) (cont'd)			rate; PRSI reduced by 1%. IR£100 million cut in business tax and improvements for small firms.	Year 3: 2.5%.
Partnership 2000 for Inclusion, Employment and Competitiveness	1997–2000	39 months	IR£900 million in tax reductions over 3 years. IR£100 million cut in business tax, including reductions in corporation tax.	Year 1: 2.5% increase. Year 2: 2.25% increase* (+ 2% local bargaining clause). Year 3: 1.5% first 9 months + 1% in last 6 months.
Programme for Prosperity and Fairness (PPF)	2000–2003	33 months (locally agreed pay pauses on last phase of agreement due to inability to pay)	IR£1.2 billion in tax breaks. Increase personal allowance by IR£800 to IR£5,500 and the PAYE allowance increased by IR£1,100 to IR£2,000; widening of the standard tax band (single tax earner from IR£17,000 to IR£20,000 and married from IR£28,000 to IR£29,000); and reductions in the rates in which tax is levied to 42% and 20%.	Year 1: 5.5% increase. Year 2: 5.5% increase (+ 2% renegotiated). Year 3: 4.0% increase (final 9 months) (+ 1% once-off lump sum).
Sustaining Progress	2003–2004	First Phase: 18 months Second Phase: 18 months (to be negotiated). 6-month pay pause	No tax concessions	3% increase for 9 months. 2% increase next 6 months. 2% increase for final

Table 13.4 (continued)				
Wage and Tax Elements of NWAs, 1987–2004				
Programme	Years	Duration (months)	Tax Provisions	Pay Terms
Sustaining Progress (cont'd)		for public sector under benchmarking agreement.		3 months. Minimum wage to increase to €7.00 per hour from 1 Feb. 2004

* Indicates the earliest date for payment of local bargaining clauses.

Note: This table simplifies the provisions in a number of ways. For instance, there were separate provisions on phasing and pay pauses in the public and private sector in some agreements.

Source: Various national agreements

Local-Level Bargaining

Two of the agreements allowed for local-level bargaining. The PESP had a three per cent local bargaining clause, which employers expressed some dissatisfaction with. Employers insisted that that the local-level increase would be paid in 'exceptional circumstances', whereas unions claimed that it was only 'in exceptional circumstances it would not be paid'. As a result of their experiences, the employers only agreed to the unions' demand for a two per cent local bargaining clause in the Partnership 2000 agreement on the basis that it would be generally paid. In effect, they considered it an integral part of the basic rise they were conceding, giving it more the appearance than the substance of a local bargaining clause.

Profit Sharing

Unlike any of the earlier agreements, Partnership 2000 contained specific provision for a two per cent profit sharing based on the establishment of partnership in the workplace. The provision in the agreement read: 'the Government and the Social Partners support more favourable tax treatment of employee share schemes and profit sharing as a means of deepening partnership and securing commitment to competitiveness at the level of the enterprise' (Partnership 2000 1997: 64).

Monitoring Agreements

The Central Review Committee was 'established under the Programme for National Recovery to review and monitor the progress in implementing the Programme and the achievement of its targets and objectives' (PESP 1991: 87). As part of the PPF agreement, a National Implementation Body (NIB) was established, which took on the role of the old ELC (Sheehan 2003c). The NIB was given a significant role in assessing the overall compliance of recommendations issued by the Labour Court and the Labour Relations Commission (Sheehan 2003c). Under Sustaining Progress, the NIB was given an enhanced role and was to meet monthly 'to ensure delivery of the stability and peace provisions of the agreement' (Sustaining Progress 2003: 68). A steering group was established under Sustaining Progress, which replaced the Central Review Committee (CRC) (Sheehan 2003a: 21). It comprises the 'government and four representatives from each of the social partner pillars' (Sustaining Progress 2003: 17). Sheehan (2003c: 3) notes that 'the Steering Group is to review, monitor and report on the progress of the implementation of the wider policy framework at quarterly plenary meetings'. In addition to formal mechanisms, under the early agreements Thomas *et al.* (2003: 33) argues that Kevin Duffy (formerly assistant general secretary, ICTU) and Turlough O'Sullivan (IBEC) acted 'as an informal Employer Labour Conference' to resolve disputes.

Sustaining Progress Agreement: Adjudication Provisions

Under the fifth agreement, the PPF, the Labour Court was given a specific role in adjudicating on the agreement. This role was strengthened in the Sustaining Progress agreement in 2003 and involved a voluntarily agreed compliance measure allowing 'the Labour Court to issue "binding recommendations on the pay agreement"' (Sheehan 2003a: 20; see also Chapter 4 on institutions). Adjudication on disputes is provided for under Section 20(2) of the Industrial Relations Act 1969. This section covers situations whereby parties in a trade dispute request the Court to investigate a specific issue involved in the dispute (mentioned below) and before the investigation undertake to accept the recommendation of the Court (Kerr 1991a: 171). The section now applies to the Sustaining Progress agreement, with the following scenarios being covered.

1. Where a breach of the agreement is claimed.
2. In a case involving 'inability to pay'.
3. Where it is claimed that cost-offsetting measures are needed to honour the deal.
4. Where there is disagreement over what constitutes 'normal ongoing' change (Sustaining Progress 2003: 75).

Table 13.5 indicates the avenue to be followed depending on which of the above scenarios arises. As this makes the agreement arbitrable, it is arguable that it represents a move in the direction of making collective agreements conform to a 'disputes of rights'-type process (see Chapter 3).

Duration of Agreements

The duration of the first five agreements varied between thirty-three and thirty-nine months (see Table 13.4). During negotiations on Sustaining Progress, difficulty was experienced in reaching agreement on a longer duration due to uncertainty over the direction of inflation and prospects for continued economic growth (Dobbins 2003a: 24). As a result, an interim agreement on wage increases was reached for an eighteen-month period, with provision for a second stage to be negotiated subsequently. Sheehan (2003b: 3) suggested that this gave the 'social partners room for some creative thinking ahead of the next set of talks'.

Table 13.5

Avenues for Dispute Resolution

Dispute resolution would follow these avenues (only if there is no resolution would the dispute move to the next level).

1. Claim → local bargaining/negotiating → refer to LRC → refer to Labour Court → issue 'binding' recommendation.

2. Claim → local bargaining/negotiating → refer to LRC → (independent assessor appointed) → refer back to LRC to review report → refer to Labour Court → issue 'binding' recommendation.

3. Claim → local bargaining/negotiating → refer to LRC → (independent assessor appointed) → refer back to LRC to review report → refer to Labour Court → three-week cooling-off period → take decided action (not binding).

4. Claim → local bargaining/negotiating → refer to LRC → refer to Labour Court → issue 'binding' recommendation.

Source: Adapted from Sustaining Progress

Renegotiation of Agreements

Two of the agreements were varied/renegotiated, a feature in common with a number of the national agreements in the 1970s. In early 1992 the government indicated that it could not meet the pay terms as a result of lower-than-expected growth (von Prondzynski 1992). Eventually, agreement was reached for the payment of the terms a year in arrears with full retrospection. This had the effect of giving an interest-free loan to the government for the period of the deferral of the increases, but retained the integrity of the increases themselves – a standard practice in public sector disputes where governments experience difficulties in implementing pay awards. The PPF had been negotiated on the prediction of a 2.5 per cent rate of inflation. However, inflation had reached 5.6 per cent by 2000 (see Figure 13.9), leading to calls from unions for the renegotiation of the agreement. As there was no provision in the agreement for such a renegotiation, employers resisted these demands. Following intense pressure, however, they conceded a two per cent additional pay rise from April 2001 and a once-off one per cent 'lump sum' increase from April 2002.

Social Provision and Involvement of the Community and Voluntary Sector

The community and voluntary sector was involved directly for the first time in the negotiation of the Partnership 2000 agreement. This was in response to criticisms that they had been excluded from negotiations and a developing view that it was insufficient to have the trade unions put forward points for this constituency, as traditionally had been the case. Groups such as The Irish National Organisation of the Unemployed (INOU), the National Youth Council, the Conference of Religious of Ireland (CORI) and Protestant Aid were among nineteen separate groups that made presentations as part of the process. Table 13.6 contains details on elements of the social provisions of the various agreements.

The PNR was generally viewed as a success in that the terms of the agreement were largely satisfied. The major successes were on the economic front. Economic growth exceeded four per cent per annum and manufacturing output and exports grew steadily, creating a major balance of trade surplus. Inflation, already at low levels at the start of the agreement, reached its lowest level in thirty years in 1988. Most significantly, the debt/GNP ratio fell from 125 per cent in 1987 to ninety-nine per cent in 1990 (see Figure 13.6 below) and net job gains were achieved, reversing the trends of the early 1980s. Amongst the trade unions there was criticism that insufficient effort was being made to tackle unemployment. The 1988 ICTU annual delegate conference saw three motions debated, all critical of the PNR. However, two years into the programme the ICTU voted to continue to support it and decided in favour of entering talks on a new agreement.

Table 13.6
Social Provisions of the NWAs

Agreement	Key Social Provisions
PNR	Emphasis on government policy on social equity, with particular attention to health services, education and housing for the disadvantaged. Maintain value in social welfare benefits and where resources are available consider increases for those receiving the lowest payments.
PESP	Seven-year health programme to improve community-based services. Education initiatives at all levels.
PCW	PESP terms for social reform will be carried over. Particular attention to improving social welfare due to 1994 budget provisions.
Partnership 2000	IR£525 million to be spent on social inclusion. Adoption of National Anti-Poverty Strategy (NAPS). Particular attention to tackling unemployment.
PPF	Investment of IR£1.5 billion on social inclusion measures. Update and review NAPS and poverty-proofing arrangements. Establishment of Housing Forum to monitor supply and affordability of housing.
Sustaining Progress	Emphasis on dealing with poverty and promoting social inclusion under NAPS, especially pensioner poverty. Structural reform of the health service. Improving employment equality, especially gender inequality and treatment of persons with disabilities.

Source: Various centralised agreements

VIEWS ON CENTRALISED AGREEMENTS

There have been a range of views on centralised agreements since their introduction in 1987. Some have suggested that they posed a challenge to democracy by taking policy decision away from the Dáil and Seanad. Others suggested that they would lead to inefficient economic outcomes, while still others welcomed the national consensus in tackling the severe economic crisis and compared this approach favourably to the social conflict that had accompanied economic restructuring in the UK in the Thatcher years. The following is a sample of some of these views.

Economic and Social Commentators

In general centralised agreements have met with approval, although there have been changes of emphases over time. Initially, there were strong reservations expressed by some economists, most noticeably those with a neo-classical perspective, with the view that agreements benefited the insiders (mostly the public sector) at the expensive of outsiders (in the exposed private sector) being a repeated theme. For example, Leddin and Walsh (1992: 267) argue that 'centralised agreements have protected the pay and conditions of work of those who have jobs in the private sector and the unionised private sector (the "insiders") at the expense of the outsiders who would work for less'. They also claim 'that social partnership has had the effect of raising the level of unemployment and emigration' (Leddin and Walsh 1992: 267).

With the boom in the Irish economy, these views were articulated less frequently. By the mid-1990s, alternative economic views, notably from the ESRI and the NESC, were expressing support for the continuation of the concept of social partnership. The NESC (1996: 280) concluded that social partnership programmes are the most effective mechanism for developing competitiveness (and social cohesion). 'Without national agreements, income determination will remain a non-competitive, highly collectivised process, with tendencies to monopoly power on both sides of industry' (NESC 1996: 280).

Following the adoption of the euro, some economists questioned the value of the continuation of agreements. Leddin (2000) argued that given the economic straitjacket of the euro, wage restraint is no longer desirable and wages should be allowed to rise, leading to a fall in competitiveness, in order to facilitate a 'soft landing' from the current exceptionally high economic growth rates. However, by 2003 the ESRI and other economists were forecasting that growth prospects were good, with 3.5 per cent being predicted by the ESRI for 2004 (ESRI 2003: 1). Support for the continuation of the social partnership process has continued within the ESRI, although there have been reservations on the impact on growth rates of the benchmarking awards in the public sector (see Fitz Gerald 2003: 12–13).

The process of social partnership came under considerable criticism from groups representing the disadvantaged, such as the Irish National Organisation of the Unemployed (INOU) and those concerned with issues of social justice, such as the Conference of Religious in Ireland (CORI). However, these criticisms revolved around seeking a greater input to the social partnership process for such groups rather than its abandonment. As noted above this led to the direct involvement of the 'community and voluntary sector' in the negotiation of the Partnership 2000 agreement.

The strongest criticism of social partnership has come from Allen (2000) in a sustained attack on the process. He claims it has presided over 'clapped-out public services', growing inequality, increased social exclusion and the transfer of wealth to the super-rich. He writes that 'originally social partnership was supposed to offer some protection from the type of deregulated market system that had been championed by the New Right ... Yet a decade after social partnership agreements were implemented, the inequalities in the Irish labour market resemble most closely those in the deregulated labour markets of the USA' (Allen, 2000: 75).

Political and Government Views

Initially, there was some political opposition to the return to centralised agreements in 1987, which took the form of assertions that they were undemocratic since they removed the Dáil and Seanad from policy formation. However, this quickly changed with the emergence of the economic boom. In 1996, the Taoiseach John Bruton, TD, who had been the most prominent political critic of centralised agreements in the late 1980s, made a strong case for a further agreement to succeed the PCW. He warned that a return to free-for-all pay bargaining would damage real living standards and hurt the most vulnerable members of society. He argued that the national programmes since 1987 had helped create a climate where companies could be confident of industrial peace, stable interest rates, low inflation and clarity about the evolution of wage costs (Sheehan 1996a: 10). All parties now appear to share in a consensus in favour of social partnership, although there are shades of opinion. Within Fianna Fáil it has been suggested that Taoiseach Bertie Ahern, TD is the strongest supporter and that the Minister for Finance, Charlie McCreevey, is less attached to the process (Frawley 2004a). It is also suggested that the Progressive Democrats may no longer be fully supportive of a continuation of the process (Frawley 2004a).

There has been strong criticism of the public sector benchmarking process by Fine Gael. In a radio interview in November 2003, Richard Bruton, TD said, 'The government was given a golden opportunity by the Benchmarking Commission to negotiate a very vigorous reform agenda ... [but] the government failed to put on the table any serious reform agenda' (*News at One* on Radio 1, 29 November 2003). He went on to advocate a renegotiation of benchmarking, thus indicating that the difficulties Fine Gael identified should be resolved within the context of centralised bargaining rather than any abandonment of the process. Direct opposition to the process of social partnership has only come from individual politicians, most noticeably independent Senator Shane Ross, who in condemning benchmarking has returned to the insider argument that public sector unions had become too powerful. Senator Mary O'Rourke is quoted as stating that 'the Senator [Ross] said the sum involved in benchmarking was vast and that the public service was a privileged group' (Seanad Debates 19 November 2003).

Trade Union Views

At an early stage Sheehan (1993) contended that many union leaders believed their best interests would be served within the context of an overall national agreement similar to the PESP. Addressing a special delegate conference of ICTU in 1990, Peter Cassells, general secretary of ICTU, advocated a prioritisation of 'jobs, tax reform and conditions of employment through national negotiations with the government and employers' (*Business and Finance* 1990).

The ICTU approach was developed in a 1990 policy document, *A Decade of Development Reform and Growth*, which advocated the 'development of a modern efficient low inflation economy ... with low levels of unemployment and high levels of social protection' (quoted in *Business and Finance* 1990). This support for national agreements held up throughout the 1990s. In a survey of civil service, employer and union elites, Wallace *et al.* (1998) found all groups strongly supportive of centralised bargaining in the context of the challenges posed by the Economic and Monetary Union (EMU). Most noticeably, of thirty employer and union elites surveyed, seventy-three per cent favoured the continuation of national agreements, while 'not a single employer or union respondent favoured a return to decentralised bargaining' (Wallace *et al.* 1998).

Despite this overall support, trade union views on the process have been expectedly diverse. This is even the case with those union leaders involved in initiating the process – the so-called '*Pepsi generation*' of union leaders. Among the issues giving rise to complaints have been the unfair sharing of the gains arising from economic success, social welfare cuts, union recognition, the continued tax burden on Pay as You Earn (PAYE) workers, a failure to extend partnership to the workplace and the inadequate provision for wage increases for low-paid workers. However, where these criticisms have arisen during agreements they have been in protest at unanticipated government cutbacks. The issue of social welfare cuts – the 'dirty dozen' in 1993 and the fourteen cuts in November 2003 – have been controversial. However, in the 1990s these were resolved through the partnership process rather than withdrawal from the process by the union leaders who complained.

Union complaints have most commonly been voiced in the period preceding negotiations on a new agreement. Due to their large size, the stance adopted by SIPTU has been crucial in the outcome of negotiations. In 1996, in the lead-up to the negotiation of the Partnership 2000 agreement, Bill Attley, general president of SIPTU, disapproved of the unresolved tax burden on the PAYE sector, declaring that the 'era of partnership is over' (IRN 1996: 18–19). Jimmy Somers, SIPTU vice-president, argued that 'it should not be necessary, in an era of partnership, that groups of workers should have to strike in order to establish their constitutional right to join and to be represented by a trade union' (IRN 1996: 19). Prior to the Partnership 2000, the PPF and Sustaining Progress agreements' concession of trade union recognition was claimed to be central to any future negotiations. In the event, the unions accepted all three agreements with less union recognition being conceded.

Viewed in retrospect, these reservations did not truly threaten the social partnership process and can be seen as part of the setting down of 'key commitments' by union leaders in an effort to influence the negotiations process. Commentators have suggested that such protestations by union leaders prior to agreements have come to be seen as having a ritual air to them – part of the 'sabre rattling' that establishes bargaining positions for the latest round. Despite the term 'social partnership' being attached to agreements, it is noteworthy that laying down 'markers' in this way is a classic feature of distributive bargaining, emphasising the point that centralised agreements conform to a 'mixed motive' rather than a pure integrative form of bargaining.

In negotiation terms this is understandable. Sheehan (2004a: 16) notes that 'SIPTU faces a major decision every time a new partnership deal comes around. The country's largest union does not want to be seen as an inevitable supporter of the deals'. Setting down markers can be seen as part of union leaders' efforts to increase their BATNA in negotiations (see Chapter 10). Sheehan (2004a: 16) suggests that there are limitations to such action and that 'SIPTU knows that it can't overplay its hand if it goes for a hardline approach [as] the union sees itself as a "defender" of the national approach'. He also notes that SIPTU has supported all six agreements (Sheehan 2004a). There has been strong support from public sector unions as well, such as IMPACT, the Irish National Teachers' Organisation (INTO) and the Teachers Union of Ireland (TUI). Thus, the majority of trade union leaders have favoured social partnership and, although critical of some of the contents of agreements or their operation, have not sought to advance an alternative strategy. Indeed, workers outside unions, such as the Gardaí, have complained at their exclusion from the process. Yet such protestations may have had a tactical air about them, perhaps designed less to gain access to the process than to justify claims in excess of those provided for in the centralised agreements.

However, a significant minority of union leaders and members have opposed the agreements. Michael O'Reilly, then district secretary of the Amalgamated Transport and General Workers Union (ATGWU), condemned the PESP and its forerunner the PNR as 'having laid the basis of marginalisation of the whole trade union movement', and argued that the 'new right' had prompted sections of the ICTU 'to advocate collaboration with employers and government in controlling workers in order to create stability'. The Association of Secondary Teachers of Ireland (ASTI) left the ICTU in early 2000 in order to pursue an independent pay policy (Frawley 2003a). Individual trade union views on social partnership have not been immutable. The Manufacturing Science and Finance Union changed from being an opponent of national agreements to being a supporter. On the other hand, the Irish Bank Officials Association (IBOA) has switched from being a supporter to an opponent and the Communications Workers Union (CWU) voted against Sustaining Progress, having previously supported the national agreements (Sheehan 2004a).

What has been most noticeable is that workers overall have supported the agreements in ballot votes. The positions adopted by SIPTU, as the largest union, and the public sector committee of ICTU have been central to the acceptance or rejection of any agreement at special ICTU delegate conferences. Sheehan (2004a: 16) suggests that 'a key factor is that the unions that voted against Sustaining Progress could all afford to do so, secure in the knowledge that the deal ensured a minimum pay rise. If it had been rejected then they felt confident that they could go out and secure at least as much'. However, it is noticeable that two unions that represent lower-paid workers have been critical of the agreements. MANDATE has been a strong critic and the Civil and Public Services Union (CPSU) voted against Sustaining Progress because of what was considered the inadequate provision for lower-paid workers. This is a somewhat surprising development, as a traditional argument in favour of centralised bargaining (especially in the 1970s) was that it protected weaker and lower-paid workers.

Shop-floor opposition has been generally muted, although there was pronounced opposition to the Partnership 2000. The data in Table 13.7 shows the vote on that agreement by the trade union delegates was the closest of any of the agreements. The modest size of the pay award in that agreement had come as a surprise to some observers given that the economy was booming at that time. In opposing that agreement, the general secretary of MANDATE, Owen Nulty, argued that under the Programme, low-paid, casual workers would benefit by around ten per cent (including tax concessions) over thirty-nine months compared with fourteen per cent or more for higher-paid workers, and the union voted against the agreement as a result (Yeates 1997). Jimmy Somers conceded that although SIPTU recommended acceptance of Partnership 2000, many SIPTU members in low-paid employments were swayed by these arguments. Carolann Duggan, a Waterford SIPTU member, summed up these feelings when she said, 'The country is booming, the employers and the banks are making a fortune in profits, up forty-five per cent according to Bill Attley. Yet the workers who created all the wealth are being told to take a rise of 7.4 per cent over three years and three months'.

Table 13.7
Voting Results at ICTU Special Delegate Congresses on National Agreements

Agreement	For	Against
PNR	181	114
PESP	224	109
PCW	256	76
Partnership 2000	217	134
PPF	251	112
Sustaining Progress	195	147*

* This result did not correspond with an *Irish Times* telephone tally the previous day, which suggested the agreement would be accepted by a margin of 231 to 150 (Sheehan 2003d: 4). Sheehan (2003d) raised a number of queries about the conduct of the balloting process.

Source: Sheehan (1997: 15); Sheehan and Hastings (2000: 16); Sheehan (2003: 4)

Employer Views

Private sector employers have generally been positive about the centralised bargaining process since 1987. Writing on the PCW agreement, Brian Geoghegan of IBEC argued that the national programme had delivered on jobs, kept inflation and interest rates low and delivered 'additional disposable income to an average employee' (Geoghegan 1996). IBEC has generally been concerned with the issues of competitiveness, taxation and the level of public expenditure. The main opposition from an employer side has come from the Irish Small and Medium Enterprises Association (ISME), which has claimed that centralised agreements place unfair burdens on small firms. Such views do not, however, seem to be representative of the broad body of employer opinion. A survey of senior personnel managers conducted in 1993 by the Institute of Personnel Management (IPM) found that ninety-five per cent of them were in favour of a further PESP-type agreement (Yeates 1993). This was significant, as the PESP was one of the less favourable agreements from an employer perspective. Even individual employers have been reticent to criticise the social partnership, although in a television interview on the *Dunphy Show* in November 2003, Michael O'Leary, chief executive of Ryanair, denounced the process.

While employers have usually been favourably disposed to the agreements, they have not foreseen any disaster if national agreements were to be abandoned, as they would have been relatively comfortable with a 'free for all' (see interview with John Dunne, Sheehan 1996c). In the absence of nationally agreed pay terms, IBEC perceives that the maintenance of pay discipline at the workplace level would be easier to achieve as a result of greater employee acceptance of the significance of external factors, such as competitive pressures and globalisation. Sheehan (2004a: 17) notes that competitiveness is the key issue for employers and that 'more and more employees are economically literate in this regard'. IBEC was strongly opposed to the renegotiation of the PPF, 'claiming that any pay increases outside the terms of the PPF will only add to inflation, erode competitiveness and threaten economic growth' (Frawley 2000a: 2). The renegotiation involved was only conceded after strong pressure. It also seemed unusual since although the agreement was predicated on a low inflation rate, there was no explicit provision for renegotiation in the event of inflation being above the predicted level. The renegotiation led to a departure from the model of modest wages increases of agreements, such as the PNR and PCW. Sheehan (2004a) suggests this may have been partly market driven and that in the private sector these market forces prompted 'employers to up pay rates to attract and retain staff'.

ECONOMIC PERFORMANCE UNDER CENTRALISED AGREEMENTS, 1987–2004

Over the period of centralised agreements since 1987 the Irish economy has undergone a remarkable transformation and has enjoyed unprecedented economic success, yet the story of the agreements is not one of continuous success. The economic trends can be broken down into three broad periods: a period of stabilisation from 1987 to 1993, a period of expansion and growth from 1994 to 2000 and a somewhat rockier period since 2000. During the period of the PNR, the public sector finances were stabilised, employment levels were maintained, unemployment decreased slightly (Figures 13.4 and 13.5) and the debt/GNP ratio was reduced (Figure 13.6).

The PESP agreement coincided with a difficult economic period caused by external factors, chiefly the first Gulf War. Until the devaluation in early 1993, interest rates rocketed but stabilised thereafter. On the positive side, growth was maintained and inflation stayed under control and at a lower level than the EU average (see Figure 13.9). Annual growth rates were extremely buoyant, with an average real GNP growth of 4.2 per cent from 1988 to 1994 (see Figure 13.7). This was almost three times as high as the EU average and more than twice the OECD average.

There was some questioning of the validity of these figures, with analysts pointing out that the growth was not being converted into employment (Murphy 1994). Unemployment was the main problem, with a substantial rise in unemployment occurring over the period of the agreement (see Figure 13.5). Barret (1993) notes the PESP had an objective of achieving a substantial increase in employment but this did not occur (see Figure 13.4). In the agreement's defence, the government argued that a significant number of jobs were saved during the term of the PESP through our improved competitiveness in wage costs relative to our main trading partners. The failure on the employment side was accompanied by an increase in the public sector pay bill of over twenty-seven per cent between 1990 and 1993.

Figure 13.4
Total Numbers Employed and Unemployed, 1987–2004

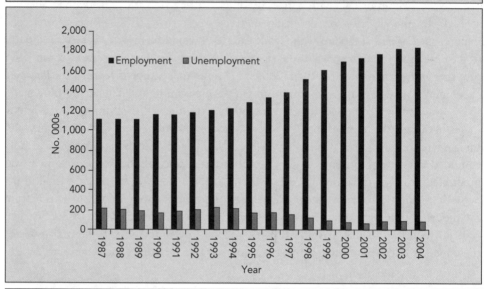

Note: 1987–1997: figure as at April of that year; 1998–2003: figure from December to November; 2004: figure only available for first quarter of that year.

Source: 1987–1989 Department of Finance (2003a); 1990–2004 CSO (2004)

Figure 13.5
Unemployment Rate, 1988–2004

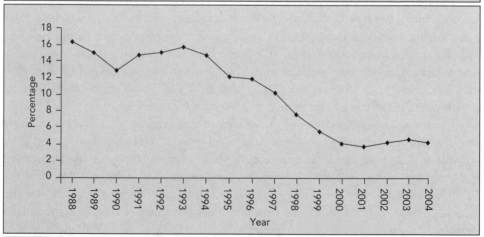

Note: 1988–1997: figure as at April of that year; 1998–2003: figure from December to November; 2004: figure only available for first quarter of that year.

Source: 1987–1989 Department of Finance (2003a); 1990–2004 CSO (2004)

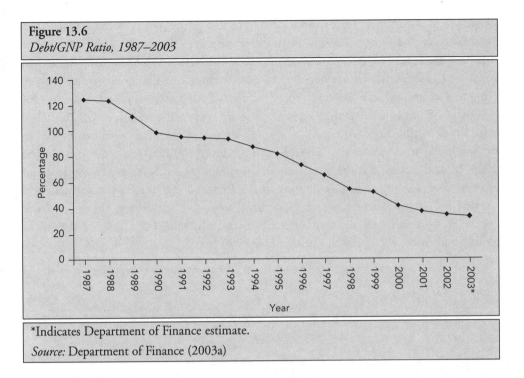

Figure 13.6
Debt/GNP Ratio, 1987–2003

*Indicates Department of Finance estimate.

Source: Department of Finance (2003a)

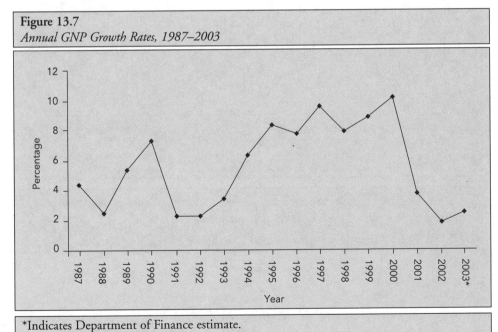

Figure 13.7
Annual GNP Growth Rates, 1987–2003

*Indicates Department of Finance estimate.

Source: Department of Finance (2003a)

After 1993 the picture changes dramatically and in an unanticipated way. Growth rates became extraordinary and consistently outstripped predictions. Budget surpluses became the norm and a massive increase in employment occurred (see Figure 13.4), led by growth in the services sector and increased female participation rates (Wallace *et al.* 2001; Wallace and Dineen 2001). Writing of the period, Hardiman (2000: 292) notes that 'real increases in disposable income were delivered, while keeping industrial conflict at low levels'. Turner and D'Art (2000) chart unambiguous evidence of an economic boom, which was delivering benefits to all participants (see Table 13.8). Sheehan (1996b) notes that the employment gains were made against a background of generally declining employment in the rest of Europe. These trends were maintained in the following years, with the debt/GNP ratio reduced to only thirty-four per cent by 2003. Most dramatic was the transformation in employment, with major employment growth being accompanied by declining unemployment. By 2000 unemployment had reached 4.1 per cent and it has been maintained around this level since then. There was even a transformation in long-term unemployment, which fell from nine per cent of the total labour force in 1994 to 2.3 per cent by 1999 (see Figure 13.8).

Figure 13.8
Long-Term Unemployment Rate, 1988–2004

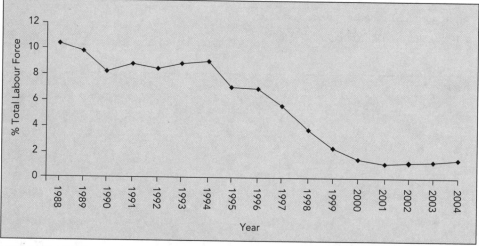

Note: 1988–1997: figure as at April of that year; 1998–2003: figure from December to November; 2004: figure only available for first quarter of that year.

Source: 1987–1989 Department of Finance (2003a); 1990–2004 CSO (2004)

Wage Outcomes

Real wages grew progressively in the period 1987–1997 in sharp contrast to the situation that had existed under decentralised bargaining in the 1980s. Turner and D'Art (2000) write that 'between 1980 and 1987, there was no real increase in the gross average industrial wage, whereas gross average earnings of industrial workers increased by 17.5 per cent between 1987 and 1998'. They go on to suggest that 'real average disposable income fell by eight to ten per cent between 1980 and 1987, while real disposable income is estimated to have increased by twenty-seven per cent between 1987 and 1998' (Turner and D'Art 2000).

Table 13.8
Economic Indicators, 1980–1998 (all figures reduced to base year 1968)

Years	National Income Change	Debt / GNP Ratio	Average Earnings Change*	Wage Bill Change **	Company Profits Change	Employment Change	Unemployment Change
1980– 1987	+7.1%	+38%	0%	+0.3%	+93.9%	–5.7%	+155%
1987– 1998	+54.2% (1987 –1996)	30% (1987 –1994)	+17.5%	+45.2% (1987 –1996)	+77.7% (1987 –1996)	+41.7%	–227%

* Refers to average industrial earnings.
** Refers to the entire wage bill for all PAYE workers minus agricultural workers.

Source: Turner and D'Art (2000)

In the same period, Sexton *et al.* (1999: 55) claim a rise in annual hourly earnings of 2.5 per cent (allowing for inflation), which suggests an even higher wage benefit. However, the relative benefit for employers has been even greater and there has been a large swing in the proportion of earnings going to profits. Company profits increased by seventy-eight per cent between 1987 and 1996, which continued a trend from the earlier period of decentralised bargaining, during which time company profits rose by an even greater percentage (see Table 13.8). EIRI Associates (2001: 27) note that 'during the 1980s, 72.5 per cent of Irish national income went to labour ... it dropped by nine percentage points, from 72.5 to 63.7 per cent'. They conclude that 'the share of national income going to labour is now the lowest in Europe' (EIRI Associates 2001: 27).

Despite the fact that national pay agreements since 1987 provided for levels of wage increases significantly lower than those agreed in the preceding twenty-five years, they have been remarkably stable. However, claims that ATN increases have not been a major feature of the agreements are not borne out by the empirical evidence, as discussed earlier. Sexton *et al.* (1999: 69) suggest that 'there has been an annual average "excess" of two per cent over the NWA provisions'. The question then arises as to why such ATN increases have not led to the controversy that existed in relation to similar awards in the 1970s. The answer may lie in the composition of the increases, which indicates that they were highest, at three per cent per annum, for managerial grades and only one per cent for those at the lower end of the skill spectrum (Sexton *et al.* 1999: 70). Wallace *et al.* (2001) claim that unlike the 1970s, this wage drift has not threatened the central agreements, as it was largely driven by market factors rather than any clauses providing for additional increases under the agreements. Sheehan (2001: 24) notes that 'many companies have had to breach the agreement [Partnership 2000] to ensure they attract or retain and pay the going rate for scarce labour in some areas'.

Causal Links between Social Partnership and Economic Performance, 1987–2004

While centralised agreements are associated with the economic success of the Celtic Tiger years, this is not sufficient to prove causality. There is considerable debate on the cause of Ireland's recent economic boom. A sense of the uncertainty surrounding this debate can be garnered from the American economist Paul Krugman's comment that Ireland, 'through a combination of good luck, good timing and good policies, has caught the crest of a geographical and technological wave, and has ridden it to a prosperity nobody expected' (see MacSharry and White 2000: 361).

There are three possible positions one can adopt in relation to the influence of the agreements on economic performance:

- the agreements have not contributed to the economic success;
- they have been one of a number of contributions; and
- they have been the sole (or main) causal variable.

In querying the causal links between centralised agreements and the recent economic success, a number of arguments can be advanced. For example, the agreements did not reduce inflation, strikes or wage increases. It can be pointed out that inflation was already at an extremely low level by 1987, strikes had dropped off during the 1980s and wage increases had also declined progressively since the abandonment of centralised agreements in 1982. In addition, arguments have been made that the national agreements were designed to 'protect the pay and conditions for work of those who have jobs in the private sector at the expense of the outsiders who work for less … This has the effect of increasing the supply of labour to the unprotected sectors of the economy where pay and conditions of work for young job-seekers have probably deteriorated, and raising the level of unemployment and emigration' (Leddin and Walsh 1992: 267). While the arguments on the trends that had emerged prior to 1987 are useful in drawing attention to developments already under way, they arguably pay insufficient attention to the fact that the PNR increase was substantially lower than that under the emerging 27th round and do not allow for the possibility that under buoyant economic conditions there would have been a return to higher strike activity. The arguments on effects on employment seem less well founded with the fall in unemployment since 1993.

While it is possible to claim that the social partnership was the sole or main cause of the boom, this is rarely encountered. However, there are many who regard the economic success as having been underpinned by the national agreements (for example, see Hardiman 2000; O'Donnell and O'Reardon 2000; MacSharry 2000). It is common to find the agreements cited as one of the *main* causes (MacSharry and White 2000: 361) or *one of a number* of causes (O'Donnell and O'Reardon 2000: 241). In recent years a consensus has emerged that the miracle was due to a confluence of favourable factors, including the following.

- The high investment in education by successive Irish governments and the quality of education (Fitz Gerald 2000).

- The growth in the labour force, particularly the higher participation rate by women (Clinch *et al.* 2002).
- The devaluations of 1986 and, more importantly, 1993, which decreased the costs of exports and increased the costs of imports, making Irish goods more competitive.
- Wage restraint combined with reductions in personal tax rates which restrained public expenditure and increased the incentive to work (Honohan and Walsh 2002).
- The growth in domestic demand, which has led to an increase in 'tax receipts and expansion of employment-intensive sectors' (Tansey 1998: 46–9).
- The attraction of an English-speaking destination within the EU for US investors.
- The very low rate of corporation profits tax, which promoted foreign direct investment (FDI), especially by US multinationals (Barry *et al.* 1999).
- The reflationary effect of EU structural funds, especially the IR£5.9 billion negotiated by the Albert Reynolds Government.
- The impact of the US boom of the Clinton years.
- The revitalisation of tourism (Deegan and Dineen 1997; Wallace and Dineen 2001).
- A range of 'soft' cultural and other such factors (Fitz Gerald 2000).

Not all these alternative variables have equal credibility. Questions arise as to why a large English-speaking and educated workforce did not produce economic success earlier and whether the growth in the labour force could have led to problems absorbing such a growing labour force. Honohan and Walsh (2002: 46) classify factors such as these as 'slowly simmering ingredients' in the success. They argue that they 'contributed to improved performance over the long run … but they did not change much during the period of the turnaround, and so cannot explain the "miracle" of the last decade'. In effect, they view such factors as facilitating rather than causing the boom. The second category of explanations they call 'cataclysmic' ones, including 'the flow of EU structural funds, the devaluations of 1986 and 1993, the revitalised promotion of tourism and inward FDI'. The third category they call 'popular explanations', of which they identify two: 'social partnership and the lowering of taxes' (Honohan and Walsh 2002: 49). The key question is if social partnership was one of a number of factors contributing to economic success, how important was it? MacSharry (2000: 144–5) claims that 'though not the only factor in the success, it [the national partnership] was undoubtedly one of the major ones'.

If centralised agreements had a causal role this requires the identification of the mechanism(s) by which it has worked. The accepted absence of any substantial development in workplace partnership up to 1997, when the boom was well under way, removes this as a possible mechanism. Not only is this the case, but Clinch *et al.* (2002: 45) reject the notion that there was a workplace 'productivity boom'. They argue that the increases in productivity were simply caused by an elastic supply of labour due to three factors: the baby boom of the 1960s and 1970s, the openness of the labour market leading to a sizeable net inflow of population and a sharp acceleration in women's labour force participation rates (Clinch *et al* 2002: 47).

The contribution which centralised bargaining made to lower inflation may be questioned on the basis that inflation was already low in 1987. However, inflation was lower than the EU average for the years 1987 to 1997 inclusive, thus delivering a competitive advantage for the Irish economy, which may be attributed to the partnership agreements (see Figure 13.9). Despite this success, Ireland has the highest cost of living in the EU, along with Finland. In addition to the possible contribution to lower inflation, the wage-tax trade-off is a further mechanism that can be identified as a driver of Ireland's economic success.

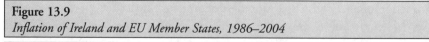

Figure 13.9
Inflation of Ireland and EU Member States, 1986–2004

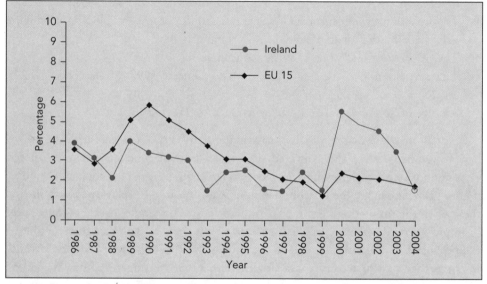

Note: 2004 data: Ireland from January to May 2004; EU 15 from January to April 2004.

Source: EU 15: Department of Finance (2003a); Ireland: Central Statistics Office (2004)

Wage determination and the tax trade-off are at the heart of the system of centralised agreements and there is undoubtedly a case to be made for this process as the central contribution of the agreements to the economic boom. Hardiman (2000: 292) suggests 'the national framework of pay bargaining made it possible for the far-reaching trade-offs between wage moderation and tax reform to take effect. Once growth began in earnest, the pay agreements helped to ensure that the gains were not dissipated by wage inflation and industrial conflicts'. Honohan and Walsh (2002: 21) write that 'the ability to lower tax rates gave the government an important bargaining chip in the centralised pay negotiations ... as credible multiyear wage agreements halted the deterioration in wage competitiveness that had been a feature of the previous ten years'. However, this seems to overstate the case for the effect of wage restraint, as unit wage costs had declined substantially in the period 1982 to 1987.

The key issues are whether pay increases since 1987 would have been higher, and if so, would this have had a negative effect. Fitz Gerald (2000: 42) suggests partnerships' 'impact on wage formation in the longer term has probably been quite limited'. The evidence available suggests that there was a change in the pattern of wage settlements from the early 1980s, before the partnership approach was implemented. However, a key point is that the PNR increase was below the level of wage rise emerging during the 27th round in 1987. Admittedly, the PESP increases were higher, but may still have been less than would otherwise have prevailed. Most tellingly, the tight increases provided for under the PCW in 1994 may have prevented the frittering away of the benefits of the 1993 devaluation. In small, open economies the policy of devaluation is difficult to operate effectively as the prices of imports increase following devaluation. This leads to inflation and as a result workers make wage demands to restore their earnings. Wage restraint limits this wasting away of the benefits of devaluation.

For those who question the importance of centralised agreements as a main causal factor in the economic success, there are a number of other factors that can be pointed to. External factors have been crucial to the relative success of the agreements. The PNR performed better than the PESP due to external factors that affected the latter, chiefly the first Gulf War. Hardiman (2000: 290), who credits the agreements with a significant role, nonetheless writes that 'fortuitous external circumstances helped the PNR to initiate a "virtuous circle" of improved domestic economic performance, which paved the way for successor agreements'. This begs the question of whether the agreements would have worked as well if the external factors were not so favourable. Similarly, the EU funds were an external injection, as was the influence of the Clinton boom years on American multinational investment in Ireland.

Turning to the wage tax trade-off, it is possible to overstate the extent to which this was due to centralised agreements. A key question in this regard is to what extent things would have differed if centralised agreements had not existed. Fitz Gerald (2000: 42) claims the impact of the 'partnership' approach 'on wage formation in the longer term has probably been quite limited. First, the evidence available suggests that there was a change in the pattern of wage settlements from the early 1980s, before the partnership approach was implemented'. It is arguable that the key factor in this reduction was the decision in 1979 to enter the European Exchange Rate Mechanism (ERM) and link the Irish currency to the strong Deutschmark. This effect would have continued to restrain wage increases after 1987. Second, the Irish boom was driven largely by foreign multinationals, which are largely non-union organisations, and the expansion of the services sector, which has low levels of unionisation. For the most part, these sectors can only have been affected in an *indirect* way by wage determination in the unionised sector. However, the extent of any such indirect effect is uncertain, as Irish collective agreements are not automatically extended to the non-union sector. It is possible that wage increases would have been determined by market factors in those sectors irrespective of the existence of centralised agreements.

It can be claimed that it is unlikely that taxes would have remained high in the absence of centralised agreements. Tax reduction was being examined long before talks began on the PNR, and by 1986 it was clear that the government would introduce such fiscal policies whether centralised agreements emerged or not (see 'Building on Reality', Ireland 1984). The corporate tax rate is likely to have been reduced due to the profile of political parties in power since 1987, notably the influence of the Progressive Democrats' neo-liberal policies. The level of corporate tax has been the major factor in attracting US companies, which have also been a major contributor to the Irish boom (Gunnigle and McGuire 2001: 44). Under a number of the agreements, much higher levels of tax cuts were delivered than were negotiated, whereas under the PESP the tax reduction targets were not met (PPF: see Frawley 2000a). While the agreements may have created an environment in which it was possible to cut taxes, they seem to have been incapable of directly determining the level of cuts that were to be delivered. Without the agreements and the wage restraint, however, it might not have been possible to deliver the full extent of the politically desired tax cuts.

Apart from the direct mechanisms through which social partnership has acted, there is also their influence on the general business climate to consider, which is readily identifiable. Honohan and Walsh (2002: 50) point to the consensus on economic policy preceding the agreements that 'the crisis in the public finances must be resolved and that the key to unemployment reduction could not be found in fiscal expansion'. This meant that companies considering investing in Ireland were faced with a stable political and social climate. However, it can plausibly be argued that the direction of causation between a stable political and social environment and economic success is not all one way and external influences may also have been at work. We have already seen how the Irish strike experience of the 1960s and 1970s was anything but unique. It may well be that just as the NWAs of the 1970s coincided with the peak of a Kondratieff wave of industrial unrest, Irish social partnership post-1987 may have been facilitated by general international influences, globalisation and increased international competition being two of the most obvious ones.

DISTRIBUTIONAL EFFECTS OF CENTRALISED AGREEMENTS

There is a broad consensus that centralised agreements since 1987 have been accompanied by greater relative social inequalities, which is commonly ascribed to the processes at work in centralised bargaining during that time. It is certain that the Irish model departs from the strongly redistributive and egalitarian neo-corporatism of the Scandinavian model post-World War II. This can be seen in an examination of trends in income inequality, wage dispersion, the universality of the welfare system, the levels of social expenditure and social mobility since 1987. The evidence on income inequality is unclear, yet there may have been a slight decrease to 1997 (see Nolan and Maître 2000: 153).

On poverty the evidence is that there was a substantial decline in absolute poverty (see Turner 2002). Clinch *et al.* (2002: 31) provocatively write that 'the rich got richer and the poor got ... richer'. However, they go on to note that measures of relative poverty are more meaningful to some economists and social scientists. Relative poverty has increased somewhat during the period of social partnership, and more tellingly, is at a high level compared to many other developed countries. Using 1994 statistics, O'Donnell and O'Reardon (2000: 245) note that 'Ireland has the highest proportion of the population living in relative poverty when defined in terms of the sixty per cent line'. The authors conclude that 'income inequality and relative poverty have remained at high levels despite social partnership, and the growth of the nineties has seen a wider dispersion of incomes' (O'Donnell and O'Reardon 2000: 245). In addition, there is evidence that measures to address poverty in Ireland have been found to be much less effective than those in other EU countries. Those who have suffered most from relative poverty are those not in work, for example, the elderly, widows and the unemployed, which means they are outside the main areas of concern to industrial relations. The increases since 1998 have not yet fed through into the analysis of relative poverty levels due to time lags in data becoming available (O'Connor 2002).

Although centralised agreements are generally claimed to protect weaker groups in the bargaining process, there has been a large growth in wage dispersion in Ireland and earnings inequality since 1987 (Barrett et al. 1999; Turner 1999). Turner (2002: 290) notes a growth in wage dispersion of seven percentage points over the period 1987 to 1997. Barrett et al. (1999: 83) note that in a comparison with other OECD countries for 1994, only Canada and the US have greater earnings inequality than Ireland (Barrett et al. 1999: 83). Turner (2002: 288) states that 'in addition to the high wage dispersion, Ireland has a high proportion of low-paid workers relative to other OECD countries'. He points out that the proportion of workers on low pay (as measured as those earning below two-thirds of the median wage) had grown from twenty-four per cent in 1987 to twenty-seven per cent by 1995 (Turner 1999: 41). The result of the weak wage solidarity provisions in the agreements have contributed to some trade unions representing lower-paid workers, notably MANDATE and the Civil and Public Services Union (CPSU), to vote against a number of the agreements. This contrasts with the approach of unions representing low-paid workers to the earlier NWAs of the 1970s.

Nolan et al. (2000: 344) note that 'social partnership has presided over a period of weakening welfare efforts, in terms of the proportion of national income going on social spending'. Turner (2002: 289) remarks that 'between 1990 and 1996 expenditure on social protection decreased from 19.1% to 18.9% of GDP' and that Ireland ranked lowest in 1995 in a comparison with eleven other EU countries. Inequality is guaranteed by reason of the fact that 'the welfare system only becomes involved in order to guarantee a minimum level of social participation by recipients' (Turner 2002: 289).

On health expenditure as a percentage of GDP, Turner (2002) observes that Ireland 'ranked lower than all the other European countries ... in the proportion spent on health, and this proportion declined by nine per cent between 1987 and 1997'. In recent years, expenditure on health as a proportion of GDP has increased and stood at 6.5 per cent in 2001. However, this is significantly less than other OECD countries such as the US (13.9 per cent), Sweden (8.7 per cent) and the UK (7.6 per cent) (OECD 2003: 1). The continuing crisis over the health service, which focuses on issues such as the two-tier nature, the long waiting lists, claims of lack of value for money and the controversial proposals for reform in the 2003 Hanley report indicate that the effects of removing 3,000 beds under the PNR continues to have reverberations over seventeen years later.

In relation to education, Turner (2002) mentions that there is no reduction on the impact of class origins on educational levels over time, with continued social class inequalities in educational outcomes.

Irish centralised bargaining since 1987 can be seen as extremely close to the liberal corporatist model. Nolan *et al.* (2000: 344) write that 'social partnership has presided over a period of weakening welfare efforts, in terms of the proportion of national income going on social spending'. Turner (2002: 275) argues that in Ireland 'the outcomes in terms of reducing inequalities between social classes still lags far behind the strongly corporatist Nordic countries. Indeed, it appears that inequality has actually increased during the present period of social partnership in Ireland'. This growth in relative inequality is not accidental and is an integral part of the wage tax trade-offs in the agreements. Nolan *et al.* (2000: 344) write that 'in addition, the impact of tax-cutting since 1987, central to the Irish social partnership exchange, has been regressive because it has been achieved largely through the reduction of tax rates which has favoured those on higher incomes'. This reduction in tax rates combined with an absence of universalistic entitlements stands in stark contrast to the Scandinavian pattern of 'welfare provision which has acted to create a solidarity between social classes and a commitment to reduced inequalities [that pervades] all areas of social policy' (Turner 2002: 289). To date, the involvement of the community and voluntary pillar since the Partnership 2000 agreement doesn't seem to have acted to redress the regressive effects of Irish social partnership.

While the partnership agreements have been central to the growth of relative inequality, it is less certain that Irish society would have been more egalitarian in the absence of such agreements. Criticising Irish social partnership on the basis of the growth in inequality masks the fact that the Irish agreements did not seek to redress social imbalances. Indeed, part of the trade-off in the agreements was an *a priori* recognition that profits would increase at the expense of wage income in order to promote employment. Second, there has been a growth in economic and social inequality in many countries since the 1970s and it is improbable that with an alternative system of wage determination Ireland would have experienced outcomes that went counter to this trend.

While one of the frequently cited reasons for the absence of social solidarity arising from Irish industrial relations is the absence of a strong left-wing party competing for power, it is pertinent to point out that countries with strong left-wing parties have seen their egalitarian systems come under pressure in recent years. A clear example is Germany, where the Social Democratic Party has come under pressure to dismantle some of the social protection and labour market regulations. Thus, the strains on social welfare and health care provision that exist in Ireland are also arising in other EU countries, though these are exerted on a much lower base for social provision in Ireland. The pressures from the regressive nature of Irish social partnership have fed back into the electoral system. There has been a growth of so-called single-issue candidates who run for election on issues like health, local hospitals and access to education facilities for intellectually disabled children.

THE FUTURE OF CENTRALISED AGREEMENTS

The economic success that has accompanied the national agreements has led to general support for their continuation. The programmes are seen to have played a role in delivering a range of favourable economic outcomes. Hardiman (2000: 307) writes that 'the process of social partnership has proved durable over quite a long time … It has adapted successfully not only to the exigencies of economic crisis, but also to the pressures of qualifying for euro membership'. She goes on to claim that 'it is hard to see what could replace social partnership given the organised nature of the workforce and the aversion built into the party political system to overt manifestations of conflict' (Hardiman 2000: 307). The latter point reflects the general political consensus that national agreements bring beneficial outcomes. Even parties with an ideological orientation that would normally be opposed to centralised agreements, such as the Progressive Democrats, have no difficulty in engaging in this new political consensus. To abandon a successful model would be likely to have certain electoral risks attached.

Within the industrial relations system there are also strong indications of a preference for a continuation of the social partnership process. Jack O'Connor, president of SIPTU, indicated shortly after his election that while he had reservations about the use of the term 'social partnership', he favoured a continuation of the agreements. For employers, they are likely to judge the merits of staying within the process by reference to the effects of wage increases on competitiveness. The LRC (2003: 1) argues that the 'nation's economic interest is best served, particularly during periods of instability, by a continuation of social partnership which has been a dominant hallmark of Irish industrial relations since 1987'. Thus, there are significant drivers to sustain the system of centralised agreements.

The reduction of inflation below two per cent in early 2004, driven by the rise in the value of the euro, decreased the importance of inflation, which Sheehan (2003a: 24) notes is always a matter of significant consideration. However, the strength of the euro creates pressures on employers to ensure wage discipline, thereby leading to the likelihood that if there is to be agreement on phase two of Sustaining Progress, it may need to provide for lower wage increases than in phase one (Sheehan 2003b: 1). Private sector employers have enjoyed the certainty that modest pay rises negotiated under the agreements have provided, but equally there is no evidence to suggest that a return to decentralised bargaining would cause them any great concern. Given the sort of competitive pressures that firms are under that act as significant restraining factors on pay demands, they would most probably be able to resist wage pressures at local level. The government will want to ensure that levels of competition in the services sector are increased (Sheehan 2003a). Some commentators have suggested that the high pay increases to the public sector under benchmarking may lead to a backlash from public sector workers. However, competitive pressures in the private sector may constrain any such effect, according to Sheehan (2004a).

Disputes over privatisation in the semi-state sector do, however, pose a source of continuing difficulty in union-government relations (Dobbins and Higgins 2003; Frawley 2004a; Sheehan 2004a). The unions also have an interest in union recognition, but it remains doubtful that this will cause a breakdown of negotiations. Sheehan (2003a: 23) suggests that 'if unions are to secure statutory rights then Europe is their best hope' (see also Wallace 2003). In the absence of European developments, legislation compelling employers to recognise trade unions is perhaps ICTU's ideal position, while 'strengthening existing "right to bargain procedures" is their realistic solution given employers' outright rejection of this issue' (Dooley 2003).

Overriding some of these concerns are relationship issues, with Frawley (2004a) suggesting that the Taoiseach Bertie Ahern, TD is the main supporter of the partnership approach and that others in the Fianna Fáil-Progressive Democrats coalition are no longer committed to the process of social partnership. Sheehan (2004: 16) suggests that 'with inflation gradually being tamed as 2003 progressed, unemployment staying below all predicted levels and healthy growth levels again in prospect, the outlook is a lot better at the start of 2004 than many believed possible when Sustaining Progress was negotiated'.

In the medium to longer term, the main challenge to Irish social partnership may be the fact that the central mechanism that contributed to its success, the wage tax trade-off, has run into the sand. This has already emerged under the Sustaining Progress agreement, which for the first time contains no formal commitment on the part of the government to reduce taxes. Sheehan (2003a: 20) also points to the 'limited scope for further tax relief' which, combined with the growth of so-called 'stealth' taxes, is likely to pose major challenges. Already the issue of the narrow tax base, which helped to derail the NWAs of the 1970s, has raised its head. David Begg, general secretary of ICTU, has indicated that the Congress has made submissions on this to government, which may bring them 'into conflict with their friends in IBEC' (radio interview, *News at One* on Radio 1, 29 November 2003). Nonetheless, many trade union leaders remain committed to the partnership process and are likely to seek to address their concerns within that process (see Sheehan 2004a). They consider that apart from pay, non-pay issues like health and welfare spending, labour legislation and programmes to combat unemployment and encourage greater social inclusion would be largely removed from the trade union sphere of influence were they to opt out of the centralised bargaining process. In the final analysis, social partnership is only likely to be abandoned if one or other of the social partners feel strongly enough that withdrawal from the process would serve their strategic interests.

CHAPTER 14

Strategy, Human Resource Management and Industrial Relations

INTRODUCTION

A notable characteristic of analyses of industrial relations over recent decades has been an increasing focus on developments at enterprise level (see Kochan *et al.* 1986). In particular, we find a greater emphasis on management strategies and polices in industrial relations. This is variously attributed to a 'new realism' among managers and trade unions/employees, the development of greater linkages between business strategy and human resource policies, the adoption of HRM approaches and a decrease in trade union membership and influence. Of particular significance is the contention that employers have taken a more proactive role in driving such change than the other key 'actors' in industrial relations. Kochan *et al.* (1986: 12) comment: 'One of the reasons why we place management values and strategies at the centre of our analysis, however, is that since 1960 union behaviour and government policy have been much slower to adapt to changes in their external environment and to changes in managerial strategies and policies'.

This chapter addresses various aspects of management's role in industrial relations, placing particular emphasis on the Irish context. In particular, we look at business strategy-industrial relations linkages and the development of human resource management (HRM) as a distinctive approach to workforce management. Before looking at these areas it is useful to consider the rationale for this greater focus on management's role and impact in industrial relations. Specifically, we explore the reasons why the management of enterprise-level industrial relations has now emerged as a significant aspect of the debate on industrial relations change.

A CHANGING ECONOMIC CONTEXT

It is generally accepted that increased product market competition, advances in technology and changes in the composition and operation of labour markets have significantly altered the context of enterprise-level industrial relations (see Kochan *et al.* 1986; Sparrow and Hiltrop 1994). Of particular significance is the requirement for increased competitiveness resulting from a range of factors, including growing market competition from late industrial starters, e.g. Singapore, greater liberalisation of trade resulting from developments under the General Agreement on Tariffs and Trade (GATT) and moves towards the Economic and Monetary Union (EMU) in the European Union (see Turner and Morley 1995). Piore and Sabel (1984) have argued that these developments represent a new industrial revolution, incorporating a major restructuring of the capitalist order. In this vein, Marshall (1992) suggests that an enterprise's commercial viability increasingly depends on their ability to effectively restructure in the face of more global competition and the fragmentation of mass markets (see also Streeck 1992).

While the advent of a new industrial revolution is open to question, there is little doubt that there have been significant changes in product markets and consumer behaviour, particularly in the goods and services produced, the way they are produced and in their delivery to the market. It is evident that such developments have directly impacted on the nature of enterprise-level industrial relations and prompted management initiatives to alter traditional approaches to workforce management. These changes have generally focused on three key aspects of enterprise-level performance, namely product quality, productivity and labour flexibility. While this text does not allow for a comprehensive analysis of the factors contributing to increased market competition, some key issues that have significantly impacted on enterprise-level industrial relations merit brief consideration. In this respect, we can point to a number of sources of increased market competition.

First, we have witnessed the *globalisation of competition*. Since the early 1980s a key development in the macroeconomic environment is the increased trend towards the greater liberalisation of world trade (Sparrow and Hiltrop 1994; Sparrow 2002). A number of issues are important in evaluating the industrial relations implications. Clearly, the trend towards greater trade liberalisation provides both opportunities and threats for firms – opportunities for greater access to new markets, but also the threat of increased market competition. In the Irish context there are competitive threats to Irish organisations from lower-cost economies and the related dangers of organisations relocating from Ireland to lower-cost regions (see Roche and Gunnigle 1997; Muller-Camen *et al.* 2001). On the positive side, greater trade liberalisation provides increased opportunities to develop new markets. However, in order to capitalise on such opportunities, it is likely that firms will have to improve their performance on dimensions such as unit costs, speed to market and customer support.

Second, we can point to the greater *intensification of competition*. Again, numerous sources may be identified – in addition to traditional sources of competition such as the US and Japan, there is the competitive threat from countries such as Singapore and South Korea. Nor are these threats lessening, as competition intensifies from fast-developing economies such as China, India and Mexico. These countries now combine a low-cost base with strong performance on dimensions such as productivity and labour skills. Nearer home, many of the Eastern European countries of the former Soviet bloc have undergone a period of restructuring and are likely to provide considerable competition as a result of their low-cost base, industrial tradition and educational systems with a strong technical and scientific foundation (Gunnigle and McGuire 2001). Ladó (2003) notes the challenges posed to established EU industrial relations systems by the low level of institutional regulation in the EU accession countries.

Third, we have the *changing nature of competitive strategies* as a stimulus for change in enterprise-level industrial relations. Key contemporary developments, such as increased product/service customisation and faster speed to market, all have important implications for industrial relations. They often require greater flexibility in employment as organisations seek to align their needs for workers with business demand with greater task flexibility in regard to the variety of tasks workers may be asked to perform.

A related factor that has also served to stimulate change in enterprise-level industrial relations is the changing role of trade unions. In particular, we have seen the decline in trade union membership and influence in many Western economies, which has prompted the union movement to seek mechanisms to increase their legitimacy and representativeness at both enterprise and national level (see Beaumont 1995a; Sparrow and Hiltrop 1994; Gunnigle et al. 2002b).

In responding to the challenges of increased product market competition, organisations appear to have followed two broad strategies. First, we witnessed widespread rationalisation, especially in Europe during the 1980s (see Sparrow and Hiltrop 1994; Sparrow 2002). Common characteristics included redundancies, contracting out or selling 'non-core' activities and 'de-layering', that is, reducing the number of hierarchical levels or grades in the organisation (see Gunnigle 1998b). A second common organisational response was a sharp increase in merger, acquisition and strategic alliance activity (see Sparrow and Hiltrop 1994). A common element in these organisational responses was an increased focus on improving workforce management at the enterprise level, specifically in seeking improvements in labour productivity and reductions in labour costs (see Chapters 11 and 12). Related enterprise-level strategies included the increased use of atypical employment forms in certain sectors, improved performance management methods and initiatives to increase task flexibility.

This brings into focus the role of management in achieving changes to industrial relations in a way that serves to enhance enterprise-level performance (see Roche 1995; Gunnigle 1998a). As noted earlier, we can identify three key areas of enterprise-level industrial relations where the role of management is seen as particularly critical. These are:

- business strategy-industrial relations linkages;
- the nature and diffusion of HRM; and
- the likely impact of HRM on industrial relations.

BUSINESS STRATEGY, INDUSTRIAL RELATIONS AND HRM

The study of strategic management has achieved increasing prominence as organisations seek to adapt to a changing business environment. Strategic management is concerned with policy decisions affecting the entire organisation and involves major resource allocation considerations, with the overall objective being to best position the organisation to deal effectively with its environment. Strategic decisions are therefore long term in nature and serve to guide subsequent decision making at lower levels. Strategic decision making incorporates strategy formulation, strategy implementation, evaluation and control. It also emphasises the monitoring and evaluation of environmental opportunities and constraints as well as the organisation's strengths and weaknesses.

Hofer and Schendel (1978) identified three levels of strategy – corporate, business and functional. *Corporate-level strategy* is essentially concerned with the question of what business one should be in. *Business-level (competitive) strategy* addresses the question of how to compete in the chosen business. Finally, *functional-level strategy* focuses on how the activities of particular functions, such as personnel management/industrial relations, come together to support business-level strategy. This conception of strategic management implies that in an organisational setting there is a hierarchy of decision choices and that key decisions on business strategy will steer more specific operational decisions on short-term problems and issues (Thurley and Wood 1983; Gunnigle *et al.* 2002a).

In this vein, Purcell (1989) differentiates between *upstream* and *downstream* strategic decisions. Upstream are *first-order decisions*, which are concerned with the long-term direction and nature of the organisation. *Second-order decisions* concern areas such as organisation structure, operating procedures and control of business unit performance. Downstream decisions deal with the implications of first-order decisions. Purcell suggests that HR policy choices are only *third-order strategic decisions*, since they will be heavily influenced by first- and second-order decisions and by broader environmental factors (see Figure 14.1). Purcell (1989) notes that diversified organisations tend to prefer decentralised structures with a clear differentiation between strategic and operational responsibilities. He also notes that organisations normally view industrial relations decisions as an operational responsibility at business-unit level.

Figure 14.1
Upstream and Downstream Strategic Decision Making

	UPSTREAM	
FIRST ORDER	Long-term direction of the firm; scope of activities, markets, location	E N V I
SECOND ORDER	Internal operating procedures; relationships between parts of the organisation	R O N M E
THIRD ORDER	Strategic choice in HRM and IR	N T
	DOWNSTREAM	

Source: Purcell (1989)

This implies that multi-business (diversified) organisations are likely to have considerable variation in industrial relations approaches as they seek to achieve some degree of 'fit' with their different business conditions and strategies. Purcell concludes that in the British and US context, a short-term stock market emphasis is often a primary characteristic of first-order strategies. Economic returns are the key yardstick and less concrete considerations, such as industrial relations, are likely to have little influence on strategic decision making at this level. He further argues that what he terms 'strategic planning' companies with integrated human resource policies, such as IBM and Hewlett-Packard, are the exceptions to a more general picture of limited strategic consideration of industrial relations and other HRM issues.

THE SIGNIFICANCE OF COMPETITIVE STRATEGY

Earlier we identified increased competitive pressures as an important source of the heightened emphasis on management's role in enterprise-level industrial relations. Of particular significance in this regard has been the notion of competitive advantage championed by Michael Porter (see Porter 1980, 1985, 1987, 1990). The concept of competitive advantage addresses the means by which competing firms seek to gain market advantage over one another and incorporates any factor(s) which allows an organisation to differentiate its product or service from its competitors to increase market share. Competitive strategy is concerned with achieving sustainable competitive advantage in particular industries or industry segments. Price and quality are common mechanisms by which organisations attempt to achieve competitive advantage. Porter identified three generic competitive strategies:

- *Cost leadership* (sometimes called *cost reduction*) involves positioning the organisation as a low-cost producer of a standard 'no frills' product or service. To succeed with a cost leadership strategy, it is suggested that the firm must become *the* cost leader and not one of several firms pursuing this strategy. Cost leadership requires an emphasis on tight managerial controls, low overheads, economies of scale and a dedication to achieving productive efficiency.
- *Product differentiation* (sometimes called *product innovation*) requires that an organisation's product or service becomes unique on some dimension, for which the buyer is willing to pay a premium price.
- A *focus strategy* involves choosing a narrow market segment and serving this either through a low-cost or a differentiation focus.

Miles and Snow (1978, 1984) developed another commonly used competitive strategy categorisation, which identifies three generic strategy types as follows.

- *Defenders*, who seek stability by producing only a limited set of products directed at a narrow segment of the total potential market. Within this niche, defenders strive to prevent competitors from entering the market. Organisations achieve this through standard economic actions, such as competitive pricing or the production of high-quality products.
- *Prospectors*, who are almost the opposite of defenders since their strength is in finding and exploiting new product and market opportunities. Innovation may be more important than high profitability. The prospector's success depends on

developing and maintaining the capacity to survey a wide range of environmental trends and maintaining a high degree of flexibility.

- *Analysers*, who try to capitalise on the best of both of the preceding types. They seek to minimise risk and maximise opportunity for profit. Their strategy is to move into new products or markets only after viability has been proven by prospectors.

An organisation's choice of generic strategy specifies its fundamental approach to achieving competitive advantage in its particular market(s) and prescribes the broad context for policies and actions in each key functional area, including industrial relations. We now consider the nature of these potential strategy-industrial relations linkages.

COMPETITIVE STRATEGY–INDUSTRIAL RELATIONS LINKAGES

A key thrust of the debate on competitive strategy and HRM is the idea that organisations should seek to achieve 'fit' between their competitive strategy and HR polices and practices. Essentially, it is argued that if an organisation is to successfully pursue a particular competitive strategy, such as cost leadership or product differentiation, it must adopt and implement a complementary set of human resources (HR) and/or industrial relations policies. Based on Porter's (1987) argument, it is expected that alternative competitive strategies need to be matched with different HR/industrial relations policy configurations. Of particular significance is the claimed need to match employee selection, workforce profile (skills, experience, etc.) and industrial relations practices with the chosen competitive strategy.

Turning to the specific links between competitive strategy and HR/industrial relations policies, it is argued that organisations will experience severe problems in strategy implementation if it is not effectively linked with appropriate P/HR/industrial relations policy choices (see Galbraith and Nathanson 1978; Fombrun *et al.* 1984; Fombrun 1986). Fombrun *et al.* (1984) attempt to address this issue by identifying three key areas of concern for strategic decision makers in organisations.

- **Mission and strategy:** Identification of an organisation's purpose and plan for how this can be achieved.
- **Formal structure:** For the organisation of people and tasks to achieve mission and strategy.
- **HR systems:** Recruitment, development, evaluation and reward of employees.

This framework is seen to differ from more traditional approaches to strategic management by incorporating workforce management considerations as an integral component of strategic decision making. Fombrun *et al.* (1984) suggest that an organisation's HR/industrial relations policies and practices are symptomatic of managerial assumptions about employees and 'appropriate' workforce management practices. Fombrun (1986) identifies four key aspects of organisational approaches to workforce management that give valuable insights into the managerial approach to employees.

1. **The nature of the psychological contract:** This may vary. At one extreme, we may find a managerial perspective that views employees in instrumental terms. This will emphasise high levels of control of both employees and the work environment. At the other extreme, we may find an approach that sees employees as intelligent and committed beings.
2. **Level of employee involvement:** Here, organisational approaches may vary from those with high levels of employee involvement in decision making to those where decisions are solely a management prerogative.
3. **Internal/external labour market:** This addresses the relative emphasis on internal versus external recruitment and related differences in employee development.
4. **Performance evaluation:** This factor focuses on the relevant managerial emphasis on group versus individual performance evaluation.

THE IMPACT OF THE PRODUCT MARKET

An organisation's product market may be simply described as the market into which a firm supplies its goods or services. Clearly, the nature of a firm's product market has considerable significance for industrial relations. In analysing these effects, Thurley and Wood (1983) identify three dimensions along which one can evaluate a product market:

* level of competitiveness;
* rate of change or stability; and
* the orientation of the market.

While the first two factors are self-explanatory, the third factor has two elements – first, the extent to which the market is geared towards particular types of customers or suppliers (many or few, large or small) and second, whether it is fashion/fad orientated or subject to steady and repeat orders. The characteristics of an organisation's particular product market will be influenced by a variety of factors, such as the cost of entry, nature of competition, technology and the customer base. Consequently, the nature of a firm's product market will be a key contextual factor influencing the choice of competitive strategy. Thurley and Wood (1983) argue that broad strategic objectives can be linked to the product market objectives, the enterprise's position in that market, the organisational characteristics and the political, social and economic influences in the community where the enterprise operates (expressed through government policy, legislation and interest group pressures). Kochan *et al.* (1986) provide a broad model of the impact of product market change on strategic decision making and on industrial relations, as outlined in Figure 14.2. This work helps to explain how changes in product market conditions can lead to critical strategic decisions on a number of different levels, namely:

* long-term strategy formulation at the top;
* human resource/industrial policy at the middle; and
* workplace and individual-organisation relationships at the shop floor level.

From this model we can see that product market change may lead to a variety of business decisions that can profoundly affect industrial relations. One such decision is to relocate to a non-union greenfield site. In evaluating the impact of increased product market competition, Kochan *et al.* (1986: 65) comment:

> When competition increases, the initial decision a firm must make is whether it wants to remain active in that line of business and compete in the new environment or withdraw and reallocate its capital resources to other opportunities. If the firm decides to remain in the market, the next decision it must make is whether to compete on the basis of low prices (costs) and high volume or to seek out more specialised market niches that will support a price premium. The central industrial relations effect of this increased sensitivity to prices and costs is that firms shift their priorities away from maintaining labour peace to controlling labour costs, streamlining work rules (so as to increase manufacturing efficiency) and promoting productivity. The pressure to control or lower costs is especially intense if a firm attempts to compete across all segments of its product market on the basis of low prices and high volume.

Figure 14.2
Product Market Change, Business Strategy and Industrial Relations

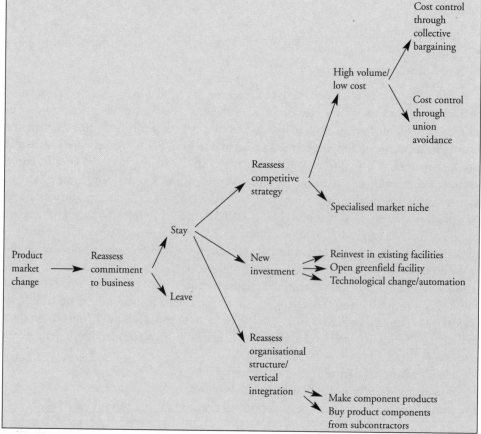

Source: Kochan *et al.* (1986: 66)

From this analysis we can see how product market context and choice of competitive strategy have important knock-on effects on HR and industrial relations strategies and practice, such as those relating to recruitment and training, remuneration and job design. It is further argued that management at the enterprise level is increasingly recognising that improved utilisation of the organisation's workforce can have a significant impact on competitive advantage (Guest 1987). Thus, we find considerable debate in the industrial relations and HR literature on the search for appropriate HR and industrial relations policies to fit particular strategic types.[1]

Marchington (1990) goes somewhat further on this theme by examining the specific links between an organisation's product market position and its approach to industrial relations. Based on four detailed case studies, Marchington develops a general model to evaluate the impact of an organisation's product market circumstances on management approaches to industrial relations at enterprise level. Marchington (1990) identifies two key dimensions along which to evaluate an organisation's product market position – the extent of *monopoly* power or *monopsony* power (see also Marchington and Parker 1990). *Monopoly* power refers to the degree to which an organisation has power to dictate market terms to customers. An organisation may have high monopoly power as a result of factors such as cartel arrangements, regulated state monopolies, high barriers to entry or unique product or technology. In such situations organisations have considerable power to dictate market terms, particularly price, to customers and therefore act as 'price makers'. In contrast, *monopsony* power refers to the extent to which customers exert power over the organisation. High monopsony power may occur as a result of high levels of market competition (numerous competitors) or because of the existence of powerful customers who can exert considerable control over price and other factors, e.g. credit terms, service. In such situations, supplying organisations may be forced to accept the market terms, particularly price, dictated by customers, i.e. become 'price takers' (see Figure 14.3).

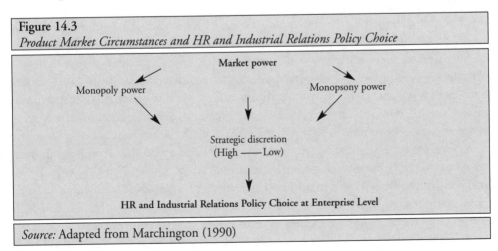

Figure 14.3
Product Market Circumstances and HR and Industrial Relations Policy Choice

Market power

Monopoly power   Monopsony power

Strategic discretion
(High ——— Low)

HR and Industrial Relations Policy Choice at Enterprise Level

Source: Adapted from Marchington (1990)

1   For a detailed consideration of particular models see, for example, Miles and Snow 1978, 1984; Schuler 1987, 1989, 1992; Schuler and Jackson 1987a, 1987b; Schuler *et al.* 1987; Huselid 1995. For a summary overview of strategy-human resource linkages see Gunnigle *et al.* 2002.

Where monopoly power is high, top management will have considerable discretion to make broad HR policy choices, including those impacting on critical aspects of industrial relations, such as wage levels or the extent of investment in training and development. Such favourable market conditions (high market share, growing market, stable demand) allow organisations greater scope to adopt 'investment-oriented styles' and are conducive to the application of more benign HRM and industrial relations practices. This does not imply that employers will always adopt 'pro-employee' policies in favourable product market conditions. Rather, such a context gives top management greater scope to pick from a range of policy choices. The actual choice will be further influenced by a complex array of factors, such as the values and ideology of top management and the organisation's preferred competitive strategy. Organisations operating under high levels of market pressure will have considerably less scope for choice and a more traditional cost and labour control approach is more likely to be used.

In evaluating Irish developments, Roche and Gunnigle (1997: 445–6) comment:

> Never before has the analysis of industrial relations practices and policies been so closely tied to an appreciation of commercial and national and international political pressures. In the past, the worlds of industrial relations practitioners and academics alike tended to be much more introverted and preoccupied with the internal dynamics of industrial relations systems, agreements and procedures. The professional preoccupations and vocabularies of industrial relations experts tended to revolve around distinctly industrial relations themes: disputes and grievance procedures, anomalies in pay structures, productivity bargaining … Currently, these concerns, though not altogether displaced, often take second place to such issues as company performance, the union's role in contributing to business success, mission statements and quality standards, business units, employment flexibility and so on.

The most widely accepted explanation of these changes is the increasingly competitive nature of product and service markets. The main sources of increased competitiveness were outlined in our introduction to this chapter and include the liberalisation of European and world trade, associated deregulation in product, service and capital markets, improved communications and transport infrastructures, developments in information technology and greater market penetration by emerging economies (see Beaumont 1995b; Roche 1995; Roche and Gunnigle 1997). These developments have significant ramifications for Ireland given that it is a small, open economy which is heavily reliant on international trade. The result of these increased competitive pressures has been to focus management attention on cost *and* product innovation/quality, which are seen as critical aspects of enterprise-level performance. It further appears that these pressures serve to create a 'flexibility imperative' whereby organisations have to be increasingly responsive to consumer demand on dimensions such as price, customer service and product quality.

It is argued that the implication of these developments has substantially diluted the premise that companies compete on either a price (low cost) or a product differentiation (premium price) basis (see Gunnigle *et al.* 1997; Marchington and Parker 1990). It appears that now the great majority of firms, not just those who compete primarily on a low-price basis, must strive to tightly control their cost structures to ensure they remain 'price competitive'. It is significant that these competitive trends are increasingly penetrating the state sector (see Hastings 1994, 2003; Hourihan 1997). A major reason for this is the erosion of state monopolies as a result of developments at European Union level. A specific example of a previously state-owned company grappling with a changing and more competitive environment is Aer Lingus. Deregulation in the airline industry meant the company faced increased competition, particularly from low-cost airlines such as Ryanair and Easyjet. Resultant restructuring has led to significant changes in employee numbers, employment patterns and reward systems. We have seen in Chapter 12 that the ESB has had to deal with significant changes in their respective product markets and this has impacted on their industrial relations strategies, policies and practices. Aer Rianta and Dublin Bus are two other state companies that in early 2004 had to grapple with market liberalisation, or what Hastings (2003) has called 'marketisation'.

HRM IN THE US

In most contemporary texts, the term '*human resource management*' is used as a generic expression to encompass that aspect of organisational management concerned with the management of an organisation's workforce. However, human resource management originally entered the management vocabulary as a term that described a distinctive, and seemingly novel, approach to workforce management. We begin by briefly reviewing the emergence of HRM in the US since the early 1980s.

In its original form, HRM was seen as a new development that contrasted with 'traditional' *personnel management*. Its apparently proactive stance was viewed as a major departure from the traditionally reactive 'industrial relations' focus associated with established approaches to 'personnel management. Tyson *et al.* (1994) write:

> The new approaches to industrial relations which adopted a managerialist rather than a pluralist stance, the restructuring possibilities, and the reduction in trade union power and influence were the backdrop to what is now perceived as a new paradigm on which to base employment relationships. In the eyes of some commentators, Human Resource Management (HRM) came to represent the new paradigm, and the critical distinction drawn was the notion that HRM placed initiatives on people management at the strategic heart of the business … The new flexibility agreements, new working practices, reorganisations, delayering activities, the flatter organisations, direct communications with the workforce, and stronger corporate cultures … could be understood as a new, more coherent approach … If this was propaganda, it was propaganda that managers themselves started to believe as the 1980s came to a close … The real challenge is to try to discover what real attempts at strategic integration there are (Tyson *et al.* 1994).

The conception of HRM as a distinctive approach to workforce management stems from two contrasting sources in the US literature. The first is the 'human resource' literature, based on the *human capital approach* of the Harvard Business School (HBS) model (Beer *et al.* 1984, 1985). This model focuses on the individual employee as *the* key organisational resource, which management must nurture and develop to maximise its contribution to the organisation. Consequently, employers are encouraged to employ a coherent range of pro-employee ('soft') HR policies to ensure the attraction, retention and development of committed, high-performing employees.

Figure 14.4
HBS Model of Human Resource Management

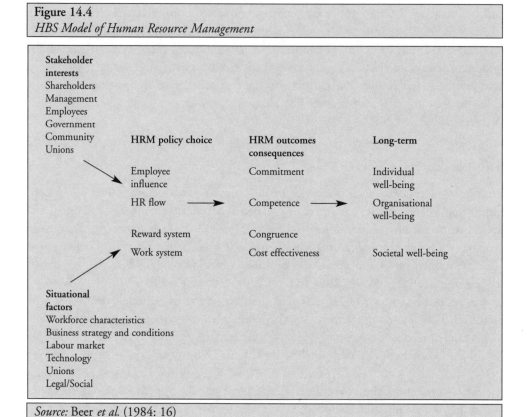

Source: Beer *et al.* (1984: 16)

The second, advocating increased strategic consideration of HRM, emanates from the broader business strategy literature, specifically the work of Fombrun *et al.* (1984). This approach suggests that organisational performance can be substantially improved by integrating HRM considerations into strategic decision making to ensure that HR policies complement business strategy. In contrast to the HBS model, this approach does not prescribe either a 'hard' or 'soft' approach to workforce management. Rather, it suggests that top management adopt those policies that best suit an organisation's particular circumstances. Because its focus is overtly managerial and focused on organisational performance, it has become associated with the concept of 'hard' HRM (see Table 14.1).

Table 14.1 *Hard and Soft HRM*	
Soft HRM	**Hard HRM**
Human Resource Management **HR Strategy as:** Series of policy choices • Total HR/management philosophy. • General management perspective. • Multiple stakeholders. • Evaluation through commitment, competence, congruence and cost effectiveness.	Human Resource **Management** **HR Strategy as:** Fit to corporate/business strategy. Emphasis on alignment and coherence. Key to strategy implementation.
Primary emphasis on management philosophy (approach to HRM)	*HR as source of competitive advantage*
Source: Adapted from Sparrow and Hiltrop (1994)	

As indicated above, the HBS model was the most influential early work on HRM and presents a broad causal map of the determinants and consequences of HRM policy choices (see Figure 14.4). Beer *et al.* (1984) describe HRM in generic terms as 'involving all management decisions and actions that affect the nature of the relationship between the organisation and its employees – its human resources'. Those in top management, particularly the chief executive, are seen as having the primary responsibility for aligning business strategy and HR policy choice. Four key components comprise the HBS model, namely stakeholder interests, HRM policy choice, HRM outcomes and long-term consequences.

The HBS model adopts an open systems perspective 'in that HRM policy choices can affect each of the other components and be affected by them' (Lundy and Cowling 1996: 1). The central contention of the HBS model is that HR outcomes are affected by policy choices made in four key areas, which are reward systems, human resource flows, work systems and employee influence. Each of these policy areas is seen as a key element of strategic choice that profoundly impacts upon employee behaviour and attitude towards the organisation. Decisions made in these policy areas are seen as affecting HR outcomes in the areas of employee commitment, congruence of employee and management interests, employee competence and cost effectiveness. These outcomes are also regarded as having broader long-term consequences for individual employee well-being, organisational effectiveness and societal well-being.

Guest's (1987) 'hard-soft, tight-loose' framework of HRM is possibly the most widely referenced European work (see Figure 14.5). The 'hard-soft' dimension refers to a continuum ranging from a resource-based 'soft' managerial perspective, characterised by benign pro-employee policies, to a more calculated 'hard' management perspective, where policy choice is driven by the need to complement business strategy and meet financial criteria. The 'tight-loose' dimension refers to a continuum where at one end HRM merely involves a 'loose' retitling of traditional personnel management, with no real change in HR practice. At the other extreme, HRM is a clearly defined and articulated approach to workforce management, with an explicit and strong ('tight') theoretical underpinning.

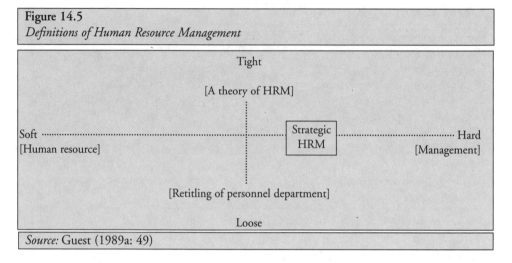

Figure 14.5
Definitions of Human Resource Management

Source: Guest (1989a: 49)

Guest then proceeds to develop a comprehensive theory of HRM, as outlined in Figure 14.6. He argues that firms will be more successful if they pursue four key HRM goals: strategic integration, employee commitment, flexibility and quality. He suggests that these HRM goals can be optimally achieved through coherent HRM policy choices in the areas of organisation/job design, management of change, recruitment, selection and socialisation, appraisal, training and development, rewards and communications. Guest identifies five necessary conditions for the effective operation of HRM, which are:

• corporate leadership, to ensure that the values inherent in HRM are championed and implemented;
• strategic vision, to ensure the integration of HRM as a key component of the corporate strategy;

Figure 14.6
A Theory of Human Resource Management

HRM policies	HR outcomes	Organisational outcomes
Organisation/job design		High job performance
Management of change	Strategic integration	High problem solving, change and innovation
Recruitment, selection and socialisation	Commitment	
Appraisal, training, development	Flexibility/adaptability	High cost effectiveness
Reward systems	Quality	Low turnover, absence, grievances
Communications		
	Leadership/Culture/Strategy	

Source: Guest (1987: 516)

- technological/production feasibility – heavy investment in short-cycle, repetitive production mitigates against the job design principles and autonomous teamworking necessary for HRM;
- industrial relations feasibility – multi-union status, low-trust management-employee relations and an adversarial industrial relations orientation mitigate against the implementation of HRM; and
- management capacity to implement appropriate policies.

CONTRASTING HRM AND 'TRADITIONAL' PERSONNEL MANAGEMENT

When HRM is contrasted with more traditional personnel management, as in Table 14.2, a number of key differences emerge. First, it is argued that workforce management considerations are fully integrated with strategic decision making in the HRM model. In the traditional personnel management model, the 'personnel' input to strategic decision making is less pronounced and more issue specific. A second contrast is that HRM is presented as proactive and long term, while the traditional personnel management is more reactive and adopts a shorter-term perspective. In terms of the desired mode of psychological contract, HRM is seen as facilitating employee commitment, while the traditional personnel management model is seen as a mode of managerial control over employees (Walton 1985). A specific contrast in the industrial relations sphere is that HRM is essentially unitarist in perspective, involving no apparent conflict of interests between employers and employees. In contrast, conventional personnel management is grounded in the pluralist tradition and much 'personnel' activity is devoted to managing the adversarial relationship between employers and workers/trade unions.

Table 14.2
Personnel Management and HRM Compared

	Personnel Management	HRM
Input into corporate planning	Issue specific	Integrated
Time and planning perspective	Short-term; reactive; marginal	Long-term; proactive, strategic
Psychological contract	Compliance	Commitment
Industrial relations	Pluralist; collective low trust; adversarial	Unitarist; individual; high-trust
Organisation structures/ systems	Bureaucratic; mechanistic	Organic; fluid
	Centralised; formal defined roles	Devolved; flexible roles
Principal delivery mechanism	Specialist personnel management function	Line management
Aims	Maximise cost effectiveness	Maximise HR utilisation

Source: Adapted from Guest (1987)

A number of *favourable* claims are made for HRM. It is suggested that HRM focuses on relations between (line) management and the individual worker, while the traditional model operates primarily between management and employee representatives. Another area of claimed contrast is that HRM operates most effectively in organic, fluid organisation structures, while personnel management is characterised by more bureaucratic and rigid organisational structures. The final perceived difference relates to the criteria utilised to evaluate effectiveness. It is claimed that HRM focuses on maximising the contribution of human resources to organisational effectiveness. In contrast, traditional personnel management is seen as having more pragmatic objectives – the maximisation of cost effectiveness. Despite these argued contrasts between HRM and traditional personnel management, Guest (1987) cautions that this does not necessarily imply that HRM is better than traditional personnel management. Rather, he suggests that traditional personnel management approaches may be more appropriate in certain organisational contexts, such as large bureaucratic organisations or heavily unionised organisations with adversarial collective bargaining traditions, while HRM may be appropriate in organisations with more organic structures and characterised by more individualist, high-trust management-employee relations.

Contradictions and Inconsistencies in HRM

In its relatively short history, HRM has attracted a great deal of attention with respect to its theoretical pedigree, empirical foundations and practical implications. Several authors have identified a number of inherent contradictions and inconsistencies in HRM, particularly the 'soft' variant advocated by the Harvard Business School model. For example, Legge (1989) highlights the apparent paradox between the traditional commodity status of labour under the capitalist framework and the essentially unitarist perspective of HRM, which sees no inherent conflict of interests between management and employees. It has generally been accepted that in the capitalist framework there is an in-built conflict of interest between management and employees over the price of labour. Indeed, this conflict of interest is the very basis for the existence of industrial relations.

However, the HRM perspective appears to ignore the 'inherency' of a conflict of interests. Rather, it focuses on the achievement of congruence of management and employee interests and on achieving high levels of employee commitment. For example, Flood (1989) suggests that HRM emphasises the need for organisations to focus on the extrinsic and intrinsic needs of employees and to develop employment practices which increase employee commitment. In a similar vein, Walton (1985) advocates that organisations should adopt policies that emphasise the mutuality of employer and employee interests to ensure employee commitment to achieve organisational goals. This focus on employee commitment not only seems incongruent with the pluralist perspective on the organisation, but also appears to conflict with another basic tenet of HRM, namely that HR policies should be integrated with business strategy. Clearly, many decisions that complement business strategy may not develop employee commitment. If an organisation's business strategy is to maximise short-term returns to owners/shareholders, this may well involve decisions that do not develop employee commitment, such as replacing labour with technology, contracting out certain tasks and making employees redundant.

A related issue on this theme is the suggestion that HRM involves the simultaneous achievement of higher levels of individualism and teamwork. These twin goals clearly have tremendous potential for conflict. For example, performance-related pay based on evaluations of the performance of individual employees may conflict with many of the underlying principles of teamworking, as indeed may individual communications.

High levels of flexibility are seen as a core objective of HRM. Guest (1987) suggests that increased flexibility involves the creation of structural mechanisms in organisations to ensure responsiveness to changing environmental conditions. However, several authors have noted the difficulties in achieving congruence in different flexibility forms in relation to numerical, functional and financial flexibility. It is clearly difficult to achieve high levels of functional flexibility, e.g. multi-skilling, where employees have a tenuous relationship with the organisation, which may result from attempts to improve numerical flexibility (Blyton and Morris 1992; Gunnigle 1992a).

Another contradiction in the HRM argument that HR policies must be internally consistent arises in relation to job security. A prominent theme in the extant literature is that for HRM to be effective, management must provide implicit job tenure guarantees for employees (Beer *et al.* 1984; Guest 1987, 1989a; Walton 1985). However, Blyton and Turnbull (1992: 10) comment that 'this is particularly problematic in highly competitive or recessionary conditions where the "needs of the business" are likely to undermine any internal "fit" with soft HRM values: shedding labour for example will severely challenge, if not destroy, an organisation's HRM image of caring for the needs and security of its employees'.

TRADE UNIONS AND HRM

The 'soft' HRM approach, as outlined by both the HBS model and Guest, places emphasis on achieving high-trust relations between management and employees. High-trust relations are pursued through managerial initiatives to increase individual employee involvement and motivation and the adoption of techniques such as performance appraisal and performance-related pay. Thus, such organisations attempt to create close management-employee ties and break down the traditional management-worker dichotomy, of which collective bargaining is seen as the principal manifestation. Such initiatives are indicative of a unitarist management perspective, albeit a very sophisticated variant, and have the potential for significant conflict with the pluralist perspective characteristic of industrial relations in many Irish organisations. This unitarist perspective is described by Guest (1989a) as follows:

HRM values are unitarist to the extent that they assume no underlying and inevitable differences of interest between management and workers ... HRM values are essentially individualistic in that they emphasise the individual-organisation linkage in preference to operating through group and representative mechanisms ... These values ... leave little scope for collective arrangements and assume little need for collective bargaining. HRM therefore poses a considerable threat to traditional industrial relations and more particularly trade unionism (Guest 1989a: 43).

In a review of American literature, Beaumont (1992) found that the most frequently cited components of HRM were a relatively well-developed internal labour market (in matters of promotion and employee development), flexible work organisations, contingent (performance-related) compensation practices, individual and group participation in task-related decisions and extensive internal communications arrangements. HRM is frequently seen as being incompatible with the collectivist ethos of trade union recognition and collective bargaining (Beer *et al.* 1984; Guest 1987, 1989a, 1989b). For example, Fiorito *et al.* (1987) argue that HRM practices are often part of employers' attempts to either substitute for or avoid trade unions.

Using a comprehensive index of twelve measures of HRM practices, Fiorito *et al.* (1987) conclude that such practices do inhibit unionisation, with those in the area of communications and participation having the greatest adverse impact on union organising success. In contrast, Milner and Richards (1991) found a significant positive association between companies that recognised unions and the greater use of employee involvement techniques. They suggest that recognising a union can facilitate the introduction of employee involvement by providing a ready-made organisational structure and, more importantly, an authority structure among employees that can be utilised to increase the chances of employee involvement techniques succeeding. Thus, we find a significant contrast in the research findings on the impact of HRM on trade unions – on the one hand, that HRM has been found to mitigate union penetration in organisations (Fiorito *et al.* 1987), and on the other hand, that HRM has been found to be both compatible with and supportive of trade unions (Storey 1989; Milner and Richards 1991).

UNION SUBSTITUTION AND SUPPRESSION

In evaluating the specific implications for industrial relations, it appears that the adoption of HRM approaches presents an explicit challenge to collective bargaining and specifically trade unions (Guest 1987; Storey 1989, 1992). The essence of such a challenge is the potentially reduced emphasis on collective bargaining and management-trade union interactions. Indeed, an area of major importance in evaluating the impact of HRM on industrial relations is the issue of trade union recognition. The term '*union substitution*' seems to have achieved widespread notoriety as a result of its association with non-union greenfield sites in the US. Probably the most widely known example in this regard was the Topeka, Kansas plant, as described by Walton (1982). This plant was seen to have two particular differentiating characteristics. It was established on a non-union basis and located outside a traditional urban/industrial centre. Beaumont and Townley (1985) suggest that in this and similar greenfield companies, work practices (such as fewer job grades, greater task flexibility, teamworking arrangements and extensive communications and grievance-handling systems) restrict the recruitment opportunities of trade unions and constitute a 'union-substitution effect'. This produces a strong employee-organisation identification process that limits the development of job dissatisfaction widely seen as precursor to unionisation (see Beaumont and Townley 1985; Foulkes 1980; Kochan *et al.* 1986).

In Ireland, the past two decades have witnessed significant growth in non-union approaches, particularly among US-owned firms (see McGovern 1989a; Gunnigle 1995a, 1995b; Gunnigle *et al.* 2001). Some of these firms, such as IBM and Intel, have adopted a 'union substitution' strategy involving the adoption of HRM policies designed to eliminate employee needs for collective representation (see Dundon 2002). A union substitution strategy is characterised by a high level of HR policy co-ordination and sophistication. To successfully implement a union substitution strategy, employers need to ensure that most of the benefits associated with union recognition still accrue in the non-union environment. Toner's work (1987) on non-union companies in Ireland identifies a range of HR practices that may be used to effect a union substitution strategy and to develop shared interests between workers and management, including lifelong employment, single status, merit pay, regular communications, gain-sharing, internal promotion and continuous development of employees.

A contrast to union substitution is *union suppression*. This is characterised by outright employer opposition to union recognition, using tactics based on fear and coercion, such as dismissals and related sanctions, and threats to close the firm and transfer operations elsewhere. Generally associated with sweatshops or exploitative small firms, this approach is characterised by low employment standards and little HR policy sophistication (see Dundon 2002; McLoughlin and Gourlay 1994).

As noted earlier, Marchington (1990) suggests that firms with high monopoly power have greater scope to choose from a wide range of HR and industrial relations policy options. In contrast, a union suppression strategy is most likely to emerge where there is little threat of unionisation. This can occur in sectors characterised by high levels of competition where most firms are quite small, where work is predominantly low skilled and where there is an unfavourable legal framework for trade unions (Roche and Turner 1998).

Commentators have identified a range of reasons as to why workers join trade unions, including pragmatic considerations such as dissatisfaction with the work environment or a critical incident, e.g. dismissal; ideological reasons, such as a deeply held belief in collective representation and solidarity; and other reasons that may relate to issues such as peer pressure (for example, see Flood and Toner 1996). Freeman and Medoff (1984) point to the benefits of union membership in providing an effective 'voice' for employees which in turn can contribute to improved worker morale and motivation, reduced rivalry between employees and a greater sense of equity through the establishment of effective procedures for handling issues such as grievances and discipline.

From an employer's perspective, there are advantages and disadvantages to union recognition. In this regard, much of the international literature has focused on the impact of unionisation on firm performance and specifically on issues such as profit levels, labour productivity and return on investment (see Freeman and Medoff 1984; Belman 1992; Huselid 1995). In evaluating this literature, Roche and Turner (1998) find the results on the impact of unionisation on productivity inconclusive but argue that the evidence from the manufacturing sector, particularly in the US, indicates that unionisation serves to reduce firm profitability. Thus, it is argued that non-union firms have a sound economic rationale for pursuing a union substitution strategy. However, there are also potential costs with such a strategy. In the Irish context, Flood and Toner's (1997) analysis identified a number of disadvantages associated with union and non-union approaches (see Table 14.3).

The disadvantages associated with union substitution are categorised by Flood and Toner (1997) as a catch-22 situation whereby firms pursuing a union substitution strategy cannot take advantage of their non-union status. For example, by reducing pay and dis-improving employment conditions or disciplining/dismissing unsatisfactory workers, there is the fear that such action will lead to union recognition. This leads Flood and Toner (1997: 270) to conclude that the major advantages of union substitution lie not in clear economic 'cost-benefit' criteria, but rather in allowing the firm greater scope to develop a unitary company culture and to foster 'warm personal relations' between management and employees (see also Toner 1987; Roche and Turner 1998). While we do not have sufficient empirical evidence to substantiate this argument, there is conclusive evidence of a substantial growth in popularity in non-union approaches, particularly among firms that have established new facilities in Ireland since the early 1980s.

Table 14.3
Disadvantages of Union Substitution and Union Recognition Strategies

Disadvantages of Union Substitution	Disadvantages of Union Recognition
Need to provide pay and employment conditions at least on par with those in similar unionised companies.	Unions make changes in work organisation more difficult.
Management is reluctant to enforce discipline.	Unions give rise to demarcation problems and impose restrictions on production.
Absence of adequate structure to deal with grievances (particularly collective issues).	Unions impose higher manning levels.
Fear of unionisation a constant concern.	Unions protect unsatisfactory workers.
Supervisors are monitored too closely.	Unions inhibit individual reward systems.
Management in non-union firms must work harder at communications.	Unions promote an adversarial industrial relations climate and can cause industrial action.
Need for expensive, well-resourced HR function.	Unions encourage the pursuit of trivial grievances.
	Unions make communication with employees more difficult.

Source: Adapted from Flood and Toner (1997)

Recent research by Gall (2001) and Dundon (2002) suggests that the union suppression or substitution dichotomy is overly simplistic and inappropriate and consequently fails to illustrate the diverse and complex array of factors that may explain and characterise non-union firms. Gall (2001) advances a more comprehensive categorisation of management control 'typologies' vis-à-vis trade unions, which acknowledges that employers may concurrently adopt approaches that are both suppressive and substitutive. Gall's categorisation was developed in the UK context and builds on earlier work by Roy (1980) in the US. He labels management control approaches in non-union firms as based on either 'fear stuff', 'sweet stuff', 'evil stuff', 'fatal stuff', 'awkward stuff', 'tame stuff' or 'harm stuff' (see Table 14.4). Despite the greater specification in the Gall/Roy typology, Dundon (2002) notes a number of problems. In particular, he claims that we are unclear as to whether employers have the capacity to consciously choose and implement one approach rather than another, suggesting that managerial approaches tend to be both 'haphazard and ad hoc'. He also argues that we have little evidence to indicate that such typologies have 'any predictive power across industrial sectors or occupational groups' (see Chapter 15).

Table 14.4
Non-union Management Control Approaches

Non-Union Approach	Type of Employer Anti-Union Behaviour and Control
Fear stuff	**Union suppression:** Includes blatant intimidation of workers, the objective to instil a 'fear' (real or otherwise) of managerial reprisals to possible unionisation.
Sweet stuff	**Union substitution:** Management claims unions are unnecessary, with better terms and conditions and sophisticated employee voice channels to resolve any grievances.
Evil stuff	**Ideological opposition to unions:** Management suggests unions are 'reds under the beds' and will be destructive to the company performance.
Fatal stuff	**Blatant refusal:** Includes refusal to recognise a union or at best a refusal to 'bargain in good faith'.
Awkward stuff	**Stonewalling:** Creation of what appear to be legitimate obstacles to union recognition, effectively employing 'delaying' tactics.
Tame stuff	**Damaged limitations:** Includes 'sweetheart' deals, partially recognising 'moderate' unions or creating internal (managerial-controlled) staff associations.
Harm stuff	**Bypassing:** Effectively marginalise employee voice, often through specific non-union communication channels.

Source: Gall (2001)

Evidence of HRM–Industrial Relations Interaction in Ireland

In Ireland we have limited empirical evidence on the impact of HRM practices on industrial relations or, more specifically, on management-trade union interactions. However, research by Turner (1993) and Roche and Turner (1998) provide some interesting insights. Turner's (1993) analysis considered the diffusion of HRM practices in Ireland and their impact on union penetration. He found that HRM practices did not significantly influence union density. He also found few significant differences between union and non-union firms in the use of HRM practices (Turner 1993). Roche and Turner (1998) outline three ways through which HRM policies impact on trade unions and collective bargaining:

- the adoption of HRM as a union substitution strategy;
- the unco-ordinated adoption of HRM policies in parallel with 'adversarial' industrial relations; and
- the adoption of HRM policies as part of a 'partnership' strategy.

Union Substitution

Roche and Turner (1998) argue that a union substitution strategy is most likely to emerge in larger firms that operate in the more profitable sectors of the economy. In such instances, firms have the financial wherewithal to provide the levels of pay, employment conditions and general working environment necessary to underpin such a strategy.

In reviewing the empirical evidence on union penetration, we noted earlier that aggregate levels of union membership and recognition in Ireland are quite high. However, union density is in decline and there is a significant increase in union avoidance in new greenfield firms. However, union de-recognition has not emerged to any great extent in Ireland, although it has become an issue of some significance in the UK. Finally, it is important to note that what is often termed '*union marginalisation*', that is, reducing the impact of trade unions in enterprise-level industrial relations, has indeed emerged as an important, if under-researched, development in Irish industrial relations. Roche and Turner (1998) suggest that a union substitution strategy can form part of either a union avoidance or a union marginalisation approach.

As noted earlier, a union substitution strategy is most commonly associated with large multinational subsidiaries that use 'employee relations' approaches that are generally characterised by good pay and conditions and influential and well-resourced HR departments. They deploy a range of sophisticated HR policies designed to enhance employee satisfaction and commitment and remove any desire or moves by workers to join trade unions (Roche and Turner 1998). Household names in this regard include Intel, Hewlett-Packard and IBM. As commented on above, there is considerable evidence to suggest that such firms have been successful both in avoiding unionisation and in meeting employee needs for voice and equity at work (see Toner 1987; Flood and Toner 1996, 1997).

However, caution is needed in interpreting this phenomenon. It would be presumptuous to generalise on industrial relations practices in non-union firms on the basis of a small number of sample companies. Gunnigle's (1995a, 1995b) study of greenfield companies found that the bulk of non-union firms did not utilise comprehensive or sophisticated HRM policies. Rather, it appeared that union avoidance was achieved through 'harder' HR practices such as outsourcing, subcontracted labour and other forms of atypical employment. This finding is in line with UK evidence which suggested that commonly used exemplar firms are the exception rather than the rule. Such findings imply that the majority of non-union firms 'do not *need*, nor could the majority *afford*, to adopt a substitution strategy' (Blyton and Turnbull 1994: 252; see also Roche and Turner 1998).

Unco-ordinated Adoption of HRM Policies in Parallel with Adversarial Industrial Relations

This second mode of HRM-industrial relations interaction, identified by Roche and Turner (1998), refers to the adoption of HRM polices in an ad hoc and unsystematic fashion within a tradition of adversarial relations between management and unions. As many commentators have noted, the empirical evidence suggests that HRM is most commonly adopted in this fashion (see Gunnigle *et al.* 1994) and Ireland is no exception in this regard.

> The most common practice in Irish companies to date, the evidence suggests, has been for managements to adopt HRM policies in an essentially piecemeal or fragmented manner, without any attempt to use these policies to promote union substitution, co-ordinate these policies with collective bargaining or to involve unions in their uptake or implementation. Unions for their part at local or plant level appear often to have been predisposed to watch management innovations from the wings, adopting an unenthusiastic, vigilant or defensive posture (Roche and Turner 1998: 76–7).

Roche and Turner (1998: 78) point to a number of studies which indicate that Irish firms have tended to adopt HRM policies 'selectively and opportunistically', with little perceptible 'concern with the overall coherence of those policies' (see also Gunnigle *et al.* 1994; Roche and Turner 1994, 1997). They conclude that is unusual to find firms that have adopted consistent sets of HRM policies 'across the spectrum of HRM policy innovations'. The more widespread pattern was the utilisation of selected HRM policies in one or a limited number of HR areas. They further argue that the uptake of HRM policy innovations was lowest in areas traditionally regulated through collective bargaining, such as payment systems and pay increases. Rather, HRM approaches were more commonly adopted in areas like communications and recruitment/deployment.

In attempting to explain such variation in the uptake of HRM policies, Roche and Turner (1998: 79–80) identify constraints emanating from Ireland's industrial relations and collective bargaining traditions:

Managements show greatest conservatism in adopting HRM innovations in the areas of pay and work organisation as these in practice tend to be most heavily regulated by trade unions. A significant change in these areas is likely to run into strong union resistance, or to require the active co-operation of trade unions. In contrast, unions are likely to be least resistant to management innovations in areas like communications, provided that they are not seen to threaten collective bargaining. In such areas management may enjoy scope to press ahead without engaging unions in their new policies. The same broadly holds for innovations in 'flow' policies. Unions have not traditionally tended to negotiate over such areas as selection policies and techniques, other than perhaps by seeking to defend established recruitment channels. Nor have they attempted to negotiate over performance appraisal systems, other than possibly by trying to regulate the use to which appraisal records are put.

In evaluating these findings, Roche and Turner (1998) conclude that the Irish evidence of fairly widespread but gradual change in the uptake of HRM approaches is similar to evidence on prevailing patterns of change in Europe and the US. They also note that such changes are most often implemented without trade unions being accorded a central role (see Roche and Kochan 1996). It therefore appears that trade unions have not generally played a prominent role in the diffusion of HRM. As such, Roche and Turner suggest that union attitudes to HRM reflect high levels of mistrust and the adoption of 'traditional adversarial' postures. This reaction probably reflects union fears that HRM approaches constitute a management-driven agenda for significant organisational change and presents a major threat to the role and influence of trade unions within the enterprise (Gunnigle 1998a).

The Adoption of HRM Policies as Part of a Strategy of Promoting 'Partnership'

This third mode or HRM-industrial relations interaction identified by Roche and Turner (1998) refers to the attempts by management and trade unions to actively co-operate in the implementation of HRM and related change initiatives. Generally captured under the rubric of 'partnership'-based industrial relations arrangements, these normally involve joint management-trade union initiatives designed to substantially change aspects of work organisation and as such inevitably involve the utilisation of HRM policies.

The nature and diffusion of partnership-based industrial relations arrangements at enterprise level was discussed in depth in Chapter 12. Of particular significance from a management and trade union perspective is the relationship between HRM initiatives and established collective bargaining arrangements. As we have seen, the adoption of partnership-based approaches requires considerable change in the role and postures of both employers and trade unions. From an employer perspective, a key concern appears to be the extent to which partnership allows the organisation to substantially change aspects of work organisation, such as work practices, manning levels and use of atypical employment forms. Such changes are often accompanied by the introduction of

particular HRM policies, especially performance management and perfo
appraisal, performance-related pay and more extensive and direct communicatio.
employees.

For trade unions, a critical concern is the extent to which they are given a m.
extensive, meaningful role in influencing key decisions on the nature of workplace
change and reorganisation. As such, they will be concerned that HRM policies are
effectively co-ordinated with established collective bargaining and collective
representation mechanisms and do not serve to undermine or diminish the role of trade
unions and collective bargaining in the enterprise (see Roche and Turner 1998).

Summary and Conclusions

In the Irish context there has been limited investigation of the linkages between
business strategy, product market conditions and developments in industrial relations.
In evaluating current developments in industrial relations in Ireland there is a danger in
confusing prominent examples of 'soft' HRM with the widespread pervasiveness of such
approaches. In the UK context, Blyton and Turnbull (1992) note that, empirically, it is
difficult to find examples of organisations that adopt coherent HRM approaches. They
argue that when firms attempt to implement HRM they run up against some key
inherent contradictions and inconsistencies between the theory and practice of HRM.
This analysis points to the significance of contextual factors on the diffusion of HRM
and its impact on industrial relations. Our review of available research points to the
considerable diffusion of *aspects* of HRM among Irish organisations and to its impact
on industrial relations practice. The chapter points to the different emergent patterns
or typologies of HRM-industrial relations interactions. This analysis illustrates the
range of management approaches or styles that employers may seek to adopt in their
approach to enterprise-level industrial relations. We turn to the issue of management
styles in the next chapter and also consider the nature and diffusion of HRM in greater
depth.

CHAPTER 15

Management Styles in Industrial Relations

INTRODUCTION

The previous chapter highlighted the marked increase in emphasis in developing linkages between business strategy, HRM and industrial relations. A critical aspect of this debate is the contention that greater strategic significance is being accorded to HRM and industrial relations considerations, which is manifest in managerial initiatives to develop particular industrial approaches or styles at enterprise level. However, there remains a reservation that the great majority of organisations do not exercise any degree of strategic choice in HRM or industrial relations management, and consequently their approach may be variously characterised as reactive, opportunist or 'fire fighting'. This chapter considers these issues, specifically:

- the nature of management styles in industrial relations;
- the possible determinants of style;
- the dimensions along which management styles in industrial relations may differ; and
- the alternative styles that may be adopted.

Particular attention is paid to the theoretical arguments and the empirical evidence at both Irish and international level.

MANAGEMENT STYLES IN INDUSTRIAL RELATIONS

In industrial relations, the concept of management style has been principally used to categorise and explain management's overall approach to industrial relations (see Fox 1966, 1974; Purcell and Sisson 1983; Poole 1986; Purcell 1987; Marchington and Parker 1990). In this vein, Rollinson (1993: 92) describes management style in industrial relations as referring to 'management's overall approach to handling the relationship between the organisation and its employees'. As such, management style in industrial relations is a dynamic concept that may be refined and changed over time. The influence and mediating effect of environmental variables on management styles is considered later in this chapter.

STRATEGIC CHOICE AND MANAGEMENT STYLES IN INDUSTRIAL RELATIONS

Earlier in this text we considered how employers may choose to organise into representative employer associations for industrial relations purposes. While employer associations clearly play an important role in industrial relations, individual employers are primarily responsible for the development and implementation of industrial relations policies and practices within their particular enterprise. Consequently, employer and management approaches to industrial relations are a critical determinant of the nature of enterprise-level industrial relations.

In our review of employer objectives in industrial relations in Chapter 6, we noted that management objectives are primarily identified with owner interests. Since control is associated with ownership, power is exercised by the owners of an enterprise through their representatives in the workplace, namely the management team. This link between ownership and the legitimacy of management authority is a critical characteristic of organisational life, despite the fact that management must also be responsible to other interest groups, such as employees and their trade unions. Consequently, management, and particularly senior management, exercise considerable power and influence by virtue of their scope to take strategic decisions.

Purcell (1987) notes the tendency to identify and contrast organisations according to their employment policies and practices and suggests that differences cannot be wholly explained by structural variables such as size, product markets and technology. Rather, he identifies strategic choice (exercised by senior management) as a key factor explaining differences in management styles in industrial relations (Purcell 1987). The notion of strategic choice infers that senior management possess some room for manoeuvre and, while environmental factors may constrain the range of choice, they retain considerable power in making decisions on 'appropriate' styles and policies. Senior management can therefore use their resources and power to make strategic choices that both influence environmental factors and affect particular management styles in industrial relations. Management styles should therefore be evaluated in terms of the interplay between environmental factors, managerial ideology/values and strategic choice. As Marchington and Parker (1990: 99) state, 'choice should be viewed as both a cause and a consequence of environmental influences ... that is, managements have some influence over the kind of markets in which they choose to operate, and in some cases over the structure of the market itself, as well as having some choice over the way in which they respond to environmental pressures'.

Management may take strategic decisions that directly influence industrial relations, such as whether or not to deal with trade unions. However, the impact of strategic decisions on industrial relations may often be indirect. For example, an organisation may decide to terminate a particular product line because of financial and market considerations, but this decision may result in redundancies and may detrimentally affect industrial relations.

As noted earlier, the question of whether senior managements actually do make strategic industrial relations decisions remains a matter for debate. A traditional view has been that senior management concentrate their strategic decision making on 'primary' business areas such as investment or production. Any attention devoted to industrial relations is secondary and somewhat incidental to the main thrust of such strategic decision making (Purcell 1987; Boxhall and Purcell 2003). On the other hand, there is evidence to suggest that some organisations adopt a particular industrial relations style or approach and take well thought-out strategic decisions to establish and sustain this style (Beer *et al.* 1984; Kochan *et al.* 1986; Guest 1987). Indeed, it would appear that practice varies widely, from a general approach of 'incidentalism', characterised by little or no strategic decision making, to a more planned approach (see Figure 15.1).

It is also possible to identify a range of issues on which employers may choose to make conscious decisions which, either directly or indirectly, impact on industrial relations at enterprise level. These are outlined in Table 15.1.

Figure 15.1
Strategic Decision Making in Industrial Relations

'Incidentalism'	Planned IR Approach
No consideration of industrial relations considerations in strategic decision making.	Key strategic decisions taken to achieve/advance a particular desired industrial relations approach.

Table 15.1
Indicative Strategic Decisions Impacting on Industrial Relations

Decisions	Impact on Industrial Relations
Location of plant	Influences labour supply, nature of labour force, labour costs, labour/employment law and prospect of unionisation.
Size of plant	Influences span of managerial control, communications, leadership/managerial style.
Recruitment and selection	By deciding on the nature of the workforce, management can influence industrial relations, e.g. propensity of workers to join trade unions.
Training and development	Nature and extent of training and development can influence management and employee approaches and attitudes to industrial relations.
Union recognition	In a greenfield situation management may be able to decide on whether or not to deal with trade unions, which will have a significant impact on the subsequent nature of enterprise-level industrial relations.
Employer association	Deciding whether or not to join an employer association may influence subsequent industrial relations decisions, such as pay negotiations.
Procedural formalisation	The extent and nature of formalisation of industrial relations procedures will impact on enterprise-level industrial relations, e.g. grievance and dispute hanling.
Use of HRM policies and/ or practices	By introducing techniques such as performance appraisal or performance-related pay, management can limit the scope of trade unions.

CONTEXTUAL INFLUENCES

To identify and explain variations in management styles it is necessary to examine the interplay of a diverse range of external and internal factors. Kochan *et al.* (1986) place particular emphasis on management values, business strategy, historical factors and the external environment as key triggers in stimulating change in industrial relations. It is argued that changes in environmental conditions affect decisions on business strategy and ultimately industrial relations. Such decisions will be conditioned by managerial values and constrained by historical factors and practice in industrial relations.

The *external environment* exerts a major influence on organisational decision making. In regard to public policy, the anti-union policies of successive Conservative Governments in the UK during the 1980s gave legitimacy and support to 'macho' management, which undermined the role of trade unions in the workplace. These factors are particularly important at an aggregate level in explaining variations in national industrial relations systems. Poole (1986) identifies the role of government and centralised control ('challenge from above') as a key constraining influence on managerial prerogative/discretion in decision making. This line of argument suggests that the greater the level of centralised control (corporatism), the more limited management's scope to develop industrial relations styles that undermine pluralist principles. Conversely, it may be argued that low levels of central intervention in industrial relations allows management greater discretion and renders the emergence of industrial relations styles that diverge from the traditional pluralist-adversarial model more likely. To date in Ireland, however, corporatist policies have not impacted greatly on management in relation to the issue of union recognition.

Technology is another key external environmental factor affecting managerial styles in industrial relations. Technology, seen in generic terms as the equipment used to perform particular tasks in the organisation and the way it is organised, is a major influence on approaches to managing industrial relations (Beer *et al.* 1984). In the previous chapter we noted Guest's (1987) analysis that identified technological/ production feasibility as a requisite condition for the successful implementation of HRM-type styles. He has suggested that the utilisation of short-cycle, repetitive, assembly line technology mitigates against the job design principles and autonomous teamworking characteristic of 'soft' HRM (Guest 1987). Technology also affects cost structure and consequently impacts upon key aspects of industrial relations, such as reward systems. Marchington (1982) suggests that in labour-intensive sectors where labour costs are high, organisations may be more constrained in developing 'soft' HRM management styles. However, in capital-intensive sectors where labour costs constitute a small proportion of total costs, organisations may have greater scope to adopt more benign management styles in industrial relations, such as attractive rewards.

The *labour market* is a particularly important influence on industrial relations, especially in relation to recruitment, employee development and reward systems. In particular, high unemployment clearly impacts the power balance in labour-management relations and can facilitate more autocratic or directive forms of management decision making. Looking at the Irish labour market, the most notable developments include the progressive decline of agricultural and industrial employment and the growth of services sector employment (Wallace *et al.* 2001), which has exercised a drag effect on union recognition due to the fact that union recognition is generally low in services. This has occurred despite the fact that union recognition in services has remained relatively stable (Wallace *et al.* 2001; Wallace and Dineen 2001). Other notable characteristics of the Irish labour market are the relatively young age profile, increased female participation rates and the growth of 'atypical' employment forms. A particularly important development over recent decades has been the rapid fall in unemployment and the consequential tightening of the labour market, particularly among certain skilled categories.

These developments clearly affect industrial relations. For example, low unemployment and a 'tight' labour market place a premium on workforce retention, factors which were evident at the height of the Celtic Tiger years. A tight labour market exerts upward pressure on wages, affects labour turnover and changes power relations in collective bargaining.

An organisation's *product market* is seen as possibly the most significant influence on strategic decision making and on management styles in industrial relations, as discussed in Chapter 14. This analysis suggested that organisations which operate from a strong product market position, e.g. high market share, growing market, stable or increasing demand, have greater scope to adopt sophisticated HR policies, which in turn can contribute to a more co-operative industrial relations climate. In contrast, firms operating under high levels of market pressure, e.g. contracting market share, high levels of price competition, may have considerably less scope for choice and be forced to adopt a more traditional 'cost and labour control' approach that may consequently contribute to the existence of adversarial industrial relations. Other external factors such as national economic performance (see Chapter 13) and cultural/societal values may impact upon business strategy. However, while an organisation's external context will serve to guide management decisions on industrial relations, it will be factors in the organisation's *internal environment*, such as managerial ideology, business strategy and organisation size/structure, that will determine the *unique* organisational responses to the external environment.

Organisation structure and size are clearly important factors impacting upon management styles in industrial relations. Numerous British studies have noted that trade union recognition and the presence of a specialised HR function are positively correlated with organisation size. In the Irish context, Gunnigle and Brady (1984) found that management in smaller organisations veer towards a unitarist frame of reference and adopt less formality in industrial relations than their counterparts in larger organisations (see MacMahon 2002; Wallace 1982). In relation to organisation structure, Purcell (1992) argues that senior (corporate) management in highly diversified organisations are primarily concerned with financial issues. As a result, HR considerations (including industrial relations) are not a concern of corporate decision making, but rather an operational concern for management at the business unit level. A corollary of this argument is that organisations with a highly diversified product range are more likely to adopt differing HR and industrial relations policies suited to the needs of constituent divisions and establishments. By comparison, 'core business' organisations with a narrow product range are more likely to integrate HR issues into strategic planning.

Several writers identify the locus of strategy formulation as a key issue influencing the nature of establishment industrial relations, including the presence or absence of trade unions (Purcell and Sisson 1983; Kochan *et al.* 1986; Poole 1986). Poole (1986: 53) argues that the growth of conglomerate multinational enterprises presents management with the opportunity to develop industrial relations policies at corporate level, 'where they are relatively unrestricted by intervention by government or by plant-level agreements with labour'. Of course, such discretion is also dependent on public policy. Some countries have developed strongly interventionist measures in relation to worker participation and union recognition, thus union recognition in Scandinavia is high by international norms and worker participation is highly developed in Germany.

Business strategy is another significant internal factor impacting upon industrial relations styles. In Chapter 14 we noted that business strategy occurs at the level of the individual business unit and is concerned with achieving competitive advantage in a particular industry or segment. It is likely that management will take steps to configure their HR policies, including industrial relations, in a way which aids strategy implementation.

Other important internal factors that impact management styles in industrial relations include *workforce profile* and *established HR and industrial relations practices*, both of which can impact on the effectiveness of change initiatives in areas such as employee involvement. In varying organisations workers may react differently to employee involvement or job enrichment initiatives. Hackman and Oldham's (1980) research found that not all employees react favourably to their suggestions for enriching jobs or for increased involvement in management decision making. They suggest that only those workers with a strong desire for achievement, responsibility and autonomy are motivated by such job redesign initiatives. These traits may in turn have been conditioned by traditional HR and industrial relations policies and practices. For example, if internal mobility and individual initiative have traditionally been discouraged, it may be difficult to quickly implement a comprehensive employee development and promotion policy.

MANAGEMENT VALUES AND IDEOLOGY

Management values and ideology incorporate senior management's deeply held beliefs, which guide decisions on various aspects of workforce management (Poole 1986; Purcell 1987; Gunnigle 1995a). As noted earlier, management's desired approach will closely reflect their underlying values, but may not necessarily translate into practice because of the mediating effect of environmental variables (Poole 1986; Rollinson 1993; Salamon 1998).

In relation to managerial values, Kochan *et al.* (1986: 14) argue that these have a tremendous impact upon industrial relations styles and strategies, acting as a 'lens' through which 'managerial decision makers weigh their options for responding to cues from the external environment'. Thus, options that are inconsistent with accepted values are discounted or not consciously considered. Freidman (1977, 1984) also places management's role at the centre of his analysis of developments in industrial relations, suggesting that the primary 'dynamic influence on the organisation of work is normally exerted through the initiatives of managers'. Freidman (1977) relates this dominance to the structure of capitalist societies, arguing that 'the fundamental structure of property rights in capitalist societies means that those with a primary claim of possession of the means of production will normally take the primary initiatives in the organisation of productive activity' (Freidman 1977: 180).

All organisations are characterised by particular values and philosophies with regard to industrial relations. In some organisations such values may be explicit, as demonstrated in statements of corporate mission or philosophy, while in others it may be implicit and inferred from management practice in areas such as supervisory style, reward systems and communications. Two cases may be highlighted. First, in a number of organisations the role of influential founders has had a determining influence on their organisation's corporate values and industrial relations style. Prominent international examples include Marks & Spencer, Hewlett-Packard and Dell Computers. The influence of entrepreneurial founders is also prominent in indigenous Irish firms. The industrial relations styles adopted over time in organisations such as Dunnes Stores, Superquinn and Ryanair have clearly been heavily influenced by the values and philosophy of their chief executives. Second, the impact of managerial values on management styles in industrial relations is associated with the notion that managerial ideology is related to broader ethnic and cultural values. Of particular significance is the suggestion that managerial opposition to pluralism, and particularly unionisation, is characteristic of American managers' value system, which HRM approaches that emphasise individual freedom and initiative, direct communications and merit-based rewards are very much in line with (Bendix 1956; Kochan et al. 1986; Jacoby 1997). This interpretation is significant in Ireland where, as we have seen, our economy is heavily dependent on foreign direct investment and where the bulk of such investment is American.

In analysing the broad links between ideology and style, Poole (1986) argues that, in the US context, the effects of values and ideologies are most obviously manifest in union avoidance practices, a pronounced 'unitary' perspective and deployment of sophisticated HRM approaches. Poole and others note that while managerial preferences have fluctuated over time, US employers have embraced a non-union approach against a more general trend in the developed world towards a tacit acceptance of trade unions (see also Kochan et al. 1986; Jacoby 1997). Several writers link the origins of this approach to the concept of 'individualism' in the wider US culture, coupled with prevalent private enterprise commitments (Rothenberg and Silverman 1973; Foulkes 1980; Guest 1989b; Jacoby 1997; Ferner 1997; Edwards and Ferner 2002).

THE SPECIALIST HR FUNCTION

A final area of HR policy choice addresses the role of the *specialist HR function*. We know that by definition all managers, supervisors and team leaders have important workforce management responsibilities, such as those dealing with staff selection, development and motivation. Many of these roles incorporate industrial relations responsibilities such as staff supervision, reward management or grievance and dispute handling. However, we also know that many medium and larger organisations tend to employ HR or industrial relations specialists to undertake particular responsibilities in workforce management, such as developing and monitoring HR/IR strategies or providing expert advice and assistance to line managers, e.g. on psychometric testing or employment legislation.

The specialist HR function plays a key role in establishing, implementing and monitoring HRM and IR in organisations. A review of the literature on the historical development of specialist personnel/HR function in Ireland identifies industrial relations as traditionally the most significant area of activity (O'Mahony 1964; Shivanath 1987; Monks 1992, 2002). This was largely due to trade unions' growth in influence up to the early 1980s, which saw many larger employers engage specialist 'personnel' managers to deal with industrial relations matters at enterprise level. Gunnigle (1998b: 4) writes:

> For the personnel function, industrial relations became *the* priority with personnel practitioners vested with the responsibility to negotiate and police agreements. Industrial harmony was the objective and personnel specialists through their negotiating, interpersonal and procedural skills had responsibility for its achievement. This industrial relations emphasis helped position the personnel function in a more central management role, albeit a largely reactive one.

It is also clear that the type and role of specialist HR function can vary considerably across organisations. For example, it is suggested that a key characteristic of organisations adopting a so-called 'strategic HRM' approach is that the major responsibility for HR activities is assumed by line managers (Beer *et al.* 1984; Monks 2002). However, Guest (1987) notes 'the well-established professional structure of HRM' in Britain, where 'professional' HR specialists undertake responsibility for a range of HR and IR issues and possess valued expertise in core HR areas such as selection, training and wage negotiations. It would seem that the issue of whether HR and IR matters are best managed by a specialist function or by line managers is a matter of emphasis, since in most larger organisations both will be involved in various aspects of HR and IR practice. For example, the 'professional' HR model involves a major role for the specialist HR function in handling HR and IR activities, with a heavy reliance on systems and procedures. Guest feels that this approach is most appropriate in stable, bureaucratic organisations. On the other hand, we have noted in Chapter 14 that more contemporary approaches place a greater emphasis on the role of line management and increased top management involvement in developing overall strategy and related HR and IR policies (Guest 1987; Boxhall and Purcell 2003).

Recognising the considerable variation in the role that the specialist HR function may play in organisations, Tyson and Fell (1986) developed a typology which identified three kinds of HR function: an administrative/support function, a systems/reactive function and a business manager function, as outlined in Table 15.2 (see also Tyson 1987).

Table 15.2
Models of the Specialist HR Function

(a) **Administrative/support function:** This type of HR function operates in an administrative support mode at a low level in the managerial hierarchy. It is responsible for basic administration, record keeping and welfare provision.

(b) **Systems/reactive function:** This type of HR function operates at a high level in the managerial hierarchy (normally at functional manager/head level) and plays a central role in handling industrial relations issues and in developing policies and procedures in other core HR areas, such as training. However, the role is largely reactive in nature, dealing with the HR and IR implications of business decisions. This model incorporates a strong 'policing' component where the HR department is concerned with securing adherence to agreed systems and procedures, particularly in the IR sphere.

(c) **Business manager function:** This type of HR function is a top-level management function involved in establishing and adjusting corporate objectives and developing strategic HR and IR policies and practices designed to facilitate the achievement of long-term business goals. HR and IR considerations are recognised as an integral component of corporate success, with the head of HR (HR director) ideally placed to assess how the organisation's human resources can best contribute to this goal. Routine HR and IR activities are delegated, allowing senior practitioners to adopt the broad strategic outlook of a 'business manager'.

Source: Tyson and Fell (1986)

A study by Shivanath (1987) considered the relevance of Tyson's typology in a cross-section of large organisations in Ireland. In relation to the *administrative/support model*, the study found that the vast majority of Irish HR practitioners were not limited to this role. While HR departments were of necessity concerned with routine clerical/administrative tasks, these were generally delegated, allowing senior practitioners to deal with more strategic matters. The description of the HR practitioner within the *systems/reactive model* seemed to Shivanath (1987) to most accurately reflect the roles of the majority of Irish practitioners. Industrial relations was identified by the majority of personnel practitioners as the most important aspect of their work. The study also found that the *business manager model* was prominent in a number of organisations, with a significant number of senior HR practitioners involved at a more strategic level.

More recent research suggests that while industrial relations remains an important aspect of the work of the specialist HR function, there has been somewhat of a reorientation that has involved a broadening of its remit so that other core areas of HR activity, particularly employee development and reward systems, are given greater priority together with an increased role in more generic management initiatives, such as quality enhancement and change management (see Heraty *et al.* 1994). In some organisations such change has led to a greater strategic role for the HR function, involving the development of closer linkages between business strategy and HR and IR practice, as discussed in Chapter 14 (see Monks 2002; Sheehan 2002; Sparrow 2002). Gunnigle (1998b) argues that up to the late 1970s, the development of the HR function in Ireland was characterised by *convergence* to a common model, which he terms 'industrial relations orthodoxy'.

> In tracing the development of the personnel function in Ireland over recent decades one can identify a predictable pattern of evolution. From somewhat humble beginnings, the specialist personnel function developed to a stage where it became accepted as an integral part of the management structure of larger organisations. This pattern of evolution saw convergence to a *prevailing orthodoxy* of the role of the personnel function. This orthodoxy was grounded in the belief that *the* key employer concern in workforce management was the establishment and maintenance of stable industrial relations … While more reactive rather than strategic, this *industrial relations* role was nonetheless significant: it served to both define what personnel work involved and position the personnel management function as an important aspect of the managerial infrastructure (Gunnigle 1998b: 17).

Gunnigle argues that this role reached its heyday in the 1970s, but by the early 1980s *industrial relations orthodoxy* as the prevailing model of the HR function began to unravel. As noted earlier, this transformation can be traced to numerous sources, but particularly to the increased competitive pressures on organisations. Thus, Gunnigle (1998b: 17) argues that 'contingency approaches are now the order of the day', with the HR role influenced by a variety of factors, such as industrial sector, managerial philosophy and market context. He outlines four *HR typologies*: the commitment model, the transaction cost model, the traditional adversarial model and the partnership model (see Table 15.3).

Table 15.3
Organisational Context-Human Resource Function Models

The Commitment Model
Generally associated with a 'soft' HRM style, this was the first HR type to seriously challenge industrial relations orthodoxy in Ireland. It is characterised by a resource perspective of employees, incorporating the view that there is an organisational pay-off in performance terms from a combination of 'sophisticated' HR and IR policies designed to develop employee commitment and emphasise the mutuality of management and employee interests. In this model, the HR function is high powered and well resourced, with a significant change agent role. This model appears to characterise core business organisations whose competitive strategy is based on a product differentiation/premium price approach, often on a 'first to market' basis. Such organisations may employ significant numbers of highly trained technical and engineering staffs whose development and retention are critical to organisational success. This model generally relies on a *union substitution* premise, although organisations with union recognition, but where the union role is somewhat peripheral, also fall within this category.

The Transaction Cost Model

While the commitment model has received much attention, its viability has increasingly come under scrutiny in recent years. In particular, exemplars of the commitment model, e.g. Wang and Digital, experienced intense competitive pressures from low-cost producers, with some going out of business. The transaction cost model places the emphasis on minimising costs. Thus, outsourcing becomes an important strategy, particularly in using contracted labour and other forms of 'atypical' employment. This approach is also associated with an intensification in the pace of work and increasing work load and employee flexibility. This approach may rely on a union suppression premise, often linked to the (management) suggestion that unions inhibit the development of flexibility levels required to ensure competitiveness. In this typology the key role of the HR function is cost-effective labour supply. The role is essentially reactive – it deals with the operational workforce management consequences of a low-cost competitive strategy.

The Traditional Adversarial Model

This approach equates to 'industrial relations orthodoxy' discussed above and, as we have seen, was traditionally the dominant type of HR function in Ireland. It is grounded in low-trust management-employee relations and primary reliance on adversarial collective bargaining – it equates to Tyson's systems/reactive manager typology.

The Partnership Model

We have earlier noted that the development of union-management partnerships has been the focus of much recent debate in Ireland (see Chapter 12). The rationale for partnership is based on so-called 'mutual gains' principles whereby workers and trade unions actively pursue, *with* management, solutions to business problems and appropriate work reorganisation in return for greater involvement in both. Within this typology, the HR function becomes an important strategic lever in developing the partnership agenda. It also assumes an important role in implementing a range of HR and IR policy initiatives to underpin this new orientation, specifically in areas such as reward systems, management-employee communications, job design and employee development.

Source: Gunnigle (1998b)

CATEGORISING MANAGEMENT STYLES IN INDUSTRIAL RELATIONS

The preceding discussion has attempted to outline the main factors that impact on variations in management styles in industrial relations. This section examines alternative management styles in industrial relations and considers their relevance for Irish industrial relations. We begin by revisiting Fox's (1966, 1974) seminal works on unitarist and pluralist perspectives on industrial relations, previously discussed in Chapters 1 and 7.

Managerial Frames of Reference

Fox (1966) argued that management approaches to industrial relations are largely determined by the frame of reference adopted by managers. A frame of reference is defined by Thelen and Withall (1949) as 'the main selective influences at work as the perceiver supplements, omits and structures what he notices'. Fox suggests that a manager's frame of reference is important because it determines how management expects people to behave and how it thinks they should behave, i.e. values and beliefs; it determines management reactions to actual behaviour, i.e. management practice; and it shapes the methods management chooses when it wishes to change the behaviour of people at work, e.g. strategies/policies.

Fox identified two alternative frames of reference to help evaluate management approaches to industrial relations, termed the *unitarist* and the *pluralist* frame of reference (see Chapters 1 and 7). These contrasting frames of reference represent dominant industrial relations orientations that may be adopted by management. In practice, one finds that most managers do not strictly adhere to one or the other of these approaches, but may adopt different approaches in different situations and/or change their approach over time. Nevertheless, these frames of reference approach provides a useful framework for evaluating management approaches to industrial relations.

Typologies of Management Styles in Industrial Relations

Moving beyond Fox's unitarist-pluralist dichotomy, several commentators have attempted to develop categorisations of management styles to explain differences in organisational approaches to industrial relations. Earlier we explored the idea of identifiable patterns or styles of industrial relations management and attempted to distinguish between organisations that operated in a strategic or reactive manner. Several writers have attempted to move beyond this crude distinction to develop ideal-typical styles of industrial relations management and classify them according to specific criteria.

While the unitarist/pluralist classification discussed above is useful in evaluating the approach of individual managers to industrial relations, it is of limited benefit in considering different organisational approaches or styles in industrial relations (Purcell and Sisson 1983). Recognising this, Fox (1974) developed a typology of industrial relations styles that was subsequently modified by Purcell and Sisson (1983) to provide a fivefold categorisation of 'ideal-typical' management styles in industrial relations. This typology, outlined in Table 15.4, is based on variations in management approaches to trade unions, collective bargaining, consultation and communications.

This categorisation of management styles in industrial relations provides a useful conceptual map. However, it is necessary to examine actual evidence on variations in management styles in industrial relations to evaluate the extent to which such categorisations provide a valid reflection of reality. To this end, Deaton (1985) attempted the first major empirical study of management styles using evidence from the UK Workplace Industrial Relations Survey. Using data from some 1,400 organisations, Deaton (1985) sought to empirically evaluate the appropriateness of Purcell and Sisson's typology. He first attempted to classify management styles in unionised companies as either 'sophisticated' or 'standard moderns'. However, Deaton (1985) found it difficult to distinguish between these two types of management styles, suggesting that it is rather tenuous to classify firms recognising trade unions into either of these groupings. Deaton

---

Table 15.4
Management Styles in Industrial Relations

Management Style	Characteristics
Traditionalist	'Orthodox unitarism': oppose role for unions, little attention to employee needs.
Sophisticated paternalist	Emphasise employee needs (training, pay, conditions, etc.), discourage unionisation, demand employee loyalty and commitment.
Sophisticated modern (two variations)	Accept trade unions' role in specific areas, emphasise role of IR procedures and consultative mechanisms. Variations: (a) *Consitutionalists:* Emphasise codification of management-union relations through detailed collective agreements. (b) *Consulters:* Collective bargaining established but management emphasises personal direct contact and problem solving, playing down formal union role at workplace level.
Standard modern	Pragmatic approach, union's role accepted but no overall philosophy or strategy developed, 'fire-fighting' approach.

Source: Adapted from Purcell and Sisson (1983)

(1985) also attempted to categorise management styles in non-union companies into 'paternalist', 'anti-union' and 'sophisticated paternalists'. He found that 'sophisticated paternalists' and 'anti-union' organisations emerged as polar opposites, while 'paternalist' organisations took the middle ground (having some characteristics common to both 'anti-union' and 'sophisticated paternalist' organisations).

Deaton (1985) concluded that attempts to classify firms into a small number of ideal styles were problematic. He argued that while the distinction between organisations that recognise trade unions and those which do not is crucial, it may not be possible to subdivide styles further in organisations where unions are recognised (Deaton 1985). However, Deaton felt that there was a greater tendency in organisations that do not recognise trade unions to adopt the 'identikit' styles suggested by Purcell and Sisson (1983).

Poole (1986) suggests that the evidence points to the existence of 'a progressively rich array' of hybrid styles rather than any convergence towards particular predominant styles or patterns. Other research studies have also identified the development of particular management styles in industrial relations. For example, we find a number of studies that point to the significance of styles designed to develop and sustain employee commitment (Walton 1985; Edwards 1987), while others have identified the development of neo-pluralist styles (Batstone 1984) and 'sophisticated' non-union styles (Foulkes 1980).

Individualism and Collectivism as Dimensions of Management Styles in Industrial Relations

More recent analyses of management styles in industrial relations have tended to focus on key dimensions of management styles rather than 'ideal-typical' style categorisations. Purcell (1987) has advanced two widely accepted dimensions of management styles in industrial relations: *collectivism* and *individualism.*

Collectivism in industrial relations incorporates the extent to which management acknowledges employees' right to collective representation and the involvement of that collective in influencing management decision making (Purcell 1987; Sisson 1987; Storey and Sisson 1994). This dimension addresses both the level of democratic employee representative structures and the extent to which management legitimises their representational and bargaining role. Thus conceived, the collectivism dimension spans a continuum from a first level of *low collectivism,* characterised by a unitarist perspective incorporating outright management opposition to employee representation. At the *second (middle) level* the managerial approach is based on adversarial IR, characterised by limited and reluctant engagement in collective bargaining, an emphasis on retaining control and the institutionalisation of conflict. The third level, *high collectivism,* is characterised by a co-operative managerial perspective involving positive engagement with employee representatives across a broad range of issues, both operational and strategic (Purcell 1987; Marchington and Parker 1990) (see Figure 15.2).

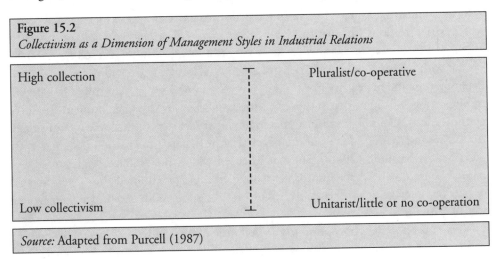

Figure 15.2
Collectivism as a Dimension of Management Styles in Industrial Relations

High collection   Pluralist/co-operative

Low collectivism   Unitarist/little or no co-operation

Source: Adapted from Purcell (1987)

Individualism, as a dimension of management styles in industrial relations, is described by Purcell (1987: 536) as 'the extent to which the firm gives credence to the feelings and sentiments of each employee and seeks to develop and encourage each employee's capacity and role at work ... Firms which have individualistically centred policies are thus expected to emphasise employees as a resource and be concerned with developing each person's talents and worth'.

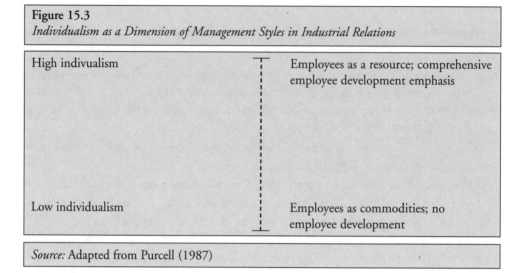

Figure 15.3
Individualism as a Dimension of Management Styles in Industrial Relations

High indivualism — Employees as a resource; comprehensive employee development emphasis

Low individualism — Employees as commodities; no employee development

Source: Adapted from Purcell (1987)

The literature identifies an increased management emphasis on the development of an individualist orientation in industrial relations as an important development over the past two decades (Beaumont 1985, 1991; Beaumont and Townley 1985; Gunnigle *et al.* 1997b; Kochan *et al.* 1986; Guest 1989b, 1992; Bacon and Storey 1993). However, beyond Purcell's (1987) and Bacon and Storey's (1993) attempts to explore the discrete components of individualism, it remains a vague concept.

Purcell identified three levels of individualism as a dimension of management styles in industrial relations (see Figure 15.4). At the first level of *low individualism,* workers are viewed in utilitarian terms: they are a factor of production to be used functionally in line with the firm's operational requirements. Within the overriding goal of profit maximisation, the management emphasis is on tight management control of labour and minimisation of labour costs, with little concern for broader human resource considerations such as job satisfaction, employment security or employee commitment. At the second, *middle level,* the managerial approach is paternalist in nature, aptly described by Salamon (2000: 236) as a situation where 'the employee is regarded as a natural subordinate deferential role whose freedom is limited by "well meant" regulation; management accept a degree of "social responsibility" to provide benevolent welfare care for *its* employees'.

The most popular conception in the literature of high individualism incorporates a strong human capital perspective, whereby workers are seen as a critical resource (Beer *et al.* 1984; Walton 1985). It is argued that managements pursuing this style will seek to develop this 'critical resource' by employing comprehensive training and development policies together with other 'individualist' policies in areas such as job design and reward systems (Kochan *et al.* 1986; Purcell 1987; Beaumont 1992, 1993). Other expected characteristics of high individualism include the use of performance-related pay systems linked to formal employee appraisals and an emphasis on extensive direct management-employee communications and involvement initiatives (Roche and Turner 1994).

Some Irish Evidence

In an Irish study of greenfield companies operating in the manufacturing and internationally traded services sectors, Gunnigle (1995b) attempts to evaluate management approaches to industrial relations on the dimensions of collectivism and individualism (see also Gunnigle *et al.* 1997b; Gunnigle *et al.* 2002b). To this end, a number of indicators were developed to evaluate the relative management emphasis on individualism and collectivism in industrial relations. These indicators were further combined to produce overall composite measures of individualism and collectivism in industrial relations (see Table 15.5).

While the findings only applied to recently established firms, they provide some interesting insights on management styles in industrial relations in Ireland. We have already noted that high levels of collectivism, and specifically trade union recognition, membership and influence, are integral to the traditional pluralist model considered characteristic of industrial relations in Ireland (Roche 1994a; Brewster and Hegewisch 1994; Roche and Turner 1994; Hillery 1994). Thus, findings on the levels of collectivism, particularly trade union recognition, are seen as critical indicators of change in management styles in industrial relations (Beaumont 1985, 1992). An important issue in evaluating the relative emphasis on collectivism and individualism is the extent to which greenfield organisations adopt what have been termed 'dualist' styles in industrial relations, namely the utilisation of a range of individualist HRM policies within a collectivist industrial relations context (see Storey 1992).

In attempting to interpret and explain the interplay of collectivism and individualism in Irish greenfield sites, Gunnigle *et al.* (1997b) developed two broad hypotheses. First, they drew on the 'non-union' literature to hypothesise that *high individualism will counterpoise low collectivism* (Foulkes 1980; Kochan *et al.* 1986; Beaumont 1991; Beaumont and Harris 1994; McLoughlin and Gourlay 1992). In this model, which was termed the '*countervailing hypothesis*', it is expected that greenfield firms characterised by low collectivism will adopt highly individualist industrial relations styles that seek to mitigate the need for collective employee representation (Beaumont 1985; Beaumont and Harris 1994; McLoughlin and Gourlay 1992; Guest and Hoque 1994).

A second and contrasting hypothesis, termed the '*dualist hypothesis*', stated that *high individualism will complement high collectivism*. This implies that greenfield firms will concurrently adopt high levels of collectivism and individualism and employ 'dualist' industrial relations styles (see Purcell 1987; Storey 1992). In the Irish context, it might plausibly be suggested that the dualist approach is the most likely pattern for industrial relations given the strong legitimacy of trade unions and collective bargaining (Gunnigle *et al.* 1994; Roche and Turner 1994).

Table 15.5
Indicators of Collectivism and Individualism

Measures of Individualism
1. **Sophistication of the employment and socialisation system:** Measured through an evaluation of the degree of sophistication and relative emphasis on individualism in the management of human resource 'flows'.
2. **Direct communications:** Based on an analysis of the level, nature and sophistication of management-employee communications.
3. **Performance-related pay:** Measured through an analysis of the incidence of performance-related pay systems and the utilisation of formal performance appraisals to aid performance-related pay decisions among non-managerial/white collar grades.
4. **Employee involvement:** Measured through an analysis of the extent to which management utilises explicit techniques to facilitate employee involvement in decision making.
5. **Employee autonomy:** Measured through an analysis of the extent to which management seeks to facilitate/promote employee autonomy.

Measures of Collectivism
1. **Trade union presence:** Measured through an analysis of levels of trade union recognition and trade union density.
2. **Pattern of trade union organisation:** Measured through an examination of the nature of trade union recognition and impact of trade unions on workplace industrial relations.
3. **Role of trade unions and other employee representative bodies:** Measured though an examination of role of trade unions and other employee representative bodies in management-employee communications/interactions.
4. **Employer association membership and utilisation:** Measured through an examination of the extent to which greenfield companies are in membership of employer associations and of the patterns of utilisation of employer association services.

Source: Gunnigle (1995b); Gunnigle *et al.* (1997b)

The findings on the indicative measures of collectivism and individualism are outlined in Table 15.6, which suggest that we should accept the 'countervailing hypothesis'. On almost all of the measures there is a negative relationship between individualism and collectivism. This negative relationship is most pronounced in the area of performance-related pay (PRP) (see Gunnigle *et al.* 1998). It is clear that PRP systems are most likely to be employed where there are low levels of union recognition and membership and where there is little or no role for collective employee representation.

As outlined earlier, 'dualist' industrial relations styles are characterised by high levels of collectivism and individualism. The data from greenfield sites provides little evidence of a positive relationship between collectivism and individualism. Thus, it appears that dualist industrial relations styles are not common in Irish greenfield companies.

Table 15.6
Measuring Collectivism and Individualism in Greenfield Sites

| | | Individualism | | | | | |
		Employee Autonomy	Direct Communications	Employment System	Employee Involvement	Performance-Related Pay	Individualism (composite measure)
Collectivism	Trade Union Presence	ns	–	–	ns	–	–
	Trade Union Organisation	ns	ns	ns	ns	–	–
	Collective Communications	ns	–	–	ns	–	–
	Employer Organisation	ns	ns	ns	–ns	–	–
	Collectivism (composite measure)	ns	–	ns	ns	–	–

ns = no significant relationship; – = significant and negative relationship

Source: Adapted from Gunnigle *et al.* (1997b)

This study also sought to establish the main explanatory factors impacting upon variations in management styles in industrial relations in the firms studied. This analysis found that company ownership, specifically US ownership, was the most significant explanatory variable. On the collectivism dimension, company ownership exerted the greatest impact. Levels of collectivism were positively associated with European ownership and negatively associated with US ownership. This was particularly the case in relation to trade union presence. Non-union companies were predominantly US owned, while all of the European companies recognised trade unions. On the individualism dimension, US ownership emerged as the most significant factor positively correlating with levels of individualism. The critical impact of ownership is illustrated in Table 15.7, which presents the mean and standard deviation scores on the dimensions of collectivism and individualism disaggregated by ownership and clearly illustrates the considerable contrast between US and other companies on the dimensions of collectivism and individualism. US companies score highest on the individualism measures and lowest on collectivism measures. Conversely, European-owned companies score highest on measures of collectivism and lowest on individualism.

As noted earlier, this study found that most significant indicators of high levels of individualism were performance-based pay systems tied to individual employee appraisals and greater direct communications with employees. An increased management focus on more extensive and direct communications with individual employees was an important feature of industrial relations management in many of the greenfield companies studied. In particular, many companies placed an especially strong emphasis on communicating information on company performance to employees. In many of these companies, such information was used to emphasise issues such as market volatility, intensity of competition and requirements for high-quality and low-cost production/service.

Table 15.7
Company Ownership, Collectivism and Individualism

Nationality	Collectivism (1–3)*		Individualism (1–3)*	
	Mean	Standard Deviation	Mean	Standard Deviation
US	1.30	0.87	2.30	0.54
Asian	1.86	0.90	1.86	0.38
Irish	2.09	0.67	1.46	0.69
European	2.88	0.35	1.25	0.46
* Legend: 1 = low; 2 = medium; 3 = high for collectivism and individualism.				

The other critical indicator of individualism identified in the greenfield study was the extent of utilisation of PRP systems based on formal appraisals of individual employee performance (Gunnigle 1995a, 1995b; Gunnigle *et al.* 1998). This research data points to significant differences between new and longer-established ('brownfield') companies in the extent of utilisation of PRP systems based on formal appraisals among non-managerial/white collar grades. The role of appraisal in aiding PRP decisions among non-managerial/white collar grades is a crucial differentiating factor, since the use of more traditional PRP systems among these grades is nothing new. However, traditional PRP systems, e.g. measured day work, were based on quantitative evaluations of employee performance and were normally the subject of collective bargaining. As such, quantitative PRP systems were integral to the collectivist tradition of Irish industrial relations. In contrast, performance appraisal is essentially an individualist management tool (Beer *et al.* 1984). By linking performance appraisals to incremental pay decisions, management in greenfield sites are posing a challenge to collectivism in industrial relations. Thus, individualism replaces collectivism at two critical phases:

• first, the process of appraisal is individualist rather than collectivist (individual appraisal rather than collective bargaining); and
• the outcome takes the form of varying PRP decisions among individual employees rather than a fixed amount that applies equally to all employees.

Another indicator of increased individualism identified in the literature is the adoption of sophisticated and highly individualist employment systems to effectively manage 'human resource flows', particularly in the areas of selection and employee development (Foulkes 1980; Beer *et al.* 1984). Another important indicator of high individualism is the incidence of extensive mechanisms to facilitate employee autonomy and involvement (Lawler 1978, 1982; Beer *et al.* 1984). It is noteworthy that Gunnigle's study did not find widespread evidence of sophisticated employment systems or mechanisms to facilitate employee involvement or autonomy in the majority of greenfield companies studied (Gunnigle 1995a, 1995b).

In considering these results it can be argued that while individualism appeared to be an important and significant aspect of management styles in industrial relations in greenfield companies, this did not necessarily imply that managements adopted a 'resource perspective' of employees (see Purcell 1987). This Irish study found little evidence of a shift from a utility perspective to a resource perspective in greenfield companies. The aggregate evidence suggests that while there is a greater emphasis on individualism in greenfield companies than has traditionally been the case with longer-established companies, this does not equate to high levels of individualism. Rather, it appears that managements in greenfield sites are adopting more individualist approaches in selected aspects of industrial relations but are not moving towards a wholly individualist approach equating to the 'soft' HRM model.

STRATEGIC INTEGRATION AS A DIMENSION OF MANAGEMENT STYLES IN INDUSTRIAL RELATIONS

Earlier in this text we considered the extent to which industrial relations and HR issues are a concern for strategic decision makers in organisations. In this section we develop this theme by examining the concept of strategic integration in industrial relations. Strategic integration as a dimension of management approaches to industrial relations refers to the extent to which industrial relations considerations impact on strategic decision making. Thus, 'high' strategic integration is characterised by the integration of industrial relations considerations into the business plan to facilitate the establishment and maintenance of competitive advantage. Such policies need not necessarily be employee centred, but may be either 'hard' or 'soft' depending on the chosen route to competitive advantage. In contrast, the traditional 'pluralist-adversarial' approach is seen as largely reactive in nature. Consequently, industrial relations considerations are not a concern of strategic decision makers, but rather an operational issue only given priority when problems arise.

We also noted earlier that a traditional perception of strategic decision making is that it concerns 'primary' business issues (such as finance) and any attention devoted to industrial relations issues is secondary and somewhat incidental. On the other hand, it is evident that some organisations incorporate human resource issues in the strategic process and take well thought-out strategic decisions. In practice, the idea of strategic integration as either total or absent does not adequately reflect the complexities of HR and industrial relations policy choice in organisations.

A more useful analysis is provided by Wood and Peccei (1990), who differentiate between *strategic human resource management*, where human resource issues are fully integrated into the strategic planning process, and *business-led human resource management*, where human resource policies are linked to the organisation's commercial imperatives. Differences between these two approaches lie in the level of strategic consideration of HR and industrial relations issues. In relation to strategic HRM, HR and industrial relations issues are integral to strategic planning and form part of the organisation's long-term business strategy. In business-led HRM, HR/industrial relations policies and practices are a lower-order strategic activity but are linked to higher-order strategic decisions in areas such as product development or market penetration. This model differs significantly from the traditional industrial relations model, where human resource considerations are not a significant top management concern, but rather a peripheral operational responsibility. Consequently, they are not strategic in nature but are ad hoc, piecemeal responses to immediate issues. These alternative approaches are represented in Figure 15.4.

Figure 15.4
Strategic Integration as a Dimension of Management Styles in Industrial Relations

High strategic integration	Strategic HRM	Industrial relations and HR issues form an integral component of the organisation's long-term strategy and mission.
	Business-led HRM	Industrial relations and HR issues are dependent upon but linked to higher-order decisions on corporate mission and objectives.
Low strategic integration	'Traditional' industrial relations/ personnel management	Industrial relations and HR issues are a peripheral management concern and handled in an essentially reactive fashion.

Factors encouraging greater strategic integration in industrial relations include:

- increased competition and greater emphasis on achieving competitive advantage;
- organisation restructuring to devolve more responsibility to strategic business units;
- increasing importance of culture and mission in focusing management effort and guiding decisions on resource allocation; and
- quality rather than price as a dominant route to competitive advantage (see Carroll 1985; Kelly and Brannick 1988b; Toner 1987; Storey and Sisson 1990).

However, there is considerable debate on the nature of these developments, as there is a wide range of factors mitigating against greater strategic integration, including the traditionally low level of consideration of HR issues in strategic decision making, the embededdness of pluralist industrial relations traditions and the probable future growth in organisation size and diversity.

Some Irish Evidence

Strategic decision making is a notoriously difficult area for researchers to analyse. Researchers often develop proxy indicators of strategic integration, which is a useful approach but requires the identification of an adequate range of robust indicators. In the Irish context, Gunnigle and Morley (1998) evaluated the nature and extent of strategic integration as a dimension of management styles in industrial relations in greenfield firms. They developed a number of variables regarded as indicative of strategic integration in industrial relations, as follows.

- **Impact on location:** Assesses the impact of industrial relations considerations on location decisions of greenfield site facilities.
- **Formal strategy development:** Addresses the capacity to engage in business strategy and whether such capacity follows through into a capacity to formulate HR and industrial relations strategy.
- **Role of HR/industrial relations function:** Assesses the incidence and role of a specialist HR and industrial relations function.
- **Impact on business policy:** Measures the impact of HR and industrial relations considerations on business policy decisions at establishment level.

The research findings on strategic integration in Irish greenfield sites provide a broad guide rather than a precise measure of the extent and direction of strategic integration as a dimension of management styles in industrial relations. Using these measures, Gunnigle *et al.* (1998) first attempted to assess the extent of strategic integration of industrial relations. They then examined the relationship between strategic integration and the other two key dimensions of management styles in industrial relations discussed above, collectivism and individualism. The study findings on the overall levels of strategic integration in Irish greenfield sites are outlined in Table 15.8.

Table 15.8
Strategic Integration in Greenfield Sites

Variable	Mean (Range 1–3*)	Standard Deviation
Location	0.87	0.59
Formal strategy development	2.08	0.76
Impact of IR on business policy decisions	1.74	0.65
Role of P/HR/IR function	2.23	0.87
Composite measure of strategic integration based on combination of the four variables above	1.91	0.69

*Legend: 1 = low; 2 = medium; 3 = high

These findings indicate that the overall extent of strategic integration is just below the mid-point (2) of the range at 1.91. This finding does not give support to the existence of a high level of strategic integration. However, there is considerable variation in the four constituent measures which make up the overall composite measure (see Table 15.8). The relationships between the study findings on strategic integration and levels of individualism and collectivism are outlined in Tables 15.9 and 15.10.

Table 15.9
Individualism and Strategic Integration in Industrial Relations

INDIVIDUALISM

		Employee autonomy	Direct communications	Employment system	Employee involvement	Performance-related pay	INDIVIDUALISM
STRATEGIC INTEGRATION	Location	ns	ns	+	+	ns	+
	Formal strategy development	ns	+	+	+	ns	+
	Impact on business policy	+	+	+	+	ns	+
	Role of IR function	ns	+	+	+	ns	+
	STRATEGIC INTEGRATION	+	+	+	+	+	+

Legend: ns = no significant relationship; + = significant and positive relationship.

Source: Adapted from Gunnigle *et al.* (1998)

Table 15.10
Collectivism and Strategic Integration in Industrial Relations

COLLECTIVISM

		Trade union presence	Trade union organisation	Collective communications	Employer organisation	COLLECTIVISM
STRATEGIC INTEGRATION	Location	−	ns	−	ns	ns
	Formal strategy development	−	−	−	ns	−
	Impact on business policy	ns	ns	−	ns	ns
	Role of IR function	−	ns	ns	ns	ns
	STRATEGIC INTEGRATION	ns	−	ns	−	−

Legend: ns = no significant relationship; − = significant and negative relationship.

Source: Adapted from Gunnigle *et al.* (1998)

These findings suggest that there is a positive relationship between individualist management styles in industrial relations and levels of strategic integration. They also indicate that management styles that are characterised by a strong strategic focus are also most likely to adopt a discernible individualist orientation. This finding is also interesting insofar as it indicates that if, as much of the literature suggests, there is a trend towards an increasing strategic focus in industrial relations, this may lead to increasingly individualist management styles in industrial relations and a concomitant diminution in collectivism.

Turning to the relationship between collectivism and levels of strategic integration, the findings in Table 15.10 suggest that where companies integrate industrial relations considerations into strategic decision making, this is most likely to lead to low levels of collectivism and in particular low levels of trade union recognition and density. These results indicate an extremely weak or negative relationship between levels of strategic integration and collectivism. Overall, it appears that the greater the strategic consideration afforded to industrial relations issues, the greater the likelihood that this will be associated with individualist industrial relations styles that exclude trade union recognition.

In relation to explanatory factors, the research findings indicate that country of origin, specifically US ownership, is the most significant variable positively impacting on levels of strategic integration. Strategic integration was also positively associated with size and location in advanced industrial sectors. The only factor that impacted negatively on levels of strategic integration was market location in predominantly indigenous/local markets.

Management Styles in Industrial Relations in Ireland: An Overview

Ever since Fox (1966) first articulated his unitarist and pluralist frames of reference, numerous attempts have been made to develop 'ideal-typical' categorisations of management styles in industrial relations. Yet it is important to note the limitations associated with such categorisations, as previous studies have identified problems in placing firms within ideal-typical management style categorisations (Deaton 1985; Salamon 1998). Ideal-typical style categorisations are inherently limiting and may not reflect organisational reality. There may be an absence of a clear and preferred management style in some companies or, indeed, companies may be in transition between styles. However, given these caveats, such style categorisations are useful in indicating dominant management orientations and therefore represent a useful analytical tool for evaluating management approaches to industrial relations and explaining variations in approaches. Style categorisations are also useful in distinguishing between companies that consciously pursue coherent industrial relations styles and those that do not.

Based on our review of typologies of management styles in industrial relations and the key dimensions of such styles, we now proffer a broad categorisation of management styles in industrial relations which draws on the available research evidence and which is considered appropriate in the Irish context. This categorisation of management styles in industrial relations in Ireland is outlined in Table 15.11 and is a variant of that developed by Purcell and Sisson (1983) and Fox (1966, 1974). This typology identifies six major management styles, with differences deriving from varying positions on the benchmark dimensions of strategic integration, individualism and collectivism and gauged through HR policy manifestations in relation to work systems, communications, reward systems, employment patterns and role of the specialist HR function.

Table 15.11
Proposed Typology of Management Styles in Industrial Relations

Anti-union Style
Organisations in this category are characterised by a commodity view of labour. In relation to the dimensions of management styles in industrial relations, such firms are distinguished by low strategic integration, low collectivism and individualism. Manifestations of this approach include a preoccupation with retaining managerial prerogative; rejection of any role for trade unions or other modes of collective representation; little or no attention to HR/industrial relations except where absolutely necessary; absence of or at best, a low-level HR function; absence of procedures for communicating or consulting with employees; and authoritarian management control, poor rewards and low levels of job security. The available research evidence suggests that 'anti-union' styles are predominantly confined to indigenous companies established and managed in the classic 'small firm/entrepreneurial' mode but may also be found in some foreign-owned firms, particularly US-owned.

Paternalist Style
In this style top management prioritises a need to 'look after' employees. The characteristics of this approach are a benevolent, welfare-oriented approach to employees. However, as in the 'anti-union' style, the management view is essentially unitarist. Little attention is paid to employee representation, involvement or development. Divergent opinions from those of management are seen as indicative of disloyalty and potentially damaging to the fabric of employer-industrial relations. Indeed, the paternalist style may incorporate a high level of management complacency about the perceived closeness of management and employee interests. In relation to the benchmark dimensions of management style, the paternalist style is characterised by little strategic integration, medium individualism, i.e. caring approach to employees but few mechanisms to enhance employee involvement or commitment, and low collectivism. HR policy manifestations include a caring supervisory style, but also a work system that limits employee involvement and discretion, limited communications mechanisms, an external labour market and extrinsic rewards emphasis and a HR function whose role is of an administrative support nature.

Traditional IR Style
The 'traditional IR' style equates to the traditional pluralist perspective characterised by adversarial industrial relations, primary reliance on collective bargaining and employer association membership and utilisation. It is characterised by low strategic integration, low/medium individualism and medium to high collectivism (of an adversarial nature). This style has many of the characteristics of Purcell and Sisson's 'sophisticated modern-constitutionalist' style, particularly in the conception of industrial relations in terms of 'conflictual terms and conditions of employment' and the codification and limiting of collective bargaining arrangements (Purcell and Sisson, 1983; Salamon, 1998). The main manifestations are trade union recognition (often incorporating multi-unionism) and reliance on collective bargaining. Management-union relations may sometimes be formalised in a procedural agreement regulating relations between the parties and encompassing issues such as union recognition (including closed shop), disciplinary, grievance and disputes procedures. However, other organisations' arrangements may not be formalised in a comprehensive written agreement but may largely be a product of custom and practice. Other manifestations include a bureaucratic organisation structure, tightly defined jobs, limited and top-down communications, a utlisation of both external and internal labour markets, extrinsic rewards

Table 15.11 (continued)
Proposed Typology of Management Styles in Industrial Relations

and a 'systems reactive'-type HR function whose primary role is to handle industrial relations (see Tyson and Fell, 1986). Information sharing and consultation are not common in these companies. In Ireland, it appears that this style is most common among longer-established and larger indigenous organisations. This style is seen as particularly characteristic of organisations in the state and semi-state sector.

'Soft' HRM Style

The 'soft' HRM style is characterised by a resource perspective of employees and a desire to create an organisational climate where individual employee needs are satisfied through a combination of positive employee-oriented policies designed (in part) to render collective representation unnecessary. This style equates to what has been termed 'union substitution' (see Chapter 14), is grounded in the unitarist perspective and is normally associated with a pronounced preference for non-union status. Manifestations of this style include competitive pay and employment conditions, extensive management–employee communications, mechanisms to facilitate direct employee involvement in work-related decisions and procedures to handle grievance and disciplinary issues. Other manifestations include an internal labour market emphasis, availability of intrinsic and extrinsic rewards (at least partially based on merit) and a highly developed and influential HR function. The hallmarks of this management style are high individualism (resource perspective of employees), high strategic integration and low to medium collectivism; however, the latter is achieved through non-union fora such as consultative committees, quality circles, etc. In the greenfield site study discussed earlier, it was found that seven of the fifty-three companies studied adopted all the hallmarks of 'soft HRM' (see Gunnigle, 1995a, 1995b; Gunnigle *et al.* 1997b). All but one of these companies were US owned and all were manufacturing companies operating from strong market positions. This seems to reflect a common consensus that soft HRM approaches are most common in US-owned firms operating in high-technology sectors.

'Hard' HRM Style

In the 'hard' HRM style the management of the company's human resources (incorporating not only employees but also subcontracted labour) is largely focused on transaction costs (see also Storey 1989; Blyton and Turnbull 1992). Thus, the management objective is to source and manage labour in as cheap and cost effective a fashion as possible to ensure achievement of the organisation's 'bottom-line' objectives. This style equates to what has been termed 'union suppression', incorporating low employment standards, and contrasts with 'union substitution', or high-standard non-union companies ('soft' HRM). The greenfield site study found that this style was particularly common among US-owned information/data processing services and electronics assembly companies operating in a subcontracting mode to major manufacturers. On the benchmark dimensions, this style is characterised by high strategic integration, low/medium collectivism and low individualism. Manifestations of this style are most obvious in the adoption of 'atypical' employment forms, particularly subcontracting and temporary/part-time employees to improve cost effectiveness while meeting required performance standards and in the use of performance management techniques designed to achieve maximum return on the organisation's investment in human resources.

Table 15.11 (continued)
Proposed Typology of Management Styles in Industrial Relations

Dualist Style

The 'dualist' style is characterised by an acceptance of the legitimacy of collective employee representation but supplemented by a strong individualist emphasis. Companies adopting this style are seen to differ from the 'soft' HRM firms on the collectivism dimension but otherwise pursue broadly similar policies. Union recognition would generally be formalised in a procedural agreement specifying management and union rights and collective bargaining arrangements. At shop-floor level, management will seek to keep formality to a minimum. The management focus is placed on minimising the extent of collective bargaining, especially that of an adversarial/distributive nature, and on emphasising more integrative/co-operative bargaining and direct dealings with employees. This style might be termed 'neo-pluralism', involving the use of selected HRM techniques such as sophisticated selection, extensive direct communications with employees and performance-related pay systems alongside established collective bargaining procedures. In the greenfield study the 'dualist' style was extremely rare and in its 'pure form' (high levels of collectivism, individualism and strategic integration) was confined to only one of the fifty-three companies studied. Manifestations include an organic organisation structure, broadly defined jobs, extensive communications fora, internal labour market emphasis, extrinsic and intrinsic rewards and a well-developed and influential HR function. Further characteristics may include careful selection and extensive employee development, employees encouraged to deal directly with management on issues of concern and line management trained in industrial relations and backed up by a well-developed HR department that on the one hand co-ordinates collective bargaining with the trade unions and on the other oversees various 'employee-oriented' HR policies.

The above typology is considered indicative of the predominant styles that might be adopted by Irish organisations. There will obviously be an overlap in management styles where companies adopt practices/polices that are common to two or more style categories. Given our earlier caveats on the limitations of 'ideal-typical' style categorisations and reflecting on the Irish situation, the most striking feature of this typology relates to the 'soft' HRM, 'hard' HRM and 'dualist' styles. These styles are significant because they indicate a planned and co-ordinated approach to industrial relations management, in contrast to the other styles, which are indicative of a more 'incidentalist' approach. The 'traditional IR' style equates to the pluralist-adversarial model and has been the most pervasive style in the majority of medium and large organisations in Ireland (Roche 1990; Hillery 1994). On the other hand, the 'anti-union' and 'paternalist' styles reflect opposition to the pluralist model as manifested through forthright attempts to curb or eliminate collective employee representation. It has traditionally been argued that these styles were confined to smaller organisations and that in the event of growth they would over time succumb to the 'traditional pluralist' model (Gunnigle 1989; Roche 1990). However, the available evidence indicates considerable change in enterprise-level industrial relations in Ireland. In terms of management styles, such developments are characterised by the increased adoption of HRM-based styles ('hard' or 'soft' variants). They suggest a strengthening of the unitarist ideology among management and greater opposition to union recognition, at least in some sectors, the emergence of a strong non-union sector and a fall in union density. Unlike the 'dualist' style (which is essentially a variant of traditional pluralism), both the 'hard' and 'soft' HRM styles contrast significantly with the traditional pluralist model and are essentially unitarist in character.

Bibliography

Ackers, P. and Black, J. (1992), 'Watching the detectives: shop stewards' expectations of their managers in the age of human resource management', in A. Sturdy, D. Knights and H. Willmott (eds), *Skill and Consent: Contemporary Studies in the Labour Process*, London: Routledge.

Adams, R.J. (30 April 1998), 'What's at stake in the battle over Australia's ports', *The Globe and Mail*.

Allen, K. (1997), *Fianna Fáil and Irish Labour: 1926 to the Present*, London: Pluto Press.

Allen, K. (2000), *The Celtic Tiger: The Myth of Social Partnership in Ireland*, Manchester: Manchester University Press.

Allen, V. (1971), *The Sociology of Industrial Relations*, London: Longman.

Anthony, P.D. (1980), *The Conduct of Industrial Relations*, London: Institute of Personnel Management.

Armstrong, M. and Murliss, H. (1994), *Reward Management: A Handbook of Remuneration Strategy and Practice*, London: Kogan Page in association with the Institute of Personnel Management.

Arrighi, G. (1990), 'Marxist century, American century: the making and the remaking of the world's labour movement', *New Left Review*, CLXXIX, 29–66.

Atkinson, A.J. (1984), *Flexible Manning: The Way Ahead*, London: Institute of Manpower Studies.

Atkinson, G. (1977), *The Effective Negotiator*, London: Quest Research Publications.

Baccaro, L. (2002), 'What is dead and what is alive in the theory of corporatism', International Institute for Labour Studies, Geneva: ILO (www.ilo.org/public/english/bureau/inst/download/dp14302.pdf)

Bacon, N. and Storey, J. (1993), 'Individualization of the employment relationship and the implications for trade unions', *Employee Relations*, XV/1, 5–17.

Baglioni, G. (2003), 'Employee involvement in the European Company Directive', *Transfer*, IX/2, 341–8.

Bain, G.S. (1970), *The Growth of White Collar Unionism*, Oxford: Clarendon Press.

Bain, G.S. and Elsheikh, F. (1980), *Union Growth and the Business Cycle*, Oxford: Basil Blackwell.

Bain, G.S. and Elsheikh, F. (1980), 'Unionisation in Britain: an inter-establishment analysis based on survey data', *British Journal of Industrial Relations*, XVIII/2, 169–78.

Bain, G.S. and Price, R. (1983), 'Union growth: dimensions, determinants and destiny', in G.S. Bain (ed.), *Industrial Relations in Britain*, Oxford: Basil Blackwell.

Barret, S. (1993), 'Don't try another PESP', *Sunday Independent*, 9 May.

Barrett, A., Callan, T. and Nolan, B. (1999), 'Rising wage inequality, returns to education and labour market institutions: evidence from Ireland', *British Journal of Industrial Relations*, XXXVII/1, 77–100.

Barrington, D. (1982), *Report of the Commission of Inquiry on Safety, Health and Welfare at Work*, Dublin: The Stationery Office.

Barry, B. (2002), 'The role of benchmarking in public service pay determination in Ireland with particular reference to the Programme for Prosperity and Fairness: The trade union perspective', unpublished MBS thesis, University of Limerick.

Barry, F. (2002), 'FDI and the Host Economy: A Case Study of Ireland', unpublished paper presented at National University of Ireland, Galway, 8 November.

Barry, F., Bradley, J. and O'Malley, E. (1999), 'Indigenous and foreign industry: characteristics and performance', in F. Barry (ed.), *Understanding Ireland's Economic Growth*, London: Macmillan.

Batstone, E. (1984), *Working Order*, Oxford: Blackwell.

Beaumont, P.B. (1985), 'New plant work practices', *Personnel Review*, XIV/5, 15–19.

Beaumont, P.B. (1990), *Change in Industrial Relations: The Organisation and the Environment*, London: Routledge.

Beaumont, P.B. (1991), 'Trade unions and HRM', *Industrial Relations Journal*, XXII/4, 300–8.

Beaumont, P.B. (1992), 'The US human resource management literature: a review', in G. Salamon (ed.), *Human Resource Strategies*, London: Sage/Open University.

Beaumont, P.B. (1993), *Human Resource Management: Key Concepts and Skills*, London: Sage.

Beaumont, P.B. (1995a), *The Future of Employment Relations*, London: Sage.

Beaumont, P.B. (1995b), 'The European Union and developments in industrial relations', in P. Gunnigle and W.K. Roche (eds), *New Challenges to Irish Industrial Relations*, Dublin: Oak Tree Press in association with the Labour Relations Commission.

Beaumont, P.B and Harris, R.I.D. (1991), 'Trade union recognition and employment contraction, 1980–1984', *British Journal of Industrial Relations*, XXIX/1.

Beaumont, P.B. and Harris, R.I.D. (1994), 'Opposition to unions in the non-union sector in Britain', *International Journal of Human Resource Management*, V/2, 457–71.

Beaumont, P.B. and Townley, B. (1985), 'Greenfield sites, new plants and work practices', in V. Hammond (ed.) *Current Research in Management*, London: Frances Pinter.

Beer, M., Spector, B., Lawrence, P.R., Quinn-Mills, D. and Walton, R.E. (1984), *Managing Human Assets: The Groundbreaking Harvard Business School Program*, New York: The Free Press/Macmillan.

Beer, M., Spector, B., Lawrence, P., Mills, D. and Walton, R. (1985), *Human Resource Management: A General Manager's Perspective*, New York: The Free Press.

Belman, D. (1992), 'Unions, the quality of labour relations and firm performance', in L. Mishel and P. Voos (eds), *Unions and Economic Competitiveness*, New York: Sharpe Economic Policy Institute.

Bendix, R. (1956), *Work and Authority in Industry*, New York: Wiley.

Bew, P., Hazelkorn, E. and Patterson, H. (1989), *The Dynamics of Irish Politics*, London: Lawrence and Wishart.

Beynon, H. (1973), *Working for Ford*, Harmondsworth: Penguin.

Biagi, M., Tiraboschi, M. and Rymkevitch, O. (2002), 'The "Europeanisation" of industrial relations: evaluating the quality of European industrial relations in a global context: a literature review', Dublin: The European Foundation for the Improvement of Living and Working Conditions (www.eurofound.ie/publications/files/EF0276EN.pdf).

Bispinck, R. and Schulten, T. (2000), 'Alliance for jobs – is Germany following the path of "competitive corporatism"?', in G. Fajertag and P. Pochet (eds), *Social Pacts in Europe – New Dynamics*, Brussels: European Trade Union Institute.

Blauner, R. (1964), *Alienation and Freedom*, Chicago: University of Chicago Press.

Blyton, P. and Morris, J. (1992), 'HRM and the limits of flexibility', in P. Blyton and P. Turnbull (eds), *Reassessing Human Resource Management*, London: Sage.

Blyton, P. and Turnbull, P. (1992), *Reassessing Human Resource Management*, London: Sage.

Blyton, P. and Turnbull, P. (1994), *The Dynamics of Employee Relations*, London: Macmillan.

Bonner, K. (1989), 'Industrial relations reform', in Department of Industrial Relations, UCD (eds), *Industrial Relations in Ireland: Contemporary Issues and Developments*, Dublin: University College Dublin.

Booth, A. (1986), 'Estimating the probability of trade union membership, a study of men and women in Britain', *Economica*, 53.

Bowey, A. (1974), *A Guide to Human Resource Planning*, London: Macmillan.

Boxhall, P. and Purcell, J. (2004), *Strategy and Human Resource Management*, Basingstoke, Hampshire: Palgrave Macmillan.

Boyd, A. (1972), *The Rise of the Irish Trade Unions, 1729–1970*, Tralee: Anvil.

Boyd, A. (1984), *Have Trade Unions Failed The North?*, Dublin: Mercier Press.

Boyle, J.W. (1988), *The Irish Labor Movement in the Nineteenth Century*, Washington, DC: The Catholic University of America Press.

Bramel, D. and Friend, R. (1981), 'Hawthorne, the myth of the docile worker, and class bias in psychology', *American Psychologist*, XXXVI/8, 867–78.

Brannick, T. and Kelly, A. (1982), 'The reliability and validity of Irish strike data and statistics', *Economic and Social Review*, XIV, 249–58.

Brannick, T. and Kelly, A. (1989), 'Voluntarism and order in trade unions: union officials' attitudes to unofficial strike action', in Department of Industrial Relations, UCD (eds), *Industrial Relations in Ireland: Contemporary Issues and Developments*, Dublin: University College Dublin.

Brannick, T., Doyle, L. and Kelly, A. (1997), 'Industrial conflict', in T.V. Murphy and W.K. Roche (eds), *Irish Industrial Relations in Practice*, Dublin: Oak Tree Press.

Braverman, H. (1974), *Labor and Monopoly Capital: The Degradation of Work in the Twentieth Century*, New York: Monthly Review Press.

Breen, R., Hannon, D., Rottman, D. and Whelan, C. (1990), *Understanding Contemporary Ireland*, Dublin: Gill & Macmillan.

Brewster, C. and Hegewisch, A. (1994), *Policy and Practice in European Human Resource Management: The Price Waterhouse Cranfield Survey*, London: Routledge.

British and Irish Legal Institute (www.bailii.org/ie/cases), downloaded on 21 January 2004.

Bristow, J. (1982), 'Wages and competitiveness', paper presented to the Institute of Personnel Management Conference, Galway.

Brown, G. (1977), *Sabotage*, Nottingham: Spokesman Books.

Brown, W. (ed.) (1981), *The Changing Contours of British Industrial Relations: A Survey of Manufacturing Industry*, Oxford: Blackwell.

Brown, W., Deakin, S. and Ryan, P. (1997), 'The effects of British industrial relations legislation 1979–1997', *National Institute Economic Review*, CLXI, 69–83.

Brown, W., Marginson, P. and Walsh, J. (2003), 'The management of pay as collective bargaining diminishes', in P. Edwards (ed.), *Industrial Relations: Theory and Practice*, 2nd ed., Oxford: Blackwell.

Browne, J. (1994), *The Juridification of the Employment Relationship*, Aldershot: Avebury.

Bullock, Lord (1977), *Report of the Committee of Inquiry on Industrial Democracy*, London: HMSO.

Business & Finance (1987), 'Dilemmas all round in tripartite talks', *Business & Finance*, 30 July, 9–10.

Business & Finance (1990), 'Leaders try to sell the new realism and tame the market', *Business & Finance*, 25 October.

Butler, N. (1997), 'Statutory employment protection', in T.V. Murphy and W.K. Roche (eds), *Industrial Relations in Practice; Revised and Expanded Edition*, Dublin: Oak Tree Press.

Butler, P. (1986), 'Employer associations: a study', unpublished BBS project, NIHE, Limerick.

Canning, L. (1979), 'Negotiating in industrial relations', unpublished paper, Dublin: Irish Management Institute.

Calmfors, L. and Driffill, J. (1988), 'Centralisation of wage policy', *Economic Policy*, VI (April), 13–61.

Carley, M. (7 January 2003), 'Industrial relations in the EU, Japan and USA, 2001', Industrial Relations Observatory Online (www.eiro.eurofound.ie).

Carroll, C. (1985), *Building Ireland's Business: Perspectives from PIMS*, Dublin: Irish Management Institute.

Carroll, C. and Byrne, R. (1992), 'EC requirements on safety and health at work: an update', *Industrial Relations News* (25 June).

Central Statistics Office (CSO) (2003a), *Quarterly National Household Survey*, Dublin: CSO August.

Central Statistics Office (CSO) (2003b), *Consumer Price Index*, Dublin: CSO November.

Central Statistics Office (CSO) (2004), *Quarterly National Household Survey*, Dublin: CSO June.

Chamberlain, N. and Kuhn, J. (1965), *Collective Bargaining*, New York: McGraw-Hill.

Chamberlain, N.W. (1948), *The Union Challenge to Management Control*, New York: Harper.

Cho, S.K. (1985), 'The labour process and capital mobility: the limits of the new international division of labour', *Politics and Society*, XIV, 185–222.

Clegg, H.A. (1975), 'Pluralism in industrial relations', *British Journal of Industrial Relations*, XIII/3, 309–16.

Clegg, H. (1976), *Trade Unionism under Collective Bargaining, A Theory Based on Comparisons of Six Countries*, Oxford: Blackwell.

Clegg, H. (1980), *The Changing System of Industrial Relations in Great Britain*, Oxford: Blackwell.

Clinch, P., Convery, F. and Walsh, B. (2002), *After the Celtic Tiger*, Dublin: O'Brien Press.

Coates, K. and Topham, A. (eds) (1968), *Industrial Democracy in Great Britain*, London: McKibbon and Kee.

Commission on Industrial Relations (1972), *Employers Organisations and Industrial Relations*, study no. 1, London: HMSO.

Commission of Inquiry on Industrial Relations (1981), *Report of the Commission of Inquiry on Industrial Relations*, Dublin: Stationery Office.

Communications, Energy and Paperworkers (CEP) Union of Canada/Bell Canada (1993), *Workplace Reorganization: Shaping the Future, Balancing the System*, August.

Connaughton, M. (1982), 'A study of the Rights Commissioners service in the Republic of Ireland', unpublished MBS dissertation, University College Dublin.

Conniffe, D. and Kennedy, K.A. (1984), *Employment and Unemployment Policy for Ireland*, Dublin: ERSI.

Coser, L. (1956), *The Functions of Social Conflict*, London: Routledge and Keegan Paul.

Costello, M. (1983), 'Ireland's experiment with worker directors', *Personnel Management*, October.

Costelloe, K. (2003), 'Liability for participation in industrial action', paper 17, *Diploma in Employment Law*, Dublin: University College Dublin.

Cox, B. and Hughes, J. (1989), 'Industrial relations in the public sector', in Department of Industrial Relations, UCD (eds), *Industrial Relations in Ireland: Contemporary Issues and Developments*, Dublin: University College Dublin.

Crepaz, M. (1992), 'Corporatism in decline? An empirical analysis of the impact of corporatism on macroeconomic performance and industrial disputes in 18 industrialised democracies', *Comparative Political Studies*, XXV/2, 139–68.

Crick, M. (1985), *Scargill and the Miners*, Middlesex: Penguin.

Crouch, C. (1982), *Trade Unions: The Logic of Collective Action*, London: Fontana.

Crouch, C. and Pizzorno, A. (1978), *The Resurgence of Class Conflict in Western Europe Since 1968*, Vols I and II, London: Macmillan.

Cutcher-Gershenfeld, J. and Verma, A. (1994), 'Joint governance in North American work-places: a glimpse of the future or the end of an era', *International Journal of Human Resource Management*, V/3, 547–80.

Dahrendorf, R. (1959), *Class and Class Conflict in Industrial Society*, London: Routledge and Keegan Paul.

Dáil Éireann (1963–1990), *Dáil Debates Collections* (various), Dublin: The Stationery Office.

Dalzell, T., Wallace, J. and Delany, B. (1997), 'The westernisation of Japanese personnel management?', in J. Wallace, T. Dalzell and B. Delany, *Continuity and Change in the Employment Relationship*, Dublin: Oak Tree Press.

Daniel, W. and Millward, N. (1983), *Workplace Industrial Relations in Britain: The DE\PSI\SSRC Survey*, London: Heinemann.

D'Arcy, F.A. (1994), 'The Irish trade union movement in the nineteenth century', in D. Nevin (ed.), *Trade Union Century*, Dublin: ICTU.

Darcy, C. (1998), *Annual Hours Report 1998*, Dublin: Employee Relations Information Unit, IBEC November.

D'Art, D. (2002), 'Managing the employment relationship in a market economy', in D. D'Art and T. Turner (eds), *Irish Employment Relations in the New Economy*, Dublin: Blackhall Publishing.

D'Art, D. and Turner, T. (2002a), *Irish Employment Relations in the New Economy*, Dublin: Blackhall Publishing.

D'Art, D. and Turner, T. (2002b), 'Union growth and recognition: the Irish case in a comparative context', Working Paper Research Series, Department of Personnel and Employment Relations, University of Limerick.

D'Art, D. and Turner, T. (2002c), 'Corporatism in Ireland: a view from below', in D. D'Art and T. Turner (eds), *Irish Employment Relations in the New Economy*, Dublin: Blackhall Publishing.

D'Art, D. and Turner, T. (2004), 'The experience of union officials with recognition and partnership at work in the Irish private sector', Working Paper Research Series, Department of Personnel and Employment Relations, University of Limerick.

Darvall, F.O. (1964), *Popular Disturbances and Public Order in Regency England*, London: Oxford University Press.

de Dreu, C.K.W. and van de Vliert, E. (1997), *Using Conflict in Organizations*, London: Sage.

Deaton, D. (1985), 'Management style and large scale survey evidence', *Industrial Relations Journal*, XVI/2, 67–71.

Deaton, D.R. and Beaumont, P.B. (1980), 'The determinants of bargaining structure: some large scale survey evidence', *British Journal of Industrial Relations*, XVIII (July), 202–16.

Deery, S. and De Cieri, H. (1991), 'Determinants of trade union membership in Australia', *British Journal of Industrial Relations*, XXIX (March), 59–74.

Deegan, J. and Dineen, D.A. (1997), *Tourism Policy and Performance*, London: International Thomson Press.

Delany, B. (1996), 'Japanese enterprise unions – success or failure?', unpublished MBS thesis, University of Limerick.

Dell'Aringa, C. and Lodovici, M. (1990), 'Industrial relations and economic performance', in R. Brunetta and C. Dell'Aringa (eds), *Labour Relations and Economic Performance*, London: Macmillan.

Department of Enterprise, Trade and Employment (2002a), *Explanatory Booklet on the Employment Appeals Tribunal*, Dublin: Department of Enterprise, Trade and Employment.

Department of Enterprise, Trade and Employment (2002b), *The Employment Appeals Tribunal, Guidelines for Persons Representing Parties before the Tribunal*, Dublin: Department of Enterprise, Trade and Employment.

Department of Finance (2003a), *Budgetary and Economic Statistics, January 2003*, Dublin: Department of Finance.

Department of Finance (2003b), *Economic Review and Outlook, 2003*, Dublin: Department of Finance.

Department of Finance (2003c), *Analysis of Exchequer Pay and Pensions Bill 1998–2003*, available at www.finance.gov.ie.

Department of Labour (1980), *Worker Participation: A Discussion Paper*, Dublin: The Stationery Office, March.

Department of Labour (1983), *Discussion Document on Industrial Relations Law Reform*, Dublin: Department of Labour.

Department of Labour (1985), *Discussion on Industrial Relations Law Reform*, Dublin: Department of Labour.

Department of Labour (1986a), *Employers' Perception of the Effect Of Labour Legislation*, Dublin: Government Publications Office.

Department of Labour (1986b), *Outline of Principal Proposals of Proposed New Trade Dispute and Industrial Relations Legislation*, Dublin: Department of Labour.

Department of Labour (1986c), *Report of the Advisory Committee on Worker Participation*, Dublin: The Stationery Office.

Department of Labour (1988), *Proposals on Industrial Relations Reform*, Dublin: Department of Labour.

Department of Labour (1991a), speech by the Minister for Labour at seminar on the Industrial Relations Act 1990, organised by the Irish Society for Labour Law on 13 July 1991, Dublin: Department of Labour.

Department of Labour (1991–1992), *Annual Reports* (various), Dublin: GPSO.

Department of the Taoiseach (1987), *Programme for Economic and Social Progress (1991)*, Dublin: The Stationery Office.

Department of the Taoiseach (1991), *Programme for National Recovery (PNR)*, Dublin: The Stationery Office.

Department of the Taoiseach (1994), *Programme for Competitiveness and Work (PCW)*, Dublin: The Stationery Office.

Department of the Taoiseach (1997), *Partnership 2000*, Dublin: The Stationery Office.

Department of the Taoiseach (2000), *Programme for Prosperity and Fairness (PPF)*, Dublin: The Stationery Office.

Department of the Taoiseach (2003), *Sustaining Progress*, Dublin: The Stationery Office.

Dineen, D. and Wallace, J. (1991), 'An overview of Irish labour market issues', paper presented at the Université Catholique de Louvain, October.

Dobbins, T. (2001a), 'Rise in union membership hides decline in density levels', *Industrial Relations News*, 26, 19–22.

Dobbins, T. (2001b), 'Implications of proposed EU information and consultation directive in Ireland', Dublin: European Foundation for the Improvement of Living and Working Conditions (www.eiro.eurofound.ie/2001/06/feature/ie0106168f.html, downloaded on 11 March 2004).

Dobbins, T. (2003a), 'Partnership has raised understanding of economic pressures – ESRI', *Industrial Relations News*, 29, 24.

Dobbins, T. (2003b), 'Long awaited public service "peace" codes may have limited impact', *Industrial Relations News*, 46, 16–20.

Dobbins, T. (2003c), 'Wellman case first to go to labour court', *Industrial Relations News*, 40, 3.

Dobbins, T. (2003d), 'Government launches consultations on implementation of EU consultation directive' (www.eiro.eurofound.ie/2003/09/feature/ie0309204f.html, downloaded on 11 March 2004).

Dobbins, T. and Higgins, C. (2003), 'SIPTU to set out stall for new pay talks', *Industrial Relations News*, 32, 12–13.

Doeringer, P. and Piore, M. (1971), *Internal Labour Markets and Manpower Analysis*, Lexington, MA: D.C. Heath.

Donovan, Lord (1968), *Report on the Royal Commission on Trade Unions and Employers' Associations 1965–1968*, London: CMND 3623, HMSO.

Dooley, C. (2003), 'Partnership talks continue but pay is stumbling block', *The Irish Times*, 11 January.

Drucker, P.F. (1950), *The New Society: The Anatomy of the Industrial Order*, New York: Harper & Bros.

Dubin, R., Kornhauser, A. and Ross, A. (eds) (1954), *Industrial Conflict*, New York: McGraw-Hill.

Duffy, K. (1993), 'Industrial Relations Act 1990 – the trade union experience', *Irish Industrial Relations Review* (January).

Dundon, T. (2002), 'Employer hostility and union avoidance in the UK', *Industrial Relations Journal*, XXXIII/3, 234–45.

Dunlop, J. (1958), *Industrial Relations Systems*, Carbondale, IL: Southern Illinois University Press.

Eaton, J. (2000), *Comparative Employment Relations: An Introduction*, Cambridge: Polity Press.

Economic and Social Research Institute (1997), *Medium Term Review: 1997–2003*, Dublin: ESRI.

Economic and Social Research Institute (2003), *Quarterly Economic Commentary – Winter 2003*, Dublin: ESRI.

The Economist (1994), 'For richer, for poorer', *The Economist*, CCCXXXIII/7888 (15 November), 19–21.

Edwards, P.K. (1986), *Conflict at Work: A Materialist Analysis of Workplace Relations*, Oxford: Blackwell.

Edwards, P.K. (1987), 'Factory managers: their role in personnel management and their place in the company', *Journal of Management Studies*, XXIV/5 (September), 479–501.

Edwards, P.K. (1992), 'Industrial conflict: themes and issues in recent research', *British Journal of Industrial Relations*, XXX, 361–404.

Edwards, P.K. (1994), 'Discipline and the creation of order', in K. Sisson (ed.), *Personnel Management: A Comprehensive Guide to Theory and Practice in Britain*, Oxford: Blackwell.

Edwards, P.K. (2003), 'The employment relationship and the field of industrial relations', in P. Edwards (ed.), *Industrial Relations: Theory and Practice*, 2nd ed., Oxford: Blackwell.

Edwards, T. and Ferner, A. (2002), 'The renewed "American challenge": a review of employment practices in US multinationals', *Industrial Relations Journal*, XXXIII/2, 94–111.

Employment Appeals Tribunal (1985–2002), *Annual Reports* (various), Dublin: Employment Appeals Tribunal/The Stationery Office.

Employment Appeals Tribunal (2002b), *Guidelines for Persons Representing Parties before the Tribunal*, www.entemp.ie/erir/guidelinebk.pdf (downloaded November 2003).

Employment Equality Agency (EEA) (1983), *Code of Practice: Equality of Opportunity in Employment*, Dublin: EEA.

Employment Equality Agency (EEA) (1986), *Transitions to Equal Opportunities at Work: Problems and Possibilities*, Dublin: EEA.

Employment Equality Agency (EEA) (1991), *A Model Equal Opportunities Policy*, Dublin: EEA.

Enderwick, P. (1986), 'Multinationals and labour relations: the case of Ireland', *Irish Business and Administrative Research*, VIII/2.

Equality Authority (2001), *Annual Report*, Dublin: The Equality Authority.

European Commission (1972), 'Proposal for a fifth directive on the structure of societies anonymes', *Bulletin of the European Communities, Supplement 10/72*, Brussels: European Economic Community.

European Commission (1997), 'Partnership for a new organization of work: green paper', *Bulletin of the European Union, Supplement 4/97*, Brussels: European Commission.

European Economic Community (EEC) (1975), 'Employee participation and company structure', *Bulletin of the European Communities, Supplement 8/75*, Brussels: European Economic Community.

European Foundation for the Improvement of Living and Working Conditions (1997), *New Forms of Work Organisation: Can Europe Realise its Potential?*, Dublin: European Foundation for the Improvement of Living and Working Conditions.

European Foundation for the Improvement of Living and Working Conditions (2004), 'Annualised hours in Europe', Dublin (www.eiro.eurofound.eu.int/2003/08/study/index.html, downloaded on 16 January 2004).

European Industrial Relations Intelligence (EIRI) Associates (2001), 'Irish social partnership at the crossroads?', *EIRI European Review* (March/April), 24–9.

European Industrial Relations Intelligence (EIRI) Associates (2004a), 'Employee involvement in a "European company"', *EIRI European Review* (March/April), 14–15.

European Industrial Relations Intelligence (EIRI) Associates (2004b), 'Proposals from the Commission which may lead to new legislation in the near future: European works councils', *EIRI European Review* (March/April), 19–22.

European Industrial Relations Intelligence (EIRI) Associates (2004c), 'Labour Court rules on collective bargaining', *EIRI European Review* (January/February), 150.

European Industrial Relations Observatory (EIRO) (2003), 'Equality Tribunal mediation facilities quicker dispute resolution" (www.eiro.eurofound.eu.int/2002/12/feature/ie0212204f.html).

Farnham, D. and Pimlott, J. (1990), *Understanding Industrial Relations,* London: Cassell.

Federated Union of Employees (1997), *FUE Annual Report 1986,* Dublin: FIE.

Federation of Irish Employers (1991), 'Accident rate is too high', *FIE Bulletin,* Dublin: FIE, May.

Fennell, C. and Lynch, I. (1993), *Labour Law in Ireland,* Dublin: Gill & Macmillan.

Ferner, A. (1997), 'Country of origin effects and HRM in multinational corporations', *Human Resource Management,* VII/1, 19–37.

Ferner, A. and Hyman, R. (1998), *Changing Industrial Relations in Europe,* 2nd ed., Oxford: Blackwell.

Finlay, I. (1996), 'The Labour Court: "not an ordinary court of law": a history of fifty years', Dublin: The Stationery Office.

Finlayson, J. (2000), 'Whither the trade unions?' http://oldfraser.lexi.net/publications/forum/2000/02/section_09.html.

Field, T. (1996), *Bullying In Sight – How to Predict, Resist, Challenge and Combat Workplace Bullying,* London: Success Unlimited.

Fiorito, J., Lowman, C. and Nelson, F.D. (1987), 'The impact of human resource policies on union organising', *Industrial Relations* (Spring), XXVI/2, 113–26.

Fisher, R. and Ury, W. (1986), *Getting to Yes,* London: Hutchinson.

Fisher, R. and Ury, W. (1997), *Getting to Yes: Negotiating Agreement without Giving In,* 2nd ed., London: Arrow Books.

Fitz Gerald, J. (2000), 'The story of Ireland's failure and belated success', in B. Nolan, J. O'Connell and C. Whelan (eds), *Bust to Boom? The Irish Experience of Growth and Inequality,* Dublin: Institute of Public Administration.

Fitz Gerald, J. (2003), *Ireland in the Medium Term: The Clockwork Mouse Runs Down,* Industrial Relations News Conference, 'No Vision No Future', University College Dublin, 27 February, 3–15.

Fitzpatrick, D. (1977), *Politics and Irish Life 1913–21,* Dublin: Gill & Macmillan.

Flanders, A. (1965), *Industrial Relations – What's Wrong with the System?,* London: Faber.

Flanders, A. (1967), *Collective Bargaining: Prescription for Change,* London: Faber.

Flanders, A. (1968a), *'Collective bargaining: a theoretical analysis'*, British Journal of Industrial Relations, VI/1, 1–26.

Flanders, A. (1968b), *Trade Unions*, London: Hutchinson.

Flood, P.C. (1989), *Human Resource Management: Promise, Possibility and Limitations*, mimeo, College of Business, University of Limerick.

Flood, P.C. and Toner, B. (1996), 'Managing without unions: a Pyrrhic victory?', in P.C. Flood, M.J. Gannon and J. Paauwe, *Managing Without Traditional Methods: International Innovations in Human Resource Management*, Wokingham: Addison-Wesley.

Flood, P.C. and Toner, B. (1997), 'How do large non-union companies avoid a Catch 22?', *British Journal of Industrial Relations*, XXXV/2, 257–77.

Fogarty, M.P., Egan, D. and Ryan, W.J.L. (1981), *Pay Policy for the 1980s*, Dublin: FUE.

Fombrun, C. (1986), 'Environmental trends create new pressures on human resources', in S.L. Rynes and G.T. Milkovich (eds), *Current Issues in Human Resource Management: Commentary and Readings*, Plano, TX: Business Publications Inc.

Fombrun, C., Tichy, N. and Devanna, M. (1984), *Strategic Human Resource Management*, New York: Wiley.

Forde, M. (1991), *Industrial Relations Law*, Dublin: Round Hall Press.

Forde, M. (2001), *Employment Law*, 2nd ed., Dublin: Round Hall Press.

Foulkes, F. (1980), *Personnel Policies in Large Non-Union Companies*, Englewood Cliffs, NJ: Prentice Hall.

Fox, A. (1966), 'Industrial sociology and industrial relations', research paper no. 3 to the Royal Commission on Trade Unions and Employers' Associations, London: HMSO.

Fox, A. (1973), 'Industrial relations: a social critique of pluralist ideology', in J. Child (ed.), *Man and Organisation*, London: Allen & Unwin.

Fox, A. (1974), *Beyond Contract: Work, Power and Trust Relations*, London: Faber.

Fox, A. (1975), 'Collective bargaining, Flanders and the Webbs', *British Journal of Industrial Relations*, XIII/2, 151–74.

Fox, A. (1977), 'The myth of pluralism and a radical alternative', in T. Clarke and L. Clements (eds), *Trade Unions under Capitalism*, London: Faber.

Franzosi, R. (1989), 'Strike data in search of a theory: the Italian case in the post war period', *Politics and Society*, XVII, 453–87.

Frawley, M. (1991), 'Labour law society reviews IR Act 1990 – "alarming possibilities" raised, recent cases reviewed', *Industrial Relations News*, 28, 14–16.

Frawley, M. (1993), 'Pat the Baker – third "recognition" dispute since '88', *Industrial Relations News*, 11, 6.

Frawley, M. (1998), 'Teachers consider revised C and A scheme', *Industrial Relations News*, 18, 6.

Frawley, M. (2000a), 'PPF – SIPTU and IMPACT press home demands for pay rise', *Industrial Relations News*, 37, 2–3.

Frawley, M. (2000b), 'Tylers shoes – pay increases could reach 16%', *Industrial Relations News*, 20, 3–4.

Frawley, M. (2001a), 'Teachers consider the options as strike suspended', *Industrial Relations News*, 14, 20–1.

Frawley, M. (2001b), 'Department breached data law by using check-off list', *Industrial Relations News*, 34, 15–16.

Frawley, M. (2002), 'Technology teachers latest group to switch to LRC, Labour Court', *Industrial Relations News*, 24, 14–15.

Frawley, M. (2003a), 'ASTI Conference – calm disintegrates as Lennon challenged, Congress snubbed', *Industrial Relations News*, 17, 15–16.

Frawley, M. (2003b), 'All Garda ranks face into major restructuring', *Industrial Relations News*, 27, 12–14.

Frawley, M. (2004a), 'Employers and unions on collision course to disaster', *Sunday Tribune*, 4 January.

Frawley, M. (2004b), 'Unions get away scot-free in costly "wildcat" strikes', *Sunday Tribune*, 22 February.

Frawley, M. (2004c), 'Sale of Eircom "a major mistake"', *Sunday Tribune*, 14 March.

Freeman, R. and Medoff, J. (1984), *What Do Unions Do*, New York: Basic Books.

Freidman, A. (1977), *Industry and Labour*, London: Macmillan.

Freidman, A. (1984), 'Management strategies, market conditions and the labour process', in R. Stephen (ed.), *Firms, Organisation and Labour*, London: Macmillan.

Freyssinet, J., Krieger, H., O'Kelly, K., Schnabel, C., Seifert, H. and Sisson, K. (1999), *Investigating Employment Pacts: Concept Paper for a Study of Collective Agreements Dealing with the Relationship Between Employment and Competitiveness*, Dublin: European Foundation for the Improvement of Living and Working Conditions.

Fröhlich, D. and Pekruhl, U. (1996), *Direct Participation and Organisational Change: Fashionable but Misunderstood?* Luxembourg: Office for Official Publications of the European Communities.

Fuerstenberg, F. (1987), 'The Federal Republic of Germany', in G.J. Bamber and R.D. Lansbury (eds), *International and Comparative Industrial Relations: A Study of Developed Market Economies*, London: Allen & Unwin.

Gall, G. (1999), 'A review of strike activity at the end of the second millennium', *Employee Relations*, XXI/4, 357–77.

Gall, G. (2001), 'Management control approaches and union tecognition in Britain', paper presented to the Work Employment and Society Conference, University of Nottingham, September.

Galvin, D. (1980), 'Worker participation survey', unpublished BBS dissertation, University of Limerick.

Geary, J. (1994), 'Task participation: employee's participation – enabled or constrained', in K. Sisson (ed.), *Personnel Management: A Comprehensive Guide to Theory and Practice in Britain*, Oxford: Blackwell.

Geary, J. (1995), 'World class manufacturing and the implications for industrial relations', in P. Gunnigle and W.K. Roche (eds), *New Challenges to Irish Industrial Relations*, Dublin: Oak Tree Press in association with the Labour Relations Commission.

Geary, J. (1996), 'Working at restructuring work in Europe: the case of team-working', *Irish Business and Administrative Research*, 17, 44–57.

Geary, J. (1998), 'New work structures and the diffusion of team working arrangements in Ireland', paper presented at the Sixth Annual John Lovett Memorial Lecture, University of Limerick, 2 April.

Geary, J. (1999), 'The new workplace: change at work in Ireland', *International Journal of Human Resource Management*, X/5, 870–90.

Geoghegan, B. (1996), 'IBEC expert defends PCW', *Sunday Business Post*, 30 August.

Gilbraith, J. and Nathanson, D. (1978), *Strategy Implementation: The Role of Structure*, St. Paul, MN: West Publishing.

Gladstone, A. (1984), 'Employers associations in comparative perspective: functions and activities', in J.P. Windmuller and A. Gladstone (eds), *Employer's Associations and Industrial Relations: A Comparative Study*, Oxford: Clarendon.

Goetschy, J. (2000), 'The European Union and national social pacts: employment and social protection put to the test of joint regulation', in G. Fajertag and P. Pochet (eds), *Social Pacts in Europe – New Dynamics*, Brussels: European Trade Union Institute.

Golden, C.S. and Parker, V.D. (eds) (1955), *Causes of Industrial Peace*, New York: Harper & Bros.

Golden, M., Wallerstein, M. and Lange, P. (1999), 'Postwar trade-union organisation and industrial relations in twelve countries', in H. Kitschelt, P. Lange, G. Marks, and J. Stephens (eds), *Continuity and Change in Contemporary Capitalism*, Cambridge: Cambridge University Press.

Goldthorpe, J. (1974), 'Industrial relations in Great Britain: a critique of reformism', *Politics and Society*, IV/4, 419–52.

Gouldner, A.W. (1954), *Wildcat Strike*, New York: Harper.

Government Publications Office (1996), *Partnership 2000 for Inclusion, Employment and Competitiveness*, Dublin: Government Publications Sales Office.

Government Social Survey (1968), *Workplace Industrial Relations*, London: HMSO.

Grafton, D. (1984), 'FUE seeks reform of JLCs to allow employers right of appeal', *Industrial Relations News*, 31, 7.

Green, G. (1991), *Industrial Relations*, London: Pitman.

Griffin, J.I. (1939), *Strikes: A Study in Quantitative Economics*, New York: Colombia University Press.

Grint, K. (1991), *The Sociology of Work: An Introduction*, Oxford: Polity Press.

Guest, D. (1987), 'Human resource management and industrial relations', *Journal of Management Studies*, XXIV/5, 503–21.

Guest, D. (1989a), 'Personnel and HRM: can you tell the difference?', *Personnel Management* (January), 48–51.

Guest, D. (1989b), 'Human resource management: its implications for industrial relations and trade unions', in J. Storey (ed.), *New Perspectives on Human Resource Management*, London: Routledge.

Guest, D. (1992), 'Right enough to be dangerously wrong: an analysis of the search of excellence phenomenon', in G. Salamon (ed.), *Human Resource Strategies*, London: Sage/Open University Press.

Guest, D. and Hoque, K. (1994), 'Employee relations in non-union greenfield sites: the good, the bad and the ugly', *Human Resource Management Journal*, V/1, 1–14.

Guest, D. and Rosenthal, P. (1992), 'Industrial relations in greenfield sites', mimeo, London: Centre for Economic Performance, Industrial Relations Conference, March.

Gunnigle, P. (1989), 'Management approaches to industrial relations in the small firm', in Department of Industrial Relations, UCD (eds), *Industrial Relations in Ireland: Contemporary Issues and Developments*, Dublin: University College Dublin.

Gunnigle, P. (1992a), 'Changing management approaches to employee relations in Ireland', *Employee Relations*, XIV/1, 17–32.

Gunnigle, P. (1992b), 'Human resource management in Ireland', *Employee Relations*, XIV/5, 5–22.

Gunnigle, P. (1992c), 'Ireland', in C. Brewster, A. Hegewisch, L. Holden and T. Lockhart (eds), *The European Human Resource Management Guide*, London: Academic Press.

Gunnigle, P. (1995a), 'Management styles in employee relations in greenfield sites: challenging a collectivist tradition', unpublished PhD thesis, Cranfield School of Management.

Gunnigle, P. (1995b), 'Collectivism and the management of industrial relations in greenfield sites', *Human Resource Management Journal*, V/4, 24–40.

Gunnigle, P. (1998a), 'More rhetoric than reality: industrial relations partnerships in Ireland', *Economic and Social Review*, XXVIII/4, 179–200.

Gunnigle, P. (1998b), 'Human resource management and the personnel function', in W.K. Roche, K. Monks and J. Walsh (eds), *Human Resource Management Strategies: Policy and Practice in Ireland*, Dublin: Oak Tree Press.

Gunnigle, P. and Brady, T. (1984), 'The management of industrial relations in the small firm', *Employee Relations*, VI/5, 21–4.

Gunnigle, P. and Flood, P. (1990), *Personnel Management in Ireland: Practice, Trends and Developments*, Dublin: Gill & Macmillan.

Gunnigle, P. and Morley, M. (1993), 'Something old, something new: a perspective on industrial relations in the Republic of Ireland', *Review of Employment Topics*, I/1, 114–42.

Gunnigle, P. and Morley, M. (1998), 'Strategic integration and industrial relations in greenfield sites', in D. Skinner, C. Mabey and T. Clark (eds), *Experiencing Human Resource Management*, London: Sage.

Gunnigle, P. and McGuire, D. (2001), 'Why Ireland? A qualitative review of the factors influencing the location of US multinationals in Ireland with particular reference to the impact of labour issues', *The Economic and Social Review*, XXXII/1, 43–67.

Gunnigle, P., Foley, K. and Morley, M. (1994), 'A review of organisational reward practices', in P. Gunnigle, P. Flood, M. Morley and T. Turner (eds), *Continuity and Change in Irish Employee Relations*, Dublin: Oak Tree Press.

Gunnigle, P., Garavan, T. and Fitzgerald, G. (1992), *Employee Relations and Employment Law In Ireland*, Limerick: The Open Business School – PMTC, University of Limerick.

Gunnigle, P., Heraty, N. and Morley, M.J. (2002a), *Human Resource Management in Ireland*, Dublin: Gill & Macmillan.

Gunnigle, P., MacCurtain, S. and Morley, M. (2001), 'Dismantling pluralism: industrial relations in Irish greenfield sites', *Personnel Review*, XXX/3, 263–79.

Gunnigle, P., Morley, M. and Heraty, N. (1997a), *Personnel and Human Resource Management: Theory and Practice in Ireland*, Dublin: Gill & Macmillan.

Gunnigle, P., Morley, M. and Turner, T. (1997b), 'Challenging collectivist traditions: individualism and the management of industrial relations in greenfield sites', *Economic and Social Review*, XXVIII/2, 105–34.

Gunnigle, P., O'Sullivan, M. and Kinsella, M. (2002b), 'Organised labour in the new economy: trade unions and public policy in the Republic of Ireland', in D. D'Art and T. Turner (eds), *Irish Employment Relations in the New Economy*, Dublin: Blackhall Publishing.

Gunnigle, P., Turner, T. and D'Art, D. (1997d), 'Counterpoising collectivism: performance related pay and industrial relations in greenfield sites', *British Journal of Industrial Relations*, XXXVI/4, 565–79.

Gunnigle, P., Turner, T. and Morley, M. (1998), 'Strategic integration and industrial relations: the impact of managerial styles', *Employee Relations*, XX/2, 115–31.

Gunnigle, P., Morley, M., Clifford, N. and Turner, T. (1997c), *Human Resource Management in Irish Organisations: Practice in Perspective*, Dublin: Oak Tree Press.

Hackman, J.R. and Oldham, G.R. (1980), *Work Redesign*, New York: Addison-Wesley.

Hall, M. (2001), 'Council of Ministers reaches political agreement on employee consultation directive', Dublin: European Foundation for the Improvement of Living and Working Conditions (www.eiro.eurofound.ie/2001/06/feature/eu0106219f.html, downloaded on 11 March 2004).

Hall, M. (2002), 'Final approval given to consultation directive', Dublin: European Foundation for the Improvement of Living and Working Conditions (www.eiro.eurofound.ie/2002/04/feature/EU0204207F.html, downloaded on 11 March 2004).

Handy, L.J. (1968), 'Absenteeism and attendance in the British coal mining industry', *British Journal of Industrial Relations*, VI/1, 27–50.

Hannigan, K. (1997), 'Partnership survey', unpublished findings of Irish Management Institute (IMI) pilot survey on Partnership conducted among participants at IMI/Department of Enterprise, Trade and Employment Conference, Workplace 2000, Dublin: IMI.

Harbison, F. (1966), *Industrial Relations: Challenges and Responses*, Toronto: University of Toronto Press.

Hardiman, N. (1988), *Pay, Politics and Economic Performance in Ireland 1970–1987*, Oxford: Clarendon.

Hardiman, N. (2000), 'Social partnership, wage bargaining, and growth', in B. Nolan, J. O'Connell and C. Whelan (eds), *Bust to Boom? The Irish Experience of Growth and Inequality*, Dublin: Institute of Public Administration.

Hastings, T. (1994), *Semi-states in Crisis: The Challenge for Industrial Relations in the ESB and Other Major Semi-state Companies*, Dublin: Oak Tree Press.

Hastings, T. (2003), *Politics, Management and Industrial Relations: Semi-State Companies and the Challenges of Marketization*, Dublin: Blackhall Publishing.

Hawkins, K. (1979), *A Handbook of Industrial Relations Practice*, London: Kogan Page.

Hebdon, R.P. and Stern, R.N. (1998), 'Trade-offs among expressions of industrial conflict: public sector strike bans and arbitrations', *Industrial and Labour Relations Review*, LI/2, 204-21.

Heraty, N., Morley, M. and Turner, T. (1994), 'Trends and developments in the organisation of the employment relationship', in P. Gunnigle *et al.* (eds), *Continuity and Change in Irish Employee Relations*, Dublin: Oak Tree Press.

Herzberg, F. (1968), *Work and the Nature of Man*, London: Staples Press.

Hibbs, D.A. (1978), 'On the political economy of long-run trends in strike activity', *British Journal of Political Science*, VIII/2, 153–75.

Higgins, C. (1996), 'Staff associations – how are they organised?', *Industrial Relations News*, 46, 17–20.

Higgins, C. (1997a), 'Howmedica and SIPTU conclude partnership agreement', *Industrial Relations News*, 40, 2–3.

Higgins, C. (1997b), 'IT sector sees rises of up to 31%', *Industrial Relations News*, 25, 11.

Higgins, C. (2000a), 'Train drivers' group not entitled to recognition, says High Court', *Industrial Relations News*, 16, 22–3.

Higgins, C. (2000b), 'European Company Statute – worker participation logjam resolved', *Industrial Relations News*, 47, 16.

Higgins, C. (2001), 'European Company Statute – details on worker participation agreed', *Industrial Relations News*, 3, 13.

Higgins, C. (2003), 'GRA approval clears way for Garda change talks', *Industrial Relations News*, 42, 11.

Hillery, B. (1994), 'The institutions of industrial relations', in T.V. Murphy and W.K. Roche (eds), *Irish Industrial Relations in Practice*, Dublin: Oak Tree Press.

Hiltrop, J.M. and Udall, S. (1995), *The Essence of Negotiation*, London: Prentice Hall.

Hirsch, B.T. and Berger, M. (1984), 'Union membership determination and industry characteristics', *Southern Economic Journal*, L/2 (January), 665–79.

Hofer, C. and Schendel, D. (1978), *Strategy Formulation: Analytical Concepts*, St Paul, MN: West Publishing.

Honohan, P. and Walsh, B. (2002), 'Catching up with the leaders: the Irish hare', in Brookings papers on economic activity, Washington, DC: Brookings Institution.

Horgan, J. (1989), 'The future of collective bargaining', in Department of Industrial Relations, UCD (eds), *Industrial Relations in Ireland: Contemporary Issues and Developments*, Dublin: University College Dublin.

Hourihan, F. (1990), 'I.R. Bill 1989 – Dáil Debate raises serious issues', *Industrial Relations News*, 15, 18–20.

Hourihan, F. (1995), 'Profit-sharing – the means to 10% greater productivity', *Industrial Relations News*, 30, 13–15.

Hourihan, F. (1996), 'Non-union policies on the increase among new overseas firms', *Industrial Relations News*, 4, 17–23.

Hourihan, F. (1997), 'The European union and industrial relations', in T.V. Murphy and W.K. Roche (eds), *Irish Industrial Relations in Practice: Revised and Expanded Edition*, Dublin: Oak Tree Press.

Huczynski, A.A. and Buchanan, D.A. (1991), *Organizational Behaviour: An Introductory Text*, London: Prentice Hall.

Huselid, M.A. (1995), 'The impact of human resource management practices on turnover, productivity, and corporate financial performance', *Academy of Management Journal*, XXXVIII/3, 635–72.

Hyman. R. (1975), *Industrial Relations: A Marxist Introduction*, London: Macmillan.

Hyman, R. (1989), *Strikes*, London: Macmillan.

Hyman, R. and Mason, B. (1995), *Managing Employee Involvement and Participation*, London: Sage.

Incomes Data Service (IDS) (1992), *Pay and Benefits*, London: IPM.

Income Data Service (IDS)/Institute of Personnel and Development (IPD) (1996), *European Management Guides: Industrial Relations and Collective Bargaining*, London: Institute of Personnel and Development.

Industrial Participation Association (IPA)/Institute of Personnel Management (IPM) (1983), *Employee Involvement and Participation: Principles and Standards of Practice*, London: IPA/IPM.

Industrial Relations News (1996), 'Rabbitte accuses employers in debate on national agreements', *Industrial Relations News*, 9, 18–19.

Industrial Relations News (2002), 'Irish Congress of Trade Unions: report of working group on trade union recognition', *Industrial Relations News*, 39, 25–8.

Industrial Relations News (2004), 'New Labour Court chair would like major overhaul of employment law', *Industrial Relations News*, 5, 21–3.

Industrial Relations Unit, Enterprise, Trade and Employment (2003), *National Information and Consultation Directive 2002/14/EC – Consultation Paper on Transposition into Irish Law*, July.

International Labour Office (ILO) (1960), *Collective Bargaining: A Workers Manual*, Geneva: ILO.

International Labour Office (ILO) (1973), *Collective Bargaining in Industrial Market Economies*, Geneva: ILO.

International Labour Office (ILO) (1975), *Collective Bargaining in Industrialised Market Economies*, Geneva: ILO.

International Labour Office (ILO) (1997), *Conciliation/Mediation: Consensus Seeking Skills for Third Parties*, Geneva: ILO.

Ireland (1984), Building on Reality 1985–1987, working paper, Dublin: The Stationery Office.

Ireland (1990), *Dáil Éireann Parliamentary Debates Official Report*, CCCXCVI, Dublin: The Stationery Office, 27 February.

Irish Business and Employers Confederation (IBEC) (1984–1998), *Annual Reports*, Dublin: IBEC.

Irish Business and Employers Confederation (1999), *Partnership at Enterprise Level: Survey Results*, Dublin: IBEC Partnership Unit.

Irish Congress of Trade Unions (ICTU) (1975–2002), *Annual Reports* (various), Dublin: ICTU.

Irish Congress of Trade Unions (ICTU) (1993), *New Forms of Work Organisation: Options for Unions*, Dublin: ICTU.

Irish Congress of Trade Unions (ICTU) (1995), *Managing Change*, Dublin: ICTU.

Irish Congress of Trade Unions (ICTU) (1996), *Minimum Standards for Atypical Work*, Dublin: ICTU.

Irish Finance, Portal (2003), www.finfacts.com/Private/personel/redundancy (downloaded on 17 January 2004).

Irish Small and Medium Enterprises (ISME) (1997), *Annual Report*, Dublin: ISME.

Irish Small and Medium Enterprises (ISME) (2003), 'ISME slams government proposals for partnership agreement', press release (available at www.isme.ie), 13 January.

The Irish Statute Book, www.irishstatutebook.ie, downloaded on 23 January 2004.

The Irish Times (1998), 'The Ryanair dispute', editorial, *The Irish Times*, 16 July.

The Irish Times (2003), 'Ireland is world's most globalised country for third year in a row', *The Irish Times*, 13 March.

Jackson, M.P. (1982), *Industrial Relations: A Textbook*, London: Kogan Page.

Jackson, M.P. (1987), *Strikes: Industrial Conflict in Britain, USA and Australia*, London: Wheatsheaf.

Jackson, M.P. (1991), *An Introduction to Industrial Relations*, London: Routledge.

Jacoby, S.M. (1997), *Modern Manors: Welfare Capitalism since the New Deal*, New Jersey: Princeton University Press.

Jensen, V. (1956), 'Notes on the beginnings of collective bargaining', *Industrial and Labour Relations Review*, IX/2, 230–2.

Kahn-Freund, O. (1977), *Labour and the Law*, London: Stevens.

Kavanagh, R. (1987), *Labour from the Beginning – 75 Years*, Dublin: The Labour Party.

Kelleher, O. (2003), 'E-mails a potential source of libels', *The Sunday Business Post* (Market section, 21 September), 14.

Keller, B. (2002), 'The European Company Statute: employee involvement – and beyond', *Industrial Relations Journal*, XXXIII/5, 424–45.

Kelly, A. (1975), 'Changes in the occupational structure and industrial relations in Ireland', *Management*, 2.

Kelly, A. (1989a), 'The Rights Commissioner: conciliator, mediator or arbitrator', in Department of Industrial Relations, UCD (eds), *Industrial Relations in Ireland: Contemporary Issues and Developments*, Dublin: University College Dublin.

Kelly, A. (1989b), 'The worker director in Irish industrial relations', in Department of Industrial Relations, UCD (eds), *Industrial Relations in Ireland: Contemporary Issues and Developments*, Dublin: University College Dublin.

Kelly, A. (undated), 'In support of the new working class thesis: the case of the Irish white collar worker', working paper no. 7, Dublin: Department of Industrial Relations, University College Dublin.

Kelly, A. and Brannick, T. (1983), 'The pattern of strike activity in Ireland, 1960–1979', *Irish Business and Administrative Research*, V/1, 65–77.

Kelly, A. and Brannick, T. (1985), 'Industrial relations practices of multinational companies in Ireland', *Irish Business and Administrative Research*, VII/1.

Kelly, A. and Brannick, T. (1986), 'The changing contours of Irish strike patterns: 1960–1984', *Irish Business and Administrative Research*, VIII, 77–88.

Kelly, A. and Brannick, T. (1988a), 'Explaining the strike proneness of British companies in Ireland', *British Journal of Industrial Relations*, XXVI/1, 37–57.

Kelly, A. and Brannick, T. (1988b), 'The management of human resources: new trends and the challenge to trade unions', *Journal of the Irish Institute of Training and Development*, (August), 11–15.

Kelly, A. and Brannick, T. (1989), 'Strikes in Ireland: measurement, indices and trends', in Department of Industrial Relations, UCD (eds), *Industrial Relations in Ireland: Contemporary Issues and Developments*, Dublin: University College Dublin.

Kelly, A. and Brannick, T. (1991), *The Impact of New Human Resource Management Policies on US MNC Strike Patterns*, mimeo, Department of Business Administration, University College Dublin.

Kelly, A. and Hourihan, F. (1997), 'Employee Participation', in T.V. Murphy and W.K. Roche (eds), *Irish Industrial Relations in Practice: Revised and Expanded Edition*, Dublin: Oak Tree Press.

Kelly, A. and Roche, W.K. (1983), 'Institutional reform in Irish industrial relations', *Studies: An Irish Quarterly Review*, LXXII/287, 221–230.

Kelly, E. (2000), 'An exploratory study on the implementation/non-implementation of section III, section V or section VI of the code of practice on dispute procedures and procedures in essential services (S.I. No. 1 of 1992) among essential service providers in Ireland', unpublished MBS thesis, University of Limerick.

Kelly, J. (1997), 'The future of trade unionism: injustice, identity and attribution', *Employee Relations*, XIX/5.

Kelly, J. (1998), *Rethinking Industrial Relations: Mobilization, Collectivism and Long Waves*, London: Routledge.

Kelly, J. (2003), 'Labour movement revitalization? A comparative perspective', Countess Markievicz Memorial Lecture, Dublin, 7 April (www.ul.ie/iair/documents/lecture0403).

Kennedy, G. (1998), *The New Negotiating Edge: A Behavioural Approach for Results and Relationships*, London: Nicholas Brearly.

Kerr, A. (1986), 'Industrial action: rights or immunities', *Journal of the Irish Society for Labour Law*, V, 7–18.

Kerr, A. (1987), 'Maternity protection – the spectre of legalism', *Industrial Relations News*, 4, 15–22.

Kerr, A. (1989), 'Trade unions and the law', in Department of Industrial Relations, UCD (eds), *Industrial Relations in Ireland: Contemporary Issues and Developments*, Dublin: University College Dublin.

Kerr, A. (1991a), *The Trade Union and Industrial Relations Acts of Ireland*, London: Sweet & Maxwell.

Kerr, A. (1991b), 'Irish industrial relations legislation: consensus not compulsion', *Industrial Law Journal* (December), XX/4.

Kerr, A. (1997), 'Collective labour law', in T.V. Murphy and W.K. Roche (eds), *Irish Industrial Relations in Practice*, Dublin: Oak Tree Press.

Kerr, A. and Whyte, G. (1985), *Irish Trade Union Law*, Abingdon: Professional Books.

Kerr, C., Harbinson, F. and Myers, H. (1962), *Industrialism and Industrial Man*, London: Heineman.

Kerr, C. and Siegel, A. (1954), 'The interindustry propensity to strike – an international comparison', in A. Kornhauser, R. Dubin and A.M. Ross (eds), *Industrial Conflict*, New York: McGraw-Hill.

Kidner, R. (1982), 'Lessons in trade union reform: the origins and passage of the Trade Disputes Act 1906', *Legal Studies*, II/1, 34–52.

Kinnie, N.J. (1986), 'Patterns of industrial relations management', *Employee Relations*, VIII/2, 17–21.

Klein, J. (1989), 'The human cost of manufacturing reform', *Harvard Business Review*, (March/April).

Kochan, T.A. and Osterman, P. (1994), *The Mutual Gains Enterprise*, Cambridge, MA: Harvard Business School Press.

Kochan, T.A., Katz, H.C. and McKersie, R.B. (1986), *The Transformation of American Industrial Relations*, New York: Basic Books.

Korpi, W. (1983), *The Democratic Class Struggle*, London: Routledge and Keegan Paul.

Krislov, J. (1972), 'Irish attitudes regarding conciliation: a survey of management, labour and conciliation officers', *Industrial Relations Journal*, III/2, 43–8.

Labour Court (1948–2002), *Annual Reports* (various), Dublin: The Stationery Office.

Labour Court, *Frequently Asked Questions*, available at www.labourcourt.ie.

Labour Court (2001), *Guide to the Labour Court*, available at www.labourcourt.ie.

Labour Court Recommendations (1995), Case Number: LCR14816 (www.labourcourt.ie/labour/labour.nsf/LookupPageLink/Recommendations).

Labour Relations Commission (1992–2002), *Labour Relations Commission Annual Report* (various), Dublin: The Stationery Office.

Labour Relations Commission (2003), 'Editorial', *LRC Review* (May), 2, 1.

Ladó, M. (2003), 'Building an enlarged Europe – challenges for industrial relations', Countess Markievicz Memorial Lecture, Dublin: www.ul.ie/iair/documents/lecture1103.pdf 24, November.

Langford, K. (2001), 'Ireland', in V. Edmunds, V. DuFeu, E. Gillow and M. Hopkins (eds), *EU and International Employment Law*, Southampton: Jordan.

Larkin, E. (1965), *James Larkin: 1876–1947 – Irish Labour Leader*, London: Routledge and Keegan Paul.

Lawler, E. (1978), 'The new plant revolution', *Organizational Dynamics* (Winter), 3–12.

Lawler, E. (1982), 'Increasing worker involvement to enhance organisational effectiveness', in P.S. Goodman (ed.), *Change in Organisations*, San Francisco: Jossey-Bass.

Leddin, A. (2000), 'Assume positions for nasty crash-landing', *The Irish Times*, 24 November.

Leddin, A. and Walsh, B. (1990), *The Macro-Economy of Ireland*, Dublin: Gill & Macmillan.

Leddin, A. and Walsh, B. (1992), *The Macro-Economy of Ireland*, 2nd ed., Dublin: Gill & Macmillan.

Leddin, A. and Walsh, B. (1998), *The Macro-Economy of Ireland*, 4th ed., Dublin: Gill & Macmillan.

Lee, J. (1980), 'Worker and society since 1945', in D. Nevin (ed.), *Trade Unions and Change in Irish Society*, Dublin: Mercier/RTÉ.

Legge, K. (1989), 'Human resource management – a critical analysis', in J. Storey (ed.), *New Perspectives on Human Resource Management*, London: Routledge.

Lehmbruch, G. (1979), 'Consociational democracy, class conflict and the new corporatism', in P.C. Schmitter and G. Lehmbruch (eds), *Trends Towards Corporatist Intermediation*, London: Sage.

Leiserson, W. (1922), 'Constitutional government in American industries', *American Economic Review*, XII, 56–79.

Lester, R.A. (1952), 'A range theory of wage differentials', *Industrial Relations Review*, V/4, 483–500.

Lewicki, R.J., Litterer, J.A., Minton, J.W. and Saunders, D.M. (1994), *Negotiation*, Burr Ridge, IL: Irwin.

Lewicki, R.J., Saunders, D.M. and Minton, J.W. (1999), *Negotiation*, 3rd ed., Boston: McGraw-Hill.

Lewicki, R.J., Saunders, D.M. and Minton, J.W. (2001), *Essentials of Negotiation*, Boston: McGraw-Hill.

Lismoen, H. (2000), 'Developments in membership of unions and employers' organisations', Industrial Relations Observatory Online (www.eiro.eurofound.ie), 28 August.

Logan, J. (1999), *Teachers' Union: The TUI and its Forerunners 1899–1994*, Dublin: A & A Farmar.

Long, P. (1988), 'A review of approved profit sharing trust schemes in Ireland and the UK', unpublished dissertation, Dublin Institute of Technology.

Lukes, S. (1974), *Power: A Radical View*, London: Macmillan.

Lundy, A. and Cowling, A. (1988), *Strategic Human Resource Management*, London: Routledge.

Macfarlane, L.J. (1981), *The Right to Strike*, Middlesex: Pelican.

MacMahon, J. (2002), 'Owner managers and employment relations in small Irish firms', unpublished PhD thesis, University of Limerick.

MacSharry, R. (2000), 'Social partnership', in R. MacSharry and P. White (eds), *The Making of the Celtic Tiger: The Inside Story of Ireland's Boom Economy*, Cork: Mercier Press.

MacSharry, R. and White, P. (2000), *The Making of the Celtic Tiger: The Inside Story of Ireland's Boom Economy*, Cork: Mercier Press.

Madden, D. and Kerr, A. (1996), *Unfair Dismissal: Cases and Commentary*, 2nd ed., Dublin: Irish Business and Employers Confederation.

Marchington, M. (1982), *Managing Industrial Relations*, London: McGraw-Hill.

Marchington, M. (1990), 'Analysing the links between product markets and the management of employee relations', *Journal of Management Studies*, XXVII/2, 111–32.

Marchington, M. and Parker, P. (1990), *Changing Patterns of Employee Relations*, Hemel Hempstead: Harvester Wheatsheaf.

Marchington, M. and Wilkinson, A. (2000), 'Direct participation', in S. Bach and K. Sisson (eds), *Personnel Management: A Comprehensive Guide to Theory and Practice*, 3rd ed., Oxford: Blackwell.

Marsh, A.I. (1973), *Managers and Shop Stewards: Shop Floor Revolution*, London: Institute of Personnel Management.

Marshall, R. (1992), 'Work organisation, unions and economic performance', in L. Mishel and P. Voos (eds), *Unions and Economic Competitiveness*, New York: ME Sharpe Inc.

Maslow, A.H. (1954), *Motivation and Personality*, New York: Harper & Row.

Mayo, E. (1949), *The Social Problems of an Industrial Civilization*, London: Routledge and Keegan Paul.

McCall, B. (2001), 'The skills we need to prosper', Commercial supplement, *The Irish Times*, 13 April.

McCarthy, C. (1973), *The Decade of Upheaval*, Dublin: Institute of Public Administration.

McCarthy, C. (1977), *Trade Unions in Ireland: 1894–1960*, Dublin: Institute of Public Administration.

McCarthy, C. (1982), 'Reform: a strategy for research', in H. Pollock (ed.), *Reform of Industrial Relations*, Dublin: O'Brien Press.

McCarthy, C. (1984), *Elements in a Theory of Industrial Relations*, Dublin: Trinity College Dublin.

McCarthy, C. and von Prondzynski, F. (1982), 'The reform of industrial relations', *Administration: Journal of the Institute of Public Administration of Ireland*, XXIX/3.

McCarthy, W.E.J., O'Brien, J.F. and O'Dowd, V.G. (1975), *Wage Inflation and Wage Leadership*, paper no. 79, Dublin: Economic and Social Research Institute.

McCartney, J. and Teague, P. (2004), 'The use of workplace innovations in Ireland: a review of the evidence', *Personnel Review*, XXXIII/1.

McCord, N. (1980), *Strikes*, Oxford: Basil Blackwell.

McGinley, M. (1989a), 'Pay in the 1980s – the issue of control', *Industrial Relations News*, XXX, 17–24.

McGinley, M. (1989b), 'Pay increases between 1981–1987', in Institute of Public Administration, *Personnel and Industrial Relations Directory*, Dublin: Institute of Public Administration.

McGinley, M. (1990), 'Trade union law – look back in anguish', *Industrial Relations News* (26 April), 16, 19–23.

McGinley, M. (1997), 'Industrial relations in the public sector', in T.V. Murphy and W.K. Roche (eds), *Irish Industrial Relations in Practice*, Dublin: Oak Tree Press.

McGinley, M. (2001), 'Benchmarking and the pursuit of a logical approach to public service pay', *Industrial Relations News*, 17, 21–5.

McGovern, P. (1989a), 'Union recognition and union avoidance in the 1980s', in Department of Industrial Relations, UCD (eds), *Industrial Relations in Ireland: Contemporary Issues and Developments*, Dublin: University College Dublin.

McGovern, P. (1989b), 'Trade union recognition – five case studies', *Industrial Relations News*, 6 (9 February), 12–16.

McKersie, R.B. (2002), 'Labour-management partnerships: US evidence and the implications for Ireland', in P. Gunnigle, M. Morley and M. McDonnell (eds), *The Lovett Lectures: A Decade of Developments in Human Resource Management*, Dublin: The Liffey Press.

McLoughlin, I. and Gourlay, S. (1992), 'Enterprise without unions: the management of employee relations in non-union firms', *Journal of Management Studies*, XXIX/5, 669–91.

McLoughlin, I. and Gourlay, S. (1994), *Enterprise without Unions: Industrial Relations in the Non-Union Firm*, Buckingham: Open University Press.

McMahon, G. (1987), 'Wage structure in the Republic of Ireland', *Advances in Business Studies*, I/1, Dublin: Dublin Institute of Technology.

McMahon, G. (1990), 'Multinationals: the labour relations experience in Ireland', *Advances in Business Studies*, II/2.

McMahon, G. (1991), 'Statutory minimum wage regulation and low pay in the Republic of Ireland', unpublished PhD thesis, Trinity College Dublin.

McMahon, G. (2000a), 'Self-managed groups are becoming more popular', *The Irish Times*, 1 May.

McMahon, G. (2000b), 'Short memories can prove fatal to the future of pay programme', *The Irish Times*, 17 April.

McMahon, G. (2001), 'Time to take the office bully by the horns', *The Irish Times*, 16 July.

McMahon, G. (2002), *Recruitment and Selection: How to Get It Right*, Dublin: Oak Tree Press.

McNamara, G., Williams, K. and West, D. (1988), *Understanding Trade Unions: Yesterday and Today*, Dublin: O'Brien Educational Press in association with the Irish Congress of Trade Unions.

McNamara, G., Williams, K. and West, D. (1994), *Understanding Trade Unions: Yesterday and Today*, Dublin: ELO Publications in association with the Irish Congress of Trade Unions.

McPartlin, B. (1997), 'The development of trade union organisation', in T.V. Murphy and W.K. Roche (eds), *Irish Industrial Relations in Practice: Revised and Expanded Edition*, Dublin: Oak Tree Press.

Meenan, F. (1991), 'Industrial Relations Act 1990 – a commentary on the trade disputes provisions, part 1 and part 2', *Industrial Relations Data Bank*, IX/207 and 208 (February).

Meenan, F. (1999), *Working Within the Law: A Practical Guide for Employers and Employees*, 2nd ed., Dublin: Oak Tree Press.

Miles, R.E. and Snow, C.C. (1978), *Organizational Strategy, Structure and Process*, New York: McGraw-Hill.

Miles, R.E. and Snow, C.C. (1984), 'Designing strategic human resources systems', *Organizational Dynamics* (Spring), 36–52.

Millis, H.A. and Brown, E.C. (1950), *From the Wagner Act to Taft-Hartley*, Chicago: University of Chicago Press.

Mills, D.Q. (1989), *Labor-Management Relations*, New York: McGraw-Hill.

Milner, S. and Richards, E. (1991), 'Determinants of union recognition and employee involvement, evidence from the London docklands', *British Journal of Industrial Relations*, XXIX/3, 377–90.

Moene, K. and Wallerstein, M. (1999), 'Social democratic labour market institutions: a retrospective analysis', in H. Kitschelt, P. Lange, G. Marks and J. Stephens (eds), *Continuity and Change in Contemporary Capitalism*, Cambridge: Cambridge University Press.

Monks, K. (1992), 'Personnel management practices: uniformity or diversity? Evidence from some Irish organisations', *Irish Business and Administrative Research*, XIII, 74–86.

Monks, K. (2002), 'Personnel or human resource management: a choice for Irish organisations?', in P. Gunnigle, M. Morley and M. McDonnell (eds), *The Lovett Lectures: A Decade of Developments in Human Resource Management*, Dublin: The Liffey Press.

Morley, M., Gunnigle, P. and Turner, T. (2001), 'The Cranfield Network on Human Resource Management (CranetE) Survey: executive report Ireland 1999/2000', Employment Relations Research Unit, College of Business, University of Limerick.

Morley, M., Moore, S., Heraty, N. and Gunnigle, P. (1998), *Principles of Organisational Behaviour*, Dublin: Gill & Macmillan.

Morrissey, T.J. (1989), 'Employee participation at sub-board level', in Department of Industrial Relations, UCD (eds), *Industrial Relations in Ireland: Contemporary Issues and Developments*, Dublin: University College Dublin.

Muller-Camen, M., Almond, P., Gunnigle, P., Quintanilla, J. and Tempel, A. (2001), 'Between home and host country: multinationals and employment relations in Europe', *Industrial Relations Journal*, XXXII/5, 435–48.

Mulligan, H. (1993), 'The Unfair Dismissals Act – day to day reality', *Industrial Relations News*, 9 (4 March), 16–18.

Mulvey, K. (1991a), 'The Potential Role of the Labour Relations Commission', paper presented to the Irish Association of Industrial Relations, Dublin: The Labour Relations Commission, 16 April.

Mulvey, K. (1991b), 'The Labour Relations Commission', paper presented to the Mid-West Chapter of the IPM, Dublin: The Labour Relations Commission, November.

Munns, V.G. (1967), 'The functions and organisation of employers associations in selected industries', in 'Employers Associations', research paper no. 7 to the Royal Commission on Trade Unions and Employers Associations HMSO.

Murphy, T.V. (1989), 'The impact of the Unfair Dismissals Act 1977 on workplace industrial relations', in Department of Industrial Relations, UCD (eds), *Industrial Relations in Ireland: Contemporary Issues and Developments*, Dublin: University College Dublin.

Murphy, A. (1994), *The Irish Economy: Celtic Tiger or Tortoise?*, Dublin: Money Markets International Stockbrokers, 1–21.

Murphy, T. and Walsh, D. (1980), *The Worker Director and His Influence On The Enterprise: Expectations, Experience and Effectiveness in Seven Irish Companies*, Dublin: Irish Productivity Centre.

Murray, M. and Keane, C. (1998), *The ABC of Bullying*, Dublin: Mercier Press.

Murray, S. (1984), *Employee Relations in Irish Private Sector Manufacturing Industry*, Dublin: Industrial Development Authority.

Myers, C.A. (1955), 'Conclusions and implications', in C.S. Golden and V.D. Parker (eds), *Causes of Industrial Peace*, New York: Harper & Bros.

National Economic and Social Council (NESC) (1986), *A Strategy for Development 1986–1990*, Dublin: NESC.

National Economic and Social Council (NESC) (1996), *Strategy into the 21st Century*, Dublin: NESC.

National Minimum Wage Commission (1998), *Report of the National Minimum Wage Commission 1*, Dublin: The Stationery Office.

NCPP/ESRI (downloaded on 24 October 2003), *Summary of NCPP/ESRI Surveys on Attitudes and Experiences in the Workplace – Anticipating and Meeting the Needs of a Changing Workforce Panel* (available at www.ncpp.ie/dynamic/docs/Note%20on%20Surveys%2010-03.doc).

Nevin, D. (1994), *Trade Union Century*, Dublin: Irish Congress of Trade Unions and RTÉ.

Nierenberg, G.I. (1968), *The Art of Negotiating*, New York: Cornerstone.

Nolan, B. and Maître, B. (2000), 'Income inequality', in B. Nolan, J. O'Connell and C. Whelan (eds), *Bust to Boom? The Irish Experience of Growth and Inequality*, Dublin: Institute of Public Administration.

Nolan, B., O'Connell, P. and Whelan, C.T. (2000), 'Conclusion: the Irish experience of growth and inequality', in B. Nolan, J. O'Connell and C. Whelan (eds), *Bust to Boom? The Irish Experience of Growth and Inequality*, Dublin: Institute of Public Administration.

O'Brien, J.F. (1981), *A Study of the National Wage Agreements in Ireland*, Dublin: Economic and Social Research Institute.

O'Brien, J.F. (1989a), 'Pay determination in Ireland', in Department of Industrial Relations, UCD (eds), *Industrial Relations in Ireland: Contemporary Issues and Developments*, Dublin: University College Dublin.

O'Brien, J.F. (1989b), 'The PNR in perspective – another round?', Eighth Annual Industrial Relations Guest Lecture, Limerick: National Institute for Higher Education.

O'Brien, J.F. (1989c.), 'The role of employer organisations in Ireland', in Department of Industrial Relations, UCD (eds), *Industrial Relations in Ireland: Contemporary Issues and Developments*, Dublin: University College Dublin.

O'Connell, P. (1998), *Astonishing Success: Economic Growth and the Labour Market in Ireland*, Geneva: International Labour Organisation.

O'Connor, E. (1988), *Syndicalism in Ireland 1917–1923*, Cork: Cork University Press.

O'Connor, K. (1982), 'The impact of the Unfair Dismissals Act 1977 on personnel management and industrial relations', *Irish Business and Administrative Research*, V/2.

O'Connor, S. (2002), *Benchmarking the Programme for Prosperity and Fairness*, Dublin: NESC February.

O'Donnell, R. and O'Reardon, C. (1996), 'Irish experiment: social partnership has yielded economic growth and social progress', Dublin: National Economic and Social Council/Economic and Social Research Institute.

O'Donnell, R. and O'Reardon, C. (2000), 'Social partnership in Ireland's economic transformation', in G. Fajertag and P. Pochett, *Social Pacts in Europe – New Dynamics*, Brussels: ETUI.

Oechslin, J.J. (1985), 'Employers organisations', in R. Blanpain (ed.), *Labour Law and Industrial Relations*, The Hague: Kluwer.

Office of Director of Equality Investigations (ODEI) – Equality Tribunal (2002), *Annual Report*, Dublin: ODEI.

Office for National Statistics (2003), *Labour Market Trends (2003)*, Cardiff: Office for National Statistics.

O'Grada, C. (1994), *Ireland: A New Economic History 1780–1939*, Oxford: Clarendon Press.

O'Grada, C. (1997), *A Rocky Road: The Irish Economy since the 1920s*, Manchester: Manchester University Press.

O'Hara, B. (1981), *The Evolution of Irish Industrial Relations: Law and Practice*, Dublin: Folens.

O'Hagan, J. (1987), *The Economy of Ireland: Policy and Performance,* 5th ed., Dublin: Irish Management Institute.

O'Hagan, J. (2000), *The Economy of Ireland: Policy and Performance of a European Region*, 8th ed., Dublin: Gill & Macmillan.

O'Keeffe, S. (1998), 'Industrial action ballots in Ireland – Nolan Transport v Halligan and others', *Industrial Law Journal*, XXVII/4, 347–52.

O'Kelly, K. and Compton P. (2003), 'Workers' participation at board level – the Irish approach', paper presented to the European Trade Union Institute and the Hans Boeckler Stiftung, Elewijt, Belgium, 27–28 June.

O'Leary, A. (2000), 'Rights Commissioners: what methods of third party intervention do they adopt?', unpublished MBS thesis, University of Limerick.

O'Malley, E. (1983), 'Late industrialisation under outward looking policies: the experience and prospects of the Republic of Ireland', unpublished PhD thesis, University of Sussex.

O'Mahony, D. (1964), *Industrial Relations in Ireland*, Dublin: Economic and Social Research Institute.

O'Muircheartaigh, C.A. (1975), *Absenteeism in Irish Industry*, Dublin: Irish Productivity Centre.

O'Regan, E. (2003), 'The European Information and Consultation Directive will have far-reaching implications for employers in Ireland', *The Sunday Business Post*, 16 March.

Organisation for Economic Co-operation and Development (OECD) (1979), *Wage Policies and Collective Bargaining Developments in Finland, Ireland and Norway*, Paris: OECD.

Organisation for Economic Co-operation and Development (OECD) (1997), *Employment Outlook*, Paris: OECD, July.

Organisation for Economic Co-operation and Development (OECD) (2003), *Health Data 2003: A Comparative Analysis of 30 Countries*, Paris: OECD.

O'Sullivan, M. (2000), 'Underlying conditions and approach efficiency as determinants of success in an advisory service investigation: an unresolved gestalt paradox', unpublished project, University of Limerick.

Palmer, G. (1983), *British Industrial Relations*, London: Allen & Unwin.

Paldam, M. and Pederson, P.J. (1982), 'The macro-economic strike model: a study of seventeen countries 1948–1975', *Industrial and Labour Relations Review*, XXXV/4, 504–21.

Panitch, L. (1979), 'The development of corporatism in liberal democracies', in P.C. Schmitter and G. Lehmbruch (eds), *Trends Towards Corporatist Intermediation*, London: Sage.

Parker, P.A.L., Hayes, W.R. and Lumb, A.L. (1971), *The Reform of Collective Bargaining at Plant and Company Level*, London: HMSO.

Pateman, C. (1970), *Participation and Democratic Theory*, Cambridge: Cambridge University Press.

Pekkarinen, J., Pohjola, M. and Rowthorn, B. (1992), 'Social corporatism and economic performance: introduction and conclusions', in J. Pekkarinen, M. Pohjola and B. Rowthorn (eds), *Social Corporatism: A Superior Economic System*, Oxford: Clarendon Press.

Pelling, H. (1976), *A History of British Trade Unionism*, Middlesex: Penguin.

Perlman, S. (1936), 'The principle of collective bargaining', *The Journal of the American Academy of Political and Social Science* (March), 154–9.

Phelps Brown, E.H. (1971), *Collective Bargaining Considered*, London: Athlone Press.

Pierson, F.C. (1961), 'Recent employer alliances in perspective', *Industrial Relations*, I (October), 39–57.

Pilger, J. (2002), *The New Rulers Of The World*, London: Verso.

Pine, M. (2003), press release, ODEI Equality Tribunal (www.odei.ie), 17 October.

Piore, M. and Sabel, C. (1984), *The Second Industrial Divide*, New York: Basic Books.

Pochet, P. and Fajertag, G. (2000), 'A new era for social pacts in Europe', in G. Fajertag and P. Pochet (eds), *Social Pacts in Europe – New Dynamics*, Brussels: European Trade Union Institute.

Pollock, H. and O'Dwyer, L. (1985), *We Can Work It Out: Relationships in the Workplace*, Dublin: O'Brien Educational Press.

Poole, M. (1986), *Industrial Relations: Origins and Patterns of National Diversity*, London: Routledge and Keegan Paul.

Porter, M. (1980), *Competitive strategy: Techniques for Analysing Industries and Competitors*, New York: The Free Press.

Porter, M. (1985), *Competitive Advantage: Creating and Sustaining Superior Performance*, New York: The Free Press.

Porter, M. (1987), 'From competitive advantage to corporate strategy', *Harvard Business Review* (May/June), 43–59.

Porter, M. (1990), *The Competitive Advantage of Nations (With New Introduction)*, London: Macmillan.

Purcell, J. (1987), 'Mapping management styles in employee relations', *Journal of Management Studies*, XXIV/5, 533–48.

Purcell, J. (1989), 'The impact of corporate strategy on human resource management', in J. Storey (ed.), *New Perspectives on Human Resource Management*, London: Routledge.

Purcell, J. (1992), 'The impact of corporate strategy on human resource management', in G. Salamon (ed.), *Human Resource Strategies*, London: Sage/Open University.

Purcell, J. and Sisson, K. (1983), 'Strategies and practice in the management of industrial relations', in G. Bain (ed.), *Industrial Relations in Britain*, Oxford: Blackwell.

Purcell, J., Marginson, P., Edwards, P. and Sisson, K. (1987), 'The industrial relations practices of multi-plant foreign owned firms', *Industrial Relations Journal* (Summer), XVIII/2.

Rabbitte, P. and Gilmore, E. (1990), *Bertie's Bill*, Dublin: The Workers Party.

Reed, M. (1989), *The Sociology of Management: Themes, Perspectives and Prospects*, London: Harvester Wheatsheaf.

Reynaud, J.P. (1978), *Problems and Prospects for Collective Bargaining in the EEC Member States*, Brussels: Commission of the European Community Document No. V/394/78-EN.

Rhodes, M. (1998), 'Globalisation, labour markets and welfare states: a future of competitive corporatism', in M. Rhodes and Y. Meny (eds), *The Future of European Welfare: A New Social Contract*, London: Macmillan.

Ridgely, P. (1988), 'How relevant is the FUE', *Irish Business*, February.

Rigby, M. and Aledo, M.L.M. (2001), 'The worst record in Europe?, A comparative analysis of industrial conflict in Spain', *European Journal of Industrial Relations*, VII/3, 287–305.

Robbins, S.P. (1983), *Organizational Theory: The Structure and Design of Organizations*, New Jersey: Prentice Hall.

Roche, W.K. (1989), 'State strategies and the politics of industrial relations in Ireland', in Department of Industrial Relations, UCD (eds), *Industrial Relations in Ireland: Contemporary Issues and Developments*, Dublin: University College Dublin.

Roche, W.K. (1990), 'Industrial relations research in Ireland and the trade union interest', paper presented to the Irish Congress of Trades Unions Conference on Joint Research between Trade Unions, Universities, Third-Level Colleges and Research Institutes, Dublin.

Roche, W.K. (1992a), 'Modelling trade union growth and decline in the Republic of Ireland', *Irish Business and Administrative Research*, XIII/1, 86–102.

Roche, W.K. (1992b), 'The liberal theory of industrialism and the development of industrial relations in Ireland', in J. Goldthorpe and C. Whelan (eds), *The Development of Industrial Society in Ireland*, Oxford: Oxford University Press.

Roche, W.K. (1994a), 'Pay determination, the State and the politics of industrial relations', in W.K. Roche and T.V. Murphy (eds), *Irish Industrial Relations in Practice*, Dublin: Oak Tree Press.

Roche, W.K. (1994b), 'The trend of unionisation', in W.K. Roche and T.V. Murphy (eds), *Irish Industrial Relations in Practice*, Dublin: Oak Tree Press.

Roche, W.K. (1995), 'The new competitive order and employee relations in Ireland', paper presented to the Irish Business and Employers IBEC conference on Human Resources in the Global Market, Dublin, November.

Roche, W.K. (1997a), 'The trend of unionisation', in W.K. Roche and T.V. Murphy (eds), *Irish Industrial Relations in Practice, Revised and Expanded Edition*, Dublin: Oak Tree Press.

Roche, W.K. (1997b), 'Pay determination, the State and the politics of industrial relations', in W.K. Roche and T.V. Murphy (eds), *Irish Industrial Relations in Practice, Revised and Expanded Edition*, Dublin: Oak Tree Press.

Roche, W.K. and Ashmore, J. (2001), 'Irish unions in the 1990s: testing the limits of social partnership', in G. Griffin (ed.), *Changing Patterns of Trade Unionism: A Comparison of English Speaking Countries*, London: Mansell.

Roche, W.K. and Geary, J.F. (1994), 'The attenuation of host-country effects? Multinationals, industrial relations and collective bargaining in Ireland', working paper, Business Research Programme, Smurfit Graduate School of Business, University College Dublin.

Roche, W.K. and Geary, J.F. (1998), 'Collaborative production and the Irish boom: work organisation, partnership and direct involvement in Irish workplaces', working paper no. 26, Smurfit Graduate School of Business, University College Dublin, December.

Roche, W.K. and Geary, J.F. (2002), 'Collaborative production and the Irish boom: work organisation, partnership and direct involvement in Irish workplaces', in D. D'Art and T. Turner (eds), *Irish Employment Relations in the New Economy*, Dublin: Blackhall Publishing.

Roche, W.K. and Gunnigle, P. (1997), 'Competition and the new industrial relations agenda', in W.K. Roche and T.V. Murphy (eds), *Industrial Relations in Practice: New and Revised Edition*, Dublin: Oak Tree Press.

Roche, W.K. and Kochan, T.A. (1996), 'Strategies for extending Social Partnership to enterprise and workplace levels in Ireland', report prepared for the National Economic and Social Council Draft, Dublin, July.

Roche, W.K. and Larragy, J. (1986), 'The formation of the Irish trade union movement and organisational developments since 1945', working paper, Department of Industrial Relations, University College Dublin.

Roche, W.K. and Larragy, J. (1989a), 'The trend of unionisation in the Irish Republic', in Department of Industrial Relations, UCD (eds), *Industrial Relations in Ireland: Contemporary Issues and Developments*, Dublin: University College Dublin.

Roche, W.K. and Larragy, J. (1989b), *The Determinants of the Annual Rate of Trade Union Growth and Decline in the Irish Republic: Evidence from the DUES Membership Series*, Dublin: University College Dublin.

Roche, W.K. and Turner, T. (1994), 'Testing alternative models of human resource policy effects on trade union recognition in the Republic of Ireland', *International Journal of Human Resource Management*, V/3, 721–53.

Roche, W.K. and Turner, T. (1997), 'The diffusion of the commitment model in the Republic of Ireland', *Review of Employment Topics*, III, 108–51.

Roche, W.K. and Turner, T. (1998), 'Human resource management and industrial relations: substitution, dualism and partnership', in W.K. Roche, K. Monks and J. Walsh (eds), *Human Resource Management Strategies: Policy and Practice in Ireland*, Dublin: Oak Tree Press.

Rojot, J. (2001), 'A European industrial relations system?', in M. Biagi (ed.), *Towards a European Model of Industrial Relations? Building on the First Report of European Commission*, The Hague.

Rollinson, D. (1993), *Understanding Employee Relations: A Behavioural Approach*, Wokingham: Addison-Wesley.

Rose, E. (2001), *Employment Relations*, Essex: Financial Times/Prentice Hall.

Rose, M. (1977), *Industrial Behaviour: Theoretical Development since Taylor*, Middlesex: Penguin.

Ross, A.M. and Hartman, P. (1960), *Changing Patterns of Industrial Conflict*, New York: Wiley.

Roth, S. (1993), 'Lean production in German motor manufacturing', *P+: European Participation Monitor*, I/5, 35–9, Dublin: European Foundation for the Improvement of Living and Working Conditions.

Rothenberg, H.I. and Silverman, S.B. (1973), *Labor Unions: How to Avert Them, Beat Them, Out-Negotiate Them, Live with Them, Unload Them*, Elkins Park, PA: Management Relations Inc.

Roy, D.F. (1980), 'Repression and incorporation. Fear stuff, sweet stuff and evil stuff: management's defences against unionization in the south', in T. Nichols (ed.), *Capital and Labour: A Marxist Primer*, Glasgow: Fontana.

Royle, T. and Towers, B. (2002), *Labour Relations in the Global Fast-food Industry*, London: Routledge.

Russell, B. (1960), *Power: A New Social Analysis*, London: Unwin Books.

Salamon, M. (1987), *Industrial Relations: Theory and Practice*, London: Prentice Hall.

Salamon, M. (1998), *Industrial Relations: Theory and Practice*, 3rd ed., London: Prentice Hall.

Salamon, M. (2000), *Industrial Relations: Theory and Practice*, 4th ed., Essex: Financial Times/Prentice Hall.

Sapsford, D., Hillery, B. and McCarthy, C. (1979), 'Symposium necessary changes in Irish industrial relations', *Journal of the Statistical and Social Inquiry Society of Ireland*, XXIV/Part 2, 29–68.

Sapsford, D., Hillery, B. and McCarthy, C. (1989), 'An overview of the Irish industrial relations system', in Department of Industrial Relations, UCD (eds), *Industrial Relations in Ireland: Contemporary Issues and Developments*, Dublin: University College Dublin.

Saville, J. (1967), 'Trade unions and free labour: the background to the Taff Vale decision', in A. Briggs and J. Saville (eds), *Essays in Labour History*, London: Macmillan.

Schmitter, P.C. and Lehmbruch, G. (eds) (1979), *Trends Towards Corporatist Intermediation*, London: Sage.

Schmitter, P.C. (1979), 'Introduction', in P.C. Schmitter and G. Lehmbruch (eds), *Trends Towards Corporatist Intermediation*, London: Sage.

Schregle, J. (1974), 'Labour relations in Western Europe: some topical issues', *International Labour Review* (January–June).

Schregle, J. (1975), 'Restructuring of the Irish trade union movement in ICTU', *Seventeenth Annual Report*, Dublin: ICTU.

Schulten, T., Seifert, H. and Zagelmeyer, S. (1999), 'Pacts for employment and competitiveness: case studies – Volkswagen AG', report to the European Foundation for the Improvement of Living and Working Conditions. (www.eurofound.eu.int/industrial/pecscstudies/pecs_volkswagen.pdf).

Scott, B. (1981), *The Skills of Negotiating*, London: Gower.

Scott, J.F. and Homans, G.C. (1947), 'Reflections on the wildcat strikes', *American Sociological Review*, XII, 278–87.

Seanad Éireann (2003), *Seanad Debates*, 19 November.

Sebenius, J.K. (2001), 'Six habits of merely effective negotiators', *Harvard Business Review*, LXXIX/4, 87–9.

Sexton, J.J., Nolan, B. and McCormick, B. (1999), 'A review of earnings trends in the Irish economy since 1987', in D. Duffy, J. Fitzgerald, K. Kennedy and D. Smyth, *Quarterly Economic Commentary*, Dublin: ESRI.

Shalev, M. (1992), 'The resurgence of labour quiescence', in M. Regini (ed.), *The Future of Labour Movements*, London: Sage.

Sheehan, B. (1983), 'Waterford tax protest – support for glass workers', *Industrial Relations News*, 17, 13–14.

Sheehan, B. (1993), 'Attley predicts difficult pay bargaining climate for trade unions', *Industrial Relations News*, 11, 2.

Sheehan, B. (1996a), 'Bruton wants new pact, asks NESC to prepare strategy', *Industrial Relations News*, 4, 10–11.

Sheehan, B. (1996b), 'Agenda for talks emerges as SIPTU's tax demands receive boost', *Industrial Relations News*, 9 (29 February).

Sheehan, B. (1996c), 'The John Dunne interview', *Industrial Relations News*, 19, 19–23.

Sheehan, B. (1997), 'Post budget votes swing majority decisively in favour of Partnership 2000', *Industrial Relations News*, 6, 13–15.

Sheehan, B. (1998a), 'Ryanair – no winners emerge from weekend of chaos as enquiry team faces unenviable task', *Industrial Relations News*, 11, 2–5.

Sheehan, B. (1998b), 'Conciliation service well regarded, change has impacted role', *Industrial Relations News*, 42, 15–19.

Sheehan, B. (1998c), 'Draft proposals on union recognition likely to face trenchant opposition', *Industrial Relations News*, 1 and 2, 3–5.

Sheehan, B. (1998d), 'Union recognition formula points to limit of partnership approach', *Industrial Relations News*, 3, 16–18.

Sheehan, B. (1998e), 'Telecom – breakthrough as talks get underway', *Industrial Relations News*, 3, 9.

Sheehan, B. (1998f), 'Employee partnership – new guide for managers', *Industrial Relations News*, 26, 18–20.

Sheehan, B. (1998g), 'Telecom - ESOP gets final seal of approval', *Industrial Relations News*, 27, 5.

Sheehan, B. (1999), 'ESB worker director's "weather alert" angers unions, challenges company', *Industrial Relations News*, 15, 14–15.

Sheehan, B. (2001), 'Social partnership and the state of industrial relations', *Industrial Relations News*, 28, 23–7.

Sheehan, B. (2002), 'Irish industrial relations and HRM: an overview of the Lovett years', in P. Gunnigle, M. Morley and M. McDonnell (eds), *The Lovett Lectures: A Decade of Developments in Human Resource Management*, Dublin: The Liffey Press.

Sheehan, B. (2003a), 'Social partners' sixth successive national deal a watershed?', *Industrial Relations News*, 14, 20–5.

Sheehan, B. (2003b), 'Gradual shift in profile of union members as density levels drift downwards', *Industrial Relations News*, 33, 20–2.

Sheehan, B. (2003c), 'Monitoring and enforcement mechanisms key features of "Sustaining Progress"', *Industrial Relations News*, 8, 18–19.

Sheehan, B. (2003d), 'Unions, employers ratify new national agreement', *Industrial Relations News*, 14, 3–4.

Sheehan, B. (2003e), 'Industrial Relations (Amendment) Bill to bolster employee representation?', *Industrial Relations News*, 27, 25–7.

Sheehan, B. (2003f), 'ESB unions prepare dispute ballot in bid to force talks on new pact', *Industrial Relations News*, 47, 3–5.

Sheehan, B. (2004a), 'Looking forward – "stage two" of national pay deal in prospect', *Industrial Relations News*, 1 and 2, 16–17.

Sheehan, B. (2004b), 'Civil service – "significant progress" ensures benchmarking pay-out, despite shortcomings', *Industrial Relations News*, 1 and 2, 21–5.

Sheehan, B. and Hastings, T. (2000), 'Strong backing for PPF, but relative pay stability may be best hope', *Industrial Relations News*, 13, 16–18.

Shivanath, G. (1987), 'Personnel practitioners 1986: their role and status in Irish industry', unpublished MBS thesis, University of Limerick.

Shorter, E. and Tilly, C. (1974), *Strikes in France 1830–68*, Cambridge: Cambridge University Press.

Siggins, L. (2004), 'Abuse of sportswear workers highlighted', *The Irish Times*, 27 March.

Silverman, J. (1970), *The Theory of Organisations*, London: Heinemann.

Sisson, K. (1983), 'Employers organisations', in G. Bain (ed.), *Industrial Relations in Britain*, Oxford: Blackwell.

Sisson, K. (1987), *The Management of Collective Bargaining: An International Comparison*, Oxford: Blackwell.

Sisson, K. (1994), 'Workplace Europe. Direct participation in organisational change: introducing the EPOC project', presented to the International Industrial Relations Association fourth European regional congress on Transformation of European Industrial Relations: Consequences of Integration and Disintegration, Helsinki.

Small Firms Association (2002), *End of Year Report on Absenteeism* (www.sfa.ie/cgi/show_press?action=ViewandReleaseID=221), downloaded on 31 December 2002.

Smith, A. (1970), *The Wealth of Nations*, London: Pelican.

Smith, S. (2003), *Labour Economics*, 2nd ed., London: Routledge.

Sparrow, P. (2002), 'Globalisation as an uncoupling force: internationalisation of the HR process?', in P. Gunnigle, M. Morley and M. McDonnell (eds), *The Lovett Lectures: A Decade of Developments in Human Resource Management*, Dublin: The Liffey Press.

Sparrow, P.R. and Hiltrop, J.M. (1994), *European Human Resource Management in Transition*, London: Prentice Hall.

Stewart, M. (1990), 'Union wage differentials, product market influences and the division of rents', *Economic Journal*, C/4 , 1122–37.

Stokke, T.A. and Thörnqvist, C. (2001), 'Strikes and collective bargaining in the Nordic countries', *European Journal of Industrial Relations*, VII/3, 245–67.

Storey, J. (ed.) (1989), *New Perspectives on Human Resource Management*, London: Routledge.

Storey, J. (1992), *Developments in the Management of Human Resources*, Oxford: Blackwell.

Storey, J. and Sisson, K. (1990), 'Limits to transformation: human resource management in the British context', *Industrial Relations Journal*, XXI, (Spring) 60–5.

Storey, J. and Sisson, K. (1994), *Managing Human Resources and Industrial Relations*, Buckingham: Open University Press.

Sturdy, A., Knights, D. and Willmott, H. (1992), 'Introduction: skill and consent in the labour process', in A. Sturdy, D. Knights and H. Willmott (eds), *Skill and Consent: Contemporary Studies in the Labour Process*, London: Routledge.

Streeck, W. (1992), 'Training and the new industrial relations: a strategic role for unions?', in M. Regini (ed.), *The Future of Labour Movements*, London: Sage.

Sweeney, P. (1998), *The Celtic Tiger – Ireland's Economic Miracle Explained*, Dublin: Oak Tree Press.

Tansey, P. (1998), *Ireland at Work*, Dublin: Oak Tree Press.

Task Force on the Prevention of Workplace Bullying (2001), *Report of the Task Force: Dignity at Work – The Challenge of Workplace Bullying*, Dublin: Government Publications.

Teague, P. (1995), 'Pay determination in the Republic of Ireland: towards social corporatism?', *British Journal of Industrial Relations*, XXXIII/2, 253–73.

Thelen, H.A. and Withall, J. (1949), 'Three frames of reference: the description of climate', *Human Relations*, II/2, 159–76.

Thomas, D., Brannick, T. and Kelly, A. (2003), 'Social Partnership and industrial conflict in Ireland: securing the peace dividend?', working paper, University College Dublin.

Thomason, G. (1984), *A Textbook Of Industrial Relations Management*, London: Institute of Personnel Management.

Thompson, L. (2001), *The Mind and Heart of the Negotiator*, 2nd ed., New Jersey: Prentice Hall.

Thurley, K. and Wood, S. (eds) (1983), *Industrial Relations and Management Strategy*, Cambridge: Cambridge University Press.

Toner, B. (1987), 'Union or non-union-employee relations strategies in the Republic of Ireland', unpublished PhD thesis, London School of Economics.

Torrington, D. and Hall, L. (1991), *Personnel Management: A New Approach*, London: Prentice Hall.

Torrington, D. and Hall, L. (1998), *Human Resource Management*, London: Prentice Hall.

Traxler, F. (1998), 'Employers and employer organisations', in B. Towers and M. Terry (eds), *Industrial Relations Journal: European Annual Review 1997*, Oxford: Blackwell.

Turner, H. (1962), *Trade Union Growth, Structure and Policy*, London: Allen & Unwin.

Turner, H. (1969), 'Is Britain really strike prone? A review of the incidence, character and costs of industrial conflict', Occasional Paper 20, Cambridge: The Cambridge University Press.

Turner, T. (1993), 'Unionisation and human resource management in Irish companies', *Industrial Relations Journal*, XXV/39, 39–51.

Turner, T. (1999), 'Income equality in the Irish labour market: changes in earnings and taxation levels, 1987 to 1995', *Irish Business and Administrative Research*, XIX/XX/1, 36–46.

Turner, T. (2002), 'Corporatism in Ireland: a comparative perspective', in D. D'Art and T. Turner (eds), *Irish Employment Relations in the New Economy*, Dublin: Blackhall Publishing.

Turner, T. and D'Art, D. (2000), 'A review of centralised wage agreements in Ireland 1987–2000', *Croner's Employee Relations Review*, 12 (February), 16–19.

Turner, T. and Morley, M. (1995), *Industrial Relations and the New Order*, Dublin: Oak Tree Press.

Turner, T. and Wallace, J. (2000), 'The Irish model of Social Partnership: achievements and limitations', paper presented to the European Congress of the International Industrial Relations Association, Oslo, 25–29 June.

Turner, T., Morley, M. and Gunnigle, P. (1994), 'Developments in industrial relations and HRM in the Republic of Ireland', *Irish Business and Administrative Research*, XV/1, 76–92.

Tyson, S. (1987), 'The management of the personnel function', *Journal of Management Studies*, XXIV/5, 523–32.

Tyson, S. and Fell, A (1986), *Evaluating the Personnel Function*, London: Hutchinson.

Tyson, S., Witcher, M. and Doherty, N. (1994), *Different Routes to Excellence*, Cranfield University School of Management, Human Resource Research Centre.

Ury, W. (1992), *Getting Past NO: Negotiating With Difficult People*, London: Century Business.

van de Vliert, E. (1985), 'Escalative intervention in small groups', *Journal of Applied Behavioural Science*, XII/1, 19–36.

von Prondzynski, F. (1985), 'The death of the pay round', *Industrial Relations News*, 16 (November).

von Prondzynski, F. (1988), 'Social partnership in Ireland and Austria', in A. Matthews and A. Sagarri (eds), *Economic Performance in Two Small European Economies: Ireland and Austria*, Dublin: Trinity College Dublin.

von Prondzynski, F. (1989), 'Collective labour law', in Department of Industrial Relations, UCD (eds), *Industrial Relations in Ireland: Contemporary Issues and Developments*, Dublin: University College Dublin.

von Prondzynski, F. (1992), 'Ireland between centralism and the market', in A. Ferner and R. Hyman (eds), *Industrial Relations in the New Europe*, Oxford: Blackwell.

von Prondzynski, F. (1998), 'Ireland: corporatism revived', in A. Ferner and R. Hyman (eds), *Changing Industrial Relations in Europe*, Oxford: Blackwell.

von Prondzynski, F. and McCarthy, C. (1984), *Employment Law*, London: Sweet & Maxwell.

von Prondzynski, F. and McCarthy, C. (1989), *von Prondzynski and McCarthy on Employment Law*, 2nd ed., London: Sweet & Maxwell.

von Prondzynski, F. and Richards, W. (1994), *European Employment and Industrial Relations Glossary: Ireland*, London: Sweet & Maxwell/Luxembourg: Office for Official Publications of the European Communities.

Waddington, J. (2003), 'What do representatives think of the practices of European works councils? Views from six countries', *European Journal of Industrial Relations*, IX/3, 303–25.

Waddington, J. and Kerckhofs, P. (2003), 'European works councils: what is the current state of play?', Transfer, 9, 322–39.

Wallace, J. (1982), *Industrial Relations in Limerick City and Environs*, Employment Research Programme, Limerick: University of Limerick.

Wallace, J. (1988a), 'Unofficial strikes in Ireland', *Industrial Relations News*, 8 (25 February), 17–21.

Wallace, J. (1988b), 'Workplace aspects of unofficial strikes', *Industrial Relations News*, 9 (3 March), 15–19.

Wallace, J. (1988c), 'A review of proposed reforms of trade disputes legislation in Ireland', *Advances in Business Studies*, I/2.

Wallace, J. (1989), 'Procedure agreements and their place in workplace industrial relations', in Department of Industrial Relations, UCD (eds), *Industrial Relations in Ireland: Contemporary Issues and Developments*, Dublin: University College Dublin.

Wallace, J. (1991), 'The Industrial Relations Act 1990 and other developments in labour law', paper presented to the Mid-West Chapter of the Institute of Personnel Management, University of Limerick November.

Wallace, J. (1999), 'Investigating employment pacts: collective agreements dealing with the relationship between employment and competitiveness', report to the European Foundation for the Improvement of Working And Living Conditions.

Wallace, J. (2000a), 'Workplace developments in collective bargaining in Ireland in the 1990s', *Croner's Employee Relations*, 13, 26–31.

Wallace, J. (2000b), 'Workplace developments in collective bargaining in Ireland in the 1990s', paper to the Irish Academy of Management Conference, Derry, 7–8 September.

Wallace, J. (2003), 'Unions in 21st century Ireland – entering the Ice Age?', Industrial Relations News Conference, 'No Vision No Future', University College Dublin, 27 February, 16–23.

Wallace, J. and Clifford, N. (1998), *Collective Bargaining and Flexibility in Ireland*, Geneva: International Labour Office.

Wallace, J. and Delany, B. (1997), 'Back to the future? – The Irish Industrial Relations Act 1990', in F. Meenan (ed.), *Legal Perspectives – The Juridification of the Employment Relationship*, Dublin: Oak Tree Press.

Wallace, J. and Dineen, D.A. (2001), 'Irish services: the industrial relations dimensions of a rapidly growing sector', *Industrielle Beziehungen*, VIII/1, 83–107.

Wallace, J. and McDonnell, C. (2000), 'The institutional provisions of the Industrial Relations Act 1990 in operation', *Irish Business and Administrative Research*, XXI/1, 169–88.

Wallace, J. and O'Shea, F. (1987), *A Study of Unofficial Strikes in Ireland*, Dublin: Government Publications Office.

Wallace, J. and O'Sullivan, M. (2002a), 'The Industrial Relations Act 1990: a critical review', in D. D'Art and T. Turner (eds), *Irish Employment Relations in the New Economy*, Dublin: Blackhall Publishing.

Wallace, J. and O'Sullivan, M. (2002b), 'Employment Protection in Ireland', paper presented at the 11th Annual Conference of the International Employment Relations Association, London, 7–11 July.

Wallace, J. and O'Sullivan, M. (2002c), 'Institutional protection for vulnerable workers in Ireland: lessons from the twentieth century', paper presented at the International Industrial Relations Association 4th Regional Congress of the Americas, Toronto, 25–28 June.

Wallace, J., Dineen, D.A. and O'Sullivan, M. (2001), 'The contribution of the services sector to the Irish employment miracle', in J.E. Dølvik (ed.), *At your Service: Comparative Perspectives on Employment and Labour Relations in the European Private Services Sector*, Brussels: PIE-Peter Lang.

Wallace, J., McDonnell, C. and Kennedy, V. (2000), 'A review of trade union rationalisation in Ireland', paper presented to the Irish Academy of Management Conference, 7–8 September.

Wallace, J., Turner, T. and McCarthy, A. (1998), 'EMU and the impact on Irish industrial relations', in T. Kauppinen (ed.), *The Impact of EMU on Industrial Relations in Europe*, publication no. 9, Helsinki: Finnish Labour Relations Association.

Walsh, B. (1985), 'Foreword', in A. Kerr and G. Whyte, *Irish Trade Union Law*, Bristol: Professional Books Ltd.

Walton, R.E. (1982), 'The Topeka work system: optimistic visions, pessimistic hypothesis and reality', in R. Zager and M. Rosow (eds), *The Innovative Organization*, New York: Pergamon.

Walton, R.E. (1985), 'From control to commitment in the workplace', *Harvard Business Review* (March/April), 77–84.

Walton, R.E. and McKersie, R.B. (1965), *A Behavioural Theory of Labour Negotiations: An Analysis of a Social Interaction System*, New York: McGraw-Hill.

Watson, T. (1987), *Sociology, Work and Industry*, London: Routledge.

Webb, S. and Webb, B. (1897), *Industrial Democracy*, Vol. I, London: Longmans & Co.

Webb, S. and Webb, B. (1920), *The History of Trade Unionism*, London: Longman.

Wedderburn, W.K. (1965), *The Worker and the Law*, London: Penguin.

Wedderburn, W.K. (1986), *The Worker and the Law*, 3rd ed., London: Penguin.

Whelan, C. (1982), *Worker Priorities, Trust in Management and Prospects for Worker Participation, Paper III*, Dublin: Economic and Social Research Institute.

Whyte, W.F. (1951), *Pattern for Industrial Peace*, New York: Harper.

Wilkinson, A. (1998), 'Empowerment', in M. Poole and M. Warner (eds), *International Encyclopaedia of Business and Management Handbook of Human Resource Management*, London: ITB Press.

Wilkinson, B. (1991), 'The Irish Industrial Relations Act 1990: corporatism and conflict control', *Industrial Law Journal*, XX/1, 21–38.

Williams, J. and Whelan, B.J. (1986), *Employers' Perceptions of the Effects of Employment Legislation*, Dublin: Economic and Social Research Institute.

Wilson, R. (2000), 'The future of unions in the year 2000', lecture given at Massey University, Albany, 23 August.

Windmuller, J.P. (1984), 'Employers associations in comparative perspective: organisation, structure and administration', in J.P. Windmuller and A. Gladstone (eds), *Employer Associations and Industrial Relations*, Oxford: Clarendon.

Womack, J.P., Jones, D.T. and Roos, D. (1990), *The Machine that Changed the World*, New York: Rawson Associates.

Wood, S. and Pecci, R. (1990), 'Preparing for 1992? Business-led versus strategic human resource management', *Human Resource Management*, I/1, 63–89.

Wood, S. (1978/1979), 'Ideology in industrial relations theory', *Industrial Relations Journal*, IX/4.

Wood, S. and Moore, S. (2002), 'In the line of fire', *People Management*, VIII/13.

Woodward, J. (1958), *Management and Technology*, London: H.M. Stationery Office.

Yeates, P. (1993), 'Personnel managers favour a new PESP', *The Irish Times*, 21 December.

Yeates, P. (1997), 'Pay agreement criticised by trade union leader', *The Irish Times*, 17 January.

Yeates, P. (2000), *Lockout Dublin 1913*, Dublin: Gill & Macmillan.

Index

MINISTERS

Mary Coughlan - Educ. & Scien
Noel Dempsey - Transport
Dermot Ahern - Justice
Michael Martin - Foreign Affairs
Eamon O Cuiv - Social & Family Af
Mary Hanafin - Arts, Sports, Touris
John Gormley - Environment Heil
                Local govt
Eamon Ryan - Comm, Energy & Nat. Res.
Brendan Smith - Agric, Fish & Food
Batt Okeeffe - Enterprise Trade & Empl.
Pat Carey - Community Rural & Gae
Tony Killeen - Defence
Barry Andrews - Children Minister

CEO of L.R.C. ⇒ Kier
set up in 1990 under the Ac
consist of a chair & 6 mem

Rights Commission
founded in 1969 IR Act
Functions ⇒ Interview/i
industrial disputes wi
view to promoting settlem
Designed to be speedy,
& cost free
① Cannot hear cases c
ing rates of pay hours
② workers must have ac
to L.C.

J.I.C ⇒ Voluntary negotiati
cy for an industry. Design
facilitate collective bar

TRADE UNIONS

IMPACT - Irish Municipal, Public & Civil Trade Union
          President - John Power /Sec. Alice Hennessy
INTO - Irish National Teachers Org.
MANDATE - The union of retail, bar & Administrative workers
ATGWU - Amalgamated Transport & General Workers Union
ITGWU - Irish   "   "   "   "
AHCPS - Association of Higher Civic & Public Servants
AUT - Association of University Teachers
ASTI - Association of Secondary Teachers Institute
BATU - Building & Allied Trade Union
CPSU - Civic & Public Service Union ⇒ Blair Horan
IFUT - Irish Federation of University Teachers
POA - Prison Officer Ass.
TUI - Teachers Union of Ireland
IBOA - Irish Bank Official Ass.
NBRU - National Bus & Rail Union
ICTU - Irish Congress of Trade Union ⇒ David Begg
P.S.EU - Public Sector Education Union
SIPTU - Service Industrial, Professional & Technical Union
          President ⇒ Jack O'Connor
INMO - Irish Nursery & Midwifery Org. secretary ⇒ Liam Doran

<u>DATES</u>

1825 ⇒ Anti Combination Acts passed by Irish legislature
failed ⇒ Due to secrecy / Social pressure on employers
scarce skills worker

1824/25 Combination Act repeal ⇒ Acts not effective / worsen relation
b/w master & worker

1834 Tolpuddle martyrs ⇒ Six farmers join Union ⇒ Sent 2 Austh.
T.u.   For 7 years, pardoned & Sent back 183

1871 ⇒ Gladstone legalised existence of trade U. T.U. Act

1875 — Disraeli T.u. Immune from law of Criminal Conspiracy

1901 ⇒ Taff vale VS ASR ⇒ case leads to 1906 / union was legal ent
                    & could be sued.

1906 ⇒ Trades Dispute Act ⇒ Immunity from tort of Civil Conspi

1911 ⇒ Unions Could not   protect peaceful picketing
                    use funds for political purposes.

1913 ⇒ T.u Act ⇒ funds allowed to be used 4 political purposes

1935 ⇒ Tu Act May own land

1941 ⇒   "   ⇒ Negotiations of Licences.

1942 ⇒ Tu Act ⇒ Exemptions from negotiation of Licences

1946 ⇒ Tu Act ⇒ Establish Labour Court

1947 – 1952 Tu Act ⇒ Six power reduce Deposit / Irish Union 75%

        <u>INDUSTRIAL RELATION ACT 1969</u>

1969 = IR Act ⇒ Enlargment of labour Court / Right Comm'ss. Intro

1971 ⇒ T.u. Act ⇒ Harder to form Union £5,000 Deposit / 500 member

1975 ⇒ T.u. Act ⇒ Encourage amalgamation by providing fund
                for successfull mergers

1976 ⇒ Ind. Rel. Act ⇒ Establish J.L.C & agric workers / access

1977 – 1988   ⇒ Allow worker Directors.

1970 2001

Trade disputes Amended 1982

1982 Act (T.d. Amended, Extend Immunities to all except
        defence force & Garda

Acts 1990 repealed 1906 & 1982 Trade disputes act provide 4
        pre strike secret ballots, Immunities restricted